CLYMER
MANUALS

HONDA
TRX250EX SPORTRAX/TRX250X • 2001-2012

WHAT'S IN YOUR TOOLBOX?

Disclaimer

There are risks associated with automotive repairs. The ability to make repairs depends on the individual's skill, experience and proper tools. Individuals should act with due care and acknowledge and assume the risk of performing automotive repairs.

The purpose of this manual is to provide comprehensive, useful and accessible automotive repair information, to help you get the best value from your vehicle. However, this manual is not a substitute for a professional certified technician or mechanic.

This repair manual is produced by a third party and is not associated with an individual vehicle manufacturer. If there is any doubt or discrepancy between this manual and the owner's manual or the factory service manual, please refer to the factory service manual or seek assistance from a professional certified technician or mechanic.

Even though we have prepared this manual with extreme care and every attempt is made to ensure that the information in this manual is correct, neither the publisher nor the author can accept responsibility for loss, damage or injury caused by any errors in, or omissions from, the information given.

More information available at haynes.com
Phone: 805-498-6703

Haynes UK
Sparkford Nr Yeovil
Somerset BA22 7JJ England

Haynes North America, Inc
859 Lawrence Drive
Newbury Park
California 91320 USA

ISBN-10: 1-59969-643-6
ISBN-13: 978-1-59969-643-0
Library of Congress: 2013932527

Author: Jon Engleman
Technical Illustrations: Steve Amos
Cover: Mark Clifford Photography at www.markclifford.com
2012 TRX250X courtesy of Bert's Mega Mall, Covina, California

© Haynes North America, Inc. 2013
With permission from J.H. Haynes & Co. Ltd.

Clymer is a registered trademark of Haynes North America, Inc.

All rights reserved. No part of this book may be reproduced or transmitted in any form or by any means, electronic or mechanical, including photocopying, recording or by any information storage or retrieval system, without permission in writing from the copyright holder.

While every attempt is made to ensure that the information in this manual is correct, no liability can be accepted by the authors or publishers for loss, damage or injury caused by any errors in, or omissions from, the information given.

M215-2, 22-336

Chapter One General Information	1
Chapter Two Troubleshooting	2
Chapter Three Lubrication, Maintenance and Tune-up	3
Chapter Four Engine Top End	4
Chapter Five Engine Lower End	5
Chapter Six Clutch and Primary Drive Gear	6
Chapter Seven Transmissions and Internal Shift Mechanism	7
Chapter Eight Fuel, Air and Exhaust Systems	8
Chapter Nine Electrical System	9
Chapter Ten Wheels, Hubs and Tires	10
Chapter Eleven Front Suspension and Steering	11
Chapter Twelve Rear Axle, Suspension and Final Drive	12
Chapter Thirteen Brakes	13
Chapter Fourteen Body	14
Supplement 2006-2012 Model Service Information	15
Index	16
Wiring Diagrams	17

Common spark plug conditions

NORMAL
Symptoms: Brown to grayish-tan color and slight electrode wear. Correct heat range for engine and operating conditions.
Recommendation: When new spark plugs are installed, replace with plugs of the same heat range.

WORN
Symptoms: Rounded electrodes with a small amount of deposits on the firing end. Normal color. Causes hard starting in damp or cold weather and poor fuel economy.
Recommendation: Plugs have been left in the engine too long. Replace with new plugs of the same heat range. Follow the recommended maintenance schedule.

TOO HOT
Symptoms: Blistered, white insulator, eroded electrode and absence of deposits. Results in shortened plug life.
Recommendation: Check for the correct plug heat range, over-advanced ignition timing, lean fuel mixture, intake manifold vacuum leaks, sticking valves and insufficient engine cooling.

CARBON DEPOSITS
Symptoms: Dry sooty deposits indicate a rich mixture or weak ignition. Causes misfiring, hard starting and hesitation.
Recommendation: Make sure the plug has the correct heat range. Check for a clogged air filter or problem in the fuel system or engine management system. Also check for ignition system problems.

PREIGNITION
Symptoms: Melted electrodes. Insulators are white, but may be dirty due to misfiring or flying debris in the combustion chamber. Can lead to engine damage.
Recommendation: Check for the correct plug heat range, over-advanced ignition timing, lean fuel mixture, insufficient engine cooling and lack of lubrication.

ASH DEPOSITS
Symptoms: Light brown deposits encrusted on the side or center electrodes or both. Derived from oil and/or fuel additives. Excessive amounts may mask the spark, causing misfiring and hesitation during acceleration.
Recommendation: If excessive deposits accumulate over a short time or low mileage, install new valve guide seals to prevent seepage of oil into the combustion chambers. Also try changing gasoline brands.

HIGH SPEED GLAZING
Symptoms: Insulator has yellowish, glazed appearance. Indicates that combustion chamber temperatures have risen suddenly during hard acceleration. Normal deposits melt to form a conductive coating. Causes misfiring at high speeds.
Recommendation: Install new plugs. Consider using a colder plug if driving habits warrant.

OIL DEPOSITS
Symptoms: Oily coating caused by poor oil control. Oil is leaking past worn valve guides or piston rings into the combustion chamber. Causes hard starting, misfiring and hesitation.
Recommendation: Correct the mechanical condition with necessary repairs and install new plugs.

DETONATION
Symptoms: Insulators may be cracked or chipped. Improper gap setting techniques can also result in a fractured insulator tip. Can lead to piston damage.
Recommendation: Make sure the fuel anti-knock values meet engine requirements. Use care when setting the gaps on new plugs. Avoid lugging the engine.

GAP BRIDGING
Symptoms: Combustion deposits lodge between the electrodes. Heavy deposits accumulate and bridge the electrode gap. The plug ceases to fire, resulting in a dead cylinder.
Recommendation: Locate the faulty plug and remove the deposits from between the electrodes.

MECHANICAL DAMAGE
Symptoms: May be caused by a foreign object in the combustion chamber or the piston striking an incorrect reach (too long) plug. Causes a dead cylinder and could result in piston damage.
Recommendation: Repair the mechanical damage. Remove the foreign object from the engine and/or install the correct reach plug.

CONTENTS

QUICK REFERENCE DATA . . . . **IX**

CHAPTER ONE **1**
GENERAL INFORMATION

    Manual organization
    Warnings, cautions and notes
    Safety
    VIN numbers
    Fasteners
    Shop supplies
    Tools
    Precision measuring tools
    Electrical system fundamentals
    Basic service methods
    Storage
    Specifications

CHAPTER TWO **32**
TROUBLESHOOTING

    Water damage
    Engine operating requirements
    Engine will not start
    Poor idle speed performance
    Poor medium and high speed performance
    Electrical testing
    Starting system
    Charging system
    Ignition system
    Lighting system
    Fuel system
    Engine overheating
    Engine
    Engine noises
    Cylinder leakdown test
    Clutch
    Transmission
    Final drive
    Handling
    Frame noise
    Brakes

CHAPTER THREE 56
LUBRICATION, MAINTENANCE AND TUNE-UP

Pre-ride check list
Maintenance schedule
Tires and wheels
Battery
Engine oil and filter
Final drive oil
General lubrication
Air and fuel system
Brake system
Clutch adjustment
Cables
Spark arrestor service
Suspension
Fastener inspection
Valve clearance
Engine compression test
Spark plug
Ignition timing inspection
Idle speed adjustment
Specifications

CHAPTER FOUR 85
ENGINE TOP END

Cylinder head cover
Rocker arms, cylinder head and pushrods
Valves and valve components
Cylinder
Piston and piston rings
Camshaft
Specifications

CHAPTER FIVE 116
ENGINE LOWER END

Engine removal/installation
Oil cooler
Alternator cover
Flywheel and starter gears
Gearshift linkage
Oil pump
Oil screen and strainer
Crankcase and crankshaft
Engine break-in
Specifications

CHAPTER SIX 151
CLUTCH AND PRIMARY DRIVE GEAR

Clutch cover
Clutch release mechanism
Centrifugal clutch and primary drive gear
Change clutch
Specifications

CHAPTER SEVEN 169
TRANSMISSION AND INTERNAL SHIFT MECHANISM

Transmission overhaul
Reverse idle gear assembly
Transmission inspection
Internal shift mechanism
Reverse selector cable replacement
Specifications

CHAPTER EIGHT 183
FUEL, AIR AND EXHAUST SYSTEMS

    Carburetor
    Carburetor adjustments
    Throttle housing
    Throttle cable replacement
    Choke cable replacement

    Fuel tank
    Fuel valve
    Air box
    Exhaust system
    Specifications

CHAPTER NINE 202
ELECTRICAL SYSTEM

    Electrical component replacement
    Electrical connectors
    Battery negative terminal
    Charging system
    Alternator
    Ignition system
    Starter

    Starter relay
    Diode
    Lighting system
    Switches
    Fuse
    Specifications

CHAPTER TEN 223
WHEELS, HUBS AND TIRES

    Front wheel
    Front hub
    Rear wheel

    Rear hub
    Tires
    Specifications

CHAPTER ELEVEN 234
FRONT SUSPENSION AND STEERING

    Handlebar
    Steering shaft
    Tie rods
    Steering knuckle

    Control arms
    Ball joint replacement
    Shock absorbers
    Specifications

CHAPTER TWELVE 248
REAR AXLE, SUSPENSION AND FINAL DRIVE

    Shock absorber
    Rear axle
    Final drive

    Driveshaft
    Swing arm
    Specifications

CHAPTER THIRTEEN 265
BRAKES

    Brake service
    Front brake pads
    Front brake caliper
    Front master cylinder
    Brake hose replacement
    Brake fluid draining

    Brake bleeding
    Rear brake drum
    Rear brake pedal and cable
    Rear brake lever/parking brake cable
    Specifications

CHAPTER FOURTEEN 290
BODY

    Retaining clips
    Retaining tabs
    Seat
    Side covers
    Fuel tank cover

    Front fender
    Front and rear guards
    Rear fender
    Footpegs and mud guards
    Handlebar cover

SUPPLEMENT
2006-2012 MODEL SERVICE INFORMATION 297

    Brake light switch adjustment
    Clutch lever adjustment
    Reverse selector cable adjustment
    Gearshift linkage
    Clutch release mechanism
    Clutch cover
    Clutch lifter arm

    Front center cover
    Front fender
    Fuel tank cover
    Rear fender
    Rear guard
    Handlebar cover
    Mud guards and footpegs

INDEX 310

WIRING DIAGRAMS 316

QUICK REFERENCE DATA

ATV INFORMATION

MODEL: _____ YEAR: _____

VIN NUMBER: _____

ENGINE SERIAL NUMBER: _____

CARBURETOR SERIAL NUMBER OR I.D. MARK: _____

TIRE PRESSURE* AND SIZE

Front tire	
Size	AT22 × 7-10
Manufacturer	Dunlop KT 171
Minimum tread depth	4 mm (0.16 in.)
Rear tire	
Size	AT22 × 10-9
Manufacturer	Dunlop KT 175
Minimum tread depth	4 mm (0.16 in.)
Inflation pressure (cold)*	
Standard	
Front	30 kPa (4.4 psi)
Rear	20 kPa (2.9 psi)
Minimum	
Front	26 kPa (3.8 psi)
Rear	17 kPa (2.5 psi)
With cargo	
Front	30 kPa (4.4 psi)
Rear	20 kPa (2.9 psi)
Maximum	
Front	34 kPa (5.0 psi)
Rear	23 kPa (3.3 psi)

*Tire inflation pressure for original equipment tires. Aftermarket tires may require different inflation pressures.

RECOMMENDED LUBRICANTS AND FLUIDS

Fuel	
Octane	Regular unleaded
Tank capacity w/reserve	
2001-2007 models	10.2 L (2.7 gal.)
2008-on models	9.5 L (2.5 gal.)
Tank reserve capacity	
2001-2007 models	2.5 L (0.66 gal.)
2008-on models	2.6 L (0.69 gal.)
Engine oil	
Grade	
2001-2005 models	API SF or SG
2006-on models	API SG or higher, or JASO MA
	(continued)

RECOMMENDED LUBRICANTS AND FLUIDS (continued)

Engine oil (continued)	
Viscosity	
2001-2005 models	10W-40
2006-on models	10W-30
Capacity	
Oil Change	1.6 L (1.7 qt.)
Disassembly	1.8 L (1.9 qt.)
Brake fluid	DOT 3 or DOT 4
Cooling system	Air cooled
Final drive oil	
Grade	Hypoid gear oil SAE 80
Capacity	
Oil change	80 ml (2.7 oz.)
After disassembly	100 ml (3.4 oz.)

MAINTENANCE AND TUNE-UP SPECIFICATIONS

Battery	
Capacity	12V-8 Ah
Current draw (maximum)	1 mA
Voltage	
Fully charged	13.0-13.2 V
Needs charging	Less than 12.3 V
Charge current	
Normal	0.9 A/5-10h
Quick*	4.0 A/1.0 h
Spark plug	
Standard	NGK DPR8EA-9 or ND X24EPR-U9
Cold climate (5° C/41° F)	NGK DPR8EA-9 or ND X24EPR-U9
For extended high-speed operation	NGK DPR8EA-9 or ND X24EPR-U9
Spark plug gap	0.8-0.9 mm (0.031-0.035 in.)
Ignition timing	14° BTDC @ 1400 rpm
Idle speed	1300-1500 rpm
Valve clearance	
Intake	0.13 mm (0.005 in.)
Exhaust	0.13 mm (0.005 in.)
Cylinder compression	1275 kPa (185 psi) @ 800 rpm

* Perform a quick charge only in an emergency. Excessive charging amperage can damage the battery.

MAINTENANCE AND TUNE-UP TORQUE SPECIFICATIONS

Item	N•m	in.-lb.	ft.-lb.
Brake bleed valve	6	53	–
Brake hose banjo bolt	34	–	25
Engine oil drain plug	25	–	18
Final drive drain bolt	12	106	–
Oil check bolt	12	106	–
Oil fill cap	12	106	–
Front hub nut	78	–	58
Rear hub nut	137	–	101
Spark plug	18-22	–	13-16
Tie rod locknut	54	–	40
Timing hole cap	10	88	–
Valve adjuster locknut	17	–	12
Wheel nut	64	–	47

CHAPTER ONE

NOTE: Refer to the Supplement at the back of this manual for procedures unique to 2006-on models.

GENERAL INFORMATION

This detailed and comprehensive manual covers the Honda TRX250EX Sportrax and TRX250X from 2001-2012.

The text provides complete information on maintenance, tune-up, repair and overhaul. Hundreds of photographs and illustrations, created during the complete disassembly of the ATV, guide the reader through every job. All procedures are in step-by-step format and designed for the reader who may be working on the machine for the first time.

MANUAL ORGANIZATION

A shop manual is a tool, and as in all Clymer manuals, the chapters are thumb-tabbed for easy reference. Main headings are listed in the table of contents and index. Frequently used specifications and capacities from the tables at the end of each chapter are listed in the *Quick Reference Data* section at the front of the manual. Specifications and capacities are provided in U.S. Standard and metric units of measure.

During some of the procedures there may be references to headings in other chapters or sections of the manual. When a specific heading is called out in a step it is *italicized* as it appears in the manual. If a sub-heading is indicated as being "in this section," it is located within the same main heading. For example, the sub-heading *Handling Gasoline Safely* is located within the main heading SAFETY.

This chapter provides general information on shop safety, tools and their usage, service fundamentals and shop supplies. General vehicle specifications are in **Tables 1-8** at the end of the chapter.

Chapter Two provides methods for quick and accurate diagnosis of problems. Troubleshooting procedures present typical symptoms and logical methods to pinpoint and repair the problem.

Chapter Three explains all routine maintenance necessary to keep the vehicle running well.

Subsequent chapters describe specific systems, such as engine, transmission, clutch, drive system, fuel system, suspension, brakes and body.

WARNINGS, CAUTIONS AND NOTES

The terms WARNING, CAUTION and NOTE have specific meanings in this manual.

A WARNING emphasizes areas where injury or death could result from negligence. Mechanical damage may also occur. WARNINGS *are to be taken seriously.*

A CAUTION emphasizes areas where equipment damage could result. Disregarding a CAUTION could cause permanent mechanical damage, though injury is unlikely.

A NOTE provides additional information to make a step or procedure easier or clearer. Disregarding a NOTE could cause inconvenience, but would not cause equipment damage or injury.

SAFETY

Professional mechanics can work for years and never sustain an injury or mishap. Follow these guidelines and practice common sense to safely service the vehicle.

1. Do not operate the vehicle in an enclosed area. The exhaust gasses contain carbon monoxide, an odorless, colorless and tasteless poisonous gas. Carbon monoxide levels build quickly in small enclosed areas and can cause unconsciousness and death in a short time. Make sure to properly ventilate the work area or operate the vehicle outside.
2. Never use gasoline or any extremely flammable liquid to clean parts. Refer to *Handling Gasoline Safely* and *Cleaning Parts* in this section.
3. Never smoke or use a torch in the vicinity of flammable liquids, such as gasoline or cleaning solvent.
4. If welding or brazing on the vehicle, remove the fuel tank to a safe distance at least 15 m (50 ft.) away.
5. Use the correct type and size of tools to avoid damaging fasteners.
6. Keep tools clean and in good condition. Replace or repair worn or damaged equipment.
7. When loosening a tight fastener, be guided by what would happen if the tool slips.
8. When replacing fasteners, make sure the new fasteners are the same size and strength as the originals.
9. Keep the work area clean and organized.
10. Wear eye protection *any time* the safety of the eyes is in question. This includes procedures that involve drilling, grinding, hammering, compressed air and chemicals.
11. Wear the correct clothing for the job. Tie up or cover long hair so it does not get caught in moving equipment.
12. Do not carry sharp tools in clothing pockets.
13. Always have an approved fire extinguisher available. Make sure it is rated for gasoline (Class B) and electrical (Class C) fires.
14. Do not use compressed air to clean clothes, the vehicle or work area. Debris may be blown into the eyes or skin. *Never* direct compressed air at anyone. Do not allow children to use or play with any compressed air equipment.
15. When using compressed air to dry rotating parts, hold the part so it does not rotate. Do not allow the force of the air to spin the part. The air jet is capable of rotating parts at extreme speed. The part may disintegrate or become damaged, causing injury.
16. Do not inhale the dust created by brake pad and clutch wear. These particles may contain asbestos. In addition, some types of insulating materials and gaskets may contain asbestos. Inhaling asbestos particles is hazardous to health.
17. Never work on the vehicle while someone is working under it.
18. When placing the vehicle on a stand, make sure it is secure before walking away.

Handling Gasoline Safely

Gasoline is a volatile, flammable liquid and is one of the most dangerous items in the shop. Because gasoline is used so often, many people forget it is hazardous. Only use gasoline as fuel for gasoline internal combustion engines. Keep in mind when working on the machine that gasoline is always present in the fuel tank and fuel lines. To avoid an accident when working around the fuel system, carefully observe the following:

1. Never use gasoline to clean parts. Refer to *Cleaning Parts* in this section.

GENERAL INFORMATION

2. When working on the fuel system, work outside or in a well-ventilated area.

3. Do not add fuel to the fuel tank or service the fuel system while the vehicle is near open flames, sparks or where someone is smoking. Gasoline vapor is heavier than air; it collects in low areas and is more easily ignited than liquid gasoline.

4. Allow the engine to cool completely before working on any fuel system component.

5. Do not store gasoline in glass containers. If the glass breaks, an explosion or fire may occur.

6. Immediately wipe up spilled gasoline with rags. Store the rags in a metal container with a lid until they can be properly disposed of, or place them outside in a safe place for the fuel to evaporate.

7. Do not pour water onto a gasoline fire. Water spreads the fire and makes it more difficult to put out. Use a class B, BC or ABC fire extinguisher to extinguish the fire.

8. Always turn off the engine before refueling. Do not spill fuel onto the engine or exhaust system. Do not overfill the fuel tank. Leave an air space at the top of the tank to allow room for the fuel to expand due to temperature fluctuations.

Cleaning Parts

Cleaning parts is one of the more difficult service jobs performed in the home garage. Many types of chemical cleaners and solvents are available for shop use. Most are poisonous and extremely flammable. To prevent chemical exposure, vapor buildup, fire and injury, observe each product warning label and note the following:

1. Read and observe the entire product label before using any chemical. Always know what type of chemical is being used and whether it is poisonous and/or flammable.

2. Do not use more than one type of cleaning solvent at a time. If mixing chemicals is required, measure the proper amounts according to the manufacturer.

3. Work in a well-ventilated area.

4. Wear chemical-resistant gloves.

5. Wear safety glasses.

6. If the instructions call for it, wear a vapor respirator.

7. Wash hands and arms thoroughly after cleaning parts.

8. Keep chemical products away from children and pets.

9. Thoroughly clean all oil, grease and cleaner residue from any part that must be heated.

10. Use a nylon brush when cleaning parts. Metal brushes may cause a spark.

11. When using a parts washer, only use the solvent recommended by the manufacturer. Make sure the parts washer is equipped with a metal lid that lowers in case of fire.

Warning Labels

Most manufacturers attach information and warning labels to the vehicle. These labels contain instructions that are important to safety when operating, servicing, transporting and storing the vehicle. Refer to the owner's manual for the description and location of labels. Order replacement labels from the manufacturer if they are missing or damaged.

VIN NUMBERS

Vehicle identification numbers are stamped on the frame and engine. Record these numbers in the *Quick Reference Data* section at the front of the book. Have these numbers available when ordering parts.

The frame number (**Figure 1**), or VIN number, is stamped on the front of the frame. The engine number (**Figure 2**) is stamped on the rear of the right side of the crankcase, just ahead of the drive shaft boot.

Refer to **Table 1** for VIN information.

FASTENERS

Proper fastener selection and installation is important to ensure the vehicle operates as designed and can be serviced efficiently. The choice of original equipment fasteners is not arrived at by chance. Make sure replacement fasteners meet all the same requirements as the originals.

Threaded Fasteners

Threaded fasteners secure most of the components on the vehicle. Most are tightened by turning them clockwise (right-hand threads). If the normal rotation of the component being tightened would loosen the fastener, it may have left-hand threads. If a left-hand threaded fastener is used, it is noted in the text.

Two dimensions are required to match the thread size of the fastener: the number of threads in a given distance and the outside diameter of the threads.

The two systems currently used to specify threaded fastener dimensions are the U.S. Standard system and the metric system (**Figure 3**). Pay particular attention when working with unidentified fasteners; mismatching thread types can damage threads.

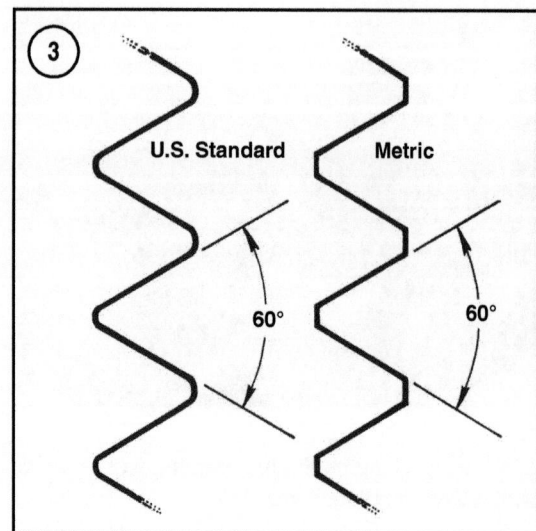

NOTE
To ensure that the fastener threads are not mismatched or cross-threaded, start all fasteners by hand. If a fastener is difficult to start or turn, determine the cause before tightening with a wrench.

The length (L, **Figure 4**), diameter (D) and distance between thread crests (pitch [T]) classify metric screws and bolts. A typical bolt may be identified by the numbers, 8 – 1.25 × 130. This indicates the bolt has a diameter of 8 mm, the distance between thread crests is 1.25 mm and the length is 130 mm. Always measure bolt length as shown in L, **Figure 4** to avoid purchasing replacements of the wrong length.

WARNING
Do not install fasteners with a strength classification lower than what was originally installed by the manufacturer. Doing so may cause equipment failure and/or damage.

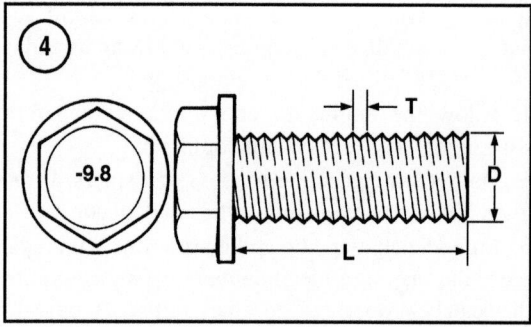

The numbers on the top of the fastener (**Figure 4**) indicate the strength of metric screws and bolts. The higher the number, the stronger the fastener. Typically, unnumbered fasteners are the weakest.

Many screws, bolts and studs are combined with nuts to secure particular components. To indicate the size of a nut, manufacturers specify the internal diameter and thread pitch.

The measurement across two flats on a nut or bolt indicates the wrench size.

Torque Specifications

The materials used in the manufacturing of the vehicle may be subjected to uneven stresses if the fasteners of the subassemblies are not installed and tightened correctly. Improperly installed fasteners or ones that became loose can cause extensive damage. It is essential to use an accurate torque wrench as described in this chapter.

GENERAL INFORMATION

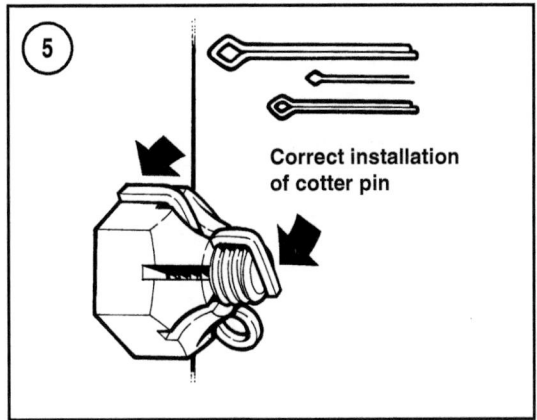

Correct installation of cotter pin

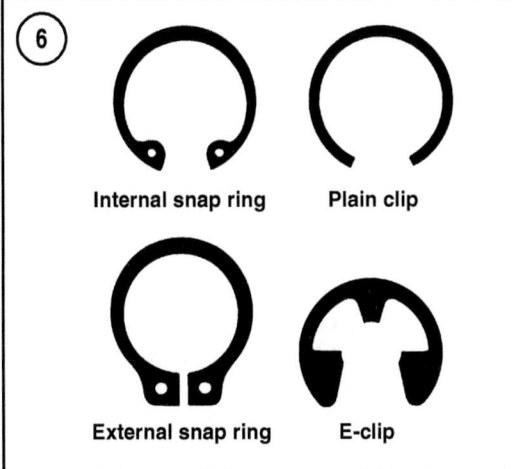

Internal snap ring   Plain clip

External snap ring   E-clip

Specifications for torque are provided in Newton-meters (N•m), foot-pounds (ft.-lb.) and inch-pounds (in.-lb.). Refer to **Table 8** for general torque specifications. To determine the torque requirement, first determine the size of the fastener as described in *Threaded Fasteners* in this section. Torque specifications for specific components are at the end of the appropriate chapters. Torque wrenches are covered in *Basic Tools* in this chapter.

Self-Locking Fasteners

Several types of bolts, screws and nuts incorporate a system that creates interference between the two fasteners. Interference is achieved in various ways, such as the nylon insert nut, or a dry adhesive coating, on the threads of a bolt.

Self-locking fasteners offer greater holding strength than standard fasteners, which improves their resistance to vibration. The materials used to form the lock become distorted after the initial installation and removal. Do not reuse or replace self-locking fasteners with standard fasteners.

Washers

The two basic types of washers are flat washers and lockwashers. Flat washers are simple discs with a hole to fit a screw or bolt. Lockwashers are used to prevent a fastener from working loose. Washers can be used as spacers and seals or can help distribute fastener load and prevent the fastener from damaging the component.

As with fasteners, when replacing washers, make sure the replacement washers are of the same design and quality.

Cotter Pins

A cotter pin is a split metal pin inserted into a hole or slot to prevent a fastener from loosening. In certain applications, such as the rear axle nut on an ATV, the fastener must be secured in this way. For these applications, a cotter pin and castellated (slotted) nut is used.

To use a cotter pin, make sure the diameter is correct for the hole in the fastener. After correctly tightening the fastener and aligning the holes, insert the cotter pin through the hole and bend the ends over the fastener (**Figure 5**). Unless instructed to do so, never loosen a tightened fastener to align the holes. If the holes do not align, tighten the fastener enough to achieve alignment.

Cotter pins are available in various diameters and lengths. Measure the length from the bottom of the head to the tip of the shortest pin.

Snap Rings and E-clips

Snap rings (**Figure 6**) are circular-shaped metal retaining clips. They are required to secure parts and gears in place on items, such as shafts, pins or rods. External-type snap rings are used to retain items on shafts. Internal-type snap rings secure parts within housing bores. In some applications, in addition to securing the component(s), snap rings of varying thickness also determine endplay. These are usually called selective snap rings.

The two basic types of snap rings are machined and stamped snap rings. Machined snap rings (**Figure 7**) can be installed in either direction because both faces have sharp edges. Stamped snap rings (**Figure 8**) are manufactured with a sharp and a rounded edge. When installing a stamped snap ring in a thrust application, install the sharp edge facing away from the part producing the thrust.

E-clips are used when it is not practical to use a snap ring. Remove E-clips with a flat blade screwdriver by prying between the shaft and E-clip. To install an E-clip, center it over the shaft groove and push or tap it into place.

Observe the following when installing snap rings:
1. Remove and install snap rings with snap ring pliers. Refer to *Basic Tools* in this chapter.
2. In some applications, it may be necessary to replace snap rings after removing them.
3. Compress or expand snap rings only enough to install them. If overly expanded, they lose their retaining ability.
4. After installing a snap ring, make sure it seats completely.
5. Wear eye protection when removing and installing snap rings.

SHOP SUPPLIES

Lubricants and Fluids

Periodic lubrication helps ensure a long service life for any type of equipment. Using the correct type of lubricant is as important as performing the lubrication service, although in an emergency the wrong type is better than not using one. The following section describes the types of lubricants most often required. Make sure to follow the manufacturer's recommendations for lubricant types.

Engine oils

Engine oil for four-stroke ATV engine use is classified by three standards: the American Petroleum Institute (API) service classification, the Society of Automotive Engineers (SAE) viscosity rating and the Japanese Automobile Standards Organization (JASO) T 903 Standard rating.

The API and SAE information is on all oil container labels. The JASO information is found on oil containers sold by the oil manufacturer specifically

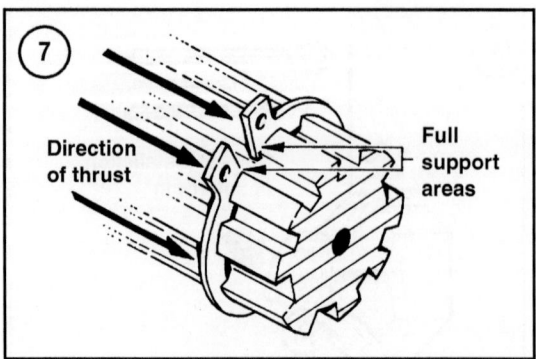

for ATV and motorcycle use. Two letters indicate the API service classification. The number or sequence of numbers and letter (10W-40 for example) is the oil's viscosity rating. The API service classification and the SAE viscosity index are not indications of oil quality.

The API service classification indicates that the oil meets specific lubrication standards. The first letter in the classification S indicates the oil is for gasoline engines. The second letter indicates the standard the oil satisfies.

The JASO certification label identifies two separate oil classifications and a registration number to ensure the oil has passed all JASO certification standards for use in four-stroke ATV and motorcycle engines. The classifications are: MA (high-friction applications) and MB (low-friction applications). Only oil that has passed JASO standards can carry the JASO certification label.

NOTE
*Refer to **Engine Oil and Filter** in Chapter Three for more information on API, SAE and JASO ratings.*

Always use oil with a classification recommended by the manufacturer. Using oil with a different classification can cause engine damage.

Viscosity is an indication of the oil's thickness. Thin oils have a lower number and thick oils have a higher number. Engine oils fall into the 5- to 50-weight range for single-grade oils.

Most manufacturers recommend multi-grade oil. These oils perform efficiently across a wide range of operating conditions. Multi-grade oils are identified by a W after the first number, which indicates the low-temperature viscosity.

Engine oils are most commonly mineral (petroleum) based, but synthetic and semi-synthetic types

GENERAL INFORMATION

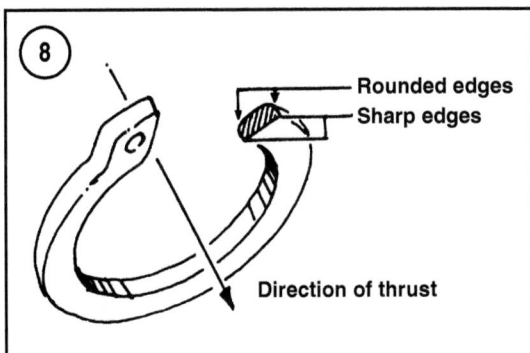

are used more frequently. When selecting engine oil, follow the manufacturer's recommendation for type, classification and viscosity.

Greases

Grease is lubricating oil with added thickening agents. The National Lubricating Grease Institute (NLGI) grades grease. Grades range from No. 000 to No. 6, with No. 6 being the thickest. Typical multipurpose grease is NLGI No. 2. For specific applications, manufacturers may recommend water-resistant type grease or one with an additive, such as molybdenum disulfide (MoS_2).

Brake fluid

Brake fluid is the hydraulic fluid used to transmit hydraulic pressure (force) to the wheel brakes. It is classified by the Department of Transportation (DOT). Current designations for brake fluid are DOT 3, DOT 4 and DOT 5. This classification appears on the fluid container.

Each type of brake fluid has its own definite characteristics. Do not intermix different types because this may cause brake system failure. DOT 5 brake fluid is silicone based and is not compatible with other brake fluids or in systems for which it was not designed. Mixing DOT 5 fluid with other fluids may cause brake system failure. When adding brake fluid, *only* use the fluid recommended by the manufacturer.

Brake fluid damages any plastic, painted or plated surface it contacts. Use extreme care when working with brake fluid and remove any spills immediately with soap and water.

Hydraulic brake systems require clean and moisture-free brake fluid. Never reuse brake fluid. Keep containers and reservoirs properly sealed.

WARNING
Never put a mineral-based (petroleum) oil into the brake system. Mineral oil causes rubber parts in the system to swell and break apart, causing complete brake failure.

Coolant

Coolant is a mixture of water and antifreeze used to dissipate engine heat. Ethylene glycol is the most common form of antifreeze. Check the manufacturer's recommendations when selecting antifreeze. Most require one specifically designed for use in aluminum engines. These types of antifreeze have additives that inhibit corrosion. Only mix antifreeze with distilled water. Impurities in tap water may damage internal cooling system passages.

Cleaners, Degreasers and Solvents

Many chemicals are available to remove oil, grease and other residue from the vehicle. Before using cleaning solvents, consider how they are used and disposed of, particularly if they are not water-soluble. Local ordinances may require special procedures for the disposal of many types of cleaning chemicals. Refer to *Safety* in this chapter.

Use brake parts cleaner to clean brake system components because it leaves no residue. Use electrical contact cleaner to clean electrical connections and components without leaving any residue. Carburetor cleaner is a powerful solvent used to remove fuel deposits and varnish from fuel system components. Use this cleaner carefully because it may damage finishes.

Generally, degreasers are strong cleaners used to remove heavy accumulations of grease from engine and frame components.

Most solvents are designed to be used with a parts washing cabinet for individual component cleaning. For safety, use only nonflammable or high flash point solvents.

Gasket Sealant

Gasket sealant is used in combination with a gasket or seal. In other applications, such as between crankcase halves, only a sealant is used. Follow the manufacturer's recommendation when using a sealant. Use extreme care when choosing a sealant different from the type originally recommended. Choose sealant based on its resistance to heat, various fluids and sealing capabilities.

A common sealant is room temperature vulcanization sealant, or RTV. This sealant cures at room temperature over a specific time period. This allows the repositioning of components without damaging gaskets.

Moisture in the air causes the RTV sealant to cure. Always install the tube cap as soon as possible after applying RTV sealant. RTV sealant has a limited shelf life and does not cure properly if the shelf life has expired. Keep partial tubes sealed and discard them if they have surpassed the expiration date.

Applying RTV sealant

Clean all old gasket residue from the mating surfaces. Remove all gasket material from blind threaded holes to avoid inaccurate bolt torque. Spray the mating surfaces with aerosol parts cleaner, and wipe with a lint-free cloth. The area must be clean for the sealant to adhere.

Apply RTV sealant in a continuous bead 2-3 mm (0.08-0.12 in.) thick. Circle all the fastener holes unless otherwise specified. Do not allow any sealant to enter these holes. Assemble and tighten the fasteners to the specified torque within the time frame recommended by the sealant manufacturer.

Gasket Remover

Aerosol gasket remover can help remove stubborn gaskets. This product can speed up the removal process and prevent damage to the mating surface that may be caused by using a scraping tool. Most of these types of products are very caustic. Follow the gasket remover manufacturer's instructions for use.

Threadlocking Compound

A threadlocking compound is a fluid applied to the threads of fasteners. After tightening the fastener, the fluid dries and becomes a solid filler between the threads. This makes it difficult for the fastener to work loose from vibration or heat expansion and contraction. Some threadlocking compounds also provide a seal against fluid leaks.

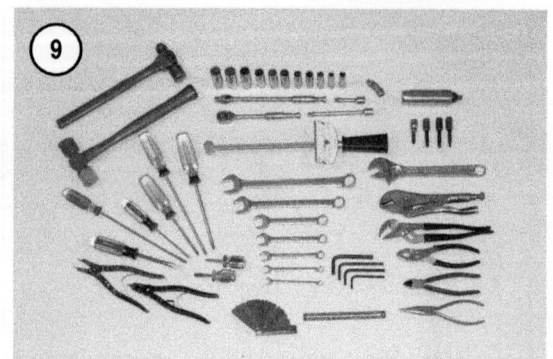

Before applying a threadlocking compound, remove any old compound from both thread areas and clean them with aerosol parts cleaner. Use the compound sparingly. Excess fluid can run into adjoining parts.

CAUTION
Threadlocking compounds are anaerobic and stress, crack and attack most plastics. Use caution when using these products in areas where there are plastic components.

Threadlocking compounds are available in a wide range of compounds for various strength, temperature and repair applications. Follow the manufacturer's recommendations regarding compound selection.

TOOLS

Most of the procedures in this manual can be carried out with simple hand tools and test equipment familiar to the home mechanic. Always use the correct tools for the job at hand. Keep tools organized and clean. Store them in a tool chest with related tools organized together.

Quality tools are essential. The best are constructed of high-strength alloy steel. These tools are light, easy-to-use and resistant to wear. Their working surface is devoid of sharp edges and carefully polished. They have an easy-to-clean finish and are comfortable to use. Quality tools are a good investment.

Some of the procedures in this manual specify special tools. In many cases the tool is illustrated in use. In some cases it may be possible to use a suitable substitute or fabricate a suitable replacement. However, the specialized equipment or expertise may make it impractical for the home mechanic to do the procedure. When necessary, such operations

GENERAL INFORMATION

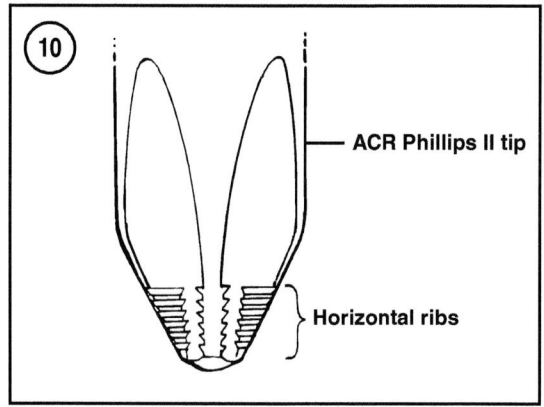

ACR Phillips II tip
Horizontal ribs

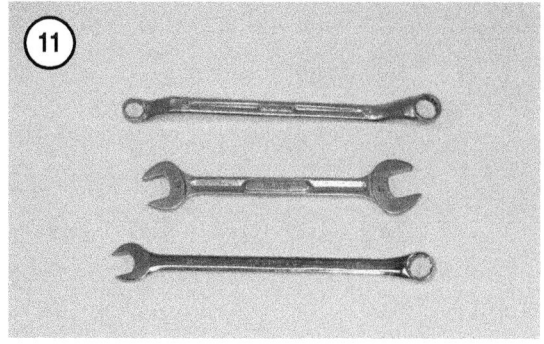

come with the recommendation to have a dealership or specialist perform the task. It may be less expensive to have a professional perform these jobs, especially when considering the cost of equipment.

The manufacturer's part number is provided for many of the tools mentioned in this manual. These part numbers are correct at the time of the first edition publication. The publisher cannot guarantee the part numbers or tools listed in this manual will be available in the future.

When purchasing tools to perform the procedures covered in this manual, consider the tool's potential frequency of use. If a tool kit is just now being started, consider purchasing a basic tool set (**Figure 9**). These sets are available in many tool combinations and offer substantial savings when compared to individually purchased tools. As work experience grows and tasks become more complicated, specialized tools can be added.

Screwdrivers

Screwdrivers of various lengths and types are mandatory for the simplest tool kit. The two basic types are the slotted tip (flat blade) and the Phillips tip. These are available in sets that often include an assortment of tip sizes and shaft lengths.

As with all tools, use a screwdriver designed for the job. Make sure the size of the tip conforms to the size and shape of the fastener. Use them only for driving screws. Never use a screwdriver for prying or chiseling metal. Repair or replace worn or damaged screwdrivers. A worn tip may damage the fastener, making it difficult to remove.

NOTE
Another way to prevent camout and to increase the grip of a Phillips screwdriver is to apply valve grinding compound or Permatex Screw & Socket Gripper onto the screwdriver tip. After loosening/tightening the screw, clean the screw recess to prevent engine oil contamination.

Phillips-head screws are often damaged by incorrectly fitting screwdrivers. Quality Phillips screwdrivers are manufactured with their crosshead tip machined to Phillips Screw Company specifications. Poor quality or damaged Phillips screwdrivers can back out (camout) and round over the screw head. In addition, weak or soft screw materials can make removal difficult.

The best type of screwdriver to use on Phillips screws is the ACR Phillips II screwdriver, patented by the Phillips Screw Company. ACR stands for the horizontal anti-camout ribs found on the driving faces or flutes of the screwdriver's tip (**Figure 10**). ACR Phillips II screwdrivers were designed as part of a manufacturing drive system to be used with ACR Phillips II screws, but they work well on all common Phillips screws. A number of tool companies offer ACR Phillips II screwdrivers in different tip sizes and interchangeable bits to fit screwdriver bit holders.

Wrenches

Open-end, box-end and combination wrenches (**Figure 11**) are available in a variety of types and sizes.

The number stamped on the wrench refers to the distance between the work areas. This size must match the size of the fastener head.

The box-end wrench grips the fastener on all sides, reducing the chance of the tool slipping. The box-end wrench is designed with either a 6- or 12-point opening. For stubborn or damaged fasteners, the 6-point provides superior holding because it contacts the fastener across a wider area at all six edges. For general use, the 12-point works well. It allows the wrench to be removed and reinstalled without moving the handle over such a wide arc.

An open-end wrench is fast and works best in areas with limited overhead access. It contacts the fastener at only two points and is subject to slipping if under heavy force or if the tool or fastener is worn. A box-end wrench is preferred in most instances, especially when breaking loose and applying the final tightness to a fastener.

The combination wrench has a box-end on one end and an open-end on the other. This combination makes it a convenient tool.

Adjustable Wrenches

An adjustable wrench, or Crescent wrench (**Figure 12**), can fit nearly any nut or bolt head that has clear access around its entire perimeter. An adjustable wrench is best used as a backup wrench to keep a large nut or bolt from turning while the other end is being loosened or tightened with a box-end or socket wrench.

Adjustable wrenches contact the fastener at only two points, which makes them more subject to slipping off the fastener. Because one jaw is adjustable and may become loose, this shortcoming is aggravated. Make sure the solid jaw is the one transmitting the force.

Socket Wrenches, Ratchets and Handles

Sockets that attach to a ratchet handle (**Figure 13**) are available with 6-point (A, **Figure 14**) or 12-point (B, **Figure 14**) openings and different drive sizes. The drive size indicates the size of the square hole that accepts the ratchet handle. The number stamped on the socket is the size of the work area and must match the fastener head.

As with wrenches, a 6-point socket provides superior-holding ability, while a 12-point socket needs to be moved only half as far to reposition it on the fastener.

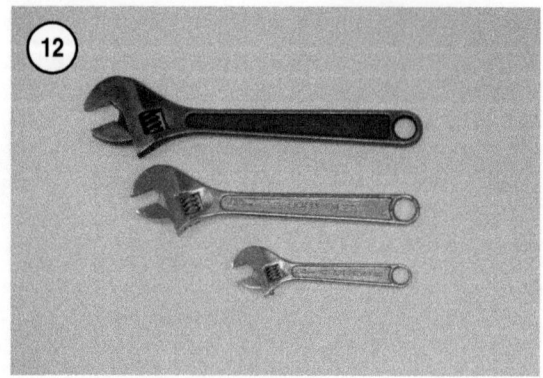

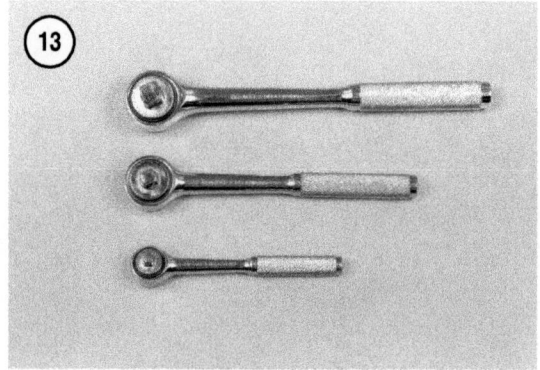

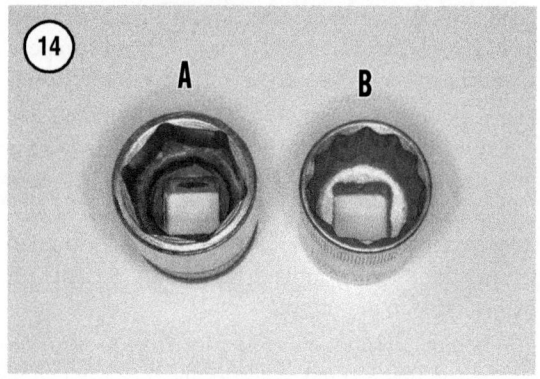

WARNING
Do not use hand sockets with air or impact tools because they may shatter and cause injury. Always wear eye protection when using impact or air tools.

Sockets are designated for either hand or impact use. Impact sockets are made of thicker material for more durability. Compare the size and wall thickness of a 19-mm hand socket (A, **Figure 15**) and the 19-mm impact socket (B). Use impact sockets when

GENERAL INFORMATION

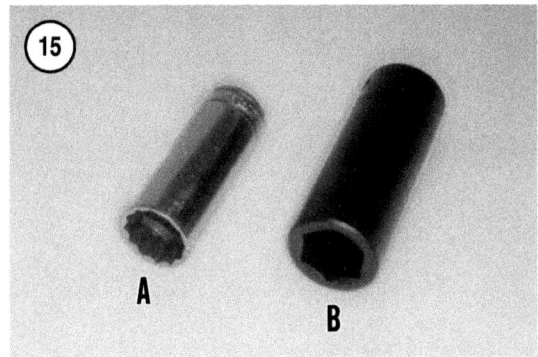

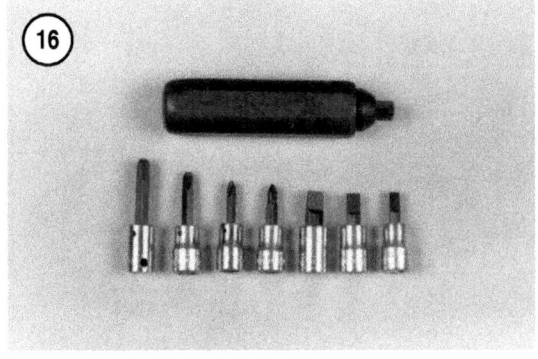

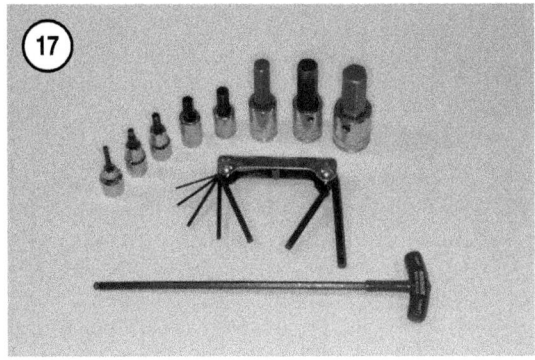

Impact Drivers

WARNING
Do not use hand sockets with air or impact tools because they may shatter and cause injury. Always wear eye protection when using impact or air tools.

An impact driver provides extra force for removing fasteners by converting the impact of a hammer into a turning motion. This makes it possible to remove stubborn fasteners without damaging them. Impact drivers and interchangeable bits (**Figure 16**) are available from most tool suppliers. When using a socket with an impact driver, make sure the socket is designed for impact use. Refer to *Socket Wrenches, Ratchets and Handles* in this section.

Allen Wrenches

Use Allen, or setscrew wrenches, (**Figure 17**) on fasteners with hexagonal recesses in the fastener head. These wrenches are available in L-shaped bar, socket and T-handle types. A metric set is required when working on most ATVs. Allen bolts are sometimes called socket bolts.

Torque Wrenches

Use a torque wrench with a socket, torque adapter or similar extension to tighten a fastener to a measured torque. Torque wrenches come in several drive sizes (1/4, 3/8, 1/2 and 3/4) and have various methods of reading the torque value. The drive size indicates the size of the square drive that accepts the socket, adapter or extension. Common methods of reading the torque value are the deflecting beam, the dial indicator and the audible click (**Figure 18**).

When choosing a torque wrench, consider the torque range, drive size and accuracy. The torque specifications in this manual provide an indication of the range required.

A torque wrench is a precision tool that must be properly cared for to remain accurate. Store torque wrenches in cases or separate padded drawers within a toolbox. Follow the manufacturer's instructions for their care and calibration.

using an impact driver or air tools. Use hand sockets with hand-driven attachments.

Various handles are available for sockets. Use the speed handle for fast operation. Flexible ratchet heads in varying lengths allow the socket to be turned with varying force and at odd angles. Extension bars allow the socket setup to reach difficult areas. The ratchet is the most versatile. It allows the user to install or remove the nut without removing the socket.

Sockets combined with any number of drivers make them undoubtedly the fastest, safest and most convenient tool for fastener removal and installation.

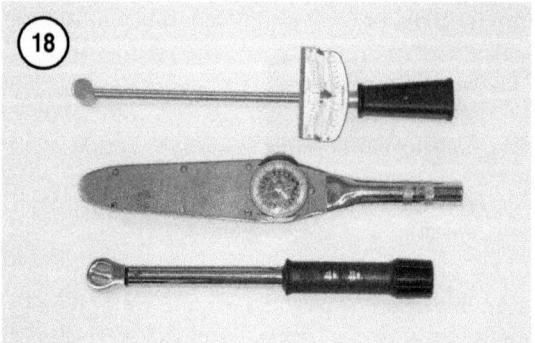

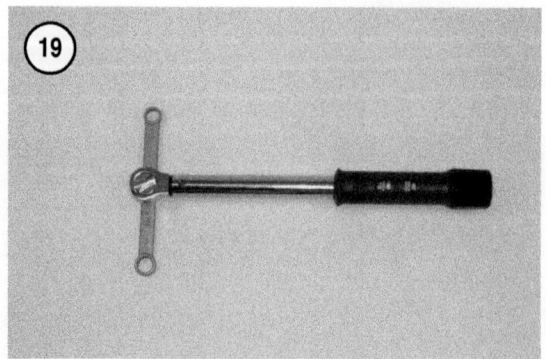

TORQUE WRENCH EFFECTIVE LEVER LENGTH

L + A = Effective length

L = Effective length

No calculation needed

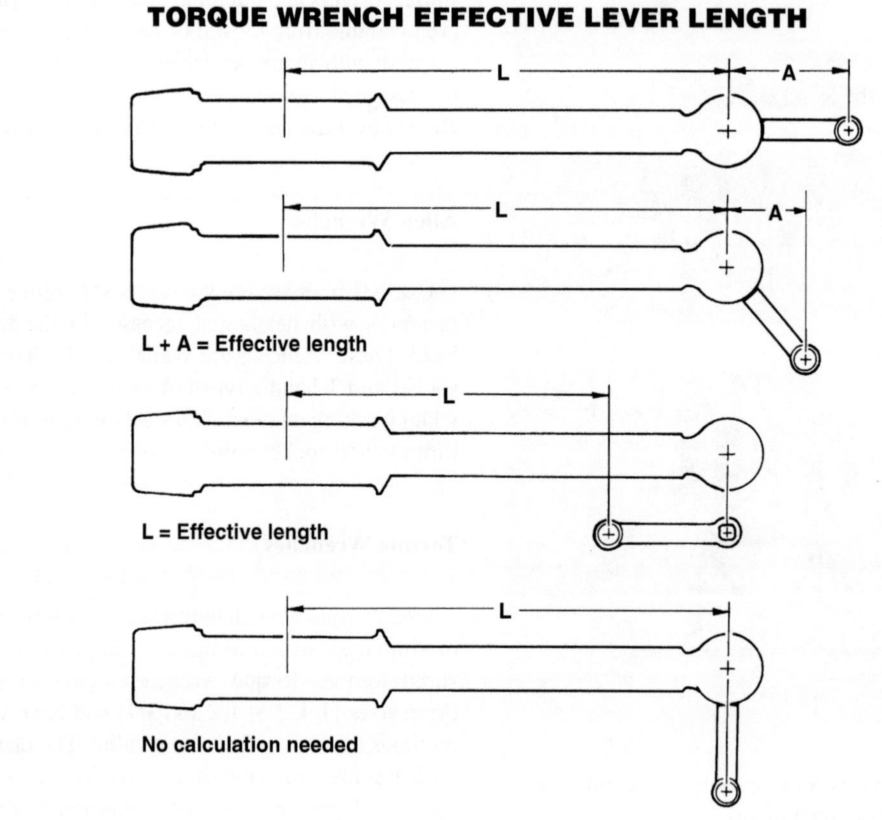

Torque Adapters

Torque adapters or extensions extend or reduce the reach of a torque wrench. The torque adapter shown in **Figure 19** is used to tighten a fastener that cannot be reached because of the size of the torque wrench head, drive and socket. If a torque adapter changes the effective lever length (**Figure 20**), the torque reading on the wrench will not equal the actual torque applied to the fastener. It is necessary to recalibrate the torque setting on the wrench to compensate for the change of lever length. When using a torque adapter at a right angle to the drive head, calibration is not required because the effective length has not changed.

To recalculate a torque reading when using a torque adapter, use the following formula and refer to **Figure 20**:

GENERAL INFORMATION

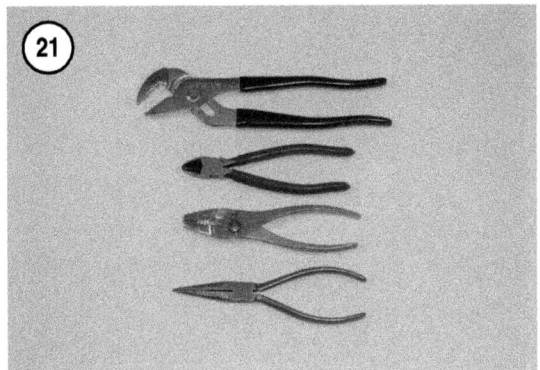

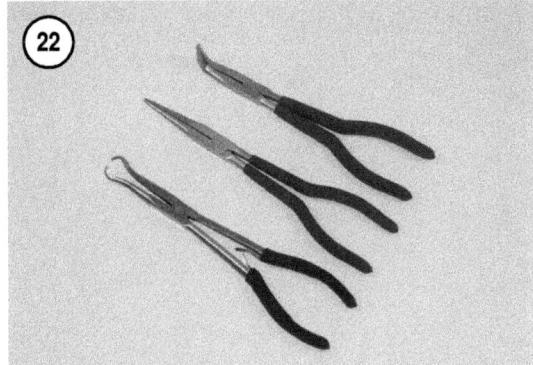

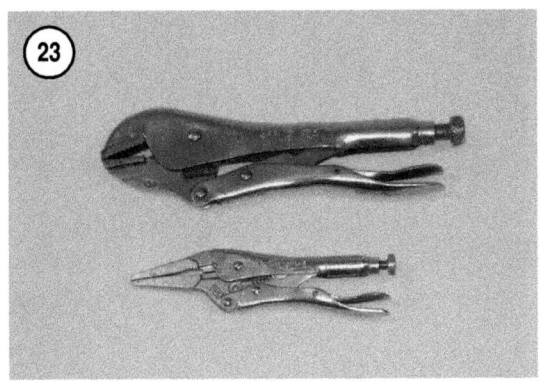

$$TW = \frac{TA \times L}{L + A}$$

TW is the torque setting or dial reading on the wrench.

TA is the torque specification and the actual amount of torque that is applied to the fastener.

A is the amount the adapter increases (or in some cases reduces) the effective lever length as measured along the centerline of the torque wrench.

L is the lever length of the wrench as measured from the center of the drive to the center of the grip.

The effective length is the sum of L and A.
Example:
TA = 20 ft.-lb.
A = 3 in.
L = 14 in.
$$TW = \frac{20 \times 14}{14 + 3} = \frac{280}{17} = 16.5 \text{ ft.-lb.}$$

In this example, the torque wrench would be set to the recalculated torque value (TW = 16.5 ft.-lb.). When using a beam-type wrench, tighten the fastener until the pointer aligns with 16.5 ft.-lb. In this example, although the torque wrench is preset to 16.5 ft.-lb., the actual torque is 20 ft.-lb.

Pliers

Pliers come in a wide range of types and sizes. Pliers are used for holding, cutting, bending and crimping. Do not use them to turn fasteners. **Figure 21** and **Figure 22** show several types of useful pliers. Each design has a specialized function. Slip-joint pliers are general-purpose pliers used for gripping and bending. Diagonal-cutting pliers are needed to cut wire and can be used to remove cotter pins. Use needlenose pliers to hold or bend small objects. Locking pliers (**Figure 23**), sometimes called Vise-Grips, are used to hold objects very tightly. They have many uses, ranging from holding two parts together, to gripping the end of a broken stud. Use caution when using locking pliers, as the sharp jaws damage the objects they hold.

Snap Ring Pliers

WARNING
Snap rings can slip and fly off when removing and installing. Also, the snap ring pliers' tips may break. Always wear eye protection when using snap ring pliers.

Snap ring pliers are specialized pliers with tips that fit into the ends of snap rings to remove and install them. Snap ring pliers (**Figure 24**) are available with a fixed action (either internal or external) or convertible (one tool works on both internal and external snap rings). They may have fixed tips or interchangeable ones of various sizes and angles. For general use, select convertible-type pliers with interchangeable tips.

Hammers

Different types of hammers (**Figure 25**) are available to fit a number of applications. Use a ball-peen hammer to strike another tool, such as a punch or chisel. Use soft-faced hammers when a metal object must be struck without damaging it. Never use a metal-faced hammer on engine and suspension components because damage occurs in most cases.

Always wear eye protection when using hammers. Make sure the hammer face is in good condition and the handle is not cracked. Select the correct hammer for the job and make sure to strike the object squarely. Do not use the handle or the side of the hammer to strike an object.

PRECISION MEASURING TOOLS

The ability to accurately measure components is essential to perform many of the procedures described in this manual. Equipment is manufactured to close tolerances, and obtaining consistently accurate measurements is essential to determine which components require replacement or further service.

Each type of measuring instrument is designed to measure a dimension with a certain degree of accuracy and within a certain range. When selecting the measuring tool, make sure it is applicable to the task.

As with all tools, measuring tools provide the best results if cared for properly. Improper use can damage the tool and cause inaccurate results. If any measurement is questionable, verify the measurement using another tool. A standard gauge is usually provided with micrometers to check accuracy and calibrate the tool if necessary.

Precision measurements can vary according to the experience of the person performing the procedure. Accurate results are only possible if the mechanic possesses a feel for using the tool. Heavy-handed use of measuring tools produces less accurate results. Hold the tool gently by the fingertips to easily feel the point at which the tool contacts the object. This feel for the equipment produces more accurate measurements and reduces the risk of damaging the tool or component. Refer to the following sections for specific measuring tools.

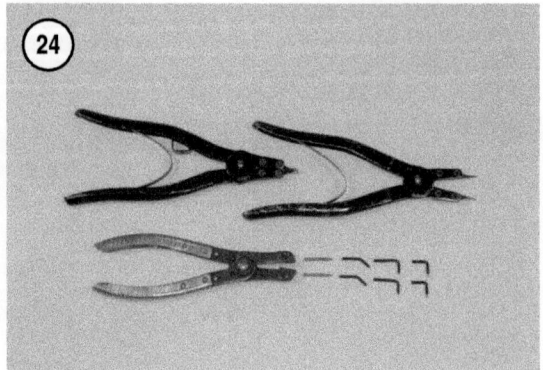

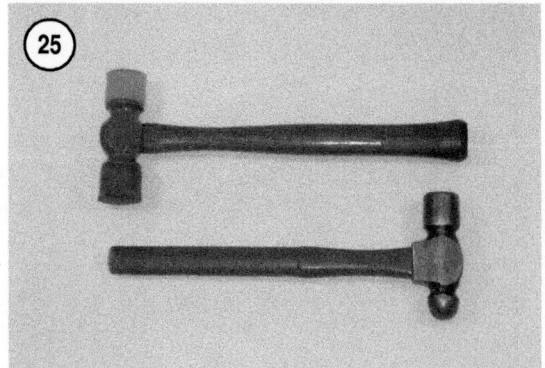

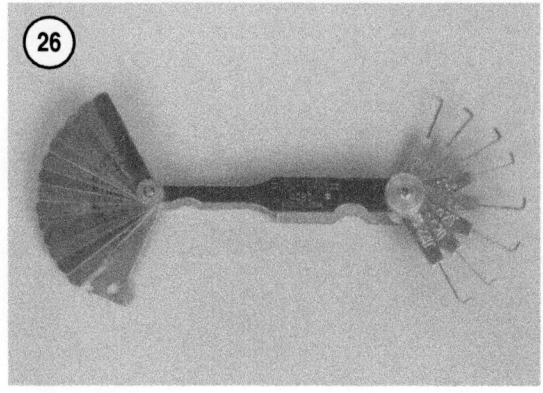

Feeler Gauge

Use feeler or thickness gauges (**Figure 26**) for measuring the distance between two surfaces. A feeler gauge set consists of an assortment of steel strips of graduated thicknesses. Each blade is marked with its thickness. Blades can be of various lengths and angles for different procedures. A common use for a feeler gauge is to measure valve clearance. Use wire (round) type gauges to measure spark plug gap.

GENERAL INFORMATION

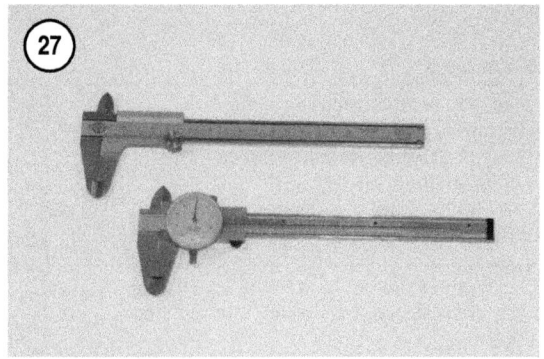

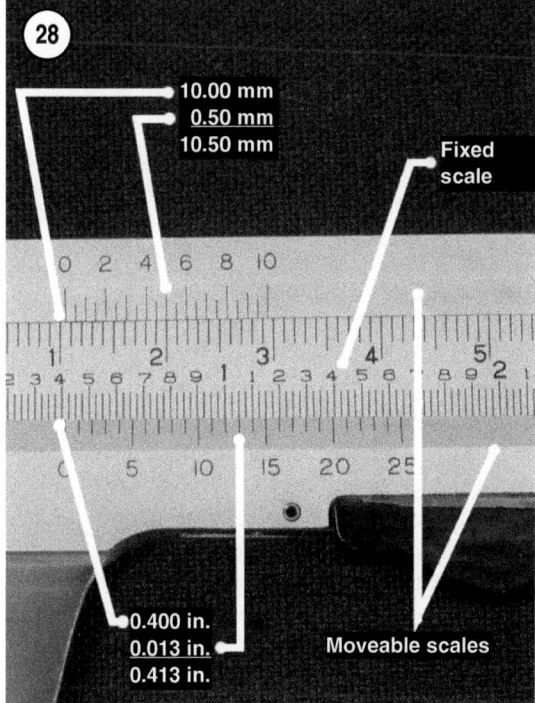

the tool and the object being measured. Never force the caliper to close around an object. Close the caliper around the highest point so it can be removed with a slight drag. Some calipers require calibration. Always refer to the manufacturer's instructions when using a new or unfamiliar caliper.

To learn how to read a vernier caliper, refer to **Figure 28**. The fixed scale is marked in 1-mm increments. Ten individual lines on the fixed scale equal 1 cm. The movable scale is marked in 0.05 mm (hundredth) increments. To obtain a reading, establish the first number by the location of the 0 line on the movable scale in relation to the first line to the left on the fixed scale. In this example, the number is 10 mm. To determine the next number, note which of the lines on the movable scale align with a mark on the fixed scale. A number of lines seem close, but only one aligns exactly. In this case, 0.50 mm is the reading to add to the first number. Adding 10 mm and 0.50 mm equals a measurement of 10.50 mm.

Micrometers

A micrometer is an instrument designed for linear measurement using the decimal divisions of the inch or meter (**Figure 29**). While there are many types and styles of micrometers, most of the procedures in this manual call for an outside micrometer. Use the outside micrometer to measure the outside diameter of cylindrical forms and the thickness of materials.

A micrometer's size indicates the minimum and maximum size of a part it can measure. The usual sizes (**Figure 30**) are 0-25 mm (0-1 in.), 25-50 mm (1-2 in.), 50-75 mm (2-3 in.) and 75-100 mm (3-4 in.).

Micrometers that cover a wider range of measurements are available. These use a large frame with interchangeable anvils of various lengths. This type of micrometer offers a cost savings, but its overall size may make it less convenient. Refer to **Figure 31** for micrometer part identification.

Adjustment

Before using a micrometer, check its adjustment as follows:
1. Clean the anvil and spindle faces.
2A. To check a 0-25 mm or 0-1 in. micrometer:

Calipers

Calipers (**Figure 27**) are used to obtain inside, outside and depth measurements. Although not as precise as a micrometer, they allow reasonable precision, typically to within 0.05 mm (0.001 in.). Most calipers have a range up to 150 mm (6 in.). Calipers are available in dial, vernier or digital versions. Dial calipers have a dial readout that provides convenient reading. Vernier calipers have marked scales that must be compared to determine the measurement. The digital caliper uses a liquid-crystal display (LCD) to show the measurement.

Properly maintain the measuring surfaces of the caliper. There must not be any dirt or burrs between

㉙	DECIMAL PLACE VALUES*
0.1	Indicates 1/10 (one tenth of an inch or millimeter)
0.010	Indicates 1/100 (one one-hundreth of an inch or millimeter)
0.001	Indicates 1/1000 (one one-thousandth of an inch or millimeter)

*This chart represents the values of figures placed to the right of the decimal point. Use it when reading decimals from one-tenth to one one-thousandth of an inch or millimeter. It is not a conversion chart (for example: 0.001 in. is not equal to 0.001 mm).

a. Turn the thimble until the spindle contacts the anvil. If the micrometer has a ratchet stop, use it to ensure the proper amount of pressure is applied.
b. If the adjustment is correct, the 0 mark on the thimble aligns exactly with the 0 mark on the sleeve line. If the marks do not align, the micrometer is out of adjustment.
c. Follow the manufacturer's instructions to adjust the micrometer.

2B. To check a micrometer larger than 25 mm or 1 in. use the standard gauge supplied by the manufacturer. A standard gauge is a steel block, disc or rod that is machined to an exact size.

a. Place the standard gauge between the spindle and anvil, and measure its outside diameter or length. If the micrometer has a ratchet stop, use it to ensure the proper amount of pressure is applied.
b. If the adjustment is correct, the 0 mark on the thimble aligns exactly with the 0 mark on the sleeve line. If the marks do not align, the micrometer is out of adjustment.
c. Follow the manufacturer's instructions to adjust the micrometer.

Care

Micrometers are precision instruments. They must be used and maintained with great care. Note the following:

1. Store micrometers in protective cases or separate padded drawers in a toolbox.
2. When in storage, make sure the spindle and anvil faces do not contact each other or another object. If

they do, temperature changes and corrosion may damage the contact faces.

3. Do not clean a micrometer with compressed air. Dirt forced into the tool causes wear.
4. Lubricate micrometers with WD-40 to prevent corrosion.

Reading Micrometers

When reading a micrometer, numbers are taken from different scales and added together. The following sections describe how to read the measurements of various types of outside micrometers.

For accurate results, properly maintain the measuring surfaces of the micrometer. There cannot be any dirt or burrs between the tool and the measured object. Never force the micrometer to close around an object. Close the micrometer around the highest point so it can be removed with a slight drag.

Metric micrometer

The standard metric micrometer is accurate to one one-hundredth of a millimeter (0.01 mm). The sleeve

GENERAL INFORMATION

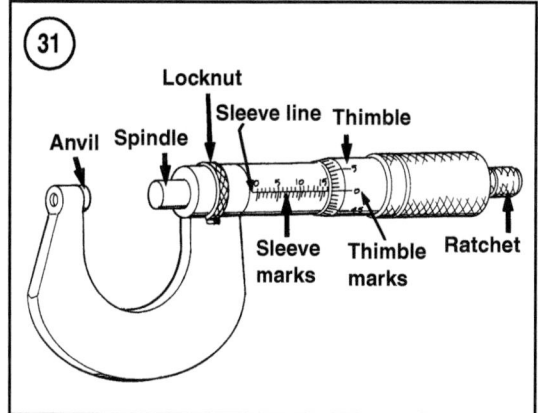

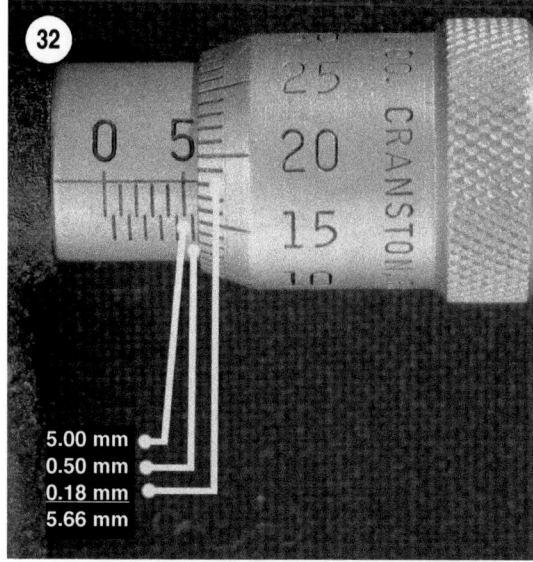

sleeve line to the number of one one-hundredth millimeters on the thimble. Perform the following steps while referring to **Figure 32**:

1. Read the upper half of the sleeve line and count the number of lines visible. Each upper line equals 1 mm.
2. Chck if the half-millimeter line is visible on the lower sleeve line. If so, add 0.50 mm to the reading in Step 1.

NOTE
If a thimble mark does not align exactly with the sleeve line, estimate the amount between the lines. For accurate readings in two-thousandths of a millimeter (0.002 mm), use a metric vernier micrometer.

3. Read the thimble mark that aligns with the sleeve line. Each thimble mark equals 0.01 mm.
4. Add the readings from Steps 1-3.

Standard inch micrometer

The standard inch micrometer is accurate to one-thousandth of an inch or 0.001. The sleeve is marked in 0.025 in. increments. Every fourth sleeve mark is numbered 1, 2, 3, 4, 5, 6, 7, 8 and 9. These numbers indicate 0.100, 0.200, 0.300 and so on.

The tapered end of the thimble has 25 lines marked around it. Each mark equals 0.001 in. One complete turn of the thimble aligns its zero mark with the first mark on the sleeve, or 0.025 in.

To read a standard inch micrometer, perform the following steps and refer to **Figure 33**.

1. Read the sleeve and find the largest number visible. Each sleeve number equals 0.100 in.
2. Count the number of lines between the numbered sleeve mark and the edge of the thimble. Each sleeve mark equals 0.025 in.

NOTE
If a thimble mark does not align exactly with the sleeve line, estimate the amount between the lines. For accurate readings in ten-thousandths of an inch (0.0001 in.), use a vernier inch micrometer.

3. Read the thimble mark that aligns with the sleeve line. Each thimble mark equals 0.001 in.
4. Add the readings from Steps 1-3.

line is graduated in millimeter and half millimeter increments. The marks on the upper half of the sleeve line equal 1.00 mm. Each fifth mark above the sleeve line is identified with a number. The number sequence depends on the size of the micrometer. A 0-25 mm micrometer, for example, has sleeve marks numbered 0 through 25 in 5 mm increments. This numbering sequence continues with larger micrometers. On all metric micrometers, each mark on the lower half of the sleeve equals 0.50 mm.

The tapered end of the thimble has 50 lines marked around it. Each mark equals 0.01 mm. One complete turn of the thimble aligns its 0 mark with the first line on the lower half of the sleeve line or 0.50 mm.

When reading a metric micrometer, add the number of millimeters and half-millimeters on the

Telescoping and Small Bore Gauges

Use telescoping gauges (**Figure 34**) and small bore gauges (**Figure 35**) to measure bores. Neither gauge has a scale for direct readings. Use an outside micrometer to determine the reading.

To use a telescoping gauge, select the correct size gauge for the bore. Compress the movable post and carefully insert the gauge into the bore. Carefully move the gauge in the bore to make sure it is centered. Tighten the knurled end of the gauge to hold the movable post in position. Remove the gauge and measure the length of the posts. Telescoping gauges are typically used to measure cylinder bores.

To use a small bore gauge, select the correct size gauge for the bore. Carefully insert the gauge into the bore. Tighten the knurled end of the gauge to carefully expand the gauge fingers to the limit within the bore. Do not overtighten the gauge because there is no built-in release. Excessive tightening can damage the bore surface and damage the tool. Remove the gauge and measure the outside dimension (**Figure 36**). Small bore gauges are typically used to measure valve guides.

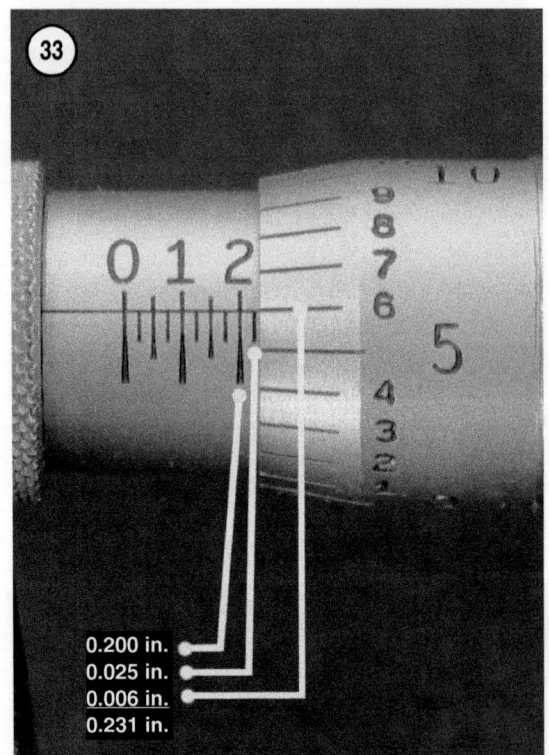

0.200 in.
0.025 in.
0.006 in.
0.231 in.

Dial Indicator

A dial indicator (A, **Figure 37**) is a gauge with a dial face and needle used to measure variations in dimensions and movements. Measuring brake rotor runout is a typical use for a dial indicator.

Dial indicators are available in various ranges and graduations and with three basic types of mounting bases: magnetic (B, **Figure 37**), clamp, or screw-in stud. When purchasing a dial indicator, select one with a continuous dial (**Figure 38**).

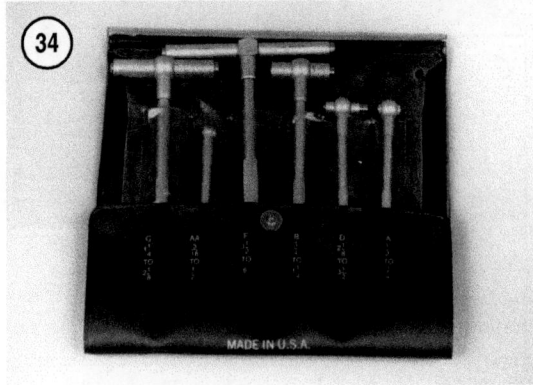

Cylinder Bore Gauge

A cylinder bore gauge is similar to a dial indicator. The gauge set shown in **Figure 39** consists of a dial indicator, handle and different length adapters (anvils) to fit the gauge to various bore sizes. The bore gauge is used to measure bore size, taper and out-of-round. When using a bore gauge, follow the manufacturer's instructions.

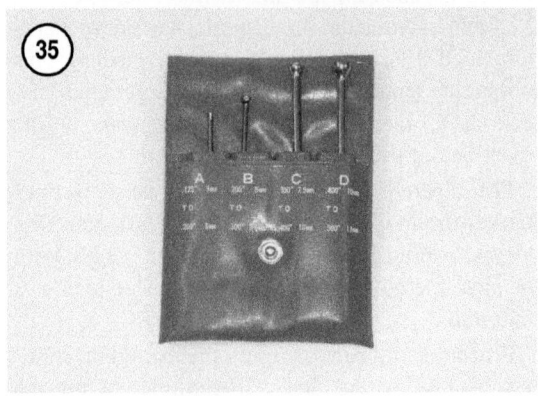

GENERAL INFORMATION

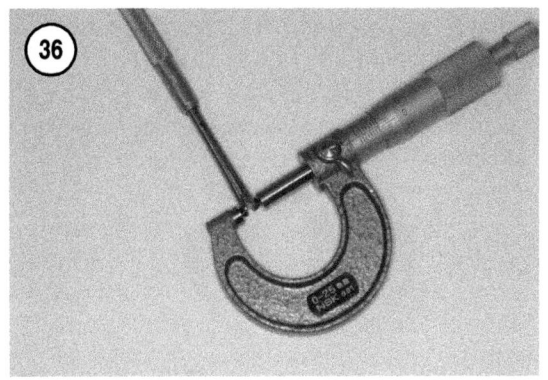

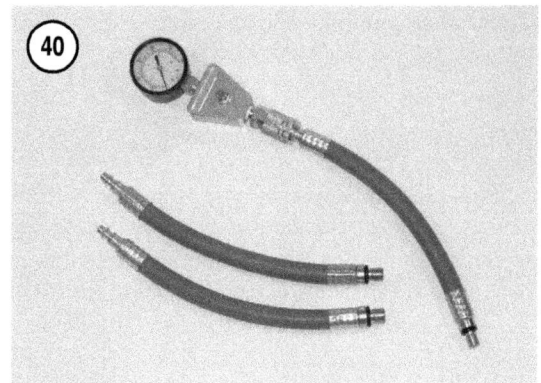

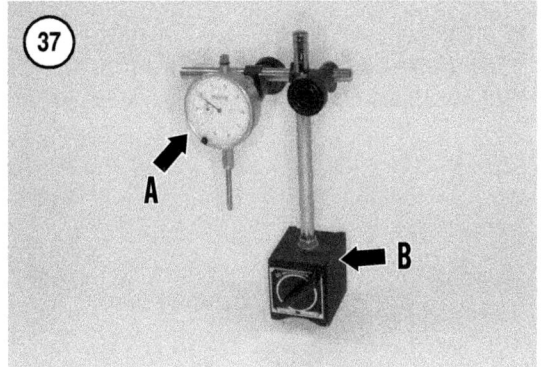

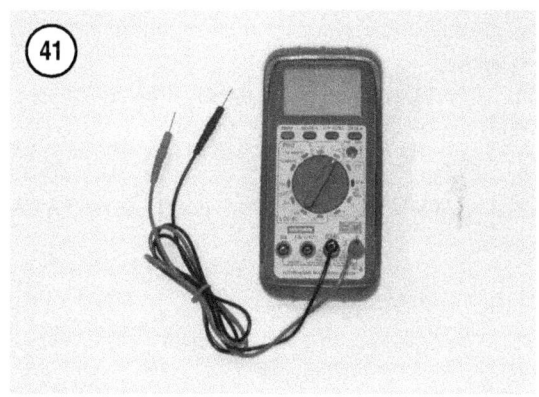

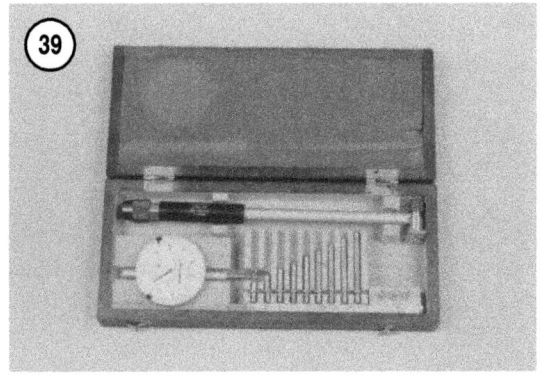

Compression Gauge

A compression gauge (**Figure 40**) measures combustion chamber (cylinder) pressure, usually in psi or kg/cm^2. The gauge adapter is either inserted or screwed into the spark plug hole to obtain the reading. Disable the engine so it does not start and hold the throttle in the wide-open position when performing a compression test. An engine that does not have adequate compression cannot be properly tuned. Refer to Chapter Three.

Multimeter

A multimeter (**Figure 41**) is an essential tool for electrical system diagnosis. The voltage function indicates the voltage applied or available to electrical components. The ohmmeter function tests circuits for continuity, or lack of continuity, and it measures the resistance of a circuit.

Some manufacturers' specifications for electrical components are based on results using a specific test meter. Results may vary if using a meter not recommended by the manufacturer. Such requirements are noted when applicable.

Ohmmeter (Analog) Calibration

Each time an analog ohmmeter is used or if the scale is changed, the ohmmeter must be calibrated.

Digital ohmmeters do not require calibration.
1. Make sure the meter battery is in good condition.
2. Make sure the meter probes are in good condition.
3. Touch the two probes together and observe the needle location on the ohms scale. The needle must align with the 0 mark to obtain accurate measurements.
4. If necessary, rotate the meter ohms adjust knob until the needle and 0 mark align.

ELECTRICAL SYSTEM FUNDAMENTALS

A thorough study of the many types of electrical systems used in today's ATV is beyond the scope of this manual. However, a basic understanding of electrical basics is necessary to perform simple diagnostic tests.

Refer to *Electrical Testing* in Chapter Two for typical test procedures and equipment. Refer to Chapter Nine for specific system test procedures.

Voltage

Voltage is the electrical potential or pressure in an electrical circuit and is expressed in volts. The more pressure (voltage) in a circuit, the more work can be performed.

Direct current (DC) voltage means the electricity flows in one direction. All circuits powered by a battery are DC circuits.

Alternating current (AC) means the electricity flows in one direction momentarily and then switches to the opposite direction. Alternator output is an example of AC voltage. This voltage must be changed or rectified to direct current to operate in a battery-powered system.

Resistance

Resistance is the opposition to the flow of electricity within a circuit or component and is measured in ohms. Resistance causes a reduction in available current and voltage.

Resistance is measured in an inactive circuit with an ohmmeter. The ohmmeter sends a small amount of current into the circuit and measures how difficult it is to push the current through the circuit.

An ohmmeter, although useful, is not always a good indicator of a circuit's actual ability under operating conditions. This is because of the low voltage (6-9 volts) the meter uses to test the circuit. The voltage in an ignition coil secondary winding can be several thousand volts. Such high voltage can cause the coil to malfunction, even though it tests acceptable during a resistance test.

Resistance generally increases with temperature. Perform all testing with the component or circuit at room temperature. Resistance tests performed at high temperatures may indicate high resistance readings and cause unnecessary replacement of a component.

Amperage

Amperage is the unit of measurement for the amount of current within a circuit. Current is the actual flow of electricity. The higher the current, the more work can be performed up to a given point. If the current flow exceeds the circuit or component capacity, it damages the system.

BASIC SERVICE METHODS

Most of the procedures in this manual are straightforward and can be performed by anyone reasonably competent with tools. However, consider personal capabilities carefully before performing any operation involving major disassembly.

1. The front of any component is the end closest to the front of the vehicle. The left and right sides refer to the position of the parts as viewed by the rider sitting on the seat facing forward.
2. When servicing an engine or suspension component, secure the vehicle in a safe manner.
3. Tag all similar parts for location and mark all mating parts for position. Record the number and thickness of any shims when removing them. Identify parts by placing them in sealed and labeled plastic sandwich bags.

GENERAL INFORMATION

4. Tag disconnected wires and connectors with masking tape and a marking pen. Do not rely on memory alone.

5. Protect finished surfaces from physical damage or corrosion. Keep gasoline and other chemicals off painted surfaces.

6. Use penetrating oil on frozen or tight bolts. Avoid using heat where possible. Heat can warp, melt or affect the temper of parts. Heat also damages the finish of paint and plastics.

7. When a part is a press fit or requires a special tool to remove, the information or type of tool is identified in the text. Otherwise, if a part is difficult to remove or install, determine the cause before proceeding.

8. To prevent objects or debris from falling into the engine, cover all openings.

9. Read each procedure thoroughly and compare the illustrations to the actual components before starting the procedure. Perform the procedure in sequence.

10. Recommendations are occasionally made to refer service to a dealership or specialist. In these cases, the work can be performed more economically by the specialist than by the home mechanic.

11. The term *replace* means to discard a defective part and replace it with a new part. *Overhaul* means to remove, disassemble, inspect, measure, repair and/or replace parts as required to recondition an assembly.

12. Some operations require using a hydraulic press. If a press is not available, have these operations performed by a shop equipped with the necessary equipment. Do not use makeshift equipment that may damage the vehicle.

CAUTION
Do not direct high-pressure water at steering bearings, fuel hoses, wheel bearings, suspension and electrical components. Water may force grease out of the bearings and possibly damage the seals.

13. Repairs are much faster and easier if the vehicle is clean before starting work. Degrease the vehicle with a commercial degreaser; follow the directions on the container for the best results. Clean all parts with cleaning solvent when removing them.

14. If special tools are required, have them available before starting the procedure. When special tools are required, they are described at the beginning of the procedure.

15. Make diagrams of similar-appearing parts. For instance, crankcase bolts are often not the same lengths. Do not rely on memory alone. Carefully laid out parts can become disturbed, making it difficult to reassemble the components correctly.

16. Make sure all shims and washers are reinstalled in the same location and position.

17. Whenever rotating parts contact a stationary part, look for a shim or washer.

18. Use new gaskets if there are any doubts about the condition of old ones.

19. If using self-locking fasteners, replace them. Do not install standard fasteners in place of self-locking ones.

20. Use grease to hold small parts in place if they tend to fall out during assembly. Do not apply grease to electrical or brake components.

Removing Frozen Fasteners

If a fastener cannot be removed, several methods may be used to loosen it. First, apply penetrating oil liberally and let it penetrate for 10-15 minutes. Rap the fastener several times with a small hammer. Do not hit it hard enough to cause damage. Reapply the penetrating oil if necessary.

For frozen screws, apply penetrating oil as described, then insert a screwdriver in the slot and rap the top of the screwdriver with a hammer. This loosens the rust so the screw can be removed in the normal way. If the screw head is too damaged to use this method, grip the head with locking pliers and twist the screw out.

Avoid applying heat unless specifically instructed. Heat may melt, warp or remove the temper from parts.

Removing Broken Fasteners

If the head breaks off a screw or bolt, several methods are available for removing the remaining portion. If a large portion of the remainder projects out, try gripping it with locking pliers. If the projecting portion is too small, file it to fit a wrench or cut a slot in it to fit a screwdriver (**Figure 42**).

If the head breaks off flush, use a screw extractor. To do this, center punch the exact center of the remaining portion of the screw or bolt (A, **Figure 43**), and then drill a small hole in the screw (B) and tap the extractor into the hole (C). Back the screw out with a wrench on the extractor (D, **Figure 43**).

Repairing Damaged Threads

Occasionally, threads are stripped because of carelessness or impact damage. Often the threads can be repaired by running a tap (for internal threads on nuts) or die (for external threads on bolts) through the threads (**Figure 44**). To clean or repair spark plug threads, use a spark plug tap.

If an internal thread is damaged, it may be necessary to install a Helicoil or some other type of thread insert. Follow the manufacturer's instructions when installing their insert.

If it is necessary to drill and tap a hole, refer to **Table 7** for metric tap and drill sizes.

Stud Removal/Installation

A stud removal tool (**Figure 45**) is available from most tool suppliers. This tool makes the removal and installation of studs easier. If one is not available, thread two nuts onto the stud and tighten them against each other. Remove the stud by turning the lower nut (**Figure 46**).
1. Measure the height of the stud above the surface.
2. Thread the stud removal tool onto the stud and tighten it, or thread two nuts onto the stud.
3. Remove the stud by turning the stud remover or lower nut.
4. Remove any threadlocking compound from the threaded hole. Clean the threads with an aerosol parts cleaner.
5. Install the stud removal tool onto the new stud or thread two nuts onto the stud.
6. Apply threadlocking compound to the threads of the stud.
7. Install the stud and tighten with the stud removal tool or the top nut.
8. Install the stud to the height noted in Step 1 or its torque specification.
9. Remove the stud removal tool or the two nuts.

Removing Hoses

When removing stubborn hoses, do not exert excessive force on the hose or fitting. Remove the hose clamp and carefully insert a small screwdriver

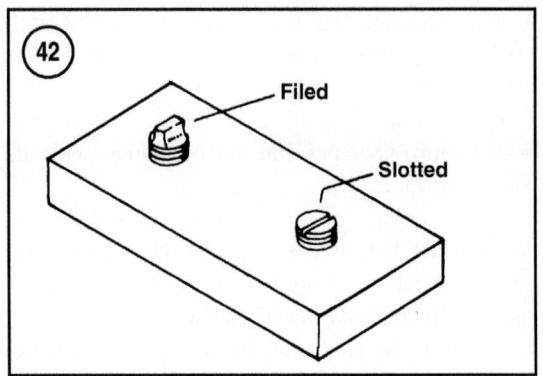

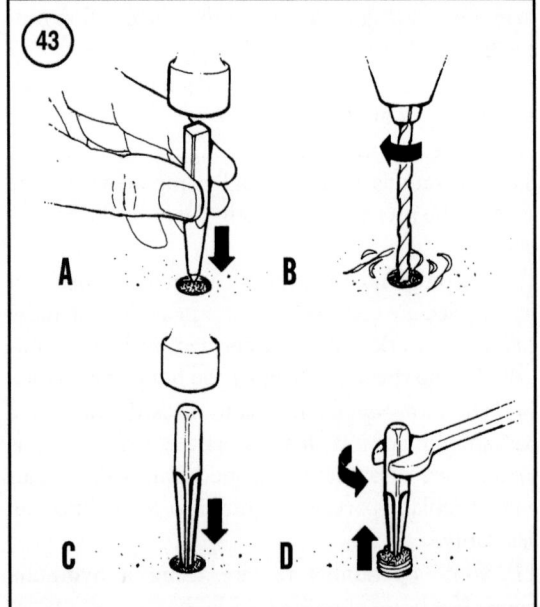

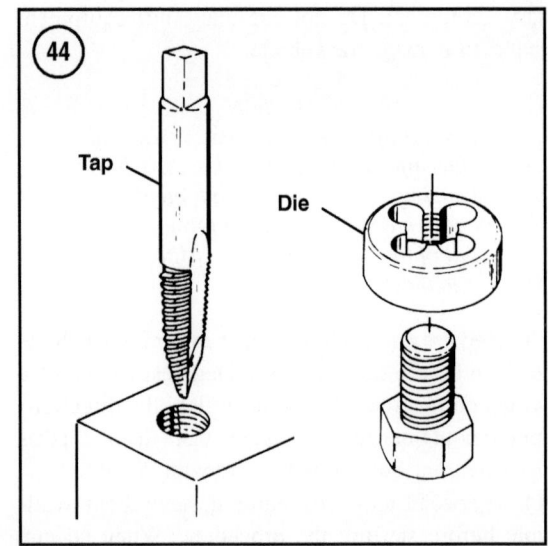

GENERAL INFORMATION

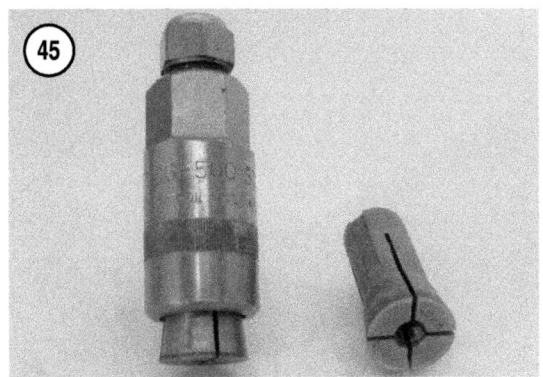

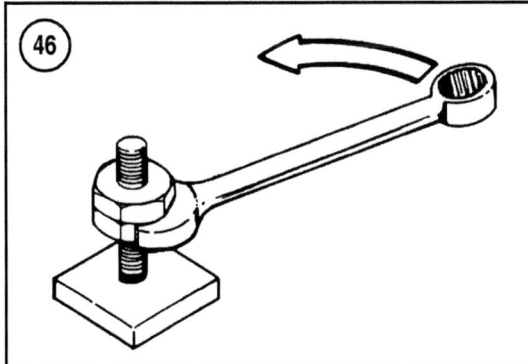

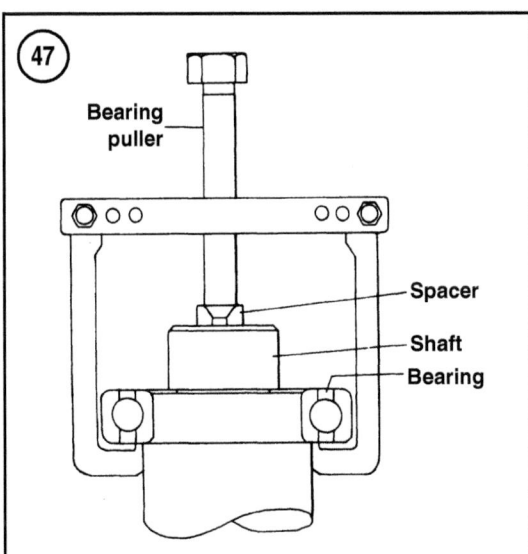

or pick tool between the fitting and hose. Apply a spray lubricant under the hose and carefully twist the hose off the fitting. Clean the fitting of any corrosion or rubber hose material with a wire brush. Clean the inside of the hose thoroughly. Do not use any lubricant when installing the hose (new or old).

The lubricant may allow the hose to come off the fitting, even with the clamp secure.

Bearings

NOTE
Unless otherwise specified, install bearings with the manufacturer's mark or number facing outward.

Bearings are used in the engine and transmission assembly to reduce power loss, heat and noise resulting from friction. Because bearings are precision parts, they must be maintained with proper lubrication and maintenance. If a bearing is damaged, replace it immediately. When installing a new bearing, take care to prevent damaging it. Bearing replacement procedures are included in the individual chapters where applicable; however, use the following sections as a guideline.

Removal

While bearings are normally removed only when damaged, there may be times when it is necessary to remove a bearing in good condition. However, improper bearing removal damages the bearing and possibly the shaft or case. Note the following when removing bearings:

1. When using a puller to remove a bearing from a shaft, make sure the shaft is not damaged. Always place a piece of metal between the end of the shaft and the puller screw. In addition, place the puller arms next to the inner bearing race. Refer to **Figure 47**.

2. When using a hammer to remove a bearing from a shaft, do not strike the hammer directly against the shaft. Instead, use a brass or aluminum rod between the hammer and shaft (**Figure 48**) and make sure to support both bearing races with wooden blocks as shown.

3. The ideal method of bearing removal is with a hydraulic press. Note the following:

   a. Always support the inner and outer bearing races with a suitable size wooden or aluminum spacer (**Figure 49**). If only the outer race is supported, pressure applied against the balls and/or the inner race damages them.

   b. Always make sure the press arm (**Figure 49**) aligns with the center of the shaft. If the arm is not centered, it may damage the bearing and/or shaft.

c. The moment the shaft is free of the bearing, it drops to the floor. Secure or hold the shaft to prevent it from falling.

Installation

1. When installing a bearing in a housing, apply pressure to the *outer* bearing race (**Figure 50**). When installing a bearing on a shaft, apply pressure to the *inner* bearing race (**Figure 51**).
2. When installing a bearing as described in Step 1, a driver is required. Never strike the bearing directly with a hammer or it damages the bearing. When installing a bearing, use a piece of pipe or a driver with a diameter that matches the bearing inner race. **Figure 52** shows the correct way to use a driver and hammer to install a bearing.
3. Step 1 describes how to install a bearing in a case half or over a shaft. However, when installing a bearing over a shaft and into the housing at the same time, a tight fit is required for both outer and inner bearing races. In this situation, install a spacer underneath the driver tool so pressure is applied evenly across both races. Refer to **Figure 53**. If the outer race is not supported as shown, the balls push against the outer bearing race and damage it.

Interference fit

1. Follow this procedure when installing a bearing over a shaft. When a tight fit is required, the bearing inside diameter is smaller than the shaft. In this case, driving the bearing on the shaft using normal methods may cause bearing damage. Instead, heat the bearing before installation. Note the following:
   a. Secure the shaft so it is ready for bearing installation.
   b. Clean all residues from the bearing surface of the shaft. Remove burrs with a file or sandpaper.
   c. Fill a suitable pot or beaker with clean mineral oil. Place a thermometer rated above 120° C (248° F) in the oil. Support the thermometer so it does not rest on the bottom or side of the pot.
   d. Remove the bearing from its wrapper and secure it with a piece of heavy wire bent to hold it in the pot. Hang the bearing in the pot so it does not touch the bottom or sides of the pot.

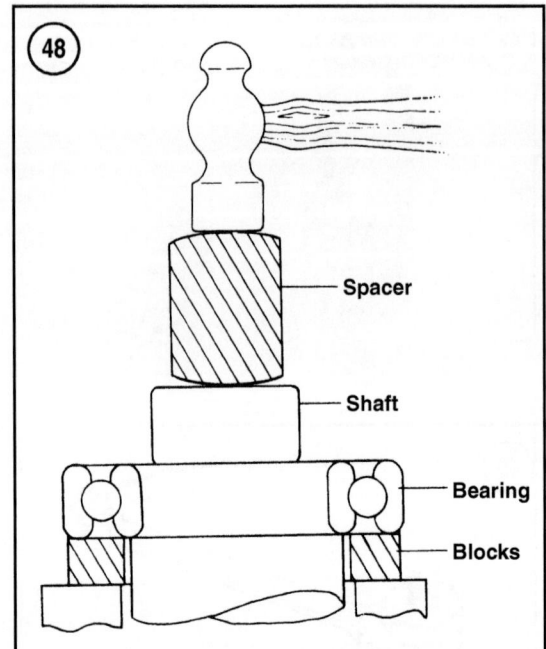

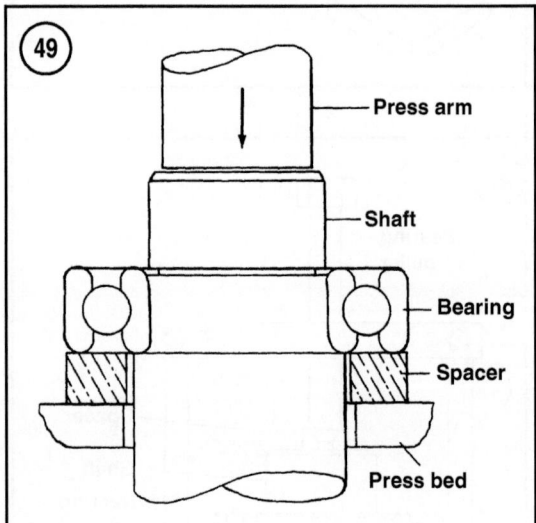

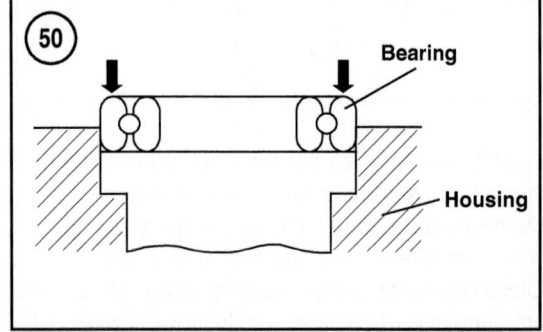

GENERAL INFORMATION

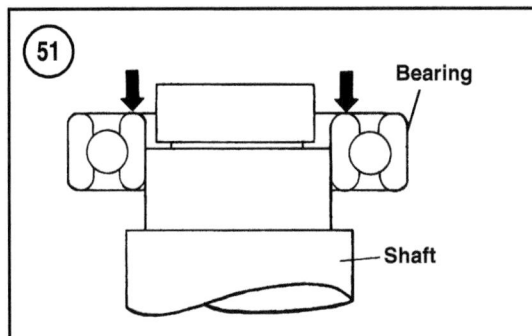

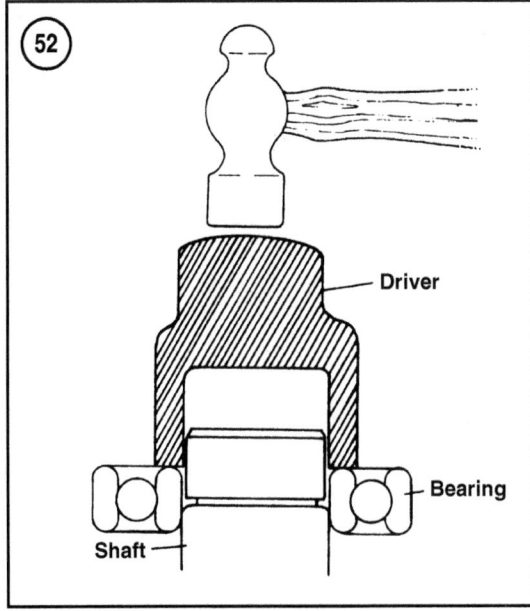

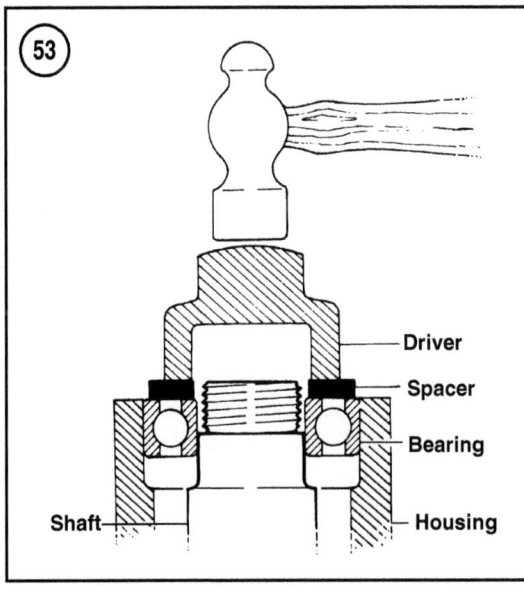

e. Turn the heat on and monitor the thermometer. When the oil temperature rises to approximately 120° C (248° F), remove the bearing from the pot and quickly install it. If necessary, place a socket on the inner bearing race and tap the bearing into place. As the bearing chills, it tightens on the shaft, so installation must be done quickly. Make sure the bearing is installed completely.

CAUTION
Before heating the housing in this procedure, wash the housing thoroughly with detergent and water. Rinse and rewash the cases as required to remove all traces of oil and other chemical deposits.

2. Follow this step when installing a bearing in a housing. Bearings are generally installed in a housing with a slight interference fit. Driving the bearing into the housing using normal methods may damage the housing or cause bearing damage. Instead, heat the housing before the bearing is installed. Note the following:

CAUTION
Do not heat the housing with a propane or acetylene torch. Never bring a flame into contact with the bearing or housing. The direct heat destroys the case hardening of the bearing and likely warps the housing.

a. Heat the housing to approximately 100° C (212° F) in an oven or on a hot plate. An easy way to check that it is the proper temperature is to place tiny drops of water on the housing; if they sizzle and evaporate immediately, the temperature is correct. Heat only one housing at a time.

b. Remove the housing from the oven or hot plate, and hold onto the housing with welding gloves. It is hot!

c. Hold the housing with the bearing side down and tap the bearing out. Remove and install the bearings with a suitable size socket and extension. Repeat for all bearings in the housing.

d. Before heating the bearing housing, place the new bearing in a freezer if possible. Chilling a bearing slightly reduces its outside diameter while the heated bearing housing assembly is slightly larger due to heat expansion. This makes bearing installation easier.

e. While the housing is still hot, install the new bearing(s) into the housing. Unless noted otherwise, install bearings with the manufacturer's mark or number facing out. Install the bearings by hand, if possible. If necessary, lightly tap the bearing(s) into the housing with a driver placed on the outerbearing race (**Figure 50**). Do not install new bearings by driving on the inner-bearing race. Install the bearing(s) until it seats completely.

Seal Replacement

Seals (**Figure 54**) contain oil, water, grease or combustion gasses in a housing or shaft. Improperly removing a seal can damage the housing or shaft. Improperly installing the seal can damage the seal. Note the following:
1. Prying is generally the easiest and most effective method of removing a seal from the housing. However, always place a rag underneath the pry tool (**Figure 55**) to prevent damage to the housing. Note the seal's installed depth or if it is installed flush.
2. Pack waterproof grease in the seal lips before the seal is installed.
3. In most cases, install seals with the manufacturer's numbers or marks facing out.
4. Install seals with a socket or driver placed on the outside of the seal as shown in **Figure 56**. Drive the seal squarely into the housing until it is to the correct depth or flush as noted during removal. Never install a seal by hitting against the top of it with a hammer.

STORAGE

Several months of non-use can cause a general deterioration of the vehicle. This is especially true in areas of extreme temperature variations. This deterioration can be minimized with careful preparation for storage. A properly stored ATV is much easier to return to service.

Storage Area Selection

When selecting a storage area, consider the following:

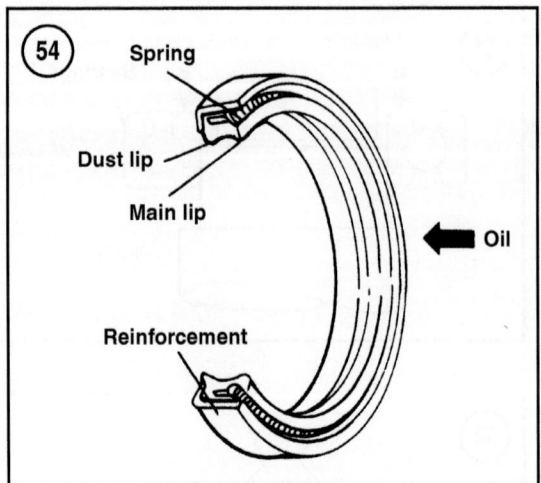

1. The storage area must be dry. A heated area is best, but not necessary. It should be insulated to minimize extreme temperature variations.
2. If the building has large window areas, mask them to keep sunlight off the vehicle.
3. Avoid buildings in industrial areas where corrosive emissions may be present. Avoid areas close to saltwater.
4. Consider the area's risk of fire, theft or vandalism. Check with an insurer regarding ATV coverage while in storage.

Preparing the Vehicle for Storage

The amount of preparation a vehicle should undergo before storage depends on the expected length of non-use, storage area conditions and personal preference. Consider the following list the minimum requirement:
1. Wash the vehicle thoroughly. Make sure all dirt, mud and road debris are removed.
2. Fill the fuel tank with a mixture of fuel and fuel stabilizer. Mix the fuel and stabilizer in the ratio recommended by the stabilizer manufacturer. Run the engine for a few minutes so the stabilized fuel can enter the fuel system. If storing the ATV for a long period, consider draining the fuel system.
3. Start the engine and allow it to reach operating temperature. Drain the engine oil regardless of the riding time since the last service. Fill the engine with the recommended type of oil.
4. Remove the spark plug and pour a teaspoon (15-20 ml) of engine oil into the cylinder. Place a

GENERAL INFORMATION

rag over the openings and slowly turn the engine over to distribute the oil. Reinstall the spark plug.

5. Remove the battery. Store the battery in a cool and dry location. Charge the battery once a month.
6. Cover the exhaust and intake openings.
7. Apply a protective substance to the plastic and rubber components. Make sure to follow the manufacturer's instructions for each type of product being used.
8. Rotate the tires periodically to prevent flat spots from developing and damaging them.
9. Cover the vehicle with old bed sheets or something similar. Do not cover it with any plastic material that traps moisture.

Returning the Vehicle to Service

The amount of service required when returning a vehicle to service after storage depends on the length of non-use and storage conditions. In addition to performing the reverse of the above procedure, make sure the brakes, clutch, throttle and engine stop switch work properly before operating the vehicle. Refer to Chapter Three and evaluate the service intervals to determine which areas require service.

Table 1 VEHICLE IDENTIFICATION NUMBER (VIN)[1,2]

Characters 1-3	Characters 4-8	Character 9	Character 10	Character 11	Characters 12-17
XXX	XXXXX	X	X	X	XXXXXX

Characters 1-3: World Manufacturing Identifier (WMI). These characters represent the manufacturer and the type of vehicle.
Characters 4-8: Vehicle attributes. These characters represent make, model and engine type.
Character 9: Check digit. This digit verifies the accuracy of the VIN transcription. The digit is mathematically determined using values assigned to the other characters in the VIN.
Character 10: Model year. The year is assigned to the model by the manufacturer and does not represent the year of manufacture. The letters I, O, Q, U, Z and the numeral 0 are not used in the model year code.
The letter X= 1999, Y=2000.
The number 1= 2001, 2= 2002, and so on until 2010.
The letter A= 2010, B=2011, and so on.
Character 11: Manufacturing plant location.
Characters 12-17: Sequential production number, as assigned by the manufacturer.

1. The VIN consists of 17 characters, with character groups representing the manufacturer and unique information about the motorcycle model.
2. VIN standards are periodically revised by the National Highway Traffic Safety Administration (NHTSA). Refer to their documentation for additional information.

Table 2 VEHICLE DIMENSIONS

Overall length	1735 mm (63.3 in.)
Overall width	1061 mm (41.8 in.)
Overall height	1073 mm (42.2 in.)
Wheelbase	1124 mm (44.3 in.)
Track	
Front	807 mm (31.8 in.)
Rear	805 mm (31.7 in.)
Ground clearance	149 mm (5.9 in.)
Seat height	794 mm (31.3 in.)
Footpeg height	319 mm (12.6 in.)

Table 3 VEHICLE WEIGHT

Dry weight	158 kg (349 lbs.)
Curb weight	166 kg (367 lbs.)
Maximum weight capacity	110 kg (243 lbs.)

Table 4 CONVERSION FORMULAS

Multiply:	By:	To get the equivalent of:
Length		
Inches	25.4	Millimeter
Inches	2.54	Centimeter
Miles	1.609	Kilometer
Feet	0.3048	Meter
Millimeter	0.03937	Inches
Centimeter	0.3937	Inches
Kilometer	0.6214	Mile
Meter	0.0006214	Mile
Fluid volume		
U.S. quarts	0.9463	Liters
U.S. gallons	3.785	Liters
U.S. ounces	29.573529	Milliliters
Imperial gallons	4.54609	Liters
Imperial quarts	1.1365	Liters
Liters	0.2641721	U.S. gallons
Liters	1.0566882	U.S. quarts
Liters	33.814023	U.S. ounces
Liters	0.22	Imperial gallons
Liters	0.8799	Imperial quarts
Milliliters	0.033814	U.S. ounces
Milliliters	1.0	Cubic centimeters
Milliliters	0.001	Liters
Torque		
Foot-pounds	1.3558	Newton-meters
Foot-pounds	0.138255	Meters-kilograms
Inch-pounds	0.11299	Newton-meters
Newton-meters	0.7375622	Foot-pounds
Newton-meters	8.8507	Inch-pounds
Meters-kilograms	7.2330139	Foot-pounds

(continued)

GENERAL INFORMATION

Table 4 CONVERSION FORMULAS (continued)

Multiply:	By:	To get the equivalent of:
Volume		
Cubic inches	16.387064	Cubic centimeters
Cubic centimeters	0.0610237	Cubic inches
Temperature		
Fahrenheit	(°F − 32) × 0.556	Centigrade
Centigrade	(°C × 1.8) + 32	Fahrenheit
Weight		
Ounces	28.3495	Grams
Pounds	0.4535924	Kilograms
Grams	0.035274	Ounces
Kilograms	2.2046224	Pounds
Pressure		
Pounds per square inch	0.070307	Kilograms per square centimeter
Kilograms per square centimeter	14.223343	Pounds per square inch
Kilopascals	0.1450	Pounds per square inch
Pounds per square inch	6.895	Kilopascals
Speed		
Miles per hour	1.609344	Kilometers per hour
Kilometers per hour	0.6213712	Miles per hour

Table 5 TECHNICAL ABBREVIATIONS

ABDC	After bottom dead center
ATDC	After top dead center
BBDC	Before bottom dead center
BDC	Bottom dead center
BTDC	Before top dead center
C	Celsius
cc	Cubic centimeter
CDI	Capacitor discharge ignition
cu. in.	Cubic inch and cubic inches
F	Fahrenheit
ft.-lb.	Foot pounds
gal.	Gallon and gallons
H/A	High altitude
hp	Horsepower
in.	Inch and inches
kg	Kilogram
kg/cm^2	Kilogram per square centimeter
kgm	Kilogram meter
km	Kilometer
L	Liter and liters
m	Meter
MAG	Magneto
mL	Milliliter
mm	Millimeter
N•m	Newton meter
oz.	Ounce and ounces
psi	Pounds per square inch
PTO	Power take off
pt.	Pint and pints
qt.	Quart and quarts
rpm	Revolution per minute

Table 6 METRIC, INCH AND FRACTIONAL EQUIVALENTS

mm	in.	Nearest fraction	mm	in.	Nearest fraction
1	0.0394	1/32	26	1.0236	1 1/32
2	0.0787	3/32	27	1.0630	1 1/16
3	0.1181	1/8	28	1.1024	1 3/32
4	0.1575	5/32	29	1.1417	1 5/32
5	0.1969	3/16	30	1.1811	1 3/16
6	0.2362	1/4	31	1.2205	1 7/32
7	0.2756	9/32	32	1.2598	1 1/4
8	0.3150	5/16	33	1.2992	1 5/16
9	0.3543	11/32	34	1.3386	1 11/32
10	0.3937	13/32	35	1.3780	1 3/8
11	0.4331	7/16	36	1.4173	1 13/32
12	0.4724	15/32	37	1.4567	1 15/32
13	0.5118	1/2	38	1.4961	1 1/2
14	0.5512	9/16	39	1.5354	1 17/32
15	0.5906	19/32	40	1.5748	1 9/16
16	0.6299	5/8	41	1.6142	1 5/8
17	0.6693	21/32	42	1.6535	1 21/32
18	0.7087	23/32	43	1.6929	1 11/16
19	0.7480	3/4	44	1.7323	1 23/32
20	0.7874	25/32	45	1.7717	1 25/32
21	0.8268	13/16	46	1.8110	1 13/16
22	0.8661	7/8	47	1.8504	1 27/32
23	0.9055	29/32	48	1.8898	1 7/8
24	0.9449	15/16	49	1.9291	1 15/16
25	0.9843	31/32	50	1.9685	1 31/32

Table 7 METRIC TAP DRILL SIZE

Metric size	Drill equivalent	Decimal fraction	Nearest fraction
3 × 0.50	No. 39	0.0995	3/32
3 × 0.60	3/32	0.0937	3/32
4 × 0.70	No. 30	0.1285	1/8
4 × 0.75	1/8	0.125	1/8
5 × 0.80	No. 19	0.166	11/64
5 × 0.90	No. 20	0.161	5/32
6 × 1.00	No. 9	0.196	13/64
7 × 1.00	16/64	0.234	15/64
8 × 1.00	J	0.277	9/32
8 × 1.25	17/64	0.265	17/64
9 × 1.00	5/16	0.3125	5/16
9 × 1.25	5/16	0.3125	5/16
10 × 1.25	11/32	0.3437	11/32
10 × 1.50	R	0.339	11/32
11 × 1.50	3/8	0.375	3/8
12 × 1.50	13/32	0.406	13/32
12 × 1.75	13/32	0.406	13/32

GENERAL INFORMATION

Table 8 GENERAL TORQUE SPECIFICATIONS

Fastener size or type	N•m	In.-lb.	ft.-lb.
5 mm screw	4	35	–
5 mm bolt and nut	5	44	–
6 mm screw	9	80	–
6 mm bolt and nut	10	88	–
6 mm flange bolt (8 mm head, small flange)	9	80	–
6 mm flange bolt (10 mm head) and nut	12	106	–
8 mm bolt and nut	22	–	16
8 mm flange bolt and nut	27	–	20
10 mm bolt and nut	35	–	26
10 mm flange bolt and nut	40	–	30
12 mm bolt and nut	55	–	41

CHAPTER TWO

TROUBLESHOOTING

Begin any troubleshooting procedure by defining the symptoms as precisely as possible. Gather as much information as possible to aid diagnosis. Never assume anything and do not overlook the obvious. Make sure there is fuel in the tank, and the fuel valve is on. Make sure the engine stop switch is in the run position and the spark plug wire is attached to the spark plug.

If a quick check does not reveal the problem, turn to the troubleshooting procedures described in this chapter. Identify the procedure that most closely describes the symptoms, and perform the indicated tests.

In most cases, expensive and complicated test equipment is not needed to determine whether repairs can be performed at home. A few simple checks could prevent an unnecessary repair charge. On the other hand, be realistic and do not attempt repairs beyond your capabilities. Many service departments do not take work that involves the re-assembly of damaged or abused equipment. If they do, expect the cost to be high.

WATER DAMAGE

Water damage is a common cause of ATV repair. If the vehicle is regularly operated in wet conditions, the brakes, cables, wheel bearings, gearcase oil and engine oil may need to be serviced more often than specified. In addition, corrosion my increase the likelihood of electrical problems. Regular cleaning and lubricating greatly extends the life of a vehicle run in these conditions.

CAUTION
If the engine oil or gearcase oil becomes contaminated with water it foams and/or has a whitish appearance. Frequently this is evident by condensation on the inside of the fill cap. Immediately flush any contamination with repeated fluid changes until all traces of moisture are gone. Oil diluted with water does not lubricate properly and quickly leads to costly repairs.

TROUBLESHOOTING

If mud is in the air box, it is usually an indicator that the vehicle has been submerged in water. If the vehicle has been submerged and no longer runs, perform the following maintenance items:
1. Drain the fuel tank.
2. Clean the carburetor.
3. Drain and replace the engine oil.
4. Remove the spark plug. Crank the engine over to remove any water.
5. Clean the air box.
6. Clean or replace the air filter.
7. Lubricate the cables.
8. Clean the brakes and check the brake fluid for contamination.
9. Drain and replace the gearcase oil.

ENGINE OPERATING REQUIREMENTS

An engine needs three basic requirements to run properly: correct air/fuel mixture, compression and a spark at the proper time. If any one element is missing, the engine does not run. **Figure 1** shows four-stroke engine operating principles.

ENGINE STARTING

CAUTION
When trying to start the engine, do not operate the starter for more than 5 seconds at a time. This can overheat the starter. Wait approximately 10 seconds before operating the starter again.

Cold Engine

1. Shift the transmission to neutral and set the parking brake.
2. Turn the ignition switch on.
3. Turn the fuel valve on.
4. Pull the choke knob all the way up (**Figure 2**).
5. With the throttle slightly open, push the starter button (A, **Figure 3**).
6A. If the ambient air temperature is normal (10-35° C [50-95° F]), perform the following after the engine has started:
   a. Move the choke knob to the halfway position.
   b. Warm up the engine by working the throttle slightly.

6B. If the ambient air temperature less than 10° C (50° F), perform the following after the engine has started:
   a. Work the throttle slightly to keep the engine running.
   b. When the engine begins to idle roughly, move the choke knob to the halfway position.
7. Idle the engine for approximately 1 minute or until the throttle responds cleanly, and move the choke knob all the way down (off).

Warm or Hot Engine

1. Shift the transmission into neutral and set the parking brake.
2. Turn the ignition switch on.
3. Turn the fuel valve on.
4. Make sure the choke knob is all the way down (off).
5. Open the throttle slightly and push the starter button.

Flooded Engine

If the engine is difficult to start and there is a strong gasoline smell, the engine is probably flooded. If so, perform the following procedure.

WARNING
Because a flooded engine smokes badly when it first starts to run, start the engine in a well-ventilated area with its muffler pointing away from all objects. Do not start a flooded engine in a closed area.

1. Make sure the choke knob is all the way down (off).
2. Turn the engine stop switch off.
3. Hold the throttle fully open.
4. Clear the engine by briefly pressing the starter button several times.
5. Wait 10 seconds, turn the engine stop switch on and perform the normal starting procedures. If the engine is flooded badly, you may have to remove the spark plug and dry off its insulator, or install a new plug. When a flooded engine first starts to run, it initially coughs and runs slowly as it burns off the excess fuel. As this excess fuel is burned off, the engine revs quickly. Release the throttle at this point

CHAPTER TWO

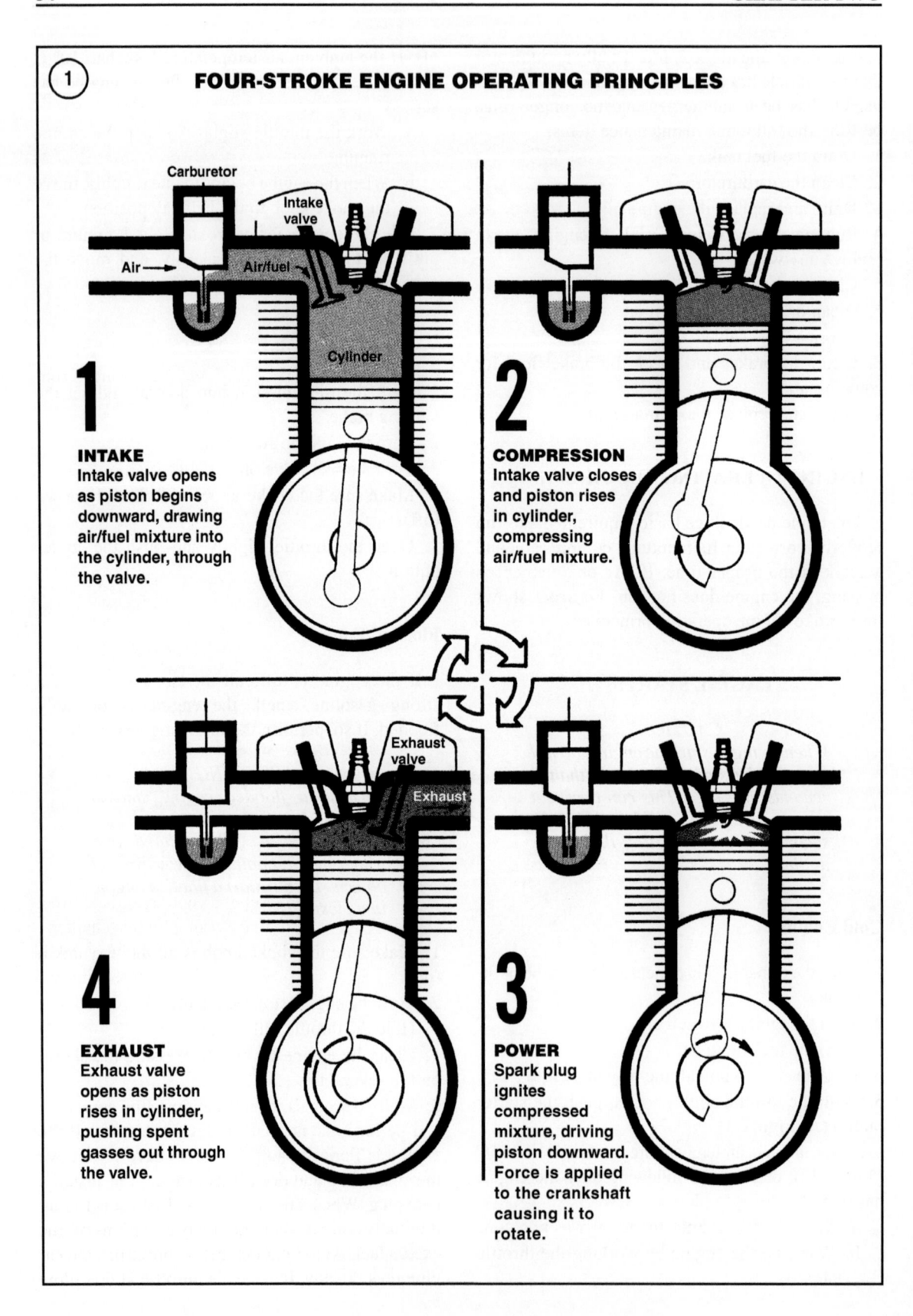

FOUR-STROKE ENGINE OPERATING PRINCIPLES

1 INTAKE
Intake valve opens as piston begins downward, drawing air/fuel mixture into the cylinder, through the valve.

2 COMPRESSION
Intake valve closes and piston rises in cylinder, compressing air/fuel mixture.

3 POWER
Spark plug ignites compressed mixture, driving piston downward. Force is applied to the crankshaft causing it to rotate.

4 EXHAUST
Exhaust valve opens as piston rises in cylinder, pushing spent gasses out through the valve.

TROUBLESHOOTING

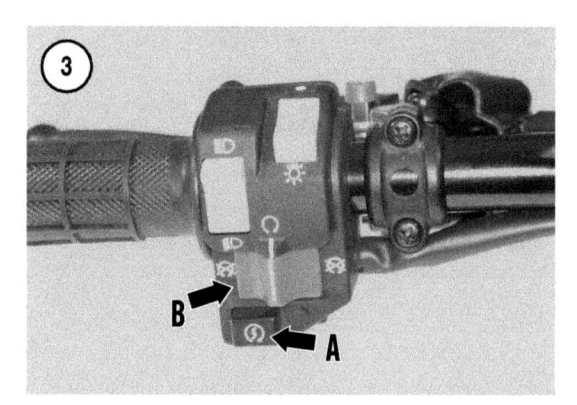

and work it slowly to make sure the engine is running cleanly.

NOTE
*If the engine refuses to start, check the carburetor overflow hose (**Figure 4**) attached to the fitting at the bottom of the float bowl. If fuel is running out of the hose, the float valve is stuck open or leaking, allowing the carburetor to overfill. If this problem exists, remove the carburetor and correct the problem as described in Chapter Eight.*

ENGINE WILL NOT START

An engine that refuses to start or is difficult to start is very frustrating. More often than not, the problem is minor and can be found with a simple and logical troubleshooting approach.

Refer to the following to isolate engine starting problems:

1. Check whether the choke knob is in the correct position. Refer to *Engine Starting* in this chapter.
2. Check whether fuel is in the tank. Fill the tank if necessary. If it has been a while since the engine has run, drain the tank and fill it with fresh fuel. Check for a clogged fuel tank vent hose (**Figure 5**). Remove the tube from the filler cap, and then wipe off one end and blow through it. Remove the filler cap and check for a plugged hose nozzle.

WARNING
Do not use an open flame to check in the tank. An explosion results.

3. Disconnect the fuel line (**Figure 6**) from the carburetor and insert the end of the hose into a clear container. Turn the fuel valve on. Fuel should flow

freely from the fuel hose. If no fuel comes out, the fuel valve may be shut off, blocked by debris, or the fuel cap vent may be plugged. Remove and clean the fuel valve (Chapter Eight) and fuel cap vent. Reconnect the fuel line to the carburetor fitting.

4. The cylinder may be flooded if there is a strong smell of gasoline, perform the procedures in *Flooded Engine* in this chapter.

5. Check the carburetor overflow hose on the bottom of the float bowl (**Figure 4**). If fuel is running from the hose, the float valve is stuck open or leaking. Turn the fuel valve off and tap the carburetor a few times. Then turn on the fuel valve. If fuel continues to run out of the hose, remove and repair the carburetor as described in Chapter Eight. Check the carburetor vent hoses to make sure they are clear. Check the end of the hoses for contamination.

> **NOTE**
> *If fuel is reaching the carburetor, the fuel system could still be the problem. The jets (pilot and main) could be plugged or the air filter could be severely restricted. However, before removing the carburetor, continue with Step 6 to check the ignition system.*

6. Make sure the engine stop switch (B, **Figure 3**) is operating correctly. Make sure the stop switch wire is not broken or shorted. If necessary, test the engine stop switch as described in *Switches* in Chapter Nine.

7. If the spark plug high-tension wire and cap (**Figure 7**) are tight on the spark plug, push and slightly rotate them to clean the electrical connection between the spark plug and the wire connector. Remove the cap from the plug, hold the high-tension wire and screw the plug cap on tightly.

8. Perform the *Spark Test* described in this section. If there is a strong spark, perform Step 9. If there is no spark, or if the spark is very weak, troubleshoot the ignition system as described in this chapter.

> **NOTE**
> *A compression problem may still exist even though it seems good in the following test. If necessary, check the engine compression using a compression gauge as described in Chapter Three.*

9. Check cylinder compression as follows:
   a. Turn the engine stop switch (B, **Figure 3**) off.
   b. Turn the fuel valve off.
   c. Remove the spark plug and ground the spark plug against the cylinder head.
   d. Place your finger over the spark plug hole.
   e. Operate the starter. When the piston comes up on the compression stroke, pressure in the cylinder should force your finger from the spark plug hole. If your finger pops off, the cylinder probably has sufficient compression to start the engine.

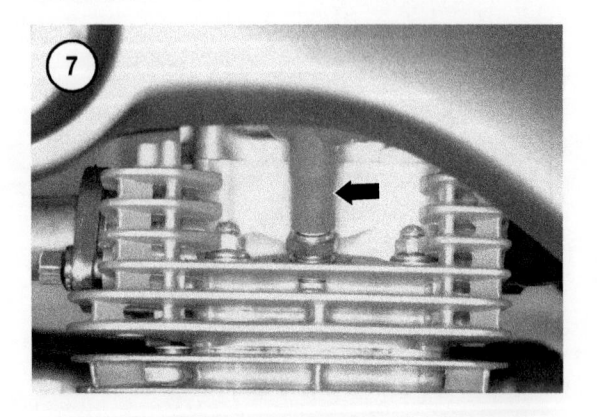

Spark Test

Perform the following spark test to determine if the ignition system is producing adequate spark. When checking spark, turn the engine stop switch to run and the ignition switch on.

> **CAUTION**
> *Before removing the spark plug in Step 1, clean all debris away from the plug base. Dirt that falls into the cylinder causes rapid engine wear.*

TROUBLESHOOTING

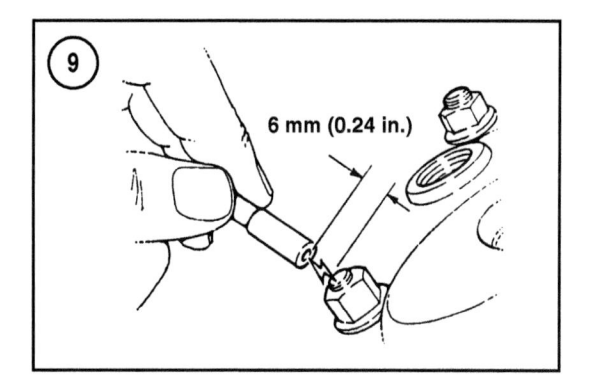

1. Disconnect the plug wire and remove the spark plug.

NOTE
*A spark tester (**Figure 8**) is a useful tool for checking the ignition system. This tool is inserted in the spark plug cap and its base is grounded against the cylinder head. Because the tool's air gap is adjustable, the intensity (sight and sound) of the spark can be observed while testing. A number of different spark testers are available through motorcycle and automotive parts stores. The spark tester shown in **Figure 8** is manufactured by Motion Pro (part No. 08-0122).*

2. If using an adjustable spark tester, set its air gap to 6 mm (0.24 in.).
3. Insert the spark plug (or spark tester) into the plug cap and touch its base against the cylinder head to ground it (**Figure 8**). Position the plug so the electrodes are in view.

WARNING
Do not hold or touch the spark plug (or spark tester), wire or connector when making a spark check. A serious electrical shock may result.

CAUTION
Mount the spark plug or spark tester away from the plug hole in the cylinder head so the spark from the plug or tester cannot ignite the gasoline vapor in the cylinder.

NOTE
*If the engine backfires when you attempt to start it, the ignition timing may be incorrect. Because the ignition timing is not adjustable, incorrect ignition timing can be caused by a loose flywheel, sheared flywheel key, loose ignition pulse generator mounting screws or connector or a damaged or defective ignition system component. Refer to **Ignition System** in this chapter.*

4. Turn the engine over with the starter button. A fat blue spark should be evident across the spark plug electrodes or across the spark tester terminals.
5. If the spark is good, check for one or more of the following possible malfunctions:
   a. Obstructed fuel line or fuel filter (if used).
   b. Low compression or engine damage.
   c. Flooded engine.
6. If the spark is weak (white or yellow in color) or if there is no spark, check for one or more of the following conditions:
   a. Fouled or wet spark plug. If there is a spark across a spark tester but not across the original spark plug, the plug is fouled. Repeat the spark test with a new spark plug.
   b. Loose or damaged spark plug cap connection. Hold the spark plug wire and turn the spark plug cap to tighten it. Install the spark plug into the cap and repeat the spark test. If there is still no spark, bypass the plug cap as described in the next step.
   c. Check for a damaged spark plug cap. Hold the spark plug wire and unscrew the spark plug cap. Hold the end of the spark plug wire 6 mm (0.24 in.) from the cylinder head as shown in **Figure 9**. If there is a strong spark, the spark plug cap is faulty. Replace the plug cap and repeat the spark test.
   d. Loose or damaged spark plug wire connections (at coil and plug cap).
   e. Faulty ignition coil or faulty ignition coil ground wire connection.
   f. Faulty ICM unit or stator coil(s).
   g. Sheared flywheel key.
   h. Loose flywheel nut.
   i. Loose electrical connections.
   j. Dirty electrical connections.

Electrical System

1. Spark plug:
   a. Fouled spark plug.

b. Incorrect spark plug gap.
c. Incorrect spark plug heat range (too cold). Refer to Chapter Three.
d. Worn or damaged spark plug electrodes.
e. Damaged spark plug.
f. Damaged spark plug cap or spark plug wire.
2. Ignition coil:
   a. Loose or damaged ignition coil leads.
   b. Cracked ignition coil body—look for carbon tracks on the ignition coil.
   c. Loose or corroded ground wire.
3. Switches and wiring:
   a. Dirty or loose fitting terminals.
   b. Damaged wires or connectors.
   c. Damaged ignition switch.
   d. Damaged engine stop switch.
4. Electrical components:
   a. Damaged ignition pulse generator.
   b. Damaged ICM unit.
   c. Faulty exciter coil.
   d. Sheared flywheel Woodruff key.

Fuel System

A contaminated fuel system causes engine starting and performance related problems. It only takes a small amount of dirt in the fuel valve, fuel line or carburetor to cause problems.
1. Air filter:
   a. Plugged air filter element.
   b. Plugged air filter housing.
   c. Leaking or damaged air filter housing-to-carburetor air boot.
2. Fuel valve:
   a. Plugged fuel hose.
   b. Plugged fuel valve filter.
3. Fuel tank:
   a. No fuel.
   b. Plugged fuel filter.
   c. Plugged fuel tank vent hose (**Figure 5**).
   d. Contaminated fuel.
4. Carburetor:
   a. Plugged or damaged choke system.
   b. Plugged main jet.
   c. Plugged pilot jet.
   d. Loose pilot jet or main jet.
   e. Plugged pilot jet air passage.
   f. Incorrect float level.
   g. Leaking or damaged float.
   h. Worn or damaged needle valve.

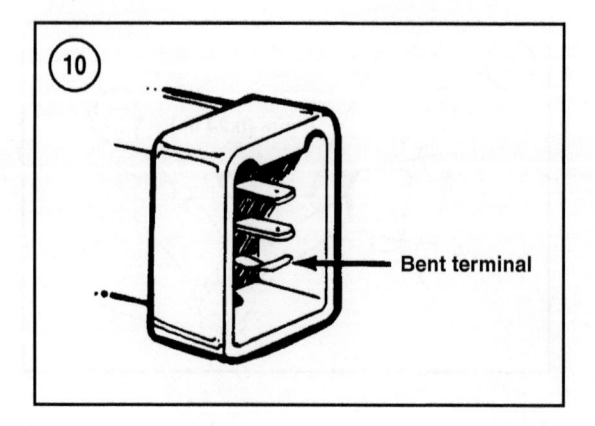

Engine Compression

Check engine compression as described in Chapter Three. To obtain a more accurate gauge of engine wear, perform an engine leakdown test as described in this chapter.
1. Cylinder and cylinder head:
   a. Loose spark plug.
   b. Missing spark plug gasket.
   c. Leaking cylinder head gasket.
   d. Leaking cylinder base gasket.
   e. Severely worn or seized piston, piston rings and/or cylinder.
   f. Loose cylinder and/or cylinder head fasteners.
   g. Cylinder head incorrectly installed and/or torqued.
   h. Warped cylinder head.
   i. Valve(s) adjusted too tightly.
   j. Bent valve.
   k. Worn valve and/or seat.
   l. Worn or damaged valve guide(s).
   m. Bent pushrod(s).
   n. Damaged cam follower.
2. Piston and piston rings:
   a. Worn piston rings.
   b. Damaged piston rings.
   c. Piston seizure or piston damage.
3. Crankcase and crankshaft:
   a. Seized connecting rod.
   b. Damaged crankcase.
   c. Damaged oil seals.

POOR IDLE SPEED PERFORMANCE

If the engine starts, but idle performance is poor, check the following:
1. Clogged or damaged air filter element.

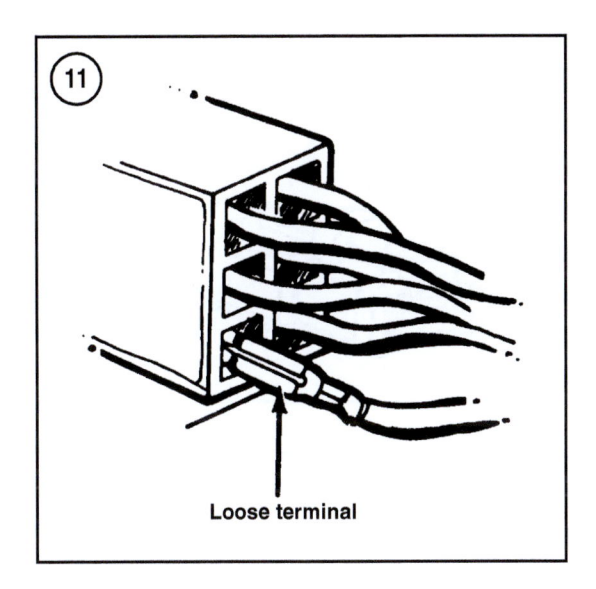

TROUBLESHOOTING

Loose terminal

2. Carburetor:
   a. Plugged pilot jet.
   b. Loose pilot jet.
   c. Damaged choke system.
   d. Incorrect throttle cable adjustment.
   e. Incorrect pilot screw adjustment.
   f. Flooded carburetor (visually check carburetor overflow hose for fuel).
   g. Throttle valve does not slide smoothly in carburetor bore.
   h. Loose carburetor.
   i. Damaged intake manifold O-ring.
   j. Incorrect idle speed.
   k. Incorrect air/fuel mixture.
3. Fuel:
   a. Water and/or alcohol in fuel.
   b. Old fuel.
4. Engine: Low engine compression.
5. Electrical system:
   a. Damaged spark plug.
   b. Open or shorted spark plug wire.
   c. Damaged ignition coil.
   d. Faulty ignition or engine stop switch.
   e. Damaged ignition pulse generator.
   f. Damaged ICM unit.
   g. Damaged exciter coil.

POOR MEDIUM AND HIGH SPEED PERFORMANCE

Check the following:
1. Carburetor:
   a. Incorrect fuel level.
   b. Incorrect jet needle clip position.
   c. Plugged or loose main jet.
   d. Plugged fuel line.
   e. Plugged fuel valve.
   f. Plugged fuel tank vent hose.
2. Plugged air filter element.
3. Engine:
   a. Incorrect valve timing.
   b. Weak valve springs.
4. Other considerations:
   a. Overheating.
   b. Clutch slip.
   c. Brake drag.
   d. Engine oil level too high.

ELECTRICAL TESTING

This section describes basics electrical testing and the use of equipment.

Preliminary Checks and Precautions

Before starting any electrical troubleshooting procedure, perform the following:
1. Check the main fuse (Chapter Nine). If the fuse is blown, replace it.
2. Inspect the battery. Make sure it is fully charged, and the battery leads are clean and securely attached to the battery terminals. Refer to *Battery* in Chapter Three.

NOTE
Always consider electrical connectors the weak link in the electrical system. Dirty, loose-fitting and corroded connectors cause numerous electrical related problems, especially on high-mileage vehicles. When troubleshooting an electrical problem, carefully inspect the connectors and wiring harness.

3. Disconnect each electrical connector in the suspect circuit. Check the terminals on both sides of the electrical connector. They should be clean and straight. A bent terminal (**Figure 10**) does not connect to its mate, causing an open circuit.
4. Make sure the terminal on the end of each wire (**Figure 11**) is pushed all the way into the connector.

If not, carefully push them in with a narrow blade screwdriver.

5. Check the wires where they enter the connectors for damage.
6. Clean and pack the connectors with a dielectric grease.
7. Push the connector halves together. Make sure the connectors are fully engaged and locked together (**Figure 12**).
8. Never pull the electrical wires when disconnecting an electrical connector—pull only on the connector plastic housing.
9. Never use a self-powered test light on circuits that contain solid-state devices. The solid-state devices may be damaged.

Electrical Component Replacement

Most ATV dealerships and parts suppliers do not accept the return of any electrical part. If the *exact* cause of any electrical system malfunction cannot be determined, have a Honda dealership retest that specific system to verify the test results. If you purchase a new electrical component(s), install it, and then find that the system still does not work properly, the unit probably cannot be returned for a refund.

Consider any test results carefully before replacing a component that tests only *slightly* out of specification, especially resistance. A number of variables can affect test results dramatically. These include the testing meter's internal circuitry, ambient temperature and conditions under which the machine has been operated. All instructions and specifications have been checked for accuracy; however, successful test results depend, to a great degree, upon individual accuracy.

Test Light or Voltmeter

A test light can be constructed from a 12-volt light bulb with a pair of test leads soldered to the bulb. To check for battery voltage in a circuit, attach one lead to ground and the other lead to various points along the circuit. The bulb lights when voltage is present.

A voltmeter is used in the same manner as the test light to find out if voltage is present in any given circuit. The voltmeter, unlike the test light, also indicates how much voltage is present at each test point.

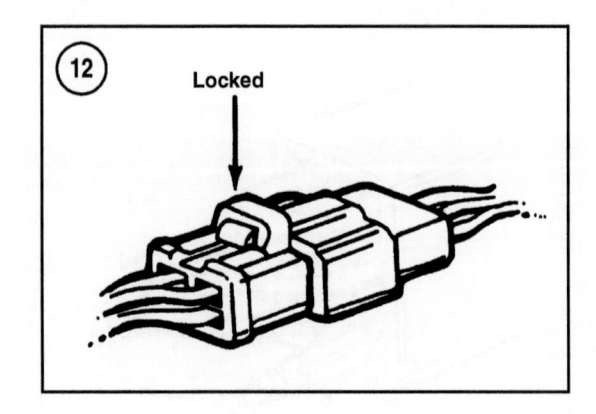

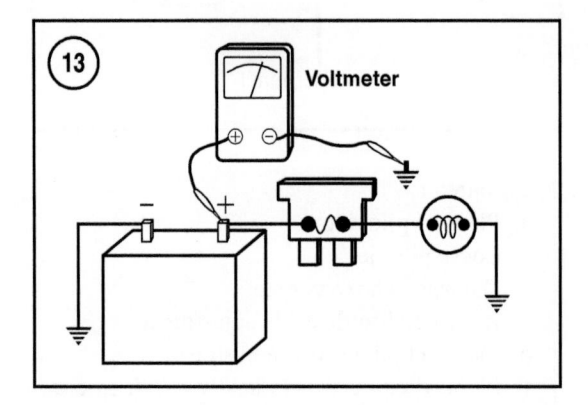

When using a voltmeter, attach the red lead to the component or wire to be checked and the negative lead to a good ground (**Figure 13**).

Ammeter

An ammeter measures the flow of current (amps) in a circuit (**Figure 14**). When connected in series in the circuit, the ammeter determines if current is flowing through the circuit and if that current flow is excessive because of a short in the circuit. Current flow is often referred to as current draw. Comparing actual current draw in the circuit or component to the manufacturer's specified current draw provides useful diagnostic information.

Self-powered Test Light

A self-powered test light can be constructed from a 12-volt light bulb, a pair of test leads and a 12-volt battery. When the test leads are touched together the light bulb should go on.

Use a self-powered test light as follows:

TROUBLESHOOTING

(14) Ammeter Connected in series — Measures current flow

(15) Ohmmeter — Component

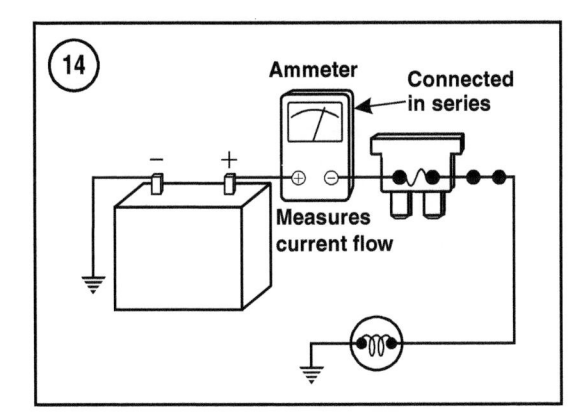

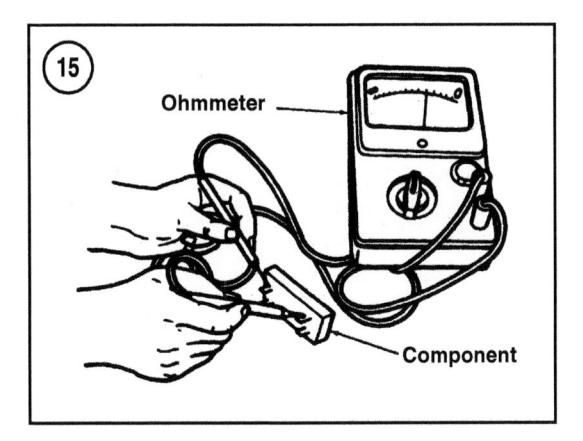

1. Touch the test leads together to make sure the light bulb goes on. If not, correct the problem before using it in a test procedure.
2. Disconnect the motorcycle's battery or remove the fuse(s) that protects the circuit to be tested.
3. Select two points within the circuit where there should be continuity.
4. Attach one lead of the self-powered test light to each point.
5. If there is continuity, the self-powered test light bulb comes on.
6. If there is no continuity, the self-powered test light bulb does not come on, indicating an open circuit.

Ohmmeter

CAUTION
Never connect an ohmmeter to a circuit that has power applied to it. Always disconnect the battery negative lead before using an ohmmeter.

An ohmmeter measures the resistance (in ohms) to current flow in a circuit or component. Like the self-powered test light, an ohmmeter contains its own power source and should not be connected to a live circuit.

Ohmmeters may be analog type (needle scale) or digital type (LCD or LED readout). Both types of ohmmeters have a switch which allows you to select different ranges of resistance for accurate readings. The analog ohmmeter also has a set-adjust control which is used to zero, or calibrate, the meter (digital ohmmeters do not require calibration).

An ohmmeter is used by connecting its test leads to the terminals or leads of the circuit or component to be tested (**Figure 15**). If an analog meter is used, it must be calibrated by touching the test leads together and turning the set-adjust knob until the meter needle reads zero. When the leads are uncrossed, the needle should move to the other end of the scale, indicating infinite resistance.

During a continuity test, a reading of infinity indicates there is an open in the circuit or component. A reading of zero indicates continuity, that is, there is no measurable resistance in the circuit or component being tested. If the meter needle falls between these two ends of the scale, this indicates the actual resistance to current flow that is present.

Jumper Wire

A jumper wire is a simple way to bypass a potential problem and isolate it to a particular point in a circuit. If a faulty circuit works properly with a jumper wire installed, an open circuit exists between the two jumper points.

To troubleshoot with a jumper wire, first use the wire to determine if the problem is on the ground or load side of a device. In the example shown in **Figure 16**, test the ground by connecting a jumper between the lamp and a good ground. If the lamp comes on, the problem is the connection between the lamp and ground. If the lamp does not come on with the jumper installed, the lamp's connection to ground is good so the problem is between the lamp and power source.

To isolate the problem, connect the jumper between the battery and the lamp. If it comes on, the problem is between these two points. Next, connect the jumper between the battery and the fuse side of the switch. If the lamp comes on, the switch is good.

By successively moving the jumper from one point to another, the problem can be isolated to a particular place in the circuit.

Note the following when using a jumper wire:

1. Make sure the jumper wire gauge (thickness) is the same as that used in the circuit being tested. Smaller gauge wire rapidly overheats and could melt.

2. Install insulated boots over alligator clips. This prevents accidental grounding, sparks or possible shock when working in cramped quarters.

3. Jumper wires are temporary test measures only. Do not leave a jumper wire installed as a permanent solution. This creates a fire hazard that could easily lead to complete loss of the ATV.

4. When using a jumper wire, always install an inline fuse/fuse holder (available at most auto supply stores or electronic supply stores) to the jumper wire. Never use a jumper wire across any load (a component that is connected and turned on). This causes a direct short and blows the fuse(s).

Voltage Test

Unless otherwise specified, all voltage tests are made with the electrical connector still connected. Insert the test leads into the backside of the connector and make sure the test lead touches the electrical terminal within the connector. If the test lead only touches the wire insulation, a false reading occurs.

Always check both sides of the connector because one side may be loose or corroded, thus preventing electrical flow through the connector. This type of test can be performed with a test light or voltmeter. A voltmeter gives the best results.

1. Attach the voltmeter's negative test lead to a good ground. Make sure the part used for ground is not insulated with a rubber gasket or rubber grommet.

2. Attach the voltmeter positive test lead to the point that needs checking (**Figure 13**).

3. Turn the ignition switch on. If using a test light, the test light comes on if voltage is present. If using a voltmeter, note the voltage reading. The reading should be within 1 volt of battery voltage. If the voltage is less, there is a problem in the circuit.

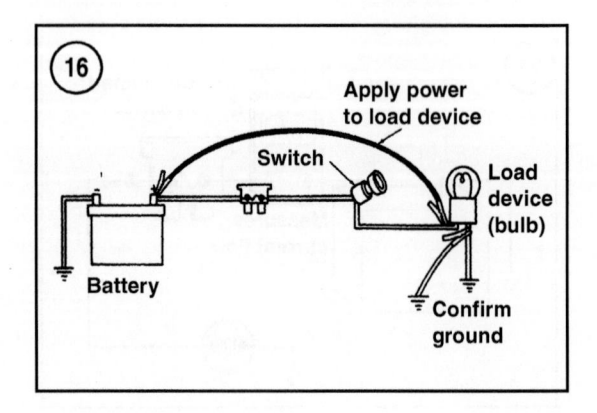

Voltage Drop Test

Because resistance causes voltage to drop, it can be determined in an active circuit using a voltmeter. This is called a voltage drop test. A voltage drop test measures the difference between the voltage at the beginning of the circuit and the available voltage at the end of the circuit while the circuit is operating. If the circuit has no resistance, there is no voltage drop and the voltmeter indicates 0 volts. The greater the resistance in a circuit, the greater the voltage drop reading. A voltage drop of 1 or more volts indicates that a circuit has excessive resistance.

It is important to remember that a 0 reading on a voltage drop test is good. Battery voltage, on the other hand, indicates an open circuit. A voltage drop test is an excellent way to check the condition of solenoids, relays, battery cables and other high-current electrical components.

1. Connect the voltmeter positive test lead to the end of the wire or switch closest to the battery.

2. Connect the voltmeter negative test lead to the other end of the wire or switch (**Figure 17**).

3. Turn the components on in the circuit.

4. The voltmeter should indicate 0 volts. If there is a drop of 1 volt or more, there is a problem within the circuit. A voltage drop reading of 12 volts indicates an open in the circuit.

Peak Voltage Test

A peak voltage test checks the voltage output at normal cranking speed. This test makes it possible to identify ignition system problems quickly and accurately.

Peak voltage testing requires the Honda peak voltage adapter (part No. 07HGJ-0020100) and

TROUBLESHOOTING 43

Voltage drop — Battery — Fan motor

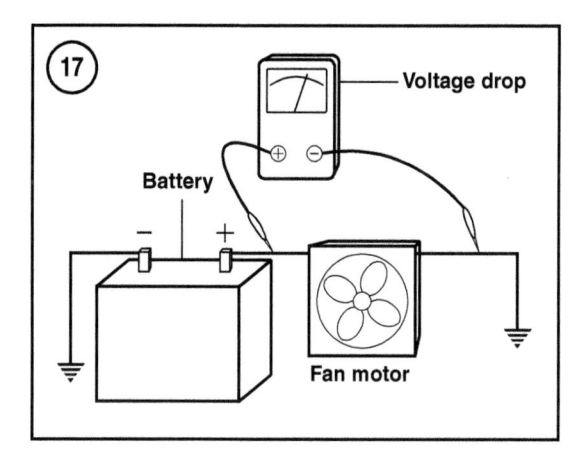

(17)

commercially available digital multimeter (minimum impedance: 10 M ohms/DCV). If these tools are not available, refer to a Honda dealership.

WARNING
High voltage is present during ignition system operation. Do not touch ignition components, wires or test leads while cranking or running the engine.

NOTE
*All peak voltage specifications are **minimum** values. If the measured voltage meets or exceeds the specification, the test results are satisfactory. On some components, the voltage may greatly exceed the minimum specification.*

Continuity Test

A continuity test is used to determine the integrity of a circuit, wire or component. A circuit has continuity if it forms a complete circuit, that is, if no opens are in either the electrical wires or components within the circuit. A circuit with an open has no continuity.

This type of test can be performed with a self-powered test light or an ohmmeter. An ohmmeter gives the best results. If using an analog ohmmeter, calibrate the meter by touching the leads together and turning the calibration knob until the meter reads zero.

1. Disconnect the negative battery cable.
2. Attach one test lead (test light or ohmmeter) to one end of the part of the circuit to be tested.
3. Attach the other test lead to the other end of the part or the circuit to be tested.
4. The self-powered test light comes on if there is continuity. An ohmmeter reads 0 or very low resistance if there is continuity. A reading of infinite resistance indicates no continuity; the circuit has an open.

Testing for a Short with a Self-powered Test Light or Ohmmeter

1. Disconnect the negative battery cable.
2. Remove the blown fuse from the fuse holder.
3. Connect one test lead of the test light or ohmmeter to the load side (battery side) of the fuse terminal in the fuse holder.
4. Connect the other test lead to a good ground. Make sure the part used for a ground is not insulated with a rubber gasket or rubber grommet.
5. With the self-powered test light or ohmmeter attached to the fuse terminal and ground, wiggle the wiring harness relating to the suspect circuit at 15.2 cm (6 in.) intervals. Start next to the fuse holder and work away from it. Watch the self-powered test light or ohmmeter as progressing along the harness.
6. If the test light blinks or the needle on the ohmmeter moves, there is a short-to-ground at that point in the harness.

Testing For a Short with a Test Light or Voltmeter

1. Remove the blown fuse from the fuse holder.
2. Connect the test light or voltmeter across the fuse terminals in the fuse holder. Turn the ignition switch on and check for battery voltage.
3. With the test light or voltmeter attached to the fuse terminals, wiggle the wiring harness relating to the suspect circuit at 15.2 cm (6 in.) intervals. Start next to the fuse holder and work away from it, watching the test light or voltmeter while progressing along the harness.
4. If the test light blinks or if the needle on the voltmeter moves, there is a short-to-ground at that point in the harness.

STARTING SYSTEM

This section describes troubleshooting procedures for the electric starting system. An ohmmeter and jumper cables are required to perform many of these procedures.

Before troubleshooting the starting circuit, make sure:
1. The battery is fully charged.
2. Battery cables are the proper size and length. Replace undersized or damaged cables.
3. All electrical connections are clean and tight.
4. The wiring harness is in good condition, with no worn or frayed insulation or loose harness sockets.
5. The fuel system is filled with an adequate supply of fresh gasoline.

Operation

An electric starter (**Figure 18**) is used on all models. The starter is mounted horizontally at the left side of the engine.

The electric starting system requires a fully charged battery to provide the large amount of current required to operate the starter. A charge coil on the stator plate and a voltage regulator, connected in circuit with the battery, keeps the battery charged while the engine is running. The battery can also be charged externally.

The starting circuit consists of the battery, starter, neutral/reverse switch, neutral indicator, starter relay, ignition switch and engine stop switch.

The starter relay (**Figure 19**) carries the heavy electrical current to the starter. Depressing the starter switch sends control current through the starter relay coil. The starter relay contacts close so load current flows from the battery through the starter relay to the starter.

When the ignition switch is turned on and the engine stop switch is in run, the starter can be operated only if the transmission is in neutral.

CAUTION
Do not operate the starter continuously for more than 5 seconds. Allow the starter to cool for at least 10 seconds between attempts to start the engine.

Starter Does Not Operate

If the starter does not operate, perform the following tests:

1. Remove the seat, side covers, upper fuel tank cover and front fender as described in Chapter Fourteen.
2. Check the 15-amp main fuse. Open the fuse holder (**Figure 20**), pull the fuse out and visually inspect it. If the fuse is blown, replace it as described in Chapter Nine. If the main fuse is good, reinstall it, and continue with Step 3.
3. Test the battery as described in Chapter Three. If the battery is damaged, replace it.
4. Check for loose, corroded or damaged battery cables. Check the cables at the battery, starter, starter relay and all cable-to-frame connections.
5. Turn the ignition switch on. Push the starter button and listen for a click at the starter relay switch (**Figure 19**).
   a. If the relay clicks, perform Step 6.
   b. If the relay does not click, go to Step 7.
6. Test the battery as follows:
   a. Park the vehicle on level ground and set the parking brake. Shift the transmission into neutral.

TROUBLESHOOTING

to the starter terminal. The starter works properly if it turns when connected directly to the battery.

e. If the starter does not turn, remove the starter and service it as described in Chapter Nine.

f. If the starter turns, check for a loose or damaged starter cable. If the cable is good, the starter relay (**Figure 19**) is faulty. Replace the starter relay and retest.

7. Check that the neutral indicator light (**Figure 22**) comes on when the transmission is in neutral and the ignition switch is on. Note the following:

   a. If the neutral indicator light does not work properly, check for a blown bulb. If the bulb works, perform Step 8.

   b. If the neutral indicator light works properly, go to Step 9.

8. Test the following items as described in Chapter Nine:

   a. Neutral/reverse switch.
   b. Ignition switch.
   c. Diode.

9. Check the voltage of the starter relay as described in Chapter Nine. Note the following:

   a. If the voltmeter shows battery voltage, continue with Step 10.

   b. If there is no voltage reading, check the ignition switch and starter switch as described in Chapter Nine. If both switches work, check the continuity of the yellow/red wire between the starter switch and the starter relay.

10. Perform the starter relay continuity test as described in Chapter Nine. Note the following:

    a. If the starter relay passes both portions of the test, continue with Step 11.

    b. If the starter relay fails either portion of the test, replace the starter relay.

11. If the starting system problem is not determined after performing these steps in order, recheck the wiring system for dirty or loose-fitting terminals or damaged wires. Clean and repair them as required.

12. Make sure all connectors disconnected during this procedure are free of corrosion and reconnected properly.

Starter Turns Slowly

If the starter turns slowly and all engine components operate normally, perform the following:

1. Test the battery as described in Chapter Three.

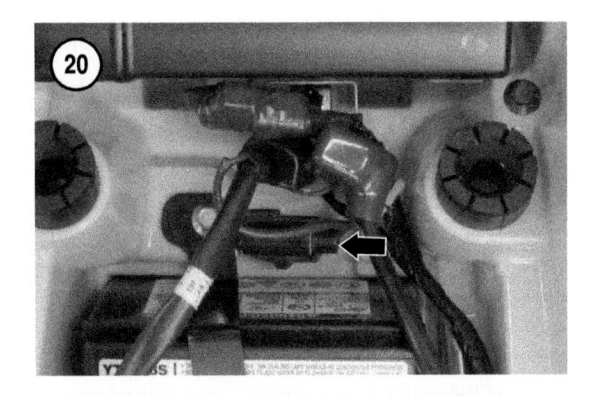

b. Remove the fuel tank as described in Chapter Eight.

c. Disconnect the cable (**Figure 21**) from the starter terminal.

WARNING
Because a spark is produced in the following steps, perform this procedure away from all open flames. Make sure there is no spilled gasoline on the ATV or gasoline fumes in the work area.

d. Momentarily connect a jumper cable (thick gauge wire) from the positive battery terminal

2. Check for the following:
   a. Loose or corroded battery terminals.
   b. Loose or corroded battery ground cable.
   c. Loose starter cable.
3. Remove, disassemble and bench test the starter as described in Chapter Nine.
4. Check the starter for binding during operation. Disassemble the starter and check the armature shaft for bending or damage. Also check the starter clutch as described in Chapter Five.

Starter Turns but the Engine Does Not

If the starter turns but the engine does not, perform the following:
1. Check for a damaged starter clutch (Chapter Five).
2. Check for damaged starter reduction gears (Chapter Five).

CHARGING SYSTEM

The charging system consists of the battery, alternator and a voltage regulator/rectifier. The 15-amp main fuse protects the circuit.

A malfunction in the charging system generally causes the battery to remain undercharged.

Battery Discharging

1. Check all connections. Make sure they are tight and free of corrosion.
2. Perform the *Regulated Voltage Test* described in Chapter Nine.
   a. If the voltage is within specification, perform Step 3.
   b. If the voltage is outside the specified range, perform Step 5.
3. Perform the *Current Draw Test* as described in Chapter Nine. Note the following:
   a. If the current draw exceeds 0.1mA, replace the battery.
   b. If the current draw is 0.1mA or less, perform Step 4.
4. Disconnect the regulator/rectifier connector, and repeat the *Current Draw Test*.
   a. If the current draw exceeds 0.1mA, check for a shorted wire harness or faulty ignition switch.
   b. If the current draw is 0.1mA or less, replace the regulator/rectifier.
5. Check the battery lead as described in *Regulator/Rectifier Harness Test* in Chapter Nine.
   a. If the voltage reading is within specification, perform Step 6.
   b. If the voltage reading is outside the specified range, check for a short in the harness or for loose, dirty connections.
6. Check the charge leads as described in *Regulator/Rectifier Harness Test* in Chapter Nine.
   a. If the resistance is within the specified range, replace the regulator/rectifier.
   b. If the resistance is outside the specified range, perform Step 7.
7. Check the resistance of the stator coil as described in Chapter Nine.
   a. If the resistance is within specification, replace the charging coil.
   b. If the resistance is outside the specified range, check for dirty or loose-fitting alternation connections.

Battery Overcharging

1. Check all connections. Make sure they are tight and free of corrosion.
2. Perform the *Regulated Voltage Test* described in Chapter Nine.
   a. If the voltage is within specification, replace the battery.
   b. If the voltage greatly exceeds the specified range, perform Step 3.
3. Check the continuity of the regulator/rectifier connector as described by *Charge Coil Resistance Test* in Chapter Nine.
   a. If the connector does not have continuity, check for a loose regulator/rectifier connector. If the connection is good, replace the regulator/rectifier.
   b. If the connector has continuity, check for a poor connection or an open in the wire harness.

IGNITION SYSTEM

Tools

Honda recommends the use of either a peak voltage tester or the Honda peak voltage adapter (part

TROUBLESHOOTING

no. 07HGJ-0020100) with a commercially available digital multimeter (minimum impedance of 10M ohms/DVC) for troubleshooting the ignition system. If these tools are unavailable, refer testing to a Honda dealership.

No Spark at the Spark Plug

1. Perform the *Spark Test* described in this chapter.
2. Check the spark plug cap and spark plug wire.
3. Perform the ignition coil primary peak voltage test, the exciter coil peak voltage test and the ignition pulse generator peak voltage test described in Chapter Nine. Write down the results of each test. If the results of any of the peak voltage test are under the specifications in **Table 1** of Chapter Nine, check the following conditions that best describe the faulty test results, and test and replace the necessary components.
4. If the ignition coil primary peak voltage is low, check the following conditions. If the test result remains low, replace the components in the order specified:
   a. Check the peak voltage adapter connections. The system is normal if the measured voltage exceeds the standard voltage at least once. A low reading may indicate reversed connections.
   b. Check the impedance of the multimeter. It must be at least 10 M ohms VDC.
   c. Check the battery state of charge. If it is low, the cranking speed may have been to slow during the test.
   d. If using a peak voltage tester, check to make sure the sampling time and measured pulse were not synchronized. The system is normal if the measured voltage exceeds the standard voltage at least once.
   e. Check for poor connections or a short in the ignition circuit as described in Chapter Nine.
   f. Check the neutral switch as described in *Switches* in Chapter Nine.
   g. Replace the neutral switch.
   h. Replace the exciter coil.
   i. Replace the ignition coil.
   j. Replace the ignition control module (ICM).
5. If there is no ignition coil primary peak voltage reading, check the following conditions. If the test result remains low, replace the components in the order specified:
   a. Check the peak voltage adapter connections. The system is normal if the measured voltage exceeds the standard voltage at least once. A low reading may indicate reversed connections.
   b. Check for a short in the engine stop switch or ignition as described in *Switches* in Chapter Nine.
   c. Check for short or poor connection in the ICM.
   d. Check for a short or a poor connection in the green/white wire of the ICM.
   e. Check for a short in the neutral switch as described in *Switches* in Chapter Nine.
   f. Replace the neutral switch.
   g. Replace the peak voltage adaptor.
   h. Replace the exciter coil.
   i. Replace the ignition pulse generator.
   j. If all other procedures test correct, or components have been replaced and there is still no reading replace the ICM.
6. If the ignition coil primary peak voltage is normal, but there is not spark at the plug, check the following conditions and replace the specified component if necessary:
   a. Check the spark plug.
   b. Check the ignition coil for leaking current in the secondary winding.
   c. Replace the ignition coil.
7. If the exciter coil peak voltage is low, check the following conditions. If the test result remains low, replace the specified component:
   a. Check the impedance of the multimeter. It must be at least 10 M ohms VDC.
   b. Check the battery state of charge. If it is low, the cranking speed was too slow during the test.
   c. If using a peak voltage tester, check to make sure the sampling time and measured pulse were not synchronized. The system is normal if the measured voltage exceeds the standard voltage at least once.
   d. Faulty exciter coil, replace the stator.
8. If there is no reading for the exciter coil peak voltage, check the following conditions. If the test result remains the same, replace the specified component:
   a. Check the peak voltage adapter or the peak voltage tester.
   b. Faulty exciter coil, replace the stator.
9. If the peak voltage reading of the ignition pulse generator is low, check the following conditions. If

the test result remains low, replace the specified component:
   a. Check the impedance of the multimeter. It must be at least 10 M ohms VDC.
   b. Check the charge of the battery. If it is low, the cranking speed was too slow during the test.
   c. If the testing is done using a peak voltage tester, make sure the sampling time and measured pulse were not synchronized. The system is normal if the measured voltage exceeds the standard voltage at least once.
   d. Replace the ignition pulse generator.

10. If there is no peak voltage reading for the ignition pulse generator, check the following conditions. If the test result remains the same, replace the specified component:
   a. Check the peak voltage adapter and peak voltage tester.
   b. Replace the ignition pulse generator.

LIGHTING SYSTEM

System Troubleshooting

If the headlight and/or taillight do not work, perform the following test procedures:
1. Check for a blown bulb as described in this section.
2. Check all lighting system connectors and wires for loose or damaged connections.
3. Check the main fuse as described in Chapter Nine. Replace a blown or damaged fuse.
4. Test the battery as described in Chapter Three. If necessary, clean and recharge the battery. If the battery is damaged or does not hold a charge, replace it. If the ATV was bought used, check the battery to make sure it is the correct type.
5. Test the ignition switch as described in Chapter Nine.
6. If the problem has not been solved, perform the *Lighting System Check* described in this section.

Faulty Bulbs

If a headlight or taillight bulb(s) continually burn out, check for one or more of the following conditions:
1. Incorrect bulb type. Refer to Chapter Nine for bulb specifications.
2. Damaged battery.

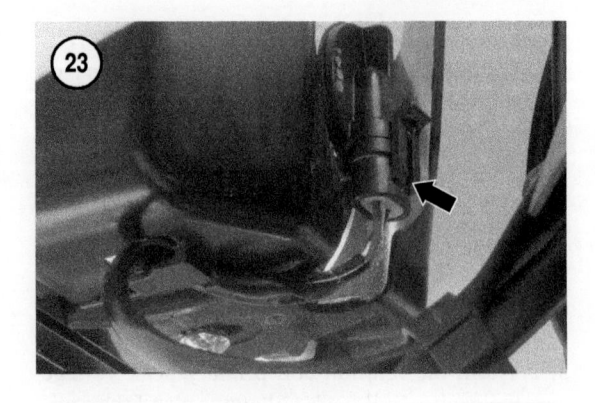

3. Damaged rectifier/regulator.
4. Damaged ignition switch and/or light switch.

Headlight Operates Darker Than Normal

Check for one or more of the following conditions:
1. Incorrect bulb type. Refer to Chapter Nine for bulb specifications.
2. Charging system problem.
3. Electric accessories added to the wiring harness. Disconnect each accessory one at a time, start the engine and check the headlight operation. If an accessory is the cause of the problem, contact the accessory manufacturer for more information.
4. Incorrect ground connection.
5. Poor main and/or light switch electrical contacts..

Lighting System Check

Headlight

If the headlights do not come on, perform the following test:
1. Remove the headlight bulb (Chapter Nine), and disconnect the headlight (**Figure 23**) from the main wiring harness.

NOTE
Two green bullet connectors are located in the same area of the frame. Follow the harness from the headlight socket so the correct bullet connector is identified during these tests. Refer to the wiring diagram at the end of this manual.

TROUBLESHOOTING

a. If the voltmeter reads 12 volts, continue with Step 5.
b. If the voltmeter does not read 12 volts, check the wiring harness from the ignition switch to the headlight socket for damage.

5. Turn the ignition switch off. Connect the voltmeter positive lead to the headlight connector blue lead and the voltmeter negative lead to the headlight connector green lead. Turn the ignition switch on and the dimmer switch to high. Note the voltmeter reading:

a. If the voltmeter reads 12 volts, continue with Step 6.
b. If the voltmeter does not read 12 volts, check the wiring harness from the ignition switch to the headlight socket for damage.

6. Turn the ignition switch off and disconnect the voltmeter leads. If the voltmeter read 12 volts for both tests (Step 4 and Step 5), the headlight wiring is good.

Taillight

If the taillight does not turn on, perform the following test:

1. Remove the taillight bulb (A, **Figure 25**) as described in Chapter Nine, and disconnect the taillight bullet connectors from the wiring harness.

   a. Connect an ohmmeter to the bulb terminals. The reading should be 0 ohms. Replace the bulb if the ohmmeter reads infinity.
   b. Check the continuity of the taillight wires. Connect an ohmmeter to one terminal in the taillight socket (B, **Figure 25**) and to the taillight side of its related bullet connector. Repeat for the other wire. Each reading should be 0 ohms. If any reading indicates an open circuit, replace the taillight socket if it cannot be repaired.

2. Install the taillight bulb into its socket and reconnect the socket bullet connectors to the main wiring harness. Do not reinstall the socket into the taillight housing (mounting position). The taillight bulb and socket must be connected to the main wiring harness when making the following tests.

3. Switch a voltmeter to its DC20V scale. In Step 4, test the taillight socket bullet connectors with the taillight connectors connected to the main wiring harness.

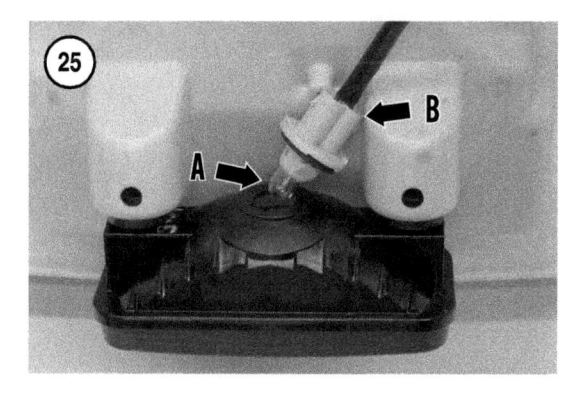

a. Connect an ohmmeter to the contacts on the back side of the bulb socket (**Figure 24**). The reading should be 0 ohms. Replace the bulb if the ohmmeter indicates an open circuit.
b. Check the continuity of the headlight socket. Remove the headlight bulb from the socket. Connect the ohmmeter to each socket terminal and it's corresponding contact on the back of the socket. Each terminal should have continuity. If a terminal does not have continuity, replace the headlight socket.

2. Install the headlight bulb into its socket and reconnect the socket bullet connectors to their mates from the wiring harness. Do not install the socket into its headlight housing. The headlight bulb and socket must be connected to the wiring harness when making the following tests.

3. Switch a voltmeter to its DC20V scale. In Step 4 and Step 5, carefully test the bullet connectors while they are connected to the main wiring harness.

4. Connect the voltmeter positive lead to the headlight connector white lead and the voltmeter negative lead to the headlight connector green lead. Turn the ignition switch on and the dimmer switch to low. Note the voltmeter reading:

4. Connect the voltmeter positive lead to the taillight connector brown lead and the voltmeter negative lead to the taillight connector green lead. Turn the ignition switch on and note the voltmeter reading:
   a. If the voltmeter reads 12 volts, continue with Step 5.
   b. If the voltmeter does not read 12 volts, check the wiring harness from the ignition switch to the taillight socket for damage.
5. Turn the ignition switch off and disconnect the voltmeter leads. If the voltmeter reads 12 volts in Step 4, the taillight wiring is good.

FUEL SYSTEM

Fuel system troubleshooting is covered in *Engine Will Not Start, Poor Idle Speed Performance* and *Poor Medium and High Speed Performance* in this chapter.

ENGINE OVERHEATING

Engine overheating can quickly cause engine seizure and damage. The following section lists the probable causes that can lead to engine overheating.
1. Ignition system:
   a. Incorrect spark plug gap.
   b. Incorrect spark plug heat range. Refer to Chapter Three.
   c. Faulty ICM incorrect ignition timing.
2. Engine compression system:
   a. Cylinder head gasket leak.
   b. Heavy carbon buildup in combustion chamber.
3. Engine lubrication system:
   a. Incorrect oil level.
   b. Incorrect oil viscosity.
   c. Faulty oil pump.
   d. Plugged oil line.
4. Fuel system:
   a. Carburetor fuel level too low.
   b. Incorrect carburetor adjustment or jetting.
   c. Loose carburetor boot clamps.
   d. Leaking or damaged carburetor-to-air filter housing air boot.
   e. Incorrect air/fuel mixture.
5. Engine load:
   a. Dragging brake(s).
   b. Damaged drive train components.
   c. Slipping clutch.
   d. Engine oil level too high.

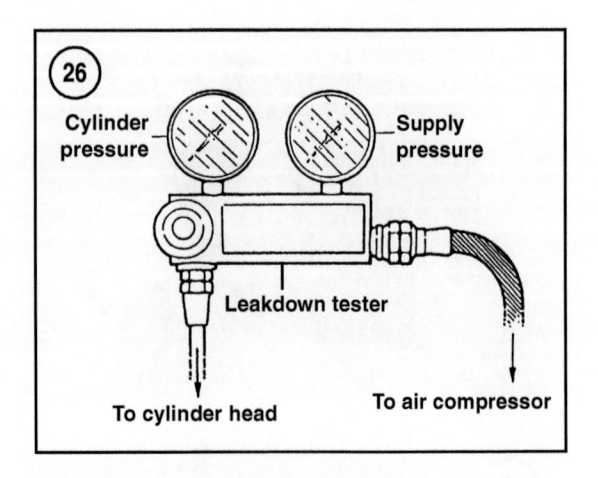

ENGINE

Preignition

Preignition is the premature burning of fuel and is caused by hot spots in the combustion chamber. The fuel ignites before spark ignition occurs. Glowing deposits in the combustion chamber, inadequate cooling or an overheated spark plug can all cause preignition. This is first noticed as a power loss but eventually causes damage to internal parts of the engine because of higher combustion chamber temperature.

Detonation

Commonly called spark knock or fuel knock, detonation is the violent explosion of fuel in the combustion chamber instead of the controlled burn that occurs during normal combustion. Severe damage can result. Use of low octane gasoline is a common cause of detonation.

Even when using a high octane gasoline, detonation can still occur. Other causes are over-advanced ignition timing, lean fuel mixture at or near full throttle, inadequate engine cooling, or the excessive accumulation of carbon deposits in the combustion chamber and on the piston crown.

Power Loss

Several factors can cause a lack of power and speed. Look for a clogged air filter or a fouled or damaged spark plug. A galled piston or cylinder, incorrect piston clearance or worn or sticking piston rings may be responsible. Look for loose bolts, defective gaskets or leaking machined mating surfaces on the cylinder head, cylinder or crankcase.

Piston Seizure

Piston seizure can be caused by incorrect piston-to-cylinder clearance, piston rings with an improper end gap, compression leak, incorrect air/fuel mixture, spark plug of the wrong heat range or incorrect ignition timing. Overheating from any cause may cause piston seizure.

Piston Slap

Piston slap is an audible slapping or rattling noise resulting from excessive piston-to-cylinder clearance. If allowed to continue, piston slap eventually causes the piston skirt to crack and shatter.

To prevent piston slap, clean the air filter element on a regular schedule. If you hear piston slap, disassemble the engine top end and measure the cylinder bore and piston diameter and check for excessive clearance. Replace parts that exceed service limits or show damage.

ENGINE NOISES

1. Knocking or pinging during acceleration can be caused by using a lower octane fuel than recommended or a poor quality of fuel. Incorrect carburetor jetting or a spark plug that is too hot can also cause pinging. Refer to *Spark Plug* in Chapter Three. Check also for excessive carbon buildup in the combustion chamber or for a faulty ICM.
2. Slapping or rattling noises at low speed or during acceleration can be caused by excessive piston-to-cylinder clearance. Check also for a bent connecting rod or worn piston pin and/or piston pin holes in the piston.
3. A knocking or rapping while decelerating usually is caused by excessive rod bearing clearance.
4. Persistent knocking and vibration or other noise—Usually caused by worn main bearings. If the main bearings are good, consider the following:
   a. Loose engine mounts.
   b. Cracked frame.
   c. Leaking cylinder head gasket.
   d. Exhaust pipe leak at cylinder head.
   e. Stuck piston ring.
   f. Broken piston ring.
   g. Partial engine seizure.
   h. Excessive connecting rod small end bearing clearance.
   i. Excessive connecting rod big end side clearance.
   j. Excessive crankshaft runout.
   k. Worn or damaged primary drive gear.
5. Rapid on-off squeal can be caused by a compression leak around cylinder head gasket or spark plug.

CYLINDER LEAKDOWN TEST

A cylinder leakdown test can determine if an engine problem is caused by leaking valves, a blown head gasket or broken, worn or stuck piston rings. A cylinder leakdown test is performed by applying compressed air to the cylinder, and then measuring the amount it leaks as a percentage. A cylinder leakdown tester (**Figure 26**) and an air compressor are required to perform this test. Follow the manufacturer's directions, along with the following information when performing a cylinder leakdown test.

1. Start and run the engine until it reaches normal operating temperature, and turn the engine off.
2. Remove the air filter element as described in Chapter Three. Open and secure the throttle in the wide-open position.
3. Set the piston to TDC on its compression stroke. Refer to *Valve Clearance* in Chapter Three.
4. Remove the spark plug.

NOTE
The engine may turn when air pressure is applied to the cylinder. To prevent this, shift the transmission into fifth gear and set the parking brake.

5. Install the cylinder leakdown tester into the spark plug hole (**Figure 27**).
6. Perform a cylinder leakdown test following the manufacturer's instructions. Listen for leaking air while noting the following:
    a. Air leaking through the exhaust pipe indicates a leaking exhaust valve.
    b. Air leaking through the carburetor indicates a leaking intake valve.
    c. Air leaking through the crankcase breather tube indicates worn piston rings.
7. A cylinder leaking 10 percent or more requires service.
8. Remove the tester and reinstall the spark plug.

CLUTCH

The TRX250EX uses two clutch assemblies: a centrifugal clutch (A, **Figure 28**) and a change clutch (B).

All clutch service, except adjustment, requires partial engine disassembly to identify and repair the problem. Refer to Chapter Six.

Clutch Slip

1. Clutch wear or damage:
    a. Incorrect clutch adjustment.
    b. Worn clutch shoe (centrifugal clutch).
    c. Loose, weak or damaged clutch spring (change and centrifugal clutch).
    d. Worn friction discs (change clutch).
    e. Warped clutch plates (change clutch).
    f. Worn clutch center and/or clutch housing (change clutch).
    g. Incorrectly assembled clutch.
2. Engine oil:
    a. Low oil level.
    b. Oil additives.
    c. Low viscosity oil.

Clutch Drag

1. Clutch wear or damage:
    a. Incorrect clutch adjustment.
    b. Damaged or incorrectly assembled clutch lever assembly.
    c. Warped clutch plates.
    d. Swollen friction discs.
    e. Warped pressure plate.
    f. Incorrect clutch spring tension.
    g. Incorrectly assembled clutch.
    h. Loose clutch nut.
    i. Incorrect clutch mechanism adjustment (change clutch).
2. Engine oil:
    a. Oil level too high.
    b. High viscosity oil.

Vehicle Creeps with Clutch Disengaged

1. Damaged centrifugal clutch.
2. Warped drive plate (centrifugal clutch).

Rough Clutch Operation

1. Damaged clutch housing slots (change clutch).
2. Damaged clutch center splines (change clutch).
3. Incorrect engine idle speed.

Transmission is Difficult to Shift

1. Clutch wear or damage:
    a. Incorrect clutch adjustment.
    b. Damaged clutch lifter mechanism.
2. Damaged shift drum shifter plate.

TRANSMISSION

Transmission symptoms can be difficult to distinguish from clutch symptoms. Make sure the clutch is not causing the trouble before working on the transmission.

Difficult Shifting

If the shift shaft does not move smoothly from one gear to the next, check the following:
1. Shift shaft:
    a. Incorrectly installed shift lever.
    b. Stripped splines on gearshift spindle, sub-gearshift spindle arm or sub-gearshift spindle.
    c. Bent sub-gearshift spindle.
    d. Damaged sub-gearshift spindle return spring.
    e. Damaged gearshift linkage assembly where it engages the shift drum.
    f. Stopper arm binding on pivot bolt.
2. Stopper arm:
    a. Seized or damaged stopper arm roller.

TROUBLESHOOTING

b. Weak or damaged stopper arm spring.
c. Loose stopper arm mounting bolt.
d. Incorrectly assembled stopper arm assembly.
3. Shift drum and shift forks:
   a. Bent shift fork(s).
   b. Damaged shift fork guide pin(s).
   c. Seized shift fork (on shaft).
   d. Broken shift fork or shift fork shaft.
   e. Damaged shift drum groove(s).
   f. Damaged shift drum bearing surfaces.

Gears Pop Out Of Mesh

If the transmission shifts into gear but then slips or pops out, check the following:
1. Gearshift linkage:
   a. Incorrectly assembled sub-gearshift spindle and gearshift A arm assembly.
   b. Stopper arm fails to move or set properly.
2. Shift drum:
   a. Incorrect thrust play.
   b. Worn or damaged shift drum groove(s).
3. Shift fork(s)
   a. Bent or damaged shift fork.
   b. Bent or damaged shift fork shaft.
4. Transmission:
   a. Worn or damaged gear dogs.
   b. Excessive gear thrust play.
   c. Worn or damaged transmission shaft circlips or thrust washers.

Transmission Overshifts

If the transmission overshifts when shifting up or down, check for a weak or broken gearshift return spring or a weak or broken stopper arm and spring assembly.

Transmission Fails to Shift into Reverse

If the transmission fails to shift into or operate in reverse properly, check the following:
1. Incorrect reverse cable adjustment.
2. Loose or damaged reverse stopper arm.
3. Damaged reverse stopper shaft.

FINAL DRIVE

Noise is usually the first indication of a final drive problem. It is not always easy to diagnose the source of the noise and the operating conditions that produce it.

Some clues may be gained by noting whether the noise is a hum, growl or knock, whether it is produced when the vehicle is accelerating under load or coasting and whether it is heard when the vehicle is going straight or making a turn.

Final drive service procedures are covered in Chapter Twelve.

CAUTION
Improperly diagnosed noises can lead to rapid and excessive final train wear and damage. If unfamiliar with the operation and repair of the final drive assembly, refer troubleshooting to a qualified repair facility.

Oil Inspection

Drain the gearcase oil (Chapter Three) into a clean container. Wipe a small amount of oil on your finger, and rub the finger and thumb together. Check for the presence of metallic particles. Also check the drain bolt for metal particles. While a small amount of particles in the oil is normal, an abnormal amount of debris is an indication of bearing or gear damage.

Excessive Noise

1. Low oil level.
2. Excessive ring gear and pinion gear backlash.
3. Worn or damaged drive pinion and splines.
4. Damaged driven flange and wheel hub.
5. Worn or damaged driven flange and ring gear shaft.

HANDLING

Poor handling reduces overall performance and may cause loss of control and a crash. Check the following items when experiencing poor handling:
1. If the handlebars are difficult to turn, check for the following:
    a. Low tire pressure.
    b. Incorrect cable routing.
    c. Damaged steering shaft bushing and/or bearing.
    d. Bent steering shaft or frame.
    e. Steering shaft nut too tight.
2. If there is excessive handlebar shake or vibration, check for the following:
    a. Incorrect tire pressure.
    b. Loose or damaged handlebar clamps.
    c. Incorrect handlebar clamp installation.
    d. Bent or cracked handlebar.
    e. Worn wheel bearing(s).
    f. Excessively worn or damaged tire(s).
    g. Damaged rim(s).
    h. Loose, missing or broken engine mount bolts and mounts.
    i. Cracked frame, especially at the steering head.
    j. Damaged shock absorber damper rod.
    k. Leaking shock absorber damper housing.
    l. Sagged shock spring(s).
    m. Loose or damaged shock mount bolts.
3. If the rear suspension is too soft, check for the following:
    a. Damaged shock absorber damper rod.
    b. Leaking shock absorber damper housing.
    c. Sagged shock spring.
    d. Loose or damaged shock mount bolts.
4. If the rear suspension is too hard, check for the following:
    a. Rear tire pressure is too high.
    b. Incorrect shock absorber adjustment.
    c. Damaged shock absorber damper rod.
    d. Leaking shock absorber damper housing.
    e. Sagged shock spring.
    f. Loose or damaged shock mount bolts.
    g. Improperly tightened swing arm pivot.
5. Frame:
    a. Damaged frame.
    b. Cracked or broken engine mount brackets.
6. Wobbling wheel:
    a. Loose wheel nuts.
    b. Loose or incorrectly installed wheel hub.
    c. Excessive wheel bearing play.
    d. Loose wheel bearing.
    e. Bent wheel rim.
    f. Bent frame or other suspension component.
    g. Improperly tightened axle.
    h. Worn swing arm bearings.
7. If vehicle pulls to one side:
    a. Incorrect tire pressure.
    b. Incorrect tie rod adjustment.
    c. Bent or loose tie rod.
    d. Incorrect wheel alignment.
    e. Bent frame or other suspension component.
    f. Weak front shock absorber.

FRAME NOISE

Noises traced to the frame or suspension are usually caused by loose, worn or damaged parts. Noises related to the frame are listed below:
1. Drum brake noise—A screeching sound during braking is the most common drum brake noise. Some other drum brake noises can be caused by:
    a. Glazed brake lining or drum surface.
    b. Excessively worn brake linings.
    c. Warped brake drum.
2. Front or rear shock absorber noise—Check for the following:
    a. Loose shock absorber mounting bolts.
    b. Cracked or broken shock spring.
    c. Damaged shock absorber.
3. Some other frame noises can be caused by:
    a. Cracked or broken frame.
    b. Broken swing arm or shock linkage.
    c. Loose engine mounting bolts.
    d. Damaged steering shaft bearings.
    e. Loose mounting bracket.

BRAKES

The front disc brakes and the rear drum brake are critical to riding performance and safety. Inspect the brakes frequently and repair any problem immediately. When replacing or refilling the front brake fluid, use only DOT 3 or DOT 4 brake fluid from a sealed container. Refer to Chapter Thirteen for additional information on brake fluid selection and brake service.

TROUBLESHOOTING

Front Disc Brake

If the front disc brakes are not working properly, check for one or more of the following conditions:
1. Air in brake line.
2. Brake fluid level too low.
3. Loose brake hose banjo bolts. Brake fluid is leaking out.
4. Loose or damaged brake hose or line.
5. Worn or damaged brake disc.
6. Worn or damaged brake pads.
7. Oil on brake disc or brake pad surfaces.
8. Worn or damaged caliper(s).

Rear Drum Brake

If the rear drum brake is not working properly, check for one or more of the following conditions:
1. Incorrect rear brake adjustment.
2. Incorrect brake cam lever position.
3. Worn or damaged brake drum.
4. Worn or damaged brake linings.
5. Oil on brake drum or brake lining surfaces.
6. Weak or damaged brake return springs.

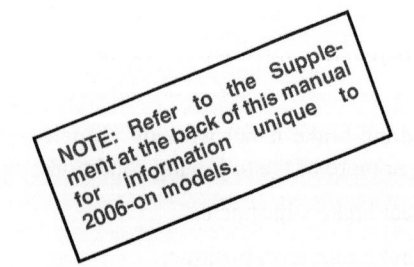

NOTE: Refer to the Supplement at the back of this manual for information unique to 2006-on models.

CHAPTER THREE

LUBRICATION, MAINTENANCE AND TUNE-UP

This chapter describes lubrication, maintenance and tune-up procedures.

Tables 1-6 are at the end of this chapter.

PRE-RIDE CHECK LIST

Perform the following checks before riding the ATV. All of these checks are described in this chapter. If a component requires service, refer to the appropriate section.

1. Inspect all fuel lines and fittings for leaks.
2. Make sure the fuel tank is full of fresh gasoline.
3. Make sure the engine oil level is correct.
4. Check the throttle for proper operation in all steering positions. Open the throttle all the way and release it. The throttle should close quickly with no binding or roughness.
5. Check that the brake levers operate properly with no binding. Replace a broken lever. Check the lever housings for damage.
6. Check the brake fluid level in the front master cylinder reservoir. Add DOT 3 or DOT 4 brake fluid if necessary.
7. Check the parking brake operation, and adjust it if necessary.
8. Inspect the front and rear suspension. Make sure they have a good solid feel with no looseness. Turn the handlebar from side to side to check steering play. Service the steering assembly if excessive play is noted. Make sure the handlebar cables do not bind.
9. Check the drive shaft boots for damage.
10. Check tire pressure.
11. Check the exhaust system for looseness or damage.
12. Check for missing or damaged skid plates.
13. Check the undercarriage for dirt, vegetation or other debris that might create a fire hazard or interfere with vehicle operation.
14. Check the tightness of all fasteners, especially engine, steering and suspension mounting hardware.
15. Make sure the headlight and taillight work properly.
16. Check that all switches work properly.
17. Check the air filter drain tube for contamination.
18. If carrying cargo, check that it is properly secured.
19. Start the engine and stop it with the engine stop switch. If the engine stop switch does not work properly, test the switch as described in Chapter Nine.

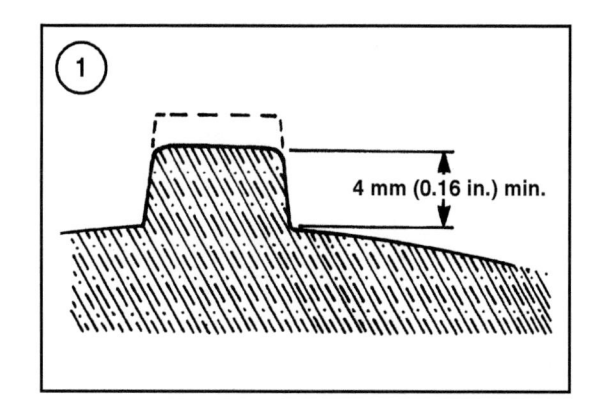

LUBRICATION, MAINTENANCE AND TUNE-UP

unequal air pressures, the vehicle may run toward one side causing poor handling.

CAUTION
Do not overinflate the tires. They can be permanently distorted and damaged.

Tire Inspection

Because ATVs operate in a variety of terrain, the tires take a lot of punishment. Inspect them daily for excessive wear, cuts, abrasions or punctures. If a nail or other object is found in the tire, mark its location with a light crayon before removing it. Service the tire as described in Chapter Ten.

To gauge tire wear, inspect the height of the tread knobs. If the average tread knob height (**Figure 1**) is less than the minimum tread depth specification in **Table 2**, replace the tire as described in Chapter Ten.

WARNING
Do not ride the vehicle with damaged or excessively worn tires. Poor tires can cause loss of control. Replace damaged or excessively worn tires immediately.

Wheel Inspection

Inspect the wheels for damage. Wheel damage can cause an air leak or knock a wheel out of alignment. Improper wheel alignment can cause vibration and an unsafe riding condition.

Make sure the wheel nuts (**Figure 2**) are tightened securely. Tighten the wheel nuts in a crisscross pattern to 64 N•m (47 ft.-lb.).

MAINTENANCE SCHEDULE

Table 1 lists the maintenance schedule for the TRX250EX. Strict adherence to these recommendations helps ensure trouble-free operation. Perform the services more often when operating the vehicle commercially and/or in dusty or other harsh conditions.

Most of the services in **Table 1** are described in this chapter. However, some procedures that require more than minor disassembly or adjustment are covered in the appropriate chapters as indicated.

TIRES AND WHEELS

Tire Pressure

Check and adjust tire pressure (**Table 2**) to maintain good traction, handling and to get the maximum life from the tire. Check tire pressure when the tires are cold.

WARNING
Always inflate the tires to the correct air pressure. If the vehicle is run with

BATTERY

Many electrical system troubles can be traced to battery neglect. Inspect and clean the battery at periodic intervals.

Type

All TRX250EX models use a maintenance-free battery. This battery is sealed at the time of service and does not require additional water. Do not remove the sealing caps to add electrolyte or water; the battery may be damaged.

Because a maintenance-free battery requires a higher voltage charging system, do not replace a maintenance-free battery with a standard battery. Always replace the battery with its correct type and designated capacity. Refer to **Table 4** for battery specifications.

Safety Precautions

When working with batteries, use extreme care to avoid spilling or splashing the electrolyte. This solution contains sulfuric acid, which can ruin clothing and cause chemical burns. If it spills or splashes on clothing or skin, immediately neutralize the affected area with a solution of baking soda and water. Flush the area with an abundance of clean water. While the TRX250EX uses a sealed battery, it vents gasses and electrolyte can leak through cracks in the battery case.

> *WARNING*
> *Battery electrolyte is extremely harmful when splashed into eyes or an open sore. Always wear safety glasses and appropriate work clothes when working with batteries. If the electrolyte gets into eyes, flush the area thoroughly with clean water and get prompt medical attention.*

When charging a battery, highly explosive hydrogen gas forms in each cell. Some of this gas escapes through filler cap openings and can form an explosive atmosphere in and around the battery. This condition can persist for several hours. Sparks, an open flame or a lighted cigarette can ignite the gas, causing an internal battery explosion and possible injury.

When servicing the battery, note the following precautions to prevent an explosion or injury:

1. Do not smoke or permit any open flame near any battery being charged or near a recently charged battery.

2. Do not disconnect live circuits at the battery terminals because a spark usually occurs when a live circuit is broken.

3. Take care when connecting or disconnecting any battery charger. Make sure its power switch is off before making or breaking connections. Poor connections are a common cause of electrical arcs that cause explosions.

4. Keep all children and pets away from charging equipment and batteries.

5. Do not open a maintenance free battery.

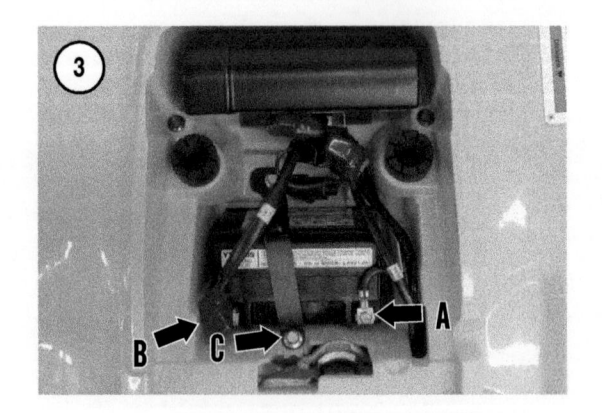

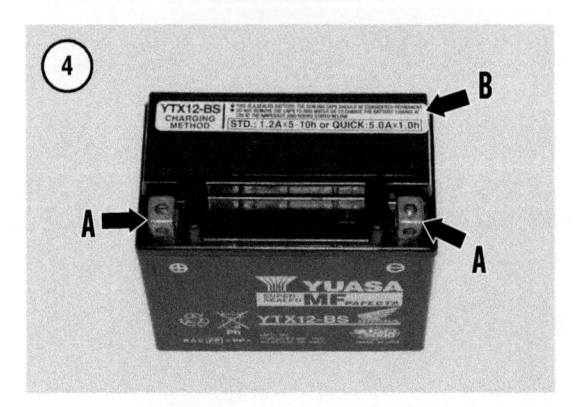

Removal/Installation

1. Turn the ignition switch off.

2. Remove the seat as described in Chapter Fourteen.

3. Disconnect the negative battery cable (A, **Figure 3**) from the battery.

4. Disconnect the positive battery cable (B, **Figure 3**) from the battery.

5. Remove the battery band (C, **Figure 3**) and lift the battery from the compartment.

6. Service the battery as described in this section.

7. Lower the battery into the battery box so its terminals face the direction shown in **Figure 3**.

8. Secure the battery in place with the battery band (C, **Figure 3**).

LUBRICATION, MAINTENANCE AND TUNE-UP

5

Digital voltmeter

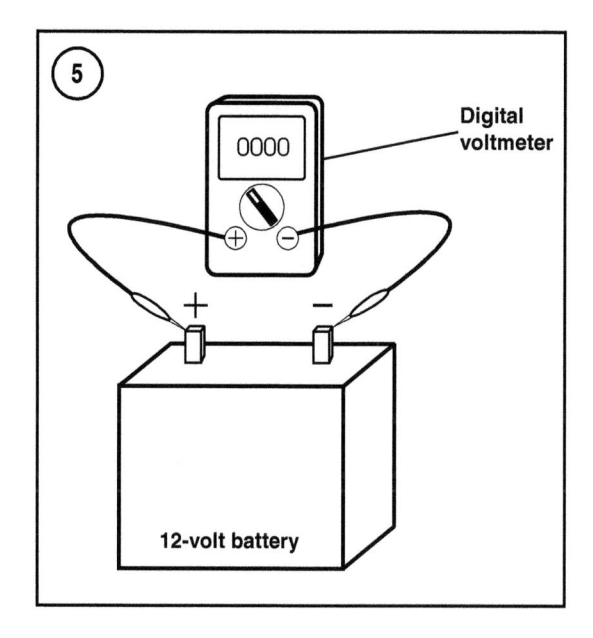

12-volt battery

9. Coat the battery terminals (A, **Figure 4**) with a thin layer of dielectric grease. This helps retard corrosion of the terminals.

10. Attach the positive battery cable (B, **Figure 3**) to the battery.

11. Attach the negative battery cable (A, **Figure 3**) to the battery.

12. Install the seat (Chapter Fourteen).

Inspection

For a preliminary test, connect a digital voltmeter to the battery negative and positive terminals and measure battery voltage (**Figure 5**). A fully-charged battery reads between 13.0-13.2 volts. If the voltmeter reads 12.8 volts or less, the battery is undercharged. If necessary, charge the battery as described in this chapter.

Table 5 lists battery state of charge readings for maintenance-free batteries.

Testing

When using a battery tester, follow the manufacturer's instructions. For best results, make sure the tester's cables are in working order and clamped tightly onto the battery terminals.

Charging

Always follow the manufacturer's instructions when using a battery charger.

> **CAUTION**
> *Always remove the battery from the vehicle before charging it. Never connect a battery charger to the battery with the electrical leads still connected to the battery.*

1. Remove the battery as described in this section.
2. Connect the positive charger lead to the positive battery terminal and the negative charger lead to the negative battery terminal.

> **CAUTION**
> *Do not exceed the recommended charging amperage rate or charging time on the label attached to the battery (B, Figure 4).*

> **CAUTION**
> *Do not charge the battery with a high-rate charger. The high current forced into the battery overheats the battery and damages the battery plates.*

3. Set the charger to 12 volts. If the amperage output is variable, select a low setting. Use the following suggested charging amperage and length of charging time:

> **CAUTION**
> *Standard charging is the preferred charging method. Quick charging should only be used in emergencies.*

  a. Standard charge: 1.2 amps at 5 to 10 hours.
  b. Quick charge: 5.0 amps at 1 hour.

4. Turn the charger on.
5. After charging the battery the specified time, turn the charger off and disconnect the charger leads.
6. Connect a digital voltmeter to the battery terminals (**Figure 5**) and measure battery voltage. A fully-charged battery reads 13.0-13.2 volts. Refer to **Table 5**.
7. If the battery voltage remains stable for 1 hour, the battery is charged.
8. Clean the battery cable connectors, battery terminals and case. Coat the terminals with a thin layer

of dielectric grease. This helps retard corrosion of the battery terminals.

9. Reinstall the battery as described in this section.

Cables

To ensure good electrical contact between the battery and the electrical cables, keep the cables clean and free of corrosion.

1. If the electrical cable terminals are badly corroded, disconnect them from the battery as described in this section.
2. Thoroughly clean each connector with a wire brush and a water and baking soda solution. Wipe the area dry with a clean cloth.
3. After cleaning, apply a thin layer of dielectric grease to the battery terminals before reattaching the cables.
4. Reconnect the battery cables as described in this section.
5. Coat the terminals with a thin layer of dielectric grease. This helps retard corrosion of the battery terminals.

Replacement

NOTE
*Recycle an old battery. When replacing the battery, turn in the old battery. Most motorcycle dealers accept old batteries in trade when purchasing a new one. **Never** place an old battery in the household trash.*

Always replace the battery with another maintenance-free battery. Before installing a new battery, make sure it is fully charged. Failure to do so shortens the useful life of the battery. Undercharging a new battery prevents a battery from ever obtaining a complete charge.

ENGINE OIL AND FILTER

Recommended Engine Oil

Honda recommends the use of Honda GN4 4-stroke oil or an equivalent 10W-40 engine oil with an API service classification of SF or SG. The classification is printed on the container. Try to use the same brand of oil at each oil change. Do not use oils with graphite or molybdenum additives. These can cause clutch slip and other clutch problems. Refer to **Figure 6** to select the correct weight oil for the anticipated ambient temperatures (not engine oil temperature).

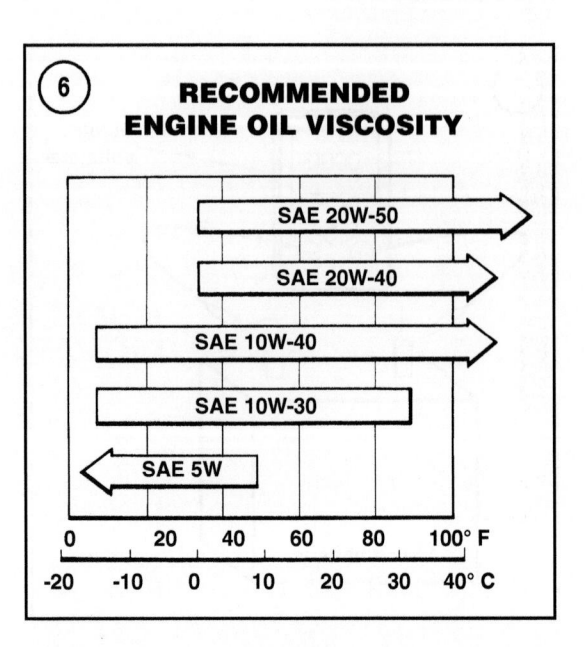

Engine Oil Level Check

Check the engine oil level with the dipstick/oil fill cap mounted on the left side of the engine.

1. Park the vehicle on level ground and set the parking brake.
2. Start the engine and let it run approximately 2-3 minutes.
3. Shut off the engine, and let the oil drain into the crankcase for a few minutes.
4. Unscrew and remove the dipstick/oil fill cap (**Figure 7**). Wipe it clean, and reinsert it onto the threads in the hole. Do not screw it in.
5. Remove the dipstick and read the oil level. The level is correct if it is between the two dipstick lines (A, **Figure 8**). If necessary, add the recommended type oil (**Table 3**) to correct the level.
6. Replace the dipstick O-ring (B, **Figure 8**) if damaged.
7. Install the dipstick/oil fill cap (**Figure 7**) and tighten it securely.

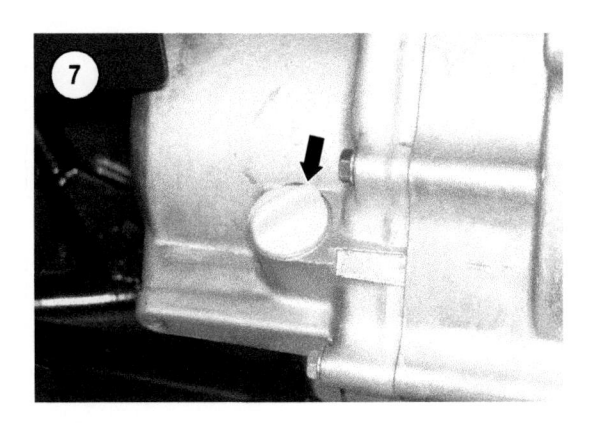

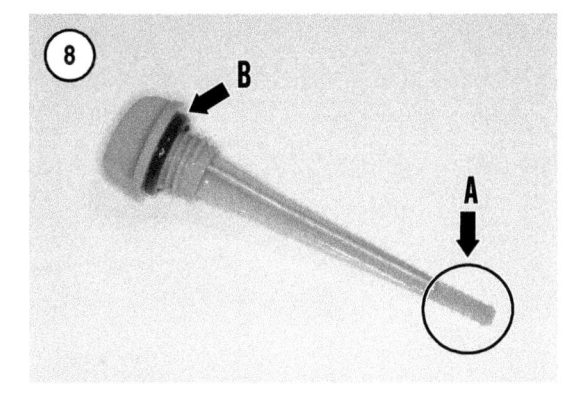

LUBRICATION, MAINTENANCE AND TUNE-UP

conditions, the oil becomes dirty more quickly and must be changed more frequently.

> *NOTE*
> *Never dispose of engine oil in the trash, on the ground or down a storm drain. Many service stations and oil retailers accept used oil for recycling. Do not combine other fluids with engine oil for recycling. To locate a recycler, contact the American Petroleum Institute (API) at **www.recycleoil.org**.*

> *NOTE*
> *Running the engine heats the oil, which enables the oil to flow more freely and carry contaminates and sludge out with it.*

1. Park the vehicle on level ground and apply the parking brake.
2. Start the engine, and let it warm to normal operating temperature. Shut the engine off.
3. Place a clean drain pan under the engine.
4. Remove the drain bolt (**Figure 9**), located in the bottom of the engine and drain the oil.
5. Remove the dipstick/oil fill cap (**Figure 7**) to help speed up the flow of oil.
6. Allow the oil to drain completely.
7. Replace the drain plug gasket if it is damaged or if the plug was leaking. Install the drain bolt (**Figure 9**), and tighten it to 25 N•m (18 ft.-lb.).
8. Insert a funnel into the oil fill hole and fill the engine with the correct weight and quantity of oil (**Table 3**).
9. Screw in the dipstick/oil fill cap (**Figure 7**) securely.
10. Start the engine and run at idle speed.
11. Turn the engine off. Check the drain bolt for leaks.
12. Check the oil level and adjust if necessary.

Engine Oil Centrifugal Filter Cleaning

Clean the centrifugal filter at the interval in **Table 1**.
1. Remove the clutch cover as described in Chapter Six.
2. Remove the mounting bolts (A, **Figure 10**) and oil filter cover (B) from the centrifugal clutch.
3. Wipe the clutch filter cover (A, **Figure 11**) and inside of the centrifugal clutch (**Figure 12**) with a clean, lint-free cloth.

Engine Oil Change

> *WARNING*
> *Prolonged contact with used oil may cause skin cancer. Wash your hands with soap and water after handling or coming in contact with motor oil.*

Table 1 lists the recommended oil and filter change intervals. This assumes the vehicle is operated in moderate climates. If it is operated in dusty

4. Inspect the gasket (B, **Figure 11**) on the back of the oil filter cover. Replace the gasket if necessary.
5. Install the oil filter cover (B, **Figure 10**). Apply ThreeBond 1333B to the threads of the mounting bolts and tighten the bolts (A, **Figure 10**) securely.
6. Install the clutch cover as described in Chapter Six.

Engine Oil screen

An oil screen is mounted inside the engine. The engine assembly must be removed and the crankcase split to service the oil screen. Honda recommends the screen be cleaned at the same interval as the centrifugal filter. However, since this is not practical, clean/inspect the screen when there are lubrication problems or when performing engine lower end repairs.

1. Access the oil screen as described in Chapter Five.
2. Simultaneously slide the oil screen (A, **Figure 13**) and oil strainer (B) from the inside of the front crankcase half.
3. Clean the oil screen (A, **Figure 14**) and oil strainer (B).
4. Place the oil screen (A, **Figure 13**) on top of the oil strainer (B), and then install the oil screen/strainer assembly. Install the screen so its narrow side slides into the crankcase half.
5. Reinstall the clutch cover as described in Chapter Six.

FINAL DRIVE OIL

Oil Level Check

1. Park the vehicle on a level surface and set the parking brake.
2. Clean the area around the oil fill cap (**Figure 15**) and oil check bolt (**Figure 16**).
3. Remove the oil check bolt.

CAUTION
If the oil level is low, inspect the final drive for leaks.

4. Oil should immediately flow from the oil-check-bolt hole once it is removed. If it does not, remove the oil fill cap (**Figure 15**), and add hypoid gear oil (**Table 3**) until oil starts to flow from the bolt hole.

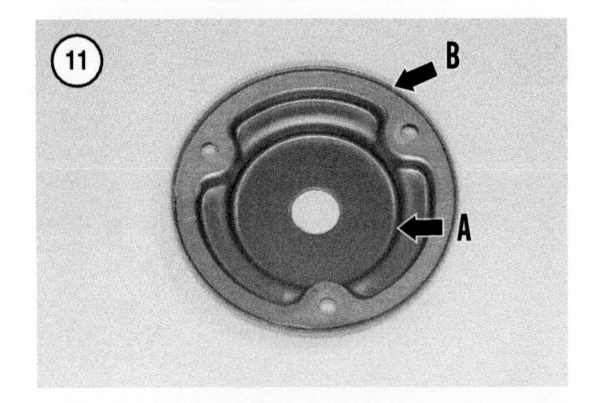

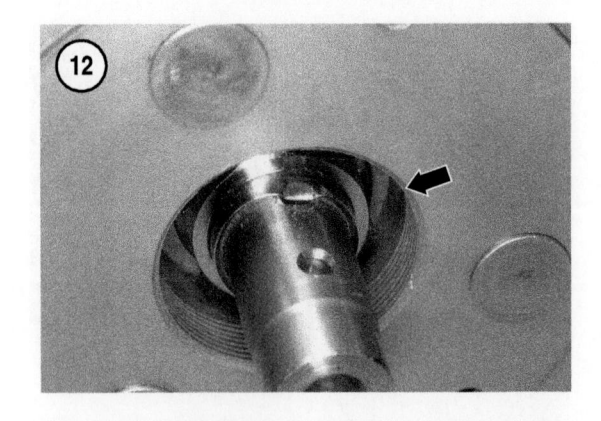

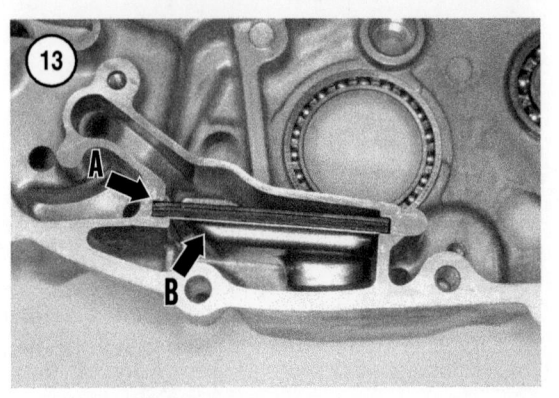

LUBRICATION, MAINTENANCE AND TUNE-UP

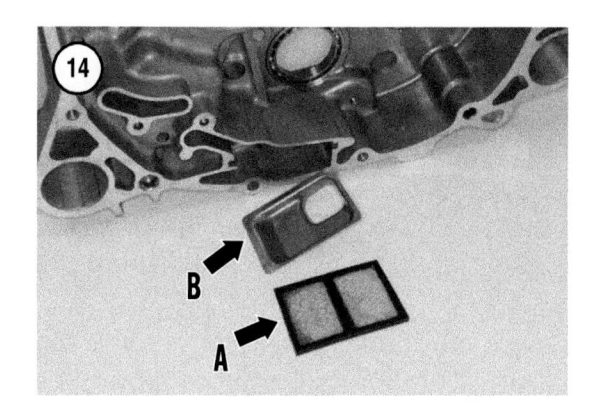

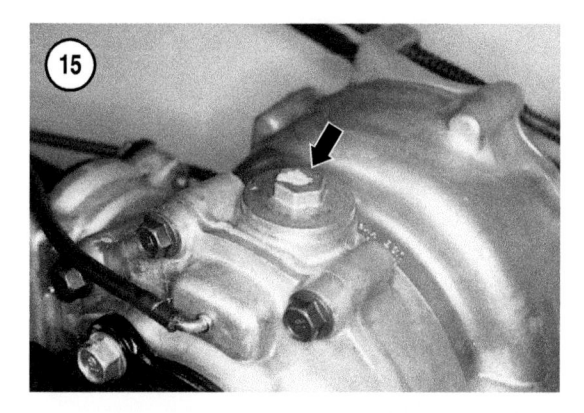

5. Install the oil check bolt, and tighten the bolt to 12 N•m (106 in.-lb.). Replace the sealing washer if necessary.

6. If removed, install the oil fill cap. Apply multipurpose lithium grease to the cap O-ring, and tighten to 12 N•m (106 in.-lb.).

Oil Change

The recommended oil change interval is in **Table 1**. Discard old oil in the same manner described in *Engine oil change* in this chapter.

NOTE
A short ride heats the final drive oil, which enables the oil to flow more freely and carry contaminates and sludge when drained.

1. Ride the vehicle until it reaches normal operating temperature.
2. Park the vehicle on a level surface and set the parking brake. Turn the engine off.

NOTE
Skid plate removal is not necessary to access the drain plug.

3. Place a drain pan underneath the final drive.
4. Remove the oil fill cap (**Figure 15**).
5. Remove the drain bolt (**Figure 17**), and drain the oil.
6. Replace the drain bolt sealing washer if it is damaged or leaking.
7. Install the drain bolt and sealing washer. Tighten the bolt to 12 N•m (106 in.-lb.).
8. Insert a funnel into the oil fill hole and add the recommended type and quantity of gear oil (**Table 3**).
9. Remove the funnel and check the oil level as described in this section. Add additional oil if necessary.
10. Inspect the oil fill cap O-ring. Replace it if damaged.
11. Apply a multipurpose lithium grease to the O-ring, and install the oil fill cap (**Figure 15**). Tighten the cap to 12 N•m (106 in.-lb.).
12. Test ride the vehicle and check for leaks. After the test ride, recheck the oil level. Adjust the oil level if necessary.

GENERAL LUBRICATION

The services in this section are not included in the maintenance schedule (**Table 1**). However, lubricate these items throughout the service year depending on vehicle use. Use a waterproof, multipurpose lithium grease or equivalent when grease is specified.

Steering Shaft

Remove the steering shaft (Chapter Eleven) and lubricate the bushing with lithium grease. At the same time, check the lower bearing and seals for damage.

Front Control Arms

Remove the pivot bolts from the upper and lower arms. Lubricate the bolts and bushings with lithium grease. Refer to Chapter Eleven for service.

Front Wheel Bearing Seals

Lubricate the front wheel bearing seals with lithium grease. If the front wheel bearings are not sealed, lubricate them. Refer to *Rear Brake Drum* in Chapter Thirteen for front wheel bearing and seal service.

Shock Absorber Pivot Bolt

Remove the front (Chapter Eleven) and rear (Chapter Twelve) shock absorbers and lubricate the mounting bolts with lithium grease.

AIR AND FUEL SYSTEM

Air Box Drain Tube

NOTE
*Non-California models use two air box drain tubes: one on the bottom of the air box (A, **Figure 18**); the other on the side (B). California models use only one drain tube.*

Remove and inspect the air box drain tube(s). If a tube is filled with water, dirt and other debris; clean and oil the air filter. Clean the air box and drain tube(s) at the same time.

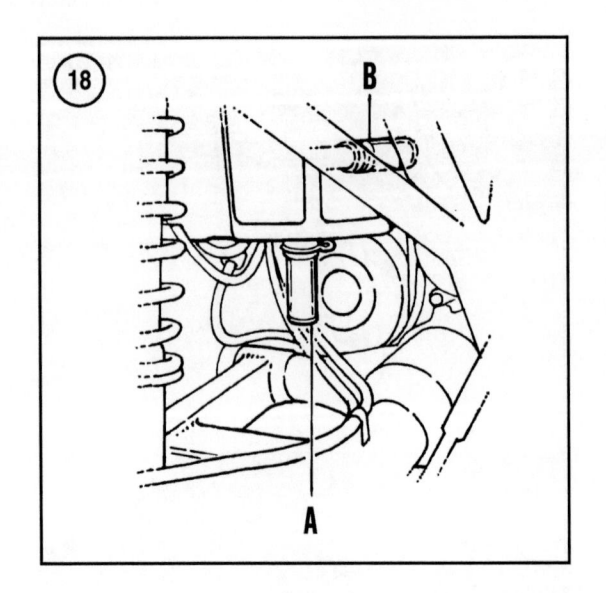

Air Filter

A clogged air filter decreases the efficiency and life of the engine. Never run the engine without a properly installed air filter. Dust that enters the engine can cause excessive engine wear and clog carburetor jets and passages.

Refer to **Figure 19**.

Removal and installation

1. Remove the seat as described in Chapter Fourteen.
2. Release the spring clips (A, **Figure 20**) and remove the air box cover (B).
3. Loosen the air filter hose clamp (A, **Figure 21**) and mounting screw (B).
4. Remove the air filter assembly (C, **Figure 21**) from the air box.
5. On California models, remove the dust cover (A, **Figure 22**) from the air box.
6. Disassemble, clean and oil the air filter as described in this section.
7. Check the air box and carburetor boot for dirt or other contaminants.
8. Wipe the inside of the air box with a clean rag. If the air box cannot be cleaned with it bolted to the frame, remove it (Chapter Eight).
9. On California models, clean the dust cover with compressed air. Install the dust cover into the air box (A, **Figure 22**) so it sits flat in its seat. Do not compress the dust cover into the seat.
10. Cover the air box opening with a clean shop rag.

LUBRICATION, MAINTENANCE AND TUNE-UP

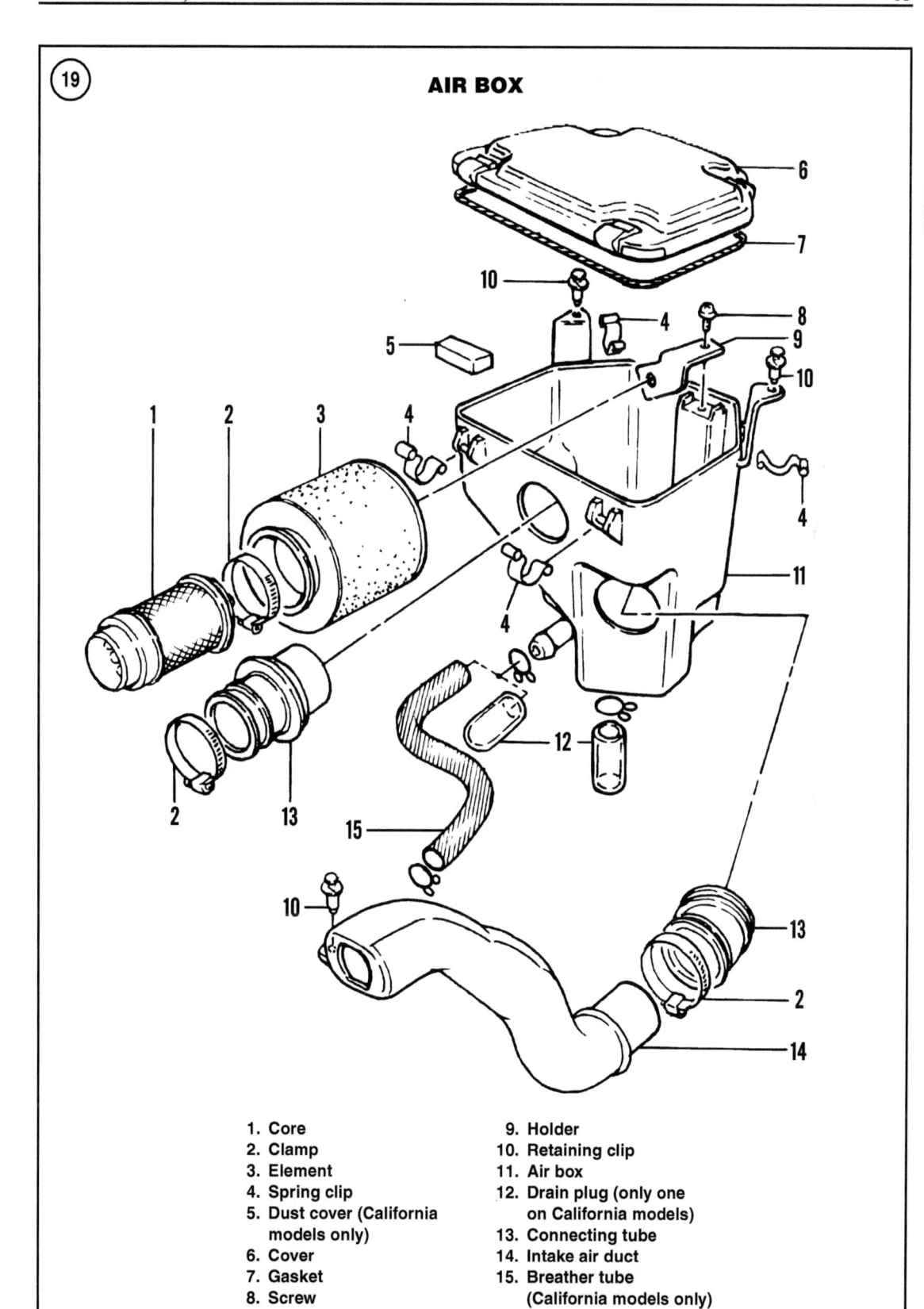

AIR BOX

1. Core
2. Clamp
3. Element
4. Spring clip
5. Dust cover (California models only)
6. Cover
7. Gasket
8. Screw
9. Holder
10. Retaining clip
11. Air box
12. Drain plug (only one on California models)
13. Connecting tube
14. Intake air duct
15. Breather tube (California models only)

11. Inspect all fittings, hoses and connections from the air box to the carburetor.

12. Install the air filter assembly into the air box so the core properly engages the duct in the front of the box (B, **Figure 22**) and the holder sits in the bracket (C) at the back of the box.

13. Secure the holder into place with the mounting screw (B, **Figure 21**) and tighten the air filter clamp (A).

14. Install the air box cover (B, **Figure 20**), and secure it with the spring clips (A).

15. Install the seat (Chapter Fourteen).

Cleaning

Service the air filter element in a well-ventilated area away from all sparks and flames.

1. Turn the holder (A, **Figure 23**) counterclockwise, and remove it from the air filter element.
2. Remove the hose clamp (B, **Figure 23**) and the core (C) from the filter element.

> **WARNING**
> *Do not clean the filter element with gasoline.*

3. Clean the filter element with a non-flammable or high flash-point solvent to remove oil and dirt.
4. Inspect the filter element. Replace the element if it is torn or broken in any area.
5. Fill a clean pan with liquid detergent and warm water.
6. Submerge the filter element in the cleaning solution and gently work the cleaner into the filter pores. Soak and squeeze (gently) the filter element to clean it.

> **CAUTION**
> *Do not wring or twist the filter element during cleaning. This could damage the filter pores or tear the filter loose at a seam. This would allow unfiltered air to enter the engine and cause excessive and rapid wear.*

7. Rinse the filter element under warm water while soaking and gently squeezing it.
8. Repeat Step 6 and Step 7 until no dirt rinses from the filter element.
9. After cleaning the element, inspect it again carefully. If it is torn or broken in any area, replace it. Do not run the engine with a damaged filter element.

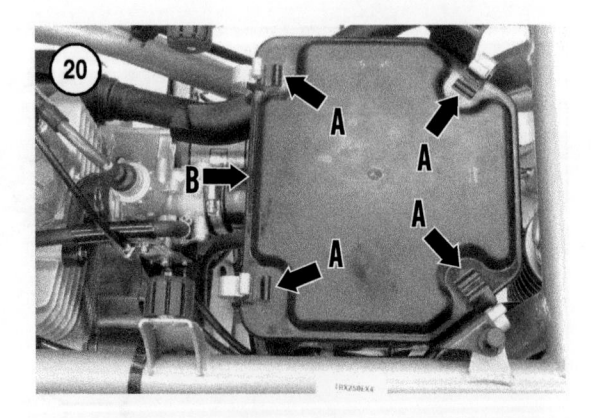

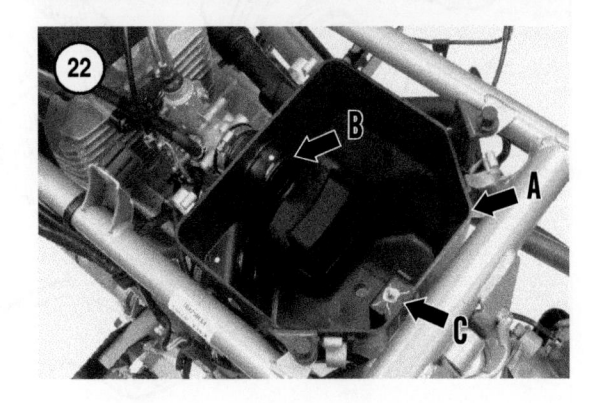

10. Set the filter element aside and allow it to dry thoroughly.
11. Clean and dry the element core (C, **Figure 23**). Check the element core for damage, and replace it if necessary.

> **CAUTION**
> *Make sure the filter element is completely dry before oiling it.*

12. Properly oiling an air filter element is a messy but important job. Wear a pair of disposable rubber gloves when performing this procedure:

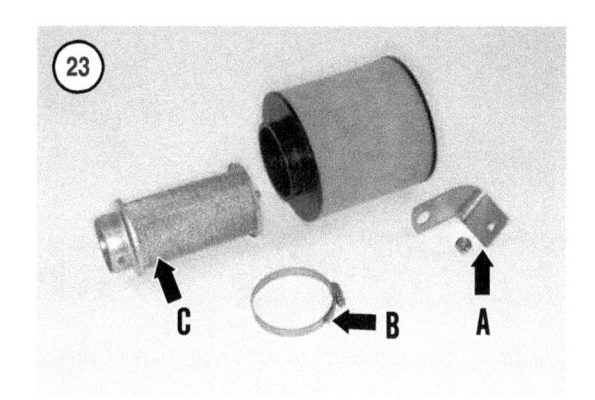

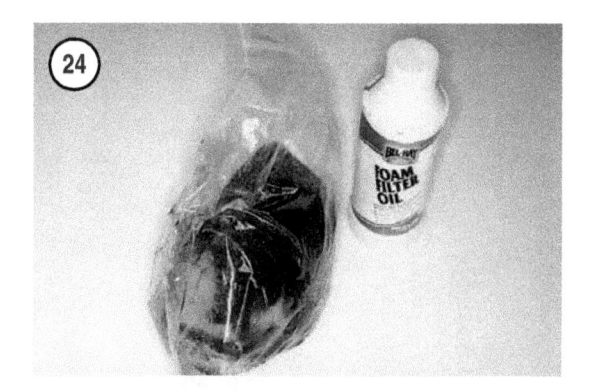

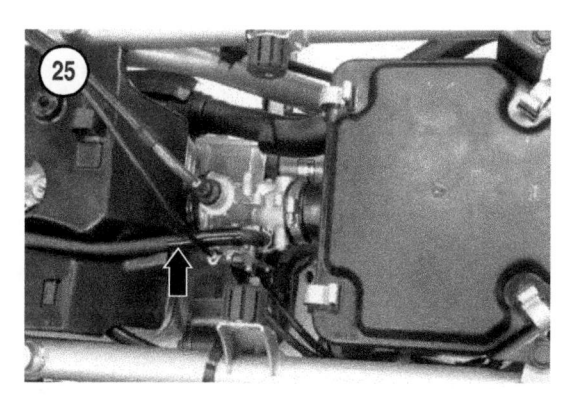

LUBRICATION, MAINTENANCE AND TUNE-UP

e. Remove the filter element from the bag and check the pores for even oiling. This is indicated by light or dark areas on the filter element. If necessary, soak the filter element and squeeze it again.

f. When the filter oiling is even, squeeze the filter element a final time.

g. Pour the leftover filter oil from the bag back into the bottle for reuse.

h. Dispose of the plastic bag.

13. Install the filter element over the element core (C, **Figure 23**). Install the clamp (B, **Figure 23**) and holder (A).

14. Install the filter element assembly as described in this section.

Fuel Line Inspection

WARNING
Some fuel may spill when performing this procedure. Because gasoline is extremely flammable, perform the following procedure away from all open flames (including appliance pilot lights) and sparks. Do not smoke or allow someone who is smoking in the work area. Always work in a well-ventilated area. Wipe up any spills immediately.

WARNING
A damaged or deteriorated fuel line presents a fire hazard to both the rider and machine.

a. Purchase a box of gallon size storage bags. The bags can be used when cleaning the filter, as well as for storing engine and carburetor parts during disassembly service procedures.

b. Place the filter element into a storage bag (**Figure 24**).

c. Pour 32-37 ml (1.1-1.3 oz.) of Honda foam filter oil or equivalent into the filter to soak it.

d. Gently squeeze and release the filter to soak filter oil into the filter's pores. Repeat this process until all the filter's pores are saturated with oil.

Remove the seat. Inspect the fuel line (**Figure 25**) for leaks, cracks, hardness, age deterioration or other damage. Make sure each end of the hose is secured with a hose clamp. Check the carburetor overflow and vent hose ends for contamination.

Fuel Tank Vent Hose Inspection

Inspect the fuel tank vent hose (**Figure 26**) for proper routing. Make sure the hose is not kinked and that its end is free of contamination.

BRAKE SYSTEM

Front Brake Pad Inspection

Inspect the brake discs and pads regularly to ensure they are in good condition. A disc can quickly become scored if the brake pads are damaged or have debris lodged in the pad material. If any damage is detected during the following checks, refer to Chapter Thirteen for brake system repair procedures and specifications.

1. Support the vehicle so the wheels are off the ground.
2. Visually inspect the front discs for:
    a. Scoring—If scoring is evident, refer to Chapter Thirteen for disc specifications and service limits.
    b. Drag—Turn each wheel and check for drag on the disc. Light drag on the disc is acceptable. If the drag substantially slows the wheel rotation, troubleshoot and repair the brake system.
    c. Runout—This is the lateral movement of the disc as it spins. It can be detected by spinning the wheel and listening for uneven drag on the disc. This pulsating drag usually indicates disc warp. If warp is suspected, it can be measured with a dial indicator. If the disc is not warped, look for loose or damaged wheel and/or axle components.
    d. Disc thickness—Measure the thickness of both discs.
3. Observe the position of the brake pad wear lug (cast into the caliper) in relation to the wear indicator pointer (**Figure 27**). If the arrow does not align with the pointer, the brake pads are worn out and must be replaced.

Rear Brake Lining Inspection

Apply the rear brake fully. The brake linings are worn to the service limit if the pointer (A, **Figure 28**) aligns to the index mark (B) on the brake panel while the rear brake is applied. If necessary, replace both rear brake shoes (Chapter Thirteen).

Rear (Parking) Brake Adjustment

1. Before adjusting the rear brake, check the brake pedal, brake cables and adjusters for loose or dam-

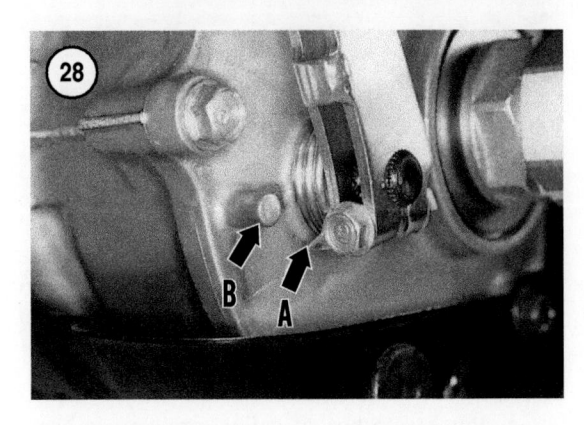

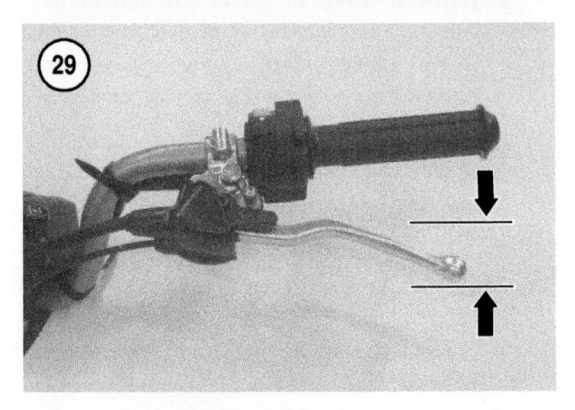

LUBRICATION, MAINTENANCE AND TUNE-UP

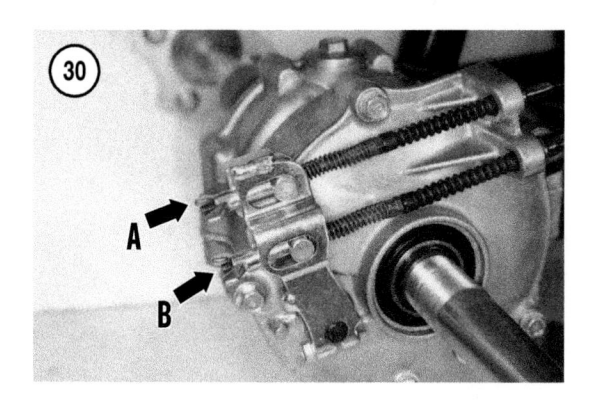

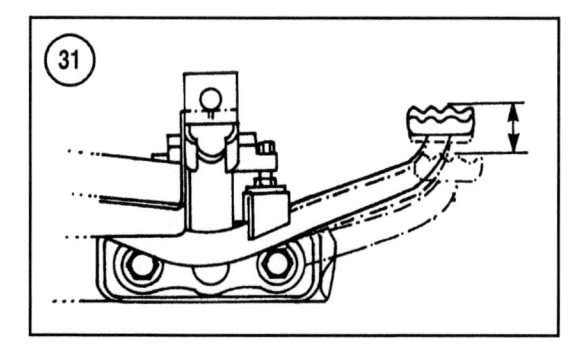

aged connections. Replace or repair any damage before continuing with Step 2.

2. Lubricate the rear brake cables as described in this chapter.

3. Release the parking brake if it is set.

4. Check the rear brake linings as described in this section. If the brake lining thickness is within specifications, continue with Step 5.

5. Apply the rear brake lever and measure the amount of free play at the end of the lever until the rear brake starts to engage (**Figure 29**). Note the following:

   a. If the rear brake lever free play is outside the range specified in **Table 4**, continue with Step 6.
   b. If the free play travel is within specification, go on to Step 7.

NOTE
Contamination inside the brake drum can cause the brakes to apply too soon. If there is dirt or other debris inside the drum, remove the brake drum and inspect the drum surface and brake linings as described in Chapter Thirteen.

6. Adjust the rear brake lever free play by turning the *upper* adjusting nut (A, **Figure 30**) in or out to achieve the correct amount of free play.

NOTE
Make sure the cutout relief in the adjust nut is properly seated on the collar.

7. Check the brake pedal free play. With the pedal in the at rest position, apply the brake pedal and check the distance it travels until the rear brake is applied (**Figure 31**). If the brake pedal free play is outside the range specified in **Table 4**, turn the lower adjusting nut (B, **Figure 30**) in or out to achieve the correct amount of free play.

NOTE
Make sure the cutout relief in the adjusting nut is properly seated on the barrel connector.

8. Support the vehicle with the rear wheels off the ground.

9. Rotate the rear wheels and make sure the brake is not dragging. If the brake is dragging, repeat this procedure until there is no drag.

NOTE
Brake drag can also be caused by dirt and other contamination in the brake drum and on the brake linings. If necessary, remove the brake drum (Chapter Thirteen) and check the brake drum and linings.

10. Lower the vehicle so all four wheels rest on the ground.

Brake Fluid Level Inspection

1. Turn the handlebar so the master cylinder is level.

2. Check the brake fluid level through the master cylinder inspection window (A, **Figure 32**). The level should be above the lower level line. If necessary, add brake fluid as follows.

CAUTION
Be careful when handling brake fluid. Do not spill it on painted, plastic or plated surfaces. Brake fluid damages these surfaces. Immediately wash the

area with soap and water and thoroughly rinse it off.

NOTE
If the brake fluid is low, check the front brake lining wear as described in this section.

3. Clean any dirt from the master cylinder cover.

4. Remove the two cover screws (B, **Figure 32**), cover and diaphragm.

WARNING
Use brake fluid clearly marked DOT 3 or DOT 4. Others may cause brake failure. Do not intermix different brands or types of brake fluid because they may not be compatible. Do not use a silicone-based (DOT 5) brake fluid. It can cause brake component damage, leading to brake system failure.

5. Add new DOT 3 or DOT 4 brake fluid to the reservoir until the fluid level rises to the limit line and raises the brake fluid level.

6. Reinstall the diaphragm and cover. Tighten the screws (B, **Figure 32**) securely.

Brake Hose Inspection

Inspect the brake hoses for cracks, cuts, bulges, deterioration and leaks. Check the metal brake lines for cracks and leaks. Refer to Chapter Thirteen for replacement procedures.

Brake Fluid Change

WARNING
Use brake fluid clearly marked DOT 3 or DOT 4. Others may cause brake failure. Do not intermix different brands or types of brake fluid because they may not be compatible. Do not use a silicone-based (DOT 5) brake fluid. It can cause brake component damage, leading to brake system failure.

WARNING
Never reuse brake fluid. Contaminated brake fluid can cause brake failure.

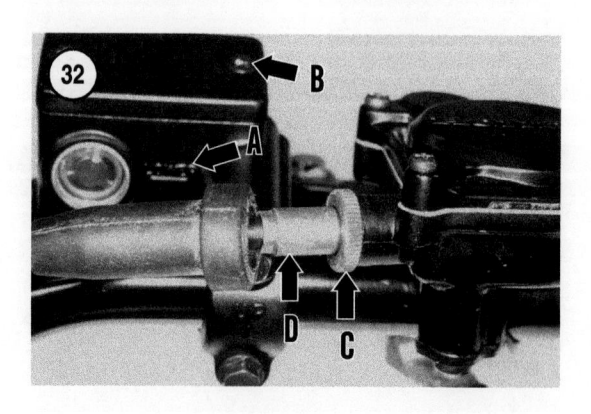

Every time the master cylinder cover is removed, a small amount of dirt and moisture can enter the brake fluid. The same thing happens if a leak occurs or if any part of the hydraulic system is loosened or disconnected. Dirt can clog the system and cause wear and brake failure. Water in the brake fluid causes corrosion inside the hydraulic system, impairing the hydraulic action and reducing the brake's stopping ability.

To maintain peak performance, change the brake fluid every two years or when rebuilding or replacing the master cylinder or a wheel cylinder. To change brake fluid, follow the brake bleeding procedure in Chapter Thirteen.

CLUTCH ADJUSTMENT

Adjust the clutch at the intervals specified in **Table 1**.

This adjustment pertains only to the change (manual) clutch. The centrifugal clutch requires no adjustment. Because there is no clutch cable, the mechanism is the only component that requires adjustment. This adjustment takes up slack due to clutch component wear.

LUBRICATION, MAINTENANCE AND TUNE-UP

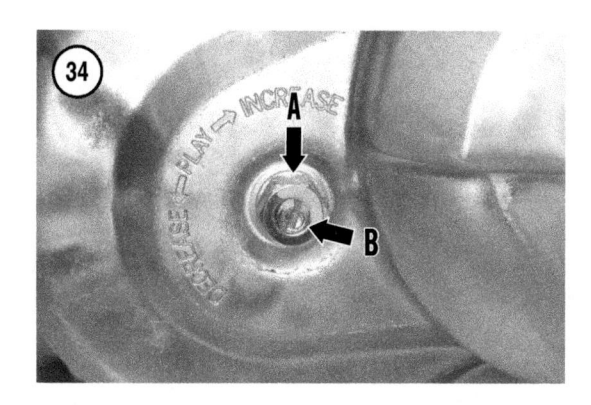

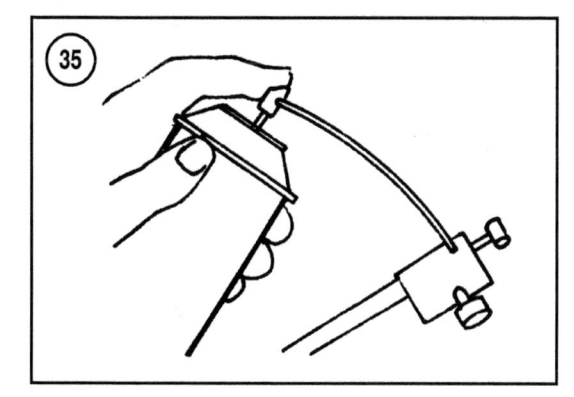

1. Loosen the clutch adjusting screw locknut (A, **Figure 34**).

2. Turn the adjusting screw (B, **Figure 34**) counterclockwise until resistance is felt, then stop.

3. From this point, turn the adjusting screw clockwise 1/4 of a turn, then stop.

NOTE
Make sure the adjusting screw does not move when tightening the locknut in Step 4.

4. Hold the adjusting screw (B, **Figure 34**) and tighten the locknut (A) securely.

NOTE
If the clutch adjustment is difficult, the friction plates may be worn. Remove the clutch cover and inspect the friction plates as described in Chapter Six.

5. Test ride the vehicle to make sure the clutch is operating correctly. Readjust if necessary.

CABLES

Lubrication

Clean and lubricate the throttle, brake, choke and reverse cables at the intervals indicated in **Table 1**. In addition, check the cables for kinks, excessive wear, damage or fraying that could cause the cables to fail or stick.

The most positive method of control cable lubrication involves the use of a cable lubricator and a can of cable lube or a general lubricant. Do not use chain lube as a cable lubricant. It is too thick and does not travel the length of the cable.

1. Disconnect the cable to be lubricated. Note the following:
   a. To service the throttle cable, refer to *Throttle Cable Replacement* in Chapter Eight.
   b. To service the brake cables, refer to *Rear Brake Pedal and Cable* and *Rear Brake Lever/Parking Brake Cable* in Chapter Thirteen.
   c. To service the choke cable, refer to *Choke Cable Replacement* in Chapter Eight.
   d. To service the reverse cable, refer to *Reverse Selector Cable Replacement* in Chapter Seven.

2. Attach a cable lubricator (**Figure 35**) to the end of the cable following its manufacturer's instructions.

NOTE
Place a shop cloth at the end of the cable to catch the oil as it runs out.

3. Inject cable lubricant into the cable until it begins to flow out of the other end of the cable.
4. Disconnect the lubricator.
5. Apply a light coat of multipurpose lithium grease to the cable ends before reconnecting them. Reconnect the cable, and adjust it as described in this chapter.
6. After lubricating the throttle cable, operate the throttle lever at the handlebar. It should open and close smoothly with no binding.
7. After lubricating the brake cable(s), check brake operation.

Throttle Cable Inspection and Adjustment

1. Before adjusting the throttle cable, operate the throttle lever and make sure it opens and closes properly with the handlebar turned in different positions.

If not, check the throttle cable for damage or improper routing. Check the throttle lever for damage. Replace or repair any damage before continuing with Step 2.

2. Lubricate the throttle cable as described in this chapter.

3. Operate the throttle lever and measure the amount of free play at the end of the lever (**Figure 36**) until the cable play is taken up and the carburetor lever starts to move. If the free play is outside the range specified in **Table 4**, continue with Step 4.

4. At the throttle housing on the handlebar, slide the rubber boot off the adjuster and loosen the cable adjuster locknut (C, **Figure 32**). Turn the adjuster (D, **Figure 32**) in or out until the free play at the throttle lever is within specification. Hold the adjuster and tighten the locknut securely. Recheck the throttle lever free play while noting the following:

  a. If the free play measurement is correct, slide the rubber boot over the adjuster, and go to Step 6.
  b. If the throttle cable free play cannot be adjusted properly, the cable has stretched excessively. Replace it as described in Chapter Eight.
  c. If the proper amount of free play cannot be achieved at the throttle housing adjuster, continue with Step 5.

5. Apply the parking brake.

WARNING
A damaged throttle cable prevents the engine from idling properly.

6. Start the engine and allow it to idle in neutral. Turn the handlebar from side to side. If the engine speed increases as the handlebar is turned, the throttle cable is routed incorrectly or there is not enough cable free play. Readjust the throttle cable, or if necessary, replace the throttle cable as described in Chapter Eight.

Choke Cable Inspection and Adjustment

1. Operate the choke knob (A, **Figure 37**). It should move smoothly from the fully closed to fully opened position and back again.

2. If necessary, lubricate the choke cable as described in this chapter.

3. Move the choke knob to its fully closed position.

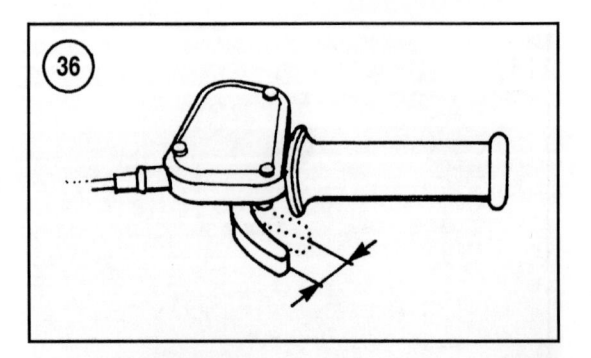

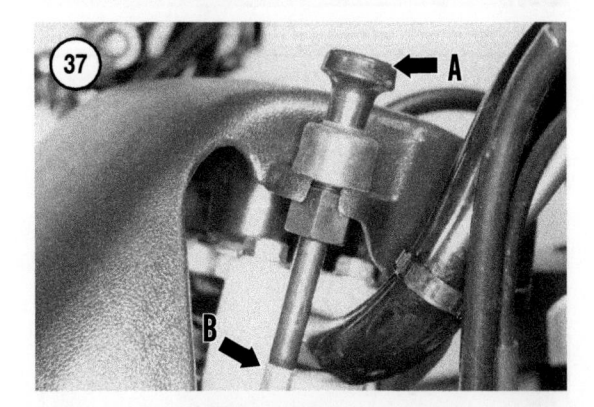

4. At the carburetor choke lever, press the inner wire cable (**Figure 38**) by hand. The wire should have a maximum of 1-2 mm (0.039-0.079 in.) of free play.

5. Adjust the free play by performing the following:

  a. Loosen the cable clamp screw (B, **Figure 37**).
  b. Turn the outer cable until the inner wire free play is 1-2 mm (0.039-0.079 in.) Tighten the cable clamp screw completely.
  c. If the free play cannot be adjusted to within specification, replace the choke knob/cable assembly as described in Chapter Eight.

LUBRICATION, MAINTENANCE AND TUNE-UP

5. Start the engine, and shift the transmission into reverse following normal operating procedures. Check that the transmission shifts into and out of reverse correctly.

SPARK ARRESTOR SERVICE

Clean the spark arrestor at the intervals in **Table 1** or sooner if a considerable amount of slow riding is done.

WARNING
To avoid burning your hands, do not perform this cleaning operation when the exhaust system is hot. Work in a well-ventilated area that is free of any fire hazards. Wear eye protection.

1. Remove the three bolts securing the end cap of the engine muffler.
2. Remove the spark arrestor and sealing gasket between it and the muffler body.
3. Use a plastic or brass brush to remove carbon deposits from the screen mesh of the spark arrester.
4. Replace the spark arrestor if the screen mesh has any breaks or holes in it.
5. Install a new gasket on the spark arrestor and insert it into the muffler. Tighten the bolts to 12 N•m (106 in.-lb.).

SUSPENSION

Steering Shaft and Front Suspension Inspection

Inspect the steering system and front suspension at the interval indicated in **Table 1**. If any of the following mentioned front suspension and steering fasteners are loose, refer to Chapter Eleven for service procedures.

WARNING
If any cotter pins are removed during inspection, replace them during assembly.

1. Park the vehicle on level ground and set the parking brake.
2. Visually inspect all components of the steering system. Repair or replace damaged components as described in Chapter Eleven.

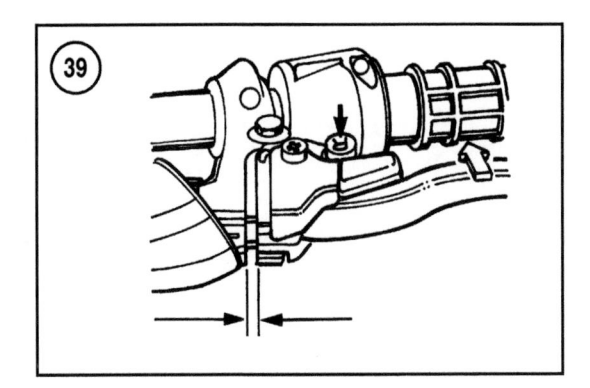

6. Visually inspect the choke cable for cracks or other damage. If necessary, replace the choke cable (Chapter Eight).

Reverse Selector Cable Inspection and Adjustment

1. Check the reverse selector cable for loose or damaged cable ends. Check the reverse lever for damage. Repair or replace any damaged parts.
2. If necessary, lubricate the reverse selector cable as described in this chapter.
3. Push the reverse selector knob (**Figure 39**) in while squeezing the rear brake lever, and measure the reverse lever free play (**Figure 39**).
4. If the free play is outside the range specified in **Table 4**, adjust the free play by performing the following:
    a. Locate the reverse stopper lever on the left side of the alternator cover.
    b. Loosen the reverse selector cable locknut (A, **Figure 40**).
    c. Turn the adjuster (B, **Figure 40**) in or out to achieve the correct amount of free play.
    d. Tighten the locknut and recheck the free play.

3. Check the shock absorbers as described in this section.

4. Remove the handlebar cover (Chapter Fourteen). Check that the handlebar holder bolts are tight. Reinstall the handlebar cover.

5. Make sure the front hub nuts are tight and that all cotter pins are in place.

6. Check that the cotter pins are in place on all steering components. If any cotter pin is missing, check the nut for looseness. Tighten the nut and install a new cotter pin as described in Chapter Eleven.

7. Check the steering shaft play as follows:
   a. Support the vehicle with the front wheels off the ground.
   b. To check steering shaft radial play, move the handlebar from side to side (without moving the wheels). If radial play is excessive, the upper bushing inside the steering shaft holder (A, **Figure 41**) is probably worn or the steering shaft holder bolts (B) are loose. Replace the upper bushing or tighten the holder bolts as necessary.
   c. To check steering shaft thrust play, lift up and then push down on the handlebar. If there is excessive thrust play, check the lower steering shaft nut (**Figure 42**) for looseness. If the nut is tightened properly, check the lower steering shaft bearing for excessive wear or damage.
   d. If necessary, service the steering shaft as described in Chapter Eleven.
   e. Lower the vehicle so all four tires are on the ground.

8. Check the steering knuckle and tie rod ends as follows:
   a. Turn the handlebar quickly from side to side. If there is appreciable looseness between the handlebar and tires, check the tie rod ends for excessive wear or damage.
   b. Service the steering knuckle and tie rods as described in Chapter Eleven.

9. Check the toe-in as described in this section.

Shock Absorber Inspection

1. Check the front and rear shock absorbers for oil leaks, a bent damper rod or other damage.

2. If necessary, replace the shock absorbers as described in Chapter Eleven (front) or Chapter Twelve (rear).

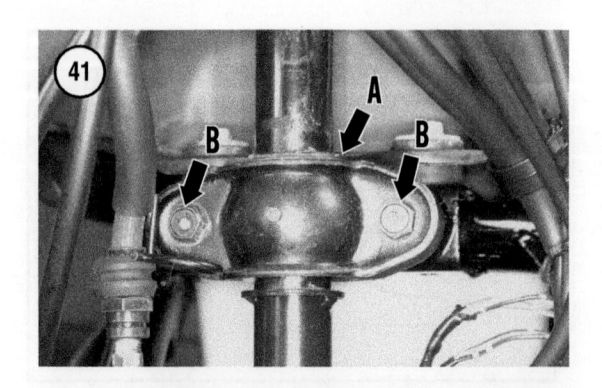

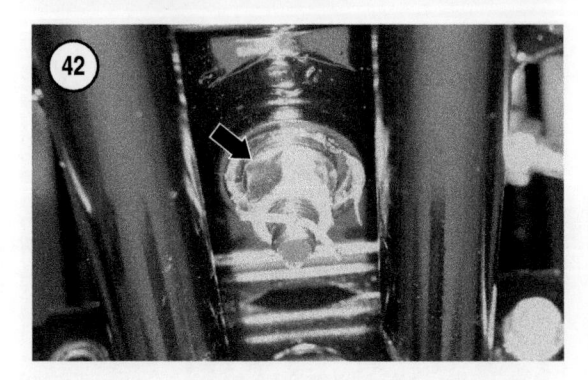

Toe-In Inspection/Adjustment

Toe-in is a condition where the front of the tires are closer together than the back (**Figure 43**). Check the toe-in whenever inspecting the suspension, after servicing the front suspension or when replacing the tie rods.

Adjust toe-in by changing the length of the tie rods.

1. Inflate all four tires to the recommended pressure specified in **Table 2**.

2. Park the vehicle on level ground and set the parking brake.

3. Raise and support the front of the vehicle so both front tires just clear the ground.

4. Turn the handlebar so the wheels are facing straight ahead.

5. Using a tape measure, carefully measure the distance between the center of both front tires at the axle height as shown in A, **Figure 43**. Mark the tires with a piece of chalk at these points. Record the measurement.

6. Rotate each tire exactly 180° so the center marks face rearward.

7. Measure the distance between the center of both front tires (B, **Figure 43**). Record the measurement.

8. Subtract the measurement taken in Step 5 (A, **Figure 43**) from the Step 7 measurement (B).

LUBRICATION, MAINTENANCE AND TUNE-UP

*remains the same on each side. If the left- and right-side tie rod lengths are different, refer to **Tie Rods** in Chapter Eleven.*

9. If the toe-in is incorrect, adjust it by performing the following:
   a. Loosen the locknut (A, **Figure 44**) at each end of both tie rods.
   b. Use a wrench on the flat portion (B, **Figure 44**) of the tie rods, and slowly turn both tie rods the same amount until the toe-in measurement is correct.
   c. When the toe-in adjustment is correct, hold each tie rod in place and tighten the locknuts to 54 N•m (40 ft.-lb.).
   d. Recheck toe-in.
10. Lower the vehicle so both front wheels are on the ground.
11. Start the engine and make a slow test ride on level ground. Ride straight while checking that the handlebar does not turn to the left or right side.

Rear Suspension Inspection

1. Support the vehicle so the rear wheels are off the ground.
2. Try to move the rear axle (**Figure 45**) sideways while checking for excessive play at the swing arm bearings.
3. If there is any play, check the swing arm pivot bolts for looseness (Chapter Twelve). If they are tightened properly, the swing arm bearings may require replacement. Refer to Chapter Twelve.
4. Lower the vehicle so all four tires are on the ground.

Skid Plate Inspection

Inspect the front, middle and rear skid plates for damage and loose fasteners. Repair or replace damaged skid plates. Replace missing or damaged mounting bolts. Tighten the mounting bolts securely.

FASTENER INSPECTION

Constant vibration can loosen many of the fasteners on the vehicle. Check the tightness of all fasteners, especially those on the following components:
1. Engine mounting hardware.

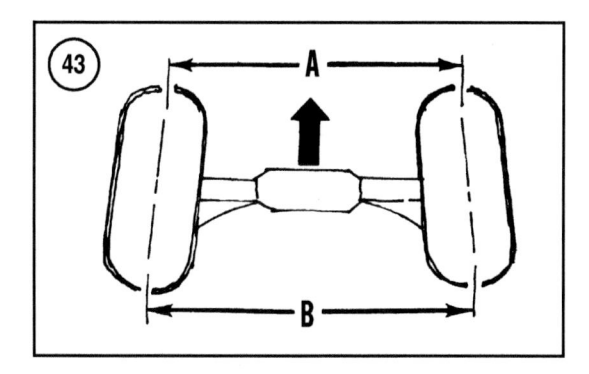

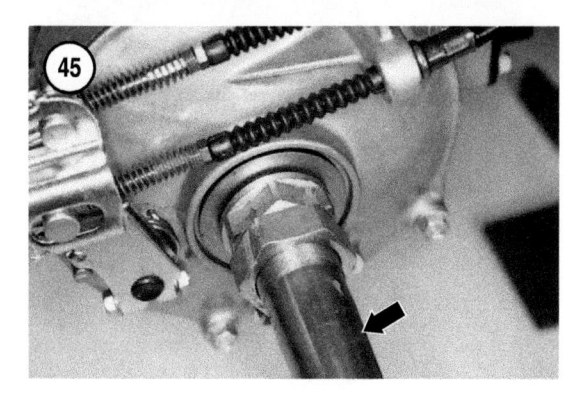

Toe-in is correct if the difference equals the specification in **Table 4**.

WARNING
If the tie rods are not adjusted equally, the handlebar is not centered while traveling straight ahead. This condition may cause loss of control. If toe-in cannot be properly adjusted, have it adjusted at a Honda dealership or other qualified shop.

NOTE
Turn both tie rods the same number of turns. This ensures the tie rod length

2. Cylinder head.
3. Alternator and clutch covers.
4. Handlebar.
5. Gearshift lever.
6. Brake pedal and lever.
7. Exhaust system.
8. Steering and suspension components.

VALVE CLEARANCE

Check and Adjustment

Check and adjust the valve clearance when the engine is cold.

1. Park the vehicle on level ground and set the parking brake.
2. Remove the fuel tank as described in Chapter Eight.
3. Remove the two bolts securing the upper motor mount, and then remove the motor mount and heat guard.
4. Remove the spark plug.
5. Remove the valve adjuster caps (**Figure 46**) and O-rings from the cylinder head cover.
6. Remove the timing hole cap (**Figure 47**) and O-ring.
7. Set the engine to TDC on the compression stroke by performing the following:
    a. Remove the three bolts and cover from the back of the engine to access the alternator bolt (**Figure 48**). Using a wrench, slowly turn the alternator bolt counterclockwise until the T-mark (**Figure 49**) on the flywheel aligns with the index mark on the rear crankcase cover.
    b. Check that the piston is at TDC on the compression stroke by moving both rocker arms by hand. Each rocker arm should have some free play. If either rocker arm is tight, turn the crankshaft one full turn and realign the flywheel T-mark with the index mark. Check that both rocker arms are loose.
8. Check the clearance of both the intake valve and exhaust valves by inserting a flat feeler gauge between the rocker arm pad and the valve stem as shown in **Figure 50**. If the clearance is correct, slight resistance is felt when the feeler gauge is withdrawn from the rocker arm pad and valve stem. Refer to **Table 4** for the intake and exhaust valve clearances.
9. To adjust the valve clearance, perform the following:
    a. Loosen the locknut (**Figure 51**) and turn the adjuster in or out until the clearance is cor-

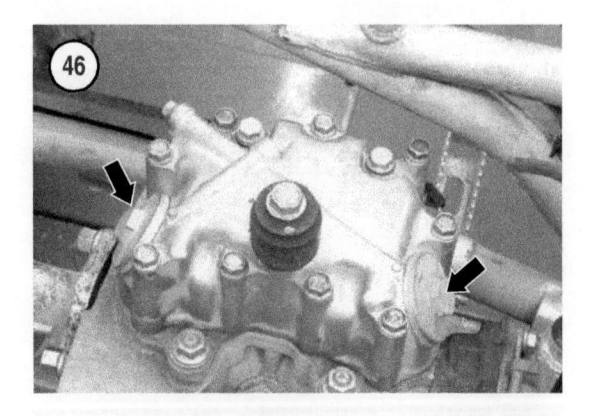

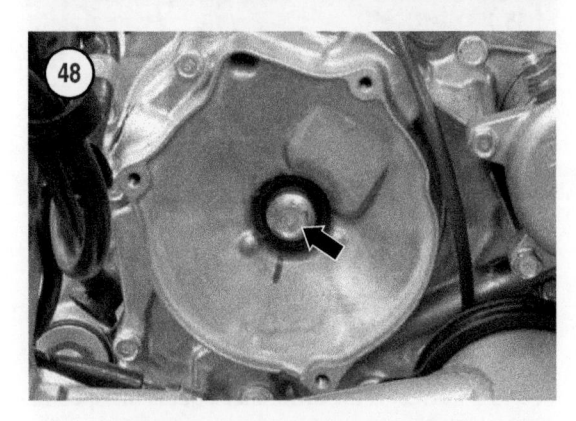

LUBRICATION, MAINTENANCE AND TUNE-UP

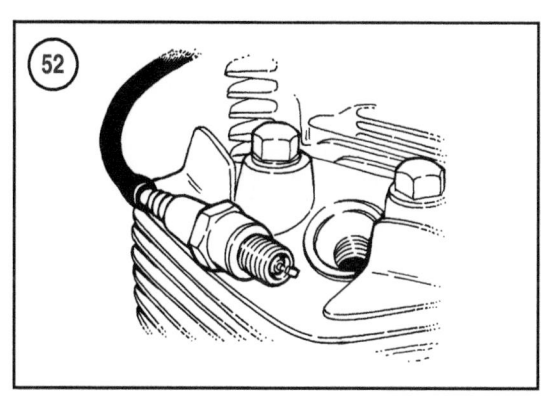

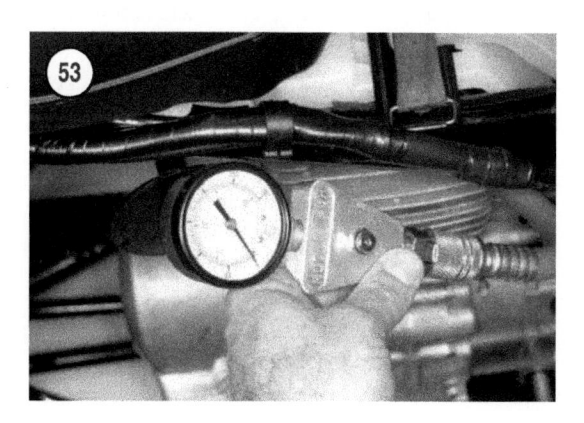

rect. Turn the square end of the adjuster with a valve adjusting tool (Honda part No. 07908-KE90200) or a 3 mm wrench. The valve is properly adjusted when slight resistance is felt as the feeler gauge is withdrawn from the rocker arm pad and valve stem.

  b. Hold the adjuster to prevent it from turning, and then tighten the locknut to 17 N•m (12 ft.-lb.).
  c. Recheck the clearance to assure the adjuster did not move when the locknut was tightened. If necessary, readjust the valve clearance.
  d. Rotate the engine one full turn counterclockwise and check the clearance of the remaining valve. If necessary, adjust the clearance as described in this section.

10. Install the spark plug and tighten it to 18-22 N•m (13-16 ft.-lb.). Install the spark plug cap.
11. Install the valve adjuster caps (**Figure 46**) and O-rings. Tighten the caps to 20 N•m (14 ft.-lb.).
12. Install the timing hole cap (**Figure 47**) and O-ring. Tighten the cap to 10 N•m (89 in.-lbs.).
13. Install the flywheel bolt cover on the back of the engine.
14. Install the engine heat shield, upper motor mount, and fuel tank (Chapter Eight).

ENGINE COMPRESSION TEST

A cylinder compression test is one of the quickest ways to check the condition of the rings, head gasket, piston and cylinder. Record the compression reading during each tune-up. Compare the current reading with those taken during earlier tune-ups. This helps to spot any developing problems.

1. Warm the engine to normal operating temperature.
2. Remove the fuel tank and heat guard (Chapter Eight).
3. Remove the spark plug. Insert the plug into the plug cap and ground the plug against the cylinder head (**Figure 52**, typical).
4. Install a compression gauge (**Figure 53**) into the cylinder head spark plug hole. Make sure the gauge is seated properly against the hole.
5. Turn the engine stop switch off.

NOTE
The battery must be fully charged or a false compression reading may be obtained. Because the engine must be turning at least 800 rpm, turn the engine over with the starter.

6. Hold the throttle wide open and crank the engine with the starter for several revolutions until the gauge stabilizes at its highest reading. Record the pressure reading and compare it to the cylinder compression specification in **Table 4**.

7. If the reading is higher than normal, there may be a buildup of carbon deposits in the combustion chamber or on the piston crown. This condition can cause detonation and overheating. Service the piston as described in Chapter Four.

8. If the reading is low, allow the engine to cool, and then adjust the valves as described in this chapter.

9. Warm up the engine to normal operating temperature, and perform another compression test. The problem has been corrected if the compression reading is within specification.

10. If the reading is still low, this indicates a leaking cylinder head gasket, a leaking valve or worn, stuck or broken piston rings. To determine which, pour about a teaspoon of engine oil through the spark plug hole onto the top of the piston. Crank the engine once to distribute the oil, then make another compression test and record the reading. If the compression increases significantly, the valves are good but the rings are worn or damaged. If compression does not increase, the valves or the cylinder head gasket is leaking. A valve could be hanging open or a piece of carbon could be on the valve seat.

NOTE
If the piston rings are worn, stuck or broken, disconnect the crankcase breather tube (Figure 54) while the engine is running. If there is smoke inside the tube, check for a stuck or damaged piston ring(s).

11. Remove the compression tester. Install the spark plug and reconnect the spark plug cap.

12. Install the heat guard and fuel tank (Chapter Eight).

SPARK PLUG

Removal

1. Grasp the spark plug cap (**Figure 55**) as near the plug as possible and pull it off the plug. If the cap is stuck to the plug, twist it slightly to break it loose.

CAUTION
When the spark plug is removed, dirt around it can fall into the plug hole. This can cause engine damage.

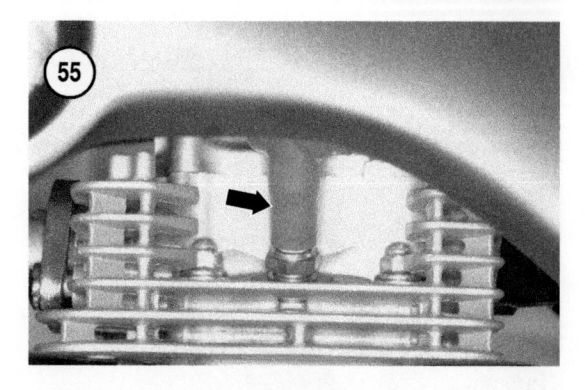

2. Blow away any dirt that has collected around the spark plug.

3. Remove the spark plug with a spark plug socket.

NOTE
If the plug is difficult to remove, apply penetrating oil around the base of the plug and let it soak about 10-20 minutes.

4. Inspect the plug carefully. Look for a broken center porcelain, excessively eroded electrodes and excessive carbon or oil fouling.

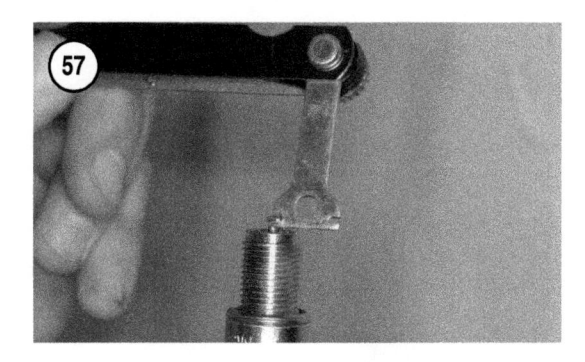

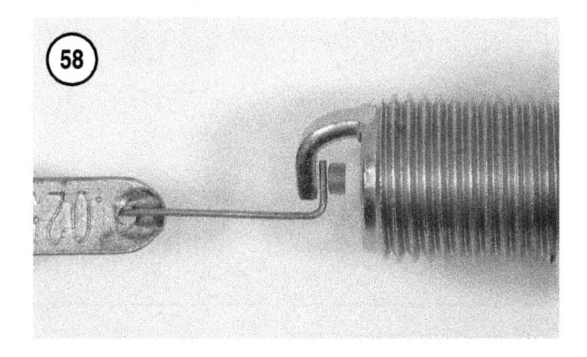

LUBRICATION, MAINTENANCE AND TUNE-UP

6. Use a spark plug wrench and tighten the new spark plug to 18 N•m (13 ft.-lb.). If a torque wrench is not available, tighten the plug an additional 1/2 turn after the gasket has made contact with the head. If installing a used spark plug, only tighten it an additional 1/8 to 1/4 turn.

Reading

Reading a plug that has been in use can provide information about spark plug operation, air/fuel mixture composition, and engine operating conditions (oil consumption due to wear for example). Before checking the spark plug, operate the ATV under a medium load for approximately 6 miles (10 km). Avoid prolonged idling before shutting off the engine. Remove the spark plug as described in this section. Examine the plug and compare it to the typical plugs shown in **Figure 59** and match it to the descriptions in this section.

When reading a plug to evaluate carburetor jetting, start with a new plug and operate the ATV at the load that corresponds to the jetting information desired. For example, if the main jet is in question, operate the ATV at full throttle; shut the engine off and coast to a stop.

Normal condition

If the plug has a light tan- or gray-colored deposit and no abnormal gap wear or erosion, good engine, carburetion and ignition condition are indicated. The plug in use is of the proper heat range. It may be serviced and returned to use.

Carbon fouled

Soft, dry, sooty deposits covering the entire firing end of the plug are evidence of incomplete combustion. Even though the firing end of the plug is dry, the plug's insulation decreases. The carbon forms an electrical path that bypasses the spark plug electrodes, causing a misfire. Carbon fouling can be caused by one or more of the following:
1. Too rich fuel mixture.
2. Spark plug heat range too cold.
3. Clogged air filter.
4. Retarded ignition timing.
5. Ignition component failure.
6. Low engine compression.
7. Prolonged idling.

Installation

Carefully adjust the electrode gap (**Figure 56**) on a new spark plug to ensure a reliable, consistent spark. Use a spark plug gapping tool (**Figure 57**) and a wire feeler gauge (**Figure 58**).
1. If using an original equipment type spark plug cap, do not install the terminal nut on the end of the new plug.
2. Select a wire feeler gauge that is within the spark plug gap range specified in **Table 4**.
3. Insert the wire feeler gauge between the center and side electrode of the plug. If the gap is correct, a slight drag is felt as the wire gauge is pulled through. If there is no drag or if the gauge does not pass through, bend the side electrode (**Figure 56**) with a gapping tool to set the proper gap.
4. Apply an antiseize compound to the plug threads before installing the spark plug. Do not use engine oil on the plug threads.
5. Screw the spark plug in by hand until it seats. Little effort should be required. If force is necessary, the plug may be cross-threaded. Unscrew it and try again.

CAUTION
Do not overtighten the plug. This only crushes the gasket and destroys its sealing ability.

Oil fouled

The tip of an oil fouled plug has a black insulator tip, a damp oily film over the firing end and a carbon layer over the entire nose. The electrodes are not worn. Common causes for this condition are:
1. Incorrect carburetor jetting.
2. Low idle speed or prolonged idling.
3. Ignition component failure.
4. Spark plug heat range too cold.
5. Engine still being broken in.

Oil fouled spark plugs may be cleaned in an emergency, but it is better to replace them. It is important to correct the cause of fouling before the engine is returned to service.

Gap bridging

Plugs with this condition exhibit gaps shorted out by combustion deposits between the electrodes. If this condition is encountered, check for an improper oil type or excessive carbon in the combustion chamber. Make sure to identify and correct the cause of this condition.

Overheated

Badly worn electrodes and premature gap wear along with a gray or white blistered porcelain insulator surface are signs of overheating. This condition is commonly caused by the use a spark plug that is too hot. If the spark plug had not been changed to a hotter one, but the plug is overheated, consider the following causes:
1. Lean fuel mixture.
2. Ignition timing too advanced.
3. Engine lubrication system malfunction.
4. Engine vacuum leak.
5. Improper spark plug installation (too tight).
6. No spark plug gasket.

Worn out

This occurs when corrosive gasses formed by combustion and high voltage sparks erode the electrodes. Spark plugs in this condition require more voltage to fire under hard acceleration. Install a new spark plug.

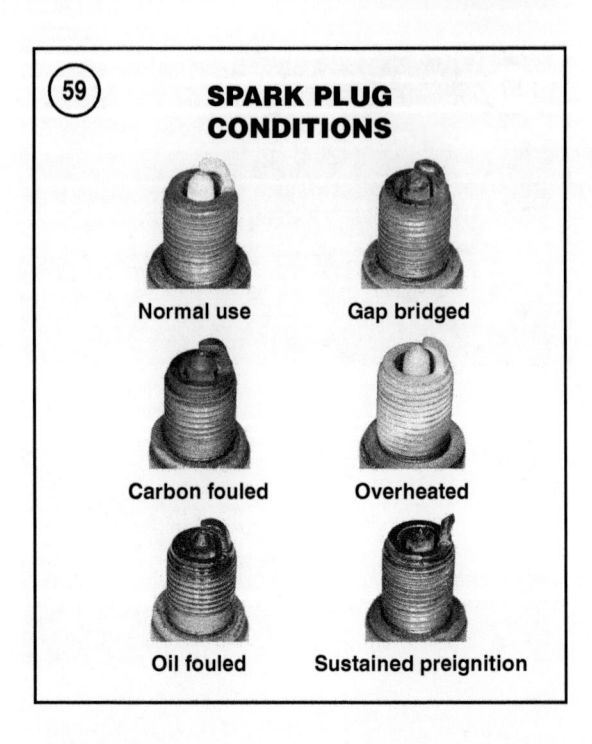

SPARK PLUG CONDITIONS

Normal use — Gap bridged — Carbon fouled — Overheated — Oil fouled — Sustained preignition

Preignition

If the electrodes are melted, preignition is almost certainly the cause. Check for carburetor mounting or intake manifold leaks and over-advanced ignition timing. A plug that is too hot can also cause this condition. Find and correct the cause of the preignition before returning the engine into service.

Heat Range

Spark plugs are available in different heat ranges, hotter or colder than the plugs originally installed. Select plugs with the heat range designed for the loads and conditions under which the ATV operates. Using a plug with an incorrect heat range can cause plug fouling or overheating and can lead to piston damage.

In general, use a hot plug for low speeds and low temperatures. Use a cold plug for high speeds, high engine loads and high temperatures. The plug should operate hot enough to burn off unwanted deposits but not so hot that it burns itself or causes preignition. To determine if the plug heat range is correct, remove the spark plug and examine the insulator.

Do not change the spark plug heat range to compensate for adverse engine or carburetion conditions. Compare the insulator to those in **Figure 58**.

When replacing the plug, make sure the reach is correct. A longer-than-standard plug can interfere

LUBRICATION, MAINTENANCE AND TUNE-UP

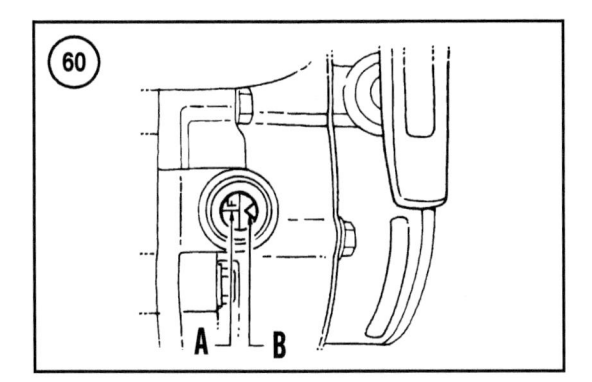

with the piston and cause engine damage. A shorter-than-standard type may foul due to the firing tip being shrouded within the spark plug hole.

Refer to **Table 4** for spark plug recommendations.

IGNITION TIMING INSPECTION

All models are equipped with a capacitor discharge ignition system (CDI). Ignition timing is not adjustable. Check the ignition timing to make sure all components within the ignition system are working correctly. If the ignition timing is incorrect, troubleshoot the ignition system as described in Chapter Two. Incorrect ignition timing can cause a loss of engine performance and efficiency. It may also cause overheating.

Before starting this procedure, check all electrical connections and grounds in the ignition system circuit. They must be tight and free from corrosion.

1. Start the engine and let it warm about 2-3 minutes.
2. Park the vehicle on level ground, apply the parking brake and shut off the engine.
3. Remove the timing hole cap (**Figure 47**) and O-ring.
4. Connect a portable tachometer following its manufacturer's instructions.
5. Connect a timing light following its manufacturer's instructions.
6. Restart the engine and let it run at the idle speed indicated in **Table 4**. Adjust the idle speed if necessary as described in this chapter.
7. Aim the timing light at the timing window and pull the trigger. The F-mark on the flywheel should align with the index mark on the rear crankcase cover (**Figure 60**). If the ignition timing is incorrect, troubleshoot the ignition system as described in Chapter Two.
8. Turn the ignition switch off, and disconnect the timing light and portable tachometer.
9. Install the timing hole cap. Lubricate the O-ring with oil and tighten the cap to 10 N•m (89 in.-lb.).

IDLE SPEED ADJUSTMENT

NOTE
The pilot screw does not require adjustment unless the carburetor is overhauled or a new pilot screw is installed. To adjust the pilot screw, refer to Chapter Eight.

1. Start the engine and let it warm up approximately 10 minutes.
2. Park the vehicle on level ground, apply the parking brake and shut off the engine.
3. Connect a portable tachometer to the engine following its manufacturer's instructions.
4. Remove the right side cover as described in Chapter Fourteen.
5. Restart the engine and turn the throttle stop screw (**Figure 61**) until the idle speed is within the range specified in **Table 4**.
6. Open and close the throttle a couple times and check for variation in idle speed. Readjust if necessary.

WARNING
With the engine idling, move the handlebar from side to side. If idle speed increases as the handlebar is moved, the throttle cable needs adjusting or may be incorrectly routed through the frame. Correct this problem immediately. Do not ride the ATV in this condition.

7. Turn the engine off and disconnect the portable tachometer.
8. Install the right side cover (Chapter Fourteen).

Table 1 MAINTENANCE SCHEDULE

After the first 20 hours or the first 100 miles (150 km) of use	Check and adjust the valve clearance. Change the engine oil. Check and adjust the engine idle speed. Inspect the reverse lock system. Clean, lubricate and adjust the cable as necessary. Inspect the clutch system. Adjust as necessary Check all fasteners. Tighten as necessary. Inspect the tires and wheels.
Every 100 hours or 600 miles (1000 km of use)	Clean the air filter. Inspect the air filter housing drain. Inspect the spark plug. Check and adjust the valve clearance. Change the engine oil. Check and adjust the engine idle speed. Inspect and adjust the brake fluid level. Inspect the brake system. Clean, lubricate and adjust the cable as necessary. Inspect the reverse lock system. Clean, lubricate and adjust the cable as necessary. Inspect the clutch. Adjust as necessary. Inspect the skid plates and engine guard. Inspect the front and rear suspension. Clean the spark arrester. Inspect the tires and wheels.
Every 200 hours or 1200 miles (2000 km) of use	Clean the air filter. Inspect the air filter housing drain. Check the fuel line. Check the operation of the throttle. Clean, lubricate and adjust the cable as necessary. Check the operation of the choke. Clean, lubricate and adjust the cable as necessary. Inspect the spark plug. Inspect the brake system. Check and adjust the valve clearance. Change the engine oil. Clean the engine oil centrifugal filter. Check and adjust the engine idle speed. Inspect the brake fluid. Add fluid as necessary. Inspect the brake shoes for wear. Inspect the brake system. Clean, lubricate and adjust the cables as necessary. Inspect the reverse lock system. Inspect the clutch. Adjust as necessary. Inspect the skid plates and engine guard. Inspect the front and rear suspension. Clean the spark arrester. Inspect all fasteners. Tighten them as necessary. Inspect the tires and wheels. Inspect the steering shaft holder bearing. Lubricate the bearing as necessary. Inspect the steering system.
Every 2 years	Replace the final drive oil.

LUBRICATION, MAINTENANCE AND TUNE-UP

Table 2 TIRE SPECIFICATIONS

Front tire	
Size	AT22 × 7-10
Manufacturer	Dunlop KT 171
Minimum tread depth	4 mm (0.16 in.)
Rear tire	
Size	AT22 × 10-9
Manufacturer	Dunlop KT 175
Minimum tread depth	4 mm (0.16 in.)
Inflation pressure (cold)*	
Standard	
Front	30 kPa (4.4 psi)
Rear	20 kPa (2.9 psi)
Minimum, (front and rear)	
Front	26 kPa (3.8 psi)
Rear	17 kPa (2.5 psi)
With cargo (front and rear)	
Front	30 kPa (4.4 psi)
Rear	20 kPa (2.9 psi)
Maximum (front and rear)	
Front	34 kPa (5.0 psi)
Rear	23 kPa (3.3 psi)

*Tire inflation pressure for original equipment tires. Aftermarket tires may require different inflation pressures.

Table 3 RECOMMENDED LUBRICANTS AND FLUIDS

Fuel	
Octane	Regular unleaded
Tank capacity w/reserve	10.2 L (2.7 gal.)
Tank reserve capacity	2.5 L (0.66 gal.)
Engine oil	
Grade	API SF or SG
Viscosity	10W-40
Capacity	
Oil change	1.6 L (1.7 qt.)
Disassembly	1.9 L (2.0 qt.)
Brake fluid	DOT 3 or DOT 4
Cooling system	Air cooled
Final drive oil	
Grade	Hypoid gear oil SAE 80
Capacity	
Oil change	80 ml (2.7 oz.)
After disassembly	100 ml (3.4 oz.)

Table 4 MAINTENANCE AND TUNE-UP SPECIFICATIONS

Battery	
Capacity	12 V – 8 AH
Current draw (maximum)	1 mA
	(continued)

Table 4 MAINTENANCE AND TUNE-UP SPECIFICATIONS (continued)

Battery (continued)	
Voltage	
Fully charged	13.0-13.2 V
Needs charging	Less than 12.3 V
Charge current	
Normal	1.2 A / 5-10 hours
Quick*	5.0 A / 1.0 hour
Spark plug	
Standard	NGK DPR8EA-9 or ND X24EPR-U9
Cold climate (5° C/41° F)	NGK DPR7EA-9 or ND X22EPR-U9
For extended high-speed operation	NGK DPR9EA-9 or ND X27EPR-U9
Spark plug gap	0.8-0.9 mm (0.031-0.035 in.)
Ignition timing	14° BTDC @ 1700 rpm
Idle Speed	1300-1500 rpm
Valve clearance	
Intake	0.13 mm (0.005 in.)
Exhaust	0.13 mm (0.005 in.)
Cylinder compression	1275 kPa (185 psi) @ 800 rpm
Front Brake pad thickness	To wear indicator
Rear drum brake lining thickness	4.5 mm (0.18 in.)
Front disc brake thickness	2.8-3.2 (0.11 - 0.13)
Rear brake lining wear limit	To wear indicator
Throttle lever free play	3-8 mm (1/8 - 5/16 in.)
Reverse selector lever free play	2-4 mm (1/16-1/8 in.)
Front brake lever free play	25-30 mm (1-1 1/4 in.)
Rear (parking) brake lever free play	15-20 mm (5/8-3/4 in.)
Brake pedal free play	15-20 mm (5/8-3/4 in.)
Toe-in	2.3 mm (3/32 in.)

*Perform a quick charge only in an emergency. Excessive charging amperage can damage the battery.

Table 5 BATTERY VOLTAGE READINGS*

State of charge	Voltage readings
100%	13.0-13.2 volts
75%	12.8 volts
50%	12.5 volts
25%	12.2 volts
0%	12.0 volts or less

*For maintenance-free batteries

Table 6 MAINTENANCE AND TUNE UP TORQUE SPECIFICATIONS

Item	N•m	in.-lb.	ft.-lb.
Brake bleed valve	6	53	–
Brake hose banjo bolt	34	–	25
Engine oil drain bolt	25	–	18
Final drive			
Drain bolt	12	106	–
Oil check bolt	12	106	–
Oil fill cap	12	106	–
Front hub nut	69	–	51
Rear hub nut	147	–	108
Spark arrester bolts	12	106	–
Spark plug	18-22	–	13-16
Tie rod locknuts	54	–	40
Timing hole cap	10	89	–
Valve adjuster cap	20	–	15
Valve adjuster locknut	17	–	12
Wheel nuts	64	–	47

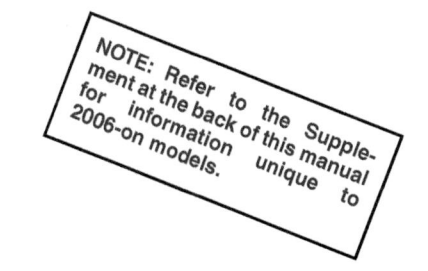

CHAPTER FOUR

ENGINE TOP END

NOTE: Refer to the Supplement at the back of this manual for information unique to 2006-on models.

The TRX250EX uses an overhead valve pushrod engine. The camshaft is mounted in the crankcase and is driven off the crankshaft by a short cam chain. The camshaft operates followers which move the pushrods against the rocker arms.

This chapter provides complete service and overhaul procedures for the engine top end components. These include the rocker arms, cylinder head, valves, cylinder, piston, piston rings and camshaft. All cylinder head components can be serviced while the engine is in the frame.

When inspecting top end components, compare any measurements to the top end specifications in **Table 2**. Replace any component that is damaged, worn to the service limit or out of specification. During assembly, tighten fasteners to the torque specifications listed in **Table 3**. **Tables 1-3** are at the end of this chapter.

Before starting any work, read the service hints in Chapter One. Make sure the engine and surrounding area is clean before working on the engine top end.

CYLINDER HEAD COVER

Removal/Installation

The cylinder head cover (**Figure 1**) can be removed with the engine in the frame. The cylinder head cover contains the rocker arm assembly. If the cylinder head cover is removed, the valves must be adjusted when the cover is reinstalled.

1. Remove the seat, fuel tank cover, side covers and front fender as described in Chapter Fourteen.
2. Disconnect the negative battery cable (**Figure 2**) from the battery.
3. Remove the fuel tank and heat guard as described in Chapter Eight.
4. Remove the two bolts securing the upper motor mount and remove the motor mount.
5. Remove the timing hole cap (**Figure 3**) and O-ring.
6. Set the engine at top dead center on the compression stroke by performing the following:
   a. Remove the valve adjuster caps (**Figure 4**) from the cylinder head cover.

CYLINDER HEAD

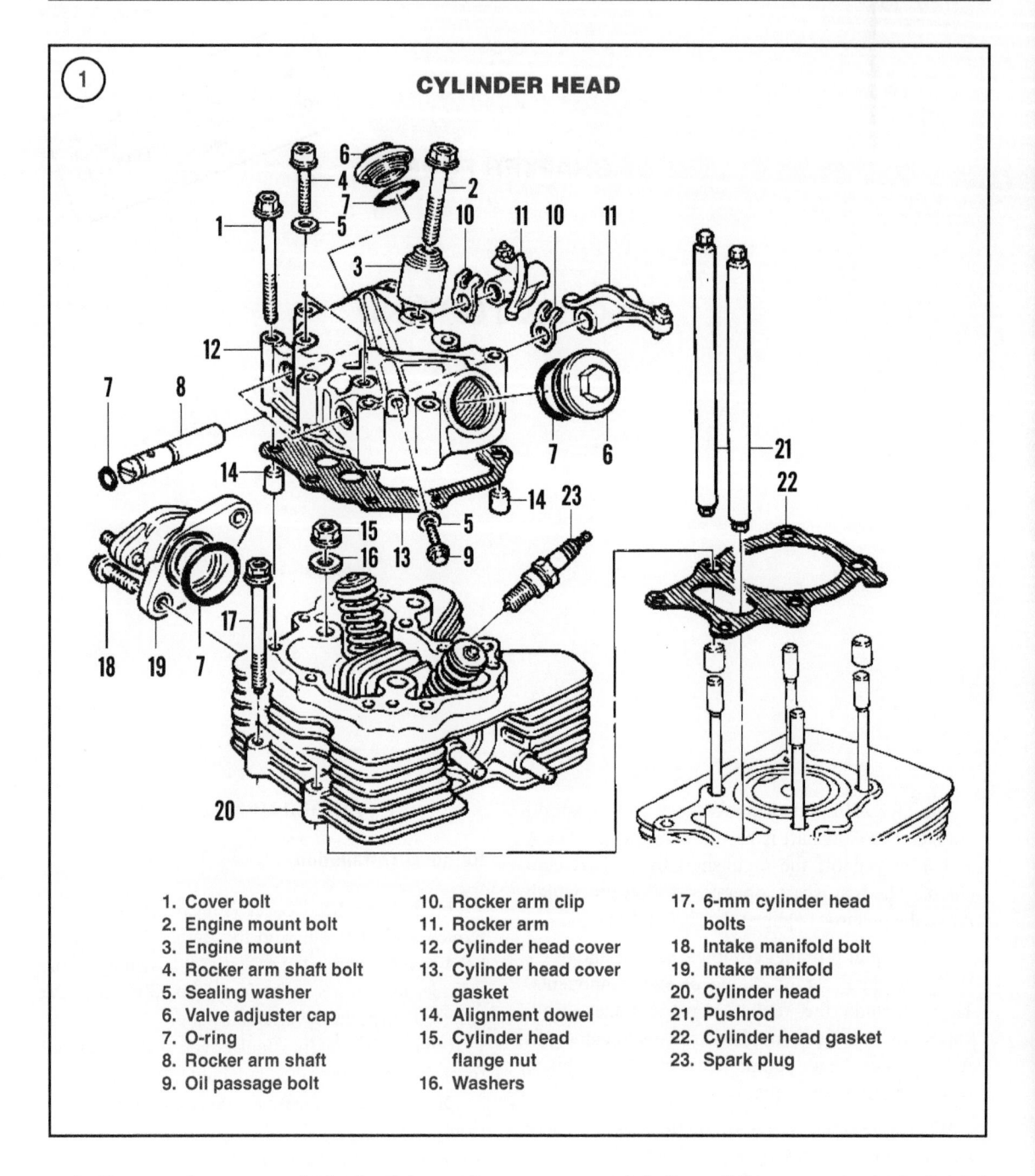

1. Cover bolt
2. Engine mount bolt
3. Engine mount
4. Rocker arm shaft bolt
5. Sealing washer
6. Valve adjuster cap
7. O-ring
8. Rocker arm shaft
9. Oil passage bolt
10. Rocker arm clip
11. Rocker arm
12. Cylinder head cover
13. Cylinder head cover gasket
14. Alignment dowel
15. Cylinder head flange nut
16. Washers
17. 6-mm cylinder head bolts
18. Intake manifold bolt
19. Intake manifold
20. Cylinder head
21. Pushrod
22. Cylinder head gasket
23. Spark plug

b. Remove the cover at the back of the engine covering the alternator bolt. Using a wrench, slowly turn the bolt counterclockwise until the T-mark (**Figure 5**) on the flywheel aligns with the index mark on the alternator cover.

c. Check that the piston is at TDC on its compression stroke by moving both rocker arms by hand. Each rocker arm should have some free play. If both rocker arms are tight, turn the crankshaft one full turn counterclockwise and realign the flywheel T-mark with the index mark. Check that both rocker arms are loose.

7. If the rocker arm assemblies will be removed from the cylinder head cover, loosen the two rocker arm shaft bolts at this time.

8. Following a crossing pattern, loosen and remove the cylinder head cover bolts (**Figure 6**). Lift the cover from the cylinder head.

ENGINE TOP END

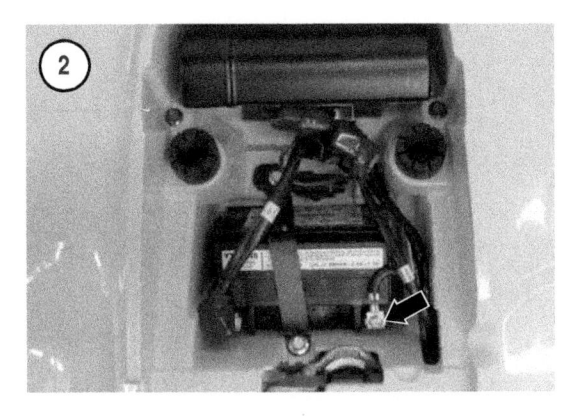

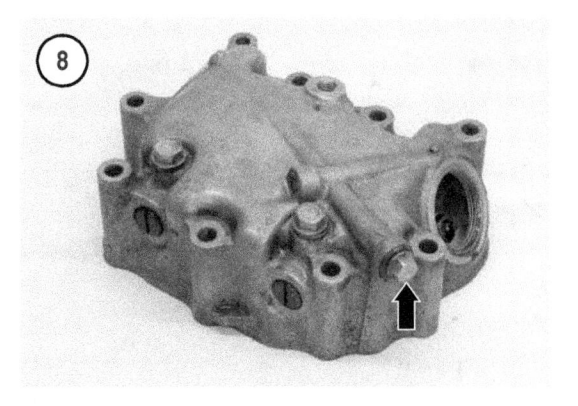

9. Remove the cylinder head cover gasket (A, **Figure 7**) and the alignment dowels (B).
10. Clean and dry the cylinder head cover. Remove the oil passage access bolt (**Figure 8**) and flush the cylinder head cover oil passages with compressed air.
11. Reverse the removal procedure to install the cylinder head cover. Note the following:
    a. Install a new cylinder head cover gasket (A, **Figure 7**).
    b. If the engine was turned over after the cylinder head cover was removed, reposition the engine at TDC by turning the alternator bolt

counterclockwise until the flywheel T-mark (**Figure 5**) aligns with the index mark on the alternator cover.

c. Lubricate the rocker arm contact surfaces (**Figure 9**) with engine oil.

d. Loosen the two valve adjuster locknuts and rocker arm adjusters, and then install the cylinder head cover.

CAUTION
The engine must remain at TDC while the cylinder head cover bolts are installed and tightened.

e. Following a crossing pattern, tighten the cylinder head cover bolts evenly in several passes to 12 N•m (106 in.-lb.).

f. If the rocker arm shaft bolts require final tightening, tighten the bolts to 10 N•m (89 in.-lbs.).

g. Adjust the valve clearance as described in Chapter Three.

ROCKER ARMS

Disassembly/Inspection/Assembly

Refer to **Table 2** when inspecting the rocker arm components. Inspect each set of parts, keeping each rocker arm with its original shaft. Replace worn or damaged parts.

CAUTION
Before removal, mark each rocker arm so it can be identified. The rocker arms must be reinstalled in their original locations.

1. Remove the cylinder head cover as described in this chapter.
2. Remove the rocker arm shaft bolts (A, **Figure 10**) from the cover.
3. Remove each rocker arm assembly as follows:
   a. Insert a small screwdriver into the bolt hole (B, **Figure 10**), and then push the rocker arm shaft (C) from the cover.
   b. Remove the rocker arm (A, **Figure 11**) and spring clip (B, **Figure 11**).
4. Clean and dry the cylinder head cover. Remove the oil passage bolt (D, **Figure 10**) and flush the oil passages with compressed air.

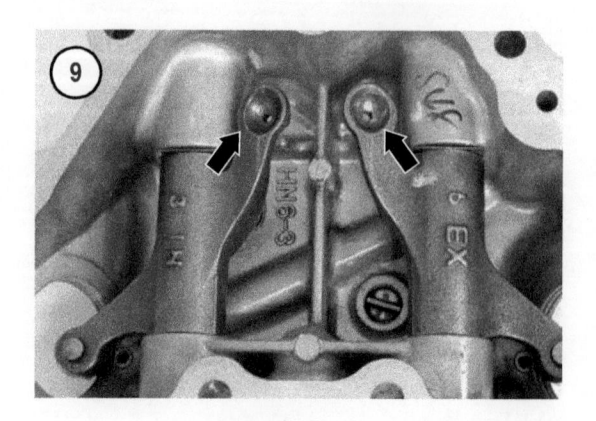

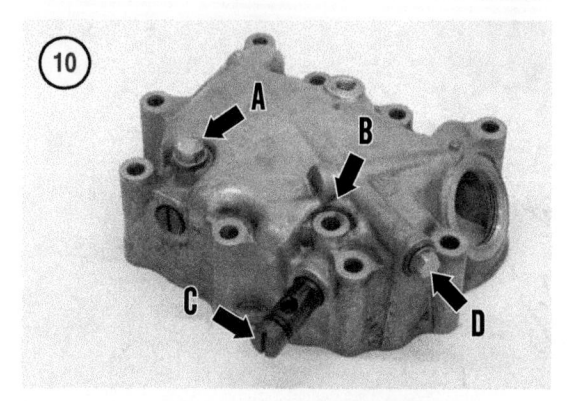

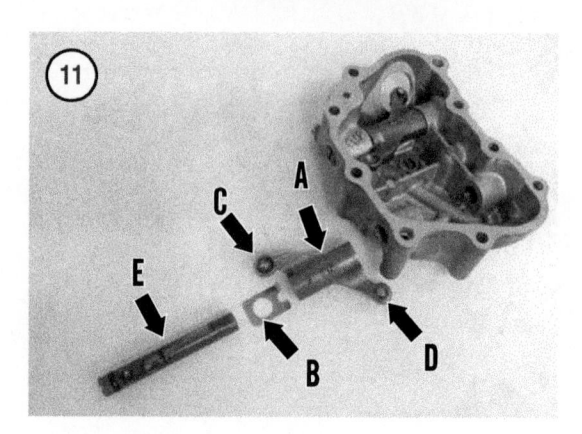

5. Inspect each rocker arm for wear and damage as follows:
   a. Inspect the rocker arm pushrod socket (C, **Figure 11**) contact point.
   b. Inspect the valve adjuster (D, **Figure 11**) contact point, threads and locknut.
6. Inspect the rocker arm shaft (E, **Figure 11**) for wear, scoring, or other damage. Replace if necessary.
7. Measure the rocker arm bore inside diameter with a small bore gauge and micrometer. If the bore

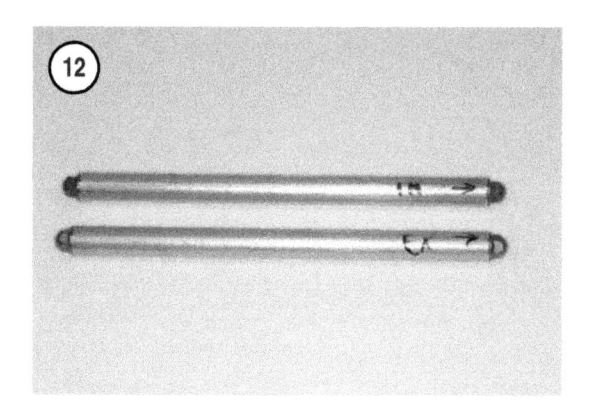

ENGINE TOP END

is within specification, record the dimension and continue the procedure.

8. Measure the rocker arm shaft outside diameter where both rocker arms pivot. If the shaft is within specification, record the dimension and continue the procedure.

9. Calculate the rocker arm-to-rocker arm shaft clearance by subtracting the rocker arm shaft outside diameter from the rocker arm bore inside diameter. Replace the rocker arms and/or the shafts if the clearance is out of specification.

10. Lubricate the rocker arm bore and shaft with engine oil. Install a new O-ring on the shaft.

11. Install each rocker arm assembly into the cylinder head cover as follows:

   a. Install the rocker arm shaft into the cylinder head cover. The slotted end of the shaft (C, **Figure 10**) must face out.
   b. Working inside the cylinder cover, slide the spring clip (B, **Figure 11**) onto the shaft. The prongs on the clip must face toward the top of the cover and point toward the rocker arm location.
   c. Install the rocker arm (A, **Figure 11**), checking that it is properly oriented.
   d. Install a new sealing washer on the rocker arm shaft bolt (A, **Figure 10**).
   e. Use a screwdriver and turn the rocker arm shaft to align the hole in the shaft with the bolt hole in the cover (B, **Figure 10**).
   f. Install the rocker arm shaft bolt and tighten it to 10 N•m (89 in.-lbs.). If desired, to keep the cover stable, the bolt can be tightened after the cylinder head cover has been installed on the engine.
   g. Check that the rocker arm pivots smoothly on the rocker arm shaft.

12. Install the cylinder head cover as described in this chapter.

CYLINDER HEAD AND PUSHRODS

The cylinder head and pushrods can be removed with the engine mounted in the frame. Some photographs show the engine removed from the frame for clarity. Refer to **Figure 1**.

Cylinder Head Removal/Installation

1. Perform Steps 1-7 of *Cylinder Head Cover Removal/Installation* (this chapter).
2. Remove the exhaust pipe and carburetor as described in Chapter Eight.
3. Remove the intake manifold and O-ring.
4. Perform Steps 8-10 of *Cylinder Head Cover Removal/Installation* (this chapter).

   NOTE
   *In the following step, identify and mark the intake and exhaust pushrods. Mark the end of the pushrod that points up (**Figure 12**). The push rods must be installed in their original locations and operating positions. Also, note the pushrod passage in the cylinder head for each pushrod.*

5. Remove the two pushrods (A, **Figure 13**).
6. Remove the 6-mm cylinder head mounting bolts (**Figure 14**), located on the right side of the head.
7. Following a crossing pattern, loosen the cylinder head flange nuts (B, **Figure 13**) evenly in two or three steps. Remove the nuts and washers.

8. Carefully raise the cylinder head. If the head is stuck to the cylinder, tap the cylinder head with a plastic mallet to break it loose.

9. Remove the cylinder head gasket.

10. Cover the cylinder with a clean shop cloth to prevent debris from entering the engine.

11. Inspect the cylinder head and pushrods as described in this section.

12. Reverse this procedure to install the cylinder head. Note the following:
   a. Clean all gasket residue from the cylinder head and cylinder mating surfaces.
   b. Install a new cylinder head gasket. Properly orient the gasket so the dowels fit correctly.
   c. Lubricate the pushrod ends with engine oil.
   d. Install the pushrods (**Figure 12**), noting their correct position and direction of installation. Check that each pushrod is seated in the center of its cam follower groove as shown in **Figure 15**.
   e. Apply engine oil to the four cylinder head flange nuts (B, **Figure 13**) and install the nuts.
   f. Following a crossing pattern, tighten the cylinder head flange nuts in 2-3 steps to 30 N•m (22 ft.-lb.).
   g. Install the two 6-mm cylinder head mounting bolts (**Figure 14**) and tighten securely.
   h. If necessary, replace the O-ring on the intake manifold to assure proper sealing.
   i. When installing the manifold, check that the "HN6" mark is facing up.

Cylinder Head Inspection

1. Remove all gasket residue from the cylinder head gasket surfaces. Do not scratch the gasket surface.

2. Without removing the valves, remove all carbon deposits from the combustion chamber. Use a fine-wire brass brush dipped in solvent or use a wood or plastic scraper. Prevent damaging the head, valves or spark plug threads.

> *CAUTION*
> *Do not clean the combustion chamber after removing the valves. Damage to the valve seat surfaces is possible, resulting in poor valve seating.*

> *CAUTION*
> *When using a tap to clean spark plug threads, coat the tap with tap-cutting fluid or kerosene.*

> *CAUTION*
> *Aluminum spark plug threads can be damaged by galling, crossthreading and overtightening. To prevent galling, apply an antiseize compound to the plug threads before installation. Do not overtighten the spark plug.*

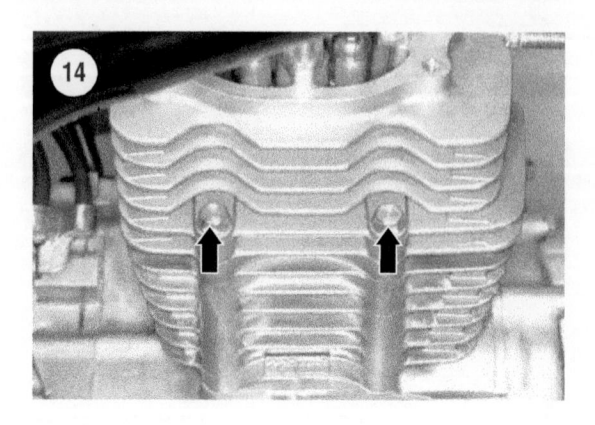

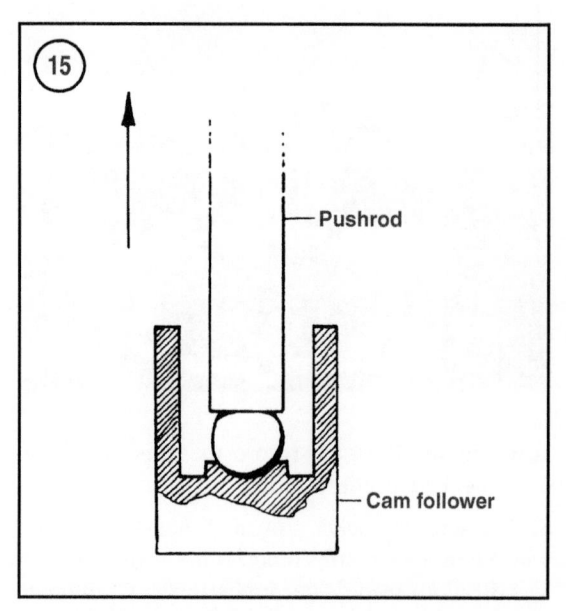

3. Examine the spark plug threads in the cylinder head for damage. If damage is minor or if the threads are dirty or clogged with carbon, use a spark plug thread tap to clean the threads. If thread damage is excessive, restore the threads with a steel thread insert.

ENGINE TOP END

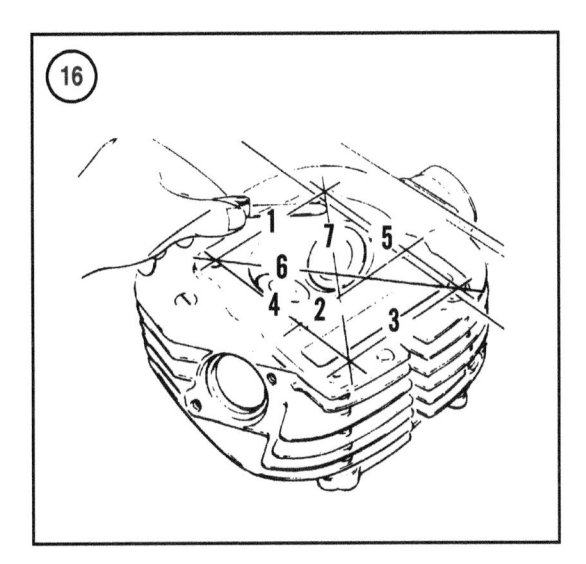

8. Inspect the intake manifold for cracks or other damage that would allow air to bypass the carburetor and cause poor fuel delivery or a lean operating condition.

9. Inspect the exhaust pipe studs for damage. If necessary, replace the studs as described in Chapter One.

10. Check the cylinder head flange nuts and washers for damage. If damage is evident, replace all the nuts and washers as a set.

11. If necessary, service the valves as described in *Valves and Valve Components* (this chapter).

Pushrod Inspection

NOTE
Although both pushrods are identical (same part number), used pushrods must be reinstalled in their original mounting positions. When cleaning and inspecting the pushrods, do not remove the identification marks made during removal.

Replace the pushrods (**Figure 12**) if they show excessive wear or damage.

1. Clean and dry the pushrods.
2. Roll each pushrod on a flat surface and check for bending.
3. Check the pushrod ends for uneven wear, cracks or signs of heat damage (discoloration).

NOTE
If the cylinder head was bead blasted, clean the head first with solvent, and then with hot soapy water. Residual grit that settles in small crevices and other areas can be hard to dislodge. Also, chase each exposed thread with a tap to remove grit trapped between the threads. Residual grit left in the engine will cause premature piston, ring and bearing wear.

4. After cleaning the combustion chamber, valve ports and spark plug thread hole, clean the entire head in solvent.

5. Examine the piston crown. The crown must show no signs of wear or damage. If the crown appears pitted or spongy, also check the spark plug, valves and combustion chamber for aluminum deposits. If these deposits are found, the cylinder is overheating due to a lean fuel mixture or preignition.

6. Check the combustion chamber and exhaust port for cracks.

7. Place a straightedge across the gasket surface and measure cylinder head warp (**Table 2**) by inserting a feeler gauge between the straightedge and cylinder head at the locations shown in **Figure 16**. Warp or nicks in the cylinder head surface could cause an air leak and overheating. If the head is warped, resurface or replace the cylinder head. Consult with a Honda dealership or a machine shop for this type of work.

VALVES AND VALVE COMPONENTS

A complete valve job, which consists of reconditioning the valve seats and replacing the valve guides, requires special tools. This section describes service procedures for checking the valve components and for determining the type of service required. Along with the special tools, considerable expertise is required to properly recondition the valves seats. Because of the cost of the equipment and their infrequent need by the typical do-it-yourselfer, valve service is generally entrusted to machine shops specializing in this type of work.

If the tools are available, follow the tool manufacturer's instruction and refer to the following procedures.

Although some of the photos in this section show the valve configuration used on an earlier version of this engine, all procedures and techniques are applicable to the current design.

Tools

A valve spring compressor is required to remove and install the valves. This tool compresses the valve springs so the valve keepers can be released from the valve stem. Do not remove or install the valves without a valve spring compressor. Because of the limited working area, most automotive type valve spring compressors do not work. Rent or purchase a valve spring compressor designed for ATV and motorcycle applications.

Solvent Test

For proper engine operation, the valves must seat tightly against their seats. Any condition that prevents the valves from seating properly can cause valve burning and reduced engine performance. Before removing the valves from the cylinder head, perform the following:
1. Remove the cylinder head as described in this chapter.
2. Support the cylinder so the exhaust port faces up (**Figure 17**) and pour solvent or kerosene into the port. Check the combustion chamber for fluid leaking past the exhaust valve seat.
3. Repeat Step 2 for the intake port and intake valve and seat.
4. If fluid leaks around a valve seat, the valve is not seating properly. The following conditions can cause poor valve seating:
   a. A bent valve stem.
   b. A worn or damaged valve seat (in the cylinder head).
   c. A worn or damaged valve face.
   d. A crack in the combustion chamber.

Valve Removal

Refer to **Figure 18**.
1. Remove the cylinder head as described in this chapter.
2. Install a valve spring compressor squarely over the valve spring seat with the other end of the tool placed against valve head (**Figure 19**). Position the head of the valve spring compressor so the valve keepers are accessible.

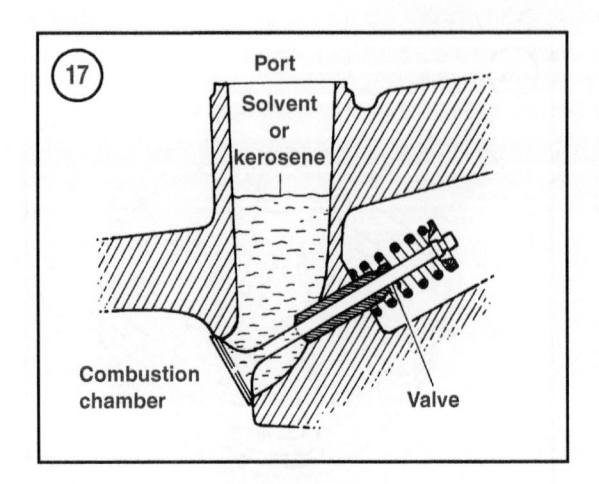

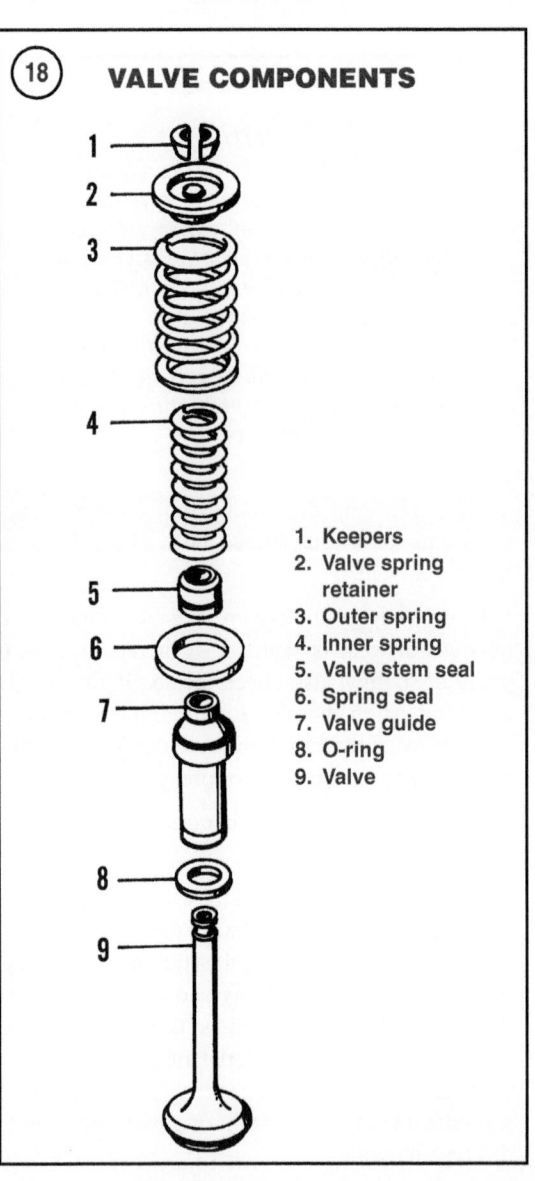

ENGINE TOP END

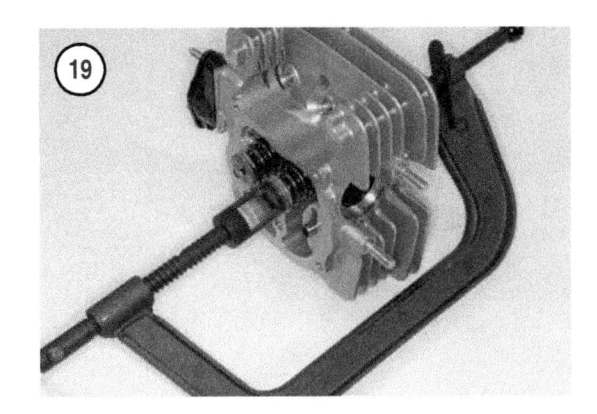

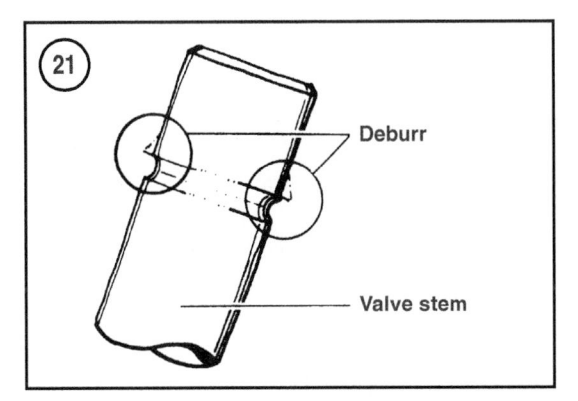

WARNING
Wear safety glasses or goggles when performing Step 3.

CAUTION
When compressing the valve springs, do not compress them any more than necessary.

3. Tighten the valve spring compressor to remove all tension from the upper spring seat and valve keepers. Remove the valve keepers (**Figure 20**) with pliers or a magnet.

4. Slowly loosen the valve spring compressor, and remove it from the head.

5. Remove the valve spring retainer and both valve springs.

CAUTION
*Remove any burrs from the valve stem groove (**Figure 21**) before removing the valve; otherwise, the valve guide can be damaged as the valve stem passes through it.*

6. Remove the valve from the cylinder head.

7. Pull the valve stem seal (**Figure 22**) from the valve guide and discard the seal.

8. Remove the lower spring seat.

CAUTION
Keep all parts of each valve assembly together. Do not mix components from the different valves assemblies. Excessive wear may result.

9. Repeat the procedure to remove the remaining valve.

10. Inspect the valves as described in this section.

Valve Installation

1. Clean and dry all parts. If the valve seats were machined, lapped or if the valve guides were replaced, thoroughly clean the valves and cylinder head in solvent, and then wash the head with hot soapy water. All lapping and grinding compound must be washed away. After drying the cylinder head, lubricate the valve guides with engine oil to prevent rust.

2. Install the spring seat (**Figure 23**).

NOTE
New valve seals must be installed whenever the valves are removed. The valve seals are color coded and not interchangeable. The intake valve seal is green; the exhaust seal is brown.

3. Install new valve seals as follows:
   a. Lubricate the inside of each new valve seal with molybdenum disulfide paste.
   b. Install the new valve seal (**Figure 22**) over the valve guide and seat it into place.
4. Coat the valve stem with molybdenum disulfide paste. Install the valve part way into the guide. Slowly turn the valve as it enters the valve seal, and continue turning the valve until it is completely installed.

NOTE
*Install each valve spring so the end with the closer wound coils (**Figure 24**) faces in toward the cylinder head.*

5. Install the inner and outer valve springs (**Figure 25**).
6. Install the valve spring retainer (**Figure 26**).

WARNING
Wear safety glasses or goggles when compressing the valve springs.

7. Install the valve spring compressor. Push down on the upper valve seat and compress the springs, and then install the valve keepers (**Figure 20**).
8. Slowly release the tension from the compressor and remove it. After removing the compressor, inspect the valve keepers to make sure they are properly seated (**Figure 27**). Tap the end of the valve stem (**Figure 28**) with a drift and hammer. This ensures the keepers are completely seated.
9. Repeat the installation procedure for the opposite valve.
10. After installing the cylinder head and rocker arm holder onto the engine, adjust the valve clearance as described in Chapter Three.

Component Inspection

When inspecting the valve components, compare the actual measurements to the specifications in **Table 2**. Replace parts that are damaged, worn to the service limit or out of specification.

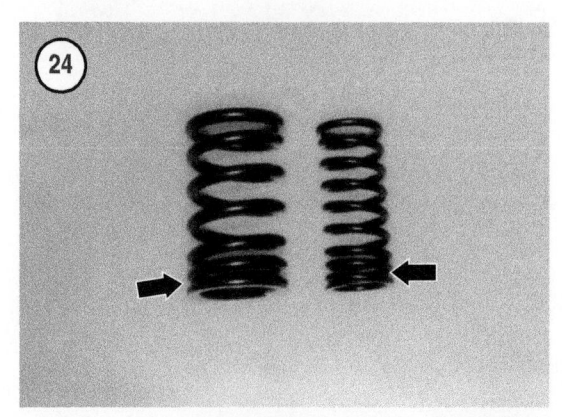

Refer to **Figure 29** when inspecting and troubleshooting the valves.

1. Clean the valves in solvent. Do not gouge or damage the valve seating surface.

2. Inspect the contact surface (**Figure 30**) of each valve for burning. Minor roughness and pitting can be removed by lapping the valve as described in this section. Excessive unevenness in the contact surface is an indication that the valve is not serviceable.

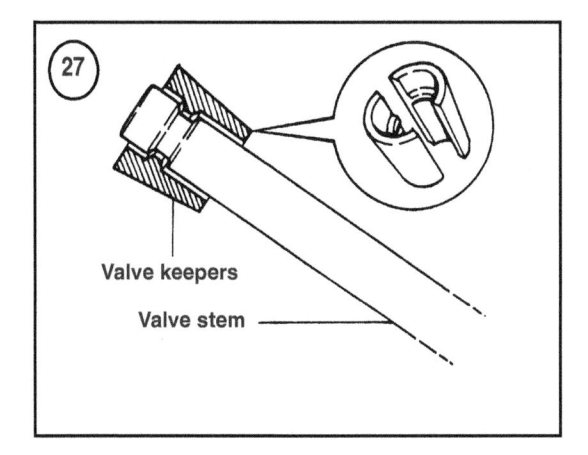

ENGINE TOP END

a micrometer (**Figure 32**) to determine the valve guide inside diameter. Record the measurement.

6. Subtract the valve stem outside diameter (Step 3) from the valve guide inside diameter (Step 5). The difference is the valve stem-to-guide clearance.

7. If the valve stem-to-guide clearance exceeds the service limit, determine if a new valve guide would bring the valve stem-to-guide clearance within specification. If it will, replace the valve guide. If it will not, replace both the valve guide and the valve. Refer to *Valve Guide Replacement* in this section.

8. Inspect the inner and outer valve springs by performing the following:
    a. Check each valve spring for visual damage.
    b. Use a square and check each spring for distortion or tilt (**Figure 33**).
    c. Measure the valve spring free length with a caliper (**Figure 34**).
    d. Replace worn or damaged springs as a set.

9. Check the valve spring seats and valve keepers for cracks or other damage.

10. Inspect the valve seats (**Figure 35**) for burning, pitting, cracks, excessive wear or other damage. If worn or burned, they may be reconditioned as described in this section. Seats and valves in near-perfect condition can be reconditioned by lapping with fine carborundum paste. Check the valve seats by performing the following:
    a. Clean the valve seat and valve mating areas with contact cleaner.
    b. Spread a thin layer of marking compound evenly on the valve seat.
    c. Install the valve into its guide and rotate it against its seat with a valve lapping tool. Refer to *Valve Lapping* in this section.
    d. Lift the valve out of the guide and measure the seat width (**Figure 36**) with a vernier caliper.
    e. Make sure the seat width is within the specification in **Table 2** all the way around the seat. If the seat width exceeds the service limit, refer to *Valve Seat Reconditioning* in this section.
    f. Remove all marking compound residue from the seats and valves.

3. Inspect the valve stems for wear and roughness. Measure the valve stem diameter (**Figure 31**) for wear. Record the measurement.

4. Remove all carbon and varnish from the valve guides with a stiff spiral wire brush before measuring wear.

5. Measure each valve guide inside diameter at its top, center and bottom of the valve guide bore with a small hole gauge. Measure the small hole gauge with

Valve Guide Replacement

A 5.5-mm valve guide reamer (Honda part No. 07984-2000001 or 07984-2000001D) and 5.5-valve guide driver (Honda part No. 07742-0010100), or

29

VALVE TROUBLESHOOTING

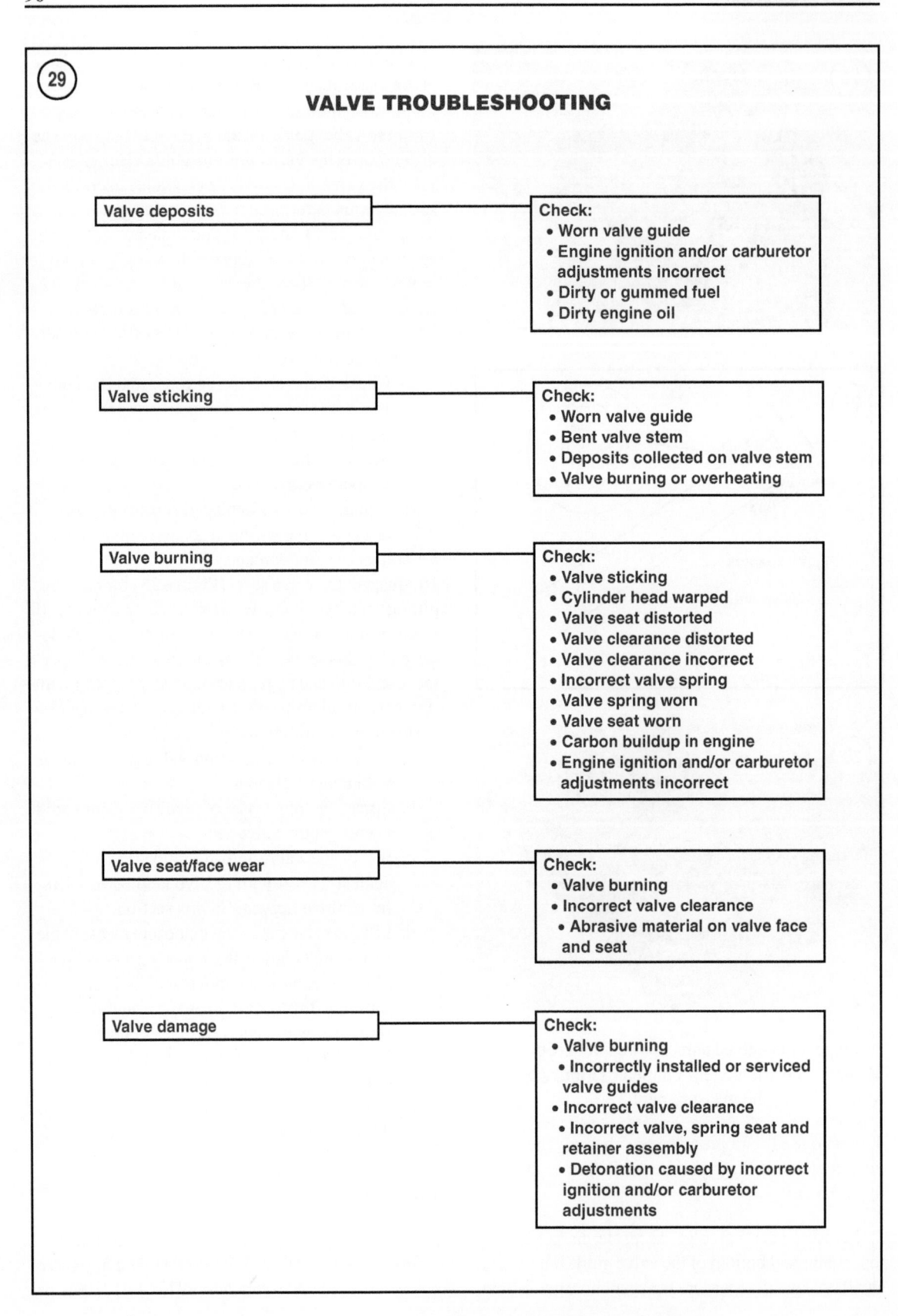

Valve deposits

Check:
- Worn valve guide
- Engine ignition and/or carburetor adjustments incorrect
- Dirty or gummed fuel
- Dirty engine oil

Valve sticking

Check:
- Worn valve guide
- Bent valve stem
- Deposits collected on valve stem
- Valve burning or overheating

Valve burning

Check:
- Valve sticking
- Cylinder head warped
- Valve seat distorted
- Valve clearance distorted
- Valve clearance incorrect
- Incorrect valve spring
- Valve spring worn
- Valve seat worn
- Carbon buildup in engine
- Engine ignition and/or carburetor adjustments incorrect

Valve seat/face wear

Check:
- Valve burning
- Incorrect valve clearance
- Abrasive material on valve face and seat

Valve damage

Check:
- Valve burning
- Incorrectly installed or serviced valve guides
- Incorrect valve clearance
- Incorrect valve, spring seat and retainer assembly
- Detonation caused by incorrect ignition and/or carburetor adjustments

ENGINE TOP END

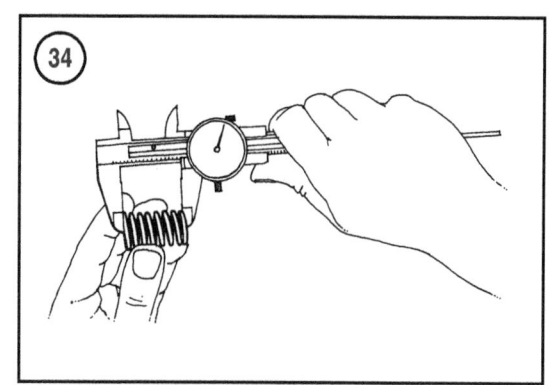

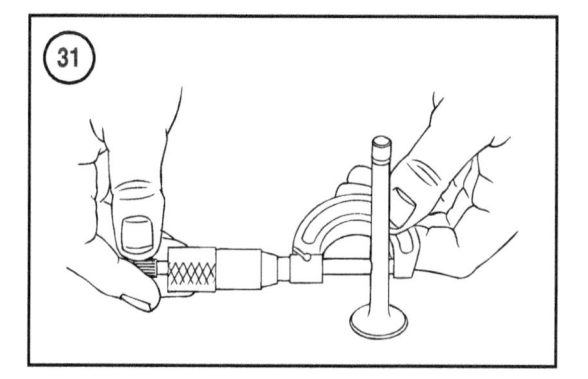

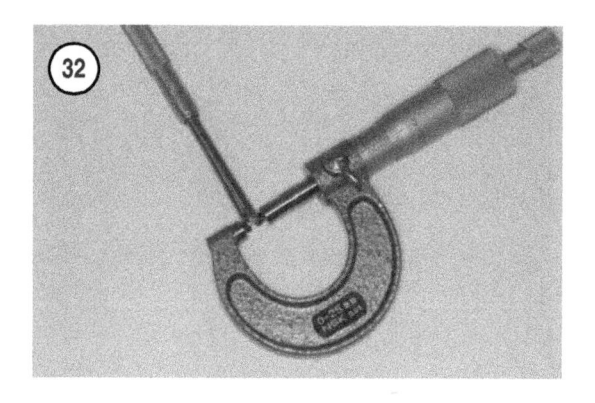

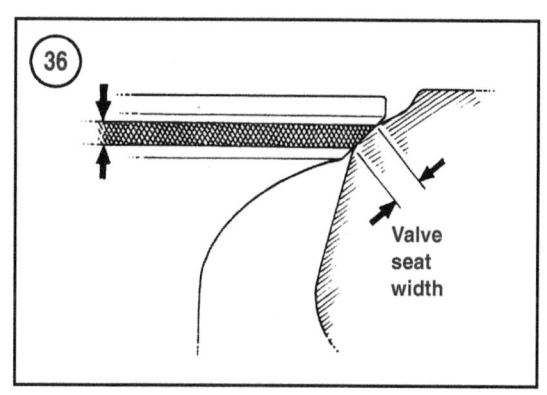

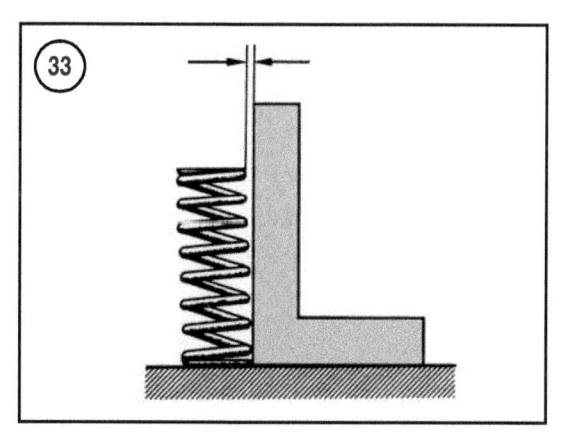

97

their equivalent, are required to replace the valve guides.

1. If still installed, remove the intake manifold and its O-ring from the cylinder head.

CAUTION
Do not heat the cylinder head with a torch (propane or acetylene). Never bring a flame into contact with the cylinder head. The direct heat destroys the case hardening and may warp the head.

2. The valve guides are installed with a slight interference fit. Heat the cylinder head in a shop oven or on a hot plate. Heat the cylinder head to 100-150° C (212-300° F). Use temperature indicator sticks, available at welding supply stores, to monitor the cylinder head temperature.

3. Place the new valve guides in the freezer overnight to reduce their outside diameters.

WARNING
Wear welding gloves when performing the following procedure. The cylinder head is hot.

4. Remove the cylinder head from the oven or hot plate. Place it on wooden blocks with the combustion chamber facing up.

CAUTION
Do not remove the valve guides if the head is not hot enough. Doing so may damage the valve guide bore.

5. From the combustion side of the cylinder head, drive out the old valve guide (**Figure 37**) with a hammer and the 5-mm valve guide driver.

6. Remove and discard the valve guide and its O-ring. Never reuse a valve guide or O-ring. They are no longer true nor within tolerance.

7. After the cylinder head cools, check the guide bore for carbon or other contamination.

8. Reheat the cylinder head to 100-150° C (212-300° F).

9. Remove the cylinder head from the oven or hot plate, and place it on wooden blocks with the combustion chamber facing down.

CAUTION
*The intake and exhaust valve guides are not interchangeable. The intake valve guide has an identification line on its lip that is not on the exhaust valve guide. Refer to **Figure 38**.*

10. Remove a new valve guide from the freezer, and install a new O-ring onto the valve guide.

11. Apply fresh engine oil to the new valve guide and to the valve guide bore in the cylinder head.

12. From the top side (valve side) of the cylinder head, drive the new valve guide into place with the valve guide driver. Drive the valve guide until the ring completely seats in the cylinder head.

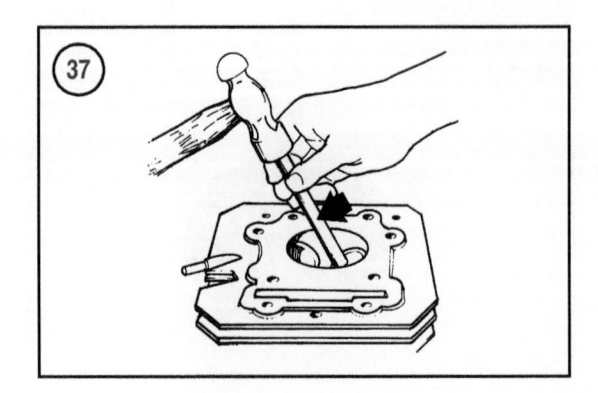

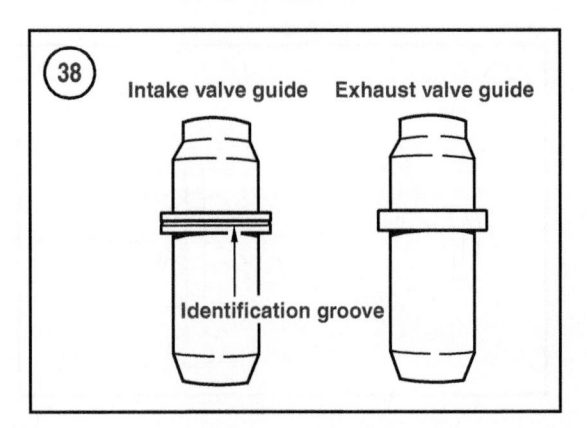

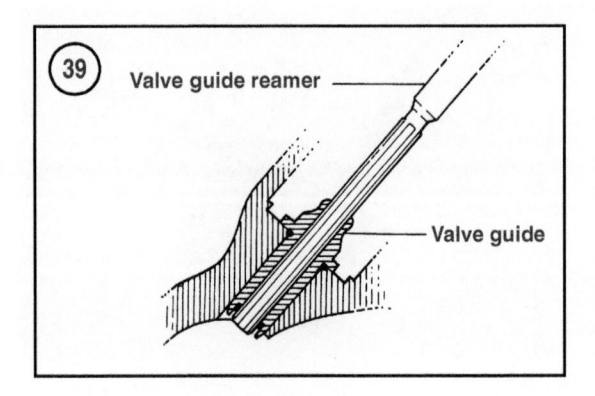

13. After installation, ream the new valve guide by performing the following:
   a. Use the valve guide reamer.
   b. Apply cutting oil to both the new valve guide and the valve guide reamer.

CAUTION
*Always rotate the reamer **clockwise**. The valve guide is damaged if the reamer is rotated counterclockwise.*

   c. Insert the reamer from the combustion chamber side and rotate it clockwise *through the*

ENGINE TOP END

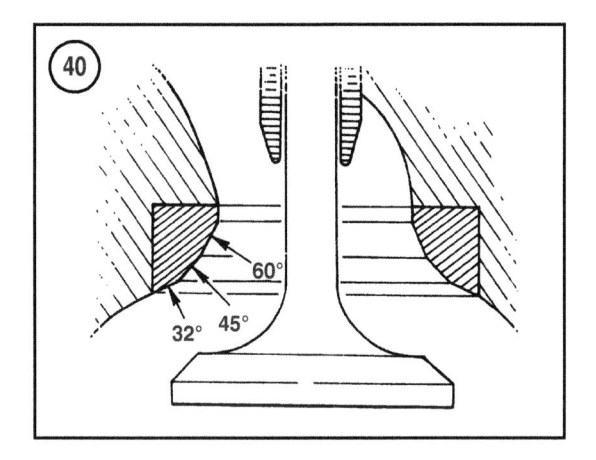

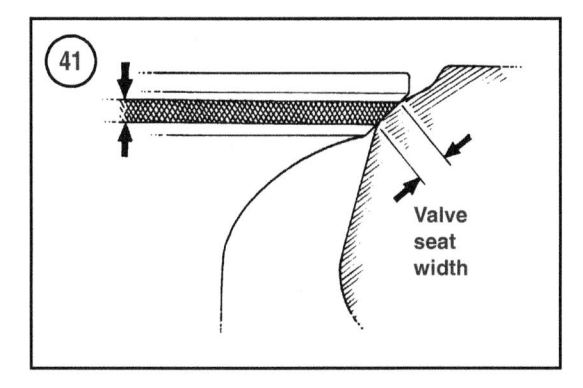

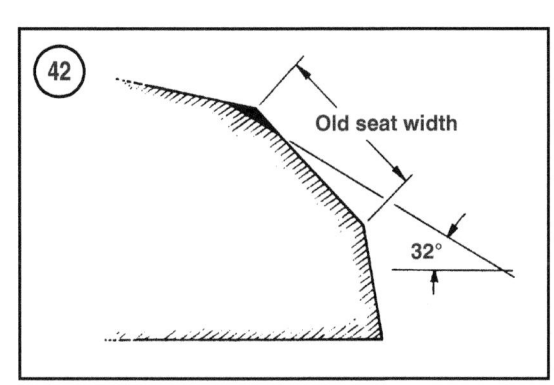

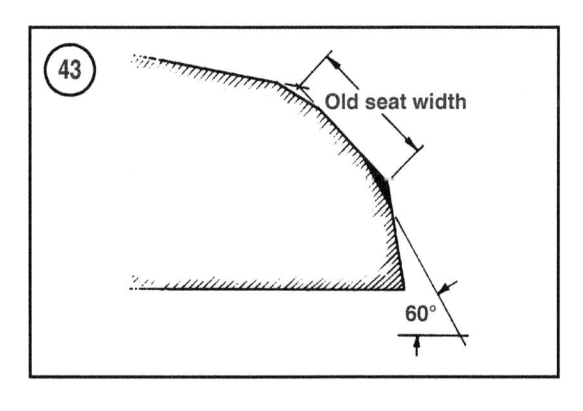

*valve guide (***Figure 39**). Continue to rotate the reamer and work it down through the entire length of the new valve guide. Apply additional cutting oil during this procedure.

d. While rotating the reamer clockwise, *withdraw the reamer from the valve guide.*

e. Measure the valve guide inside diameter with a small hole gauge. This measurement must be within the specification in **Table 2**.

14. Repeat for the other valve guides.

15. Thoroughly clean the cylinder head and valve guides with solvent to remove all metal particles. Clean the cylinder head with hot, soapy water, rinse the head completely and thoroughly dry it with compressed air.

16. Lubricate the valve guides with engine oil.

Valve Seat Reconditioning

Reconditioning the valve seats requires special valve cutting tools with the angles shown in **Figure 40**.

CAUTION
When cutting valve seats, work slowly to avoid removing too much material. An overcut seat moves the valve farther into the head, which reduces valve clearance and may make it impossible to obtain the correct clearance.

1. Install a 45° cutter onto the T-handle. Use the 45° cutter to descale and clean the valve seat with one or two turns.

2. Measure the valve seat width (**Figure 41**) with a vernier caliper, and record the measurement. Use it as a reference during the remainder of the procedure.

CAUTION
The 32° cutter removes material quickly. Work carefully and check the progress often.

3. Use the 32° cutter to lightly remove the top 1/4 of the existing valve seat (**Figure 42**).

4. Use the 60° cutter too lightly remove the lower 1/4 of the existing valve seat (**Figure 43**).

5. Measure the valve seat width (**Figure 41**) with a vernier caliper. Use the 45° cutter to cut the valve seat to the specified width in **Table 2**. Refer to **Figure 44**.

6. Once the valve seat width is within specification, check the valve seating by performing the following:
   a. Clean the valve seat with contact cleaner.
   b. Evenly spread a thin layer of marking compound on the valve face.
   c. Once the compound is dry, insert the valve into its guide.
   d. Support the valve by hand (**Figure 45**), and tap the valve up and down in the cylinder head. Do not rotate the valve. This yields a false reading.
   e. Remove the valve, and examine the impression left by the marking compound. Measure the valve seat width (**Figure 41**). The valve contact area should be approximately in the center of the valve seat area and within specification.
7. If the valve contact area is too high or too low, perform the following:
   a. If the contact area is too high on the valve or if it is too wide, use the 32° cutter to remove a portion of the top area of the valve seat, which lowers and narrows the contact area (**Figure 42**).
   b. If the contact area is too low on the valve or if it is too wide, use the 60° cutter to remove a portion of the lower area of the valve seat, which raises and narrows the contact area (**Figure 43**).
8. Once the desired valve seat position and width is obtained, use the 45° cutter to very lightly clean off any burrs that may have been caused by previous cuts.
9. Lap the valve to the seat as described in this section.
10. Repeat Steps 1-9 for the other valve.
11. Clean the cylinder head and all valve components in solvent or detergent and hot water. Dry all parts thoroughly.
12. Once the components are completely dry, apply a light coat of engine oil to all bare metal surfaces to prevent rust.

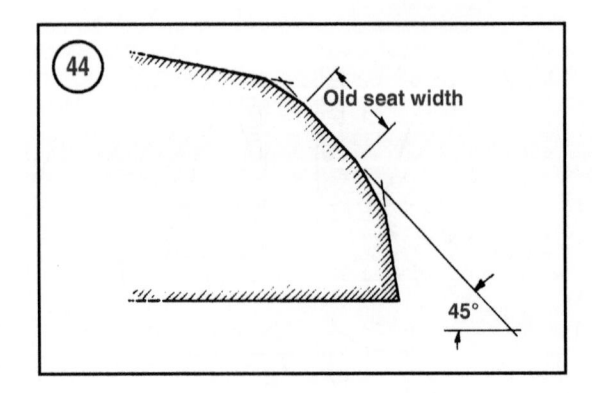

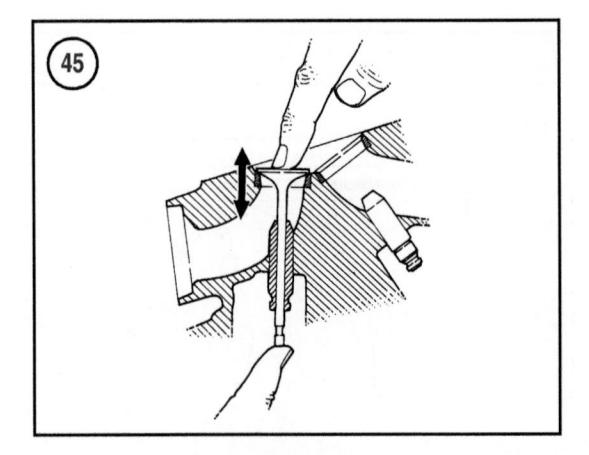

Valve Lapping

Valve lapping can restore the valve seat without machining, if the amount of wear or distortion is not too great.

Perform this procedure after determining that the valve seat width and outside diameter are within specification. Refer to the *Component Inspection* procedure in this section.

1. Smear a light coating of fine grade valve lapping compound on the valve face.
2. Insert the valve into the head.
3. Wet the suction cup of the lapping stick and stick it onto the head of the valve. Lap the valve to the seat by spinning the lapping stick in both directions. Every 5 to 10 seconds, rotate the valve 180° in the valve seat. Continue this action until the mating surfaces on the valve and seat are smooth and equal in size.
4. Closely examine the valve seat in the cylinder head. It should be even with a smooth, polished seating ring.
5. Thoroughly clean the valves and cylinder head in solvent and then with hot soapy water to remove all lapping compound. Any compound left on the valves or the cylinder head contaminates the engine oil and causes excessive wear and damage. After drying the cylinder head, lubricate the valve guides with engine oil to prevent rust.
6. After installing the valves into the cylinder, test the valve seat seal as described in *Solvent Test*. If

ENGINE TOP END

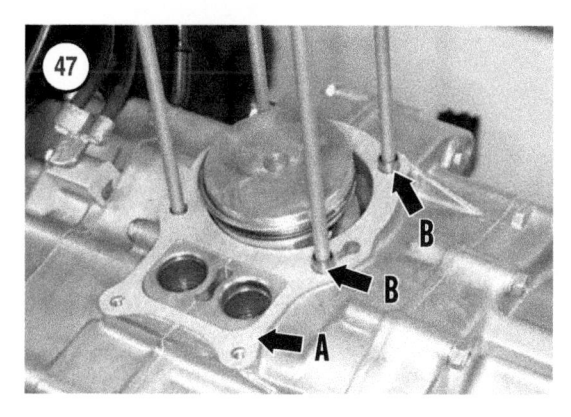

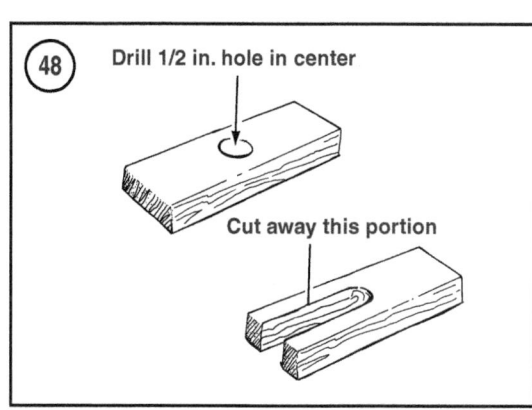

46

47

48 Drill 1/2 in. hole in center
Cut away this portion

fluid leaks past the seat, remove the valve assembly and repeat the lapping procedure until there are no leaks. When there are no leaks, remove both valve sets and reclean the cylinder head assembly.

CYLINDER

The alloy cylinder has a pressed-in cast iron cylinder liner. Oversize piston and ring sizes are available through Honda dealerships and aftermarket piston suppliers.

The cylinder and piston can be serviced with the engine mounted in the frame. Because of the engine's mounting position in the frame, the following photographs are shown with the engine removed for clarity.

Removal

1. Remove the pushrods and cylinder head as described in this chapter.
2. Loosen the cylinder by tapping around the perimeter with a rubber or plastic mallet.
3. Lift the cylinder (**Figure 46**) straight up and off the crankcase studs.
4. Remove the gasket (A, **Figure 47**) and two dowels (B).
5. If necessary, remove the piston as described in this section.
6. If necessary, remove the cam followers as described in *Camshaft* in this chapter.
7. Cover the crankcase opening to prevent objects from falling into the crankcase.

Installation

1. Check that the top and bottom cylinder surfaces are clean of all gasket residue.
2. If removed, install the cam followers as described in *Camshaft* in this chapter.
3. If removed, install the piston and rings as described in this chapter.

CAUTION
Make sure to install and secure the piston pin circlips.

4. Install a new base gasket (A, **Figure 47**) and the two dowels into the crankcase (B). Make sure all holes in the gasket align with their mating holes in the crankcase.

NOTE
*A piston holding fixture can be made from wood as shown in **Figure 48**.*

5. Install a piston holding fixture under the piston.
6. Lubricate the cylinder wall, piston and rings with engine oil.

CAUTION
Install the cylinder over the piston by compressing the rings with a ring

compressor. As the cylinder is installed over the piston, the compressed rings pass into the cylinder and then expand out once they are free of the ring compressor. A hose clamp works well for this. Before using a ring compressor or hose clamp, lubricate its ring contact side with engine oil. Do not overtighten the ring compressor or hose clamp. The tool should be able to slide freely as the cylinder pushes against it.

7. Compress the rings with a ring compressor or appropriate size hose clamp. Align the cylinder with the piston and *carefully* slide it down past the rings. When all the rings are installed in the cylinder, hold the cylinder and remove the ring compressor or hose clamp.

8. Remove the piston holding fixture, and slide the cylinder (**Figure 46**) all the way down until it seats on the crankcase.

CAUTION
If the piston does not move smoothly, one of the piston rings may have slipped out of its groove when the cylinder was installed. Lift the cylinder and piston up together so there is space under the piston. Install a clean rag under the piston to catch any pieces from a broken piston ring, and then remove the cylinder.

9. While holding the cylinder down with one hand, turn the engine over by rotating the alternator bolt clockwise. The piston must move up and down in the bore with no binding or roughness.

10. Install the cylinder head and pushrods as described in this chapter.

Inspection

Refer to **Table 2** when inspecting the cylinder. Replace parts that are damaged or out of specification.

1. Remove all gasket residue from the top and bottom cylinder gasket surfaces.
2. Wash the cylinder in solvent, and dry it with compressed air.
3. Check the dowel pin holes for cracks or other damage.
4. Check the cylinder for warp with a feeler gauge and straightedge as shown in **Figure 49**. Check for warp at several places on the cylinder. If warp exceeds the service limit, refer service to a Honda dealership.

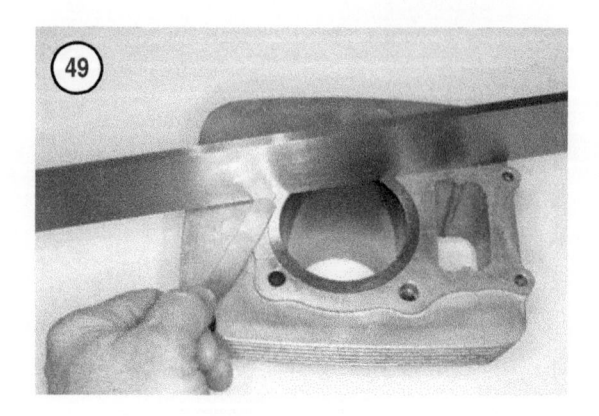

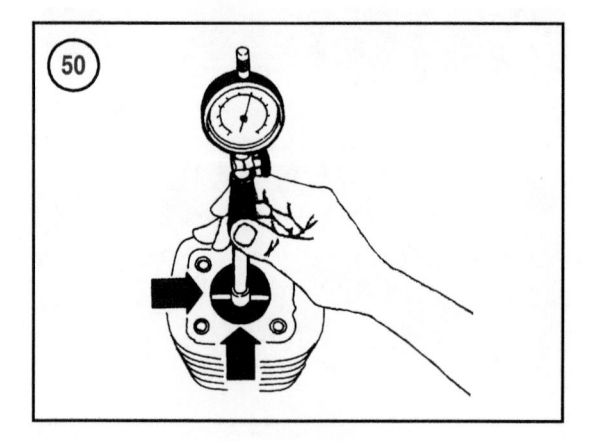

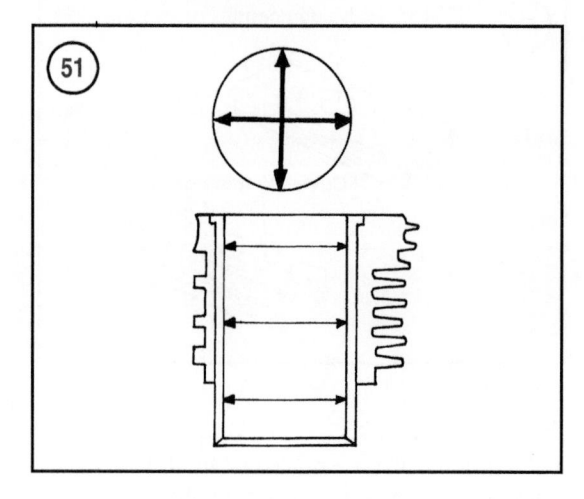

5. Measure the cylinder bore inside diameter with a bore gauge or inside micrometer (**Figure 50**) at the top, middle and bottom of the cylinder. At each lo-

ENGINE TOP END

6. If the cylinder is not worn past the service limit, check the bore for scratches or gouges. The bore still may require boring and reconditioning.

CAUTION
The soap and water described in Step 7 is the only solution that can wash the fine grit residue out of the cylinder crevices. Solvent and kerosene cannot do this. Grit residue left in the cylinder causes rapid and premature wear to the new rings and cylinder bore surface.

7. After servicing the cylinder, wash the bore in hot, soapy water. This is the only way to clean the cylinder wall of the fine grit material left from the bore or honing job. After washing the cylinder wall, run a clean white cloth through it. The cylinder must be free of all grit and other residue. If the rag is dirty, rewash the cylinder wall again and recheck with the white cloth. Repeat until the cloth comes out clean. When the cylinder is clean, lubricate it with engine oil to prevent the cylinder liner from rusting.

PISTON AND PISTON RINGS

The piston is made of an aluminum alloy. The piston pin is made of steel and is a precision fit in the piston. The piston pin is held in place by a circlip at each end.

Piston Removal

1. Remove the cylinder as described in this chapter.
2. Use rags to block the crankcase below the piston to prevent the piston pin circlips from falling into the crankcase.
3. Before removing the piston, hold the rod and rock the piston (**Figure 52**). Any rocking motion (do not confuse with the normal sliding motion) indicates wear on the piston pin, rod bore, pin bore or a combination of all three.

WARNING
Wear safety glasses when removing the circlips in Step 4.

4. Remove the circlips (**Figure 53**) from the piston pin bore grooves.
5. Push the piston pin (A, **Figure 54**) out of the piston by hand. If the pin is tight, fabricate a tool (**Figure 55**) to remove it. Do not drive the piston pin out.

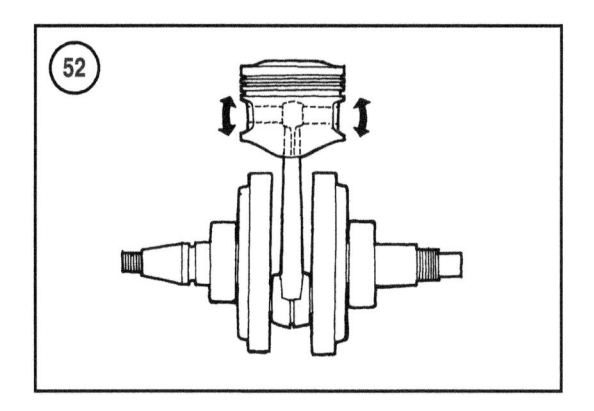

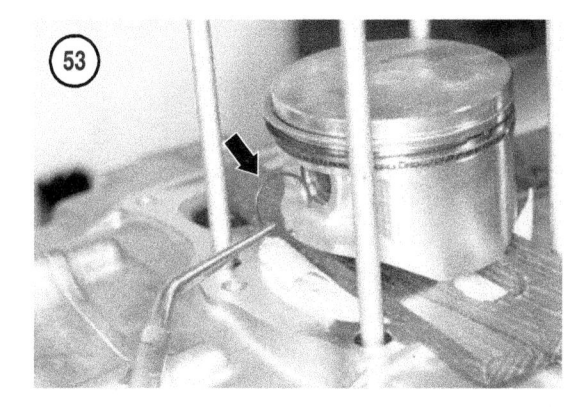

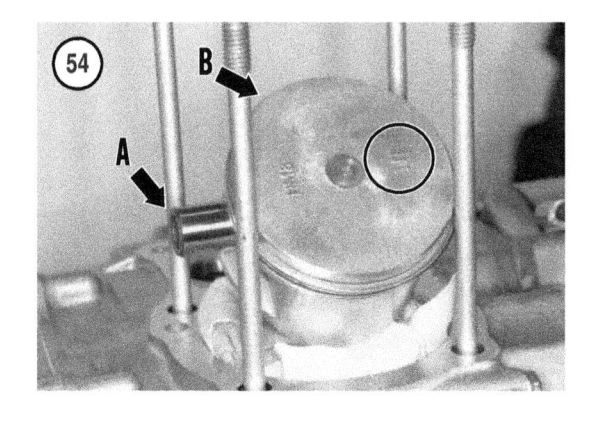

cation, measure the bore in-line with the piston pin and at 90° to the pin. Refer to **Figure 51**. If the bore inside diameter, taper or out-of-round exceeds the service limit, the cylinder must be rebored to the next oversize and a new piston and ring assembly installed. Refer this service to a Honda dealership or a qualified machine shop.

NOTE
*To determine piston clearance, refer to **Piston and Piston Rings** in this chapter.*

The driving force could damage the piston pin, connecting rod or piston.

6. Lift the piston (B, **Figure 54**) off the connecting rod.
7. Inspect the piston as described in this section.

Piston Installation

1. Install the piston rings onto the piston as described in this section.
2. Install a *new* piston pin circlip into one piston pin bore. The circlip ends must not align with the cutout in the piston (**Figure 56**).
3. Cover the crankcase opening with clean rags.
4. Coat the connecting rod bore, piston pin and piston with engine oil.
5. Slide the piston pin into the piston until its end is flush with the piston pin boss as shown in **Figure 57**.
6. Place the piston over the connecting rod so the IN mark (**Figure 54**) on the piston crown faces the intake side (rear) of the engine.
7. Align the piston pin with the hole in the connecting rod. Push the piston pin (A, **Figure 54**) through the connecting rod until the pin clears the circlip groove or until it bottoms against the circlip on the opposite side of the piston.

WARNING
Wear safety glasses or goggles when installing the piston pin circlips in Step 8.

8. Install a *new* piston pin circlip (**Figure 53**) into the remaining piston pin bore. Make sure the circlips seat in the grooves completely. Turn the circlip so its end gap does not align with the cutout in the piston (**Figure 56**).

Piston Inspection

1. Remove the piston rings as described in this section.
2. Clean the carbon from the piston crown (**Figure 58**) with a soft scraper. Large carbon accumulations reduce piston cooling and cause detonation and piston damage.

CAUTION
Do not wire brush the piston skirt.

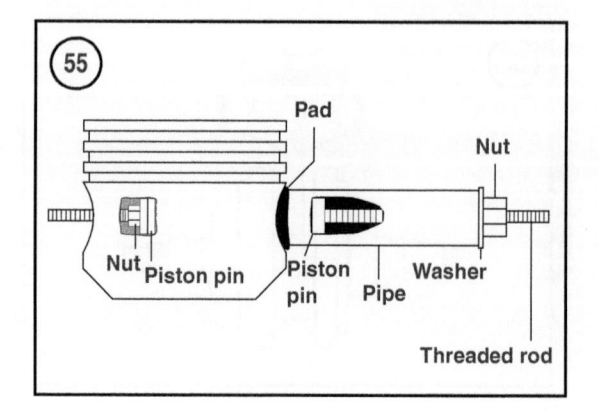

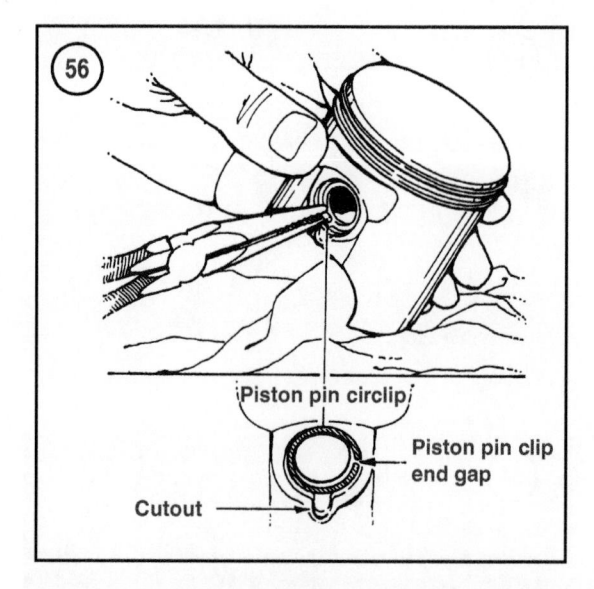

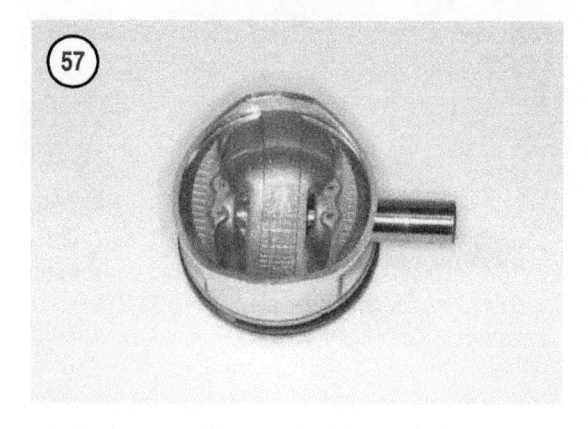

3. After cleaning the piston, examine the crown. The crown must show no signs of wear or damage. If the crown appears pecked or spongy-looking, also check the spark plug, valves and combustion chamber for aluminum deposits. If these deposits are found, the engine is overheating.

ENGINE TOP END

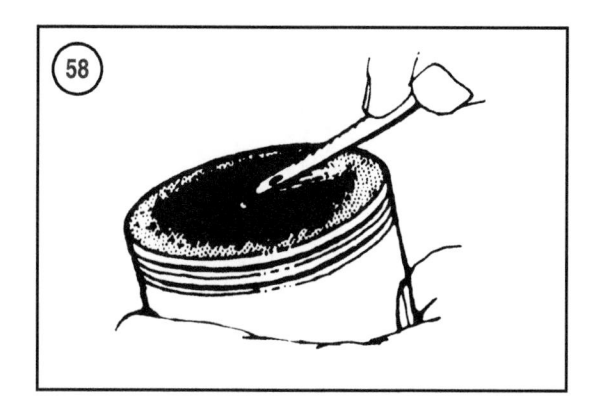

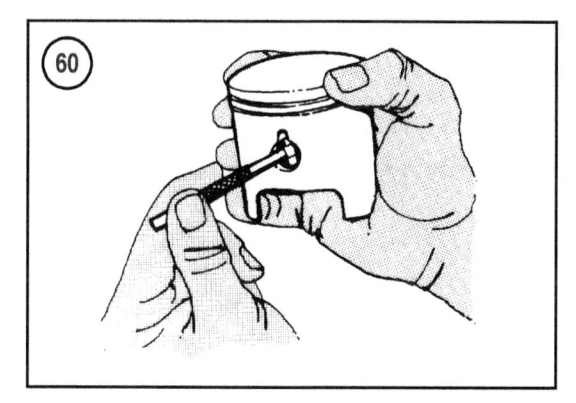

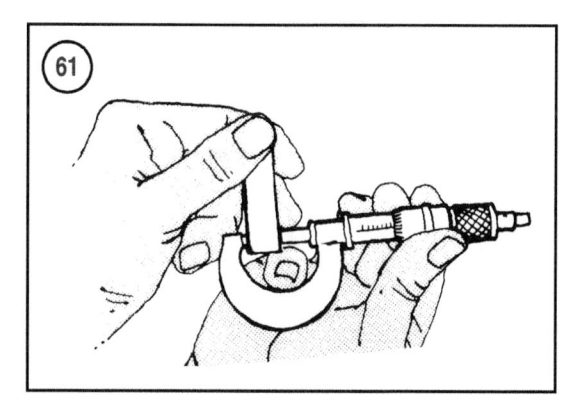

4. Examine each ring groove for burrs, dented edges or other damage. Pay particular attention to the top compression ring groove because it usually wears more than the others. Because the oil rings are bathed in oil, the rings and grooves wear less than compression rings and their grooves. If there is evidence of oil ring groove wear or if the oil ring is tight and difficult to remove, the piston skirt may have collapsed due to excessive heat. Replace the piston.

5. Check the piston oil control holes for carbon or oil sludge buildup. Clean the holes with wire.

6. Check the piston skirt (**Figure 59**) for cracks or other damage. If the piston shows signs of partial seizure (bits of aluminum buildup on the piston skirt), replace the piston and bore the cylinder (if necessary) to reduce the possibility of engine noise and further piston seizure.

NOTE
If the piston skirt is worn or scuffed unevenly from side to side, the connecting rod may be bent or twisted.

7. Check the piston circlip grooves for wear, cracks or other damage. If a circlip groove is worn, replace the piston.

8. Measure piston-to-cylinder clearance as described in this section.

9. If damage or wear indicates piston replacement is necessary, select a new piston as described in *Piston Clearance* in this section. If the piston, rings and cylinder are not damaged and are dimensionally correct, they can be reused.

Piston Pin Inspection

Refer to **Table 2** when inspecting the piston pin components in this section. Replace parts that are out of specification or show damage.

1. Clean and dry the piston pin.
2. Inspect the piston pin for chrome flaking, cracks or signs of heat damage.
3. Measure the piston pin bore inside diameter (**Figure 60**).
4. Measure the piston pin outside diameter (**Figure 61**).
5. Subtract the piston pin outside diameter (Step 4) from the piston pin bore inside diameter (Step 3) to determine the piston-to-piston pin clearance. Replace the piston and/or piston pin if the clearance is excessive.

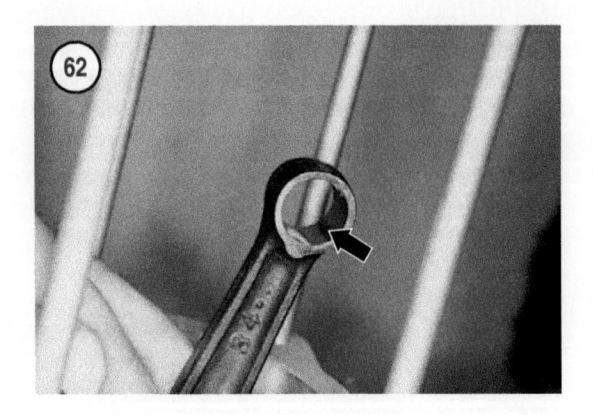

Connecting Rod Small End Inspection

1. Inspect the connecting rod small end (**Figure 62**) for cracks or signs of heat damage.
2. 2Measure the small end inside diameter with a snap gauge (**Figure 63**). Measure the snap gauge with a micrometer. If the small end inside diameter exceeds the service limit in **Table 2**, replace the crankshaft assembly. The connecting rod cannot be replaced separately.

Piston Clearance

1. Make sure the piston and cylinder walls are clean and dry.
2. Measure the cylinder bore inside diameter as described in *Cylinder Inspection*. Record the largest bore inside diameter measurement.
3. Measure the piston diameter with a micrometer at a right angle to the piston pin bore. Measure piston diameter at the specified distance (**Table 2**) from the bottom edge of the piston skirt as shown in **Figure 64**. Record the piston diameter measurement.
4. Subtract the piston diameter from the largest bore diameter. This difference is piston-to-cylinder clearance. If clearance exceeds the service limit in **Table 2**, the cylinder must be bored to the next oversize and a new piston/ring assembly installed.

Piston Ring Inspection and Removal

The piston uses a three-ring assembly (**Figure 65**). The top and second rings are compression rings. The lower ring is an oil control ring assembly, which consists of two ring rails and an expander spacer.

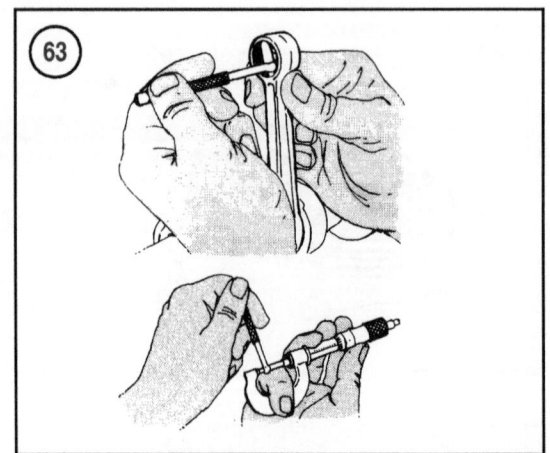

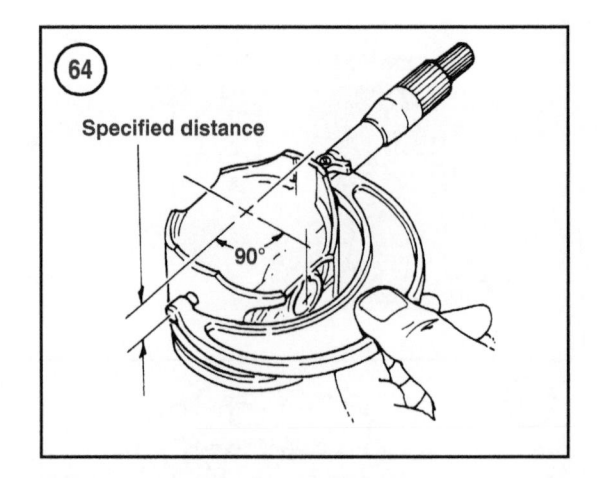

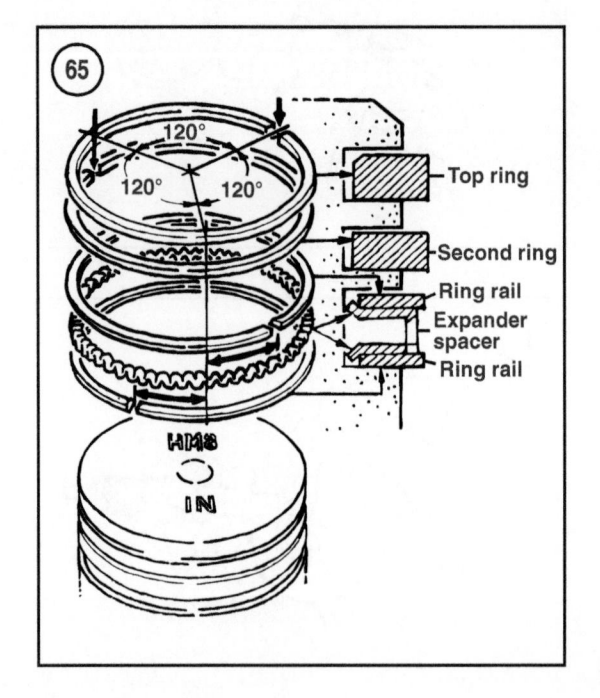

ENGINE TOP END

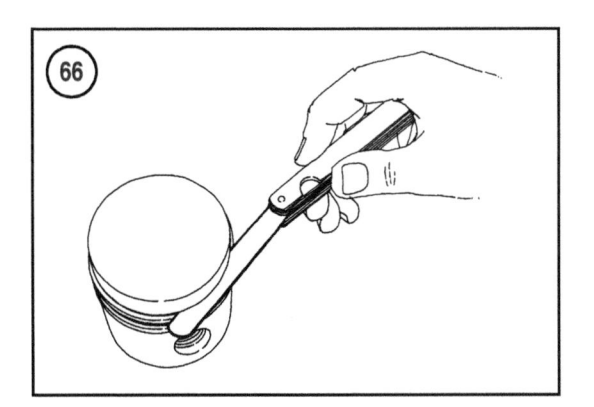

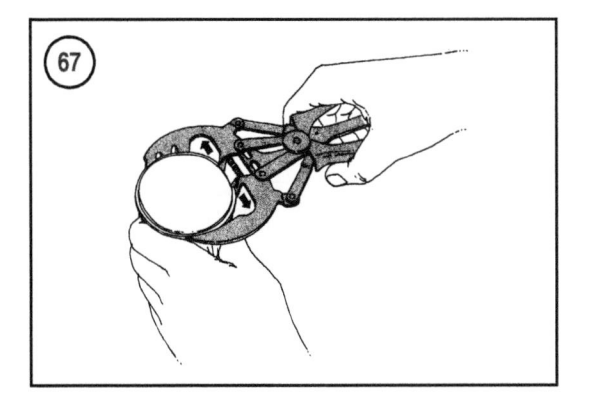

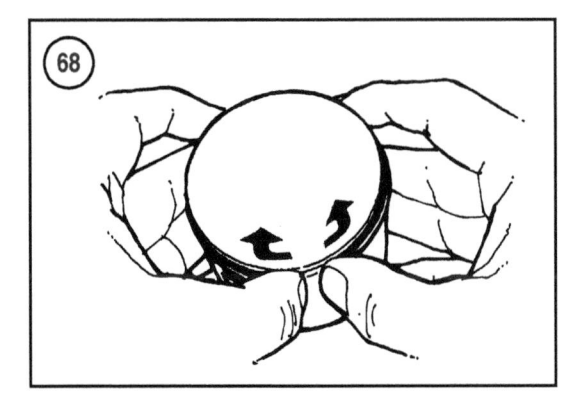

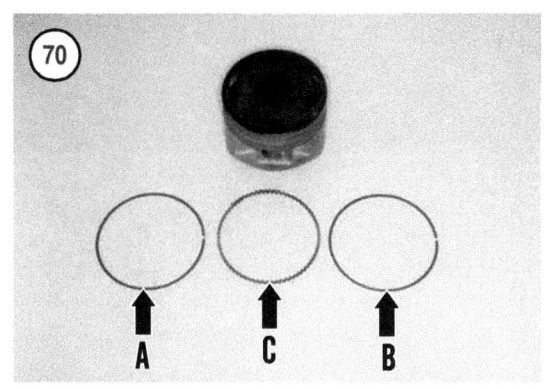

1. Measure the piston-to-groove clearance of each compression ring with a flat feeler gauge (**Figure 66**). If the clearance is greater than specified, replace the rings. If the clearance is still excessive with the new rings, replace the piston.

> *WARNING*
> *The piston rings are very sharp. Be careful when handling them.*

2. Remove the compression rings with a ring expander tool (**Figure 67**) or spread the ring ends by hand (**Figure 68**). Lift the rings out of their grooves and up, over the piston.

3. Remove the oil ring assembly (**Figure 69**) by first removing the upper (A, **Figure 70**) and then the lower (B) ring rails. Remove the expander spacer (C, **Figure 70**).

> *CAUTION*
> *When cleaning the piston ring grooves in Step 4, use the same type of ring that operates in the groove. Using a dissimilar ring damages the groove.*

4. Using a broken piston ring, remove carbon and oil residue from the piston ring grooves (**Figure 71**).

> *CAUTION*
> *Do not remove aluminum material from the ring grooves because this increases ring side clearance.*

5. Inspect the ring grooves for burrs, nicks or broken or cracked lands. Replace the piston if necessary.

> *NOTE*
> *When measuring the oil control ring end gap, measure the upper and lower*

ring rail end gaps only. Do not measure the expander spacer (C, Figure 70).

6. Check the end gap of each ring compression ring and both oil ring side rails. Perform the following:
   a. Insert each ring into the bottom of the cylinder bore and square it with the cylinder wall by tapping it with the piston (**Figure 72**).
   b. Measure the end gap with a feeler gauge. Replace the rings if the end gap exceeds the service limit in **Table 2**.
   c. If the gap on the new ring is smaller than specified, hold a fine-cut file in a vise. File the ends of the ring to enlarge the gap (**Figure 73**).
7. Roll each ring around its piston groove (**Figure 74**) to check for binding. Repair minor binding with a fine-cut file.

Piston Ring Installation

1. Hone or deglaze the cylinder before installing new piston rings. This machining process helps the new rings seat in the cylinder. If necessary, refer this job to a Honda dealership or machine shop. After honing, measure the end gap of each ring.
2. Thoroughly clean the piston and rings. Dry them with compressed air.

NOTE
The top and second compression rings are different. Refer to Figure 65 to identify the rings.

3. Install the piston rings as follows:

CAUTION
Install the piston rings—first the bottom, then the middle and then the top ring—by carefully spreading the ends by hand and slipping the rings over the top of the piston. Remember that the piston rings must be installed with the manufacturer's marks facing up. Incorrectly installed piston rings can wear rapidly and/or allow oil to escape past them.

   a. Install the oil control ring assembly into the bottom ring groove. Install the oil ring expander spacer first (A, **Figure 75**), and then install each ring rail (B). Make sure the ends

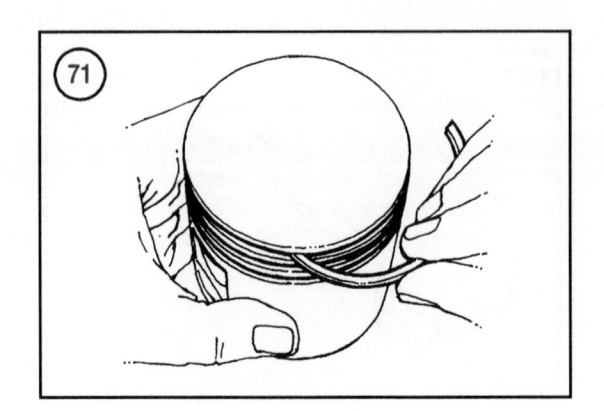

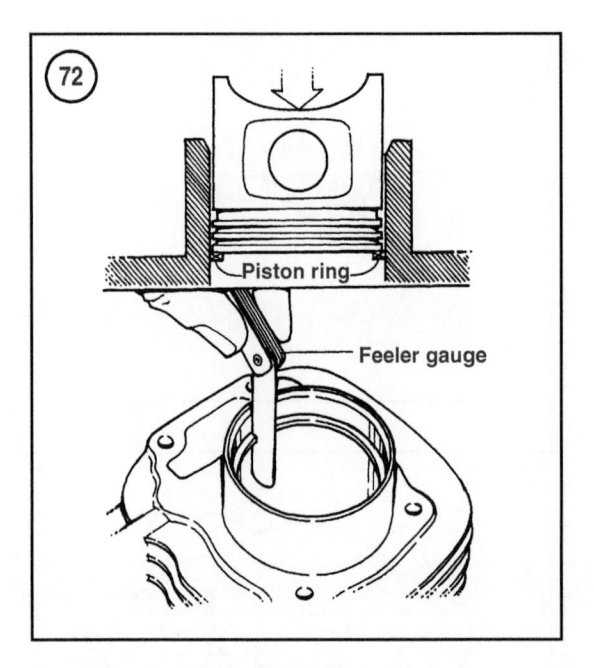

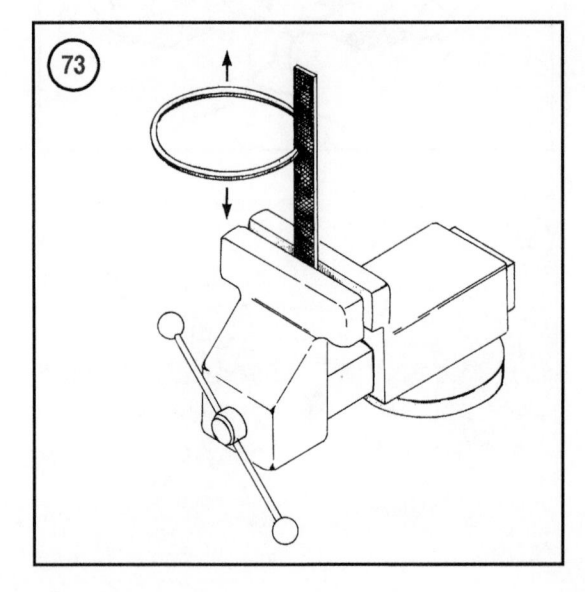

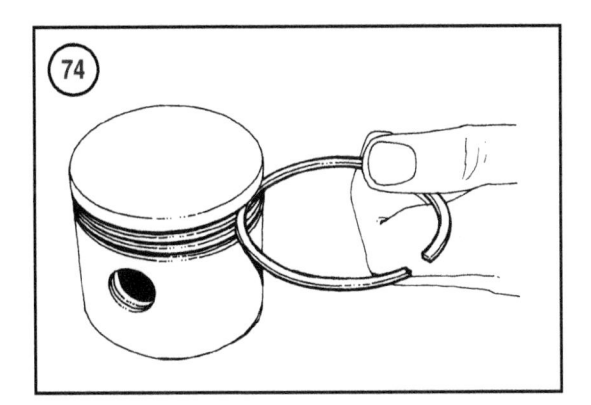

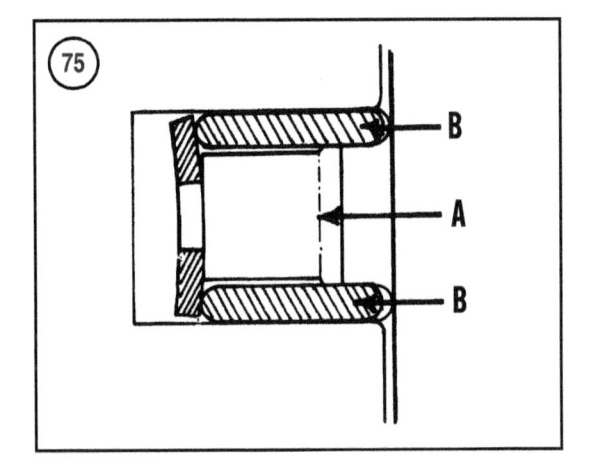

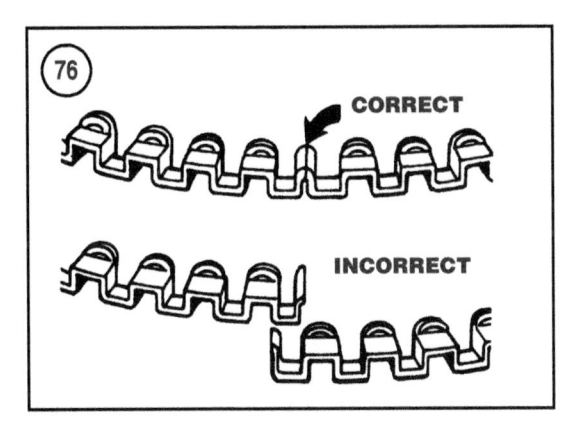

ENGINE TOP END

b. Install the 2nd, or middle, compression ring with the manufacturer's reference mark facing up. This ring has square edges (**Figure 65**).

c. Install the top compression ring with the manufacturer's reference mark facing up.

4. Make sure the rings are seated completely in their grooves all the way around the piston. Also position the rings so their end gaps are distributed around the piston as shown in **Figure 65**. The ring gaps must not align with each other. This prevents compression pressures from escaping past them.

CAMSHAFT

The camshaft and cam chain tensioner assembly can be removed with the engine mounted in the frame. Because of the engine's position in the frame, the following photographs show the engine removed for clarity.

Refer to **Figure 77** when servicing the camshaft and its components. During inspection, compare measurements to the specifications in **Table 2**. Replace any components that are damaged, worn to the service limit or out of specification. During assembly, tighten fasteners to the torque specifications.

Removal

1. Remove the cylinder head and cylinder as described in this chapter.
2. Remove the centrifugal clutch and the change clutch as described in Chapter Six.
3. Remove the cam followers (**Figure 78**) from the crankcase. Mark each cam follower as it is removed so it can be reinstalled in its original location.
4. Remove the mounting bolts (A, **Figure 79**) and cam chain tensioner (B).
5. Remove the pivot bolt, washer (A, **Figure 80**), and tensioner arm (B).
6. Remove the camshaft bearing retainer bolt (**Figure 81**) and retainer.
7. Align the timing mark on the camshaft sprocket with the index mark on the crankcase (**Figure 82**).
8. Slightly pull the camshaft from the crankcase. Disengage the cam chain from the camshaft sprocket and remove the camshaft.
9. Remove the cam chain from the crankshaft timing sprocket.

of the expander spacer butt together (**Figure 76**). They should not overlap. If reassembling used parts, install the ring rails as they were removed.

NOTE
When installing aftermarket piston rings, follow the manufacturer's directions.

CAMSHAFT ASSEMBLY

1. Cam chain
2. Camshaft assembly
3. Bolt
4. Bearing retainer
5. Cam follower
6. Dowel
7. Circlip
8. Piston
9. Piston pin
10. Timing hole cap
11. O-ring
12. Cam chain tensioner
13. Washer
14. Tensioner arm

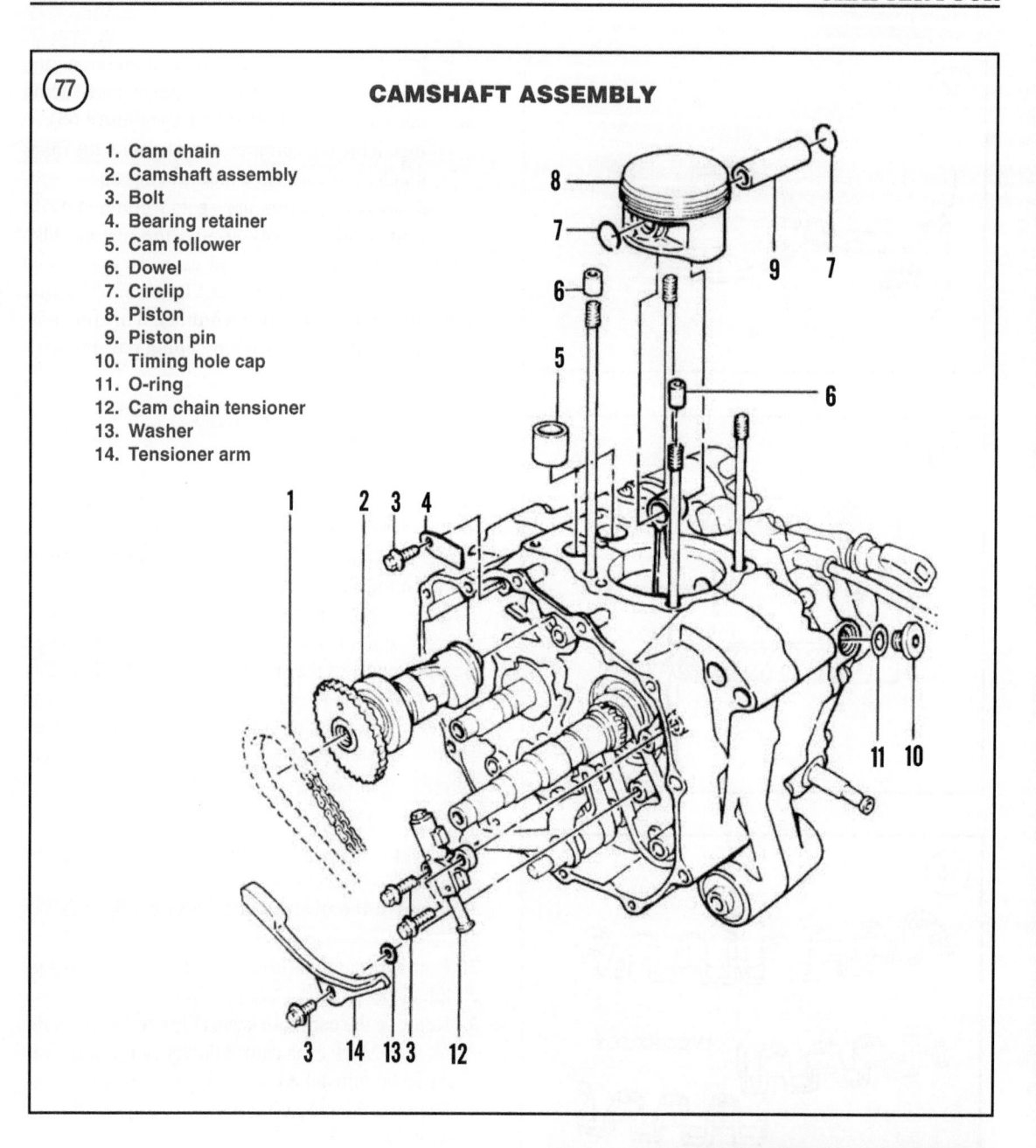

Installation

1. Check that the engine is still set to top dead center. If necessary, turn the flywheel bolt to rotate the crankshaft so the T-mark on the flywheel aligns with the index mark (**Figure 83**).

2. Install the cam chain onto the crankshaft timing sprocket.

3. Apply molybdenum-disulfide oil to the cam lobes and journals on the camshaft.

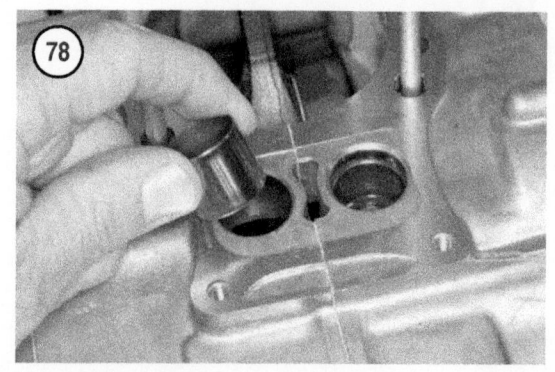

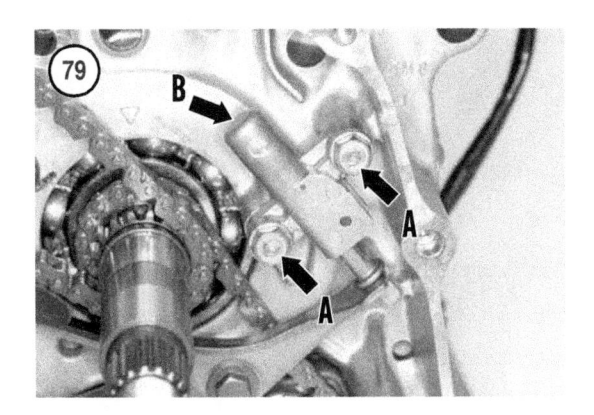

ENGINE TOP END

CAUTION
Do not rotate the crankshaft during camshaft and cam chain installation.

4. Position the camshaft so the cam lobes point down. Fit the camshaft through the cam chain, and slide the camshaft into the crankcase. Align the timing mark on the camshaft sprocket (**Figure 82**) with the index mark on the crankcase.

5. Install the cam chain onto the camshaft sprocket, and press the camshaft into place in the crankcase. Make sure the timing mark on the camshaft sprocket still aligns with the index mark on the crankcase.

6. Place the bearing retainer onto the crankcase boss, and secure the retainer with the mounting bolt (**Figure 81**).

7. Install the cam chain tensioner arm (B, **Figure 80**). Apply ThreeBond 1333B, or equivalent, to the threads of the tensioner arm pivot bolt. Install the bolt along with its washer. Tighten the cam-chain-tensioner-arm pivot bolt (A, **Figure 80**) to 12 N•m (106 in.-lb.).

8. Check the operation of the tensioner arm by rotating the arm. If the tensioner arm binds, the bolt was installed incorrectly. Remove the tensioner arm and reinstall it.

CAUTION
*Check that the engine is still set to top dead center (**Figure 83**) and that the camshaft sprocket still aligns with the index mark on the crankcase (**Figure 82**).*

9. Press the tensioner release with a screwdriver (**Figure 84**). Push the pushrod into the tensioner body and hold it in place with your finger.

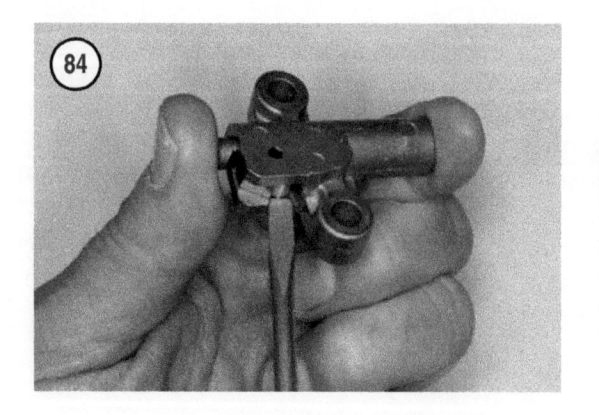

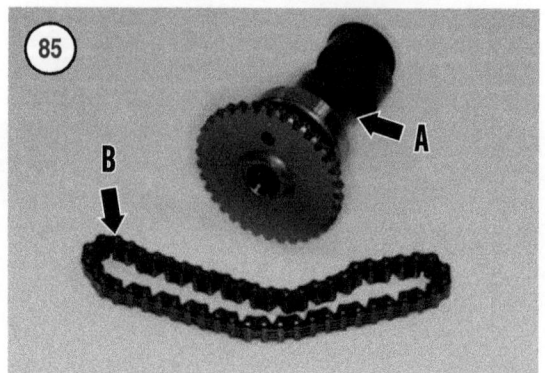

10. Install the cam chain tensioner (B, **Figure 79**), and secure it in place with the mounting bolts (A).

11. Apply engine oil to the inner and outer surfaces of the cam followers, and install each cam follower (**Figure 78**) into its original location in the crankcase.

12. Install the change clutch and the centrifugal clutch as described in Chapter Six.

13. Install the cylinder and cylinder head as described in this chapter.

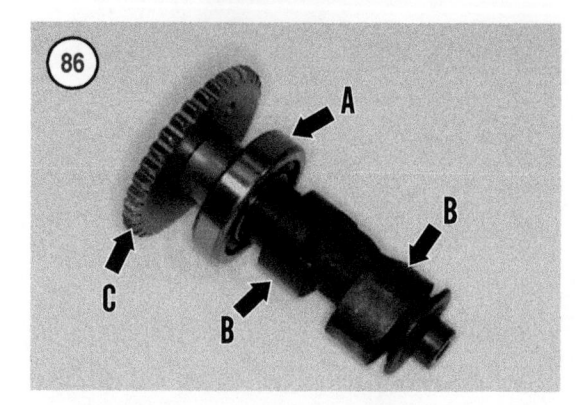

Camshaft and Cam Chain Inspection

Refer to **Table 2** when inspecting camshaft components. Replace parts that are out of specification or damaged.

1. Clean and dry the camshaft assembly (A, **Figure 85**). Lubricate the bearing with engine oil.

2. Check that the camshaft bearing (A, **Figure 86**) fits tightly on the camshaft. If the bearing is loose, replace the camshaft assembly.

3. Turn the camshaft bearing by hand. The bearing must turn smoothly. If the bearing is damaged, replace the camshaft assembly.

4. Check the cam lobes (B, **Figure 86**) for scoring or other damage.

5. Measure each cam lobe height with a micrometer (**Figure 87**). Replace the camshaft if either lobe is out of specification.

6. Inspect the camshaft sprocket (C, **Figure 86**) for broken or chipped teeth. Also check the teeth for cracking or rounding. If the camshaft sprocket is damaged, replace the camshaft. Also inspect the timing sprocket mounted on the crankshaft as described in Chapter Five.

7. Inspect the cam chain (B, **Figure 85**) for excessive wear, loose or damaged pins, cracks or other damage. Replace if damaged.

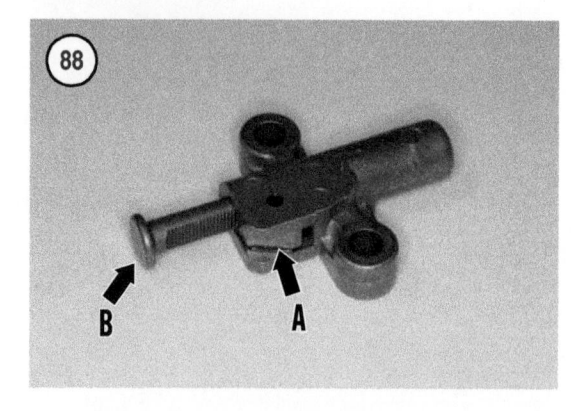

ENGINE TOP END

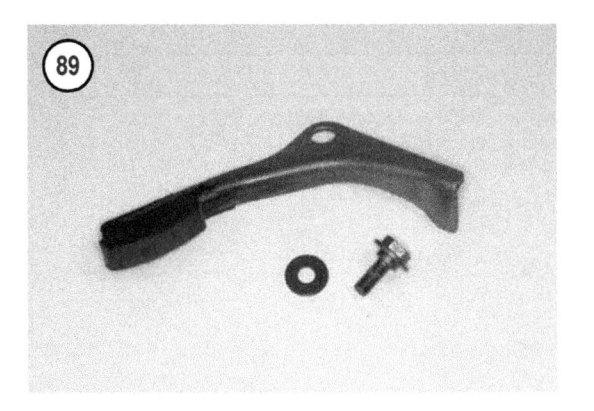

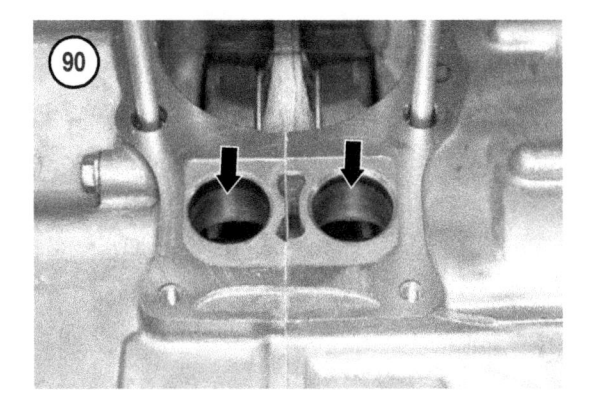

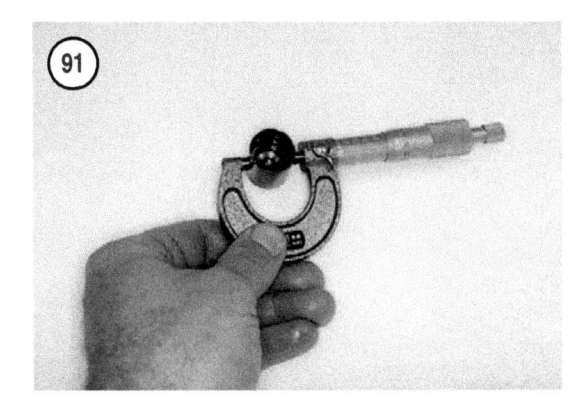

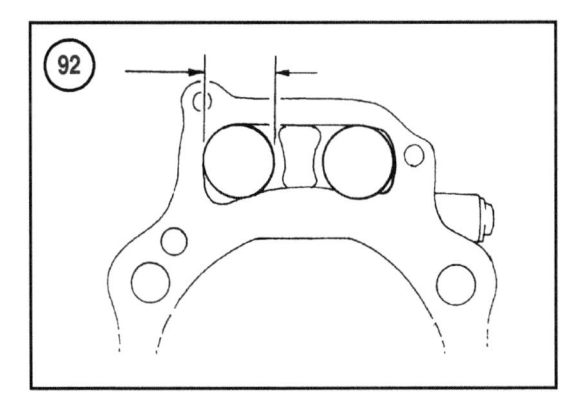

Cam Chain Tensioner Inspection

1. Press the stopper (A, **Figure 88**) into the tensioner body with a screwdriver (**Figure 84**), and check the movement of the pushrod (B, **Figure 88**). If it does not slide smoothly in and out of the housing, replace the tensioner body.

2. Inspect the sliding surface of the cam chain tensioner arm (**Figure 89**). Replace the tensioner arm if necessary.

Cam Follower Inspection

Refer to **Table 2** when inspecting the cam followers. Replace parts that are out of specification or show damage.

CAUTION
Each cam follower must be installed in its original location. Do not mix the cam followers during inspection. If necessary, reapply the identification marks made during removal.

1. Clean and dry the cam followers.

2. Inspect the cam followers for scoring, cracks or other damage.

3. Inspect the cam follower bores (**Figure 90**) in the crankcase for scoring, excessive wear or other damage.

4. Measure the cam follower outside diameter (**Figure 91**). Record the dimension. Replace the cam follower if out of specification.

5. Measure the cam follower bore inside diameter (**Figure 92**). Record the dimension. Replace the crankcase half if the bore is out of specification.

6. If the cam follower outside diameters and cam follower bore inside diameters are within specifications, calculate the cam follower-to-bore clearance as follows:

   a. Subtract the cam follower outside diameter (Step 4) from the cam follower bore inside diameter (Step 5). The result is cam follower-to-bore clearance.

   b. Repeat for both cam followers.

   c. If the clearance exceeds the service limit, replace the cam follower and then remeasure. If the clearance is still out of specification, replace the crankcase half.

Table 1 GENERAL ENGINE SPECIFICATIONS

	Specification
Type and number of cylinders	4-stroke, OHV, air-cooled single
Bore × stroke	68.4 × 62.2 mm (2.70 × 2.45 in.)
Displacement	229 cc (14.0 cu. in.)
Compression ratio	9.0:1
Valve timing	
Intake	
Open	8° BTDC
Closed	38° ABDC
Exhaust	
Open	34° BBDC
Close	4° ATDC

Table 2 ENGINE TOP END SPECIFICATIONS

	Specification mm (in.)	Service limit mm (in.)
Camshaft		
Cam lobe height		
Intake	35.764-35.924 (1.408-1.414)	35.6 (1.40)
Exhaust	35.292-35.452 (1.389-1.396)	35.1 (1.38)
Cam follower outside diameter (intake/exhaust)	22.467-22.482 (0.8845-0.8851)	22.46 (0.884)
Cam follower bore inside diameter (intake/exhaust)	22.510-22.526 (0.8862-0.8868)	22.54 (0.887)
Cam follower-to-bore clearance	0.028-0.059 (0.0011-0.0023)	0.07 (0.003)
Rocker arm inside diameter	12.000-12.018 (0.4724-0.4731)	12.05 (0.474)
Rocker arm shaft outside diameter	11.964-11.984 (0.4710-0.4718)	11.92 (0.469)
Rocker arm-to-shaft clearance	0.016-0.054 (0.0006-0.0021)	0.08 (0.003)
Cylinder head warp	–	0.10 (0.004)
Cylinder compression	1275 kPa (185 psi) @ 800 rpm	–
Valves and valve springs		
Valve clearance (intake/exhaust)	0.13 (0.005)	–
Valve stem outside diameter		
Intake	5.475-5.490 (0.2156-0.2161)	5.45 (0.215)
Exhaust	5.455-5.470 (0.2148-0.2154)	5.43 (0.214)
Valve guide inside diameter (intake/exhaust)	5.500-5.512 (0.2165-0.2170)	5.525 (0.2175)
Stem-to-guide clearance		
Intake	0.010-0.037 (0.0004-0.0015)	0.12 (0.005)
Exhaust	0.030-0.057 (0.0012-0.0022)	0.14 (0.006)
Valve seat width (intake/exhaust)	1.2 (0.05)	1.5 (0.06)
Valve spring free length		
Inner (intake/exhaust)	42.4 (1.67)	41.2 (1.62)
Outer (intake/exhaust)	44.2 (1.74)	43.0 (1.69)
Valve seat surface angle	45°	
Valve seat cutting angle	32, 45, 60°	
Cylinder		
Bore inside diameter	68.500-68.510 (2.6968-2.6972)	68.6 (2.70)
Out of round	–	0.10 (0.004)
Taper	–	0.10 (0.004)
Warp	–	0.10 (0.004)
Oversize pistons and rings	+ 0.25, 0.50, 0.75 or 1.00	
Piston-to-cylinder clearance	0.018-0.048 (0.0007-0.0019)	0.10 (0.004)

(continued)

ENGINE TOP END

Table 2 ENGINE TOP END SPECIFICATIONS (continued)

	Specification mm (in.)	Service limit mm (in.)
Pistons		
Outside diameter	68.462-68.482 (2.6953-2.6961)	68.4 (2.69)
Outside diameter measuring point	6-14 (0.2-0.6) from bottom of skirt	
Piston pin bore inside diameter	15.002-15.008 (0.5906-0.5909)	15.04 (0.592)
Piston pin outside diameter	14.994-15.000 (05903-0.5906)	14.96 (0.589)
Piston-to-piston pin clearance	0.002-0.014 (0.0001-0.0006)	0.020 (0.0008)
Piston rings		
Ring-to-groove clearance		
Top	0.015-0.045 (0.0006-0.0018)	0.09 (0.0004)
Second	0.015-0.045 (0.0006-0.0018)	0.09 (0.0004)
Ring end gap		
Top	0.20-0.35 (0.008-0.014)	0.5 (0.02)
Second	0.40-0.55 (0.016-0.022)	0.7 (0.03)
Oil ring side rail	0.20-0.70 (0.008-0.028)	–
Connecting rod		
Small end inside diameter	15.010-15.028 (0.5909-0.5917)	15.06 (0.593)
Rod-to-piston pin clearance	0.010-0.034 (0.0004-0.0013)	0.10 (0.004)

Table 3 ENGINE TOP END TORQUE SPECIFICATIONS

Item	N•m	in.-lb.	ft.-lb.
Cam chain tensioner arm pivot bolt*	12	106	–
Cylinder head flange nuts	30	–	22
Cylinder head cover bolts	12	106	–
Cylinder head studs	6	53	–
Engine mounting bolts and nuts			
Lower engine mount	54	–	40
Cylinder head cover mount	32	–	24
Engine oil drain plug	25	–	18
Exhaust pipe protector bolt	22	–	16
Muffler clamp bolt	23	–	17
Rocker arm shaft bolt	10	89	–
Valve adjuster caps	20	–	14
Valve adjuster locknut	17	–	12

*Apply threadlocking compound.

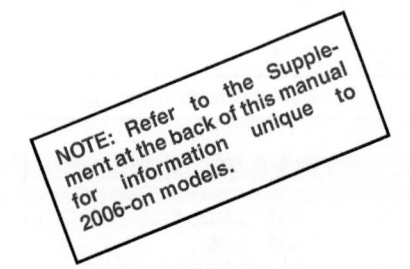

NOTE: Refer to the Supplement at the back of this manual for information unique to 2006-on models.

CHAPTER FIVE

ENGINE LOWER END

This chapter describes service procedures for the lower end components.

The following components can be serviced with the engine mounted in the frame:
1. Cylinder head.
2. Cylinder and piston.
3. Clutch.
4. Oil pump.
5. Oil cooler.
6. Carburetor.
7. Alternator.

The text frequently mentions the front and rear sides of the engine. These terms refer to the engine in the vehicle's frame, not how it may sit on the workbench.

When inspecting lower end components, compare measurements to the engine lower end specifications in **Table 1**. Replace any component that is damaged, worn to the service limit or out of specification. During assembly, tighten fasteners to the torque specifications. **Table 1** and **Table 2** are at the end of this chapter.

ENGINE REMOVAL/INSTALLATION

Refer to **Figure 1**.

1. Park the vehicle on a level surface and set the parking brake.
2. Drain the engine oil as described in Chapter Three.
3. Remove the seat, both side covers, front fender and rear mudguards as described in Chapter Fourteen.
4. Disconnect the negative battery cable (**Figure 2**).
5. Remove the fuel tank and heat guard as described in Chapter Eight.
6. Remove the air box, carburetor and exhaust pipe as described in Chapter Eight.
7. Remove the spark plug cap.
8. Remove the cable (**Figure 3**) from the starter.
9. Remove the bolt (A, **Figure 4**) and disconnect the two ground cables (B) from the crankcase.
10. Disconnect the 3-pin alternator connector (A, **Figure 5**) and the 2-pin pulse generator connector (B).
11. Loosen the clamp bolt and remove the shift pedal (**Figure 6**) from the gearshift spindle. Note that the punch mark on the pedal aligns with the mark on the spindle. These marks must align during assembly.
12. Disconnect the crankcase breather hose (**Figure 7**) from the port on the crankcase.

ENGINE LOWER END

ENGINE REMOVAL

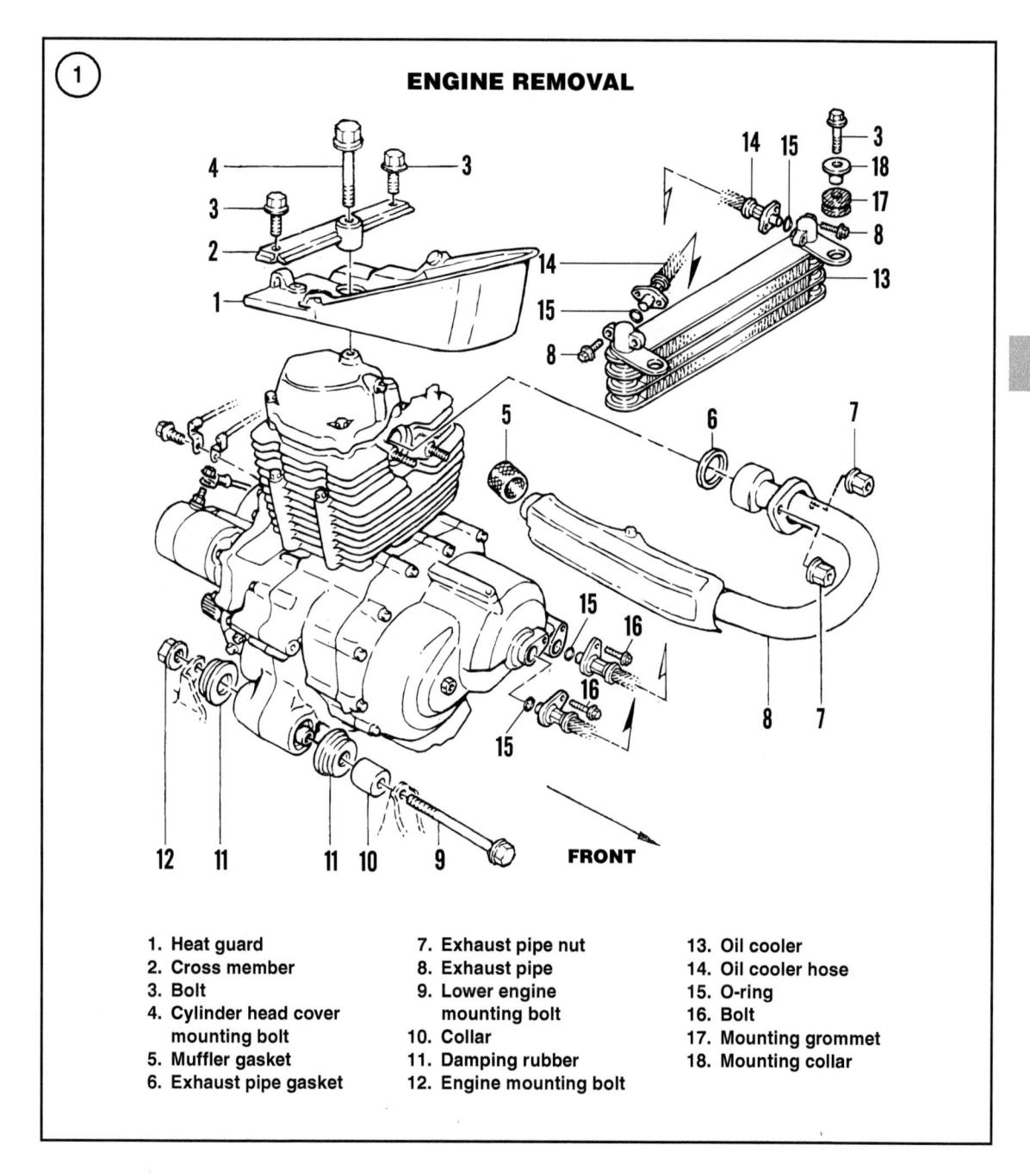

1. Heat guard
2. Cross member
3. Bolt
4. Cylinder head cover mounting bolt
5. Muffler gasket
6. Exhaust pipe gasket
7. Exhaust pipe nut
8. Exhaust pipe
9. Lower engine mounting bolt
10. Collar
11. Damping rubber
12. Engine mounting bolt
13. Oil cooler
14. Oil cooler hose
15. O-ring
16. Bolt
17. Mounting grommet
18. Mounting collar

13. Loosen the clamp bolt (**Figure 8**) on the swing arm boot.

14. On the left side of the alternator cover, remove the mounting bolts (A, **Figure 9**) and remove the cover (B) from the reverse stopper lever.

15. Remove the cable bracket mounting bolt (C, **Figure 9**), and disconnect the reverse selector cable from the reverse stopper lever (A, **Figure 10**).

16. Disconnect the electrical connectors.

a. On 2001-2002 models, disconnect the reverse switch connector (B, **Figure 10**) and the neutral switch connector (C) directly from the externally mounted switches (**Figure 11**).

b. On 2003-on models, disconnect the reverse and neutral switch connector from the switches mounted inside the alternator cover.

17. Place a jack under the engine and support the engine to remove tension from the lower engine

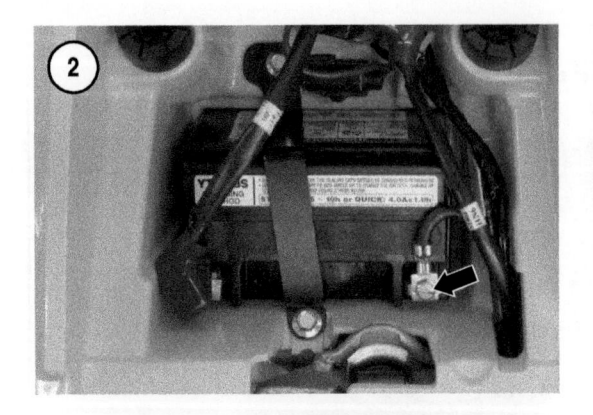

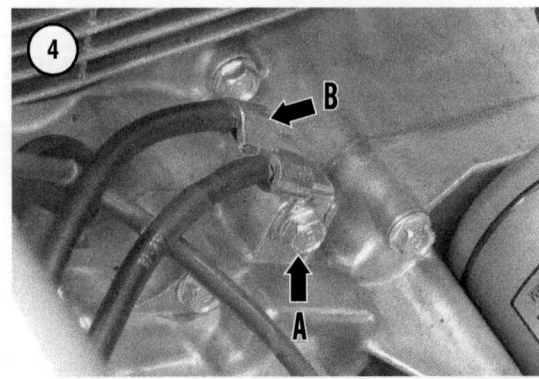

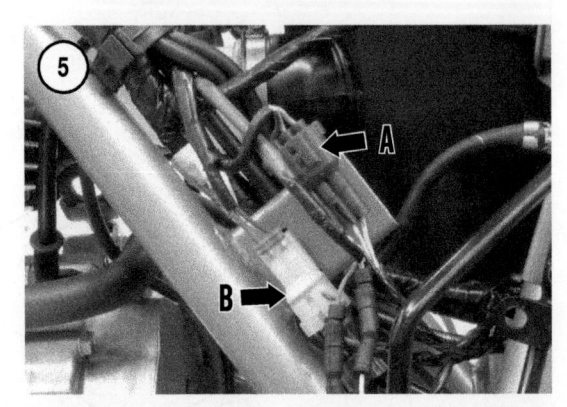

hanger mounting bolts. Place a block of wood between the jack pad and engine to protect the crankcase.

18. Remove the cylinder head cover mounting bolt.
19. Remove the right lower engine mounting nut (A, **Figure 12**). Pull the engine hanger bolt (B, **Figure 12**) from the mount, and remove the collar (C) and both damping rubber (D).
20. Remove the left lower engine mounting nut (A, **Figure 13**). Remove the hanger bolt (B, **Figure 13**) from the mount, and remove the collar (C) and both damping rubber (D).

WARNING
If removing an assembled engine, the following steps requires the aid of a helper to remove the engine from the frame.

21. Move the engine forward and disconnect the countershaft from the universal joint. Remove the engine from the left side of the frame. Support the engine on a workbench.
22. Install the engine in the frame by reversing these steps. Note the following:

ENGINE LOWER END 119

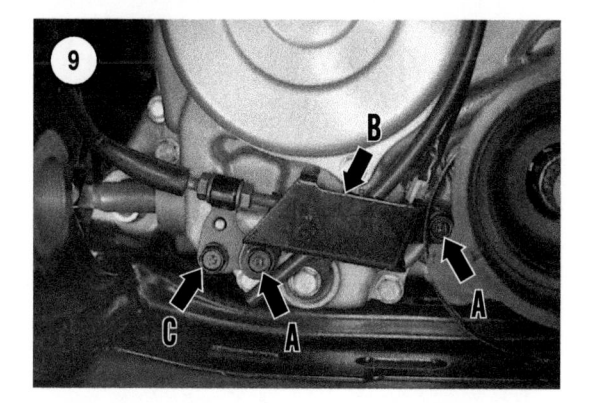

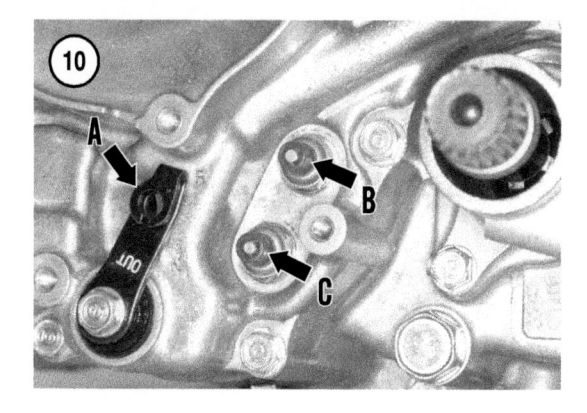

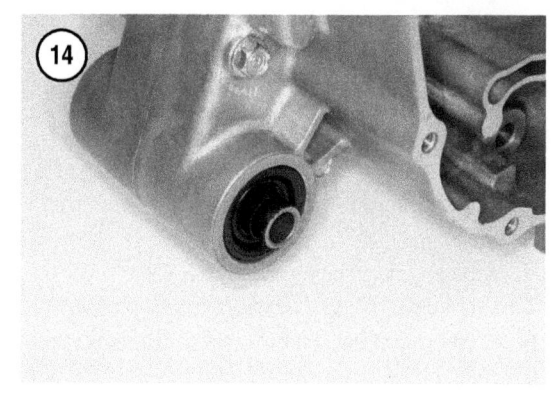

a. Replace damaged engine mount fasteners.

b. Apply an antiseize compound to the shoulders on each engine mount bolt. This helps to prevent rust and corrosion.

c. Lubricate the universal joint and countershaft splines with molybdenum disulfide grease.

d. Make sure the damping rubber is in place on each side of the hanger bushings (**Figure 14**). The larger diameter end must face in (11, **Figure 1**).

e. Tighten the lower engine mounting nuts (A, **Figure 12** and A, **Figure 13**) to 54 N•m (40 ft.-lb.).
f. Tighten the cylinder head cover mounting bolt to 32 N•m (24 ft.-lb.).
g. When installing the shift pedal, align the punch mark on the shift pedal with the mark on the gearshift spindle. Tighten the shift pedal clamp bolt to 18 N•m (13 ft.-lb.).
h. Check the electrical connectors for corrosion. Pack the connectors with dielectric grease before reconnecting them.
i. Fill the engine with the recommended type and quantity of oil. Refer to Chapter Three.
j. Check the throttle operation. If necessary, adjust the throttle cable as described in Chapter Three.
k. Adjust the reverse selector cable as described in Chapter Three.

OIL COOLER

The oil cooler plays an important role in maintaining the engine temperature within acceptable limits. Keep the oil cooler fins clean and straight so airflow can remove excess engine heat.

Removal/Installation

1. Drain the engine oil as described in Chapter Three.
2A. If the engine is being removed, disconnect the oil cooler hoses (**Figure 15**) from the clutch cover.
2B. If only removing the oil cooler, disconnect the oil cooler hoses from the oil cooler. Remove the joint bolts that secure each pipe (A, **Figure 16**).
3. Remove the O-ring from the joint at the pipe fittings.
4. Remove the mounting bolts (B, **Figure 16**) that secure the oil cooler.
5. Inspect the oil cooler as described in this section.
6. Reverse this procedure to install the oil cooler, and observe the following:
   a. Install *new*, lubricated O-rings in the oil pipe connections (**Figure 17**).
   b. After refilling with oil, start the engine and check all its fittings for leaks.

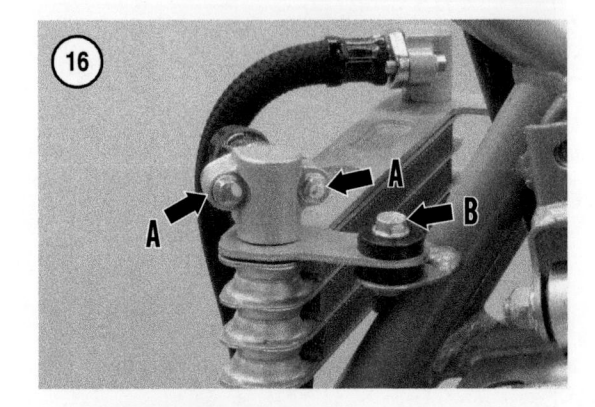

Inspection

1. Drain any remaining oil out of the oil cooler. Cover the oil cooler inlet and outlet holes to prevent the entry of dirt during the cleaning and inspection procedure.
2. Blow all debris from the cooling fins, and then wipe the oil cooler clean.
3. Inspect the cooling fins for damage. Straighten bent fins with a flat-blade screwdriver.
4. Inspect the oil cooler for pin holes and cracks. If damage is evident, take the oil cooler to a dealership

ENGINE LOWER END

ALTERNATOR COVER

ALTERNATOR COVER (2001-2002)

ALTERNATOR COVER (2003-ON)

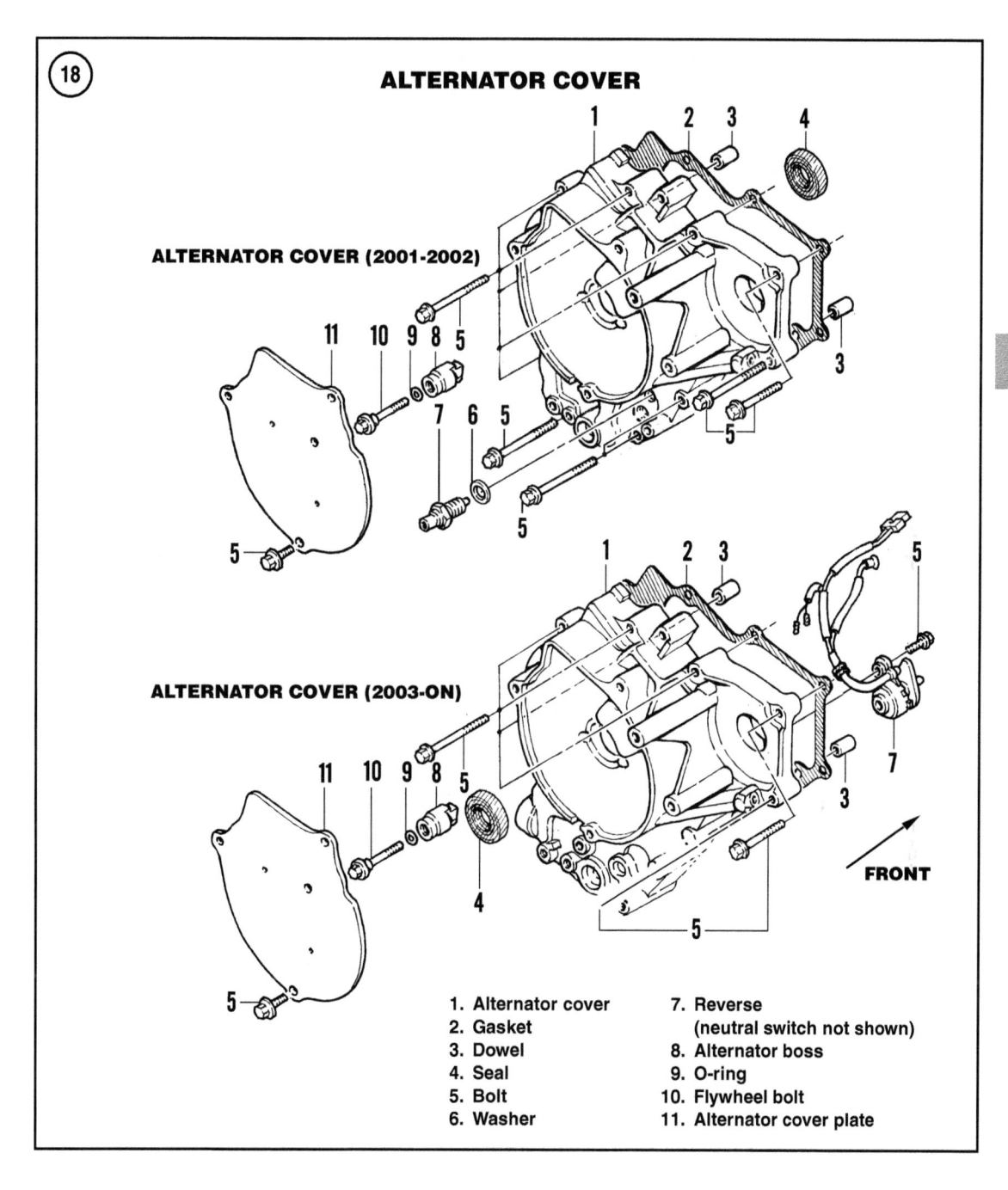

1. Alternator cover
2. Gasket
3. Dowel
4. Seal
5. Bolt
6. Washer
7. Reverse (neutral switch not shown)
8. Alternator boss
9. O-ring
10. Flywheel bolt
11. Alternator cover plate

or radiator shop to see if repairs are possible. If not, replace the oil cooler.

5. Blow through the oil cooler inlet to check for plugging. If plugging is evident or suspected, take the oil cooler to a dealership or radiator repair shop to see if cleaning is possible. If not, replace the oil cooler.

6. Install the oil cooler as described in this section.

ALTERNATOR COVER

There are two different alternator covers (**Figure 18**). The 2001-2002 model covers have the neutral and reverse switches mounted externally. The 2003-on models have a combined reverse/neutral switch mounted internally to the inside of the cover. Both switches are tested the same.

122 CHAPTER FIVE

The following components are mounted to the alternator cover:
1. Ignition pulse generator/stator assembly.
2. Neutral and reverse switches.
3. Gearshift A-arm/gearshift spindle assembly (**Figure 19**).
4. Reverse stopper lever.

Removal

1. If the engine is mounted in the frame, perform the following:
   a. Remove the seat, side covers and rear mudguards as described in Chapter Fourteen.
   b. Disconnect the negative battery cable as described in Chapter Three.
   c. Drain the engine oil as described in Chapter Three.
   d. Remove the oil cooler as described in this chapter.
   e. Remove the starter as described in Chapter Nine.
   f. Remove the bolt (A, **Figure 4**) and disconnect the two ground cables (B) from the crankcase.
   g. Disconnect the 3-pin alternator connector (A, **Figure 5**) and the 2-pin pulse generator connector (B).
   h. Loosen the clamp bolt and remove the shift pedal (**Figure 6**) from the gearshift spindle. Note that the punch mark on the pedal aligns with the mark on the spindle. These marks must align during assembly.
   i. On the left side of the alternator cover, remove the mounting bolts (A, **Figure 9**) and cover (B) from the reverse stopper lever.
   j. Remove the cable bracket mounting bolt (C, **Figure 9**), and disconnect the reverse selector cable from the reverse stopper lever (A, **Figure 10**).
   k. Remove the mounting bolt and remove the reverse stopper lever (A, **Figure 10**) from the reverse stopper shaft.
   l. Disconnect the electrical connectors.
   m. On 2001-2002 models, disconnect the reverse switch connector (B, **Figure 10**) and the neutral switch connector (C) directly from the externally mounted switches (**Figure 11**).
   n. On 2003-on models, disconnect the reverse and neutral switch connector from the switches mounted inside the alternator cover.

2. Remove the three bolts (**Figure 20**) that secure the flywheel bolt plate cover.

3. Remove the alternator cover bolts (**Figure 21**) and the alternator cover. Do not lose the washer (A, **Figure 22**) from the end of the reverse stopper shaft.

4. Remove the alternator cover gasket (A, **Figure 23**) and the dowels (B).

ENGINE LOWER END

b. Hold the flywheel with a strap wrench, and tighten the flywheel bolt (**Figure 24**) to 74 N•m (54 ft.-lb.).

c. Remove the flywheel bolt from the crankshaft.

2. Install the two dowels (B, **Figure 23**) and a new alternator cover gasket (A) onto the crankcase.

3. Check that the washer (A, **Figure 22**) is in place on the reverse stopper shaft.

NOTE
*The pin on the gearshift A-arm (**Figure 19**) must engage the slot in the sub-gearshift spindle (B, **Figure 22**). The transmission cannot be shifted if these parts do not properly engage.*

4. Align the pin on the gearshift A-arm (**Figure 19**) with the slot in the sub-gearshift spindle (B, **Figure 22**), and fit the alternator cover into place on the crankcase.

5. Install the alternator cover bolts (**Figure 21**). Evenly tighten the bolts in a crisscross pattern.

6. Set the reverse stopper lever (A, **Figure 10**) onto the reverse stopper shaft so the OUT on the lever faces away from the crankcase. Install the mounting bolt, and tighten it securely.

7. Once the cover is in place, perform the following:

a. Check the gearshift linkage engagement by turning the gearshift spindle. Turning play should be minimal. If play is noted, the engagement was probably not made. Confirm this by installing the shift pedal onto the gearshift spindle, and then try to shift the transmission. If the engine is out of the frame, turn the countershaft while shifting. If the engine is in the frame and connected to the drive shaft, support the vehicle with the rear wheels off the ground and turn the rear wheels while shifting.

b. Move the reverse stopper lever by hand. The reverse stopper shaft should engage and disengage its groove in the shift drum.

c. If either linkage is not working correctly, remove the alternator cover and correct the problem.

8. Install the flywheel bolt and tighten to 74 N•m (54 in.-lb.).

9. If the engine is installed in the frame, perform the following:

Installation

CAUTION
The flywheel must be properly seated on the crankshaft taper. If it is not, the magnetic force pulls the flywheel off the taper when the alternator cover is installed.

1. Seat the flywheel onto the crankshaft by performing the following:

a. Apply oil to the O-ring, threads of the flywheel bolt, and bolt flange. Install the bolt into the crankshaft.

a. Connect the electrical connectors (**Figure 11**) to the reverse switch (B, **Figure 10**) and the neutral switch (C) on the left side of the alternator cover.
b. Connect the reverse selector cable to the reverse stopper lever (A, **Figure 10**), and secure the cable bracket in place with the mounting bolt (C, **Figure 9**).
c. Place the cover (B, **Figure 9**) over the reverse stopper lever, and secure it in place with the mounting bolts (A).
d. Install the shift pedal onto the gearshift spindle. Make sure the punch mark on the pedal aligns with the mark on the spindle, and tighten the shift pedal clamp bolt to 20 N•m (14 ft.-lb.).
e. Connect the 3-pin alternator connector (A, **Figure 5**) and the 2-pin pulse generator connector (B) to their mates on wiring harness.
f. Secure the two ground cables (B, **Figure 4**) to the crankcase with the mounting bolt (A).
g. Install the starter as described in Chapter Nine.
h. Add engine oil as described in Chapter Three.
i. Connect the negative battery cable as described in Chapter Three.
j. Install the seat and side covers as described in Chapter Fourteen.

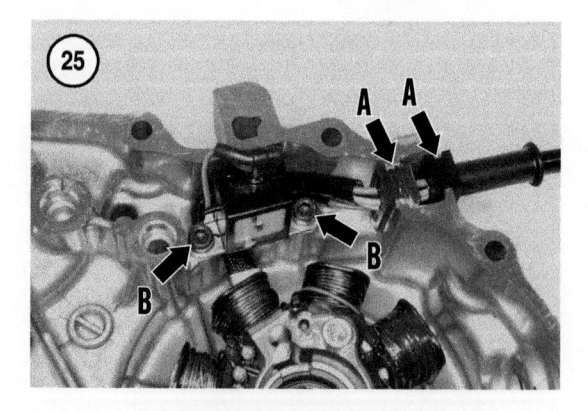

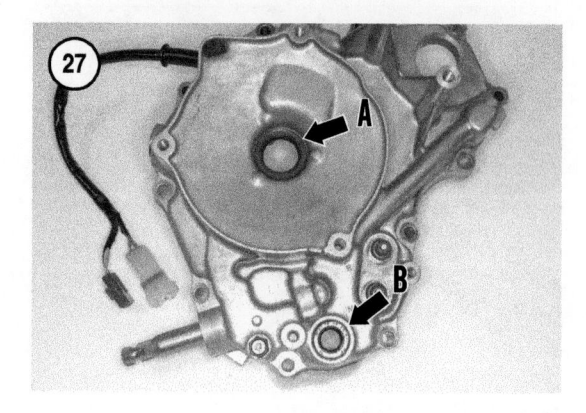

Disassembly/Assembly

Perform these steps to remove the ignition pulse generator/stator assembly from the alternator cover.
1. Note how the alternator cable is routed through the cover. It must be rerouted along the same path during assembly.
2. Lift the alternator cable, and remove the grommets (A, **Figure 25**) from the alternator cover.
3. Remove the ignition pulse generator mounting bolts (B, **Figure 25**).
4. Remove the stator mounting bolts (**Figure 26**).
5. Lift the ignition pulse generator/stator assembly from the cover, and remove the ignition pulse generator/stator assembly..
6. Assembly is the reverse of disassembly. Note the following:
   a. Apply ThreeBond 1342, or its equivalent, to the threads of the ignition pulse generator bolts. Tighten the bolts to 6 N•m (53 in.-lb.).
   b. Apply a non-hardening sealant to the cable grommets (A, **Figure 25**) before installing them into the alternator cover.

Oil Seal Inspection/Replacement

1. Inspect the alternator cover seal (A, **Figure 27**) and the reverse stopper shaft seal (B) for oil leaks, wear or damage.
2. Replace either seal as necessary by performing the following:

ENGINE LOWER END

FLYWHEEL AND STARTER GEARS

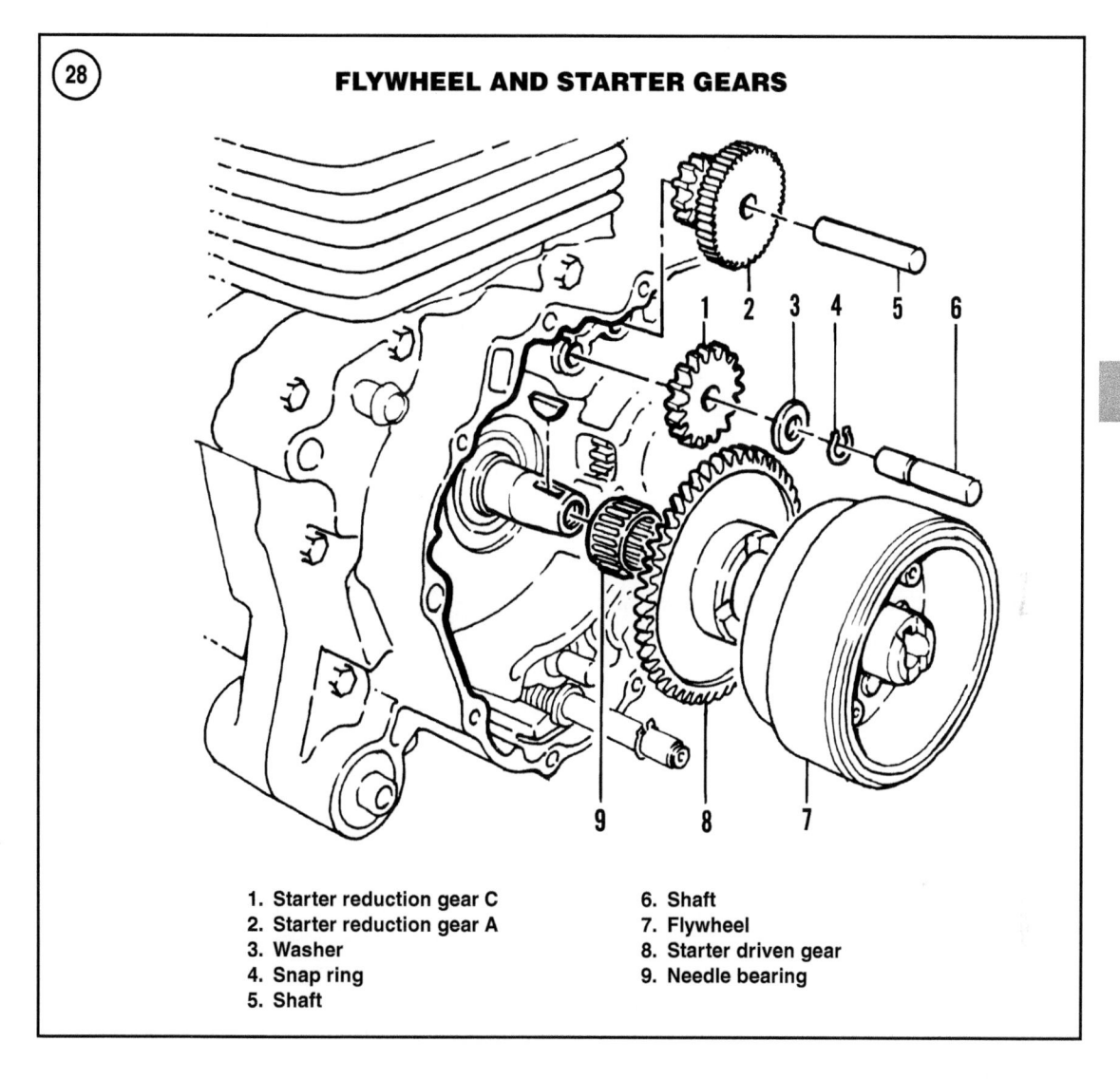

1. Starter reduction gear C
2. Starter reduction gear A
3. Washer
4. Snap ring
5. Shaft
6. Shaft
7. Flywheel
8. Starter driven gear
9. Needle bearing

a. Pry the seal out of the cover with a seal remover. Pad the bottom of the tool to prevent it from damaging the alternator cover.

b. Pack the lips of the new seal with lithium grease.

c. Drive the seal into place with an appropriate size bearing driver or socket that matches the outside diameter of the seal. Install the seal with the manufacturer's marks facing out.

FLYWHEEL AND STARTER GEARS

This section describes service to the starter gears, flywheel and starter clutch assembly. These assemblies can be serviced with the engine installed in the frame. The engine is shown removed from the frame for clarity.

Flywheel Removal

A flywheel puller is required to remove the flywheel from the crankshaft. Use either a Honda flywheel puller (part No. 07733-0010000 or 07933-2000000) or a K&L rotor puller (part No. 35-0829).

Refer to **Figure 28**.

1. Remove the alternator cover as described in this chapter.

2. Remove the reduction gear A (**Figure 29**) and its shaft from the boss in the crankcase.

3. Remove the reduction gear C assembly (**Figure 30**) from the crankcase.

4. Slide reduction gear C (A, **Figure 31**) and its washer (B) off the shaft (C).

> *CAUTION*
> *Do not remove the flywheel without a puller. Doing so damages the crankshaft and flywheel.*

5. Turn the flywheel puller (**Figure 32**) into the flywheel.

> *CAUTION*
> *If normal flywheel removal attempts fail, do not force the puller. Excessive force strips the flywheel threads, causing expensive damage. Take the engine to a dealership and have it remove the flywheel.*

6. Hold the flywheel and gradually tighten the flywheel puller until the flywheel pops off the crankshaft taper.
7. Remove the puller from the flywheel.
8. Remove the flywheel/starter clutch assembly (**Figure 33**) from the crankshaft.
9. Remove the needle bearing (A, **Figure 34**) and the Woodruff key (B).
10. Inspect the flywheel, starter clutch and starter gears as described in this section.

Flywheel Installation

1. Clean any oil from the crankshaft taper.
2. Apply engine oil onto the needle bearing, and install the bearing (A, **Figure 34**) onto the crankshaft.
3. Seat the Woodruff key (B, **Figure 34**) into the crankshaft.
4. Align the flywheel key way with the Woodruff key in the crankshaft, and install the flywheel/starter clutch assembly (**Figure 33**).

> *CAUTION*
> *The flywheel must be properly seated on the crankshaft taper. If it is not, the magnetic force pulls the flywheel off the taper when the alternator cover is installed.*

5. Seat the flywheel onto the crankshaft by performing the following:
   a. Apply oil to the O-ring, the threads of the alternator bolt and the bolt flange. Install the bolt into the crankshaft.   
   b. Hold the flywheel with a strap wrench and tighten the bolt (**Figure 24**) to 74 N•m (54 ft.-lb.).
   c. Remove the flywheel bolt from the crankshaft.

6. Install the thrust washer (B, **Figure 31**) and reduction gear C (A) onto the shaft. Make sure the thrust washer sits against the snap ring.
7. Align the teeth of reduction gear C with the teeth of the starter driven gear, and install reduction gear C assembly into the crankcase (**Figure 30**). Make

ENGINE LOWER END

2. Check the flywheel for cracks or breaks.

WARNING
Replace a cracked or chipped flywheel. A damaged flywheel can fly apart, throwing metal fragments into the engine. Do not repair a damaged flywheel.

3. Check the flywheel tapered bore and the crankshaft taper for damage.
4. Replace damaged parts as required.

Starter Reduction Assembly Inspection

Replace parts that show damage as described in this section.
1. Clean and dry all parts (**Figure 31**).
2. Inspect the reduction gears for the following conditions:
    a. Excessively worn or damaged gear teeth.
    b. Excessively worn or damaged bearing surfaces.
3. Inspect the reduction gear shafts for excessive wear.
4. Check the snap ring in the shaft (C, **Figure 31**) for reduction gear C. If the snap ring was removed, install a new one during installation.

Starter Clutch Disassembly/Inspection/Assembly

Refer to **Figure 35**.
1. Check the one-way clutch operation by performing the following:
    a. Place the flywheel and starter clutch on the workbench so the driven gear faces up as shown in **Figure 36**.
    b. Hold the flywheel and try to turn the driven gear clockwise and then counterclockwise. The driven gear should turn counterclockwise but not clockwise.
    c. If the driven gear turns clockwise, the one-way clutch is damaged and must be replaced.
2. Rotate the driven gear (**Figure 36**) counterclockwise while pulling up, and remove the driven gear from the starter clutch.
3. Inspect the driven gear for the following conditions:
    a. Worn or damaged gear teeth (A, **Figure 37**).

sure the shaft is properly seated in the crankcase mounting boss.

8. Install the reduction gear A assembly (**Figure 29**) into its mounting boss in the crankcase. Make sure the teeth of the inboard gear mesh with those of reduction gear C.
9. Install the alternator cover as described in this chapter.

Flywheel Inspection

1. Clean and dry the flywheel.

b. Worn or damaged bearing shoulder (B, **Figure 37**).

4. Inspect the needle bearing (C, **Figure 37**). The needles should be smooth and polished with no flat spots, cracks or other damage. Inspect the bearing cage for cracks or other damage. Replace the bearing if necessary.

5. Inspect the one-way clutch rollers for uneven or excessive wear.

6. If the one-way clutch needs replacement, perform the following:

CAUTION
Do not let the jaws of the vise clamp onto the flywheel. This damages the flywheel.

a. Hold the flywheel assembly by securing the outer race in a vise with soft jaws. Protect the outer race with a rag so it is not damaged by the vise.

b. Remove the one-way clutch mounting bolts (**Figure 38**), and separate the flywheel from the one-way clutch assembly.

c. Note how the flange of the one-way clutch (4, **Figure 35**) fits in the recess of the outer race (3). Install the new one-way clutch in the same manner.

d. Remove the one-way clutch from the outer race. Install the new one-way clutch so its flange fits in the recess of the outer race.

e. Set the one-way clutch assembly into the back of the flywheel so the flange side of the one-way clutch faces in toward the flywheel.

f. Apply ThreeBond 1333B, or its equivalent, to the threads of the one-way clutch bolts, and evenly tighten the bolts.

g. Tighten the one-way clutch bolts to 16 N•m (12 ft.-lb.). Hold the rotor assembly by securing the outer race in a vise with soft jaws as described in substep a. Protect the outer race with a rag so it is not damaged by the vise.

7. Assemble the starter clutch by performing the following:

a. Place the flywheel on the workbench so the one-way clutch (**Figure 39**) faces up.

b. Set the driven gear onto the one-way clutch.

c. Press the driven gear (**Figure 36**) down while rotating it counterclockwise.

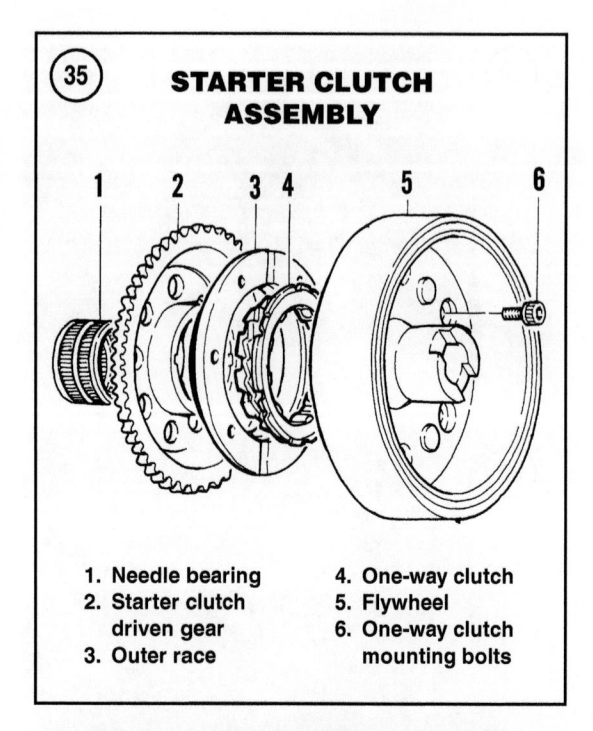

STARTER CLUTCH ASSEMBLY

1. Needle bearing
2. Starter clutch driven gear
3. Outer race
4. One-way clutch
5. Flywheel
6. One-way clutch mounting bolts

GEARSHIFT LINKAGE

Removal

Refer to **Figure 40**.

1. Park the ATV on level ground and set the parking brake.

2. Shift the transmission into neutral.

3. Loosen the clamp bolt, and remove the shift pedal from the gearshift spindle. Note that the punch mark in the pedal aligns with the punch mark on the spindle. These marks must align during assembly.

4. Remove the alternator cover as described in this chapter.

ENGINE LOWER END

10. If the pin does not come out with the drum shifter, remove it from the shift drum (A, **Figure 45**).
11. Remove the bolt (B, **Figure 45**) and stopper arm (C) along with the stopper arm washer and return spring.
12. Remove the sub-gearshift spindle (**Figure 46**) and washer from the rear side of the crankcase.
13. If still in place, remove the washer (A, **Figure 22**) from the reverse stopper shaft.
14. Pry the reverse arm (A, **Figure 47**) from behind the boss on the crankcase, and remove the reverse stopper shaft (B).
15. If necessary, remove the gearshift A-arm (A, **Figure 48**) from the alternator cover by performing the following:
   a. Bend the lock tab (B, **Figure 48**) away from the bolt flat, and remove the bolt from the gearshift A-arm.
   b. Slide the gearshift spindle (C, **Figure 48**) from the gearshift A-arm.
   c. Remove the gearshift A-arm and its washers from the alternator cover.
   d. Discard the lockwasher. A new one must be installed during assembly.

Installation

1. Slide the reverse stopper shaft into place in the crankcase so the reverse arm (A, **Figure 47**) sits behind the boss in the crankcase. Make sure the spring tang (C, **Figure 47**) engages the stiffening rib in the crankcase.
2. Install the washer (A, **Figure 22**) onto the reverse stopper shaft.
3. Install the washer (A, **Figure 49**) onto the sub-gearshift spindle, and slide it up against the snap ring (B).
4. Slide the sub-gearshift spindle (**Figure 46**) into the crankcase until it bottoms.
5. If the gearshift-A arm was removed from the alternator cover, install it by performing the following:
   a. Pack the gearshift-spindle seal (**Figure 50**) in the cover with lithium grease.

NOTE
The washer with the tabs sits on the pin side of the A-arm. Refer to **Figure 40**.

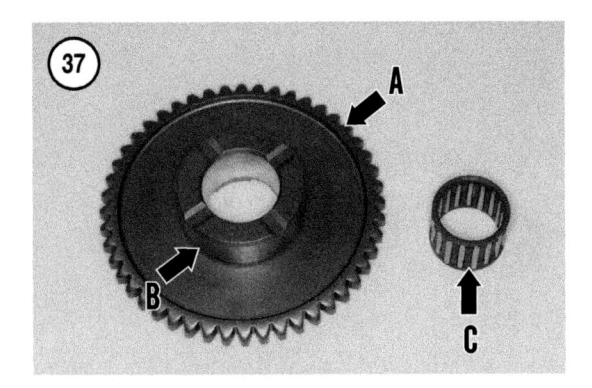

5. Remove the clutch cover, centrifugal clutch and change clutch as described in Chapter Six.
6. Unhook the spring (A, **Figure 41**) from the gearshift plate on the front side of the crankcase, and then remove the master arm and return spring (B).
7. Remove the guide plate bolt (A, **Figure 42**) and guide plate (B).
8. Remove the gearshift plate (A, **Figure 43**), and then remove the washer (A, **Figure 44**) from the sub-gearshift spindle.
9. Pry the stopper arm away from the drum shifter (B, **Figure 44**) with a screwdriver, and remove the drum shifter and pin (C).

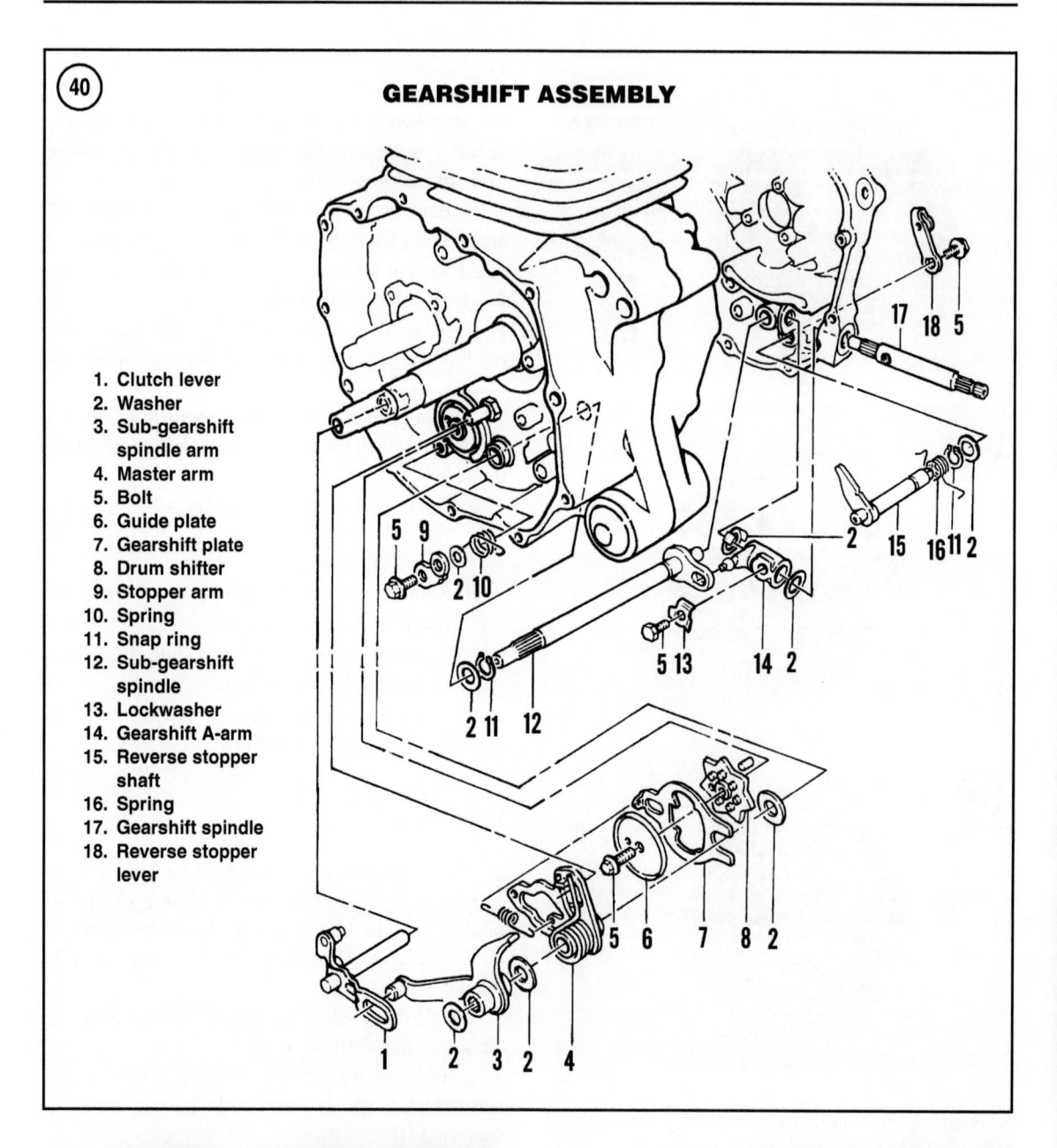

CHAPTER FIVE

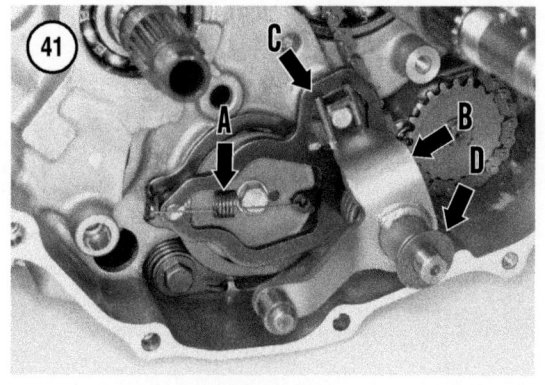

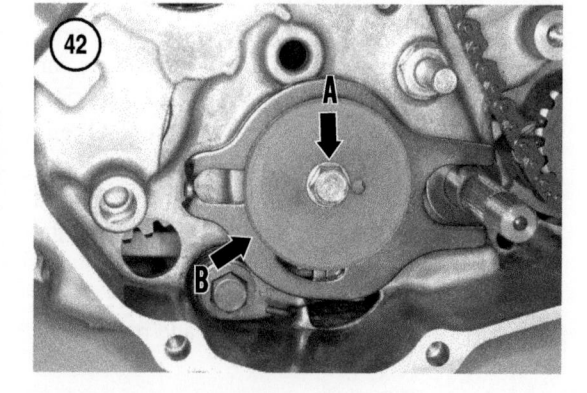

④ GEARSHIFT ASSEMBLY

1. Clutch lever
2. Washer
3. Sub-gearshift spindle arm
4. Master arm
5. Bolt
6. Guide plate
7. Gearshift plate
8. Drum shifter
9. Stopper arm
10. Spring
11. Snap ring
12. Sub-gearshift spindle
13. Lockwasher
14. Gearshift A-arm
15. Reverse stopper shaft
16. Spring
17. Gearshift spindle
18. Reverse stopper lever

ENGINE LOWER END

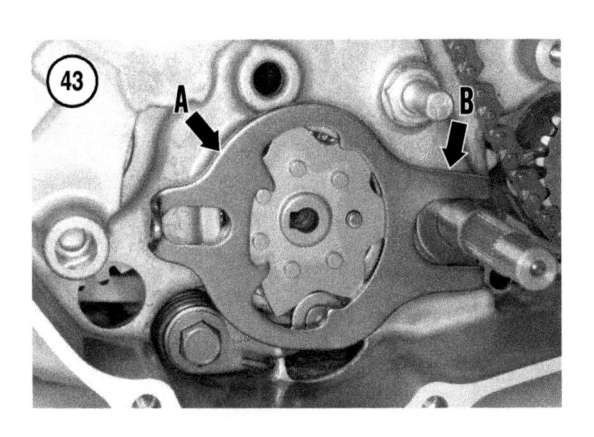

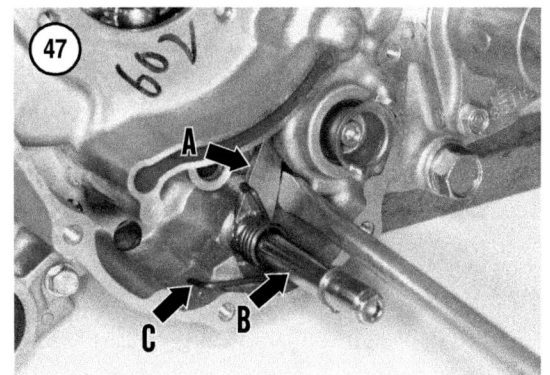

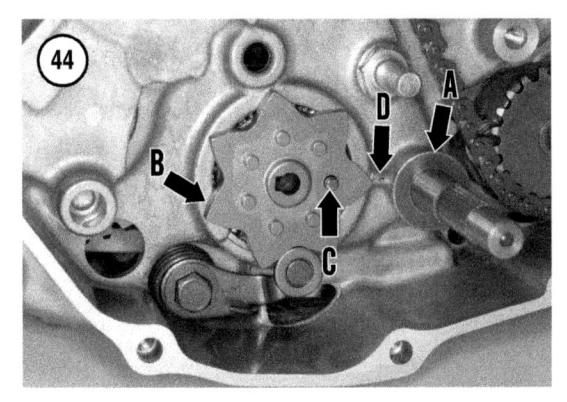

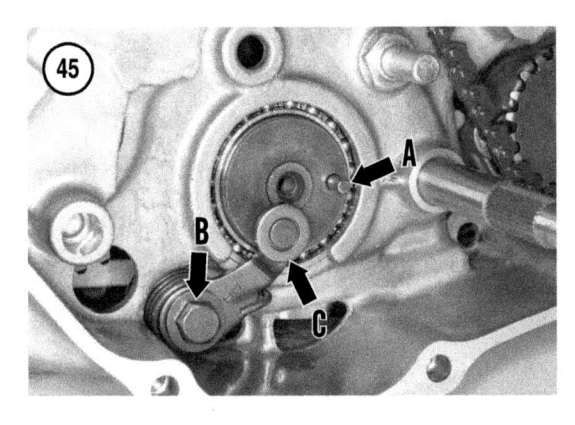

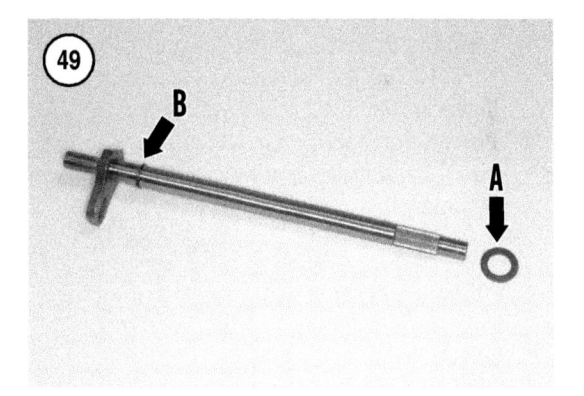

131

b. Make sure the washers are in place on either side of the A-arm, and set the gearshift A-arm (A, **Figure 48**) into place in the alternator cover.

c. Align the master splines on the gearshift spindle with those of the gearshift A-arm, and install the gearshift spindle (C, **Figure 48**) through the seal and into the A-arm.

d. Apply ThreeBond 1333B, or its equivalent, to the threads of the gearshift A-arm bolt, and install the bolt with a new lockwasher.

e. Tighten the gearshift A-arm bolt to 25 N•m (18 ft.-lb.), and bend a lock tab against a bolt flat (B, **Figure 48**).

f. Pivot the gearshift spindle to make sure it moves smoothly with no binding or roughness.

6. Install the stopper arm by performing the following:

a. Install the stopper arm bolt through the mounting hole in the stopper arm, and then install the washer onto the bolt.

b. Hook the return spring onto the stopper arm.

c. Apply ThreeBond 1333B, or its equivalent, to the threads of the stopper arm bolt.

d. Fit the stopper arm into place in the crankcase, and tighten the bolt (B, **Figure 45**) to 12 N•m (106 in.-lb.). Make sure the return spring hooks around the stopper arm.

e. Press the stopper arm down, and release it. It must move under spring pressure with no binding.

NOTE
If the stopper arm does not move, the bolt is not centered through the stopper arm, washer or spring. Loosen the bolt, and reinstall it.

7. Install the pin (A, **Figure 45**) into the shift drum.

8. Press the stopper arm with a screwdriver, and install the drum shifter (B, **Figure 44**) onto the shift drum. Make sure the drum shifter engages the pin (C, **Figure 44**) in the shift drum.

NOTE
The transmission is in neutral when the pin (C, Figure 44) aligns with indexing mark on the crankcase (D).

9. Install the washer (A, **Figure 44**) onto the end of the sub-gearshift spindle.

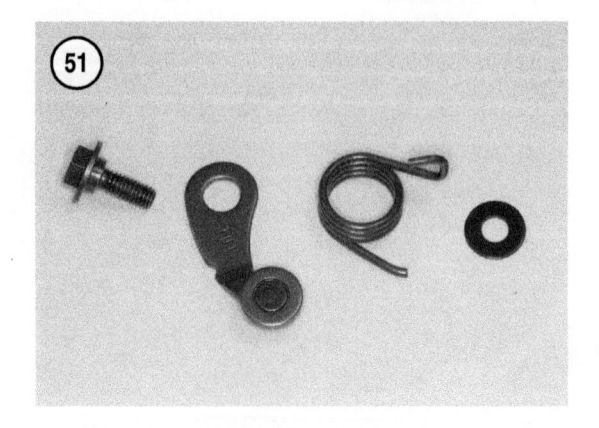

10. Install the gearshift plate so its arms (B, **Figure 43**) straddle the sub-gearshift spindle.

11. Install the gearshift plate (B, **Figure 42**). Apply ThreeBond 1333B to the threads of the guide plate bolt (A, **Figure 42**), and tighten the bolt to 16 N•m (12 ft.-lb.).

12. Slide the master arm (B, **Figure 41**) onto the sub-gearshift spindle so the arms of the spring (C) straddle the stopper bolt, and then install the washer (D).

13. Hook the return spring (A, **Figure 41**) to the master arm and gearshift plate.

14. Install the change clutch, centrifugal clutch and the clutch cover as described in Chapter Six.

15. Install the alternator cover as described in this chapter.

16. If the engine is installed in the frame, install the shift pedal onto the gearshift spindle. Make sure the punch mark on the pedal aligns with the punch mark on the spindle. Tighten the shift pedal clamp bolt to 20 N•m (14 ft.-lb.).

ENGINE LOWER END

8. Check the gearshift spindle dust seal in the alternator cover. Replace the seal if it is brittle or showing signs of leaking. Refer to Chapter One. Install the seal with the manufacturer's marks facing out.
9. Inspect the reverse stopper shaft (**Figure 53**) for:
    a. Weak or damaged spring.
    b. Bent or damaged reverse shaft.
    c. Damaged snap ring groove.
    d. To replace the spring, remove the snap ring and spring. Install the spring over the reverse stopper shaft as shown in **Figure 53**. Install a new snap ring.

OIL PUMP

The oil pump assembly is mounted on the clutch side of the engine. The oil pump can be removed with the engine mounted in the frame. The following steps are shown with the engine removed for clarity.

Removal/Installation

1. Remove the clutch cover and the centrifugal clutch as described in this chapter.

NOTE
The oil pump can be removed and installed with the cam chain mounted on the engine. Do not perform Step 2 unless the oil pump chain must be serviced.

2. If the oil pump chain requires service, set the engine to top dead center and remove the cam chain tensioner, tensioner arm and cam chain as described in Chapter Four.
3. Remove the snap ring (A, **Figure 54**) from the end of the pump shaft, and remove the oil pump sprocket (B).
4. Remove the oil pump bolts (A, **Figure 55**), and pull the oil pump assembly (B) from the crankcase.
5. Remove the dowels (**Figure 56**) from the crankcase.
6. If the oil pump is not going to be serviced, store it in a plastic bag.
7. Service the oil pump as described in this section.
8. Install the oil pump by reversing these removal steps, plus the following:
    a. Make sure the oil pump engages the dowels (**Figure 56**) in the crankcase.

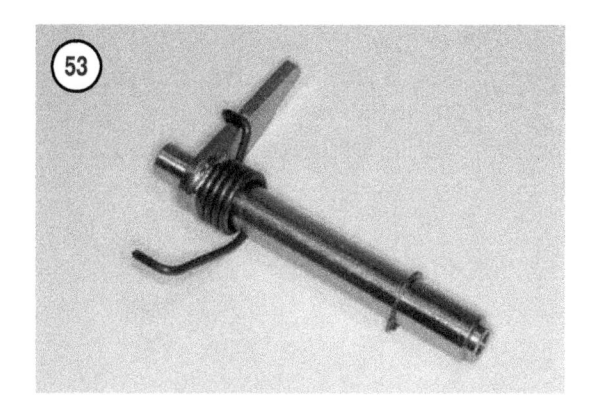

Inspection

Replace parts that show excessive wear or damage as described in this section.
1. Clean and dry all parts.
2. Check the splines on the master arm, sub-gearshift spindle and gearshift spindle.
3. Check the sub-gearshift spindle and the gearshift spindle for bending or other damage.
4. Check the snap ring groove in the sub-gearshift spindle for cracks or damage. If the snap ring is removed (B, **Figure 49**), install a new one during assembly.
5. Check the drum shifter for wear, cracks or other damage.
6. Check the stopper arm assembly (**Figure 51**) for:
    a. Damaged stopper arm.
    b. Worn or damaged roller.
    c. Weak or damaged return spring.
7. Check the master arm assembly (**Figure 52**) for:
    a. Damaged master arm.
    b. Weak or damaged return spring.

b. Install the oil pump sprocket so the flat on the mounting hole engages the boss on the oil pump shaft. Refer to **Figure 57**.
c. Make sure the oil pump chain properly engages the oil pump sprocket and the oil pump drive sprocket on the crankshaft.
d. Check pump engagement by turning the crankshaft back and forth. When doing so, the pump shaft (visible on the outside of the pump) should turn.

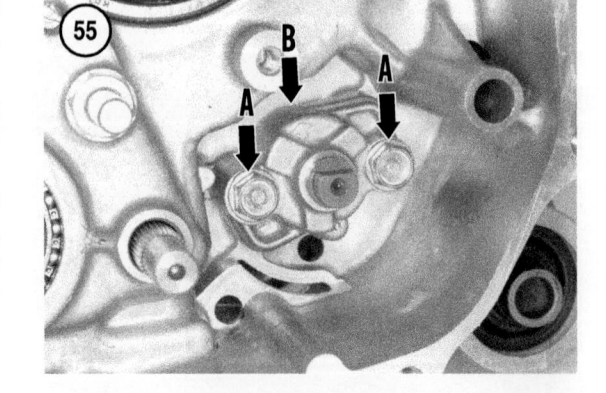

Disassembly

Refer to **Figure 58**.
1. If still installed, remove the dowels (A, **Figure 59**) from the pump side plate.
2. Remove the E-clip (B, **Figure 59**) and washer (C) from the pump shaft.

CAUTION
The oil pump screw is very tight. Loosen the screw with a hand impact driver and No. 2 Phillips bit. If the head is damaged, the screw must be drilled out.

3. Use an impact driver to loosen the oil pump screw (D, **Figure 59**), and then remove the screw from the pump body. Remove the side plate from the pump body.

NOTE
If the rotors are not marked, mark their up sides so the rotors can be reinstalled with the same side facing out toward the side plate.

4. Remove the pump shaft (A, **Figure 60**) and both rotors (B).
5. Inspect the oil pump assembly (**Figure 61**) as described in this section.

Assembly

1. If necessary, clean the parts again as described in this section. Lubricate the rotors and body rotor bore with fresh engine oil when installing them in the following steps.
2. Install the outer and inner rotors (B, **Figure 60**). If installing the original rotors, install them with their marked sides facing up as noted during disassembly.

3. Install the pump shaft (A, **Figure 60**).
4. Install the dowels (A, **Figure 59**) and the side plate.
5. Install the washer (C, **Figure 59**) and the screw (D). Finger-tighten the screw.
6. Install the E-clip (B, **Figure 59**) with its chamfered side facing the washer. Make sure the clip is completely seated in the pump shaft groove.
7. Tighten the screw securely.

ENGINE LOWER END

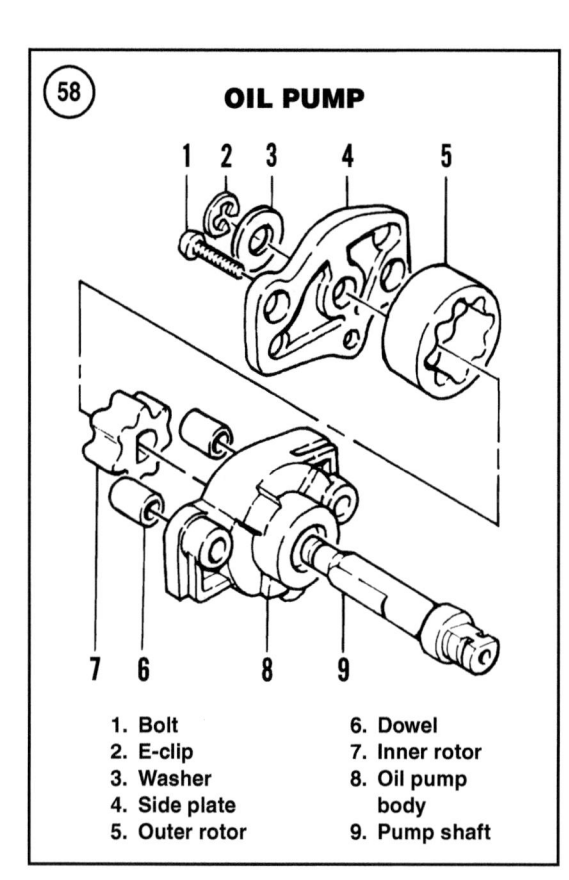

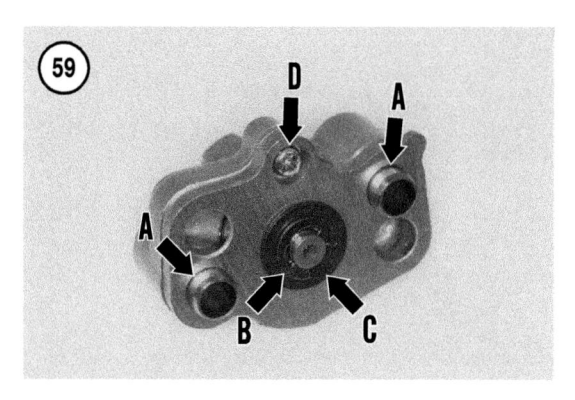

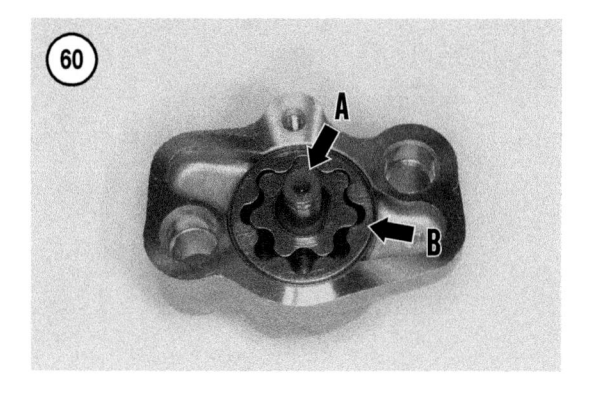

58 OIL PUMP

1. Bolt
2. E-clip
3. Washer
4. Side plate
5. Outer rotor
6. Dowel
7. Inner rotor
8. Oil pump body
9. Pump shaft

8. Turn the pump shaft. If there is any roughness or binding, disassemble the oil pump and check it for damage.

9. Store the oil pump in a plastic bag until installation.

Cleaning and Inspection

An excessively worn or damaged oil pump does not maintain oil pressure and should be repaired or replaced before it causes engine damage. Inspect the oil pump carefully when troubleshooting a lubrication or oil pressure problem.

Refer to **Figure 58** when inspecting the oil pump components in this section. Replace parts that are out of specification or damaged.

1. Clean and dry all parts. Place the parts on a clean, lint-free cloth.
2. Check the pump shaft for scoring, cracks or signs of heat discoloration. Check the E-clip groove for damage.
3. Check the oil pump body for:
   a. Warped or cracked mating surfaces.
   b. Rotor bore damage.
4. Check the oil pump rotors for:
   a. Cracked or damaged outer surface.
   b. Worn or scored inner mating surfaces.
5. If the oil pump side plate, body and both rotors are in good condition, check their operating clearances as described in Step 6 and Step 7.

NOTE
The pump rotors are sold separately. The pump body, pump shaft and side plate are not.

6. Install the inner and outer rotors (B, **Figure 60**) and pump shaft (A) into the pump body.

7. Using a flat feeler gauge, measure the clearance between the outer rotor and the oil pump body (**Figure 62**). If the oil pump body clearance exceeds the service limit, replace the outer rotor and remeasure. If it is still out of specification, replace the oil pump assembly.

8. Using a flat feeler gauge, measure the clearance between the inner rotor tip and the outer rotor (**Figure 63**). If the oil pump tip clearance exceeds the service limit, replace the inner and outer rotors.

9. Using a flat feeler gauge and straightedge, measure the side clearance between the body surface and rotors (**Figure 64**). If the oil pump side clearance exceeds the service limit, replace the oil pump assembly.

CRANKCASE AND CRANKSHAFT

The crankcase is made in two halves of thin-wall, precision diecast aluminum alloy. To avoid damage, do not hammer or pry on any of the interior or exterior projected walls. A gasket seals the crankcase mating surfaces while dowels align the halves when they are bolted together. A crankcase half can be replaced separately.

The crankshaft assembly consists of two full-circle flywheels pressed together on a crankpin. Two ball bearings in the crankcase support the crankshaft assembly.

The procedure which follows is presented as a complete, step-by-step major lower end overhaul. If only servicing the transmission, disassemble and reassemble the crankcase without removing the crankshaft.

An oil screen and oil strainer are installed inside the crankcase. Thoroughly clean these parts whenever the crankcase halves are separated.

References to the front and rear sides of the engine refer to the engine in the frame, not how it may sit on the workbench.

Tools

The following Honda tools are required to install the crankshaft into the rear crankcase half. Have these tools or their equivalent on hand if removing the crankshaft.

1. Assembly shaft (A, **Figure 65**): part No. 07965-VM00200 or 07931-ME4010B.

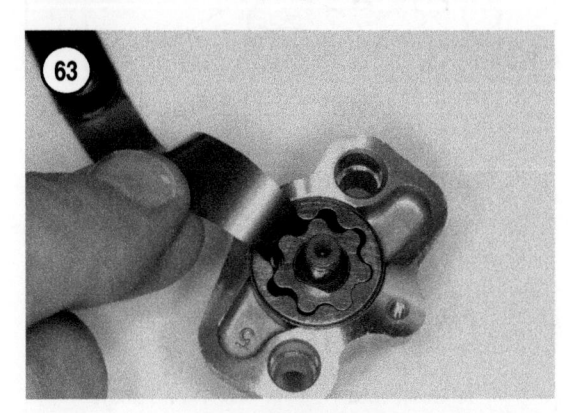

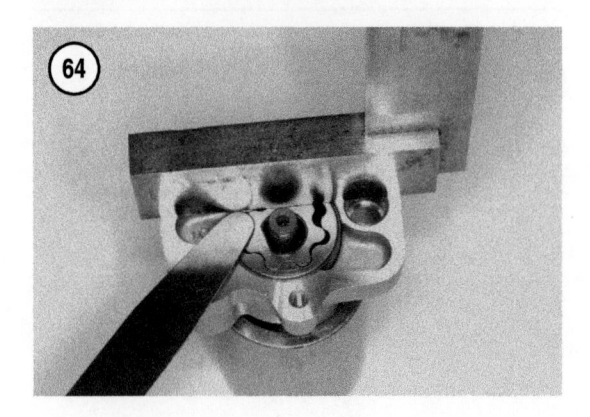

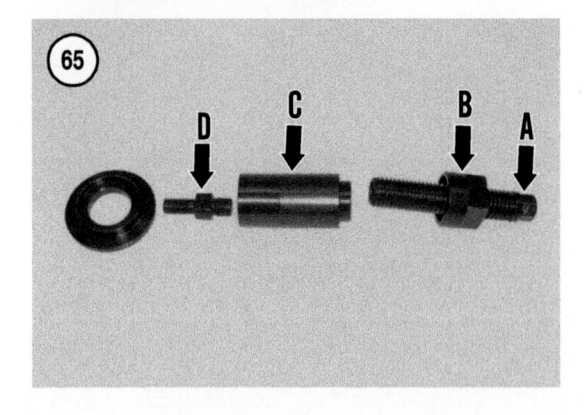

ENGINE LOWER END   137

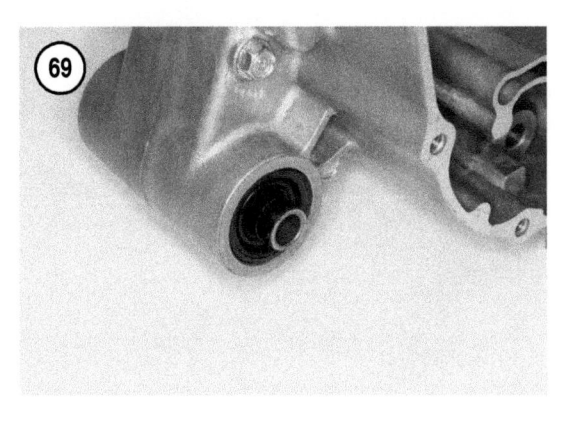

2. Special nut (B, **Figure 65**): part No. 07931-HB3020A.
3. Assembly collar (C, **Figure 65**): part No. 07965-VM00100.
4. Threaded adapter (D, **Figure 65**): part No. 07965- KA30000 or 07VMF-HM8010A.

Crankcase Disassembly

This procedure describes disassembly of the crankcase halves and removal of the transmission and internal shift mechanism. Crankshaft removal is covered in a separate procedure in this section. Refer to Chapter Seven for transmission and internal shift mechanism service.

1. Remove all exterior engine assemblies as described in this chapter and other related chapters:
   a. Cylinder head, cylinder and piston (Chapter Four).
   b. Remove the centrifugal and change clutch (Chapter Six).
   c. Oil cooler.
   d. Flywheel and starter clutch.
   e. Starter (Chapter Nine).
   f. Gearshift linkage.
   g. Oil pump.
2. Remove the engine from the frame as described in this chapter. Set it on wooden blocks.
3. Remove the mounting bolts (**Figure 66**) and remove the countershaft protector and its O-ring (**Figure 67**).
4. Remove the mounting bolt (A, **Figure 68**), and remove the neutral switch rotor (B) from the shift drum.
5. Remove the damping rubber from each engine hanger (**Figure 69**), and drive out each hanger bushing (**Figure 70**).

> *NOTE*
> *To prevent loss and to ensure proper bolt location during assembly, draw the crankcase outline on cardboard (**Figure 71**). Punch holes into this template that correspond to bolt locations. Insert the crankcase bolts in their appropriate locations after removing them.*

6. Loosen and remove the three front crankcase bolts (**Figure 72**), and place them in the cardboard template.

138   **CHAPTER FIVE**

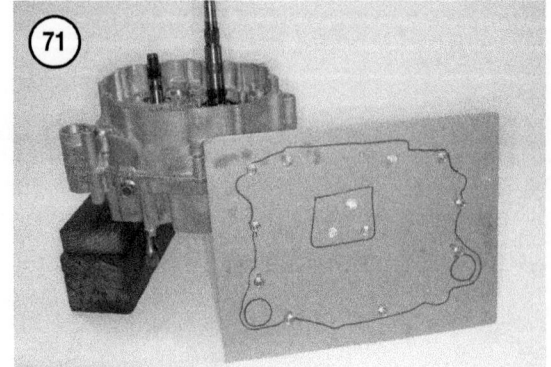

7. Turn the engine over so the rear side faces up.
8. Evenly loosen each rear crankcase mounting bolts (**Figure 72**) 1/4 turn and in a crisscross pattern. Repeat this until all the mounting bolts are loose.
9. Remove all the bolts loosened in Step 8, and set them in the cardboard template. Make sure to remove all the crankcase mounting bolts.
10. Turn the engine over so the front side (**Figure 73**) faces up.

CAUTION
*Perform this operation over and close to the work bench because the crankcase halves may easily separate. Do **not** hammer directly on the crankcase halves. This damages the case halves.*

CAUTION
Do not pry between the crankcase mating surfaces when separating the crankcase halves. Doing so may cause an oil leak.

11. Tap on the front crankcase while lifting it off the engine. Tap the transmission shafts if they bind with the crankcase and prevent disassembly. Lift the front crankcase from the rear case.

NOTE
The oil screen is not quite rectangular. One side is narrower than the other. Note how the narrow side fits in toward the front crankcase half. It must be reinstalled with this same orientation during assembly.

12. Simultaneously slide the oil screen (A, **Figure 74**) and the oil strainer (B) from the inside of the front crankcase half.

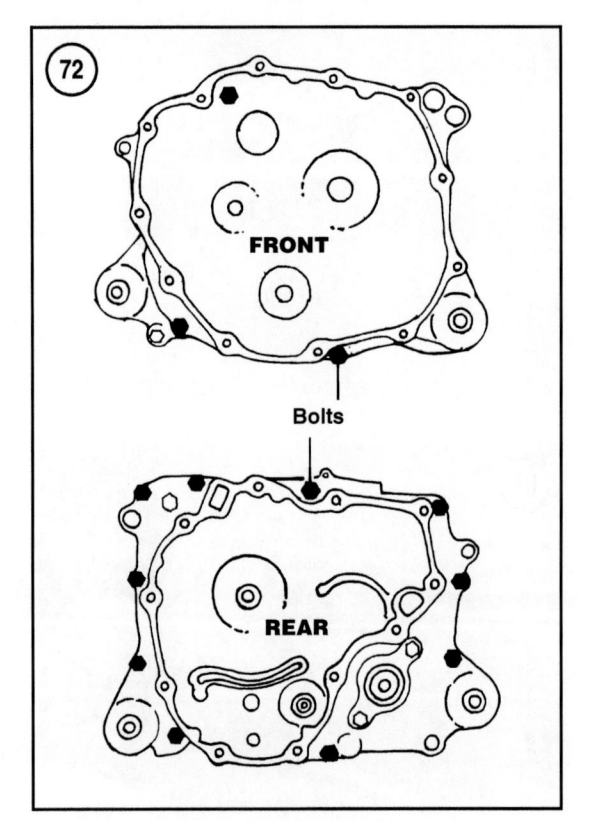

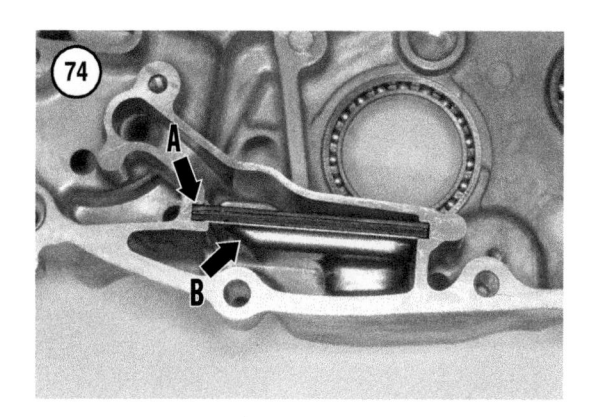

ENGINE LOWER END

13. Remove the gasket (A, **Figure 75**) and dowels (B) from the rear crankcase.

NOTE
Steps 14-17 describe removal of the transmission.

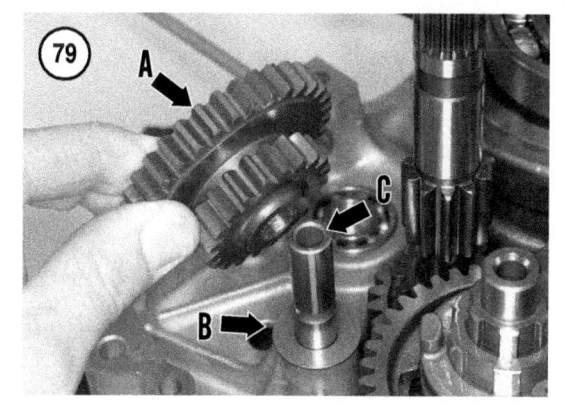

14. Remove the thrust washer (A, **Figure 76**), countershaft first gear (B) and first gear bushing (**Figure 77**) from the countershaft.

15. Remove the thrust washer (**Figure 78**) and the reverse idle gear (A, **Figure 79**) from the reverse idle shaft.

16. Remove the second thrust washer (B, **Figure 79**) and reverse idler shaft (C).

17. Grasp the mainshaft (A, **Figure 80**), countershaft (B) and shift drum/shift fork (C) assemblies together, and remove all three assemblies from the rear crankcase half as a single unit.

NOTE
Steps 18-20 describe crankshaft removal.

18. Install the threaded adapter onto the rear of the crankshaft (**Figure 81**).

19. Set the rear crankcase half into a press, and press the crankshaft from the case half.

> *CAUTION*
> *The rear crankshaft bearing must be replaced whenever the crankshaft is removed.*

20. Remove the rear crankcase bearing as described in this section.

Crankcase Assembly

1. Install the rear crankshaft bearing into the rear crankcase half as described in this section.

2. Install the crankshaft into the rear crankshaft bearing by performing the following:
   a. Apply engine oil to the bearing and to the crankshaft bearing journal.
   b. Slide the crankshaft through the bearing until the bearing journal bottoms against the bearing inner race.
   c. Use a rubber band to support the connecting rod in an upright position as shown in **Figure 82**.
   d. Install the threaded adapter onto the rear crankshaft end (**Figure 81**).
   e. Slide the assembly collar (A, **Figure 83**) over the crankshaft, and seat it against the bearing.
   f. Thread the special nut (B, **Figure 83**) down onto the assembly shaft (C).
   g. Slide the assembly shaft into the assembly collar and thread it onto the threaded adapter on the crankshaft end. Run the special nut down against the assembly collar.
   h. Hold the special nut (B, **Figure 83**) and turn the assembly shaft (C) to pull the crankshaft into the bearing. Frequently check that the crankshaft is going straight into the bearing and not binding to one side.
   i. Turn the assembly shaft until the crankshaft is pulled into the bearing. Remove the tool and check the operation of the crankshaft. It must turn smoothly.

3. Set the rear crankcase half onto wooden blocks (**Figure 84**).

ENGINE LOWER END

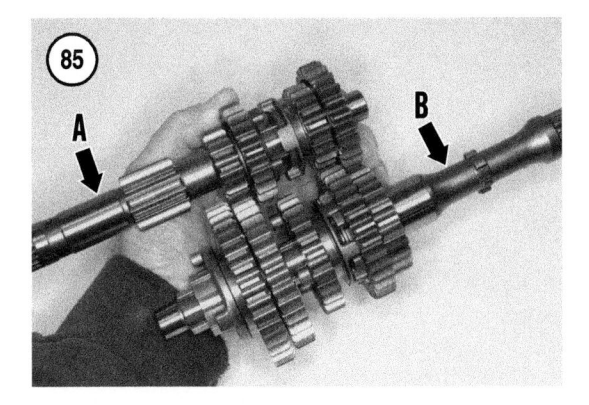

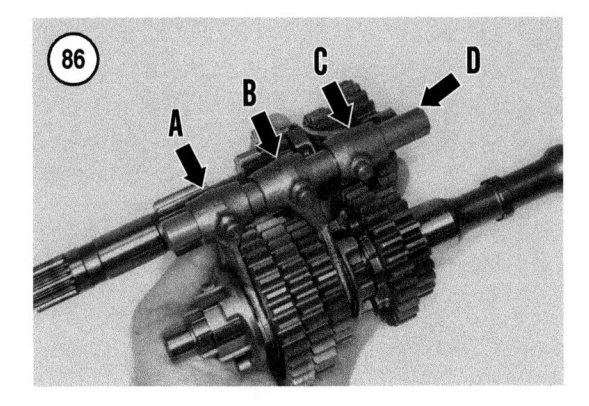

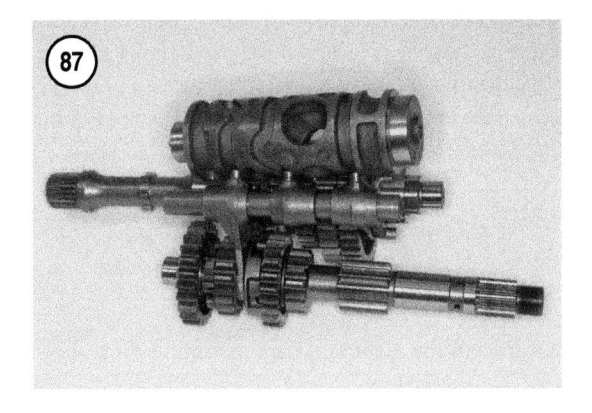

NOTE
Setting the mainshaft washer into the crankcase half is easier than trying to install the transmission shafts while this washer is installed on the mainshaft. The washer could easily fall from the end of the mainshaft without being heard.

4. Apply grease to the mainshaft washer, and center the washer over the mainshaft bearing in the rear crankcase half. The grease helps hold the washer in place while the transmission is installed.

NOTE
The transmission is assembled on the bench and then the entire transmission assembly (mainshaft, countershaft, shift forks and shift drum assemblies) is installed as one unit.

5. Mesh the mainshaft (A, **Figure 85**) and the countershaft assemblies (B) together.

NOTE
Install each shift fork so the side with stamping faces the clutch end of the mainshaft. Apply engine oil to the shift forks and to the groove in the related shifter gear before installing each shift fork.

6. Install the shift fork marked HB3R (A, **Figure 86**) into the shift groove in the reverse shifter on the countershaft.
7. Install the shift fork marked HB3C (B, **Figure 86**) into shift groove on countershaft fourth gear.
8. Install the shift fork marked HB3L (C, **Figure 86**) into shift groove on mainshaft third gear.
9. Rotate the shift forks as necessary to align their guide pins, and install the shift fork shaft (D, **Figure 86**) through the forks.
10. Set the shift drum onto the assembly so each shift fork guide pin engages a groove in the shift drum. Refer to **Figure 87**.
11. Grasp the entire transmission assembly and lower it into place in the rear crankcase half. Make sure the countershaft seats in the countershaft bearing (A, **Figure 88**), the mainshaft passes through the washer and seats in the mainshaft bearing (B), the shift drum seats in the shift drum bushing (C) and the shift fork shaft seats in the crankcase boss (D).

12. Install the reverse idle shaft (B, **Figure 79**), and install the thrust washer (B) onto the reverse idler shaft. The flat side of the thrust washer must face in toward the crankcase.

13. Install the reverse idle gear (A, **Figure 79**) onto the reverse idle shaft, and then install the another thrust washer (**Figure 78**). The flat side of this thrust washer must face out away from the reverse idle gear.

14. Install the countershaft first gear bushing (**Figure 77**) onto the countershaft so the oil hole in the bushing aligns with the hole in the shaft.

15. Install the countershaft first gear (B, **Figure 76**) and the thrust washer (A).

16. Check the operation of the transmission by turning the countershaft and shifting the shift drum through the gears. Note the following:
    a. Make sure the guide pin on each shift fork properly engages its groove in the shift drum.
    b. Visually inspect the movement of each shift fork.

17. Place the oil screen (A, **Figure 74**) on top of the oil strainer (B), and then install the oil screen/strainer assembly (**Figure 89**). The narrow side of the oil screen must go into the crankcase half.

18. Install a new gasket (A, **Figure 75**) and the dowels (B) into the rear crankcase half.

CAUTION
When the shafts align properly, the front crankcase half installs easily without the use of force. If the crankcase halves do not fit together, do not pull them together with the crankcase bolts. Remove the front crankcase half and look for the source of interference. If the crankshaft was removed, make sure it is seated properly in the rear crankcase main bearing. If the transmission was removed, make sure each shaft was properly assembled and installed in the rear crankcase half.

19. Lubricate all shafts and gears with engine oil.

20. Lower the front crankcase half over the crankshaft and transmission assemblies, and install it onto the rear crankcase half. Press the front crankcase down until it engages the dowels and seats completely against the rear crankcase half.

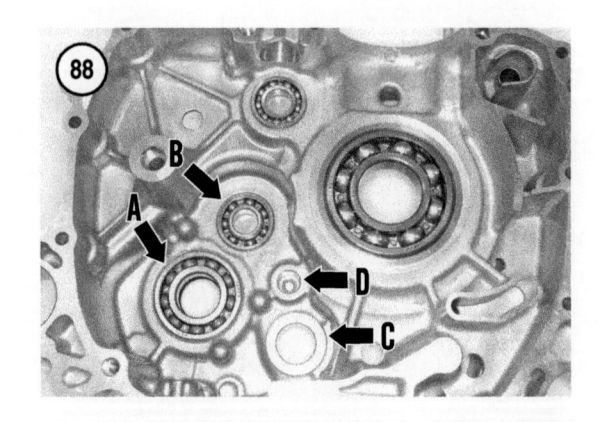

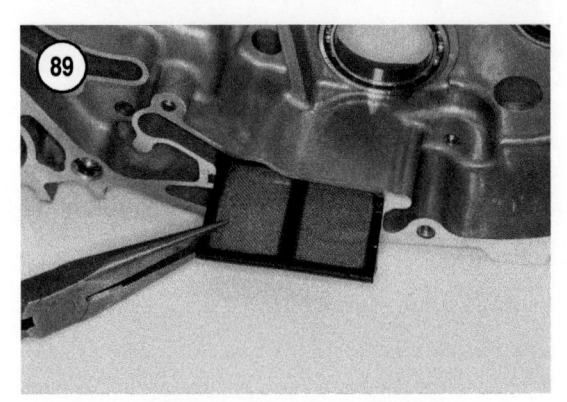

21. Check the operation of the crankshaft and transmission by turning all exposed shafts and the shift drum. Each component must turn smoothly.

22. Turn the engine over so the rear side (**Figure 90**) faces up.

NOTE
Use the cardboard template (Figure 71) to identify the proper location for each crankcase bolt.

23. Install the rear crankcase mounting bolts (**Figure 72**) finger-tight. Make sure the bolts are clean

ENGINE LOWER END

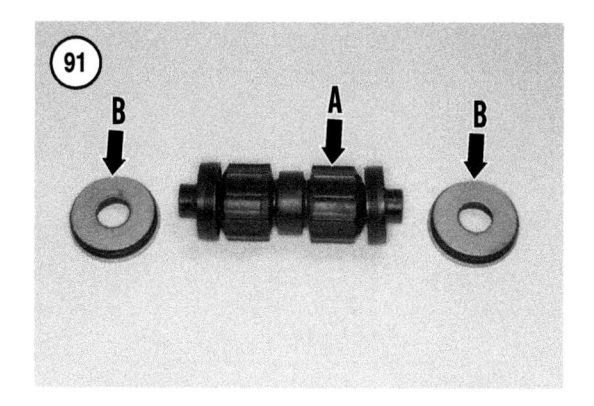

91

92

and dry. Following a crisscross pattern, evenly tighten the crankcase bolts in 1/4 turns until all are secure. Tighten the bolts to 12 N•m (106 in.-lb.).
24. Turn the engine over so the front side (**Figure 73**) faces up.
25. Install the front crankcase mounting bolts (**Figure 72**). Make sure the bolts are clean and dry. Evenly tighten the bolts until they are secure, and then tighten the bolts to 12 N•m (106 in.-lb.).
26. Perform the *Transmission Shifting Check* described in this section.
27. Rotate the crankshaft and transmission shafts to ensure they turn without binding. If any binding is noted, separate the crankcase halves and correct the problem.
28. Install the neutral switch rotor (B, **Figure 68**) onto the shift drum. Make sure the holes in the rotor engage the pins on the end of the shift drum. Apply ThreeBond 1333B, or its equivalent, to the threads of neutral switch rotor bolt (A, **Figure 68**), and tighten the bolt to 10 N•m (89 ft.-lb.).
29. Install a new O-ring (**Figure 67**) onto the countershaft protector, and install the protector onto the rear crankcase half. Tighten the mounting bolts (**Figure 66**) securely.

30. Drive each hanger bushing (A, **Figure 91**) into place so the bushing shafts are centered in the engine crankcase mount (**Figure 92**). Do not install the damper rubbers (B, **Figure 91**) at this time. They are installed just before the engine is installed into the frame.
31. Install the engine as described in this chapter.
32. Install all removed exterior assemblies as described in this and other chapters:
    a. Oil pump.
    b. Gearshift linkage.
    c. Starter (Chapter Nine).
    d. Flywheel and starter clutch.
    e. Oil cooler.
    f. Centrifugal clutch and the change clutch (Chapter Six).
    g. Cylinder head, cylinder and piston (Chapter Four).

Crankcase Inspection

1. Remove all sealer and gasket residue from the gasket surfaces.

WARNING
When drying the crankcase bearings, do not allow the inner races to spin. The bearings are not lubricated and damage may result. When drying the bearings with compressed air, do not allow the air jet to spin the bearing. The air jet can rotate the bearings at excessive speeds. The bearing could fly apart causing injury.

2. Clean both crankcase halves and all crankcase bearings with solvent. Thoroughly dry them with compressed air.
3. Flush all crankcase oil passages with compressed air.
4. Lightly oil all the crankcase bearings with engine oil before checking the bearings.
5. Check the bearings for roughness, pitting, galling and play by rotating them slowly by hand. Replace any bearing that turns roughly or has excessive play (**Figure 93**).
6. Replace any worn or damaged bearings as described in this section.

NOTE
Always replace the opposing bearing at the same time.

7. Carefully inspect the case halves for cracks and fractures, especially in the lower areas where they are vulnerable to rock damage.

8. Check the areas around the stiffening ribs, bearing bosses and threaded holes for damage. Refer crankcase repair to a shop specializing in the repair of precision aluminum castings.

9. Check the threaded holes in both crankcase halves for thread damage, dirt or oil buildup. If necessary, clean or repair the threads with the correct size metric tap. Coat the tap threads with kerosene or an aluminum tap fluid before use.

10. Check the gearshift stopper bolt (**Figure 94**) for looseness or damage. During installation, apply ThreeBond 1333B, or its equivalent, to the bolt threads and tighten the stopper bolt to 22 N•m (16 ft.-lb.).

Rear Crankshaft Bearing Replacement

The rear crankshaft bearing must be replaced when the crankcase halves are separated.

1A. If the rear crankshaft bearing came out with the crankshaft, perform the following:
  a. Install a bearing separator onto the crankshaft as shown in **Figure 95**. Make sure the separator is between the bearing and the crankweb.
  b. Support the bearing separator in a hydraulic press (**Figure 96**). Center the crankshaft beneath the press ram, and press the crankshaft from the bearing.
  c. If a hydraulic press is not available, remove the bearing with a puller (**Figure 97**).
  d. Remove the separator and bearing from the crankshaft.

1B. If the rear crankshaft bearing remains in the rear crankcase half, drive the bearing from the outside of the case half.

2. Discard the bearing, and install a new bearing into the crankcase half.

3. Place the new bearing in the freezer, and heat the crankcase half in an oven as described in Chapter One.

WARNING
Hold onto the crankcase with a kitchen pot holder, heavy gloves or a heavy shop cloth because it is hot.

4. Apply oil to the bearing and its seat in the crankcase half.

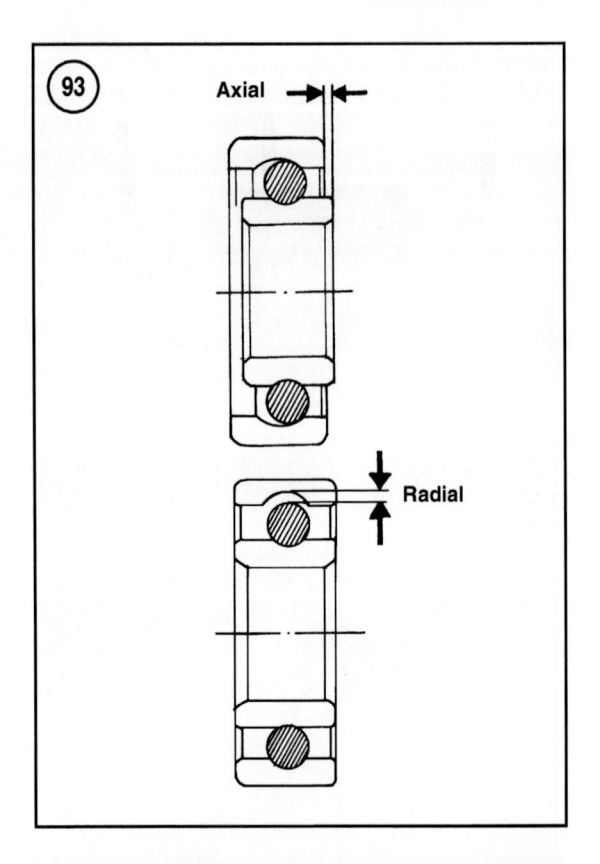

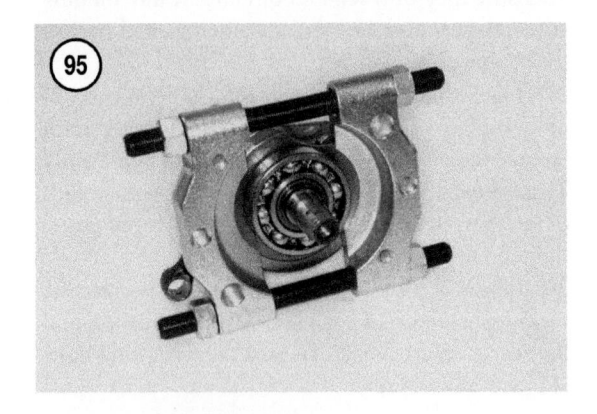

ENGINE LOWER END

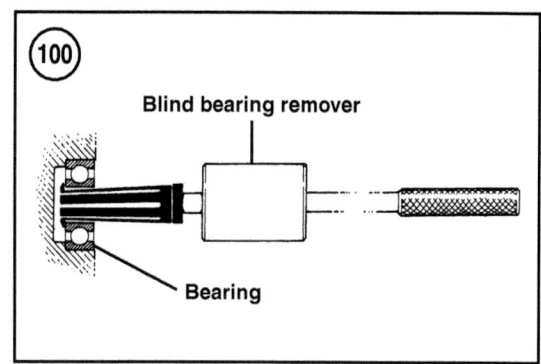

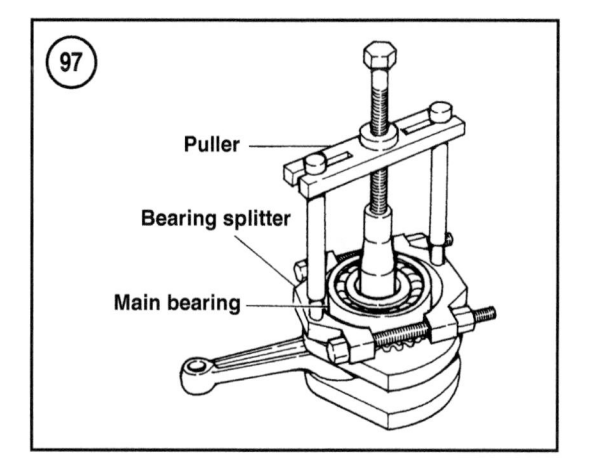

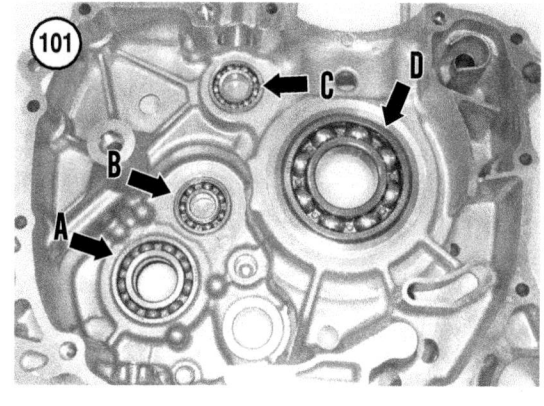

5. Set the bearing into the rear crankcase half (**Figure 98**).

6. Install the bearing into the crankcase with an appropriate size bearing driver or socket that matches the outside diameter of the bearing. Drive the bearing until it bottoms in the crankcase (**Figure 99**).

Crankcase Bearing Replacement

When replacing bearings in the following steps, note the following:

1. Because of the number of bearings used in the front and rear crankcase halves, identify the bearings before removing them. Identify each bearing by referring to its size code marks.

2. Before removing the bearings, note and record the direction in which the bearings' size codes face for proper reinstallation.

3. Replace the bearings as described in Chapter One. Use a blind bearing remover to remove bearings installed in blind holes (**Figure 100**).

4. Refer to **Figure 101** to identify the bearings installed in the rear crankcase half:

    a. Countershaft (A).

b. Mainshaft (B).
c. Camshaft (C).
d. Crankshaft (D)

5. Refer to **Figure 102** to identify the bearings installed in the front crankcase half:
   a. Mainshaft (A).
   c. Shift drum (C).

Rear countershaft bearing replacement

Perform the following to replace the countershaft bearing in the rear crankcase half (A, **Figure 101**):

1. Use an oil seal remover to pry the countershaft oil seal (**Figure 103**) from the outside of the rear crankcase half. Protect the crankcase with a rag so it is not marred.
2. Use a blind bearing puller to remove the countershaft bearing (**Figure 104**) from the inside of the rear crankcase half.
3. Apply engine oil to the bearing and crankcase.
4. Drive the new bearing into the crankcase with an appropriate size bearing driver of socket.
5. Pack the lips of a new countershaft seal with lithium grease, and install the oil seal (**Figure 103**).

Front mainshaft bearing replacement

Perform the following to replace the mainshaft bearing in the front crankcase half (A, **Figure 102**).

1. Remove the retainer bolts (A, **Figure 105**) and bearing retainer (B) from the crankcase half.
2. Remove the bearing from the crankcase with a blind bearing puller.
3. Lubricate the new bearing and crankcase with engine oil. Use the appropriate size bearing driver or socket that matches the outside diameter of the bearing to drive the bearing into the crankcase until the bearing bottoms.
4. Secure the bearing retainer (B, **Figure 105**) in place with the retainer bolts (A). Apply ThreeBond 1333B, or its equivalent, to the threads of the retainer bolts, and tighten the bolts securely.

Crankcase Stud Replacement

The crankcase studs are different lengths. When replacing the studs, measure their length before removal. Install the new stud, and tighten it to 12 N•m (106 in.-lb.).

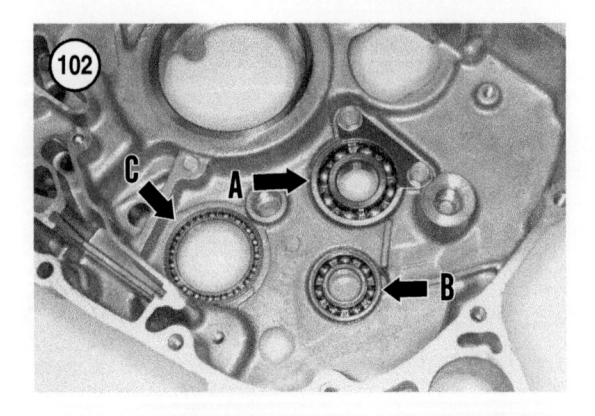

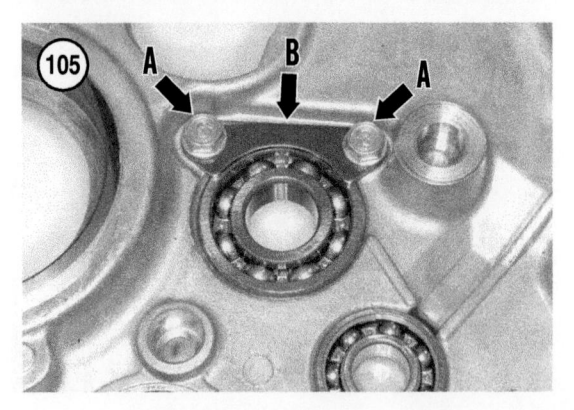

ENGINE LOWER END

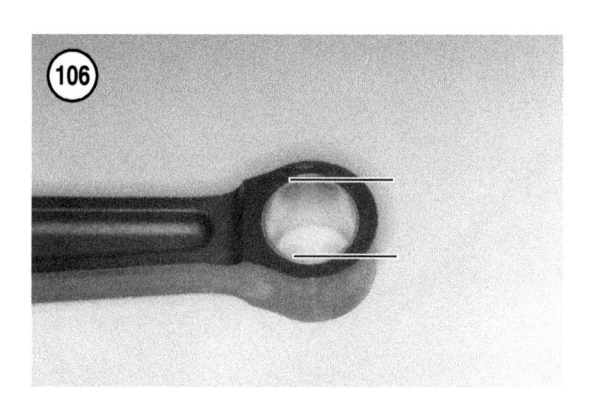

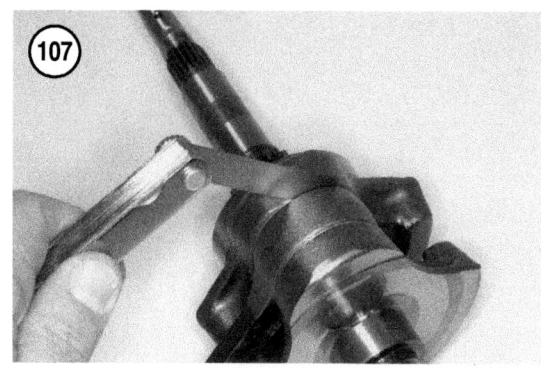

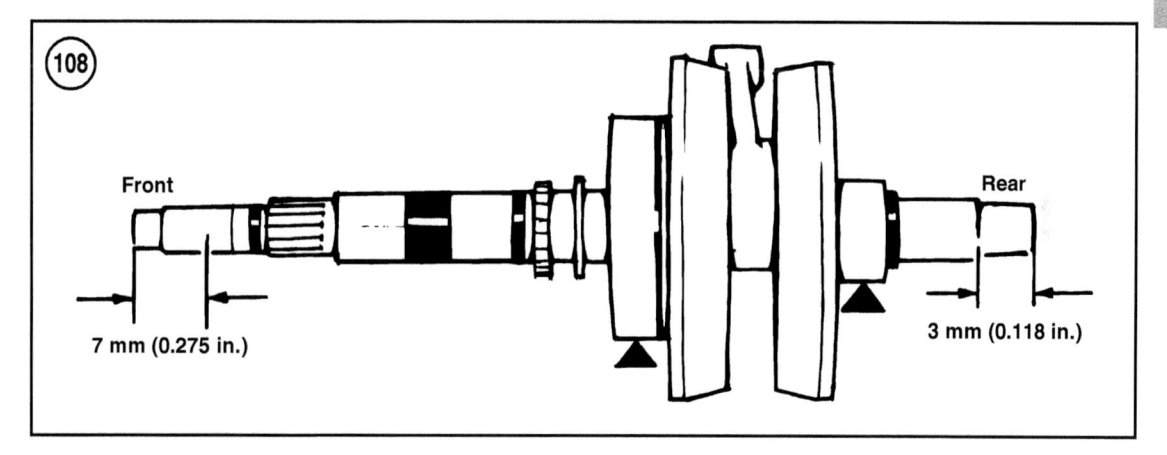

106

107

108

Front — 7 mm (0.275 in.)

Rear — 3 mm (0.118 in.)

Crankshaft Inspection

Handle the crankshaft carefully when performing the following cleaning and inspection procedures. Compare any measurements to the lower end specification in **Table 1**. If any part is excessively worn, damaged or out of specification, the crankshaft must be replaced or overhauled.

1. Clean the crankshaft thoroughly with solvent. Clean the crankshaft oil passageway with compressed air. Dry the crankshaft with compressed air, and lubricate all bearing surfaces with a light coat of engine oil.
2. Check the crankshaft journals for scratches, heat discoloration or other defects.
3. Check the flywheel taper, threads and keyway for damage.
4. Inspect the teeth on the timing sprocket and on the oil pump drive sprocket.
5. Check the connecting rod big end for signs of damage, as well as bearing or thrust washer damage.
6. Check the connecting rod small end for signs of excessive heat (blue coloration) or other damage.
7. Measure the connecting rod small end inside diameter (**Figure 106**) with a snap gauge or an inside micrometer.
8. Slide the connecting rod to one side and check the connecting rod side clearance with a flat feeler gauge (**Figure 107**).
9. Place the crankshaft on V-blocks at the points shown in **Figure 108**. Use a dial indicator to measure front runout at a point 7 mm (0.275 in.) from the end of the crankshaft. Measure rear runout at a point 3 mm (0.118 in.) from the end of the crankshaft. Replace or overhaul the crankshaft if either end of the crankshaft is worn to the service limit.
10. Place the crankshaft on a set of V-blocks and measure the connecting rod big end radial clearance with a dial indicator (**Figure 109**). Measure in the two directions shown in **Figure 110** and compare to the dimension in **Table 1**.

Crankshaft Overhaul

Crankshaft overhaul requires a number of special tools: a hydraulic press with a 20-ton capacity (minimum), holding jigs, crankshaft alignment jig, dial indicators and a micrometer or vernier caliper. For this reason, refer crankshaft overhaul to a Honda dealer or motorcycle repair shop familiar with crankshaft rebuilding.

Transmission Shifting Check

Transmission shifting can be checked with the engine mounted in the frame or sitting on the workbench. Always check transmission shifting after reassembling the crankcase.

1. Install the stopper arm assembly (A, **Figure 111**) and the drum shifter (B) as described in *Gearshift Linkage* in this chapter.
2. Turn the drum shifter so the dowel pin (C, **Figure 111**) aligns with the crankcase index mark (D). The transmission is now in neutral. Turn the countershaft or mainshaft. When the transmission is in neutral, the countershaft and mainshaft turn independently of each other. That is, when you turn one shaft, the other shaft does not turn.
3. To check the forward gears, turn the mainshaft or countershaft while turning the shifter drum counterclockwise. The transmission is in gear when the stopper arm roller seats into one of the drum shifter segment ramps. When the transmission is in gear, the countershaft and mainshaft are engaged. They should turn together. Refer to **Figure 112**.
4. To check the reverse gear, move the reverse stopper shaft (**Figure 113**) down (to disengage it from the shift drum), and then turn the drum shifter (B, **Figure 111**) clockwise. The transmission should shift into reverse.
5. If the transmission does not shift properly into each gear, disassemble the engine and check the transmission and internal shift mechanism.

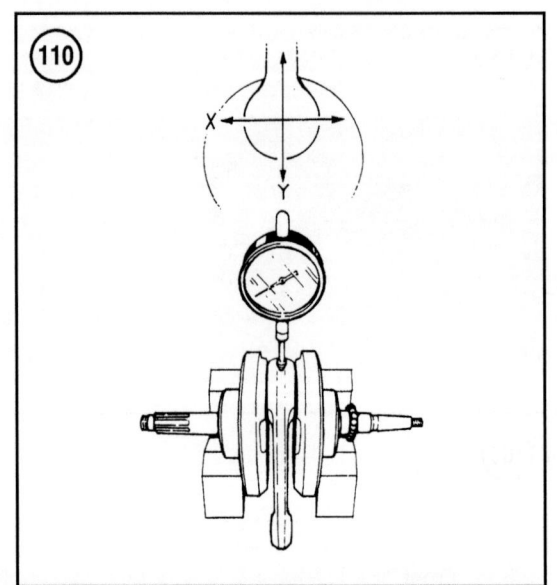

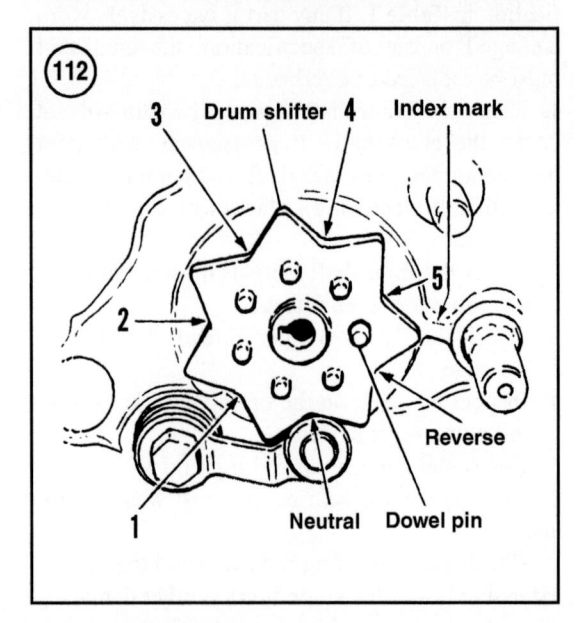

ENGINE LOWER END

113

ENGINE BREAK-IN

If you replaced the piston rings, installed a new piston, honed or rebored the cylinder or performed major lower end work, the engine must be broken in as if new. The performance and service life of the engine depends greatly on a careful and sensible break-in.

For the first 5-10 hours of operation, use no more than one-third throttle and vary the speed as much as possible within the one-third throttle limit. Avoid prolonged or steady running at one speed as well as hard acceleration.

Table 1 ENGINE LOWER END SPECIFICATIONS

	Specification mm (in.)	Service limit mm (in.)
Crankshaft runout		
Front	–	0.06 (0.002)
Rear	–	0.03 (0.001)
Connecting rod		
Small end inside diameter	15.010-15.028 (0.5909-0.5917)	15.06 (0.593)
Big end side clearance	0.05-0.50 (0.002-0.020)	0.80 (0.031)
Big end radial clearance	0.004-0.012 (0.0002-0.0005)	0.05 (0.002)
Oil pump		
Tip clearance	0.15 (0.006)	0.20 (0.008)
Body clearance	0.15-0.21 (0.006-0.008)	0.25 (0.010)
Side clearance	0.05-0.13 (0.002-0.005)	0.15 (0.006)

Table 2 ENGINE LOWER END TORQUE SPECIFICATIONS

Item	N•m	in.-lb.	ft.-lb.
Crankcase bolts	12	106	–
Crankcase studs	12	106	–
Engine mounting bolts and nuts			
Lower engine mount	54	–	40
Cylinder head cover mount	32	–	24
Engine oil drain bolt	25	–	18
Exhaust pipe protector bolt	22	–	16
Flywheel bolt	74	–	54
Gearshift A-arm bolt*	25	–	18
(continued)			

Table 2 ENGINE LOWER END TORQUE SPECIFICATIONS (continued)

Item	N•m	in.-lb.	ft.-lb.
Gearshift bolt	25	–	18
Gearshift stopper bolt	22	–	16
Guide plate bolt*	16	–	12
Ignition pulse generator bolts*	6	53	–
Muffler clamp bolt	23	–	17
Neutral switch rotor bolt*	10	89	–
One-way clutch bolts*	16	–	12
Shift pedal clamp bolt	20	–	14
Skid plate bolt	32	–	24
Stopper arm bolt*	12	106	–

*Apply threadlocking compound.

> NOTE: Refer to the Supplement at the back of this manual for information unique to 2006-on models.

CHAPTER SIX

CLUTCH AND PRIMARY DRIVE GEAR

This chapter describes service procedures for the following assemblies:
1. Clutch cover.
2. Clutch lever.
3. Centrifugal clutch and primary drive gear.
4. Change clutch.

The clutch cover, clutch and primary drive gear assemblies can be serviced with the engine mounted in the frame. However, because of the engine's mounting position in the frame, the photographs in this chapter show the engine removed from the frame for clarity.

When inspecting clutch components, compare all measurements to the clutch specifications in **Table** 1. Replace any component that is damaged, worn to the service limit or out of specification. During assembly, tighten fasteners as specified. **Table 1** and **Table 2** are at the end of this chapter.

CLUTCH COVER

Removal

1. Park the vehicle on level ground and set the parking brake.
2. Remove the seat, both side covers and front fender as described in Chapter Fourteen.
3. Drain the engine oil as described in Chapter Three.
4. Remove the oil line flange bolts and disconnect the oil cooler hoses (**Figure 1**) from the clutch cover.
5. Evenly loosen and then remove the clutch cover bolts (**Figure 2**).

NOTE
*Watch for the clutch lever (A, **Figure** 3). It may fall out when the clutch cover is removed.*

6. Remove the clutch cover from the front of the crankcase. Do not lose the washer (B, **Figure 3**) from the master arm shaft.
7. Remove the gasket (A, **Figure 4**) and dowels (B).
8. Disassemble and inspect the clutch cover as described in this section.

Installation

1. Remove all gasket residue from the clutch cover and crankcase gasket surfaces.
2. If the clutch lever was removed, perform the following:
   a. Lubricate the clutch lever roller with engine oil.
   b. Install the clutch lever so its shaft seats in the boss in the crankcase (A, **Figure 5**).
   c. Make sure the clutch lever roller engages the arm of the lifter cam (B, **Figure 5**) and the roller on the master arm sits inside the slot in the clutch lever arm (C).
3. Make sure the washer (B, **Figure 3**) is in place on the end of the master arm shaft.
4. Install a new clutch cover gasket (A, **Figure 4**) and the dowels (B).
5. Install the clutch cover and secure it in place with the clutch cover bolts (**Figure 2**). Follow a crisscross pattern, and evenly tighten the clutch cover bolts securely.
6. Adjust the clutch as described in Chapter Three.
7. Install the front fender, side covers and seat as described in Chapter Fourteen.

Disassembly/Inspection/Assembly

The clutch cover houses the crankshaft end bearing and the clutch adjuster mechanism. The bearing supports the front end of the crankshaft so it must operate smoothly and fit tightly in the mounting bore.

1. Carefully remove any gasket residue from the gasket mating surfaces on the clutch cover and on the crankcase. Do not scratch the surfaces, cover or crankcase. An oil leak could result.
2. Remove the adjuster locknut (A, **Figure 6**) from the adjuster bolt (B).
3. Remove the adjusting plate (A, **Figure 7**) from the inside of the cover, and then remove the adjuster bolt (B) and its O-ring.

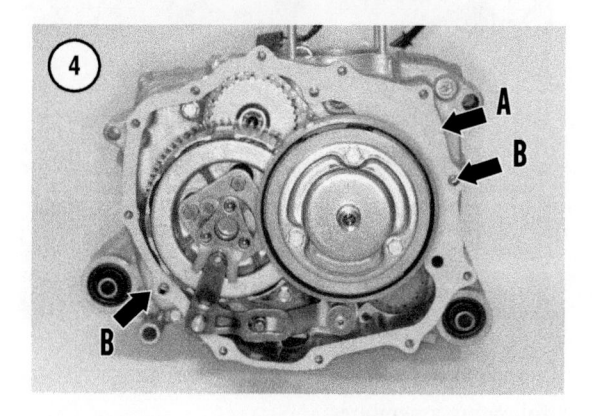

CLUTCH AND PRIMARY DRIVE GEAR

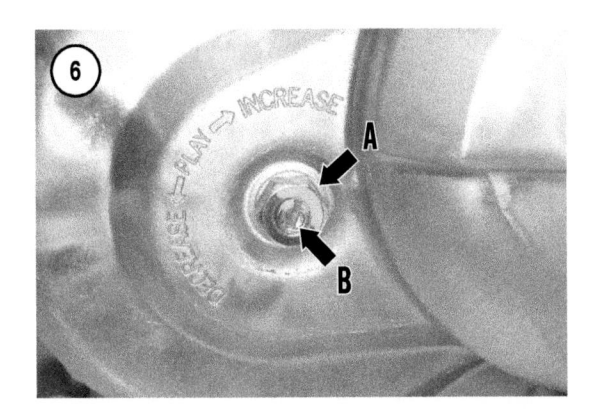

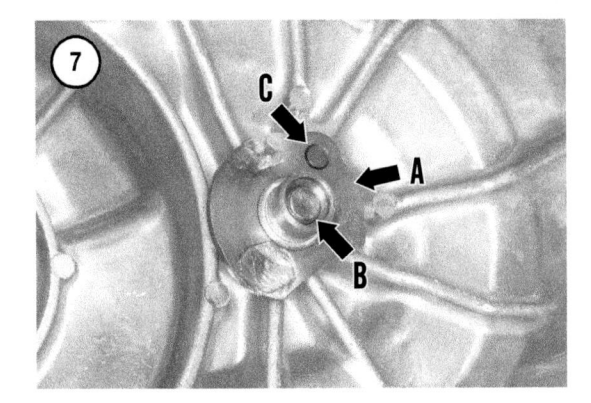

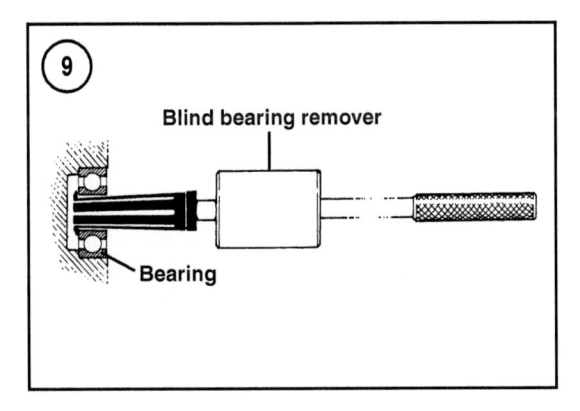

WARNING
Do not spin the bearing with compressed air when drying it. Doing so may cause the bearing to fly apart.

4. Clean the clutch cover and its oil passages with solvent. Clean the crankshaft end bearing while it is submerged in solvent. Dry the clutch cover, oil passages and bearing with compressed air.
5. Lubricate the crankshaft end bearing with engine oil.
6. Hold the clutch housing and slowly turn the crankshaft end bearing (**Figure 8**) inner race. Check the crankshaft end bearing for roughness, pitting, noise and play. Replace the bearing if it turns roughly or has excessive play as follows:
    a. Set the clutch cover on the bench with the bearing facing up.
    b. Use a blind bearing puller (**Figure 9**) to remove the crankshaft end bearing from the clutch cover.
    c. Apply engine oil to the new bearing outer race and to the mounting bore in the clutch cover.
    d. Drive the new bearing into place with an appropriate bearing driver or socket that matches the outside diameter of the bearing. Install the bearing so its sealed side faces the outside of the clutch cover.
7. Check that the bearing outer race fits tightly in its mounting bore. If the bearing fits loosely in the clutch cover, the mounting bore is probably cracked or excessively worn. Replace the clutch cover. Inspect the crankshaft end bearing by turning it by hand.
8. Assembly is the reverse of removal. Note the following:
    a. Apply engine oil to a new O-ring and fit in on the adjuster bolt. Make sure the side with the O-ring faces away from the adjusting plate.
    b. Install the adjusting plate so its stopper pin (C, **Figure 7**) sits in the boss on the inside of the clutch cover.
    c. Install and finger-tighten the clutch adjuster locknut (A, **Figure 6**). The nut is tightened once the clutch is adjusted.

CLUTCH RELEASE MECHANISM

The clutch release mechanism (**Figure 10**) engages and disengages the change clutch as the gearshift pedal is moved during gear changes.

CLUTCH RELEASE MECHANISM

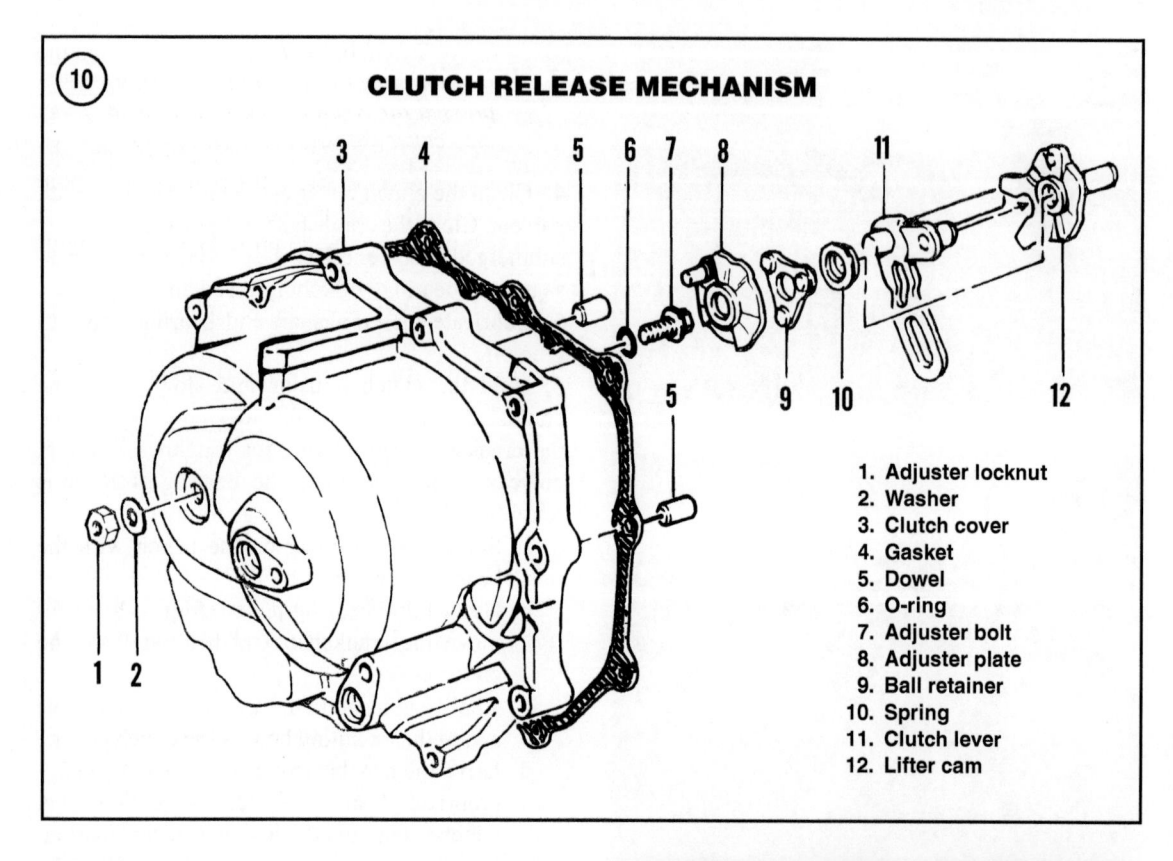

1. Adjuster locknut
2. Washer
3. Clutch cover
4. Gasket
5. Dowel
6. O-ring
7. Adjuster bolt
8. Adjuster plate
9. Ball retainer
10. Spring
11. Clutch lever
12. Lifter cam

Removal

1. Remove the clutch cover as described in this chapter.

2. Remove the clutch lever (A, **Figure 3**) from the crankcase. Note that the clutch lever roller engages the arm of the lifter cam (B, **Figure 5**) and the bearing on the master arm sits inside the slot in the clutch lever arm (C).

3. Remove the ball retainer (A, **Figure 11**) and spring (B) from the lifter cam (C).

4. Remove the lifter cam assembly (A, **Figure 12**) from the lifter plate (B).

5. If necessary, remove the adjusting plate from the clutch cover as described in *Clutch Cover, Disassembly/Inspection/Assembly*.

Installation

1. If removed, install the adjusting plate into the clutch cover as described in *Clutch Cover, Disassembly/Inspection/Assembly*.

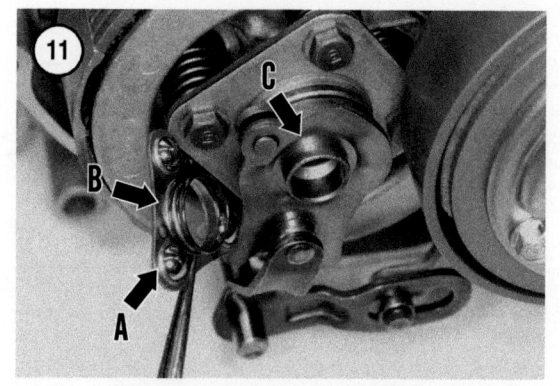

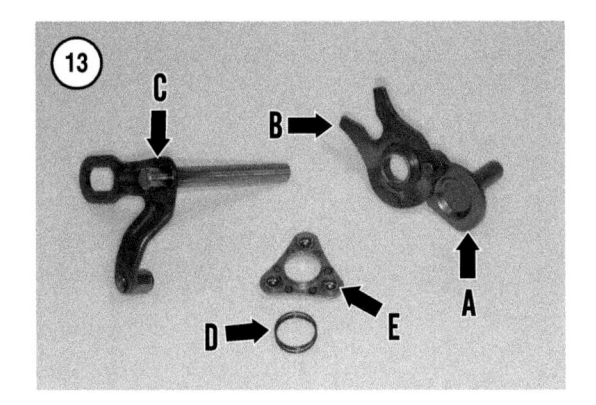

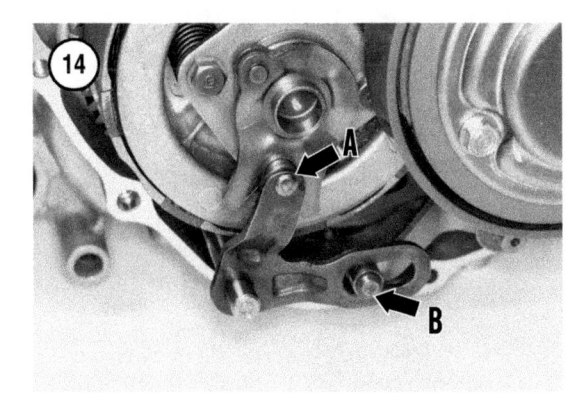

CLUTCH AND PRIMARY DRIVE GEAR

b. Install the clutch lever so its shaft seats in the boss in the crankcase (A, **Figure 5**).
c. Make sure the clutch lever roller engages the arm of the lifter cam (A, **Figure 14**) and the roller on the master arm sits inside the slot in the clutch lever arm (B).

5. Install the spring (B, **Figure 11**) onto the shoulder of the ball retainer (A).
6. Install the spring and ball retainer onto the lifter cam shoulder (**Figure 15**).
7. Install the clutch cover as described in this chapter.

Inspection

Replace parts that show excessive wear or damage.

1. Clean and dry all parts.
2. Check the clutch lever (C, **Figure 13**) for cracks or wear. Make sure the roller turns freely.
3. Check the arms of the lifter cam (B, **Figure 13**) where the arms engage the clutch lever roller.
4. Check the lifter cap (A, **Figure 13**) for excessive wear or damage. Check its pivot pin for excessive wear.
5. Check the spring (D, **Figure 13**) for stretched or damaged coils.
6. Check the ball retainer (E, **Figure 13**) for a cracked ball cage. The balls must turn smoothly in the retainer and not fall out. Check the balls for cracks or flat spots.
7. Check the adjuster bolt for stripped threads. Replace the O-ring if it is cracked or damaged.
8. Check the adjusting plate for damaged or excessively worn engagement arm tabs.

CENTRIFUGAL CLUTCH AND PRIMARY DRIVE GEAR

The TRX250EX uses two clutch assemblies: a centrifugal clutch (C, **Figure 3**) on the crankshaft and a change clutch (D) on the mainshaft. The centrifugal clutch must be removed first.

The centrifugal clutch can be removed with the engine installed in the frame. Refer to **Figure 16**.

2. The lifter cap is attached to the lifter cam with a pivot pin. Lubricate the lifter cap bore (A, **Figure 13**) with lithium grease.

3. Install the lifter cam assembly (A, **Figure 12**) onto the lifter plate (B) so the lifter cap is seated in the bearing bore.

4. Install the clutch lever (A, **Figure 3**) by performing the following:

   a. Lubricate the clutch lever roller with engine oil.

Tools

Before removing the centrifugal clutch nut, note the following:

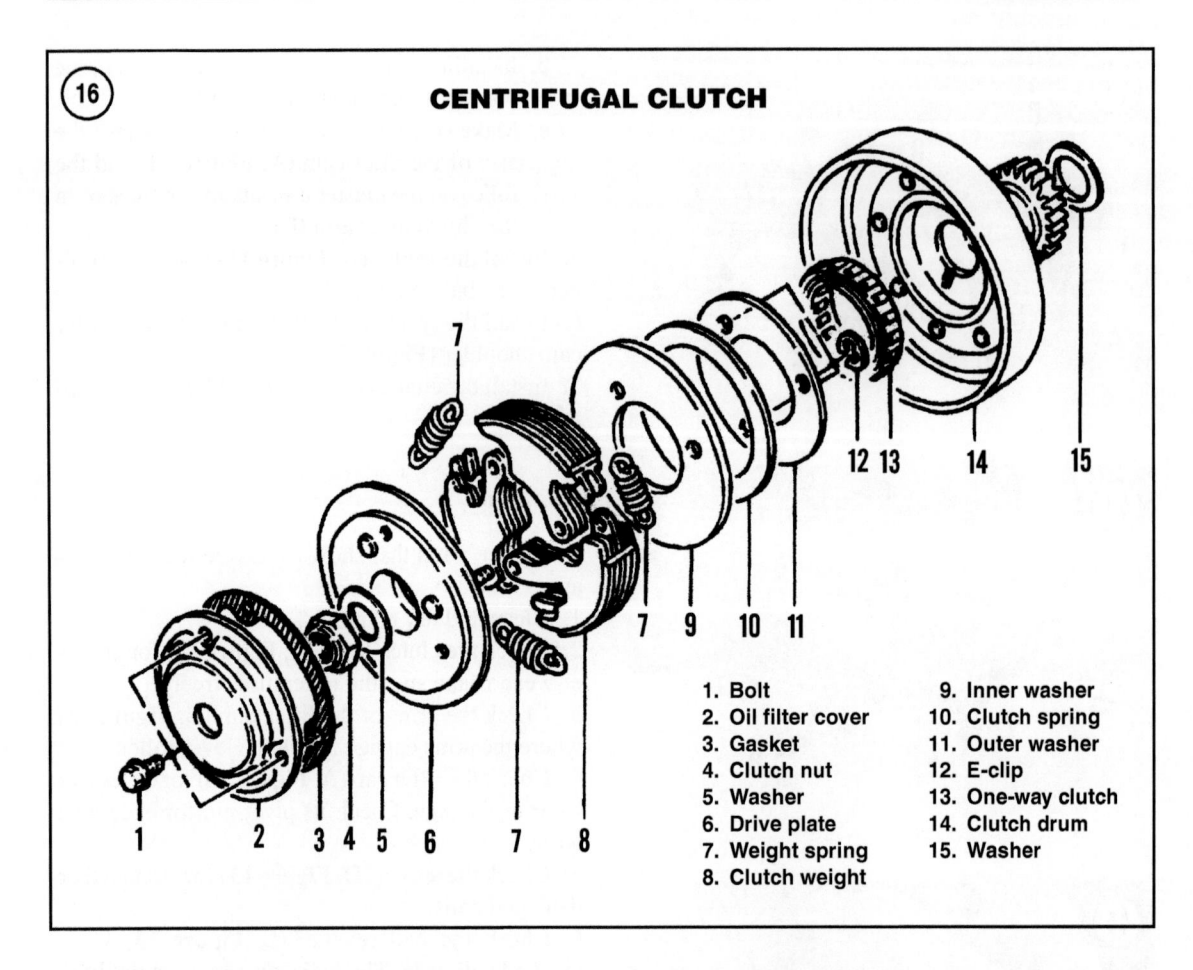

CHAPTER SIX

CENTRIFUGAL CLUTCH

1. Bolt
2. Oil filter cover
3. Gasket
4. Clutch nut
5. Washer
6. Drive plate
7. Weight spring
8. Clutch weight
9. Inner washer
10. Clutch spring
11. Outer washer
12. E-clip
13. One-way clutch
14. Clutch drum
15. Washer

1. The clutch drum must be locked in place when loosening and tightening the clutch locknut. The following two tools can be used to do this:
   a. Honda clutch holder (part No. 07HMB-HB70100 or 07923-HB3000B [**Figure 17**]).
   b. Universal flywheel holder (**Figure 18**).

NOTE
If the engine is mounted in the frame, it may be difficult to hold the clutch drum with a flywheel holder.

2. The clutch nut (**Figure 19**) is staked to a notch in the crankshaft. Purchase a new locknut before removing the centrifugal clutch.

Centrifugal Clutch Removal

1. Remove the clutch cover as described in this chapter.
2. Remove the mounting bolts (A, **Figure 20**) and oil filter cover (B) from the centrifugal clutch. 
3. Inspect the gasket (**Figure 21**) on the back of the oil filter cover. Replace the gasket if necessary.

CAUTION
Make sure to unstake the clutch nut where it contacts the crankshaft. This prevents the nut from damaging the crankshaft threads as the nut is being removed.

CLUTCH AND PRIMARY DRIVE GEAR

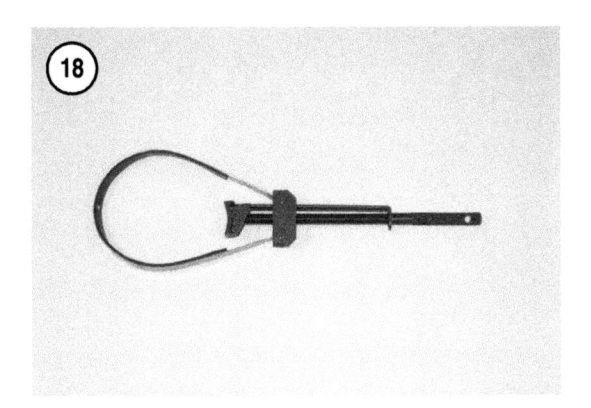

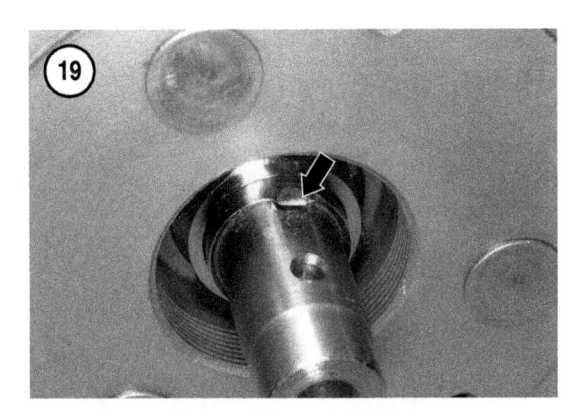

4. Using a die grinder, unstake the clutch nut from the groove in the crankshaft (**Figure 19**). Cover exposed parts so metal particles do not enter the clutch or engine.

NOTE
The centrifugal clutch nut has left-hand threads.

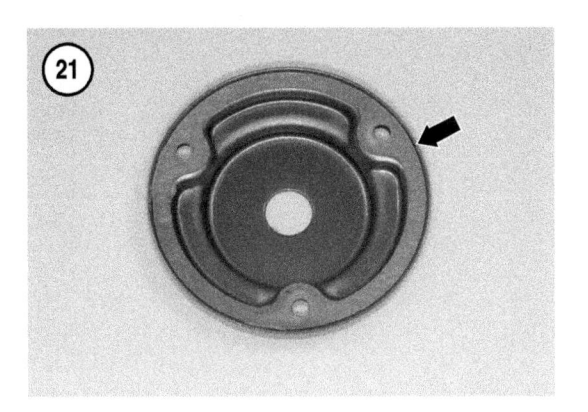

5. Hold the clutch drum with a clutch holder (**Figure 22**). Loosen and remove the centrifugal clutch nut (A, **Figure 23**) and washer (B). Discard the clutch nut.

6. Thread the clutch puller onto the drive plate threads. Hold the clutch puller body with a wrench and then turn its end bolt to pull the drive plate assembly off the crankshaft. Refer to **Figure 24**.

7. Rotate the change clutch, and align its cutout (A, **Figure 25**) with the primary drive gear (B). Remove the clutch drum (C, **Figure 25**) from the crankshaft.

8. Remove the washer (**Figure 26**) from the crankshaft.

9. Inspect the clutch drum and drive plate assemblies as described in this section.

Centrifugal Clutch Installation

1. Set the clutch drum on the bench so the one-way clutch side faces up (**Figure 27**).
2. Set the drive plate assembly into the clutch drum so the drive plate boss sits in the one-way clutch. Turn the drive plate assembly clockwise (**Figure 28**) and press it into the one-way clutch until it bottoms.
3. Lubricate the crankshaft, primary drive gear bore and washer with engine oil.
4. Install the washer (**Figure 26**) onto the crankshaft.
5. Align the splines of the drive plate with those of the crankshaft, and slide the centrifugal clutch (C, **Figure 25**) onto the crankshaft. Rotate the change clutch as necessary so the primary drive gear (B, **Figure 25**) aligns with the cutout in the change clutch (A).
6. Install the washer (B, **Figure 23**) onto the crankshaft.

NOTE
The centrifugal clutch nut has left-hand threads.

7. Apply engine oil to the threads and flange of a new centrifugal clutch nut, and install the nut (A, **Figure 23**).
8. Hold the centrifugal clutch with the same tool used during removal (**Figure 22**), and tighten the centrifugal clutch nut to 88 N•m (65 ft.-lb.).
9. Stake the edge of the clutch nut (**Figure 19**) to the notch in the crankshaft.
10. Clean the oil filter cover as described in *Engine Oil and Filter* in Chapter Three.
11. Install the oil filter cover (B, **Figure 20**). Apply ThreeBond 1333B to the threads of the mounting bolts and tighten the bolts (A, **Figure 20**) securely.
12. Install the clutch cover as described in this chapter.

Clutch Drum Inspection

Refer to **Table 1** when inspecting the clutch drum components. Replace parts that are out of specification or damaged.
1. Check the one-way clutch operation by performing the following:
   a. Set the clutch drum on the bench so the one-way clutch side faces up (**Figure 27**).

CLUTCH AND PRIMARY DRIVE GEAR

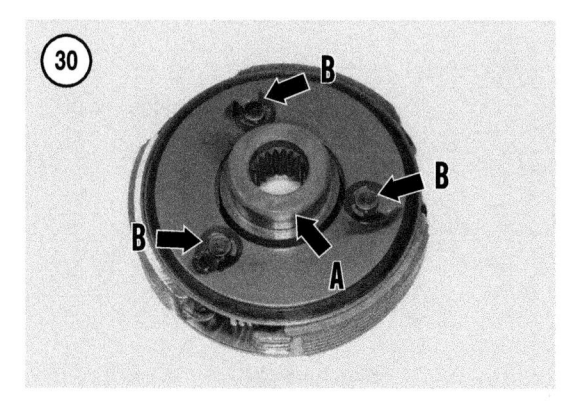

b. Set the drive plate assembly into the clutch drum so the drive plate boss sits in the one-way clutch. Turn the drive plate assembly (**Figure 28**) clockwise and press it into the one-way clutch until it bottoms.

c. Hold the clutch drum and turn the drive plate assembly. If should turn *clockwise* within the clutch drum but not counterclockwise.

2. Remove the drive plate assembly from the clutch drum.

3. Mark the one-way clutch (**Figure 27**) so its up side can be identified. The one-way clutch must be reinstalled with the same orientation during assembly.

4. Remove the one-way clutch (**Figure 29**) from the clutch drum. Inspect the one-way clutch for signs of heat damage, cracks or other damage. Replace the one-way clutch if there is visible damage or if it failed to operate as described in Step 1.

5. Inspect the drive plate bearing boss (A, **Figure 30**) for excessive wear or damage. Check for signs of overheating.

6. Check the exterior of the clutch drum for cracks or damage, and check the inside diameter for excessive wear or damage. Measure the clutch drum inside diameter with a vernier caliper (**Figure 31**).

7. Measure the inside diameter of the clutch drum bushing (**Figure 32**).

8. Check the clutch drum bushing (A, **Figure 33**) for burning, scoring or other signs of damage.

9. Inspect the primary drive gear (B, **Figure 33**) for broken or excessively worn teeth.

10. Measure the outside diameter of the crankshaft at the two points shown in **Figure 34**.

11. Lubricate the one-way clutch and its housing in the clutch drum with engine oil. Install the one-way

clutch in the housing so the side marked during removal faces out (**Figure 27**).

12. Inspect and service the centrifugal weight assembly as described in this section.

Drive Plate Disassembly/Inspection/Assembly

Refer to **Table 1** when inspecting drive plate assembly components. Replace parts that are out of specification or damaged.

1. Disassemble the drive plate assembly (**Figure 16**) by performing the following:

> *CAUTION*
> *Apply just enough pressure to expose the clip grooves in the drive plate pins. Excessive pressure could damage the drive plate assembly.*

   a. Secure the drive plate assembly in a vise by applying just enough pressure to expose the groove in the end of each drive plate pin.
   b. Remove the E-clips (B, **Figure 30**), and then remove the drive plate assembly from the vise.
   c. Remove the outer washer, clutch spring and inner washer.
   d. Remove the weight springs (7, **Figure 16**) and clutch weights (8).

2. Measure the lining thickness of each weight at the points shown in **Figure 35**. If any lining is out of specification, replace all the clutch weights as a set.

3. Check the clutch spring (10, **Figure 16**) for cracks or signs of heat damage. Measure the height of the clutch spring with a vernier caliper (**Figure 36**).

4. Check the weight springs (7, **Figure 16**) for cracks or stretched coils. Measure the free length of each spring (**Figure 37**) with a vernier caliper. If any weight spring is out of specification, replace all of the weight springs as a set.

5. Check the outer and inner washers. Replace them as necessary.

6. Inspect the drive plate for damaged splines, warp or damaged clutch weight pins. Check the E-clip groove in the end of each pin for damage.

7. Reassemble the drive plate assembly by performing the following:

   a. Lubricate the drive plate pins with engine oil.   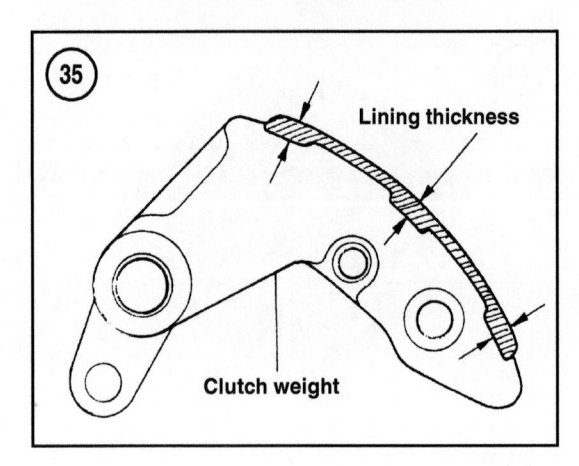
   b. Install the clutch weights and weight springs. Install the weight springs with their open ends facing down.
   c. Install the inner washer (9, **Figure 16**).
   d. Install the clutch spring (10, **Figure 16**) so its cupped side faces down toward the inner washer.
   e. Install the outer washer (11, **Figure 16**) so its locating pins face out.

CLUTCH AND PRIMARY DRIVE GEAR

Tools

Before removing the change clutch, note the following:

1. The clutch nut (**Figure 39**) is staked to a notch in the mainshaft. Purchase a new clutch nut before removing the change clutch.

2. When loosening and tightening the clutch nut, some means of holding the change clutch is required. The following list suggests methods for the home mechanic:

   a. A clutch center holder (Honda part No. 07GMB-KT70101 or 07HGB001010B [**Figure 40**] or its equivalent).

   b. An impact wrench can be used to loosen the clutch nut. However, when tightening the nut during clutch assembly, a separate tool setup is required to hold the clutch so the clutch nut can be tightened with a torque wrench.

   c. A spare gear (**Figure 41**) can be used to lock the clutch outer gear to the primary drive gear for tightening the clutch nut.

Removal/Disassembly

1. Remove the clutch release mechanism as described in this chapter.

2. Remove the centrifugal clutch as described in this chapter.

3. Evenly loosen the four lifter plate bolts (A, **Figure 42**) 1/4 turn at a time in a crisscross pattern. Remove the bolts (A, **Figure 42**), the lifter plate (B) and each clutch spring (**Figure 43**).

CAUTION
Make sure to unstake the clutch nut where it contacts the mainshaft. This prevents the nut from damaging the mainshaft threads as the nut is being removed.

4. Using a die grinder, unstake the clutch nut from the groove in the mainshaft (**Figure 39**). Cover the exposed parts so metal particles do not enter the clutch or engine.

5. If the clutch plate assembly is not being serviced, install two clutch springs, washers and clutch spring bolts so the clutch plate assembly (the clutch center, clutch plates, friction plates and pressure

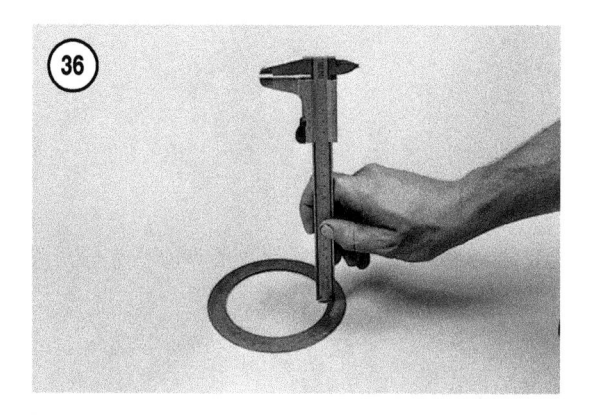

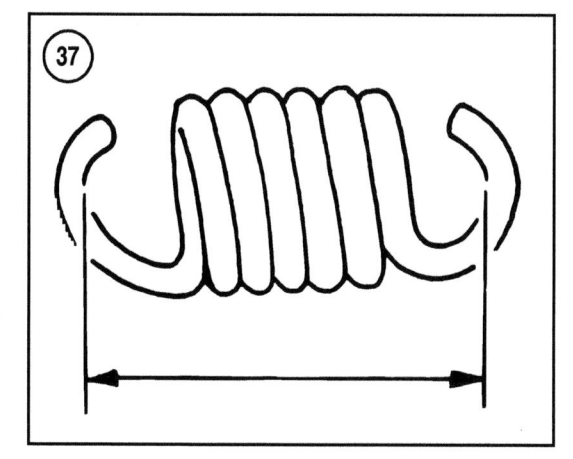

CAUTION
Apply just enough pressure to expose the clip groove in the drive plate pins. Excessive pressure could damage the drive plate assembly.

f. Secure the drive plate in a vise by applying just enough pressure to compress the clutch spring and expose the clip grooves in the end of each drive plate pin. Install the E-clips with the open end of each E-clip against its corresponding locating pin on the outer washer. Check that each E-clip seats in its groove completely.

g. Remove pressure from the drive plate and check that the outer washer seats evenly against each E-clip.

CHANGE CLUTCH

The change clutch (**Figure 38**) can be removed with the engine installed in the frame.

CHANGE CLUTCH

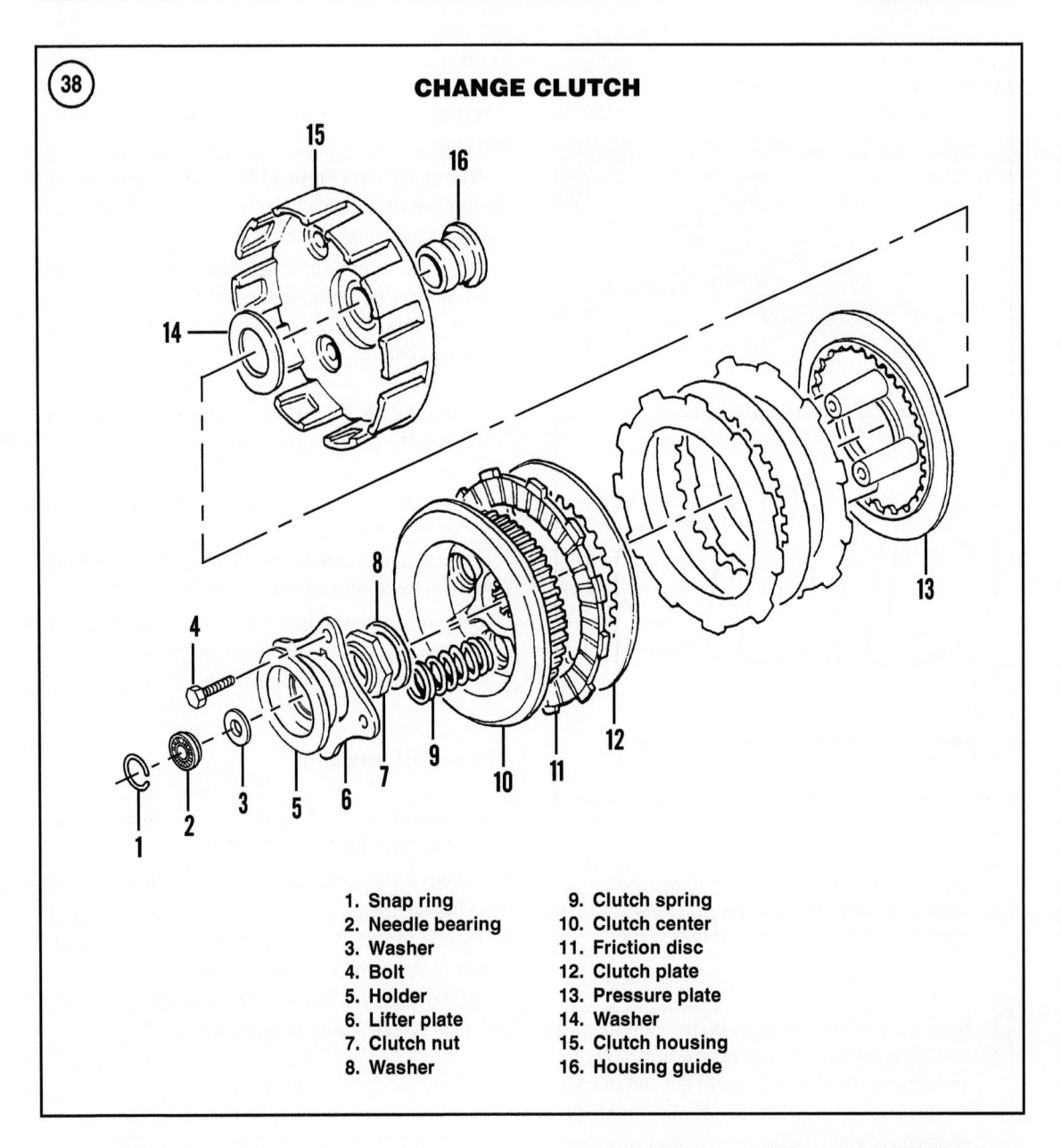

1. Snap ring
2. Needle bearing
3. Washer
4. Bolt
5. Holder
6. Lifter plate
7. Clutch nut
8. Washer
9. Clutch spring
10. Clutch center
11. Friction disc
12. Clutch plate
13. Pressure plate
14. Washer
15. Clutch housing
16. Housing guide

plate) are not disassembled during removal. Refer to A, **Figure 44**.

NOTE
*If a clutch center holder is unavailable, remove the clutch nut with an air or electric impact wrench Refer to **Tools** in this section.*

6. Hold the clutch center with the clutch center holder (**Figure 45**). Loosen and remove the change clutch nut (B, **Figure 44**) and washer (C). If a clutch

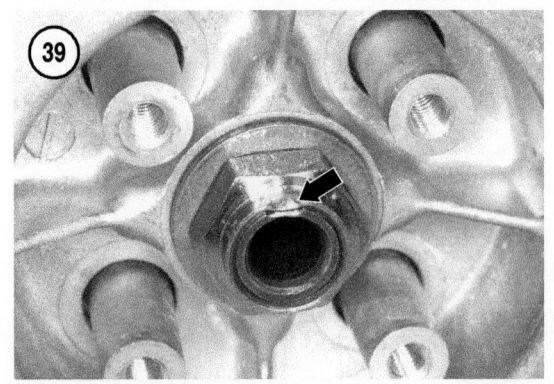

CLUTCH AND PRIMARY DRIVE GEAR

163

40 — Nut, Slots numbered 4, 5 and 6, Holder plate, Collars

41

42 A, B

43

44 A, B, C

45 Clutch center holder

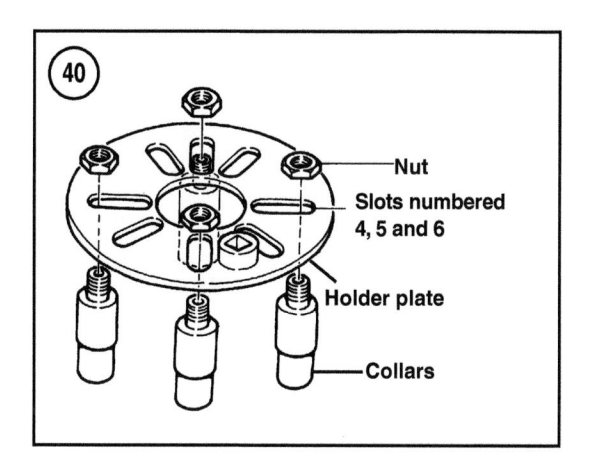

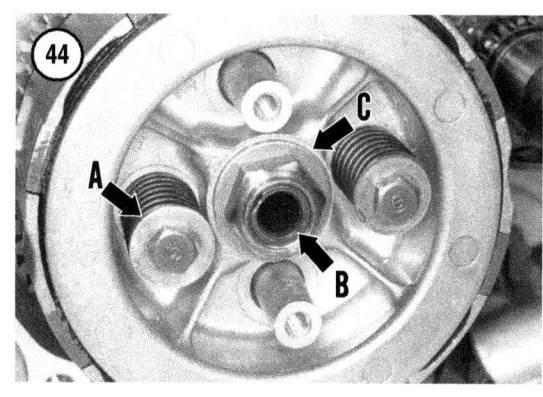

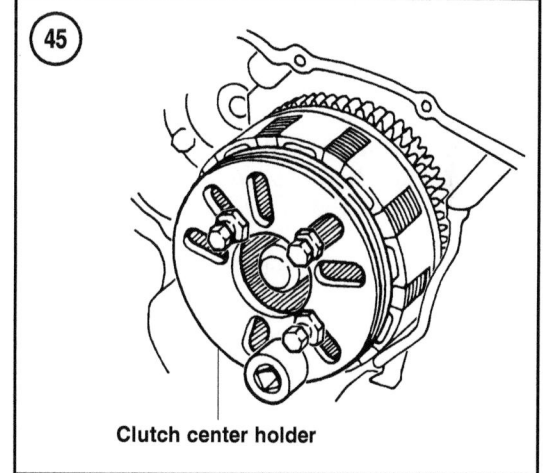

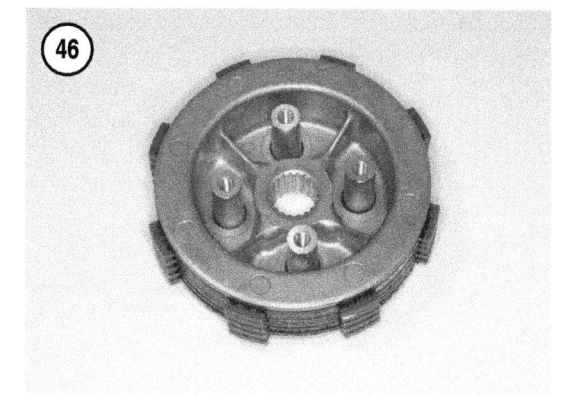

46

center holder is not available, use an impact wrench to remove the clutch nut.

7. Remove the clutch center, clutch plates, friction discs and the pressure plate as an assembly (**Figure 46**).

8. Remove the washer (A, **Figure 47**) and the clutch housing (B).

9. Remove the clutch housing guide (**Figure 48**) from the mainshaft.

10. Inspect the change clutch as described in this section.

Assembly/Installation

Refer to **Figure 38**.

1. Lubricate the mainshaft and all clutch parts with engine oil.

> *CAUTION*
> *Never assemble the clutch without lubricating the clutch plates and friction discs with oil, especially if the clutch was cleaned in solvent or new discs and plates are being installed. Otherwise, these plates may grab and lock up when the engine is first started and cause clutch damage.*

2. Install the clutch housing guide (**Figure 48**) onto the mainshaft.

3. Install the clutch housing (B, **Figure 47**) and then install the washer (A).

4. Assemble the clutch plate assembly by performing the following:

   a. Place the clutch center (**Figure 49**) on the workbench.

   b. Lubricate the friction discs and clutch plates with engine oil.

   c. Install a friction disc and clutch plate. Continue to alternately install a friction disc and then a clutch plate until all the discs and plates are installed. A friction disc should be installed last (A, **Figure 50**).

   d. Install the pressure plate (B, **Figure 50**) and seat it against the outer friction disc (**Figure 51**). Check that the clutch plate inner tabs engage the clutch center splines and that the clutch center sits flush against the friction disc as shown in **Figure 52**.

   e. Turn the assembly over so the clutch center (A, **Figure 53**) faces up. Adjust the friction discs as necessary so all their tabs align (B, **Figure 53**).

   f. If not using a clutch center holder, install two clutch springs, washers and clutch spring bolts as shown in C, **Figure 53**. Tighten the bolt to hold the clutch plate assembly to-

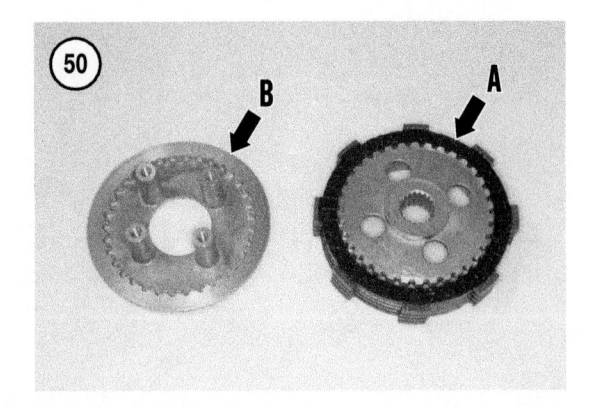

CLUTCH AND PRIMARY DRIVE GEAR

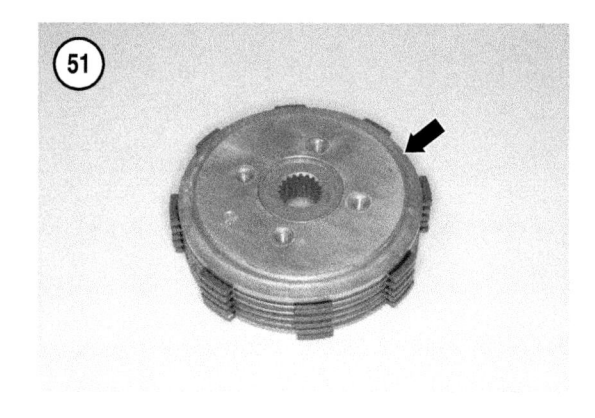

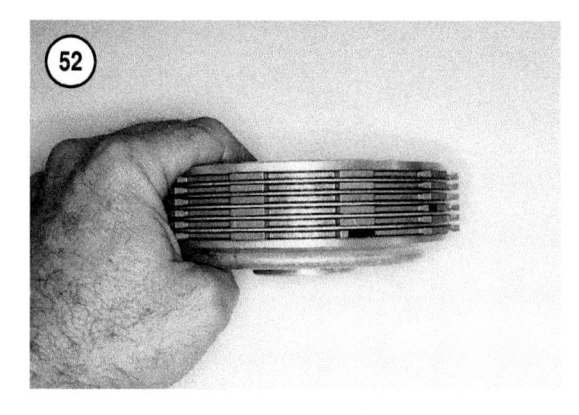

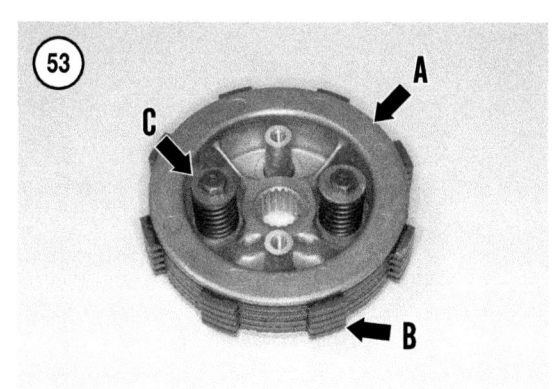

gether. This keeps the clutch center from slipping when tightening the clutch nut.

5. Align the splines of the clutch center with those on the mainshaft, and install the clutch plate assembly (A, **Figure 54**) into the clutch housing. Make sure the friction plate tabs (B, **Figure 54**) sit inside the slots in the clutch housing.
6. Install the washer (C, **Figure 54**) onto the mainshaft.
7. Apply oil to the threads and flange of a new clutch nut, and install the nut (B, **Figure 44**).
8. Using one of the methods described in *Tools*, lock the clutch center to the clutch housing. Note the following:
    a. If using a gear (**Figure 41**) to lock the clutch outer gear to the primary drive gear, install two or more clutch springs, flat washers and bolts. This prevents the clutch center from slipping when tightening the clutch locknut.
    c. When using the clutch center holder (**Figure 45**), remove any clutch spring bolts, washers and clutch springs that were installed in Step 4.
9. Tighten the change clutch nut to 79 N•m (58 ft.-lb.).
10. Remove the tools used to hold the clutch.
11. Using a punch, stake the clutch nut shoulder into the mainshaft notch. Refer to **Figure 39**.
12. If installed, remove the clutch spring bolts and flat washers.
13. Install the clutch springs (**Figure 43**).
14. Install the lifter plate (B, **Figure 42**) and the four clutch spring bolts (A). Finger-tighten the bolts.
15. Evenly tighten the bolts in a crisscross pattern in 2-3 steps, and then tighten the bolts to 12 N•m (106 in.-lb.).
16. Install the clutch release mechanism and the centrifugal clutch as described in this chapter.

Inspection

When inspecting the change clutch components (**Figure 38**), compare any measurements to the clutch specifications in **Table 1**. Replace parts that are out of specification or damaged.

1. Clean all parts in solvent and dry with compressed air.
2. Measure the free length of each clutch spring (**Figure 55**) with a vernier caliper.

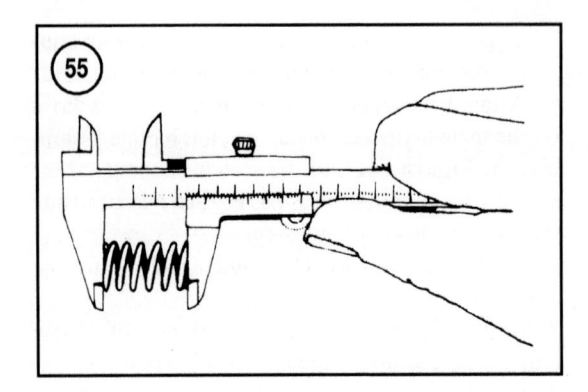

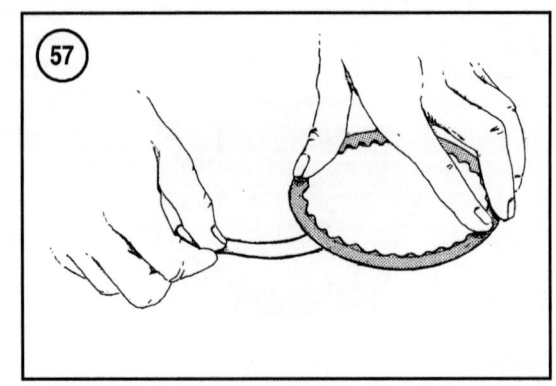

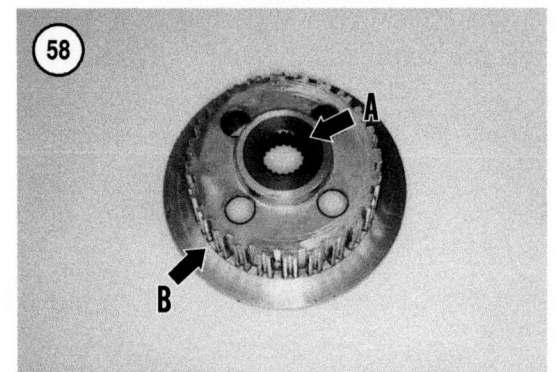

3. Measure the thickness of each friction disc at several places around its circumference (**Figure 56**). Replace the friction discs as a set if any one is too thin or damaged. Do not replace only one or two friction discs.

4. Place each clutch plate on a surface plate or a thick piece of glass, and measure for warp with a feeler gauge (**Figure 57**). Replace all the clutch plates as a set if one is out of specification.

5. Check the clutch center splines (A, **Figure 58**) and plate grooves (B) for cracks or excessive wear.

6. Check the clutch housing slots (A, **Figure 59**) for grooves, steps, cracks or other damage. These slots must be smooth for proper clutch operation. Repair light damage with a fine-cut file or oilstone. Replace the clutch housing if the damage is non-repairable.

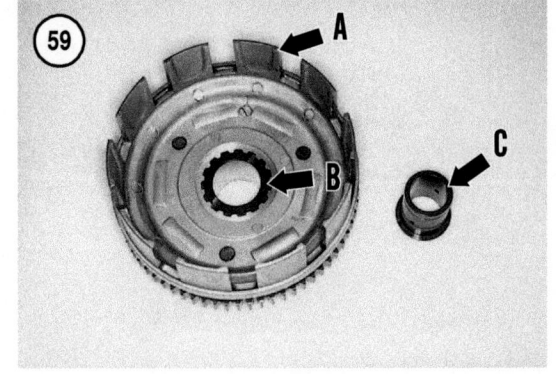

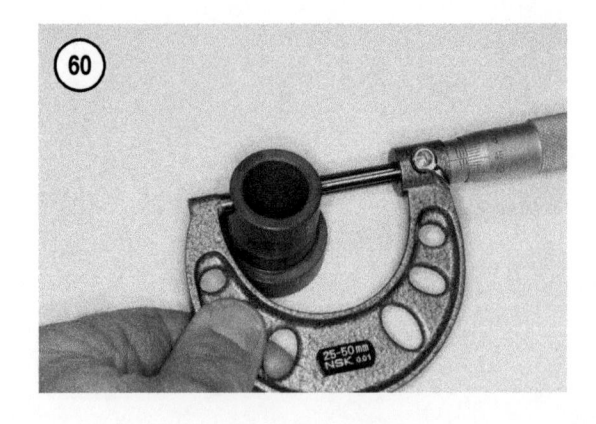

CLUTCH AND PRIMARY DRIVE GEAR

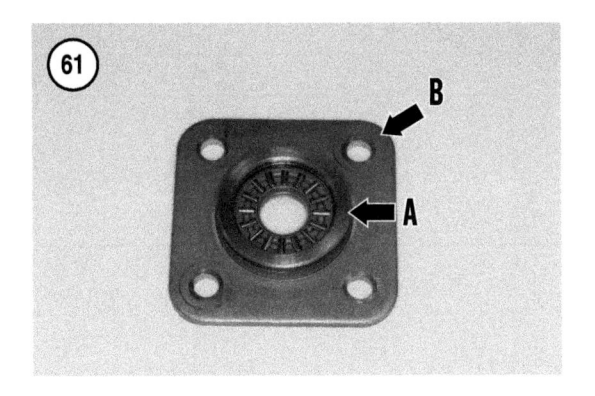

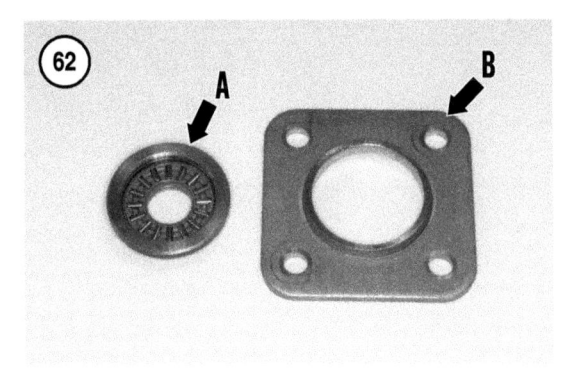

7. Check the clutch housing bore (B, **Figure 59**) for excessive wear or damage. Measure the inside diameter of the clutch housing bore.
8. Check the clutch housing outer gear for damaged gear teeth.
9. Check the clutch housing guide (C, **Figure 59**) inside and outside surfaces for cracks, deep scoring or other damage. If there is no visible damage, measure the outside diameter of the clutch outer guide (**Figure 60**).
10. Check the pressure plate (B, **Figure 50**) for thread damage, cracked spring towers or other damage.
11. Remove the holder (A, **Figure 61**) from the lifter plate (B) and perform the following:

   a. Check the lifter bearing by turning it within the holder (A, **Figure 62**). The bearing should turn smoothly with no signs of roughness or noise.

   b. Visually inspect the holder (A, **Figure 62**) and lifter plate (B) for damage.

   c. Install the holder (A, **Figure 61**) into the lifter plate (B).

Table 1 CLUTCH SPECIFICATIONS

Item	Standard mm (in.)	Service limit mm (in.)
Crankshaft outside diameter (at primary drive gear)	23.959-23.980 (0.9433-0.9441)	23.93 (0.942)
Centrifugal clutch		
Clutch drum inside diameter	116.00-116.20 (4.567-4.575)	116.5 (4.59)
Clutch drum bushing inside diameter	24.000-24.021 (0.9449-0.9457)	24.05 (0.947)
Weight lining thickness	2.0 (0.08)	1.2 (0.05)
Clutch spring height	3.0 (0.12)	2.85 (0.112)
Clutch weight spring free length	30.75 (1.211)	31.6 (1.24)
Change Clutch		
Spring free length	35.2 (1.39)	34.5 (1.36)
Friction disc thickness	2.9-3.0 (0.11-0.12)	2.6 (0.10)
Clutch plate warp	–	0.20 (0.008)
Clutch housing guide outside diameter	27.959-27.980 (1.1007-1.1016)	27.92 (1.099)
Clutch housing bore inside diameter	28.000-28.021 (1.1024-1.1032)	28.05 (1.104)

Table 2 CLUTCH TORQUE SPECIFICATIONS

Item	N•m	in.-lb.	ft.-lb.
Centrifugal clutch nut	88	–	65
Change clutch nut	79	–	58
Change clutch spring bolts	12	106	–
Clutch cover bolt	12	106	–
Oil line flange bolts	9	80	

CHAPTER SEVEN

TRANSMISSION AND INTERNAL SHIFT MECHANISM

This chapter describes service to the forward and reverse transmission assemblies identified in **Figure 1**:

1. Mainshaft (A).
2. Reverse idle gear assembly (B).
3. Countershaft (C).
4. Shift drum (D).
5. Shift fork shaft and shift forks (E).

All TRX250EX models use a 5-speed transmission with reverse. The engine must be removed and the crankcase disassembled (Chapter Five) to service the transmission and internal shift mechanism.

When inspecting transmission components, compare measurements to the specifications in **Tables 1-5**. Replace any component that is damaged, worn to the service limit or out of specification. During assembly, tighten fasteners as specified.

Tables 1-6 are at the end of this chapter.

TRANSMISSION OVERHAUL

Removal/Installation

Remove and install the transmission and internal shift assemblies as described in *Crankcase and Crankshaft* in Chapter Five.

Preliminary Inspection

After the transmission shaft assemblies have been removed from the crankcase, clean and inspect each assembly before disassembling it. Place a shaft assembly into a large can or plastic bucket, and thoroughly clean the assembly with a stiff brush and a petroleum-based solvent, such as kerosene. Dry the assembly with compressed air, or let it drip dry on rags.

1. After the shaft assemblies have been cleaned, visually inspect the components of each assembly for excessive wear. Any burrs, pitting or roughness on

the teeth of a gear causes wear on its mated gear. Minor roughness can be cleaned up with an oilstone, but there is little point in attempting to remove deep scars.

> **CAUTION**
> *Replace defective gears. It is best to replace its mated gear on the other shaft as well, even though the mate may not show as much wear or damage.*

2. Carefully check the engagement dogs. If any is chipped, worn, rounded or missing, replace the affected gear.
3. Rotate the transmission bearings by hand. Check for roughness, noise and radial play. Replace any suspect bearing.
4. If the transmission assemblies are in satisfactory condition and are not being disassembled, apply assembly or engine oil to all components, and reinstall the assemblies into the crankcase as described in Chapter Five.

> **NOTE**
> *Watch for any additional shims not shown in the illustrations or photographs. During a previous repair additional shims may have been installed to take up excess clearance created by worn components. If the transmission is being reassembled with the old parts, install these shims in their original locations because the shims have developed a wear pattern. If new parts are being used, discard the additional shims.*

Service Notes

1. As each part is removed from its shaft, set it in an egg crate in the exact order of removal and with the same orientation it had when installed on the shaft.
2. The snap rings fit tightly on the transmission shafts. Replace all snap rings during assembly.
3. Snap rings turn and fold over making removal and installation difficult. To ease the removal, open a snap ring with a pair of snap ring pliers. At the same time grasp the back of the snap ring with another pair of pliers, and slide the snap ring off the shaft. Repeat this process during installation.

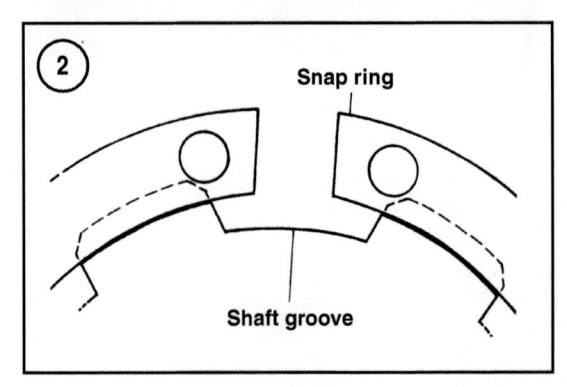

4. When installing a snap ring, align the end gap in the snap ring with a groove in the shaft (**Figure 2**).
5. When installing a bushing, align the hole in the bushing with the oil hole in the shaft.

Mainshaft Disassembly

Refer to **Figure 3**.

1. Clean and dry the assembled mainshaft (**Figure 4**).
2. Remove the thrust washer.
3. Remove fifth gear and its bushing.
4. Remove the second thrust washer.
5. Remove third gear.
6. Remove the snap ring and splined washer. Discard the snap ring.
7. Remove fourth gear and its bushing.
8. Remove the thrust washer.

> **NOTE**
> *Mainshaft second and first gears are an integral part of the mainshaft. They cannot be removed.*

TRANSMISSION AND INTERNAL SHIFT MECHANISM

MAINSHAFT

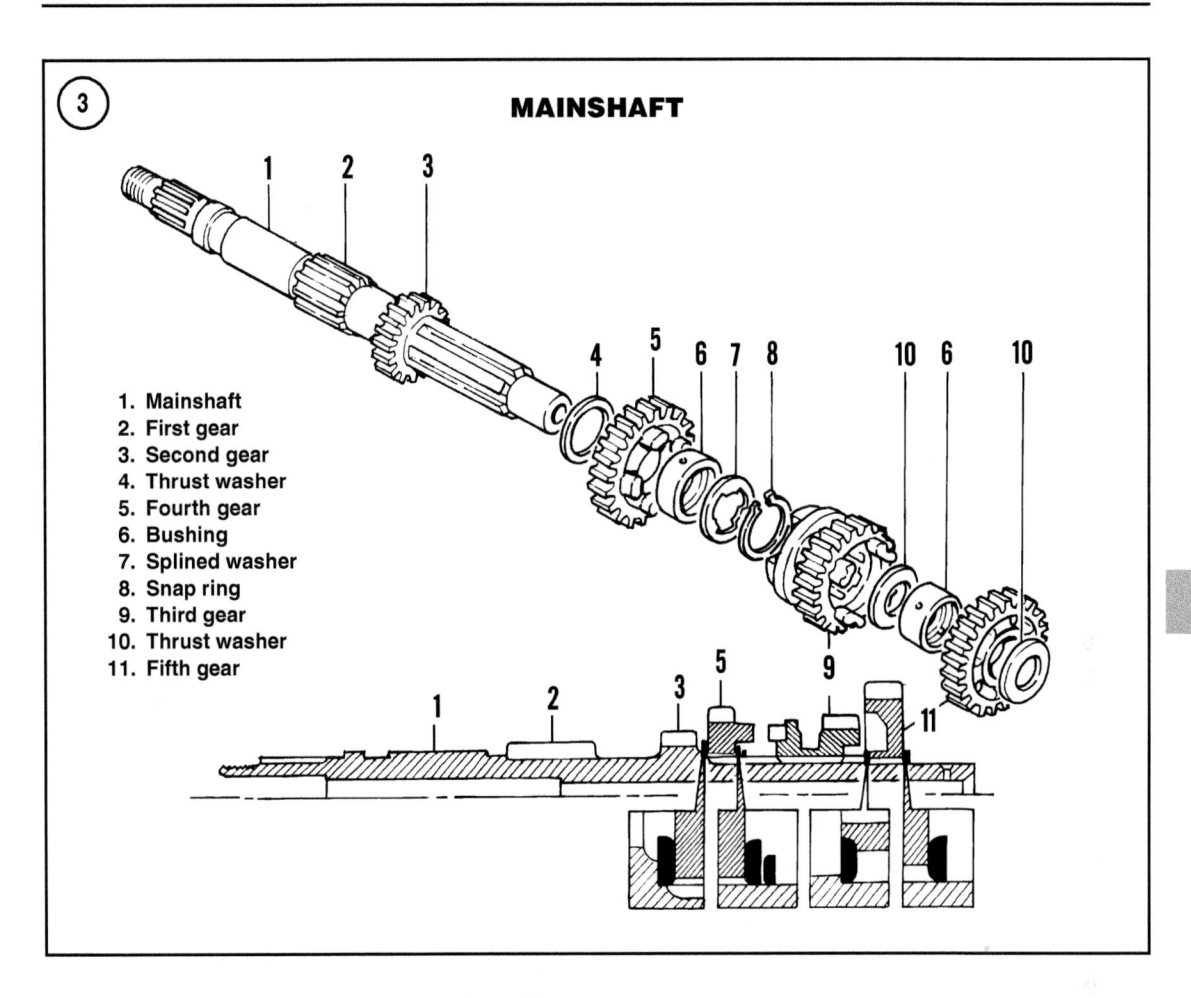

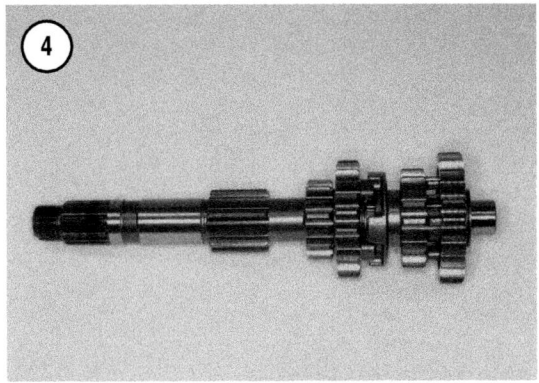

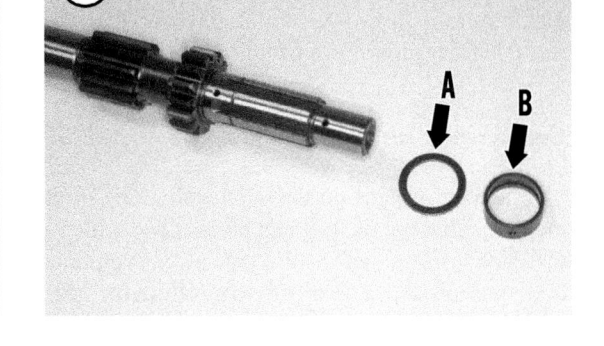

1. Mainshaft
2. First gear
3. Second gear
4. Thrust washer
5. Fourth gear
6. Bushing
7. Splined washer
8. Snap ring
9. Third gear
10. Thrust washer
11. Fifth gear

9. Inspect the mainshaft assembly as described in *Transmission Inspection* in this chapter.

Mainshaft Assembly

Refer to **Figure 3**.

1. Lubricate all sliding surfaces with engine oil.

2. Install the thrust washer (A, **Figure 5**) and slide it against second gear. The flat side of the thrust washer must face in toward second gear.

3. Align the hole in the fourth gear bushing (B, **Figure 5**) with the oil hole in the mainshaft, and slide the bushing up against the thrust washer (**Figure 6**).

4. Install fourth gear over the shaft and onto the fourth gear bushing. The gear's engagement dogs

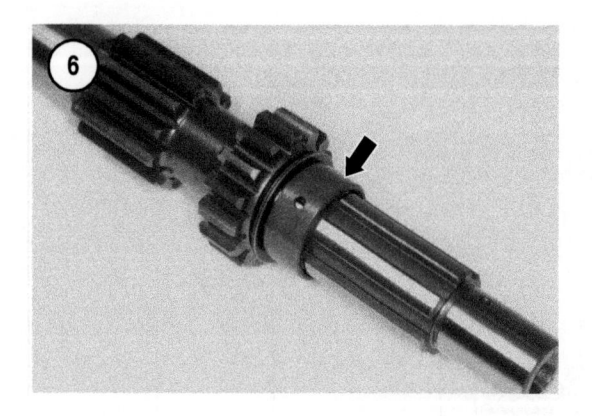

must face out away from second gear as shown in A, **Figure 7**.

5. Install the splined washer (A, **Figure 8**) and slide it against fourth gear. The flat side of the washer must face away from fourth gear.

6. Install a new snap ring (B, **Figure 8**) so its flat side faces away from the splined washer. Seat the snap ring in the snap ring groove, and rotate the snap ring as necessary so its end gap aligns with a shaft groove. Refer to B, **Figure 7**.

7. Install third gear (A, **Figure 9**) so its shift fork groove faces toward fourth gear.

8. Install the thrust washer (B, **Figure 9**) so its flat side faces toward third gear and install the fifth gear bushing (C).

9. Install fifth gear (A, **Figure 10**) onto the bushing so the flat side of the gear faces away from third gear.

10. Install the thrust washer (B, **Figure 10**) so its flat side faces away from fifth gear.

Countershaft Disassembly

A number of parts on the countershaft are symmetrical. This means they can be installed with either side facing in either direction. However, on a used transmission, a wear pattern develops on some of these parts. To prevent excessive wear or transmission noise after assembly, mark the spline collar, reverse shifter and spline bushings with a grease pencil so they can be installed in their original operating positions.

Refer to **Figure 11**.

NOTE
*The countershaft first gear (A, **Figure** 12), first gear bushing (B) and thrust*

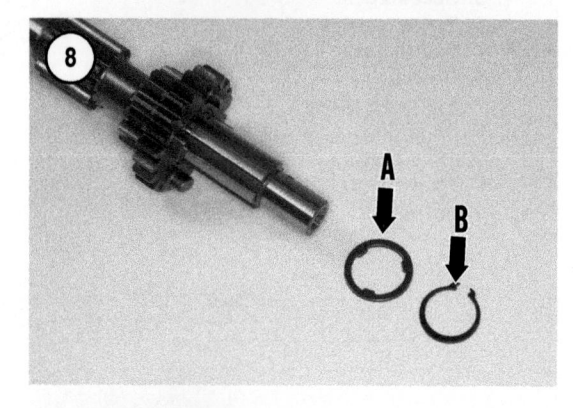

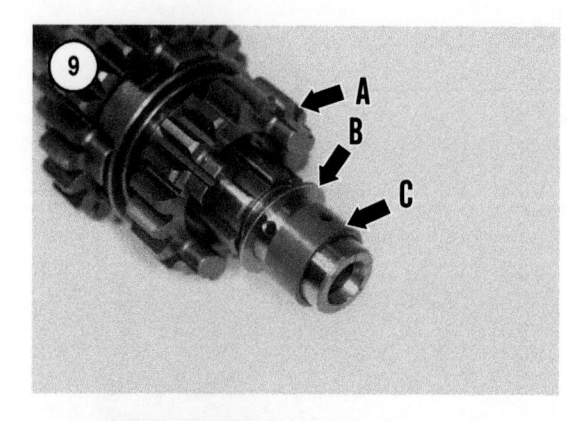

TRANSMISSION AND INTERNAL SHIFT MECHANISM

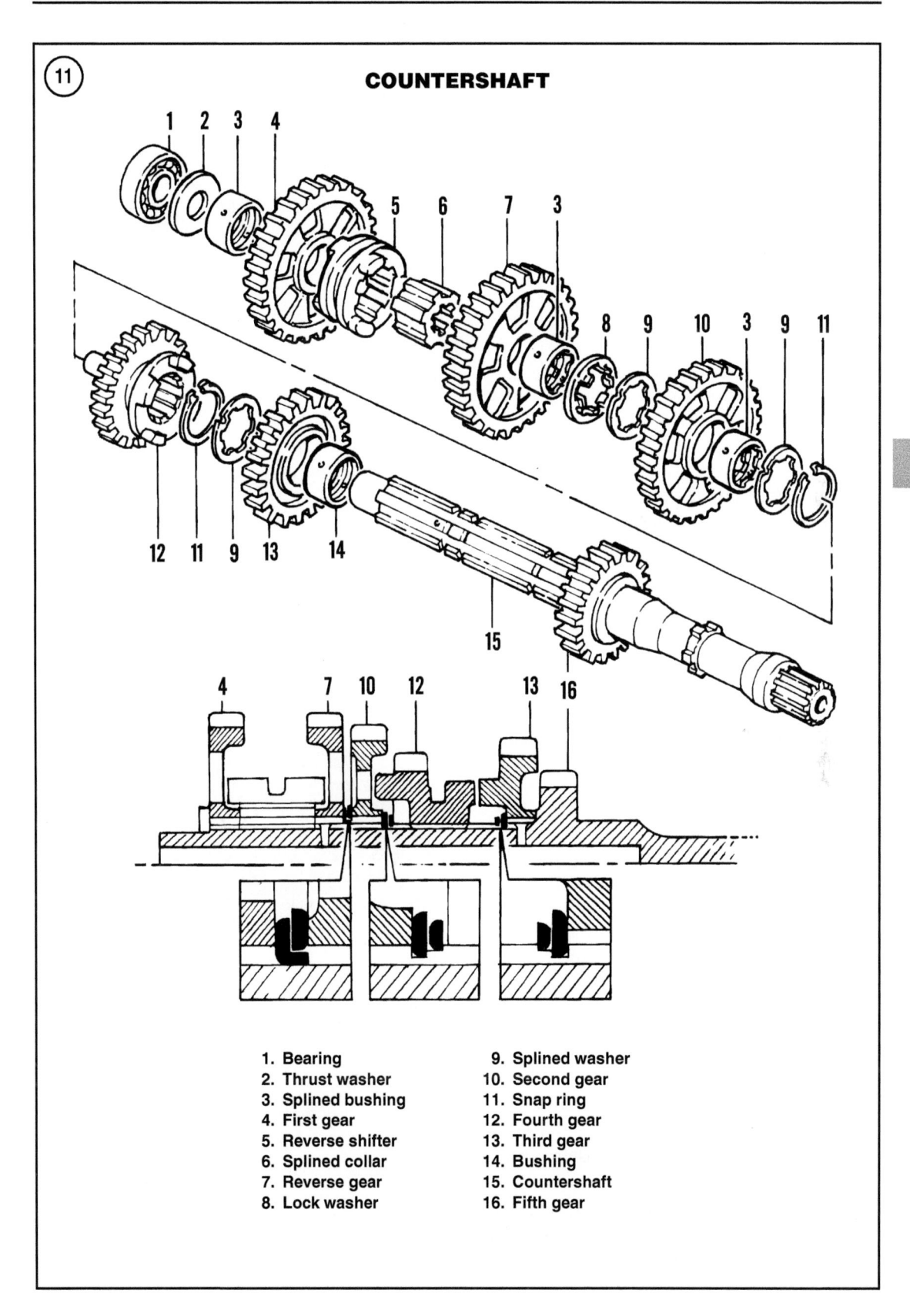

COUNTERSHAFT

1. Bearing
2. Thrust washer
3. Splined bushing
4. First gear
5. Reverse shifter
6. Splined collar
7. Reverse gear
8. Lock washer
9. Splined washer
10. Second gear
11. Snap ring
12. Fourth gear
13. Third gear
14. Bushing
15. Countershaft
16. Fifth gear

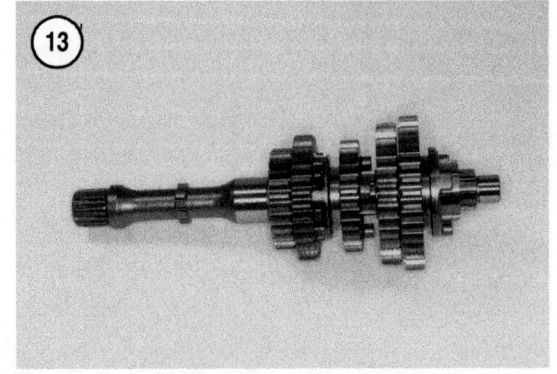

washer (C) were removed during transmission removal (Chapter Five).

1. Clean and dry the assembled countershaft (**Figure 13**).
2. Remove the reverse shifter and its splined collar.
3. Remove the reverse gear and its splined bushing.
4. Disengage the lockwasher teeth from the splined washer. Remove the lockwasher and the splined washer.
5. Remove the second gear and its splined bushing.
6. Remove the splined washer and snap ring. Discard the snap ring.
7. Remove fourth gear.
8. Remove and discard the snap ring, and then remove the splined washer.
9. Remove third gear and its bushing.

NOTE
Fifth gear is an integral part of the countershaft. It cannot be removed.

10. Inspect the countershaft assembly as described in *Transmission Inspection* in this chapter.

Countershaft Assembly

Refer to **Figure 11**.

1. Lubricate all sliding surfaces with engine oil.
2. Install the third gear bushing (A, **Figure 14**) onto the countershaft, and slide the bushing against fifth gear.
3. Install third gear (B, **Figure 14**) onto the countershaft and over the third gear bushing. The engagement dogs on third gear must face away from fifth gear. Refer to A, **Figure 15**.

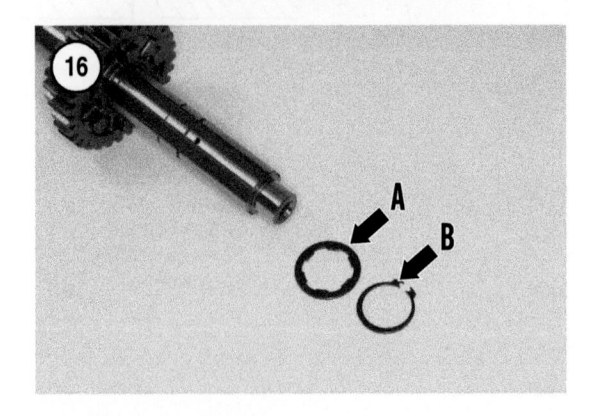

TRANSMISSION AND INTERNAL SHIFT MECHANISM

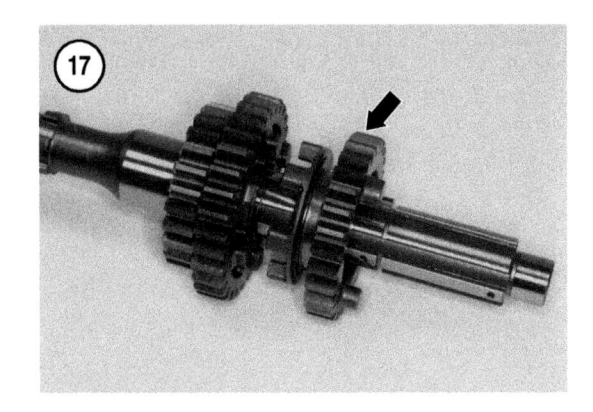

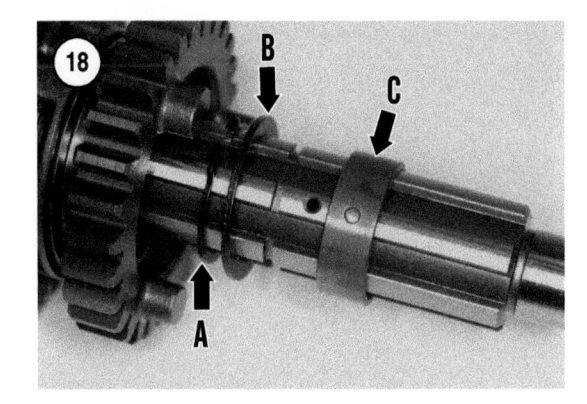

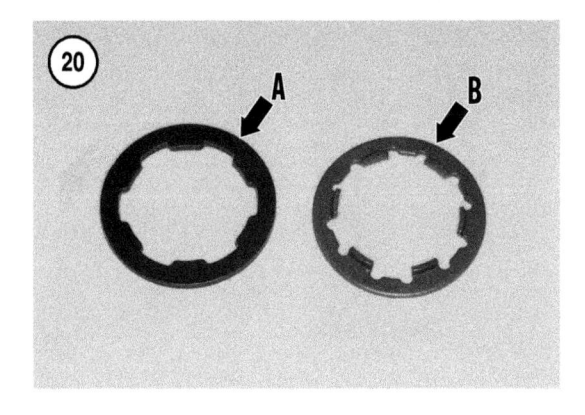

4. Install the splined washer (A, **Figure 16**), and slide it against third gear. The flat side of the splined washer must face away from third gear.

5. Install a new snap ring (B, **Figure 16**) and seat it in the snap ring groove next to the third gear splined washer. The flat side of the snap ring must face away from the washer. Rotate the snap ring as necessary so its end gap aligns with a groove in the shaft. Refer to B, **Figure 15**.

6. Install fourth gear (**Figure 17**) so the side with the shift fork groove faces toward third gear.

7. Install a new snap ring (A, **Figure 18**) and seat it in the snap ring groove closest to fourth gear. The flat side of the snap ring must face in toward fourth gear, and the snap ring end gap must align with a groove in the countershaft (**Figure 2**).

8. Install a splined washer (B, **Figure 18**), and slide it against the snap ring. The flat side of splined washer must face toward the snap ring.

9. Align the hole in the second gear splined bushing (C, **Figure 18**) with the oil hole in the countershaft, and slide the bushing against the splined washer.

10. Install second gear (**Figure 19**), and seat it onto the second gear splined bushing. The flat side of the gear must face away from fourth gear.

11. Install the lockwasher assembly by performing the following:

   a. Install the splined washer (A, **Figure 20**) onto the countershaft and seat it against second gear.

   b. Rotate the splined washer (**Figure 21**) so its splines align with the countershaft splines.

   c. Position the lockwasher (B, **Figure 20**) with its teeth pointing toward the splined washer.

d. Slide the lockwasher over the countershaft, and insert its teeth into the grooves in the splined washer (**Figure 22**).

12. Align the hole in the reverse gear splined bushing (**Figure 23**) with the oil hole in the countershaft, and slide the bushing against the lockwasher assembly.

13. Install the reverse gear (A, **Figure 24**) onto the shaft, and seat the gear on the bushing. The flat side of reverse gear must face toward second gear.

14. Install the splined collar (B, **Figure 24**) onto the countershaft, and seat it against the reverse gear.

15. Install the reverse shifter (**Figure 25**). Make sure its engagement dogs properly engage the reverse gear.

16. The countershaft assembly is complete. First gear (A, **Figure 12**), the first gear bushing (B) and the thrust washer (C) are installed during transmission installation (Chapter Five).

REVERSE IDLE GEAR ASSEMBLY

Disassembly/Assembly

1. The reverse idle gear assembly (**Figure 26**) is disassembled when it is removed from the crankcase. Follow the procedure described in *Crankcase and Crankshaft* in Chapter Five.

2. Clean the reverse idle gear components in solvent. Dry them with compressed air.

3. Inspect the reverse idle gear assembly as described in *Transmission Inspection* in this chapter.

NOTE
*During crankcase assembly, install both thrust washers with their chamfered sides facing toward the reverse idle gear. Refer to **Figure 26**.*

4. The reverse idle gear assembly is assembled when installed into the crankcase. Follow the procedures in *Crankcase and Crankshaft* in Chapter Five.

TRANSMISSION INSPECTION

Mainshaft

When inspecting mainshaft components (**Figure 27**), compare measurements to the mainshaft specifications in **Table 2** at the end of this chapter. Re-

TRANSMISSION AND INTERNAL SHIFT MECHANISM

REVERSE IDLE GEAR ASSEMBLY

1. Thrust washer
2. Reverse idle gear
3. Shaft

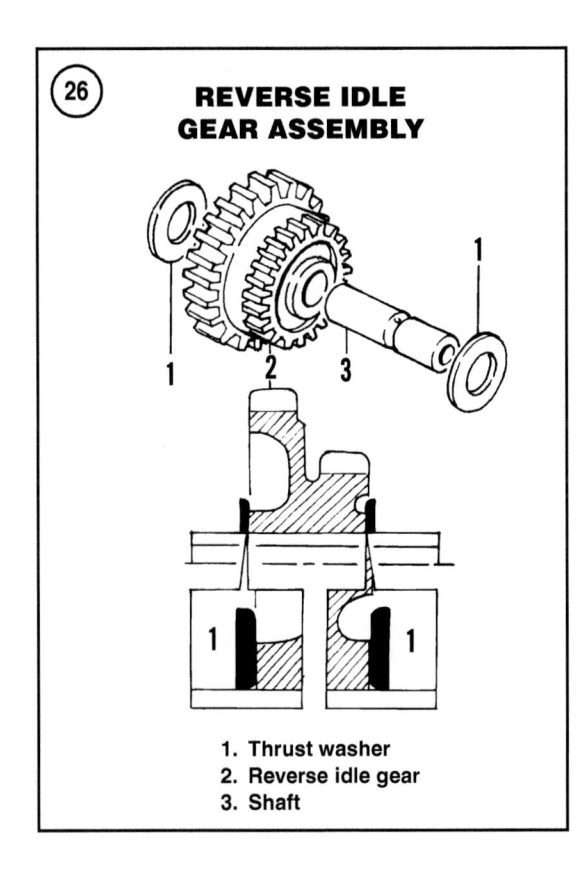

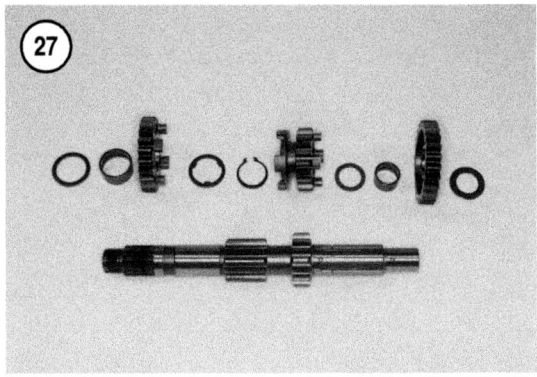

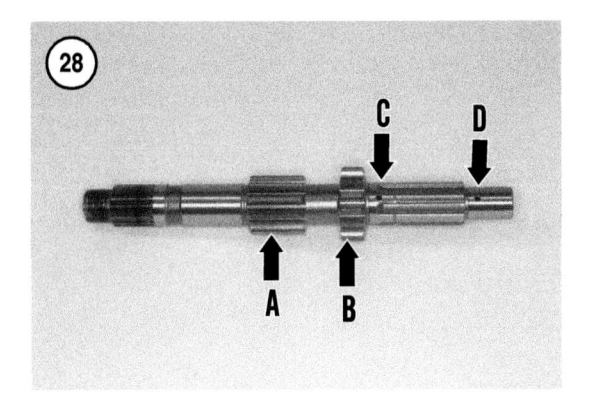

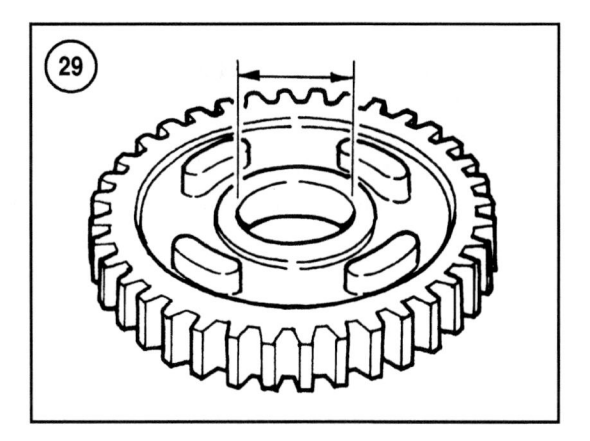

place parts that are damaged or out of specification. When replacing a gear, also replace its mated gear on the countershaft, even though the mate may not show as much wear or damage.

1. Clean and dry the mainshaft components. Flush the shaft and bushing oil holes with compressed air.
2. Inspect the mainshaft (**Figure 28**) for:
    a. Worn or damages splines.
    b. Missing, broken or chipped first (A, **Figure 28**) and second (B) gear teeth.
    c. Excessively worn or damaged bearing surfaces.
    d. Cracked or rounded-off snap ring groove.
    e. Plugged oil holes.
3. Check each mainshaft gear (**Figure 27**) for:
    a. Missing, broken or chipped teeth.
    b. Worn, damaged or rounded engagement dogs.
    c. Worn or damaged splines.
    d. Cracked or scored gear bore.
4. Check each mainshaft bushing for:
    a. Excessively worn or damaged bearing surfaces.
    b. Worn or damaged splines.
    c. Cracked or scored gear bore.
5. Measure the mainshaft outside diameter at the fourth (C, **Figure 28**) and fifth (D) gear operating positions, and record the dimensions.
6. Measure the inside diameter of the mainshaft fourth and fifth gears (**Figure 29**), and record the dimensions.
7. Measure the inside and outside diameters of the mainshaft fourth- and fifth-gear bushings (**Figure 30**), and record the dimensions.

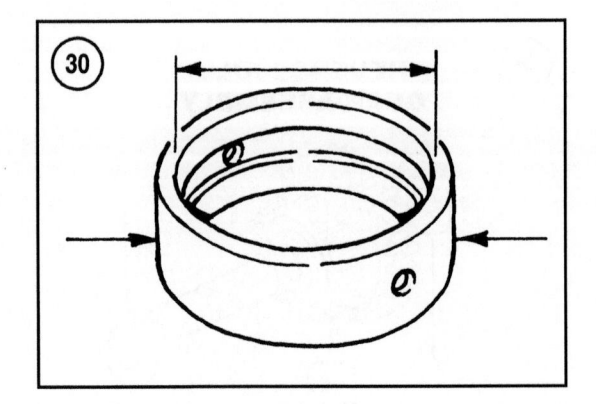

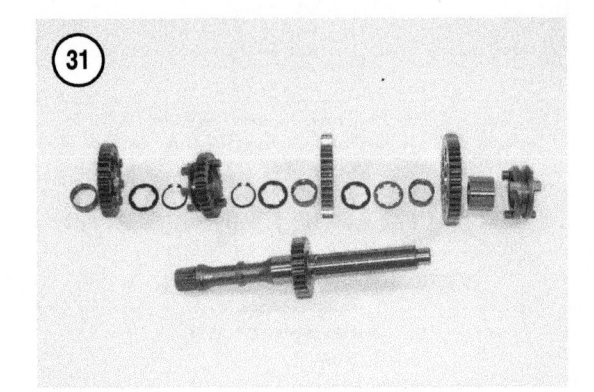

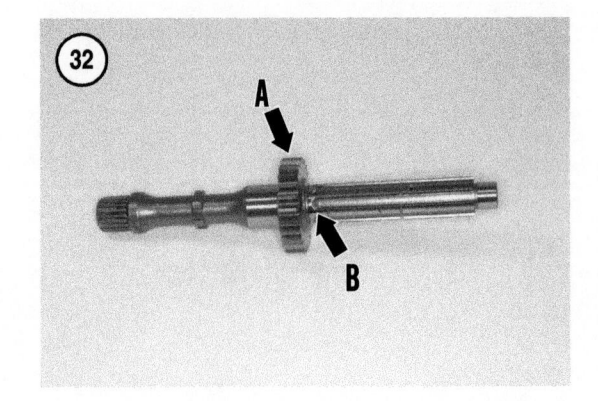

8. Determine the gear-to-bushing clearance by subtracting a bushing outside diameter (Step 7) from its related gear's inside diameter (Step 6).

9. Determine the bushing-to-shaft clearance by subtracting a mainshaft outside diameter (Step 5) from the related bushing's inside diameter (Step 7).

Countershaft

When inspecting countershaft components (**Figure 31**), compare measurements to the countershaft specifications in **Table 3**. Replace parts that are damaged or out of specification. When replacing a gear, also replace its mated gear on the mainshaft even though the mate may not show as much wear or damage.

1. Clean and dry the countershaft components. Flush the shaft and bushing oil holes with compressed air.
2. Inspect the countershaft (**Figure 32**) for:
    a. Worn or damaged splines.
    b. Missing, broken or chipped fifth gear teeth (A, **Figure 32**).
    c. Excessively worn or damaged bearing surfaces.
    d. A cracked or rounded-off snap ring groove.
    e. Plugged oil holes.
3. Check each countershaft gear (**Figure 31**) for:
    a. Missing, broken or chipped teeth.
    b. Worn, damaged or rounded engagement dogs.
    c. Worn or damaged splines.
    d. A cracked or scored gear bore.
4. Check each countershaft bushing for:
    a. Excessively worn or damaged bearing surfaces.
    b. Worn or damaged splines.
    c. A cracked or scored gear bore.
5. Inspect the reverse shifter for worn, damaged or rounded engagement dogs. Check the splines for excessive wear or damage.
6. Inspect the splined collar for excessive wear or damage.
7. Measure the inside diameter of the countershaft first, second, third and reverse gears (**Figure 29**). Record the dimensions.
8. Measure the outside diameter of the countershaft first-, second-, third- and reverse-gear bushings (**Figure 30**). Record the dimensions.

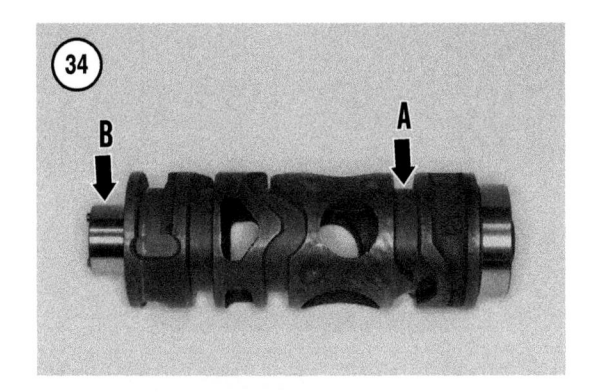

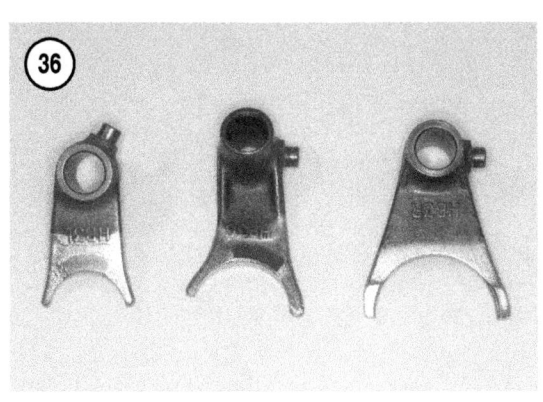

TRANSMISSION AND INTERNAL SHIFT MECHANISM

10) from the third-gear bushing inside diameter (Step 11).

Reverse Idle Gear

When inspecting reverse idle gear components (**Figure 33**), compare measurement to the specification in **Table 4** at the end of this chapter. Replace parts that are damaged or out of specification.
1. Clean and dry the reverse idle gear assembly.
2. Check the reverse idle gear shaft (A, **Figure 33**) for cracked, scored or damaged bearing surfaces.
3. Check the reverse idle gear (B, **Figure 33**) for:
   a. Missing, broken or chipped teeth.
   b. A cracked or scored gear bore.
4. Check each reverse idle gear thrust washer (C, **Figure 33**) for scoring or other signs of damage.
5. Measure the outside diameter of the reverse idle gear shaft, and record the dimension.
6. Measure the inside diameter of the reverse idle gear (**Figure 29**), and record the dimension.
7. Determine the gear-to-shaft clearance by subtracting the shaft outside diameter (Step 5) from the gear inside diameter (Step 6).

INTERNAL SHIFT MECHANISM

Removal/Installation

The internal shift mechanism is removed and installed with the transmission shaft assemblies. Perform the procedure described in Chapter Five.

Shift Drum Inspection

1. Clean and dry the shift drum.
2. Check the shift drum for excessively worn or damaged guide pin grooves (A, **Figure 34**) or bearing surfaces (B). Replace the shift drum if necessary.
3. Inspect each pin on the end of the shift drum (**Figure 35**). Replace as necessary.

Shift Fork Inspection

During inspection, compare shift fork measurements to the specifications in **Table 5** at the end of this chapter. Replace parts that are damaged or out of specification.
1. Inspect each shift fork (**Figure 36**) for signs of wear or damage. Examine the shift forks fingers

9. Determine the gear-to-bushing clearances by subtracting the bushing's outside diameter (Step 8) from its related gear's inside diameter (Step 7).

10. Measure the countershaft outside diameter at the third gear operating position (B, **Figure 32**), and record the dimension.

11. Measure the inside diameter of the countershaft third gear bushing (**Figure 30**), and record the dimension.

12. Determine the bushing to shaft clearance by subtracting the countershaft outside diameter (Step

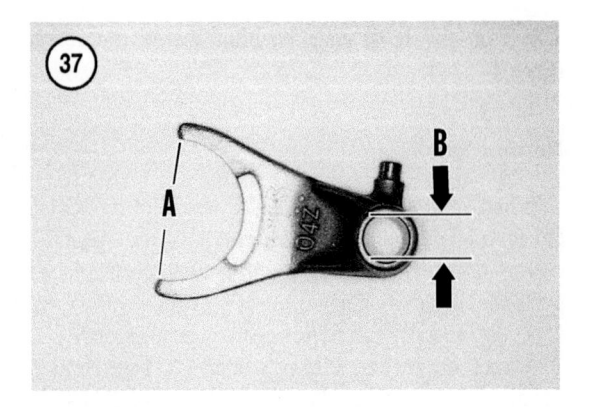

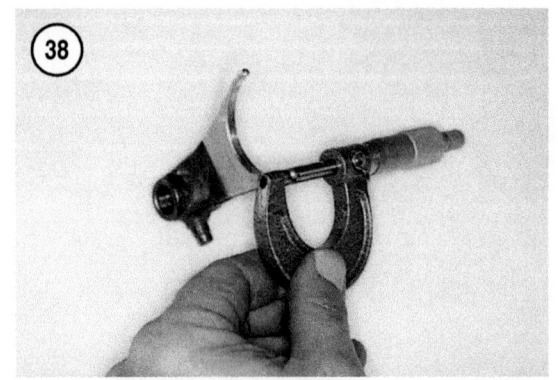

where they contact the slider gear (A, **Figure 37**). These surfaces must be smooth with no signs of wear, bending, cracks, heat discoloration or other damage.

2. Check each shift fork for arc-shaped wear or burn marks. These marks indicate that the shift fork has contacted the gear.
3. Check the shift fork shaft for bending or other damage. Install each shift fork onto the shaft, and slide it back and forth. Each shift fork must slide smoothly with no binding or tight spots. If there is binding with all three shift forks, check the shaft closely for bending. If there is binding with only one shift fork, check the shift fork closely.
4. Measure each shift fork finger thickness (**Figure 38**).
5. Measure the shift fork inside diameter (B, **Figure 37**) with a small bore gauge. Measure the gauge with a micrometer.
6. Measure the shift fork shaft outside diameter at three different points on the shaft.

REVERSE SELECTOR CABLE REPLACEMENT

1. Remove the handlebar cover (Chapter Fourteen).
2. Remove the fuel tank as described in Chapter Eight.
3. Make a diagram of the reverse selector cable routing path from the handlebar to the reverse stopper lever.
4. Remove any cable guides from the reverse selector cable.
5. On the left side of the alternator cover, remove the mounting bolts (A, **Figure 39**) and cover (B) from the reverse stopper lever.

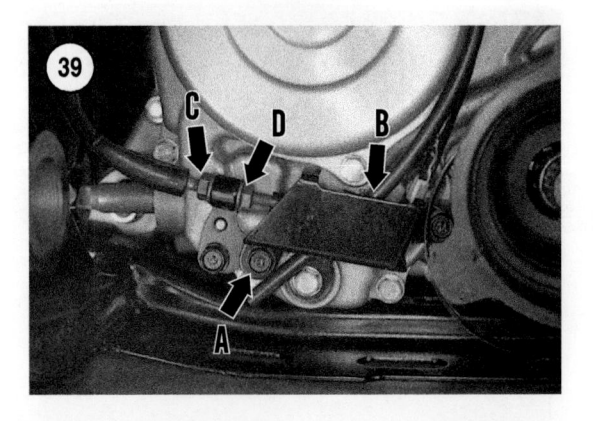

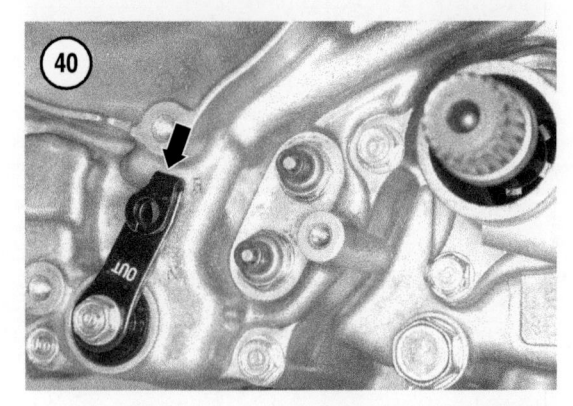

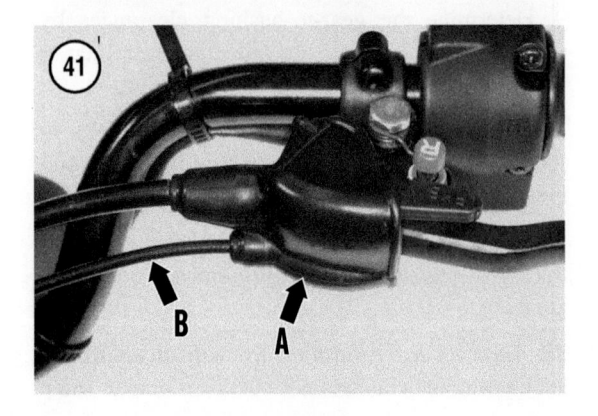

TRANSMISSION AND INTERNAL SHIFT MECHANISM

6. Loosen the cable locknut (C, **Figure 39**) and cable adjuster (D).
7. Disconnect the cable end from the reverse stopper lever (**Figure 40**), and release the cable from the bracket on the alternator cover.
8. At the handlebar, pull back the boot (A, **Figure 41**) and disconnect the reverse selector cable (B).
9. Remove the reverse selector cable. Note the path it follows.
10. Reverse these steps to install the reverse selector cable, plus the following:

    a. Lubricate the new cable as described in Chapter Three.

    b. Apply grease to the barrel connector at the cable end.

    c. Adjust the reverse selector cable as described in Chapter Three.

Table 1 TRANSMISSION SPECIFICATIONS

Item	Specifications
Primary reduction ratio	3.087 (71/23)
Final reduction ratio	3.692 (48/13)
Transmission	5-speed plus reverse, constant mesh
Shift pattern	R-N-1-2-3-4-5
Gear ratios	
1st gear	2.846 (37/13)
2nd gear	1.933 (29/15)
3rd gear	1.444 (26/18)
4th gear	1.130 (26/23)
5th gear	0.913 (21/23)
Reverse	4.769 (31/16 × 32/13)

Table 2 MAINSHAFT SPECIFICATIONS

Item	New mm (in.)	Service limit mm (in.)
Gear inside diameter		
Fourth gear	23.000-23.021 (0.9055-0.9063)	23.04 (0.907)
Fifth gear	18.000-18.021 (0.7087-0.7095)	18.04 (0.710)
Mainshaft outside diameter		
Fourth gear	19.959-19.980 (0.7858-0.7866)	19.93 (0.785)
Fifth gear	14.966-14.984 (0.5892-0.5899)	14.94 (0.588)
Gear bushing		
Fourth gear		
Inside diameter	20.000-20.021 (0.7874-0.7882)	20.04 (0.789)
Outside diameter	22.959-22.979 (0.9039-0.9047)	22.94 (0.903)
Fifth gear		
Inside diameter	15.000-15.018 (0.5906-0.5913)	15.04 (0.592)
Outside diameter	17.959-17.980 (0.7070-0.7079)	17.94 (0.706)
Gear-to-bushing clearance		
Fourth gear	0.021-0.062 (0.0008-0.0024)	0.10 (0.004)
Fifth gear	0.020-0.062 (0.0008-0.0024)	0.10 (0.004)
Bushing-to-shaft clearance		
Fourth gear	0.020-0.062 (0.0008-0.0024)	0.10 (0.004)
Fifth gear	0.016-0.052 (0.0006-0.0024)	0.10 (0.004)

Table 3 COUNTERSHAFT SPECIFICATIONS

Item	New mm (in.)	Service limit mm (in.)
Gear inside diameter		
First, second, third and reverse gears	25.000-25.021 (0.9843-0.9851)	25.04 (0.986)
Gear bushing		
First, second and reverse gears		
Outside diameter	24.959-24.980 (0.9826-0.9835)	24.94 (0.982)
Third gear		
Inside diameter	22.000-22.021 (0.8661-0.8670)	22.04 (0.868)
Outside diameter	24.959-24.980 (0.9826-0.9835)	24.94 (0.982)
Gear-to-bushing clearance		
First, second, third and reverse gears	0.020-0.062 (0.0008-0.0024)	0.10 (0.004)
Bushing-to-shaft clearance		
Third gear	0.020-0.062 (0.0008-0.0024)	0.10 (0.004)

Table 4 REVERSE IDLE GEAR SPECIFICATIONS

Item	New mm (in.)	Service limit mm (in.)
Reverse idle gear shaft outside diameter	12.996-12.984 (0.5105-0.5112)	12.94 (0.509)
Gear inside diameter	13.000-13.018 (0.5118-0.5125)	13.04 (0.513)
Gear-to-shaft clearance	0.016-0.052 (0.0006-0.0020)	0.10 (0.004)

Table 5 SHIFT FORK SPECIFICATIONS

Item	New mm (in.)	Service limit mm (in.)
Shift fork finger thickness	4.93-5.00 (0.194-0.197)	4.60 (0.181)
Shift fork inside diameter	13.000-13.021 (0.5118-0.5126)	13.04 (0.513)
Shift fork shaft outside diameter	12.996-12.984 (0.5105-0.5112)	12.96 (0.510)

Table 6 TRANSMISSION TORQUE SPECIFICATIONS

Item	N•m	in.-lb.	ft.-lb.
Gearshift A arm bolt	25	–	18
Shift cam plate bolt	16	–	12
Shift drum stopper arm bolt	12	106	–
Shift shaft return spring pin	22	–	16

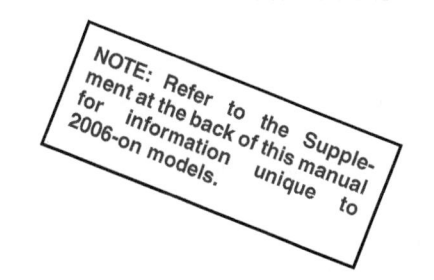

> NOTE: Refer to the Supplement at the back of this manual for information unique to 2006-on models.

CHAPTER EIGHT

FUEL, AIR AND EXHAUST SYSTEMS

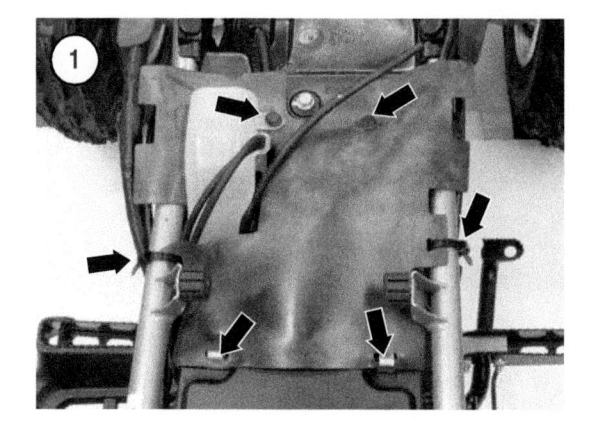

1

This chapter includes service procedures for all parts of the fuel system, as well as the exhaust system. Routine air filter service is covered in Chapter Three.

The fuel system consists of the carburetor, fuel tank, fuel valve, air box and air filter.

Table 1 lists carburetor specifications; **Table 2** lists fuel and exhaust system torque specifications. During assembly, tighten fasteners to the specifications in **Table 2**. **Table 1** and **Table 2** are at the end of the chapter.

CARBURETOR

Carburetor Removal/Installation

NOTE
Mark each hose and its fitting during removal so each hose is installed onto the correct fitting during installation.

1. Park the vehicle on level ground and set the parking brake.
2. Remove the seat and both side covers (Chapter Fourteen).
3. Disconnect the negative battery cable from the battery (Chapter Three).
4. Remove the rear heat protector from the frame (**Figure 1**).
5. Remove the air box as described in this chapter.
6. Place a suitable container beneath the drain hose (A, **Figure 2**). Open the drain screw (B, **Figure 2**), and drain the fuel from the float bowl.
7. Unscrew the throttle valve cover (A, **Figure 3**), and remove the throttle valve assembly from the carburetor (**Figure 4**).
8. Disconnect the fuel hose (B, **Figure 3**) from the carburetor.

CHAPTER EIGHT

9. Loosen the clamp screw (A, **Figure 5**), and disconnect the choke cable (B) from the choke lever.
10. Remove the mounting nut (**Figure 6**) on each side of the carburetor, and remove the carburetor from the intake manifold.
11. Install the carburetor by reversing these removal steps, while noting the following:
   a. Install a new O-ring (**Figure 7**) into the groove in the carburetor mounting boss.
   b. If removed, install the boot (C, **Figure 3**) onto the throttle valve cover. Align the boot tab with the groove in the cover.
   c. Adjust the throttle cable free play and engine idle speed as described in Chapter Three.
   d. If necessary, adjust the pilot screw as described in this chapter.

Throttle Valve Disassembly

1. Pull the spring out of the throttle valve (**Figure 8**).
2. Push the throttle cable into the throttle valve, and disengage the cable end from its seat in the throttle valve.
3. Slide the throttle cable end (A, **Figure 9**) out the throttle valve cutout, and remove it from the throttle valve (B).
4. Remove the throttle valve spring from the throttle valve cover (**Figure 10**).
5. Pinch the retainer knob (**Figure 11**) to release it from the throttle valve bore, and remove the retainer. Watch for the small spring in the bottom of the retainer. Refer to **Figure 12**.
6. Remove the jet needle from the throttle valve. Note the position of the jet needle clip. If removed, record the clip position so it can be reinstalled in the same groove.

FUEL, AIR AND EXHAUST SYSTEMS 185

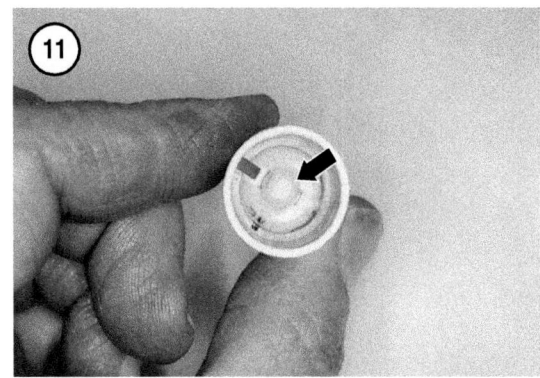

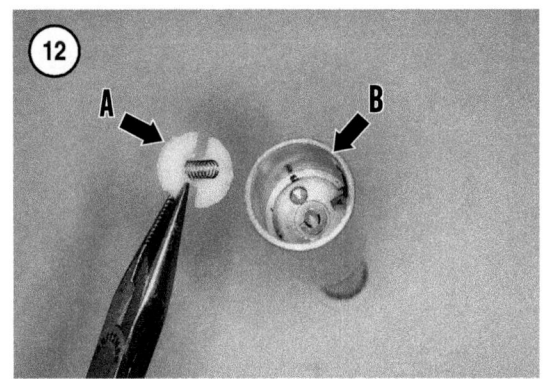

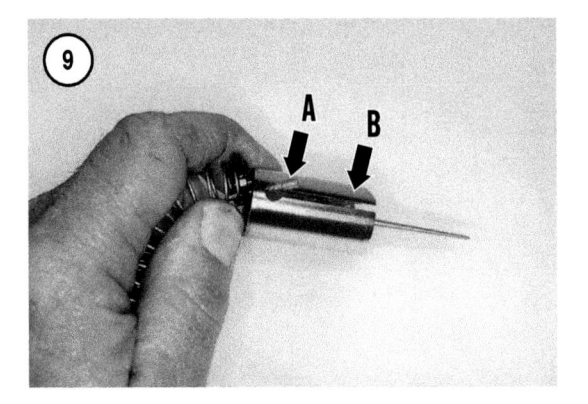

7. Inspect the throttle valve assembly as described in this section.

8. If necessary, adjust the jet needle clip as described in this chapter.

Throttle Valve Assembly

1. If removed, install the jet needle clip onto the position noted during removal or to the specified position.

2. Install the jet needle into the throttle valve assembly.

3. Pinch the retainer knob (**Figure 11**), and seat it in the throttle valve. Make sure the locating tab on the retainer (A, **Figure 12**) sits in the cutout on the throttle valve (B).

4. Install the throttle valve spring into the throttle valve cover (**Figure 10**).

5. Compress the throttle valve spring. Feed the throttle cable end (A, **Figure 9**) along the throttle valve cutout and through the slot in the retainer (**Figure 8**). Make sure the cable end engages the seat in the throttle valve.

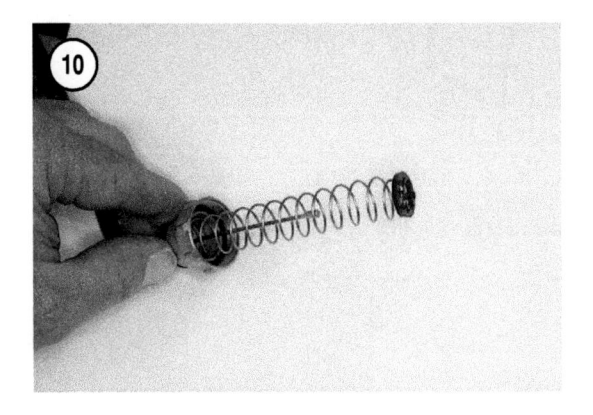

CHAPTER EIGHT

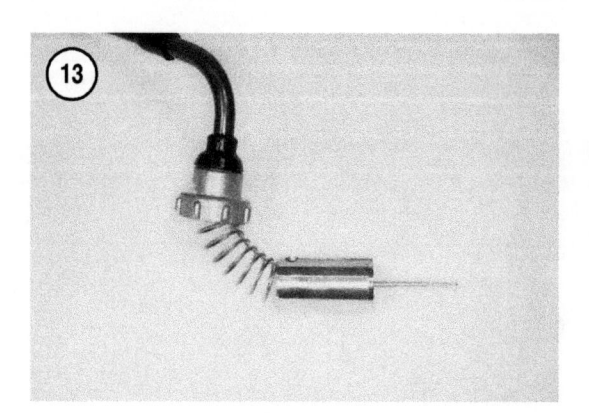

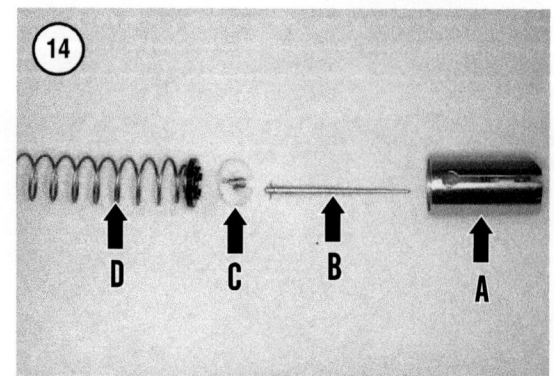

CARBURETOR

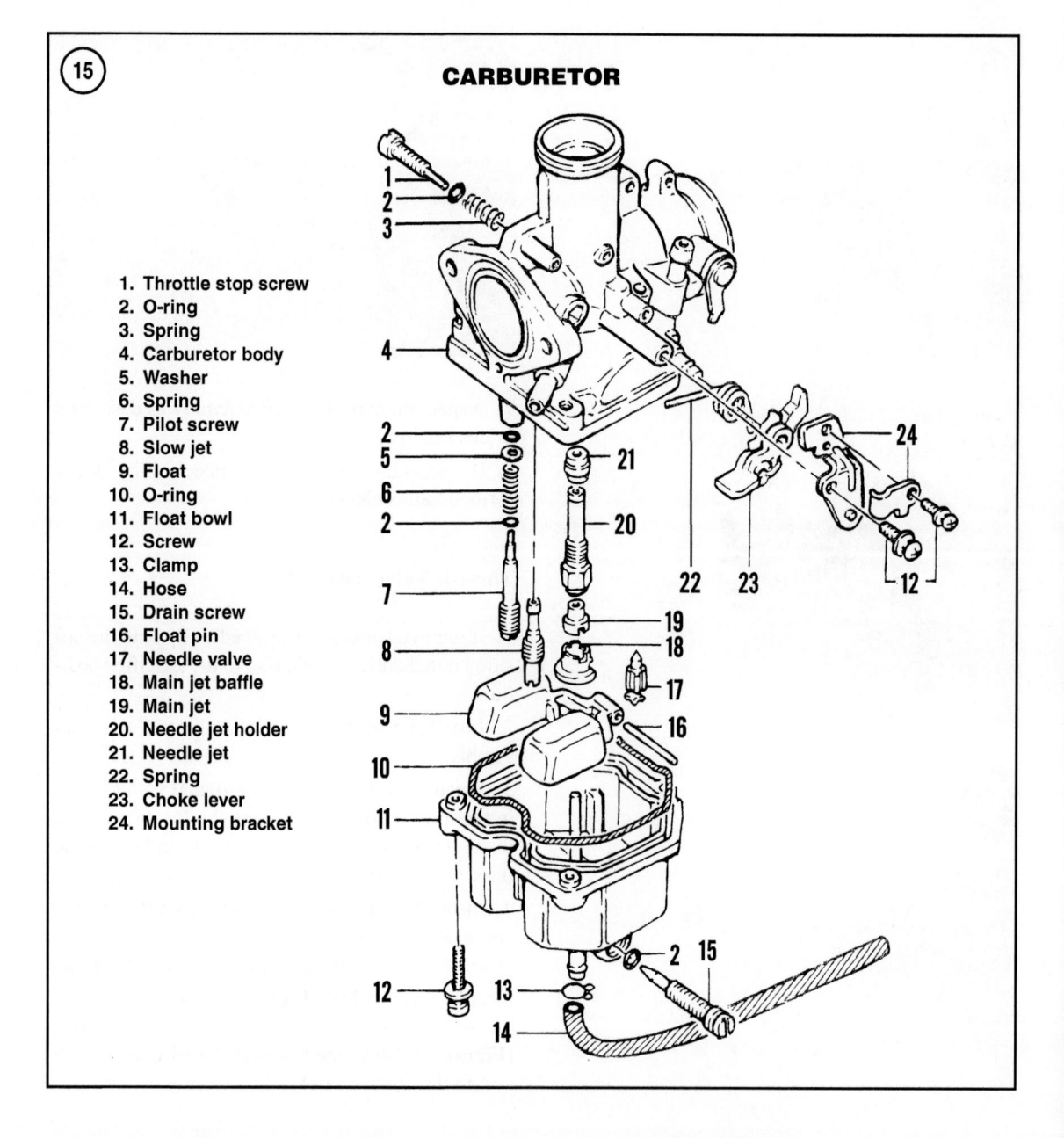

1. Throttle stop screw
2. O-ring
3. Spring
4. Carburetor body
5. Washer
6. Spring
7. Pilot screw
8. Slow jet
9. Float
10. O-ring
11. Float bowl
12. Screw
13. Clamp
14. Hose
15. Drain screw
16. Float pin
17. Needle valve
18. Main jet baffle
19. Main jet
20. Needle jet holder
21. Needle jet
22. Spring
23. Choke lever
24. Mounting bracket

FUEL, AIR AND EXHAUST SYSTEMS

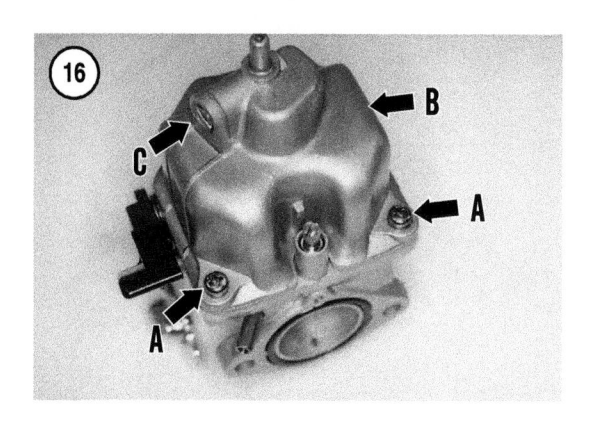

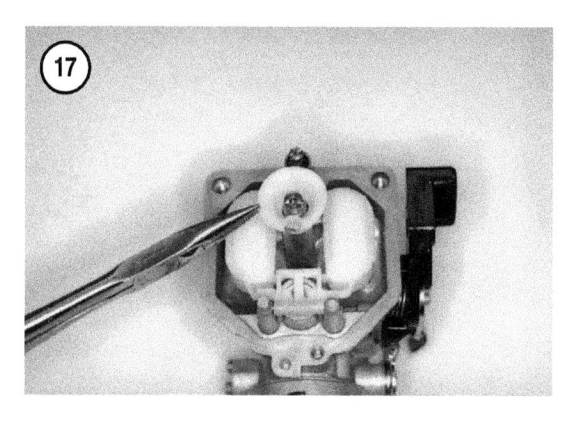

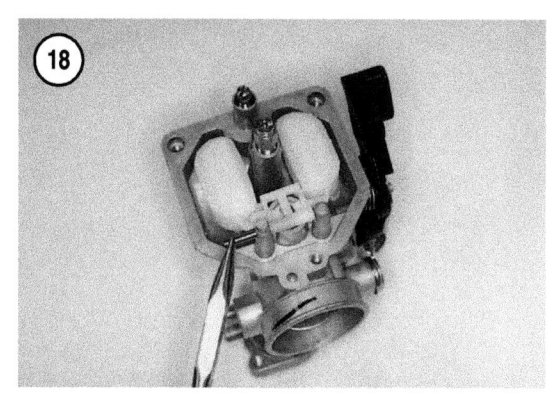

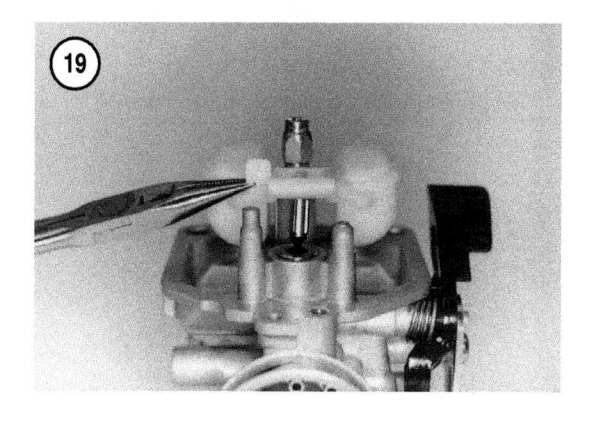

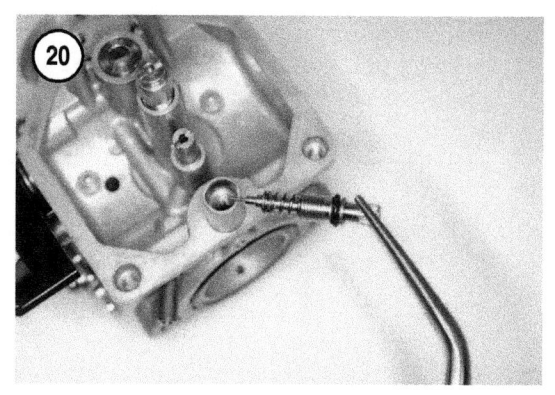

6. Release the spring and seat it in the bottom of the throttle valve (**Figure 13**).

Throttle Valve Inspection

1. Inspect the throttle valve (A, **Figure 14**) for signs of abrasion.
2. Inspect the jet needle (B, **Figure 14**) for nicks, steps and other signs of wear.
3. Inspect the retainer (C, **Figure 14**) for cracks or signs of deterioration.
4. Inspect the spring seat and the throttle valve spring (D, **Figure 14**) for signs of fatigue or damage.

Carburetor Disassembly

Refer to **Figure 15**.
1. Remove the drain hose from the float bowl.
2. Remove the float bowl screws (A, **Figure 16**) and float bowl (B) from the carburetor body.
3. Remove the main jet baffle (**Figure 17**).
4. Remove the float pin (**Figure 18**) from the posts in the float bowl.
5. Lift the float and the needle valve (**Figure 19**) from the carburetor.
6. While counting the number of turns, turn the pilot screw in until it *lightly* seats. Record the number of turns for assembly. Back the pilot screw out, and remove it from the carburetor (**Figure 20**). A washer, spring and O-ring should come out with the pilot screw (**Figure 21**). Watch for a second O-ring. It may remain in the pilot screw bore.
7. Remove the slow jet (**Figure 22**).
8. Remove the main jet (**Figure 23**).
9. Remove the needle jet holder (**Figure 24**).

10. Turn the carburetor so its top side faces up, and tap the body to remove the needle jet (**Figure 25**). If the needle jet does not fall out, gently push it out with a plastic rod.
11. Remove the throttle stop screw (**Figure 26**).
12. Remove the drain screw (C, **Figure 16**) and O-ring from the float bowl.

NOTE
Further disassembly is neither necessary nor recommended.

13. Clean and inspect all parts as described in this section.

Carburetor Assembly

Refer to **Figure 15** when assembling the carburetor body.
1. Install the drain screw (C, **Figure 16**) and O-ring into the float bowl. Tighten the drain screw securely.
2. Install the throttle stop screw (**Figure 26**) and spring.
3. Install the needle jet (**Figure 25**) with its chamfered end facing into the carburetor.
4. Install the needle jet holder (**Figure 24**) and tighten it securely.
5. Install the main jet (**Figure 23**).
6. Install the slow jet (**Figure 22**).
7. Install a new O-ring, the spring and washer onto the pilot screw (**Figure 21**).
8. Carefully seat a second new O-ring into the pilot screw bore, and install the pilot screw (**Figure 20**). Turn it in until it *lightly* seats in the carburetor. Back the screw out the number of turns recorded during removal, or set it to the number of turns in **Table 1**.
9. Hook the float valve onto the float, and install the float/valve assembly (**Figure 19**) so the float valve sits in the float valve seat.
10. Insert the float pin (**Figure 18**) through the posts and float.
11. Check the float level as described in this chapter.
12. Install the main jet baffle (**Figure 27**).
13. Install the O-ring into the float bowl groove (**Figure 28**). Install the float bowl, and secure it with the three mounting screws (A, **Figure 16**).
14. Connect the drain hose to the float bowl of the carburetor.

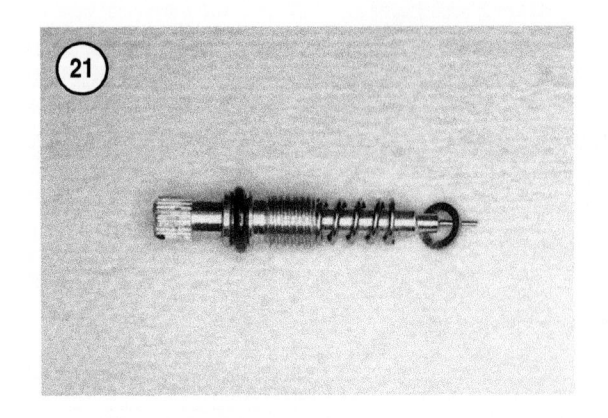

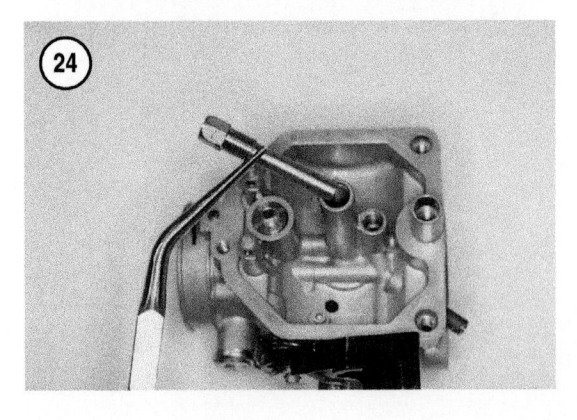

FUEL, AIR AND EXHAUST SYSTEMS

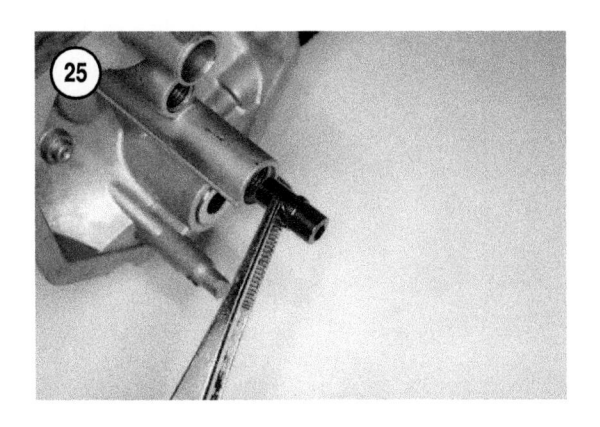

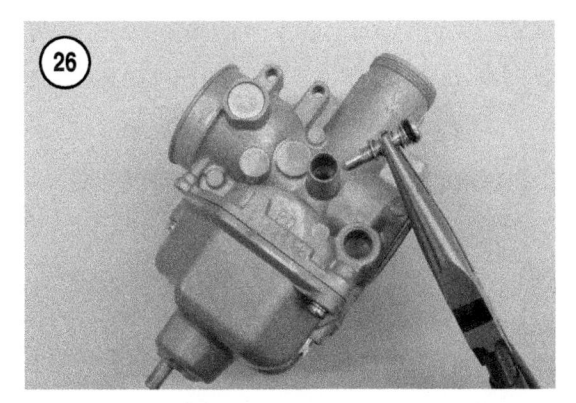

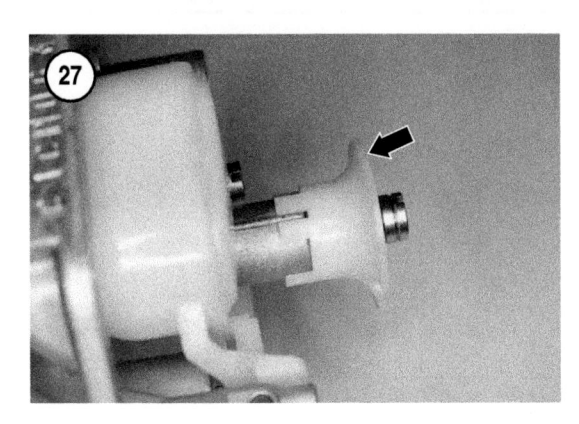

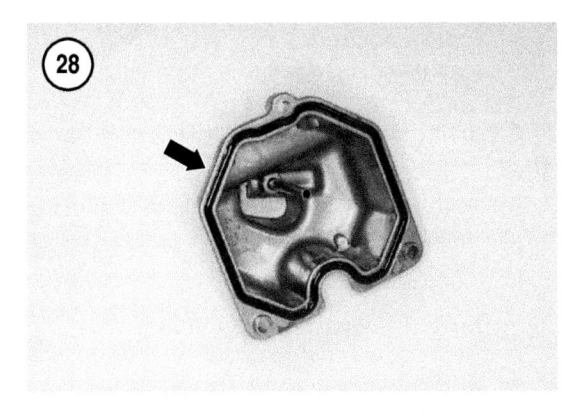

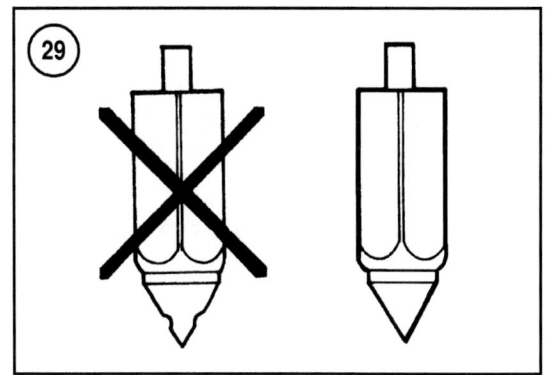

15. Install the carburetor as described in this section.
16. Adjust the pilot screw as described in this chapter.

Carburetor Cleaning and Inspection

1. Clean and dry the carburetor parts.

CAUTION
Do not dip the carburetor body or any of the O-rings in a carburetor cleaner or other solution that damages the rubber parts and seals.

CAUTION
Do not use wire or drill bits to clean jets. Even minor gouges in a jet can change the air/fuel mixture.

2. Clean the float bowl drain tube with compressed air.
3. Replace the float bowl O-ring if it leaks, is damaged or starts to harden.
4. Inspect the float valve assembly as follows:
    a. Check the end of the needle valve (**Figure 29**) for steps, excessive wear or damage.
    b. At the opposite end, push the needle in and release it. If the needle does not spring out, replace the needle valve.
5. Check the valve seat in the carburetor (**Figure 30**) for steps, uneven wear or other damage.
6. Inspect the pilot screw (**Figure 21**) and spring for damage. Replace the screw if damaged. Replace both pilot screw O-rings.
7. Inspect the float for deterioration or damage. Check the float by submersing it in a container of water. If water enters the float, replace it.

190

CHAPTER EIGHT

8. Make sure all openings in the carburetor body are clear. Clean them with compressed air.
9. Inspect all jets (**Figure 31**). Clean their openings with compressed air. Replace any jet that cannot be cleaned.

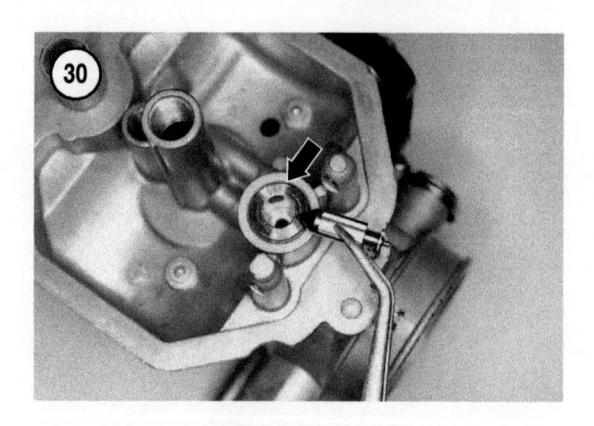

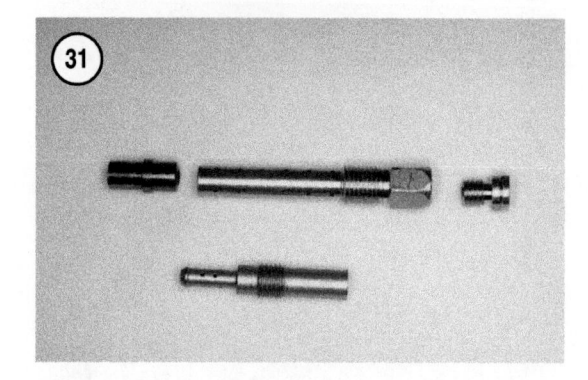

CARBURETOR ADJUSTMENT

Idle Speed

Refer to Chapter Three.

Float Level

The float valve and float maintain a constant fuel level in the float bowl. Because the float level affects the air/fuel mixture throughout the engine's operating range, this level must be maintained within specification.

The carburetor must be removed and partially disassembled for this adjustment.

1. Remove the carburetor as described in this chapter.
2. Remove the float bowl mounting screws (A, **Figure 16**) and remove the float bowl (B) from the carburetor body.
3. Hold the carburetor so the needle valve just touches the float arm without pushing it down. Measure the distance from the carburetor body sealing surface to the top of the float with a float level gauge (**Figure 32**), ruler or vernier caliper.
4. The float is non-adjustable. If the float level is incorrect, check the float pin and float valve for damage. If these parts are in good condition, replace the float, and remeasure the float level.
5. Install the O-ring (**Figure 29**) onto the float bowl, and install the float bowl. Tighten the mounting screws securely (A, **Figure 16**).
6. Install the carburetor as described in this chapter.

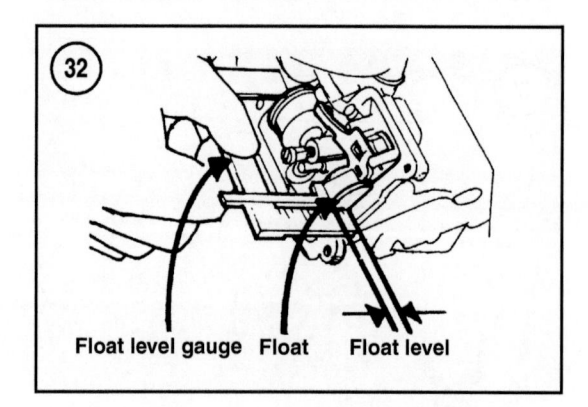

Pilot Screw

The pilot screw is preset. Routine adjustment is not necessary unless the pilot screw was removed, replaced or the carburetor was overhauled.

WARNING
Do not run the engine in an enclosed area when adjusting the pilot screw. Doing so fills the area with carbon monoxide gas. Dangerous levels of carbon monoxide cause loss of consciousness and death in a short time.

1. Clean the air filter as described in Chapter Three.
2. Connect a tachometer to the engine following the manufacturer's instructions.

CAUTION
Table 1 *contains two specifications for the initial pilot screw setting: standard and high altitude. Use the stan-*

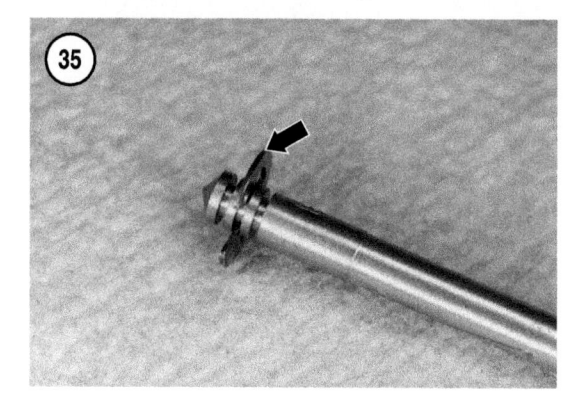

FUEL, AIR AND EXHAUST SYSTEMS

3. Turn the pilot screw (**Figure 33**) clockwise until it *lightly* seats, and then back it out to the initial setting for the model and operating altitude.

4. Start the engine and warm it to operating temperature.

5. Open and release the throttle lever a few times, making sure it returns to its closed position. If necessary, turn the engine off and adjust the throttle cable as described in Chapter Three.

6. With the engine idling, turn the throttle stop screw (**Figure 34**) to set the idle speed to specification.

7. Slowly turn the pilot screw in or out to obtain the highest engine idle speed.

8. Turn the throttle stop screw to reset the idle speed to specification.

9. While reading the tachometer, slowly turn the pilot screw clockwise until the engine speed drops 100 rpm.

10. Slowly turn the pilot screw counterclockwise the number of turns indicated by the secondary setting for the model.

11. Readjust the idle speed with the throttle stop screw. Open and close the throttle lever a few times while checking the idle speed reading. The engine must idle within the speed range in **Table 1**. If necessary, readjust the idle speed with the throttle stop screw.

12. Turn the engine off and remove the tachometer.

Jet Needle

The jet needle (**Figure 35**) controls the air/fuel mixture in the mid-throttle range (between 1/4- and 3/4-throttle). The jet needle can be raised or lowered to adjust the mid-throttle mixture.

1. Remove and disassemble the throttle valve as described in this chapter.

NOTE
*Record the jet needle clip position before removing it. Refer to **Table 1** for the standard jet needle clip position.*

2. Remove the jet needle clip (**Figure 35**) and reposition it on the needle. Lowering the clip raises the needle in the bore and richens the mid-throttle mixture. Raising the clip lowers the needle in the bore and leans the mixture. Refer to **Figure 36**. Move the clip one groove at a time, and then test the engine.

dard setting if the vehicle is operated below 1500 m (5000 ft.) for sustained periods of time. An engine tuned to the high altitude settings can be damaged if it is run below 1500 m (5000 ft.) for sustained periods of time.

NOTE
To accurately detect speed changes during this adjustment, use a tachometer with graduations of 100 rpm or smaller.

3. Assemble and install the throttle valve assembly as described in this chapter.

High Altitude

There are two different jetting specifications: standard and high altitude. Use the standard jetting when operating the vehicle below 1500 m (5000 ft.). Use the high altitude jetting when operating the vehicle between 1500-2500 m (3000-8000 ft.).

1. Remove the carburetor as described in this chapter.
2. Remove the mounting screws (A, **Figure 16**) and float bowl (B).
3. Remove the standard main jet (**Figure 23**), and install the correct size main jet for high altitude operation. Refer to **Table 1**.
4A. If the pilot screw (**Figure 33**) is set to the standard setting, turn it clockwise 1/8 turn.
4B. If the status of the pilot screw setting is unknown, turn the pilot screw (**Figure 33**) clockwise until it *lightly* seats. Back the screw out the number of turns indicated for the high altitude specification.
5. Reassemble and install the carburetor.
6. Adjust the idle speed as described in Chapter Three. The idle speed is the same for standard and high altitude carburetor settings.

CAUTION
If the engine has been tuned to high altitude specifications, avoid sustained operation at elevations below 1500 m (5000 ft.). Sustained running at these elevations with high altitude jetting may cause overheating and engine damage. For sustained operation at sub-1500 m (5000 ft.) elevations, reset the carburetor to the standard settings by installing the standard main jet and turning the pilot screw counterclockwise 1/8 turn.

THROTTLE HOUSING

Disassembly/Inspection

Refer to **Figure 37**.

1. Park the vehicle on level ground and set the parking brake.

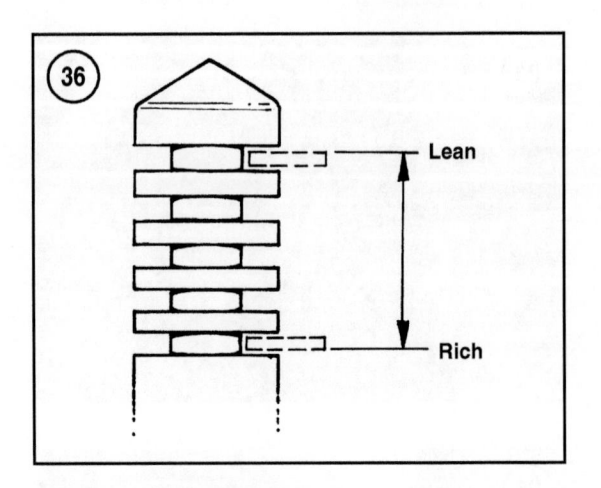

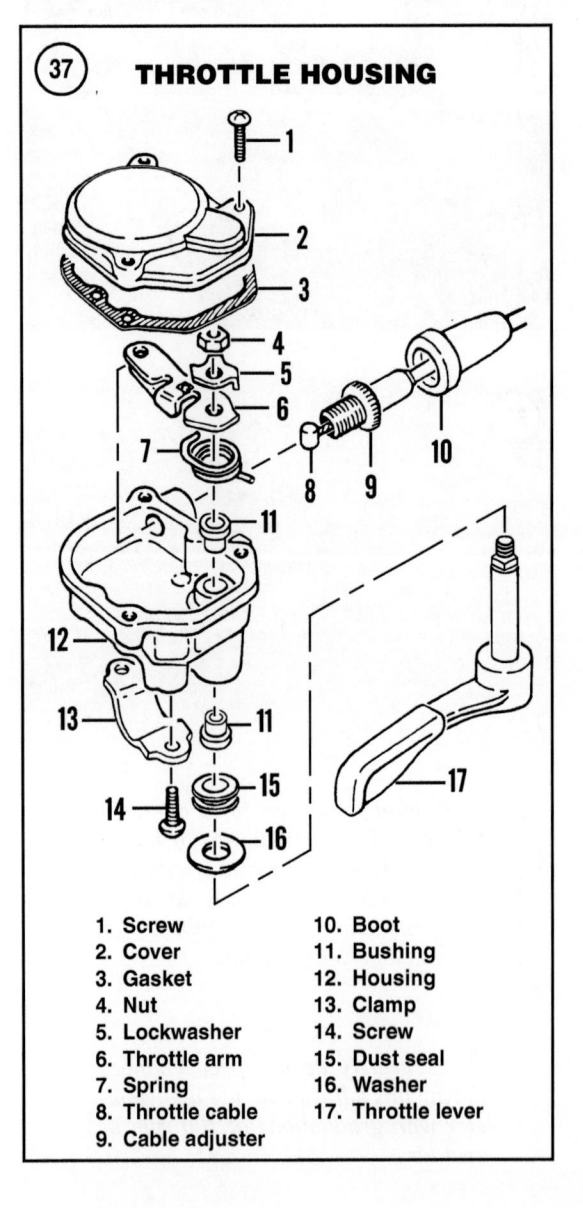

---

36 Lean / Rich

37 THROTTLE HOUSING

1. Screw
2. Cover
3. Gasket
4. Nut
5. Lockwasher
6. Throttle arm
7. Spring
8. Throttle cable
9. Cable adjuster
10. Boot
11. Bushing
12. Housing
13. Clamp
14. Screw
15. Dust seal
16. Washer
17. Throttle lever

FUEL, AIR AND EXHAUST SYSTEMS

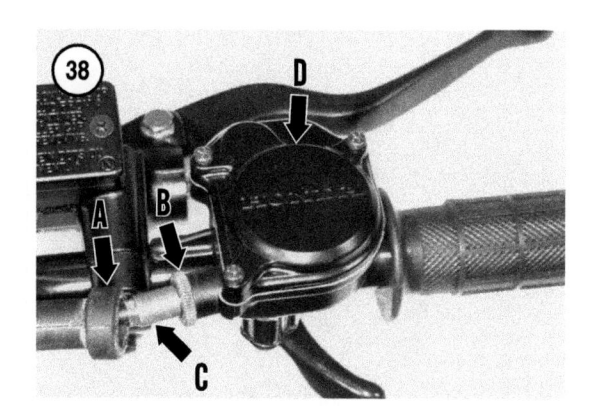

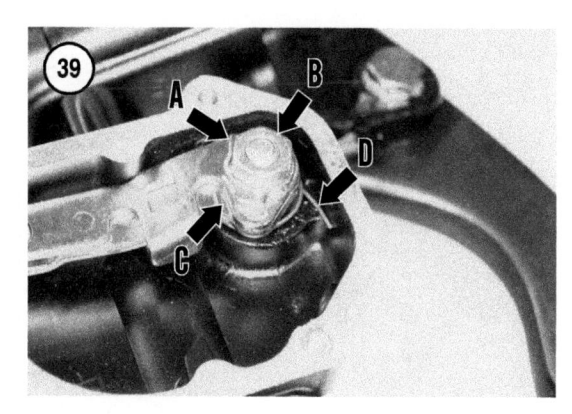

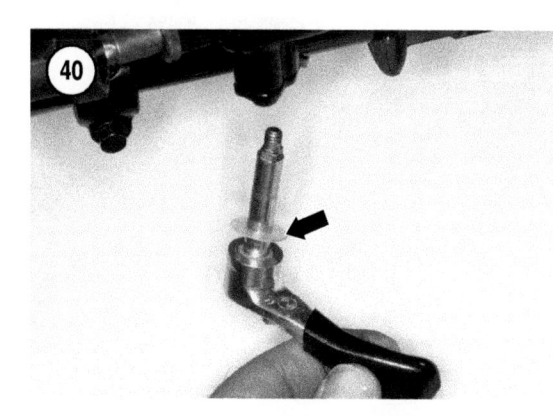

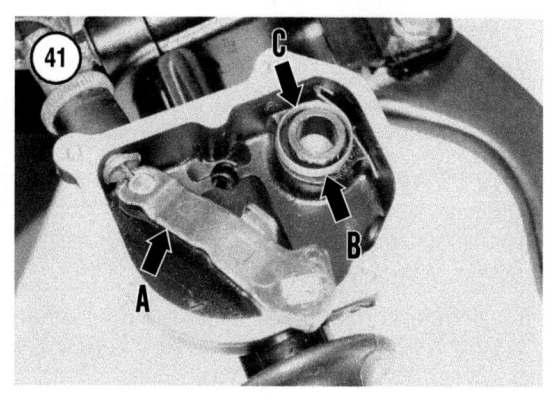

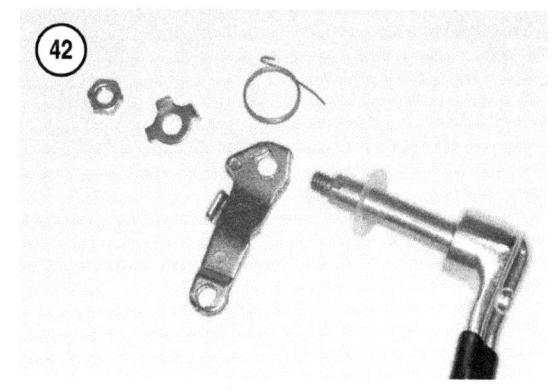

2. Slide the rubber boot (A, **Figure 38**) off the cable adjuster. Loosen the throttle cable adjuster locknut (B, **Figure 38**) and loosen the adjuster (C).

3. Remove the three cover screws, and remove the cover (D, **Figure 38**) from the throttle housing. Discard the cover gasket. A new one must be installed during assembly.

4. Pry the lock tab (A, **Figure 39**) away from the throttle arm nut (B).

5. Remove the throttle arm nut and lockwasher, and then remove the throttle lever (**Figure 40**) from the housing pivot.

6. Disconnect the throttle cable from the throttle arm (A, **Figure 41**). Remove the throttle arm and spring (B).

7. Clean and dry the throttle housing and all its parts.

8. Inspect the throttle housing assembly (**Figure 42**) as follows:

   a. Check for a weak or damaged spring.

   b. Check the throttle arm. It must not be damaged or corroded.

   c. Check the bushing on the inside (C, **Figure 41**) of the housing. Remove the dust seal (**Figure 43**) and inspect the bushing on the outside of the housing. Replace both bushings if either is worn.

   d. Inspect the dust seal and replace it if any damage is noted.

   e. Inspect the housing cover and body for cracks, a nicked gasket surface or other damage that could admit dirt or water.

Assembly

NOTE
Use a multipurpose lithium grease (NLGI #2, or an equivalent) when grease is called for in the following procedure.

1. Install a bushing on the outside and inside of the housing pivot (C, **Figure 41**).
2. Lubricate a new dust seal with grease, and install the seal (**Figure 43**).
3. Connect the throttle cable ball onto the end of the throttle arm (A, **Figure 41**).
4. Hook the spring around the throttle arm, and install the spring and throttle arm onto the housing pivot. The return spring must be centered around the pivot. Also, make sure the hooked end of the spring engages the throttle arm (C, **Figure 39**) and the straight end (D) sits against the throttle housing.
5. If removed, install the washer (**Figure 40**) onto the throttle lever.
6. Lubricate the throttle lever post with grease.
7. Install the throttle lever post through the bushing/dust seal, into the pivot and out through the throttle arm.
8. Install a new lockwasher over the throttle lever post.
9. Install and tighten the throttle arm nut (B, **Figure 39**).
10. Check the operation of the throttle lever.
    a. If its movement is rough or sluggish, the return spring is not centered on the pivot post. Remove and reinstall the throttle arm so the spring remains centered.
    b. Once the throttle lever movement is smooth, bend the lock tab against the nut.
11. Install the throttle housing cover (D, **Figure 38**) with a new gasket. Tighten the cover screws to 4 N•m (35 in.-lb.).
12. Adjust the throttle cable free play as described in Chapter Three.
13. Tighten the throttle cable adjuster locknut (B, **Figure 38**) and slide the rubber boot (A) over the adjuster.

THROTTLE CABLE REPLACEMENT

1. Park the vehicle on level ground and set the parking brake.   
2. Remove the handlebar cover (Chapter Fourteen).
3. Remove the fuel tank and heat guard as described in this chapter.
4. Note how the throttle cable is routed through the frame. Make a diagram of the cable's route from the handlebar to the carburetor. The new cable must follow the same route.
5. Disconnect the throttle cable from the throttle arm by performing Steps 1-6 of *Throttle Housing, Disassembly/Inspection* in this chapter.

FUEL, AIR AND EXHAUST SYSTEMS

11. Install the new throttle cable through the frame, routing it along the original path from the handlebar to the carburetor. Secure the cable with its frame clips.
12. Connect the throttle cable to the throttle valve as described in *Throttle Valve Assembly* in this chapter.
13. Insert the throttle valve assembly (**Figure 45**) into the carburetor and screw the throttle valve cover (**Figure 44**) into place.
14. Reconnect the throttle cable to the throttle arm and assemble the throttle housing as described in *Throttle Housing, Assembly* in this chapter.
15. Operate the throttle lever and make sure the carburetor throttle valve operates correctly. If throttle operation is sluggish, check that the cable is attached correctly and there are no tight bends in the cable.
16. Adjust the throttle cable free play as described in Chapter Three.
17. Test ride the vehicle and make sure the throttle is operating correctly.

CHOKE CABLE REPLACEMENT

NOTE
The choke cable and knob are only available as an assembly.

1. Park the vehicle on level ground and set the parking brake.
2. Remove the fuel tank and heat guard as described in this chapter.
3. Remove the choke knob (A, **Figure 46**) by turning the large plastic nut (**Figure 47**) securing it to the handlebar cover. Remove the handlebar cover (B, **Figure 46**) as described in *Handlebar Cover* in Chapter Fourteen.
4. Note how the choke cable is routed through the frame. Make a diagram of the cable's route from the choke knob to the carburetor. The new cable must follow the same route.
5. Remove any cable guides securing the choke cable to the frame.
6. At the carburetor, loosen the clamp screw (A, **Figure 48**), and disconnect the choke cable (B) from the choke lever.
7. Pull the choke knob/cable from the frame.
8. Lubricate the new choke cable assembly as described in Chapter Three.
9. Reverse these steps to install the choke cable.

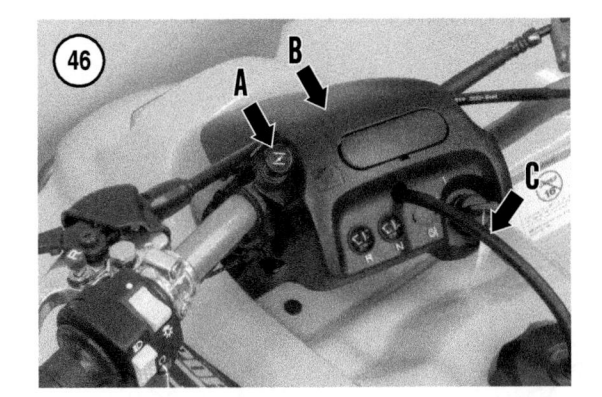

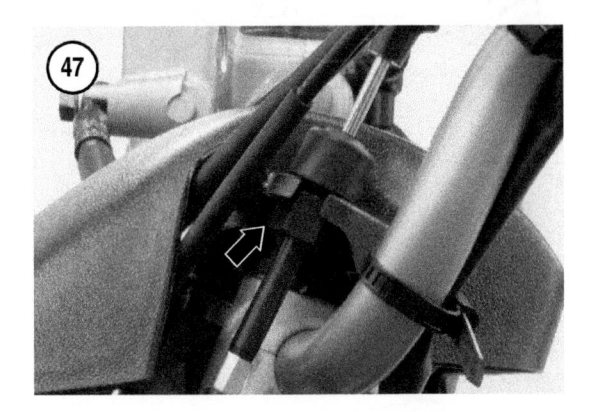

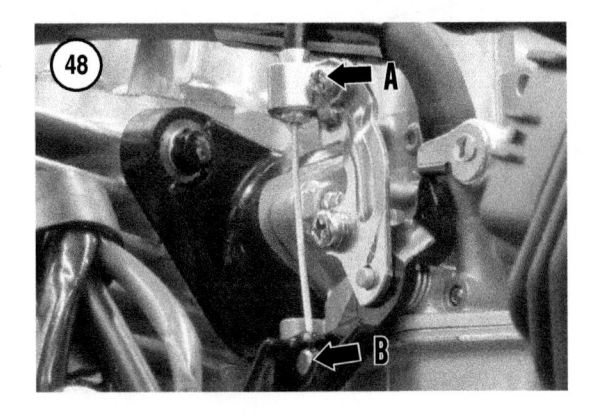

6. Unscrew the throttle valve cover (**Figure 44**), and remove the throttle valve assembly from the carburetor (**Figure 45**).
7. Disconnect the throttle cable from the throttle valve as described in *Throttle Valve Disassembly* in this chapter.
8. Disconnect the throttle cable from any clips holding the cable to the frame.
9. Pull the throttle cable from the frame.
10. Lubricate the new throttle cable as described in Chapter Three.

196 CHAPTER EIGHT

FUEL TANK

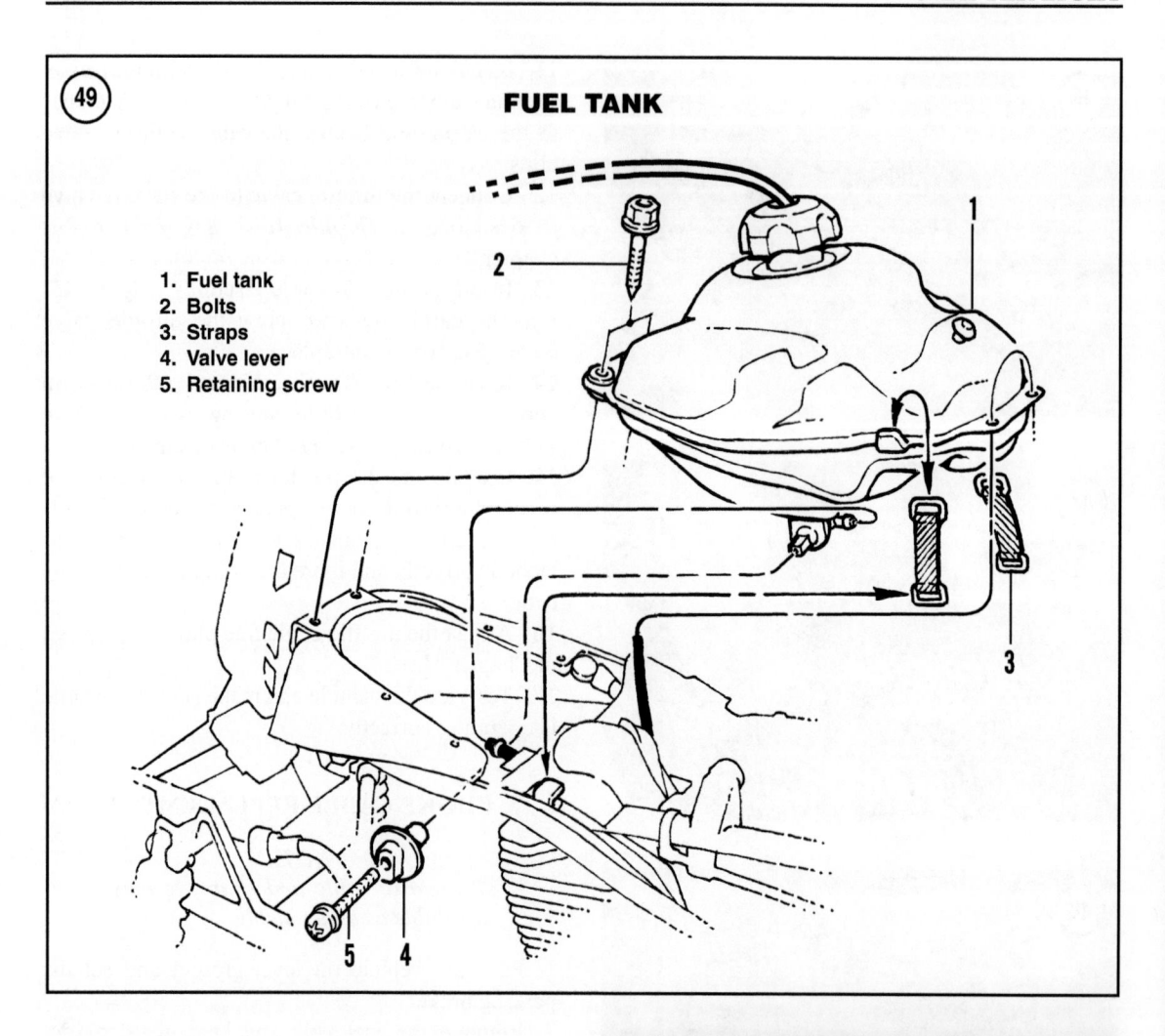

1. Fuel tank
2. Bolts
3. Straps
4. Valve lever
5. Retaining screw

10. Test ride the vehicle and check the choke operation.

FUEL TANK

Removal/Installation

Refer to **Figure 49**.

1. Park the vehicle on level ground and set the parking brake.
2. Turn the fuel valve off.
3. Remove the seat, side panels, fuel tank cover and front fender as described in Chapter Fourteen.
4. Disconnect the negative battery cable (Chapter Three).
5. Remove the mounting screw (**Figure 50**) and knob from the fuel valve.
6. Remove the front fuel tank mounting bolts (A, **Figure 51**).
7. Remove the fuel tank holder bands (B, **Figure 51**).
8. Lift the fuel tank up slightly and disconnect the fuel hose from the fuel valve (A, **Figure 52**).
9. Remove the fuel tank vent hose (C, **Figure 46**) from the handlebar cover, and remove the fuel tank.

FUEL, AIR AND EXHAUST SYSTEMS

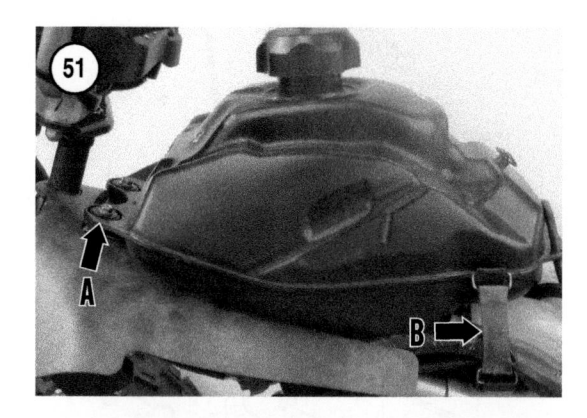

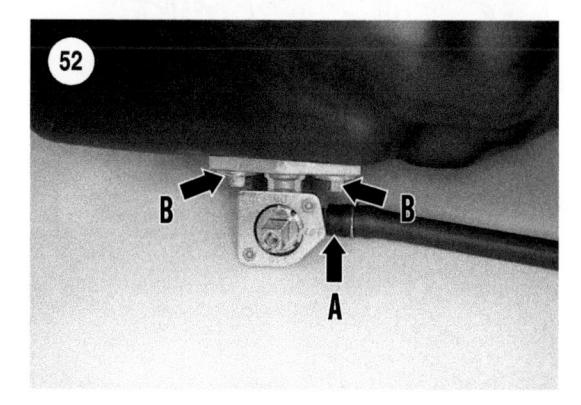

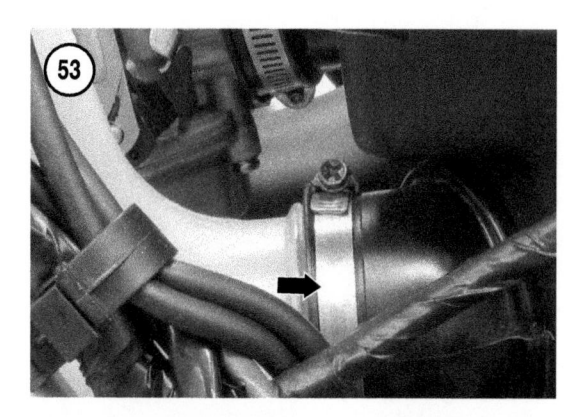

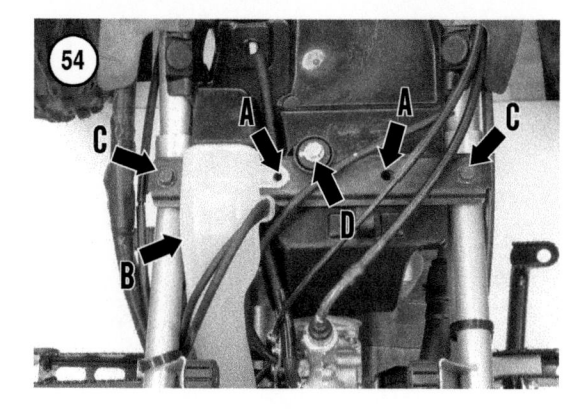

10. Remove the heat guard by performing the following:
    a. Loosen the intake-air-duct clamp (**Figure 53**).
    b. Remove the retaining clips (A, **Figure 54**), and intake air duct (B).
    c. Remove the bracket bolts (C, **Figure 54**) and cylinder head cover bolt (D).
    d. Remove the heat guard bracket and heat guard.
11. Install the fuel tank by reversing these removal steps, plus the following:
    a. Replace the front fuel tank collars if they are missing or damaged.
    b. Replace missing or damaged fuel tank dampers or holder bands.
    c. If the intake-air-duct connecting tube is pulled out from the air box during disassembly, reinstall the tube by aligning the arrow on the connecting tube with the index mark on the air box.
    d. Secure the fuel hose to the fuel valve with its hose clamp.
    e. Tighten the fuel tank mounting bolts securely.
    f. Tighten the cylinder head cover bolt to 32 N•m (24 ft.-lb.).
    g. Turn the fuel valve on and check for leaks.

FUEL VALVE

Removal/Installation

1. Remove the fuel tank as described in this chapter.
2. Drain all gasoline from the fuel tank. Store the gas in a can approved for gasoline storage.
3. Remove the fuel valve bolts (B, **Figure 52**) and fuel valve from the fuel tank.
4. Remove the O-ring and strainer screen from the fuel valve.
5. Clean the strainer screen in a high-flash point solvent. Replace the strainer screen if it shows any damage.
6. Install a new fuel valve O-ring.
7. Install the fuel valve by reversing the preceding removal steps, plus the following:
    a. Tighten the fuel valve mounting bolts securely.
    b. After turning on the fuel valve, check the fuel valve and hose for leaks.

CHAPTER EIGHT

AIR BOX

55

1. Core
2. Clamp
3. Element
4. Spring clip
5. Dust cover (California models only)
6. Cover
7. Gasket
8. Screw
9. Holder
10. Retaining clip
11. Air box
12. Drain plug (only one on California models)
13. Connecting tube
14. Intake air duct
15. Breather tube (California models only)

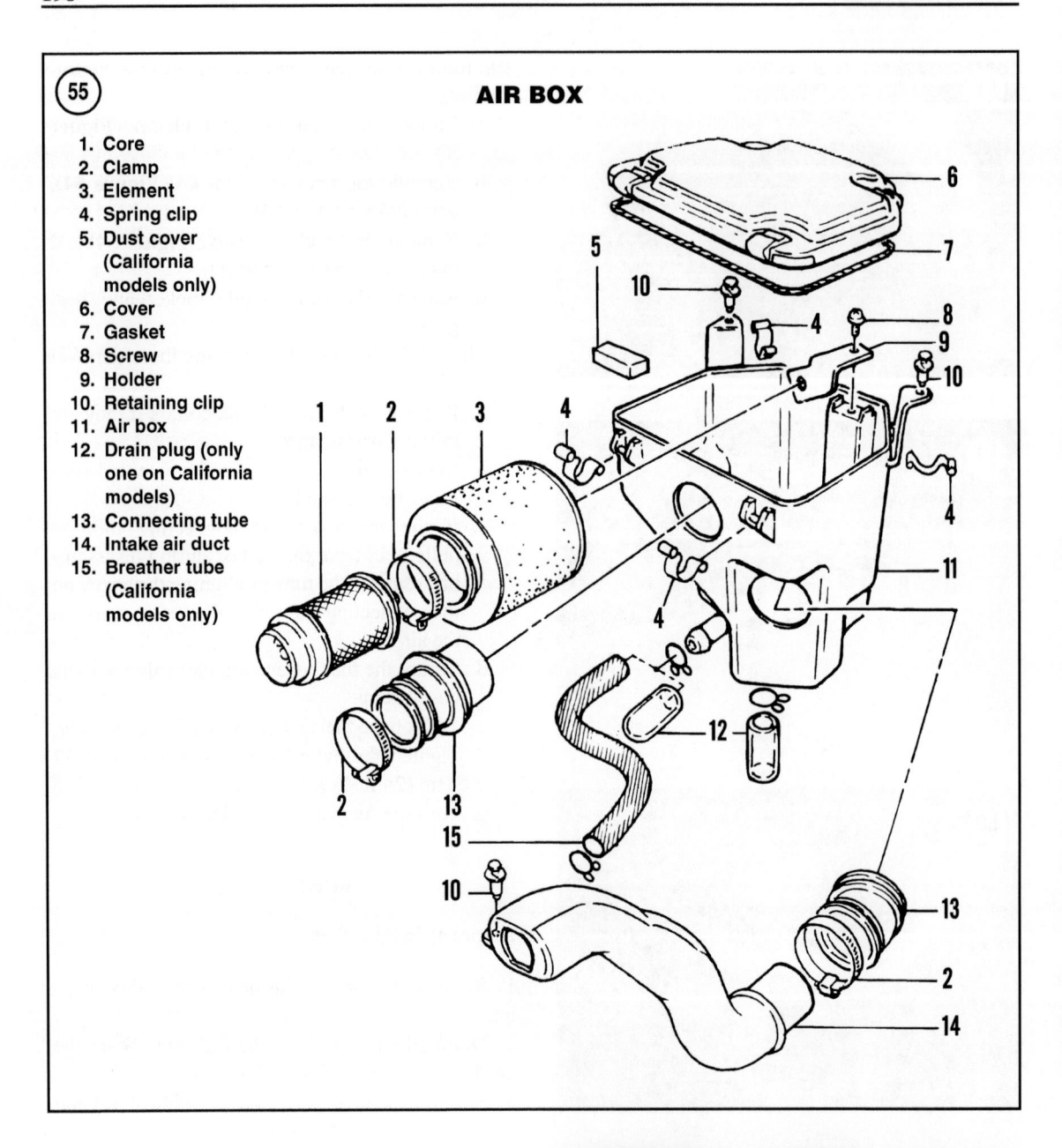

AIR BOX

Removal/Installation

Refer to **Figure 55** when servicing the air box assembly. Refer to Chapter Three when servicing the air filter element.

1. Park the vehicle on level ground and set the parking brake.

2. Remove the seat and side covers as described in Chapter Fourteen.

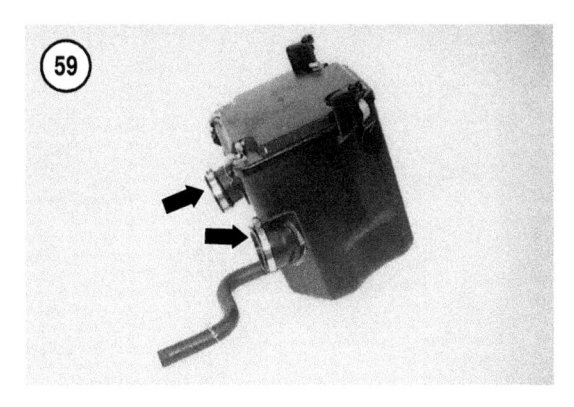

FUEL, AIR AND EXHAUST SYSTEMS

57

58

59

3. Loosen the carburetor clamp screw (**Figure 56**) and the intake-air-duct clamp screw (**Figure 53**).

4. Remove the breather hose (**Figure 57**) from the crankcase.

5. Remove the air box retaining clips (**Figure 58**).

6. Move the air box rearward, and disconnect the connecting tubes from the carburetor and intake air duct.

7. Lift the air box from the frame.

8. Stuff a clean rag into the carburetor intake so dust and dirt cannot enter.

9. Install the air box by reversing the removal procedure. Note the following:
   a. Check the carburetor connector tube for loose parts or other debris before connecting it to the carburetor.
   b. If either connecting tube (**Figure 59**) is pulled out from the air box during disassembly, reinstall the tube by aligning the arrow on the connecting tube with the index mark on the respective air box opening.
   c. Make sure the drain plugs are securely installed on the air box.
   d. On California models, make sure the breather tube is secured to the crankcase breather fitting (**Figure 57**).

EXHAUST SYSTEM

Check the exhaust system for deep dents and fractures. Repair them or replace parts immediately. Check the muffler mounting flanges on the frame for fractures and loose bolts. Check the cylinder head mounting flange for tightness. A loose exhaust pipe connection causes excessive exhaust noise and robs the engine of power. Before removing the exhaust system, check for leaks at the exhaust port and at the muffler clamp.

Refer to **Figure 60**.

Removal/Installation

NOTE
The exhaust system can be removed with the front and rear fenders installed on the vehicle. The fenders have been removed in the following photographs for clarity.

1. Park the vehicle on level ground and set the parking brake.

2. Remove the front fender and side covers as described in Chapter Fourteen.

3. Loosen the muffler clamp bolt (**Figure 61**).

4. Remove the muffler hanger bolts (**Figure 62**).

5. Withdraw the muffler from the exhaust pipe, and remove the muffler.

6. Remove the exhaust pipe nuts (A, **Figure 63**), and slide the clamp (B) off the studs and down the exhaust pipe.

7. Pull the exhaust pipe fitting from the exhaust port, and remove the exhaust pipe.

200

CHAPTER EIGHT

EXHAUST SYSTEM

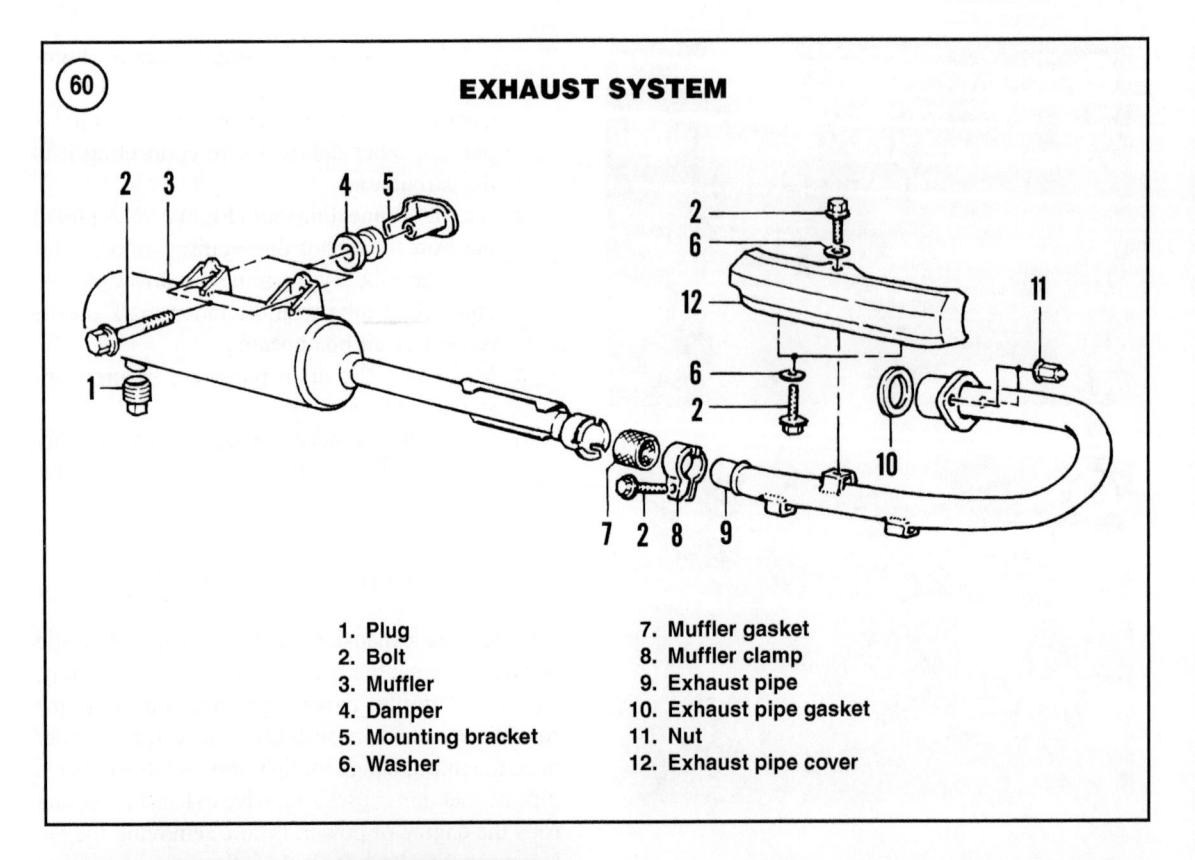

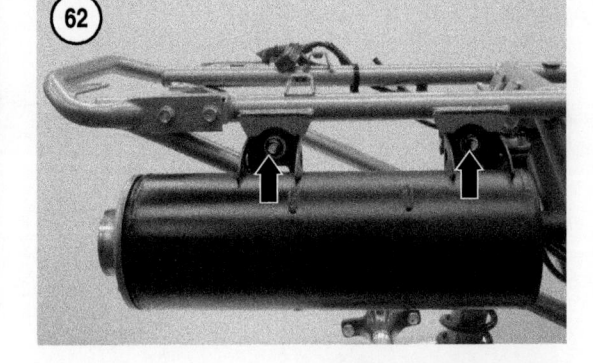

1. Plug
2. Bolt
3. Muffler
4. Damper
5. Mounting bracket
6. Washer
7. Muffler gasket
8. Muffler clamp
9. Exhaust pipe
10. Exhaust pipe gasket
11. Nut
12. Exhaust pipe cover

8. Remove the exhaust pipe gasket from the exhaust port, and discard the gasket. The exhaust pipe must be reinstalled with a new gasket.

9. If necessary, remove the mounting screws and exhaust pipe cover (**Figure 64**) from the exhaust pipe.

10. Install the exhaust system by performing the following:

   a. Install a new exhaust header gasket. Apply a small amount of grease to the gasket to hold it

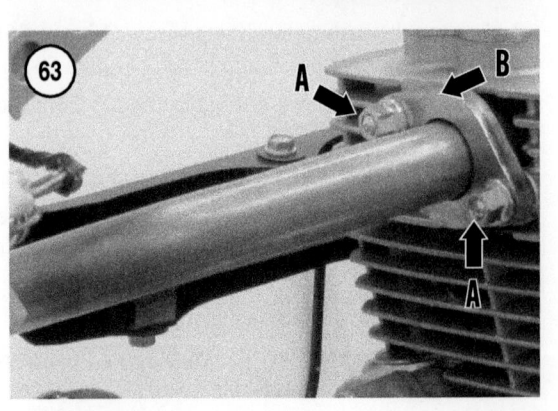

FUEL, AIR AND EXHAUST SYSTEMS

in place, and fit the gasket into the exhaust port.

b. Fit the exhaust pipe into the exhaust port, and slide the clamp (B, **Figure 63**) over the header studs. Loosely install the exhaust pipe nuts (A, **Figure 63**).

c. Install a new muffler gasket into the muffler.

d. From the rear of the vehicle, slide the muffler forward and into the exhaust pipe. Make sure the muffler pipe is inboard of the frame member.

e. Slide the muffler clamp over the pipe joint, and loosely install the muffler hanger bolts (**Figure 62**).

11. To minimize the chances of an exhaust leak, tighten the bolts in the following order:

a. Exhaust pipe nuts (A, **Figure 63**).

b. Muffler clamp bolt (**Figure 61**). Tighten the muffler clamp bolt to 23 N•m (17 ft.-lb.).

c. Muffler hanger bolts (**Figure 62**).

12. If removed, install the exhaust pipe cover. Tighten the cover mounting bolts to 22 N•m (16 ft.-lb.).

13. After installation is complete, start the engine and check for exhaust leaks.

14. Install the front fender (Chapter Fourteen).

Spark Arrester Cleaning

Refer to Chapter Three.

Table 1 CARBURETOR SPECIFICATIONS

Carburetor type	Piston valve
Identification number	PDC1D
Throttle bore	20 mm (0.8 in.)
Main jet	#95
Standard[1]	#95
High-altitude[2]	#92
Slow jet (pilot jet)	#38
Jet needle clip position	3rd groove from top
Pilot screw setting	
Initial setting[1]	1 7/8 turns out
High altitude[2]	1 3/4 turns out
Final setting	7/8 turns out
Float level	14 mm (0.6 in.)
Idle speed	1300-1500 rpm
Throttle lever free play	3-8 mm (1/8-5/16 in.)

1. Below 1500 m (5000 ft.)
2. 1000-2500 m (3000-8000 ft.)

Table 2 FUEL AND EXHAUST SYSTEM TORQUE SPECIFICATIONS

Item	N•m	in.-lb.	ft.-lb.
Carburetor intake manifold stud	10	89	–
Cylinder head cover bolt	32	–	24
Exhaust pipe cover bolts	22	–	16
Muffler clamp bolt	23	–	17
Throttle housing cover screws	4	35	–

NOTE: Refer to the Supplement at the back of this manual for information unique to 2006-on models.

CHAPTER NINE

ELECTRICAL SYSTEM

This chapter contains service and test procedures for most electrical and ignition components. Information regarding the battery and spark plug is in Chapter Three.

Tables 1-3 are located at the end of this chapter. When inspecting a component, compare measurements to the electrical specifications in **Table 1**. Replace any component that is damaged or out of specification. During assembly, tighten fasteners to the specifications in **Table 3**.

ELECTRICAL COMPONENT REPLACEMENT

Most motorcycle dealerships and parts suppliers do not accept the return of any electrical part. If you cannot determine the *exact* cause of any electrical system malfunction, have a Honda dealership retest that specific system to verify your test results. If you purchase a new electrical component(s), install it, and then find that the system still does not work properly, you probably cannot return the unit for a refund.

Consider any test results carefully before replacing a component that tests only *slightly* out of specification, especially resistance. A number of variables can affect test results dramatically. These include the testing meter's internal circuitry, ambient temperature and conditions under which the machine has been operated. All instructions and specifications have been checked for accuracy; however, successful test results depend to a great degree upon individual accuracy.

ELECTRICAL CONNECTORS

TRX250EX models are equipped with a variety of electrical components, connectors and wires. Corrosion-causing moisture can enter these connectors and cause poor electrical connections, which ultimately leads to component failure. Troubleshooting an electrical circuit with one or more corroded electrical connectors can be time-consuming and frustrating.

To prevent corrosion, pack electrical connectors with dielectric grease when reconnecting them. Dielectric grease is especially formulated for sealing and waterproofing electrical connectors, and it does not interfere with the current flow. Only use this compound or an equivalent designed for this specific purpose. Other materials may interfere with the current flow. Do not use silicone sealant.

Thoroughly clean and dry both the male and female connector halves. Pack one of the halves with dielectric grease compound before joining the two connector halves.

In addition to packing electrical connectors, make sure the ground connections are tight and free of corrosion.

ELECTRICAL SYSTEM

1

2

Voltmeter

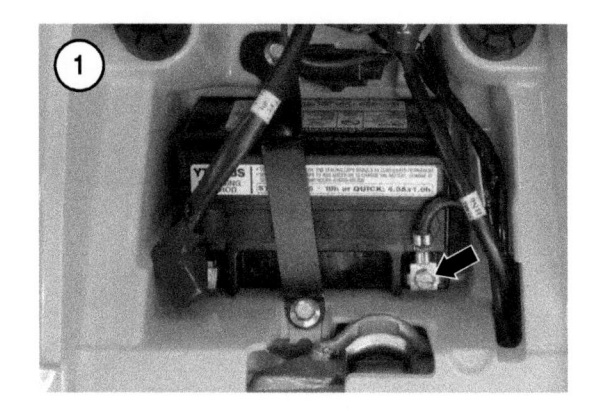

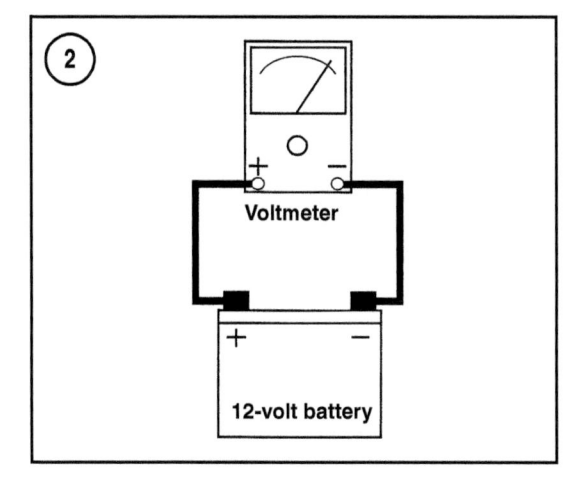

12-volt battery

The location of electrical connectors can vary between model years. If the ATV has been worked on by someone else, this person may have repositioned the connector. Always check the connector wire colors to make sure it is the correct electrical connector. To double check, follow the electrical cable from the specific component to where it connects to the wiring harness or to another electrical component within that system.

BATTERY NEGATIVE TERMINAL

Some of the procedures in this chapter require disconnecting the negative battery cable as a safety precaution.
1. Turn the ignition switch off.
2. Remove the seat as described in Chapter Fourteen.
3. Disconnect the cable from the negative battery terminal (**Figure 1**).
4. Move the cable out of the way so it does not accidentally make contact with the terminal.

5. Once the procedure is completed, connect the battery negative cable to the terminal, and tighten the bolt securely.
6. Install the seat as described in Chapter Fourteen.

CHARGING SYSTEM

The charging system consists of the battery, alternator and a voltage regulator/rectifier. A 15-amp main fuse protects the circuit. Refer to the wiring diagram in the back of the manual.

Alternating current generated by the alternator is rectified to direct current. The voltage regulator maintains the voltage to the battery and additional electrical loads at a constant level despite variations in engine speed and load.

Troubleshooting

Refer to Chapter Two.

Battery Voltage Check

To obtain accurate charging system test results, the battery must be fully charged. Check battery voltage as follows:
1. Remove the seat (Chapter Fourteen).
2. Connect a digital voltmeter across the battery negative and positive terminals and measure the battery voltage (**Figure 2**). A fully-charged battery reads between 13.0-13.2 volts. If the voltage reading is less than this amount, recharge the battery as described in Chapter Three.

Current Draw Test

Perform this test before performing the charging voltage test.
1. Remove the seat (Chapter Fourteen).
2. Turn the ignition switch off.
3. Disconnect the negative battery cable from the battery (**Figure 1**).

CAUTION
Before connecting the ammeter to the circuit, set the meter to its highest amperage scale. This prevents a large current flow from damaging the meter or blowing the meter's fuse, if so equipped.

4. Connect an ammeter between the battery negative lead and the negative terminal of the battery (**Figure 3**). Switch the ammeter from its highest to lowest amperage scale while reading the meter. If the needle swings even the slightest amount, current is draining from the system.
5. A current draw higher than 1.0 mA indicates a continuous battery discharge. Dirt and/or electrolyte on top of the battery or a crack in the battery case can cause this type of problem by providing a path for battery current to flow. Remove and clean the battery as described in Chapter Three. Reinstall the battery and retest.
6. If the current draw is still excessive, the battery is damaged or the system contains a short circuit.
7. To find the short circuit, refer to the wiring diagram at the end of this manual. Measure the current draw while disconnecting system connectors one by one. When the current rate returns to normal, the circuit just disconnected contains the short. Test that circuit further to find the problem.
8. Disconnect the ammeter from the battery and battery cable.
9. Reconnect the negative battery cable to the battery.
10. Install the seat (Chapter Fourteen).

Regulated Voltage Test

This procedure tests charging system operation. It does not measure maximum charging system output. **Table 1** lists charging system specifications.

To obtain accurate test results, the battery must be fully charged. Check the battery voltage as described in this section. Charge the battery if necessary.
1. Start and run the engine until it reaches normal operating temperature, and then turn the engine off.
2. Connect a tachometer to the engine following its manufacturer's instructions.
3. Connect a 0-20 DC voltmeter to the battery terminals as shown in **Figure 2**.
4. Start the engine and let it idle.
5. Turn the headlight to HI beam.
6. Gradually increase engine speed from idle to 5000 rpm and note the reading on the voltmeter. It should equal the regulated voltage specification.
   a. If the regulated voltage is less than specified, the wiring harness may have an open or short, the alternator may have an open or short or the regulator/rectifier may be faulty.
   b. If the regulated voltage exceeds specification, the regulator/rectifier may be poorly grounded, the battery may be faulty or the regulator/rectifier is faulty.
7. Shut off the engine and disconnect the voltmeter and tachometer.
8. Install the seat (Chapter Fourteen).

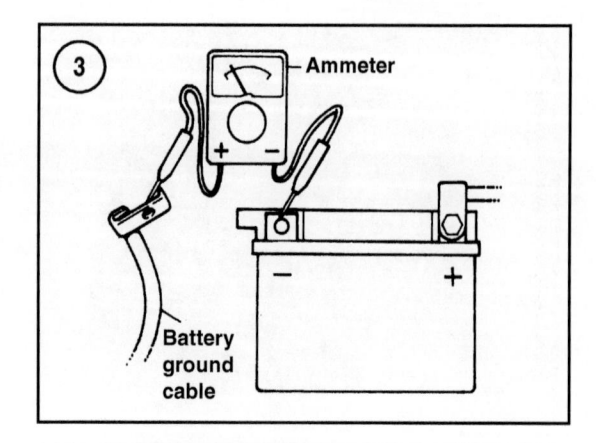

Regulator/Rectifier Harness Test

1. Remove the seat and the left side cover as described in Chapter Fourteen.
2. Disconnect the 5-pin connector (A, **Figure 4**) from the regulator/rectifier.
3. Check the connector for loose or corroded terminals.

NOTE
Perform all tests (Steps 4-6) on the harness side of the connector, not on the regulator/rectifier side.

4. Check the battery lead by performing the following:
   a. Connect a voltmeter between the red and green terminals in the connector.
   b. With the ignition switch off, the voltmeter should read 13.0-13.2 volts (battery voltage).
   c. If the reading is less than battery voltage, check both wires for damage.
   d. Disconnect the voltmeter leads.
5. Check the ground wire continuity by performing the following:.
   a. Connect an ohmmeter between the green wire and a good engine ground.
   b. The ohmmeter should indicate continuity (zero or low resistance).

ELECTRICAL SYSTEM

3. Disconnect the 5-pin connector (A, **Figure 4**) from the regulator/rectifier.
4. Remove the bolts securing the regulator/rectifier (B, **Figure 4**) to the frame and remove it.
5. Install by reversing the preceding removal steps.

ALTERNATOR

The alternator consists of the flywheel and stator coil assembly. Flywheel and stator removal/installation procedures are in Chapter Five.

Flywheel Testing

The flywheel is permanently magnetized and cannot be tested except by replacing it. A rotor can lose magnetism over time or from a sharp blow. Replace the flywheel if it is defective or damaged.

Charge Coil Resistance Test

NOTE
The stator coil is also referred to as the charge coil.

The charge coil (**Figure 5**) is part of the stator assembly, which is mounted inside the alternator cover. This test can be performed with the alternator cover mounted on the engine.

1. Remove the seat and the left side cover as described in Chapter Fourteen.
2. Check the regulator/rectifier connector by performing the following:
   a. Disconnect the regulator/rectifier 5-pin connector (A, **Figure 4**).
   b. Measure the resistance across the two yellow wire terminals in the harness side of the connector. It should equal the specified charge coil resistance (**Table 1**).
   c. Check the continuity between each yellow terminal in the connector and a good ground. There should be no continuity (infinite resistance).
   d. If either yellow wire has continuity to ground (low resistance), perform Step 3.
3. Check the charge coil resistance and continuity at the alternator connector by performing the following:
   a. Disconnect the red, 3-pin alternator connector (A, **Figure 6**).

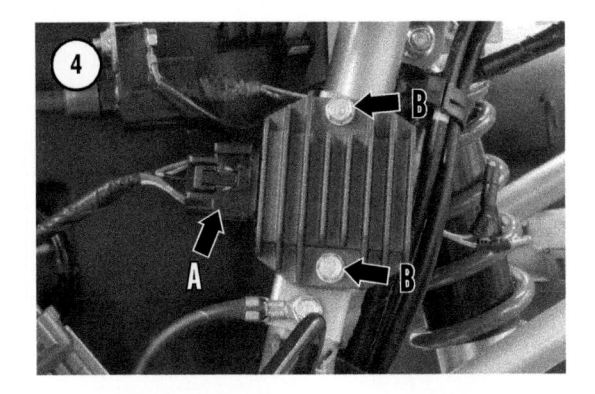

   c. If there is no continuity (infinite resistance), check the green wire for damage.
6. Check the charge leads by performing the following:
   a. Measure resistance across the two yellow terminals in the connector. It should equal the specified charge coil resistance (**Table 1**).
   b. A reading of infinity indicates an open circuit. Test the stator coil resistance as described in this chapter.
   c. If the resistance reading is excessive, check for dirty or loose-fitting terminals or damaged wires.
7. If all the tests are within specification, the harness is working properly. Replace the regulator/rectifier as described in this section.
8. Reconnect the regulator/rectifier electrical connector (A, **Figure 4**).

Regulator/Rectifier Removal/Installation

1. Remove the seat and the left side cover (Chapter Fourteen).
2. Disconnect the negative battery cable from the battery.

b. Measure the resistance across the two yellow wire terminals in the alternator side of the connector. The charge coil is faulty if the resistance exceeds specification.

c. Check the continuity between each yellow terminal in the alternator side of the connector and a good engine ground. There should be no continuity. If either terminal has continuity to ground, the charge coil is shorted and must be replaced.

NOTE
Before replacing the stator assembly, check the electrical wires to and within the electrical connector for any open or poor connections.

4A. If the charge coil fails either test at the alternator connector (Step 3), the charge coil is faulty. Replace the stator assembly as described in *Alternator Cover* in Chapter Five.

4B. If the charge coil fails a test at the regulator/rectifier connector (Step 2) but passes the tests at the alternator connector (Step 3), replace the regulator/rectifier harness.

5. Apply a dielectric grease to the alternator connector before reconnecting it. This helps seal out moisture.

IGNITION SYSTEM

All models are equipped with a capacitor discharge ignition system. Refer to the wiring diagram at the end of this manual.

Tools

Various peak voltage tests are used to test the ignition system. These tests require either a peak voltage tester or the Honda peak voltage adapter (part No. 07HGJ-0020100) used with a commercially available digital multimeter (minimum impedance: 10 M ohms/DCV). If these tools are not available, refer the tests to a Honda dealership.

Precautions

When working on the ignition system, protect the system by taking the following precautions:

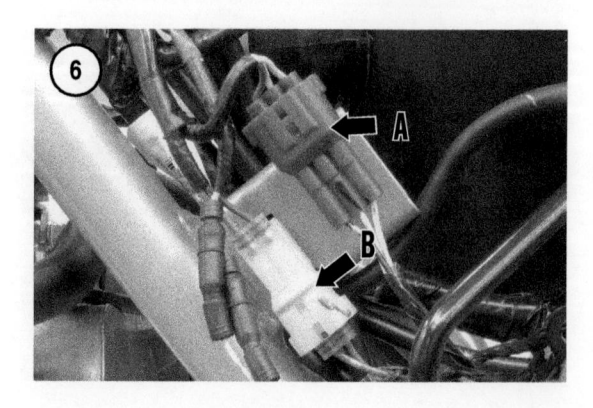

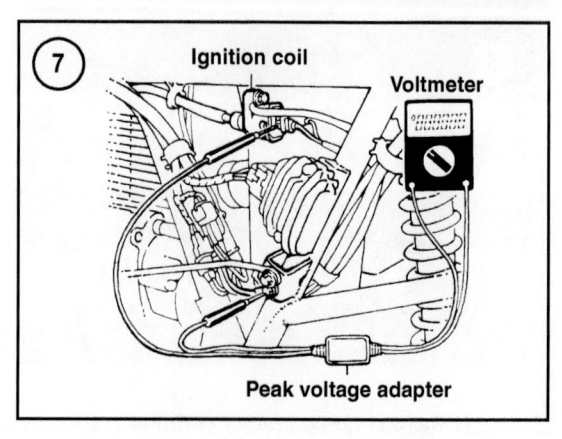

1. Never disconnect any electrical connection while the engine is running.

2. Apply dielectric grease to all electrical connectors before reconnecting them. This helps seal out moisture.

3. The electrical connectors must be free of corrosion and properly connected.

4. The ignition control module (ICM) is mounted in a rubber mount. The ICM must always be reinstalled into its rubber mount after service or testing.

Troubleshooting

Refer to Chapter Two.

Ignition Coil Primary Peak Voltage Test

1. Check the engine compression as described in Chapter Three. The following test results are inaccurate if engine compression is low.

2. Check all electrical connections in the ignition system. They must be clean and tight.

ELECTRICAL SYSTEM

tem in Chapter Two. Locate the description that best describes the results obtained from this peak voltage test, and perform the indicated checks.

Ignition Pulse Generator Peak Voltage Test

1. Check the engine compression as described in Chapter Three.
2. Confirm that the spark plug and plug cap are correctly installed.
3. Remove the seat and left side cover as described in Chapter Fourteen.
4. Shift the transmission into neutral.
5. Connect a peak voltage adapter to the multimeter following the manufacturer's instructions.
6. Measure the peak voltage at the ICM connector by performing the following:
   a. Disconnect the 4-pin ICM connector (A, **Figure 8**) from the ICM.
   b. Connect the peak voltage adapter's positive lead to the black/yellow terminal on the 4-pin ICM connector, and connect the adapter's negative lead to green/white terminal. Refer to **Figure 9**.
   c. Turn the ignition on and the engine stop switch to RUN.
   d. Press the starter button and read the peak voltage on the voltmeter. The reading should exceed the pulse generator peak voltage specification in **Table 1**. Record the peak voltage reading.
7. If the peak voltage reading is less than specified, measure the peak voltage at the ignition pulse generator connector by performing the following:
   a. Disconnect the 2-pin ignition pulse generator connector (B, **Figure 6**).
   b. Connect the peak voltage adapter's positive lead to the blue/yellow terminal on the 2-pin connector, and connect the adapter's negative lead to a good ground. Refer to **Figure 10**.
   c. Turn the ignition on and the engine stop switch to RUN.
   d. Press the starter button and read the peak voltage on the voltmeter. The reading should exceed the pulse generator peak voltage specification. Record the peak voltage reading.
8. Compare the two test readings.
   a. If the peak voltage at the 2-pin ignition pulse generator connector is within specification

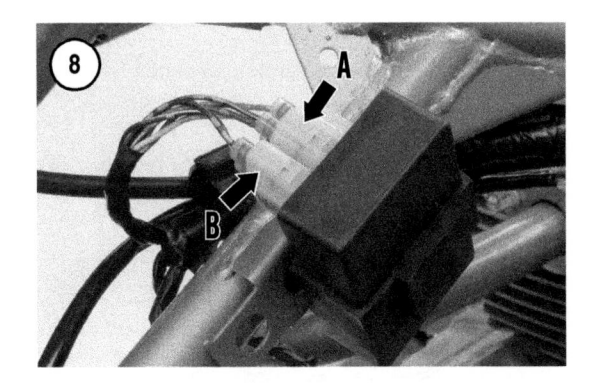

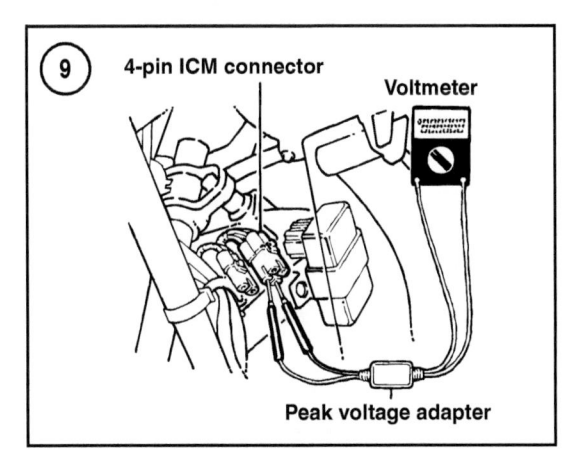

3. Disconnect the spark plug cap from the spark plug.
4. Install a known good spark plug into the plug cap, and ground the spark plug against the cylinder or cylinder head.
5. Connect the peak voltage adapter to the multimeter following the manufacturer's instructions.
6. Connect the peak voltage adapter's positive lead to the black/yellow terminal on the ignition coil, and connect the adapter's negative lead to a good ground. Make sure the ignition coil primary wire is still connected to the ignition coil. Refer to **Figure 7**.
7. Turn the ignition on and the engine stop switch to RUN.
8. Shift the transmission into neutral.
9. Press the starter button and read the peak voltage on the voltmeter. The reading should exceed the ignition coil peak voltage specification in **Table 1**. Record the peak voltage reading.
   a. If the peak voltage reading is less than specified, check for an open or a poor connection on the black/yellow wire. If this is not the source of the problem, refer to *Ignition Sys-*

but the peak voltage at the 4-pin ICM connector is less than specified, the wiring harness is faulty. Check for an open or loose connection.
b. If both peak voltage readings are less than specified, refer to *Ignition System* in Chapter Two. Locate the description that best describes the results obtained from this peak voltage test, and perform the indicated checks.

Exciter Coil Peak Voltage Test

1. Check the engine compression as described in Chapter Three.
2. Confirm that the spark plug and plug cap are correctly installed.
3. Remove the seat and left side cover as described in Chapter Fourteen.
4. Shift the transmission into neutral.
5. Connect a peak voltage adapter to the multimeter following the manufacturer's instructions.
6. Measure the peak voltage at the ICM connectors by performing the following:
    a. Disconnect the 4-pin connector (A, **Figure 8**) and the 2-pin connector (B) from the ICM.
    b. Connect the peak voltage adapter's positive lead to the black/red terminal in the 2-pin connector, and connect the adapter's negative lead to green/white terminal in the 4-pin ICM connector. Refer to **Figure 11**.
    c. Turn the ignition on and the engine stop switch to RUN.
    d. Press the starter button and read the peak voltage on the voltmeter. The reading should exceed the exciter coil peak voltage specification. Record the peak voltage reading.
7. If the peak voltage reading is less than specified, measure the peak voltage at the alternator connector by performing the following:
    a. Disconnect the 3-pin alternator connector (A, **Figure 6**).
    b. Connect the peak voltage adapter's positive lead to the black/red terminal on the alternator connector, and connect the adapter's negative lead to a good ground. Refer to **Figure 12**.
    c. Turn the ignition on and the engine stop switch to RUN.
    d. Press the starter button and read the peak voltage on the voltmeter. The reading should exceed the exciter coil peak voltage specification. Record the peak voltage reading.

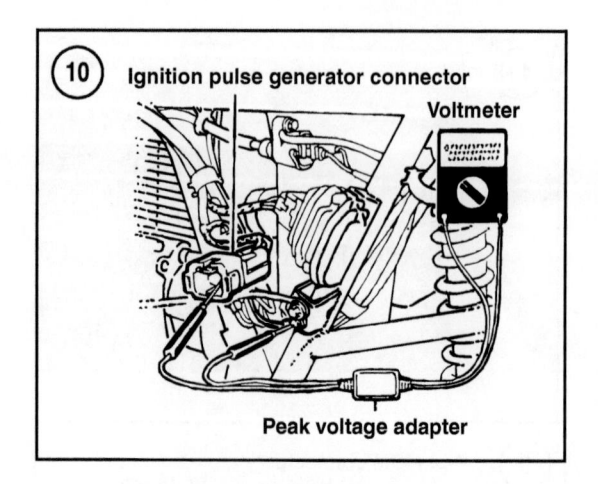

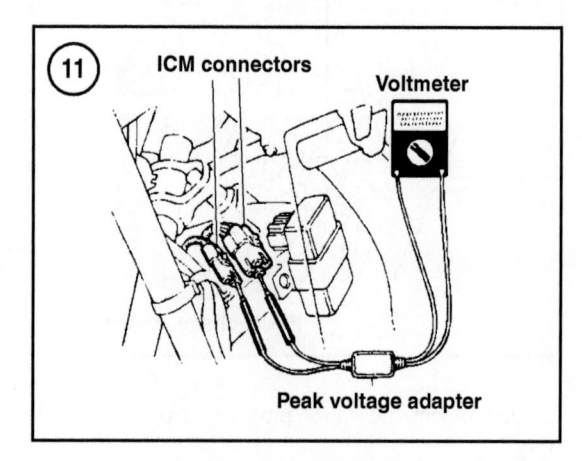

8. Compare the two test readings.
    a. If the peak voltage at the alternator connector is within specification but the peak voltage at the ICM connectors is less than specified, the wiring harness is faulty. Check for an open or loose connection.
    b. If both peak voltage readings are less than specified, refer to *Ignition System* in Chapter Two. Locate the description that best describes the results obtained from this peak voltage test, and perform the indicated checks.

Ignition Control Module (ICM) Removal/Installation

1. Remove the front fender as described in Chapter Fourteen.
2. Remove the 4-pin (A, **Figure 8**) and 2-pin (B) ICM connectors from the ignition control unit.
3. Pull the ICM unit from its rubber mount.

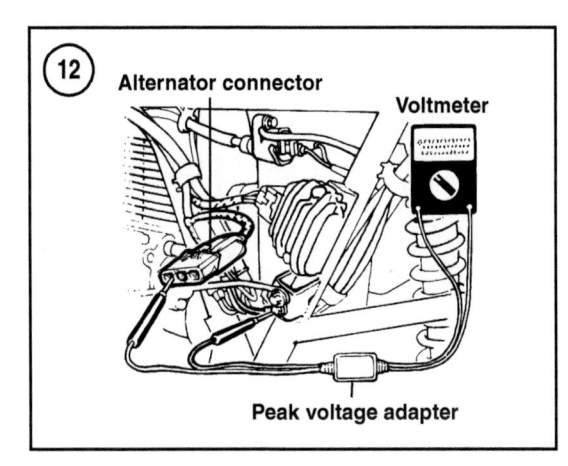

ELECTRICAL SYSTEM

12 Alternator connector / Voltmeter / Peak voltage adapter

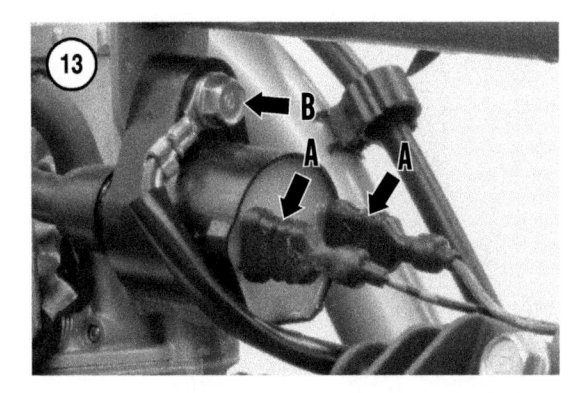

13 B, A, A

4. Install the new unit in the rubber mount, and connect both connectors.
5. Reinstall the front fender (Chapter Fourteen).

Ignition Coil Removal/Installation

1. Remove the fuel tank and heat guard as described in Chapter Eight.
2. Remove the spark plug cap from the spark plug, and release the spark plug wire from its clamp.
3. Disconnect the primary wires (A, **Figure 13**) from the ignition coil terminals.
4. Remove the mounting bolt (B, **Figure 13**) and ignition coil/wire assembly.
5. Installation is the reverse of removal.

Stator/Ignition Pulse Generator Removal

The ignition pulse generator and the stator form an assembly that mounts to the inside of the alternator cover. Neither can be replaced separately. Refer to *Alternator Cover Disassembly/Assembly* in Chapter Five for replacement procedures.

STARTER

The starting system consists of the starter, starter gears, starter relay and the starter button.

Starter gear service is covered in Chapter Five.

Troubleshooting

Refer to Chapter Two.

Removal/Installation

1. Park the vehicle on level ground and set the parking brake.
2. Remove the seat, side covers and rear fender as described in Chapter Fourteen.
3. Disconnect the negative battery cable from the battery.
4. Remove the boot from the starter terminal, and disconnect the starter cable (A, **Figure 14**) from the starter.

> *CAUTION*
> *Do not operate the starter for more than 5 seconds at a time. Let the starter cool approximately 10 seconds, and then try again.*

5. Remove the two starter mounting bolts (B, **Figure 14**) and remove the starter.
6. If necessary, service the starter as described in this chapter.
7. Install the starter by reversing the preceding removal steps. Pay attention to the following:
   a. Lubricate the starter O-ring (A, **Figure 15**) with grease.
   b. Clean any rust or corrosion from the round terminal on the starter cable.
   c. Tighten the starter mounting bolts securely.

Disassembly

Refer to **Figure 16**.

1. Find the alignment marks (B and C, **Figure 15**) across the armature housing and both covers. If necessary, make your own marks.
2. Remove the two throughbolts, washers, lockwashers and O-rings (**Figure 17**).

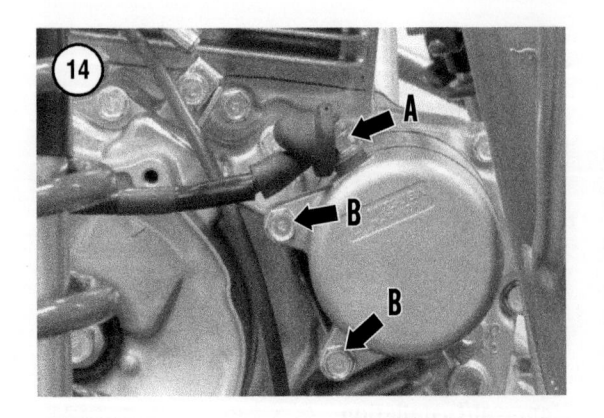

210 CHAPTER NINE

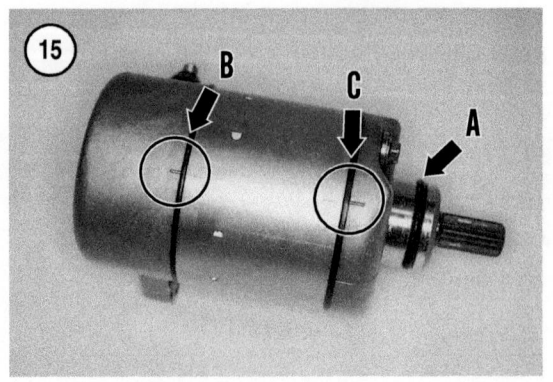

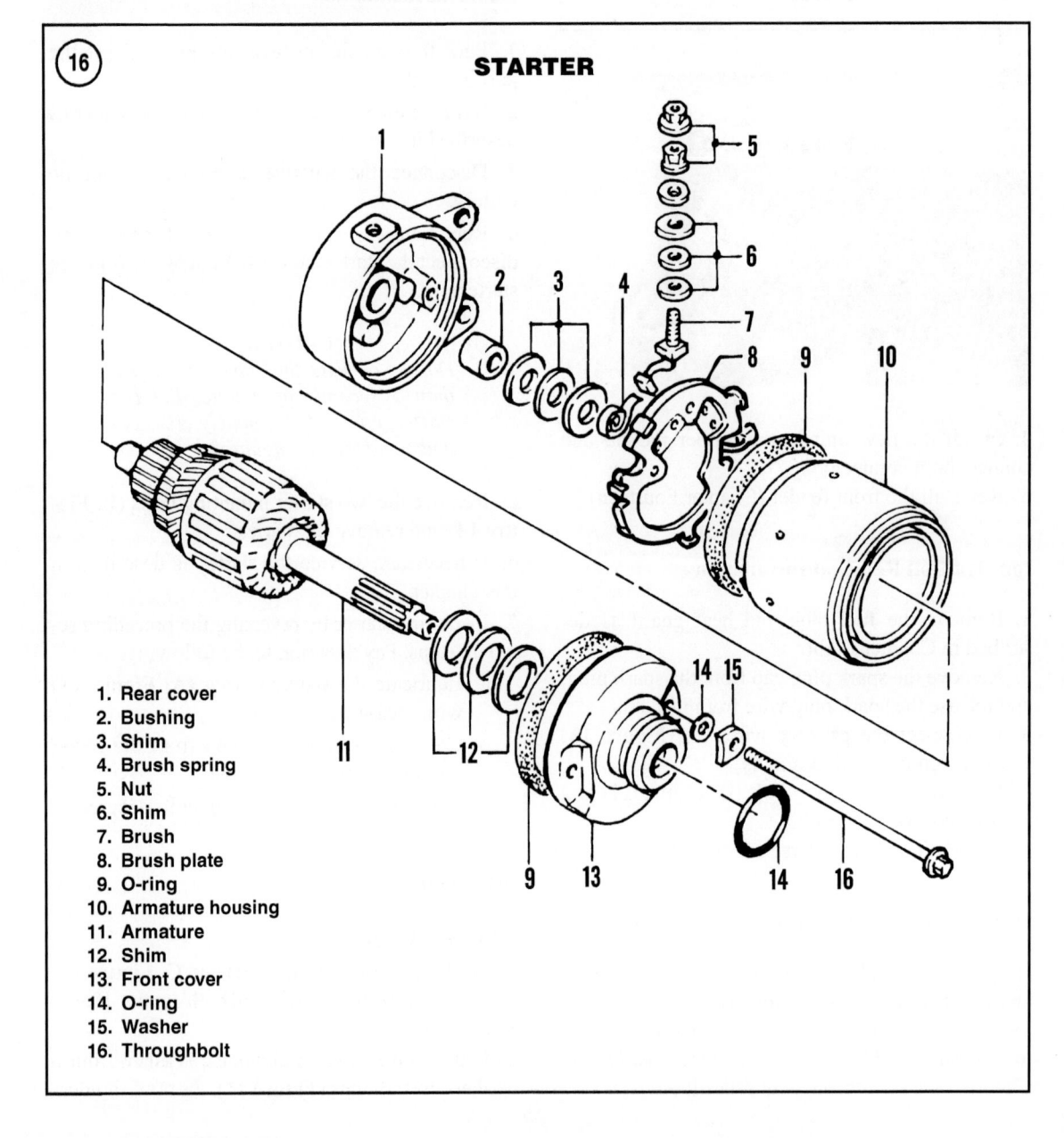

STARTER

1. Rear cover
2. Bushing
3. Shim
4. Brush spring
5. Nut
6. Shim
7. Brush
8. Brush plate
9. O-ring
10. Armature housing
11. Armature
12. Shim
13. Front cover
14. O-ring
15. Washer
16. Throughbolt

ELECTRICAL SYSTEM

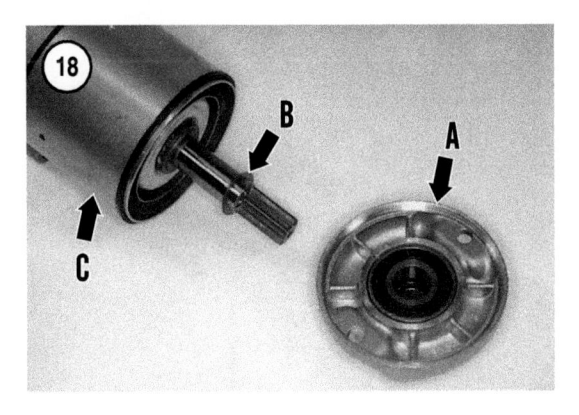

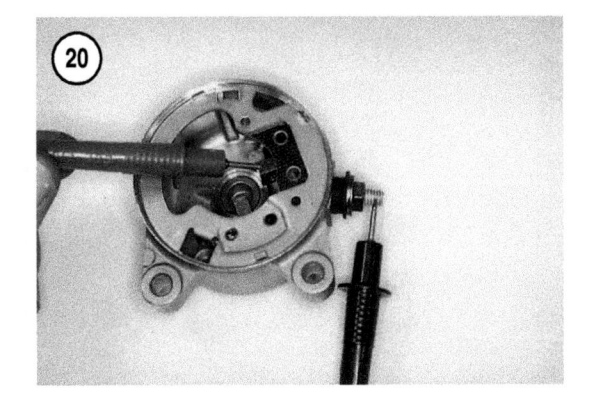

NOTE
Record the thickness and alignment of each shim and washer removed during disassembly.

NOTE
The number of shims used in each starter varies. The starter you are working on may use a different number of shims from that shown in the following photographs.

3. Remove the front cover (A, **Figure 18**).
4. Remove the front shims (B, **Figure 18**) from the armature shaft.
5. Remove the rear cover (A, **Figure 19**) from the armature housing.
6. Remove the rear shim set (B, **Figure 19**).

CAUTION
Wipe the windings with a cloth lightly moistened with solvent. Do not immerse the wire windings in the case or the armature in solvent. This could damage the insulation.

7. Clean all grease, dirt and carbon from the armature, housing and covers.

Inspection

1. Use an ohmmeter to perform the following:
   a. Check the continuity between the terminal bolt and the brush wire (the indigo-colored wire or the insulated brush holder). Refer to **Figure 20**. There should be continuity (low resistance).
   b. Check the continuity between the rear cover and the brush wire (the indigo-colored wire or the insulated brush holder). Refer to **Figure 21**. There should be no continuity (infinite resistance).
   c. Replace the starter if the rear cover fails either test.
2. Remove the nut and washers from the terminal bolts in the rear cover (**Figure 22**). Note the order of the parts as they are removed. The washers must be reinstalled in their original positions.
3. Pull the brush plate (**Figure 22**) out of the end cover.
4. Pull each spring (A, **Figure 23**) away from its brush, and pull the brush (B) from its brush holder.

5. Measure the length of each brush (**Figure 24**). If the length of either brush is less than the service limit in **Table 1**, replace both brushes as a set. When replacing the brushes, note the following:
   a. The starter brushes do not require soldering during replacement.
   b. Replace the terminal bolt and its brush (A, **Figure 25**) as an assembly.
   c. Replace the brush plate and its brush (B, **Figure 25**) as an assembly.
   d. Install the terminal bolt washer set (**Figure 22**) in the order noted during removal.
6. Inspect the brush springs. Replace them both if either is weak or damaged. To replace the brush springs, perform the following:
   a. Make a drawing that shows the location of the brush springs on the brush holder. Also indicate the direction in which each spring coil turns.
   b. Remove and replace both brush springs as a set.
7. Inspect the armature shaft (A, **Figure 26**) for excessive wear, scoring or other damage.
8. Inspect the commutator (B, **Figure 26**). The mica must be below the surface of the copper bars. On a worn commutator the mica and copper bars may be worn to the same level (**Figure 27**). If necessary, have the commutator serviced by a dealership or electrical repair shop.
9. Inspect the commutator copper bars for discoloration. A discolored pair of bars indicates grounded armature coils.
10. Use an ohmmeter and perform the following:
    a. Check for continuity between the commutator bars (**Figure 28**). There should be continuity (low resistance) between pairs of bars.
    b. Check for continuity between the commutator bars and shaft (**Figure 29**). There should be no continuity (infinite resistance).

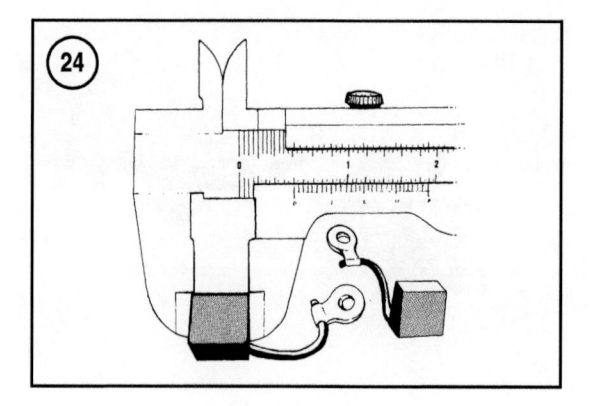

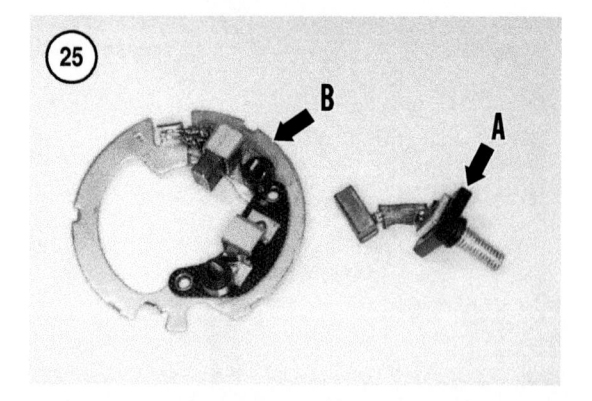

ELECTRICAL SYSTEM

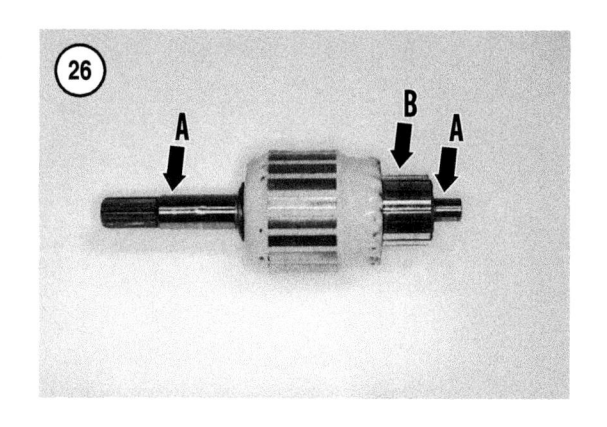

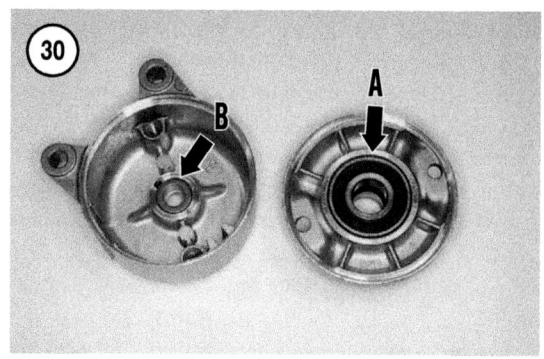

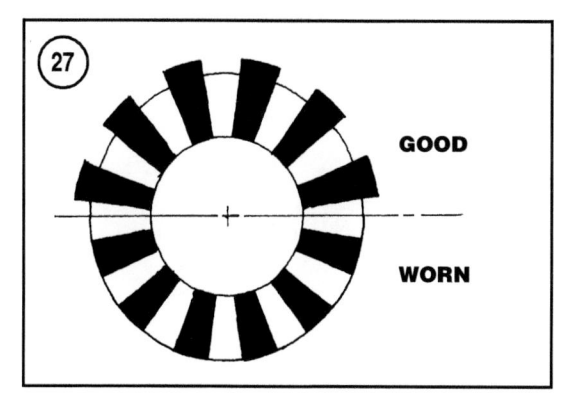

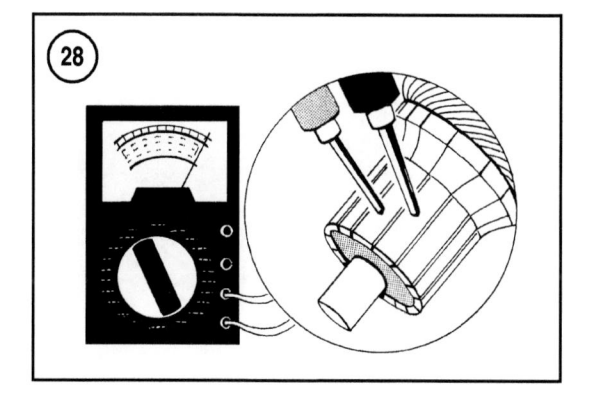

NOTE
The covers and armature housing are not available separately. If either part is worn or damaged, replace the starter.

    c. If the armature fails either of these tests, replace the starter.

11. Inspect the front cover bearing (A, **Figure 30**). Also inspect the dust seal behind the bearing. Replace the starter if either part is excessively worn or damaged.

12. Inspect the rear cover bushing (B, **Figure 30**). Replace the starter if the bushing is damaged.

13. Inspect the armature housing (**Figure 31**) for cracks or other damage. Then inspect for loose, chipped or damaged magnets.

14. Inspect all O-rings. Replace any that is worn or starting to harden.

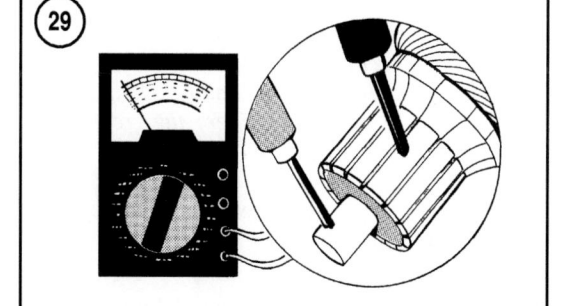

Assembly

1. If removed, install the brushes into their holders. Secure the brushes in place with the springs.

2. Align the tab on the brush plate with the notch in the rear cover, and install the brush plate (A, **Figure 32**) into the cover.

3. Install the rear shims (B **Figure 32**) onto the commutator end of the armature shaft.

4. Insert the armature into the rear cover (**Figure 33**). Turn the armature during installation so the brushes engage the commutator properly. Do not damage the brushes. During assembly, keep the commutator end of the armature up. If it is angled downward, the shims could slide off the armature shaft.

5. Install the two O-rings onto the armature housing. Then slide the housing (C, **Figure 18**) over the armature. Align the indexing marks on the housing and rear cover (B, **Figure 15**).

6. Install the front shims (B, **Figure 18**) onto the armature shaft.

7. Install the front cover (A, **Figure 18**) over the armature shaft. Align the indexing marks on the front cover and the armature housing (C, **Figure 15**).

NOTE
If one or both throughbolts do not pass through the starter, the covers and/or brush plate are installed incorrectly.

8. Lubricate the throughbolt O-rings with oil.
9. Install the bolts, washers and O-rings (**Figure 17**) and tighten the bolts securely.

STARTER RELAY

System Test

System testing of the starter relay switch is described in *Starting System* in Chapter Two.

Operation Check

1. Remove the seat (Chapter Fourteen).
2. Turn the ignition switch on and depress the starter button. The starter relay (**Figure 34**) should click. If the starter relay does not click, perform the *Voltage Test* described in this section.
3. Turn the ignition switch off and install the seat (Chapter Fourteen).

Voltage Test

1. Remove the seat (Chapter Fourteen).
2. Disconnect the two starter relay bullet connectors (**Figure 35**).

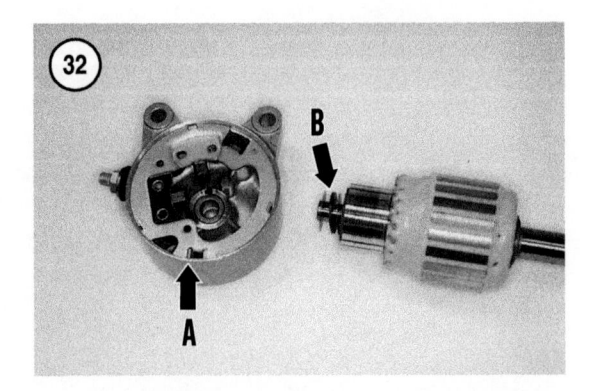

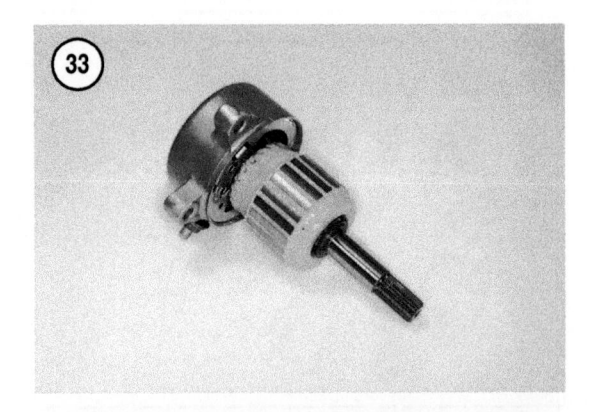

NOTE
This test can be performed with the fender installed. The starter relay bullet connectors (light green and yellow/red wires) are located beside the regulator/rectifier, under the rear fender on the left side of the vehicle.

3. Connect a voltmeter between the starter relay connector yellow/red and light green terminals on the harness side of the connectors.
4. Shift the transmission into neutral and turn the ignition switch on. Press the starter button and read

ELECTRICAL SYSTEM

2. Connect an ohmmeter to the battery and starter terminals (**Figure 36**) on the starter relay.
3. Momentarily connect a fully-charged 12-volt battery to the starter relay switch terminals as shown in **Figure 36** while reading the resistance on the ohmmeter.
4. The relay must have continuity when battery voltage is applied and no continuity when the battery is disconnected from the relay.
5. If either reading is incorrect, replace the starter relay and retest.

Removal/Installation

1. Remove the seat (Chapter Fourteen).
2. Disconnect the negative battery cable from the battery (Chapter Three).
3. Slide the rubber boots back from the starter relay terminals.
4. Remove the mounting nuts and disconnect the starter lead (A, **Figure 37**) and battery lead (B) from the starter relay.

NOTE
The starter relay bullet connectors (light green and yellow/red wires) are found beside the regulator/rectifier. Look underneath the rear fender on the left side of the vehicle.

5. Disconnect the two starter relay bullet connectors (**Figure 35**).
6. Pull the starter relay harness from the fender (**Figure 38**).
7. Pull the starter-relay rubber mount (C, **Figure 37**) from the mounting bracket, and remove the starter relay.
8. Install the starter relay by reversing the removal procedures.

DIODE

A diode is installed in the starting circuit (**Figure 39**). Test the diode when troubleshooting a neutral indicator circuit problem.

Removal/Installation

1. Remove the seat (Chapter Fourteen).
2. Disconnect the negative battery cable from the battery (Chapter Three).

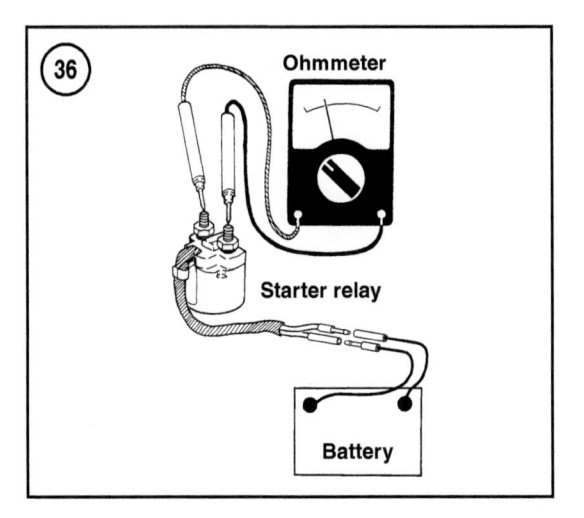

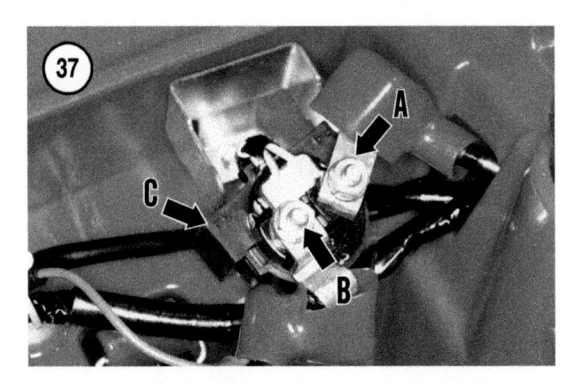

the voltage on the meter. It should read battery voltage. If the voltmeter reading is incorrect, perform the *Continuity Test* described in this section.
5. Turn the ignition switch off.
6. Reverse Steps 1-3 to complete installation.

Continuity Test

1. Remove the starter relay (**Figure 34**) as described in this section.

3. Remove the tape from around the diode (**Figure 39**), and disconnect the diode from the wiring harness.
4. Reverse Steps 1-3 to install the diode.

Continuity Test

1. Remove the diode as described in this chapter.
2. Check for continuity between the two terminals of the diode as shown in **Figure 40**.
3. Reverse the ohmmeter leads and recheck for continuity.
4. The diode should have continuity during Step 2 but no continuity (infinite resistance) with the leads reversed. Refer to the wiring diagrams at the end of the manual.
5. Replace the diode if it fails the continuity test.

LIGHTING SYSTEM

The lighting system consists of a headlight, taillight and indicator lights. Always use the correct bulb (**Table 2**). Using the incorrect wattage produces a dim light or causes the bulb to burn out prematurely. It is possible to replace both bulbs without removing the fenders or housings. They are removed here for clarity.

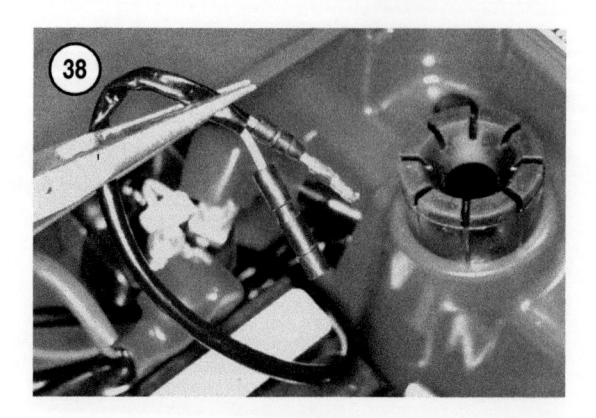

Headlight Bulb Replacement

WARNING
If the headlight just burned out or if it has just been turned off, it is hot. Do not touch the bulb until it cools.

1. Disconnect the wiring harness from the back of the headlight (**Figure 41**).
2. Twist the bulb holder to the left to remove it from the housing (**Figure 42**).
3. Remove the bulb from the socket.
4. Installation is the reverse of removal. The headlight bulb socket can only go into the housing one way. Make sure to correctly align the tabs before installing the socket.
5. Check headlight operation.

Headlight Housing Removal/Installation

1. Disconnect the wiring harness from the back of the headlight (**Figure 41**).

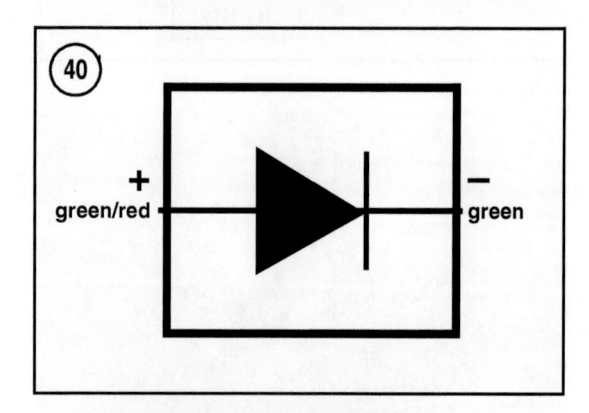

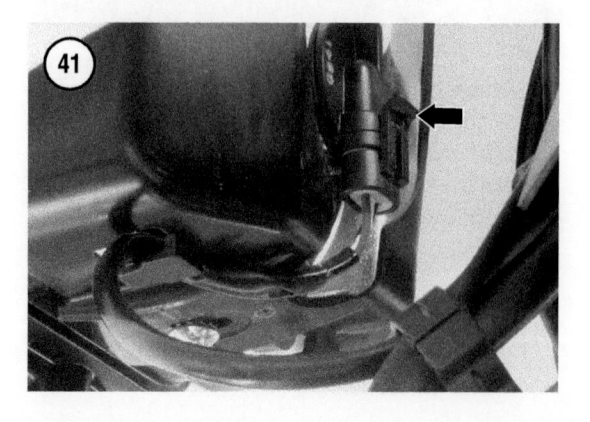

ELECTRICAL SYSTEM

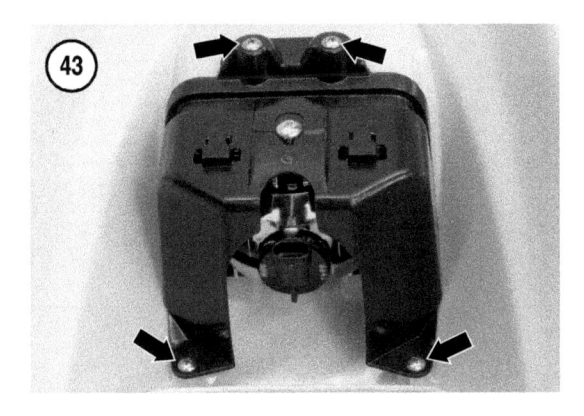

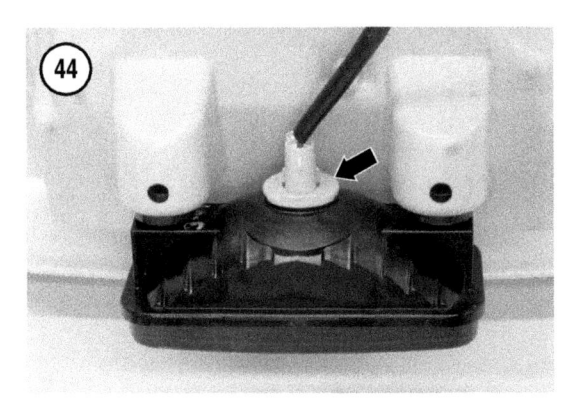

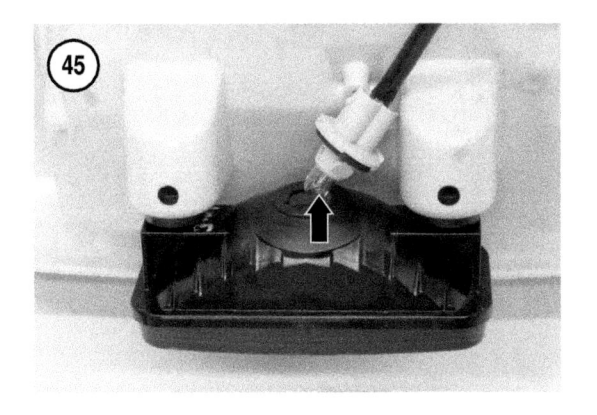

2. Remove the front fender as described in Chapter Fourteen.
3. Remove the four screws securing the housing to the fender (**Figure 43**).
4. Installation is the reverse of removal.

Taillight Bulb Replacement

1. Turn the bulb socket (**Figure 44**) counterclockwise, and remove it from the lens housing.
2. Remove the old bulb (**Figure 45**).
3. Reverse these steps to install a new bulb.
4. Start the engine and check taillight operation.

Indicator Bulb Replacement

The indicator bulbs are mounted in the handlebar cover. The bulbs can be removed with the handlebar cover in place.

1. Remove the lens (**Figure 46**) from the socket.
2. Pull the socket (**Figure 47**) from the handlebar cover and then remove the bulb.
3. Reverse these steps to install the new bulb. When installing the socket, align the tab on the socket with the groove in the handlebar cover.
4. Start the engine and check bulb operation.

SWITCHES

Testing

Test the switches by performing a continuity test with an ohmmeter (see Chapter Two) or a test light. Disconnect each switch connector and check the continuity while operating the switch in each of the positions shown in the continuity diagram.

For example, **Figure 48** shows a continuity diagram for the ignition switch. When the ignition switch is on, there should be continuity between the black and red terminals. This is indicated by the line on the continuity diagram connecting these two terminals. An ohmmeter connected across the black and red terminals should indicate little or no resistance, or a test light should light when the switch is turned on. When the ignition switch is off, there should be no continuity between these two terminals.

Before testing a switch, note the following:

1. Check the fuse (**Figure 49**) as described in *Fuse* in this chapter.
2. Check the battery as described in *Battery* in Chapter Three. Charge the battery if required.
3. Disconnect the negative battery lead from the battery if the switch connectors are not disconnected from the circuit.

CAUTION
Do not start the engine with the battery disconnected.

4. When separating two connectors, pull the connector housings and not the wires.
5. After locating a defective circuit, check the connectors to make sure they are clean and properly connected. Check all wires going into a connector housing to make sure each wire is properly positioned and that the wire end is not loose.
6. When reconnecting electrical connector halves, push them together until they click or snap into place.

Left Handlebar Switch Replacement

NOTE
The switches mounted in the left handlebar switch housing are not available separately. If one switch is damaged, replace the switch housing assembly.

1. Remove the handlebar cover and front fender as described in Chapter Fourteen.
2. Remove any clamps securing the switch wiring harness to the handlebar. Note how the switch harness is routed through the frame. The harness on the new switch must follow the same path.
3. Disconnect the handlebar switch red, 3-pin connector (**Figure 50**) and the two handlebar switch bullet connectors. These connectors are located behind the ICM on the left frame member.

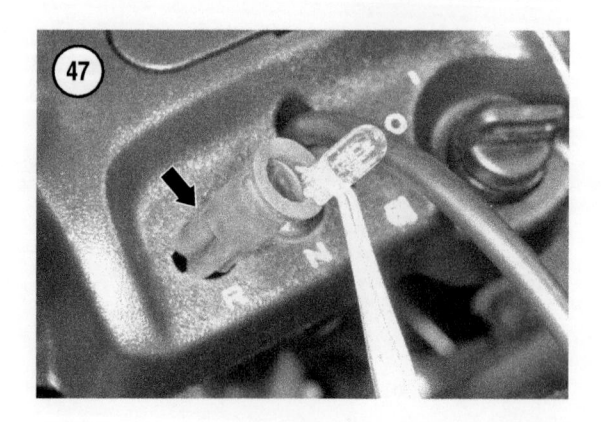

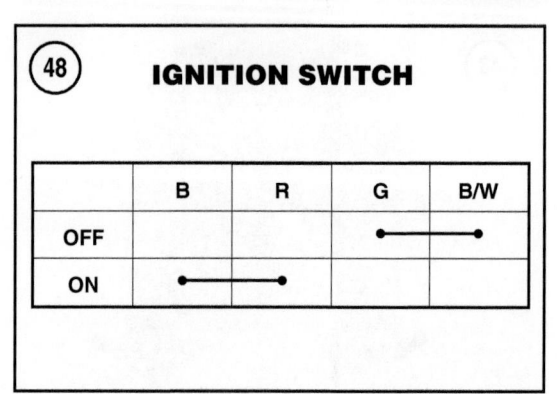

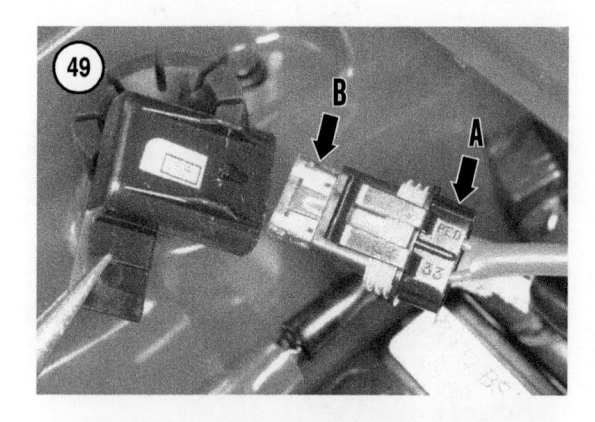

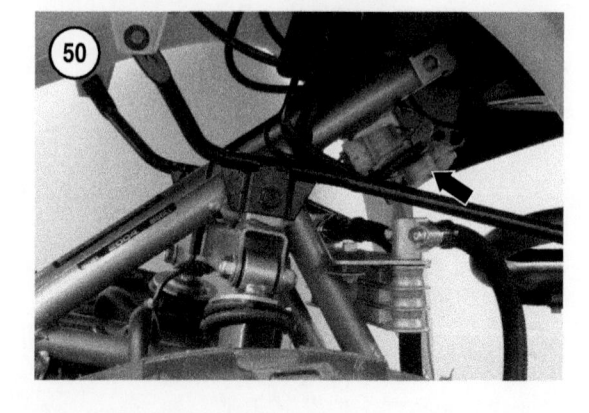

IGNITION SWITCH

	B	R	G	B/W
OFF			•—	—•
ON	•—	—•		

ELECTRICAL SYSTEM

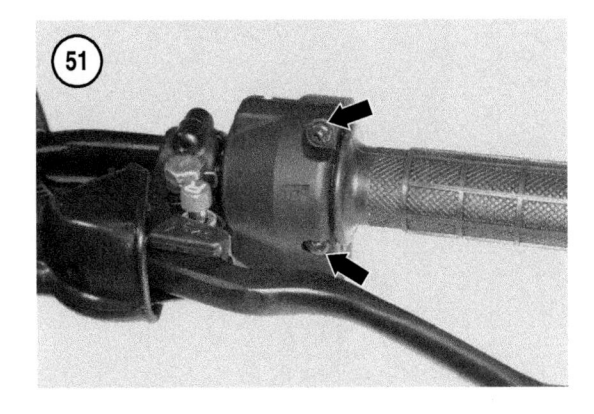

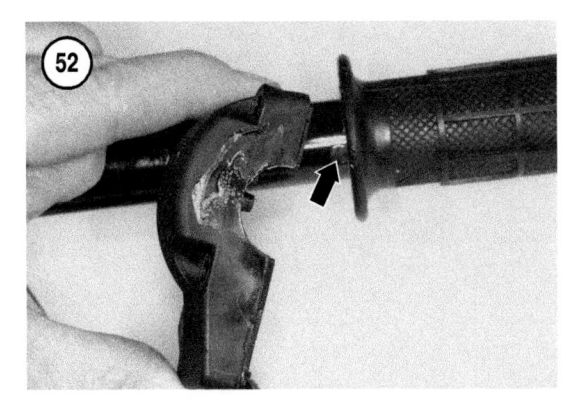

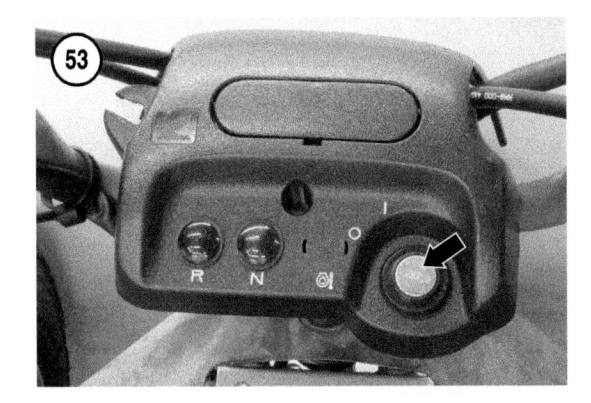

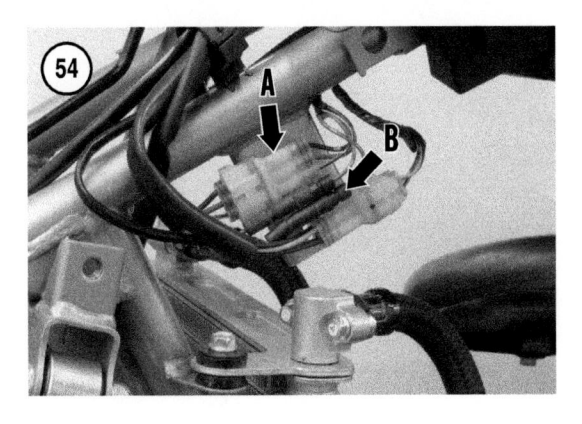

4. Remove the switch housing screws (**Figure 51**) and separate the switch halves. Remove the switch and its wiring harness from the frame.

5. Install the switch housing by reversing these removal steps. Note the following:

   a. Fit the pin on the rear switch housing half into the hole in the handlebar (**Figure 52**), and then install the switch housing.

   b. Tighten the upper switch housing screw first and then the lower screw.

6. Start the engine and check the switch in each of its operating positions.

Ignition Switch Replacement

The ignition switch mounts to the handlebar cover (**Figure 53**).

1. Remove the handlebar cover and front fender as described in Chapter Fourteen.

2. Disconnect the ignition switch wiring harness from the clamp on the bottom of the handlebar cover. Note how the harness is routed through the frame. The new harness must follow the same path.

3. Disconnect the ignition switch 3-pin connector (A, **Figure 54**) and its bullet connector (B, green wire). These connectors are located on the left frame member, just forward of the ICM.

4. Press the switch arms together (**Figure 55**), and push the ignition switch out the bottom side of the cover. Remove the switch and its harness.

5. Install the ignition switch by reversing the preceding steps, plus the following:

   a. Install the new switch by aligning its two tabs with the notch in the switch mounting hole, and then push the switch in place. Make sure the arms lock the ignition switch into place in the handlebar cover (**Figure 56**).

   b. Turn the ignition switch on and check its operation.

Neutral/Reverse Switch Continuity Test

The neutral and reverse switches are mounted on the outside of the alternator cover for 2001-2002 models. 2003-on models have the switch mounted on the inside of the cover.

CHAPTER NINE

2001-2002 models

1. Remove the seat, left side cover and left rear mudguard as described in Chapter Fourteen.

2. On the left side of the alternator cover, remove the mounting bolts (A, **Figure 57**) and cover (B) from the reverse stopper lever.

3. Disconnect the electrical connectors (**Figure 58**) from the neutral switch (A, **Figure 59**) and the reverse switch (B) on the left side of the alternator cover.

4. Connect ohmmeter leads between the terminal in the center of the neutral switch body and a good ground. The switch should have continuity (low resistance) when the transmission is in neutral and have no continuity (infinite resistance) when the transmission is in gear. Replace the neutral switch if it fails either test.

5. Connect the ohmmeter leads to the terminal in the center of the reverse switch body and a good ground. The switch should have continuity (low resistance) when the transmission is in reverse and have no continuity (infinite resistance) when the transmission is in any other gear or neutral. Replace the reverse switch if it fails either test.

6. Installation is the reverse of removal. Reconnect the neutral/reverse switch electrical connector securely.

2003-on models

The neutral/reverse switch is mounted internally on these models. It is only possible to test the switch at the bullet connectors.

1. Remove the seat and the left side cover as described in Chapter Fourteen.

2. Follow the harness from the alternator cover to the bullet connectors.

3. Connect ohmmeter leads between the bullet connector of the light green neutral switch wire and a good ground. The switch should have continuity (low resistance) when the transmission is in neutral and have no continuity (infinite resistance) when the transmission is in gear.

4. Connect the ohmmeter lead between the bullet connector of the green neutral switch wire and a good ground. The switch should have continuity (low resistance) when the transmission is in neutral and have no continuity (infinite resistance) when the transmission is in any forward gear or neutral.

5. If the switch fails either continuity test, replace it.

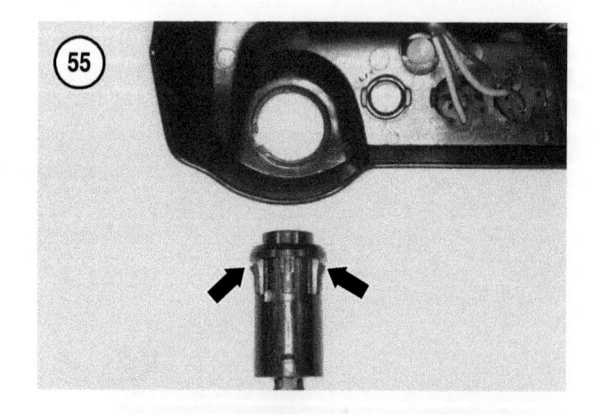

ELECTRICAL SYSTEM

a. Tighten the neutral or reverse switch to 13 N•m (115 in.-lb.).
b. Reconnect the neutral/reverse switch electrical connector (**Figure 58**) securely.
c. Start the engine and check the neutral/reverse switch indicator light operation.

2003-on models

The neutral and reverse switches are combined into a single switch that is mounted inside the alternator cover. This switch has the same leads and is tested the same as earlier models using two separate switches. To replace this switch, it is necessary to remove the alternator cover.

Refer to *Alternator Cover* in Chapter Five.

FUSE

When the fuse blows, determine the reason for the failure before replacing the fuse. Usually the trouble is a short circuit in the wiring, which may be caused by worn-through insulation or a disconnected wire touching ground.

Refer to **Table 2** for fuse specifications.

Main Fuse

The fuse box (**Figure 60**) mounts to the battery compartment.

1. Remove the seat (Chapter Fourteen).

CAUTION
If the main fuse is replaced with the ignition switch turned on, an accidental short circuit could damage the electrical system.

2. Make sure the ignition switch is turned off.
3. Unlock the clasp on the fuse box and separate the halves of the fuse box (A, **Figure 61**).
4. Remove the main fuse (B, **Figure 61**) from the connector.
5. Install by reversing the removal steps.

WIRING DIAGRAMS

The wiring diagrams are located at the end of this manual.

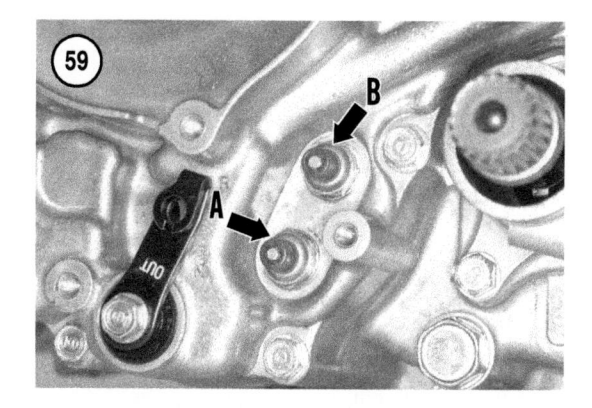

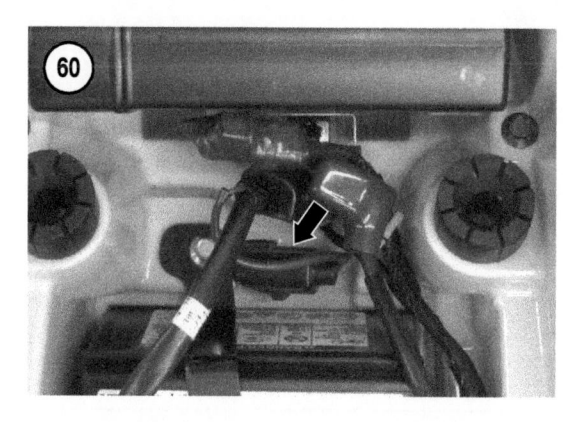

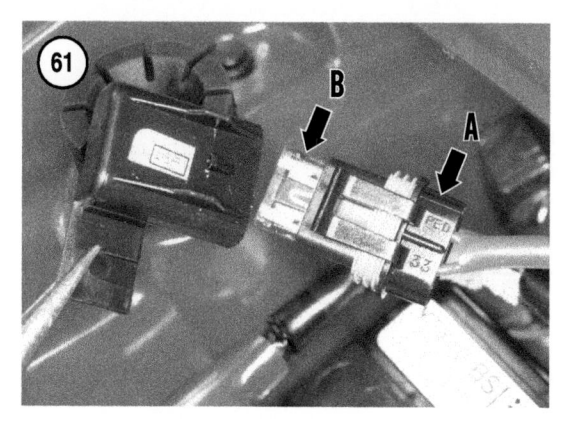

Neutral/Reverse Switch Replacement

2001-2002 models

1. Remove the reverse stopper lever cover and the neutral/reverse connectors as described in *Neutral/Reverse Switch Continuity Test* in this section.
2. Unthread and remove the neutral switch (A, **Figure 59**) or reverse switch (B). Make sure the sealing washer comes out with the switch.
3. Installation is the reverse of removal. Not the following:

Table 1 ELECTRICAL SYSTEM SPECIFICATIONS

Battery	Specification
Capacity	12 V – 8 AH
Current draw (maximum)	1.0 mA
Voltage	
Fully charged	13.0-13.2 V
Needs charging	Less than 12.3 V
Charge current	
Normal	0.9 A / 5-10 h
Fast[1]	4.0 A / 1.0 h
Alternator	
Capacity	0.13 kW @ 5000 rpm
Charge coil resistance (20° C [68° F])	0.1-1.0 ohms
Regulator/rectifier	Single phase, full-wave rectification
Regulated voltage	14.0-15.0 V @ 5000 rpm
Ignition system	AC CDI
Ignition timing[2]	14° BTDC @1700 rpm
Ignition coil peak voltage	100 V minimum
Ignition pulse generator peak voltage	0.7 V minimum
Exciter coil peak voltage	100 V minimum
Spark plug	
Standard	NGK DPR8EA-9 or ND X24EPR-U9
Cold climate (5° C [41° F])	NGK DPR7EA-9 or ND X22EPR-U9
For extended high-speed operation	NGK DPR9EA-9 or ND X27EPR-U9
Spark plug gap	0.8-0.9 mm (0.031-0.035 in.)
Starter brush length	
Standard	12.5 mm (0.49 in.)
Service limit	9.0 mm (0.35 in.)

1. Fast charging should be performed only in an emergency.
2. Not adjustable.

Table 2 BULB AND FUSE SPECIFICATIONS

Item	Specification
Headlight (high/low beam)	12 V-35/35 W × 2
Taillight	12V-5W
Reverse/Neutral Indicator	12V-1.7W × 2
Main fuse	15 A

Table 3 ELECTRICAL SYSTEM TORQUE SPECIFICATIONS

Item	N•m	in.-lb.	ft.-lb.
Ignition pulse generator	6	53	–
Neutral and reverse switches	13	115	–

CHAPTER TEN

WHEELS, HUBS AND TIRES

This chapter describes repair and maintenance of the front and rear wheels, hubs and tires.

When inspecting components, compare any measurements to the tire and wheel specifications in **Table 1**. Replace any part that is damaged or out of specification. Tighten all wheel and hub fasteners to the specifications in **Table 2**. **Table 1** and **Table 2** are at the end of this chapter.

FRONT WHEEL

Removal/Installation

1. Park the vehicle on level ground and set the parking brake.

NOTE
Mark the tires for location and direction before removing them.

2. Loosen the four front wheel nuts (**Figure 1**).
3. Raise the front of the vehicle with a jack so the front wheels are off the ground. Support the vehicle with safety stands or wooden blocks in the event the jack fails. Make sure the stands are properly placed before beginning work.
4. Remove the wheel nuts and pull the front wheel off the hub.
5. Clean the wheel nuts in solvent and dry them thoroughly. Inspect the nuts, and replace them if necessary.
6. Inspect the wheel. Replace it if it is damaged.
7. Install the front wheel by reversing these removal steps. Note the following:
   a. Install each wheel nut with its curved side facing toward the wheel (**Figure 2**). Finger-tighten the wheel nuts, and check that the wheel sits squarely against the hub.
   b. Lower the vehicle so both front wheels are on the ground.
   c. Tighten the wheel nuts in a crisscross pattern to 64 N•m (47 ft.-lb.).
   d. Support the vehicle again so both front wheels are off the ground.

224 CHAPTER TEN

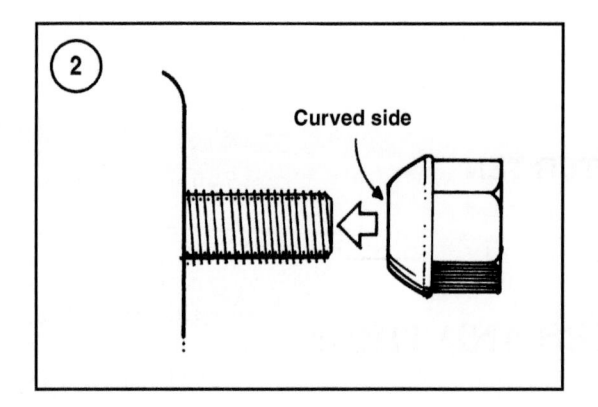

e. Rotate the wheels and apply the front brake. Repeat this step several times to make sure each wheel rotates freely and that its brake is working properly.

FRONT HUB

Removal/Installation

1. Remove the front wheel as described in this chapter.

> *CAUTION*
> *Do not allow the caliper to hang by the brake hose. Tape or wire the caliper to another location on the frame.*

2. Remove the brake caliper as described in Chapter Twelve.
3. Remove the retaining bolts and disc guard (**Figure 3**).
4. Remove the cotter pin and hub nut (**Figure 4**).
5. Remove the hub and brake disc (**Figure 5**) from the axle.
6. If necessary, remove the brake disc as described in the Chapter Twelve.
7. Inspect and repair the front hub as described in this section.
8. Reverse these steps to install the front hub and perform the following:
   a. Inspect the steering knuckle (**Figure 6**) condition before installing the hub. Check for cracks and damage on bearing surfaces and threads. Repair or replace if necessary.
   b. Tighten the hub nut to 69 N•m (51 ft.-lb.). After tightening the nut, continue turning it until the nut is aligned with the cotter pin hole. Do not loosen the nut to align the cotter pin hole.

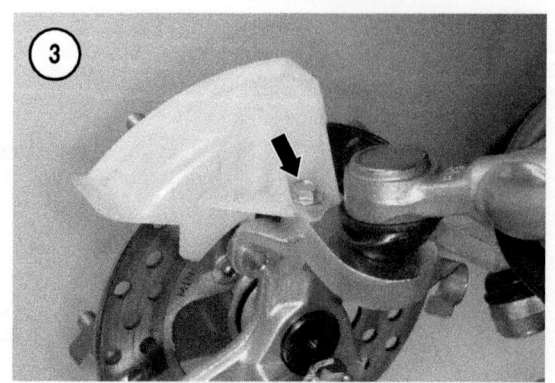

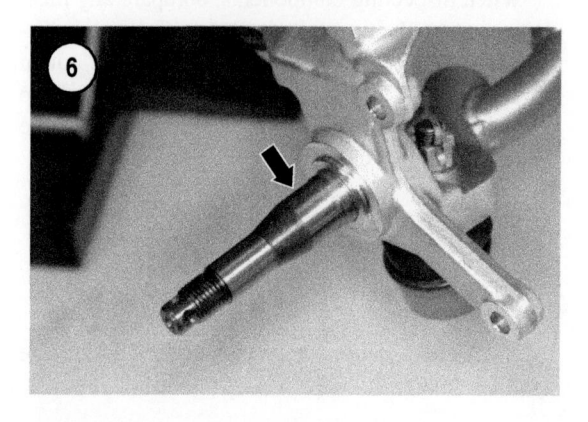

WHEELS, HUBS AND TIRES

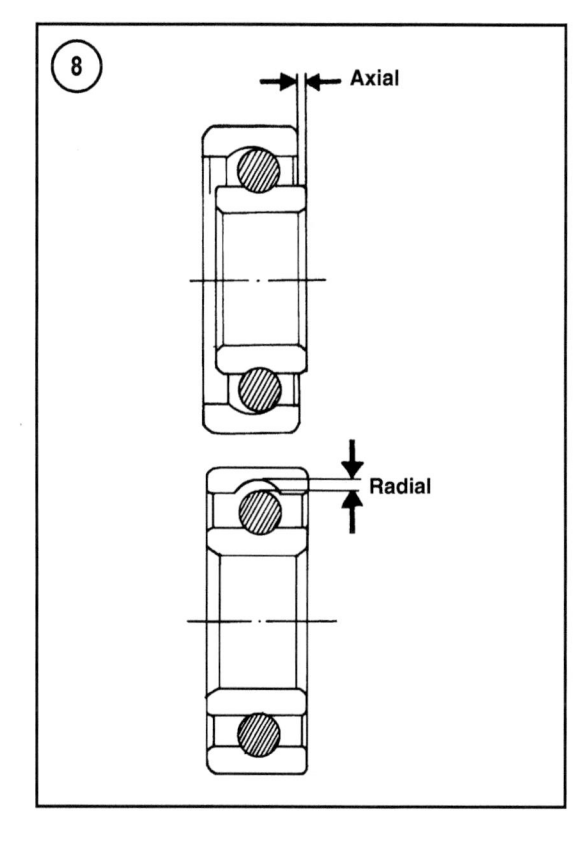

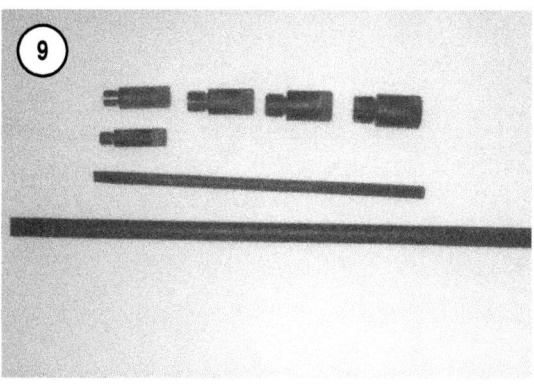

c. Install a *new* cotter pin.

Inspection

1. Remove the collars (**Figure 7**) from both sides of the hub.
2. Inspect the seals for damage.
3. Turn each bearing inner race by hand. The bearing should operate smoothly and quietly. If binding or roughness is detected, replace both bearings.
4. Check each bearing for axial and radial play (**Figure 8**). If play does not exist or is barely noticeable, the bearing is still in usable condition. Replace both bearings if either has excessive play.
5. Check the tightness of the bearings in the hub. Replace the bearings if they feel loose.
6. Install the collars if the bearings and seals are in good condition. Leave the collars out if replacing the bearings and/or seals.

Bearing and Seal Replacement

The difficulty in bearing removal is getting the first bearing out of the hub. In the following procedure, two methods are given for removing the first bearing.

The first method uses special tools, while the second method (Step 2B) uses common shop tools.

The tools shown in the procedure are part of the Kowa Seiki Wheel Bearing remover set (**Figure 9**). The set is distributed by K&L Supply Co., Santa Clara, CA. The set is designed so a properly-sized remover head can be wedged against the inner bearing race. The bearing can then be driven from the hub.

A similar set can be ordered from Honda dealership. The parts required are the: bearing remover shaft (part No. 07746-0050100) and bearing remover head, 15mm (part No. 07746-0050400).

1. Pry out the seals from both sides of the hub (**Figure 10**). Protect the hub and disc as shown.
2A. Remove the hub side bearing (**Figure 11**) using special tools as follows:
   a. Select the appropriate-size remover head (A, **Figure 12**). The small split end of the remover shaft must fit inside the bearing race (B, **Figure 12**).
   b. Insert the small end of the remover head into the outer bearing (**Figure 13**).

c. Insert the tapered end of the driver (C, **Figure 12**) through the back side of the hub (**Figure 13**). Fit the tapered end into the slot of the remover head.
d. Position the hub so the remover head is against a solid surface, such as a concrete floor.
e. Strike the end of the driver so it wedges firmly in the remover head. The remover head should now be jammed tight against the inner bearing race.
f. Reposition the assembly (**Figure 14**) so the remover head is free to move and the driver can be struck again.
g. Strike the driver, forcing the bearing and remover head from the hub.
h. Remove the driver from the remover head.
i. Remove the spacer from the hub, noting the direction that it is installed.

2B. To remove the outer bearing from the hub without special tools:
a. Insert a long driver into the hub from the brake side (**Figure 15**).
b. Carefully wedge the spacer to one side so the edge of the bearing race is exposed.
c. Tap the bearing out of the hub, working around the race. Work slowly to avoid damaging the smooth surface of the spacer.
d. Remove the spacer from the hub.

3. Drive the inner bearing on the brake side with a bearing driver or a large socket.
4. Clean and dry the hub and spacer.
5. Before installing the new bearings and seals, note the following:
a. Inspect the new bearings and determine which side faces out. This is usually the side with the manufacturer's marks and numbers.

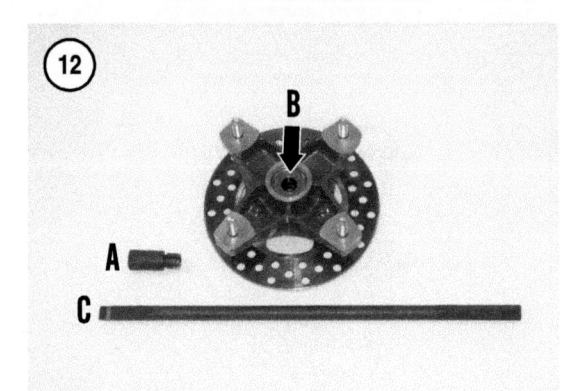

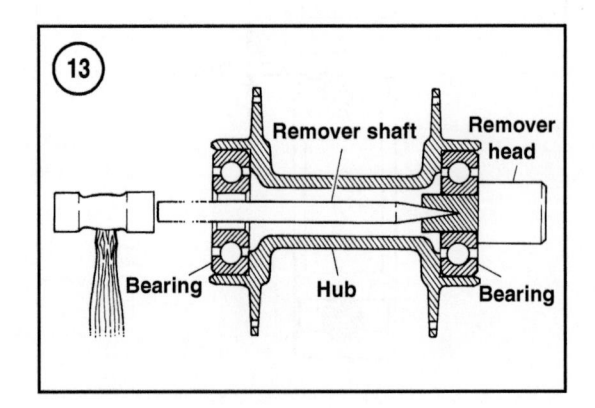

WHEELS, HUBS AND TIRES

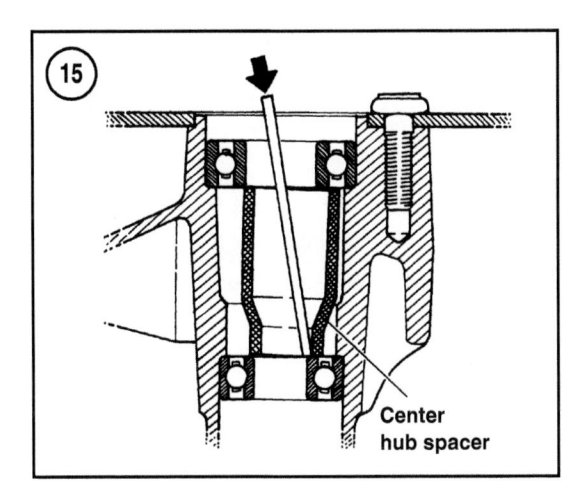

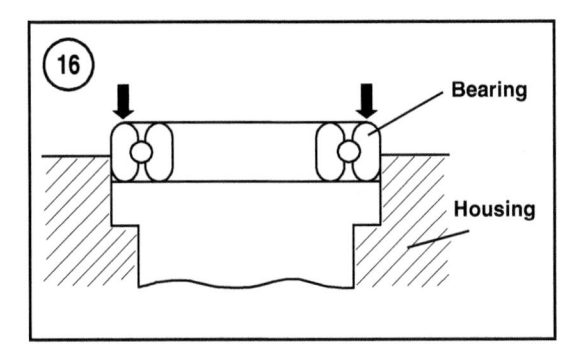

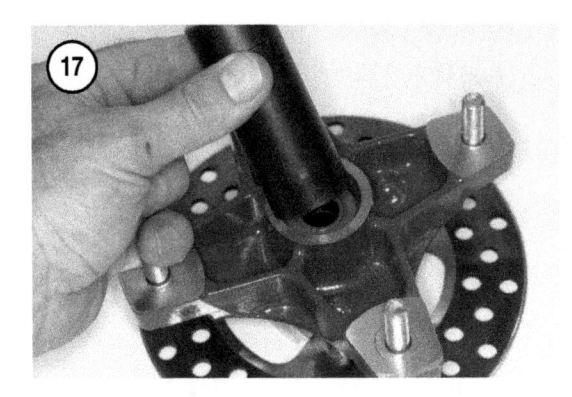

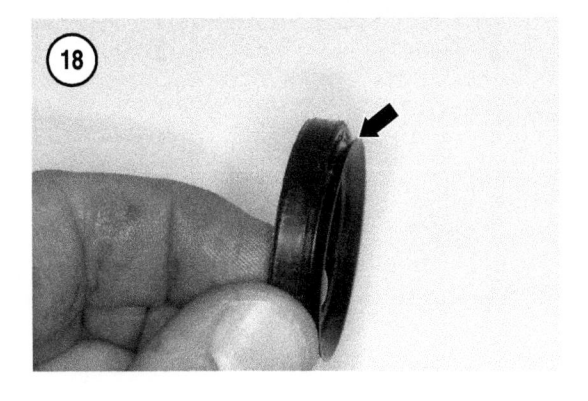

Center hub spacer

Bearing

Housing

If a shield is on one side of the bearing, the shield should face out.

   b. Apply grease (NLGI #2) to bearings that are not lubricated by the manufacturer. Work the grease into the cavities between the balls and races.

   c. Always support the bottom side of the hub, near the bore, when installing bearings.

6. Place the outer bearing *squarely* over the bearing bore.

7. Place a suitably-sized driver or socket over the bearing. The driver should seat against the outside diameter of the bearing (**Figure 16**).

> *CAUTION*
> *Do not press or strike the bearing directly. Bearing damage occurs.*

8. Drive the inner bearing into place, seating it in the hub (**Figure 17**).

9. Turn the hub over and install the spacer so the small diameter is next to the outer bearing.

10. Place the inner bearing *squarely* over the bearing bore. Make sure the manufacturer's marks face up. Drive in the bearing, seating it in the hub.

11. Install the seals as follows:

   a. Pack grease into the inner lips of the new seals.

   b. Lubricate the seal bores.

   c. Place a seal *squarely* over the bore.

> *NOTE*
> *The inner seal (brake side) has an outer lip (**Figure 18**).*

> *NOTE*
> *When installed in the hub, the inner seal lip is above the edge of the hub (**Figure 19**).*

   d. Press the seal into place by hand (**Figure 20**).

12. Install the collars on both sides of the hub (**Figure 21**).

REAR WHEEL

Refer to **Figure 22**.

Removal/Installation

1. Park the vehicle on level ground and set the parking brake. Block the front wheels so the vehicle cannot roll in either direction.

WARNING
The tread pattern is directional on the rear tires. The V-pattern in the tire tread must point in the direction of the wheel's forward rotation. Each rear wheel must be installed on the correct side of the vehicle. Mark each wheel before removing it to make sure it gets installed on the correct side.

2. Identify the rear tires with an L (left side) or R (right side) mark. Refer to these marks to install the wheels on their correct sides.
3. Loosen the wheel nuts (**Figure 23**) securing the wheel to the hub.
4. Raise the rear of the vehicle so the rear wheels are off the ground. Support the vehicle with safety stands or wooden blocks in the event the jack fails. Make sure the stands are properly placed before beginning work.
5. Remove the wheel nuts and rear wheel.
6. Clean the wheel nuts in solvent and dry them thoroughly. Inspect the nuts, and replace them as necessary.
7. Inspect the wheel for cracks, bending or other damage. If necessary, replace the wheel.
8A. If reinstalling a wheel, reinstall it onto its original side.
8B. If installing a rear wheel with new original equipment tires, install the wheel so the V-pattern in the tire tread points in the direction of the wheel's forward rotation.
9. Install the wheel nuts with their curved end (**Figure 3**) facing toward the wheel. Finger-tighten the nuts to center the wheel squarely against the hub.
10. Lower the vehicle so both rear wheels are on the ground.

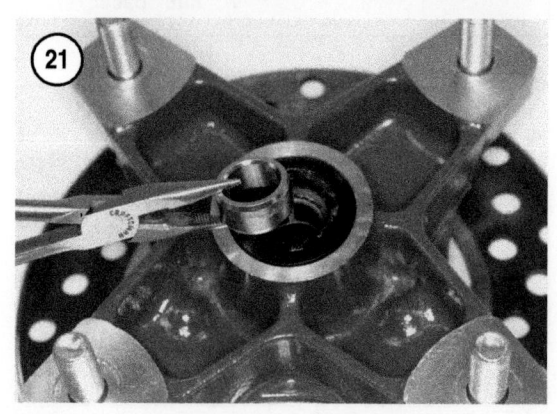

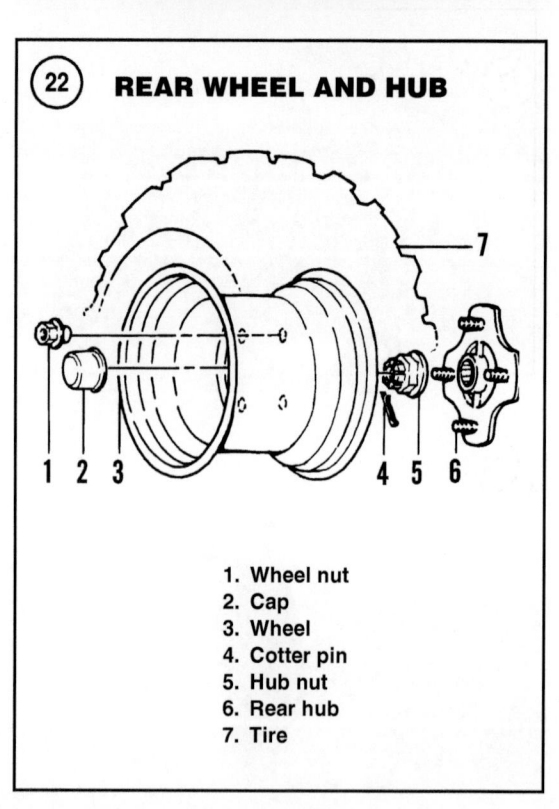

REAR WHEEL AND HUB

1. Wheel nut
2. Cap
3. Wheel
4. Cotter pin
5. Hub nut
6. Rear hub
7. Tire

WHEELS, HUBS AND TIRES

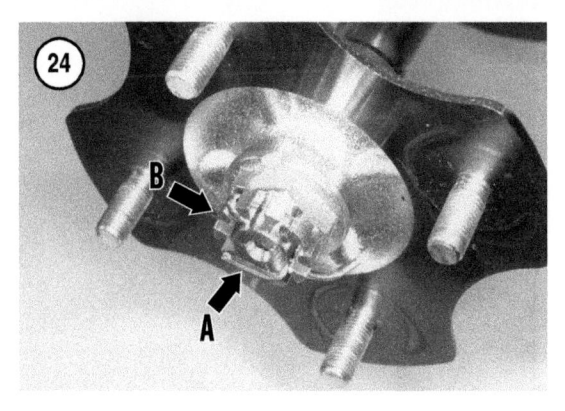

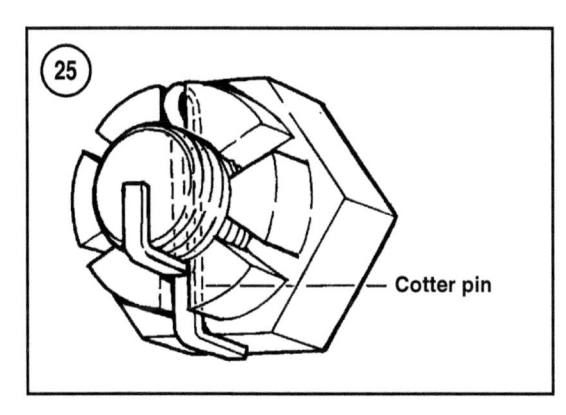

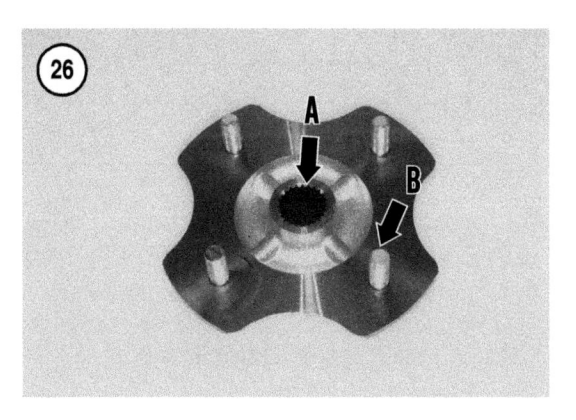

11. Tighten the wheel nuts (**Figure 23**) in a criss-cross pattern to 64 N•m (47 ft.-lb.).

12. Support the vehicle again so both rear wheels are off the ground.

13. Rotate the wheels and apply the rear brake. Repeat this step several times to make sure wheels rotates freely and the brake is working properly.

REAR HUB

Refer to **Figure 22**.

Removal/Installation

1. Remove the rear wheel as described in this chapter.
2. Remove and discard the hub nut cotter pin (A, **Figure 24**).
3. Remove the hub nut (B, **Figure 24**), and pull the rear hub off the axle.
4. Inspect the rear hub as described in this section.
5. To install the rear hub, reverse these removal steps and perform the following:
   a. Apply molybdenum disulfide grease to the axle splines.
   b. Tighten the hub nut (B, **Figure 24**) to 147 N•m (108 ft.-lb.). If necessary, tighten the hub nut to align it with the cotter pin hole in the axle. Do not loosen the hub nut to align it with the hole.
   c. Install a *new* cotter pin, and bend the ends over completely as shown in **Figure 25**.

Inspection

1. Inspect the hub inner splines (A, **Figure 26**) for wear or damage. Replace the hub if necessary.
2. Inspect the wheel studs (B, **Figure 26**). Replace a damaged stud.
3. Check the hub for cracks or other damage.

TIRES

TRX250EX models are equipped with tubeless, low pressure tires designed specifically for off-road use. Rapid tire wear occurs if it is driven on paved surfaces.

Tire Replacement

A bead breaker, tire irons and rim protectors are needed to change the tires.

> **CAUTION**
> *If the tire is difficult to remove or install, do not take a chance on damaging the tire or rim sealing surface. Take the tire and rim to a dealership for service.*

1. Remove the valve stem cap and core, and deflate the tire. Do not reinstall the core at this time.

> **WARNING**
> *Only use water to lubricate the tire during removal and installation. Soap or other types of tire lubricants can leave a residue, which can lead to tire slip, rapid pressure loss and a possible accident.*

2. Lubricate the tire bead and rim flanges with water. Press the tire sidewall/bead down so the water can run into and around the bead area. Also apply water to the area where the bead breaker arm contacts the tire sidewall.
3. Position the wheel into the bead breaker tool (**Figure 27**).
4. Slowly work the bead breaker tool, making sure the tool arm seats against the inside of the rim, and break the tire bead away from the rim.
5. Using your hands, press the tire on either side of the tool to break the rest of the bead free from the rim.
6. If the rest of the tire bead cannot be broken loose, raise the tool, rotate the tire/rim assembly and repeat Step 4 and Step 5 until the entire bead is broken loose from the rim.
7. Turn the wheel over and repeat the preceding steps to break the bead on the opposite side of the rim.

> **CAUTION**
> *When using tire irons, work carefully so the tire or rim sealing surfaces are not damaged. Any damage to these areas may cause an air leak and require replacement of the tire or rim.*

8. Lubricate the tire beads and rim flanges as described in Step 2. Pry the bead over the rim with two tire irons (**Figure 28**). Work with small sections of the tire and place rim protectors between the tire irons and the rim.
9. When the upper tire bead is free, lift the second bead up into the center rim well. Remove the second bead from the rim as described in Step 8.
10. Clean and dry the rim.

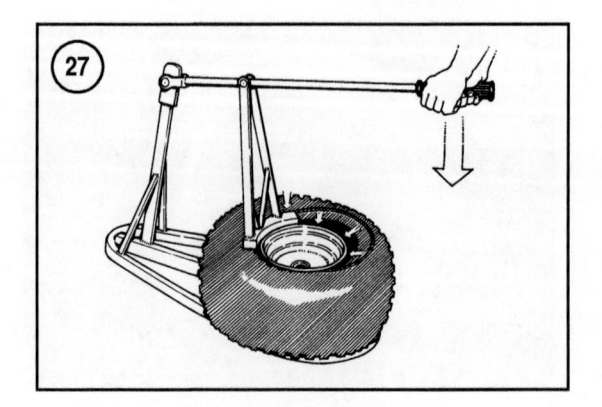

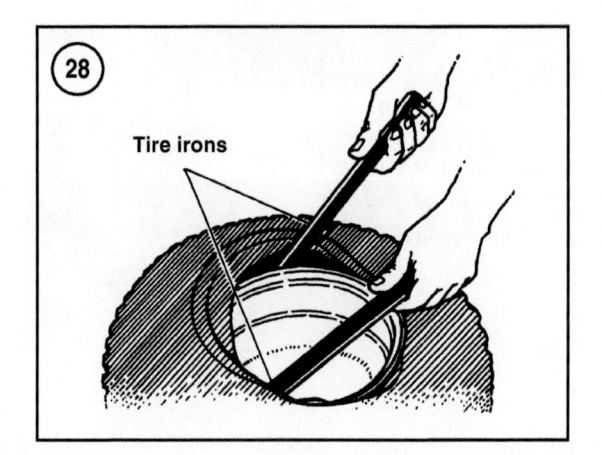

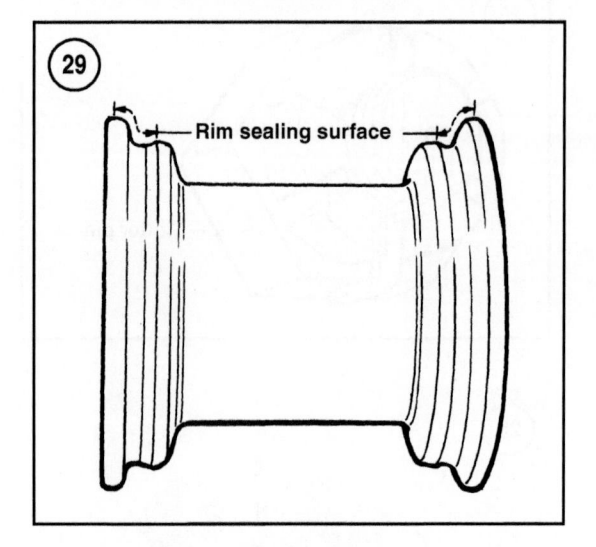

WHEELS, HUBS AND TIRES

Figure 30 (Pull)

Figure 31

Figure 32

b. Lubricate the new valve stem with water.
c. Pull a new valve stem into the rim, from the inside out, until it snaps into place (**Figure 30**).

13. Inspect the tire for cuts, tears, abrasions or any other defects.

WARNING
Only use only clean water as a lubricant during tire mounting. Soap or other tire lubricants can leave a residue, which could cause the tire to slip on the rim and lose air pressure during operation.

14. Clean the tire and rim of any lubricant used during removal.

NOTE
The tread pattern is directional on the rear tires. Position the tire onto the rim so the chevron on the tire tread points in the direction of rear wheel's forward rotation.

NOTE
If the tire is difficult to install, place the tire outside in the sun (or in the trunk of a car). The higher temperatures soften the tire and help ease installation.

15. Install the tire onto the rim from the side with the narrower rim shoulder. If this cannot be determined, start with the side opposite the valve stem. Push the first bead over the rim flange. Force the bead into the center of the rim to help installation (**Figure 31**).
16. Install the rest of the bead with tire irons (**Figure 32**).
17. Repeat the preceding steps to install the second bead onto the rim.
18. Install the valve stem core, if necessary.
19. Apply water to the tire bead and inflate the tire to seat the tire onto the rim. Check that the rim lines on both sides of the tire are parallel with the rim flanges as shown in **Figure 33**. If the rim flanges are not parallel, deflate the tire and break the bead. Lubricate the tire with water again and reinflate the tire.
20. When the tire is properly seated, deflate the tire and wait 1 hour before putting the tire into service. After 1 hour, inflate the tire to the standard inflation pressure in **Table 1**.
21. Check for air leaks and install the valve cap.

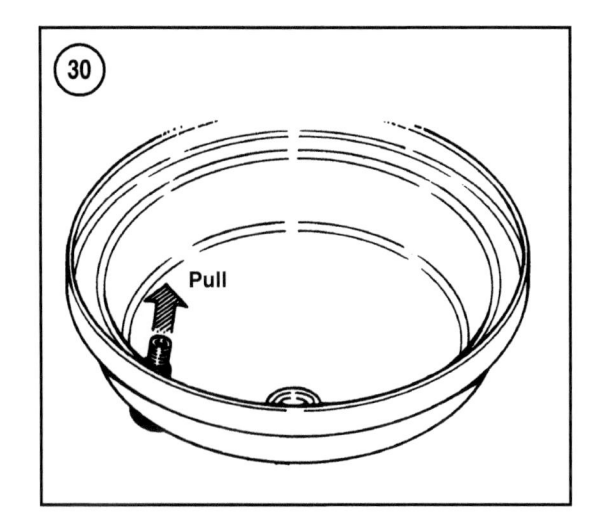

11. Inspect the sealing surface on both sides of the rim (**Figure 29**). If the wheel is bent, it may leak air.
12. To replace the valve stem, perform the following:
    a. Support the rim and pull the valve stem out of the rim. Discard the valve stem.

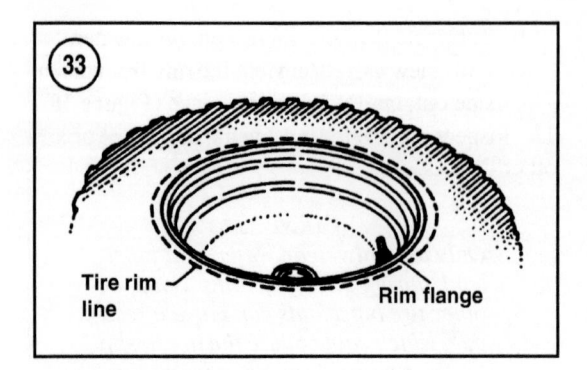

Cold Patch Repair

Use the manufacturer's instructions for the tire repair kit being used. If there are no instructions, use the following procedure.
1. Remove the tire as described in this chapter.
2. Before removing the object that punctured the tire, mark the puncture location with chalk or a crayon. Remove the object (**Figure 34**).
3. Working on the inside of the tire, roughen an area around the hole that is larger than the patch (**Figure 35**). Use the cap from the tire repair kit or a pocket knife. Do not scrape too vigorously or additional damage may occur.
4. Clean the area with a non-flammable solvent. Do not use an oil base solvent. It leaves a residue, rendering the patch useless.
5. Apply a small amount of special cement to the puncture and spread it evenly.
6. Allow the cement to dry until tacky—usually 30 seconds or so.

> *CAUTION*
> *Do not touch the newly exposed rubber with your fingers or the patch does not stick firmly.*

7. Remove the backing from the patch.
8. Center the patch over the hole. Hold the patch firmly in place for about 30 seconds to allow the cement to dry. Use a roller, if available, to press the patch into place (**Figure 36**).
9. Dust the area with talcum powder.

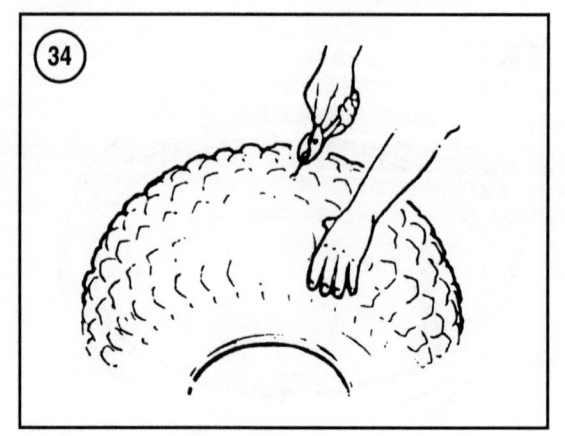

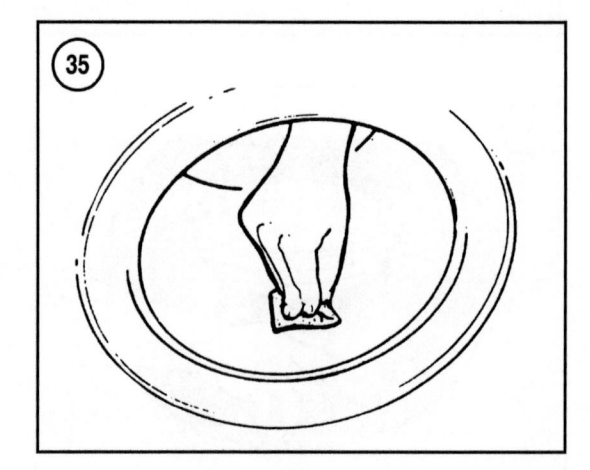

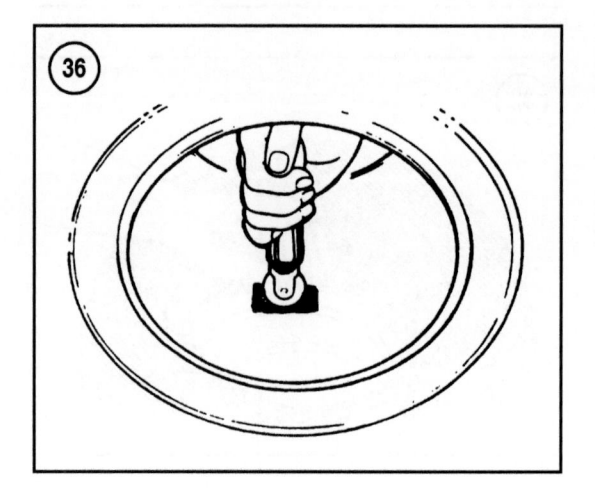

Table 1 TIRE AND WHEEL SPECIFICATIONS

Front tire	
Size	AT22 × 7-10
Manufacturer	Dunlop KT 171
Minimum tread depth	4 mm (0.16 in.)
Rear tire	
Size	AT22 × 10-9
Manufacturer	Dunlop KT 175
Minimum tread depth	4 mm (0.16 in.)
Inflation pressure (cold)*	
Standard	
Front	30 kPa (4.4 psi)
Rear	20 kPa (2.9 psi)
Minimum (front and rear)	
Front	26 kPa (3.8 psi)
Rear	17 kPa (2.5 psi)
Maximum (front and rear)	
Front	34 kPa (5.0 psi)
Rear	23 kPa (3.3 psi)
With cargo (front and rear)	
Front	30 kPa (4.4 psi)
Rear	20 kPa (2.9 psi)
Wheel size	
Front	10 × 5.5 AT
Rear	9 × 8.0 AT

*Tire inflation pressure for original equipment tires. Aftermarket tires may require different inflation pressures.

Table 2 WHEEL AND HUB TORQUE SPECIFICATIONS

Item	N•m	in.-lb.	ft.-lb.
Front hub nut	69	–	51
Rear hub nut	147	–	108
Wheel nuts	64	–	47

CHAPTER ELEVEN

FRONT SUSPENSION AND STEERING

This chapter contains repair and replacement procedures for the front suspension and steering components. During inspection, compare measurements to the specifications in **Table 1**. Replace any part that is damaged or out of specification. During assembly, tighten fasteners as specified. **Table 1** and **Table 2** are at the end of this chapter.

HANDLEBAR

Removal

CAUTION
Cover the seat, fuel tank and front fender with plastic to protect it from brake fluid spills. Brake fluid damages the finish on any painted, plated or plastic surface. Clean up any spilled brake fluid immediately. Wash the area with soapy water and rinse thoroughly.

1. Remove the handlebar cover as described in Chapter Fourteen.
2. Remove the wire bands securing the wiring harness to the handlebar.
3. Remove the two throttle housing clamp screws (A, **Figure 1**) and the clamp. Remove the throttle housing (B, **Figure 1**) and lay it over the front fender. Make sure the throttle cable is not kinked.
4. Remove the clamp bolts (C, **Figure 1**) from the front master cylinder. Remove the front master cylinder, and lay it over the front fender. Keep the reservoir in an upright position to minimize loss of brake fluid and to keep air from entering the brake system. The hydraulic brake line does not have to be removed from the master cylinder.
5. Remove the clamp screws (A, **Figure 2**) from the rear brake lever housing. Remove the housing (B, **Figure 2**) and lay it over the front fender. Make sure the cables are not kinked.

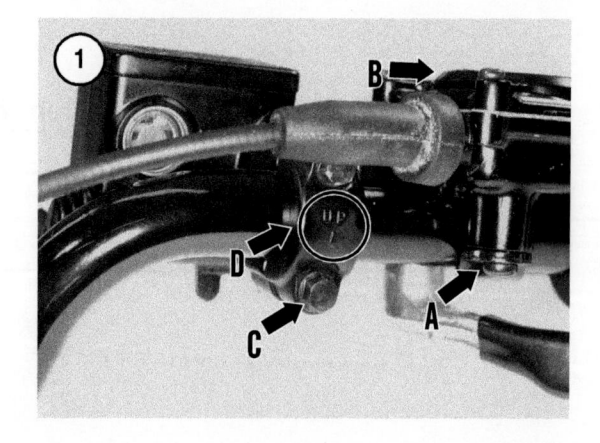

FRONT SUSPENSION AND STEERING

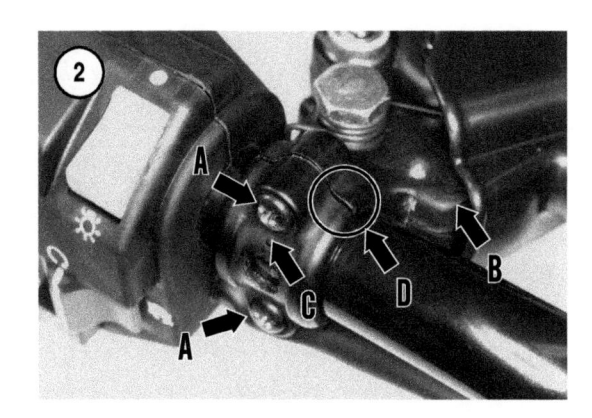

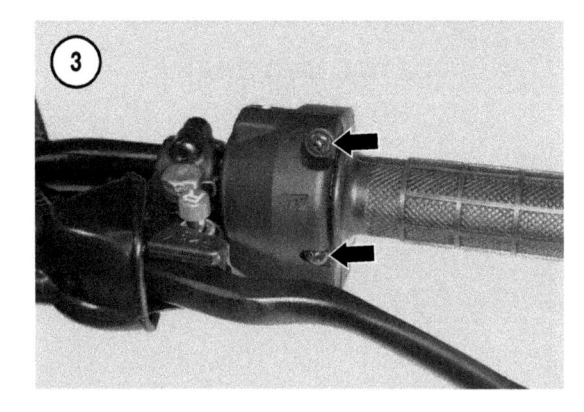

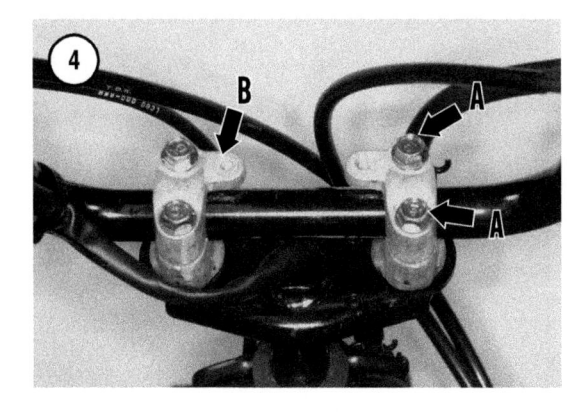

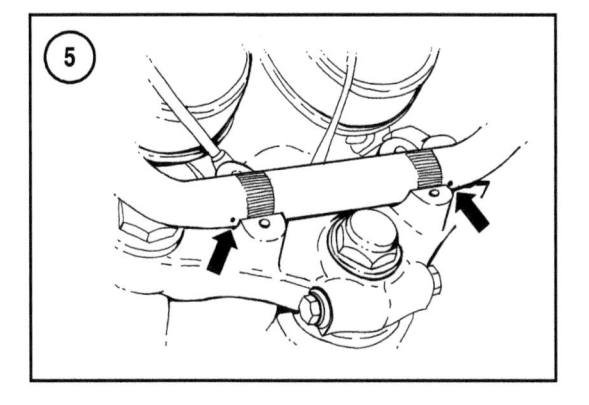

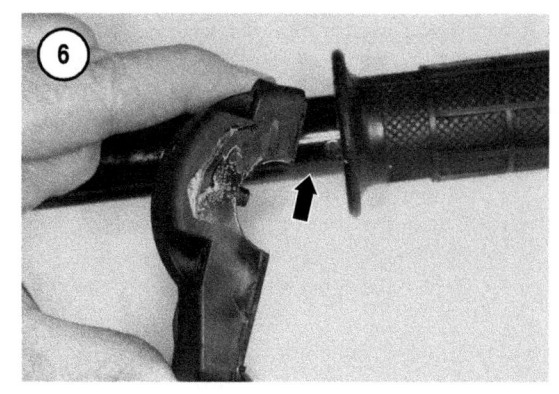

6. Remove the switch housing screws (**Figure 3**). Separate the switch halves, and set the assembly aside.
7. Remove the upper handlebar holder mounting bolts (A, **Figure 4**) from each handlebar holder. Remove the upper holders and handlebar.

Installation

1. Position the handlebar on the lower handlebar holders and hold it in place.
2. Set each upper handlebar holder in place so its cover boss faces forward as shown in B, **Figure 4**.
3. Align the punch mark on the handlebar with the top surface of the lower holders (**Figure 5**).
4. Install the handlebar holder bolts (A, **Figure 4**). Tighten the forward bolts first and then the rear bolts. Tighten each bolt securely.
5. Install the left switch housing by performing the following:
   a. Fit the pin on the rear switch housing half into the hole in the handlebar (**Figure 6**) and then install the switch housing.
   b. Tighten the upper switch housing screw first and then the lower screw (**Figure 3**).
6. Install the rear brake lever housing by performing the following:
   a. Fit the rear brake lever housing and its clamp into place on the handlebar. Position the clamp so its punch mark (C, **Figure 2**) faces up.
   b. Align the edge of the housing with the punch mark (D, **Figure 2**) on the handlebar.
   c. Install the clamp screws. Tighten the upper screw first and then the lower screw.
7. Install the master cylinder by performing the following:

a. Fit the master cylinder and its clamp into place on the handlebar. Position the clamp so its UP mark (D, **Figure 1**) faces up.
b. Align the edge of the master cylinder housing with the punch mark (A, **Figure 7**) on the handlebar.
c. Install the master cylinder clamp bolts. Tighten the bolts to 12 N•m (106 in.-lb.). Tighten the upper bolt first and then the lower bolt.

8. Install the throttle housing by aligning the line on the throttle housing (B, **Figure 7**) with the edge of the master cylinder. Install the clamp and tighten the clamp screws securely (A, **Figure 1**).
9. Secure the wiring harness to the handlebar with the wire bands.
10. Check all cable adjustments as described in Chapter Three.
11. Check that the front brake works properly.
12. Check that each handlebar switch works properly.
13. Install the handlebar cover (Chapter Fourteen).

STEERING SHAFT

Refer to **Figure 8**.

Removal

1. Remove the front fender as described in Chapter Fourteen.
2. Open the wire clamp (A, **Figure 9**) on the steering shaft holder, and release the wires.
3. Release the brake hose (B, **Figure 9**) from the clamp on the steering shaft holder.
4. Remove the lower handlebar holder nuts and washers (**Figure 10**). Discard the lower handlebar holder locknuts. New ones must be installed during assembly.
5. Pull the handlebar assembly back so the brake hose, cables or wiring harness are not damaged. Support the handlebar so the master cylinder remains upright. This minimizes the loss of brake fluid and keeps air from entering the brake system.
6. Disconnect the tie rods from the steering arm by performing the following:
    a. Remove the cotter pin (A, **Figure 11**) from each inner tie rod end.
    b. Hold the flats of each ball joint (C, **Figure 11**) with a wrench, and remove the tie rod nut (B).

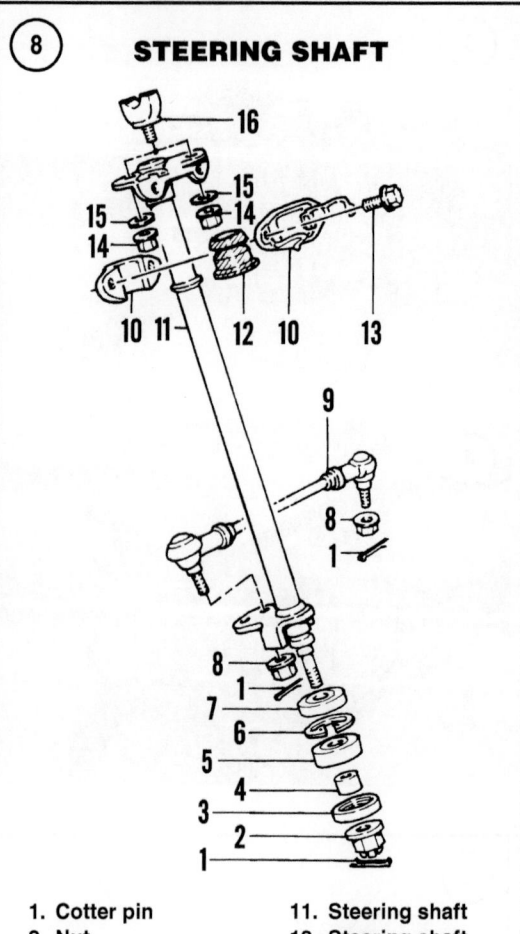

STEERING SHAFT

1. Cotter pin
2. Nut
3. Lower dust seal
4. Collar
5. Bearing
6. Snap ring
7. Upper dust seal
8. Tie rod nut
9. Tie rod
10. Steering shaft holder
11. Steering shaft
12. Steering shaft bushing
13. Steering shaft holder bolt
14. Handlebar holder nut (self-locking)
15. Washer
16. Lower handlebar holder

FRONT SUSPENSION AND STEERING

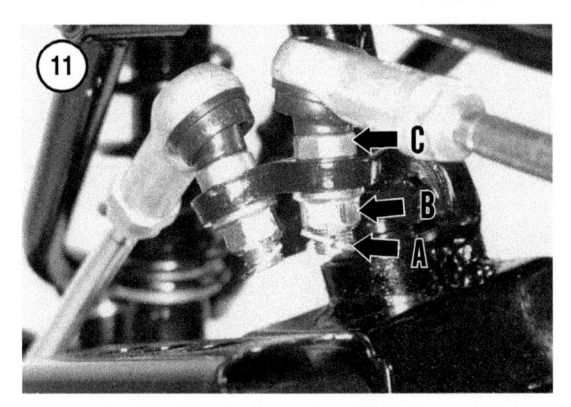

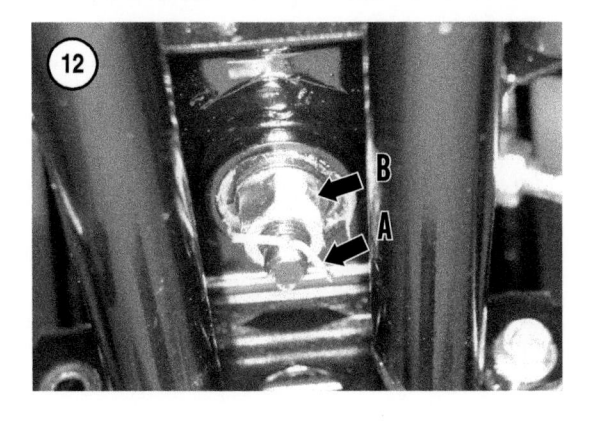

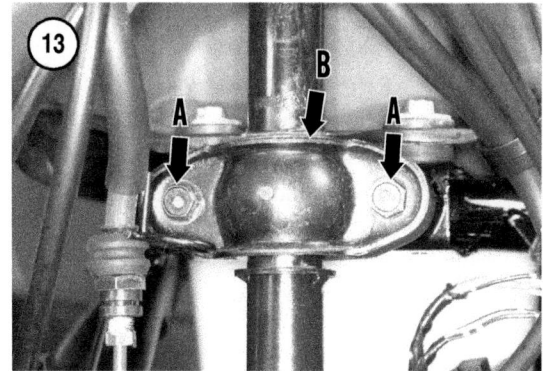

c. Disconnect the tie rod from the steering arm.
7. Remove the cotter pin (A, **Figure 12**) from the bottom of the steering shaft.
8. Remove the steering shaft nut (B, **Figure 12**) from the steering shaft.
9. Remove the steering shaft holder bolts (A, **Figure 13**) and the holder assembly (B).
10. Remove the steering shaft from the frame.

Installation

1. Pack the lips of the steering shaft bushing with lithium grease, and install the bushing onto the steering shaft so its UP mark faces toward the handlebar.
2. Install the steering shaft into the frame.
3. Install the steering shaft holder (B, **Figure 13**) over the bushing and install the bolts (A). Tighten the steering shaft holder bolts to 32 N•m (24 ft.-lb.).
4. Apply lithium grease to the flange and threads of the steering shaft nut. Install the steering shaft nut (B, **Figure 12**), and tighten the nut to 108 N•m (80 ft.-lb.). Secure the nut with a *new* cotter pin and bend the ends over completely.
5. Install the tie rods by performing the following:
    a. Fit each inner tie rod end (**Figure 11**) into its mounting boss on the steering arm.
    b. Install the tie rod nut onto each tie rod. Tighten each tie rod nut to 54 N•m (40 ft.-lb.).
    c. Install a *new* cotter pin through the hole in the stud and bend the ends over completely.
6. Set the handlebar assembly into place on the steering shaft. Check the routing of the brake hose, cables and wiring harness.
7. Install the washers and secure the handlebar with *new* handlebar lower holder nuts (**Figure 10**). Tighten the nuts to 39 N•m (29 ft.-lb.).

8. Secure the brake hose (B, **Figure 9**) to the clamp on the steering shaft holder.
9. Secure the wires with the wire clamp (A, **Figure 9**) on the steering shaft holder.
10. Install the front fender (Chapter Fourteen).
11. Check that the handlebar turns properly and that the throttle returns to its closed position after releasing it.
12. Adjust the toe-in as described in Chapter Three.

Inspection

Replace parts that are excessively worn or damaged as described in this section.
1. Clean and dry all parts.
2. Remove the steering shaft bushing from the steering shaft. Check the bushing for excessive wear or damage.
3. Check the steering shaft for bending or thread damage.
4. Check the cotter pin hole at the end of the steering shaft. Make sure no fractures or cracks lead out toward the end of the steering shaft. If any are present, replace the steering shaft.
5. Check the steering arm for cracks, spline damage or other damage.
6. Inspect the steering bearing by turning its inner race by hand. Replace the bearing if it turns roughly or has excessive play.
7. Inspect the dust seals for excessive wear or other damage.
8. Replace the dust seals and bearing as described in this section.

Dust Seal and Bearing Replacement

The steering shaft bearing is pressed into the frame. Do not remove the bearing unless it requires replacement.
1. Remove the collar from the lower dust seal.

NOTE
The upper (27 × 40 × 6) and lower (23 × 35 × 7) dust seals are not interchangeable. Have both seals on hand before removing them. New seals must be installed during assembly.

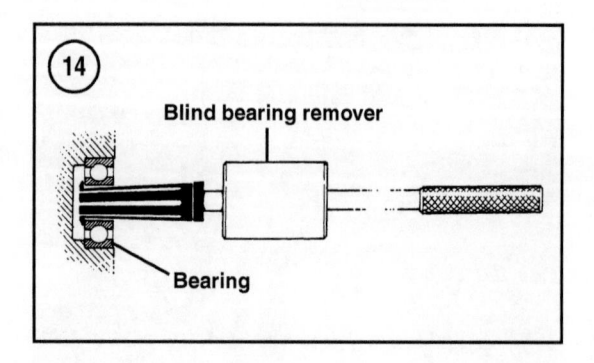

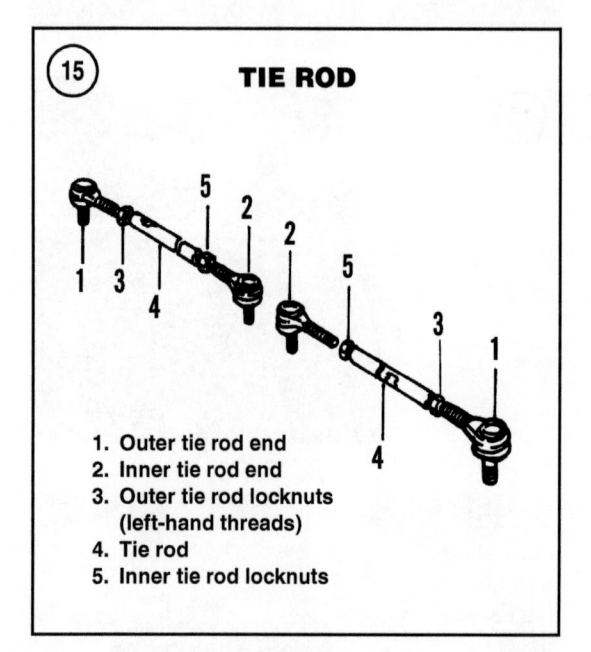

NOTE
If only replacing the dust seals, go to Step 10.

2. Pry the upper and lower dust seals from the bearing bore. Discard both seals.
3. Remove the snap ring from the bearing bore groove.
4. Before removing the bearing, check that its outer race fits tightly in the bearing bore. If the bearing is loose, check the bearing bore for cracks or other damage.
5. Remove the bearing from the top side of the frame. Either pull the bearing from the bore with a blind bearing remover (**Figure 14**) or drive the bearing from the bottom side with the appropriate size socket or bearing driver.
6. Clean the bearing bore and check it for cracks or other damage.

FRONT SUSPENSION AND STEERING

TIE RODS

The tie rods (**Figure 15**) consist of an inner end and outer end. All the parts of the tie rod assembly are available separately.

Removal

1. Support the vehicle with the front wheels off the ground.
2. Disconnect the inner tie rod end from the steering arm by performing the following:
   a. Remove the cotter pin (A, **Figure 11**) from each tie rod end.
   b. Hold the flats of each ball joint (C, **Figure 11**) with a wrench, and remove the tie rod nut (B).
   c. Disconnect the tie rod from the steering arm.
3. Repeat the subteps and disconnect the outer tie rod end (**Figure 16**) from the steering knuckle.
4. Remove the tie rod.

Installation

1. Install the tie rod so the end with the adjusting flat (A, **Figure 17**) sits on the steering knuckle.
2. Secure the tie rod assembly to the steering arm (**Figure 11**) and steering knuckle (**Figure 16**) by performing the following:
   a. Thread a new tie rod nut (B, **Figure 11**) onto the stud.
   b. Hold the ball joint flats (C, **Figure 11**) with a wrench, and tighten the tie rod nut (B) to 54 N•m (40 ft.-lb.).
   c. Install a *new* cotter pin (A, **Figure 11**) through the hole in the stud. Spread the cotter pin arms to lock them in place.
3. Check the toe-in adjustment as described in Chapter Three. If the tie rod ends were replaced, their locknuts are tightened during the adjustment procedure.

Inspection

> *CAUTION*
> *When cleaning the tie rods, do not immerse the ball joints in any chemical that could contaminate the internal lubricating grease and/or damage the protective rubber boots.*

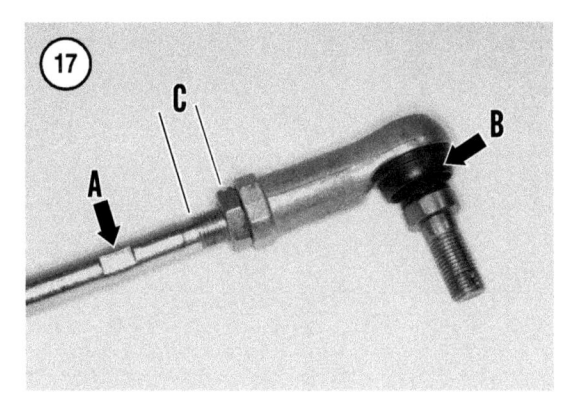

7. The replacement bearing is sealed on one side. Pack the open bearing side with lithium grease (or an equivalent waterproof bearing grease). Thoroughly work the grease in between the balls. Turn the bearing by hand to make sure the grease is distributed evenly inside the bearing.
8. Install the new bearing with its sealed side facing out. Note the following:
   a. Use a bearing driver or socket that matches the diameter of the outer bearing race.
   b. Drive the bearing squarely into place until it bottoms the bearing bore. The snap ring groove must be visible above the top of the bearing.
   c. Do not tap on the inner race or the bearing might be damaged.
9. Install the snap ring into the bearing bore groove. Make sure the snap ring seats in the groove completely.
10. Pack the lips of the new seals with grease.
11. Install the upper (27 × 40 × 6) and lower (23 × 35 × 7) dust seals into place in the bearing bore. The closed side of each seal must face out.
12. Install the collar into the lower dust seal.

1. Inspect the tie rod shaft. Replace it if damaged.

2. Inspect the rubber boot (B, **Figure 17**) of the ball joint on each tie rod end. The ball joints are permanently packed with grease. If a rubber boot is damaged, dirt and moisture can enter the ball joint and damage it. If a boot is damaged in any way, disassemble the tie rod and replace the tie rod end(s) as described in this section.

3. Pivot the ball joint stud back and forth by hand. If it moves roughly or with excessive play, replace it as described in the following procedure.

Disassembly/Assembly

Refer to **Figure 15**.

1. Loosen the tie-rod locknuts (A, **Figure 18**). The locknut securing the inner tie rod end uses left-hand threads.

2. Unscrew the tie rod end(s) (B, **Figure 18**).

3. Clean the mating shaft and tie rod end threads with contact cleaner.

4. The inner tie rod end is marked with the letter L (**Figure 19**). Install this tie rod end onto the end of the shaft without the adjusting flat on it. This tie rod end uses a silver-colored locknut.

5. The outer tie rod end is not marked but uses a gold-colored locknut.

6. Set the tie rod length by performing the following:

   a. Turn each tie rod end so the amount of exposed thread equals 5.5 mm (0.22 in.) when the locknut is seated against the tie rod end. Refer to C, **Figure 17**.

   b. Position the tie rod ends so the studs are parallel (**Figure 18**).

   c. Tighten the locknut securely. The locknut is tightened to specification during toe-in adjustment.

   d. Adjust the toe-in as described in Chapter Three.

   e. Measure the amount of exposed thread at each tie rod end (**Figure 20**). The tie rod length is within specification if the difference between these two measurements is less than or equal to 3 mm (0.1 in.).

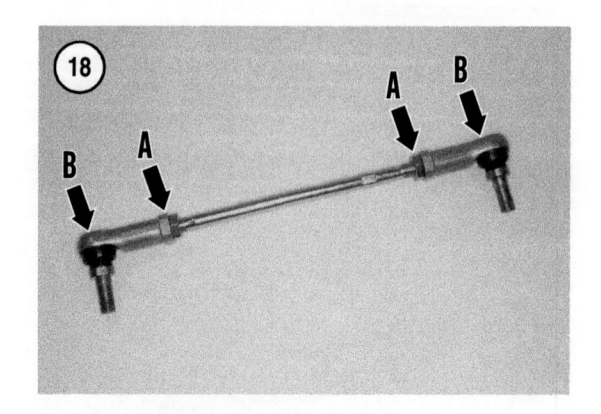

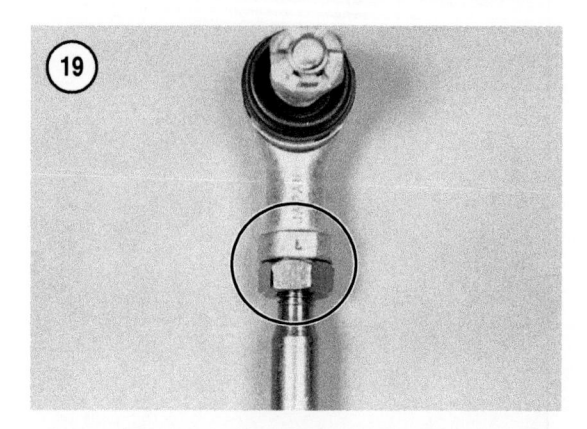

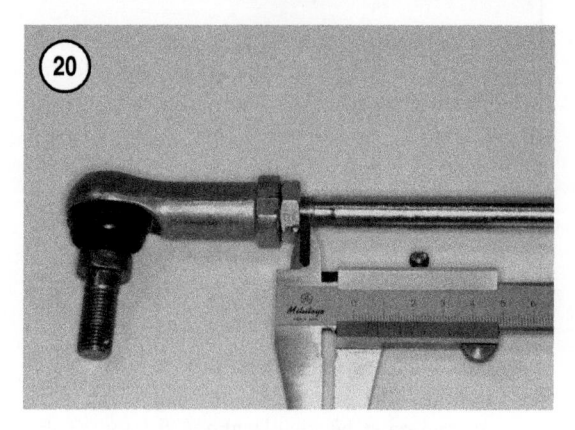

STEERING KNUCKLE

Removal/Installation

Refer to **Figure 21**.

1. Remove the front wheel as described in this chapter.

2. Remove the brake drum as described in Chapter Thirteen.

3. Remove the brake hose guide mounting bolt (A, **Figure 22**) and disc brake cover bolt (B).

FRONT SUSPENSION AND STEERING

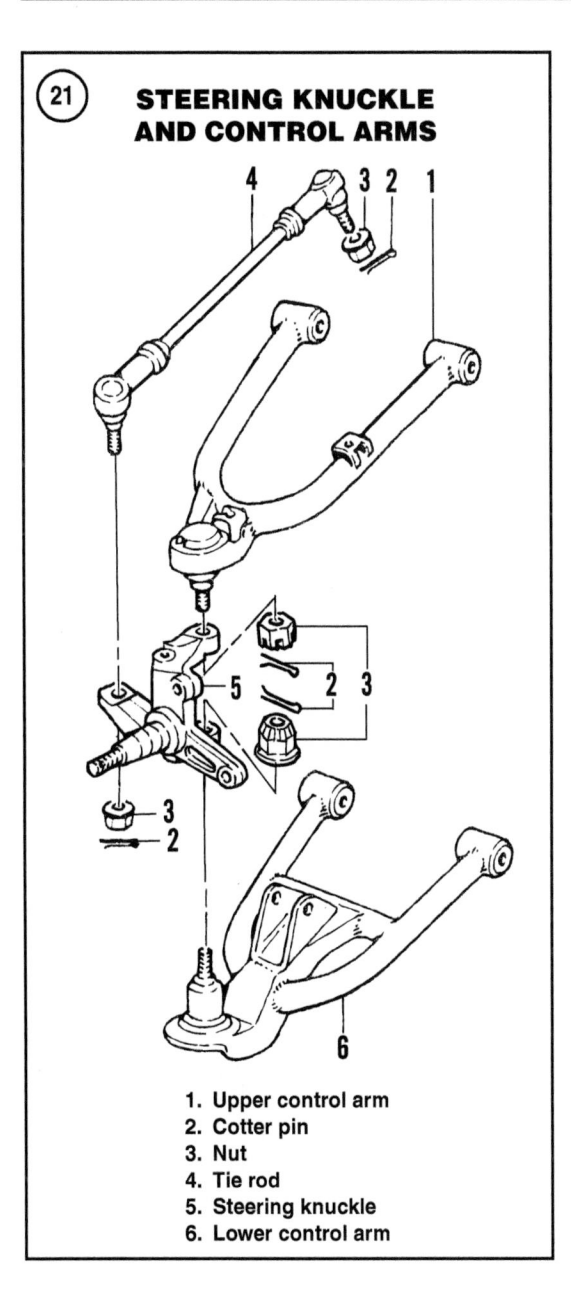

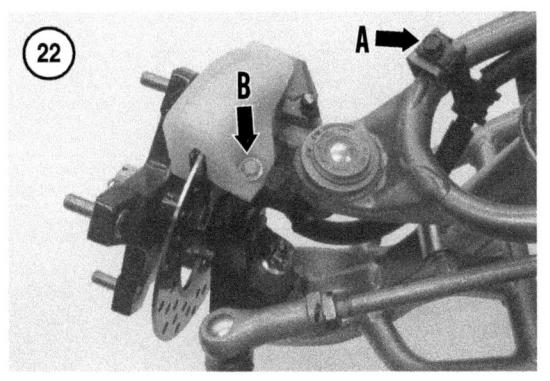

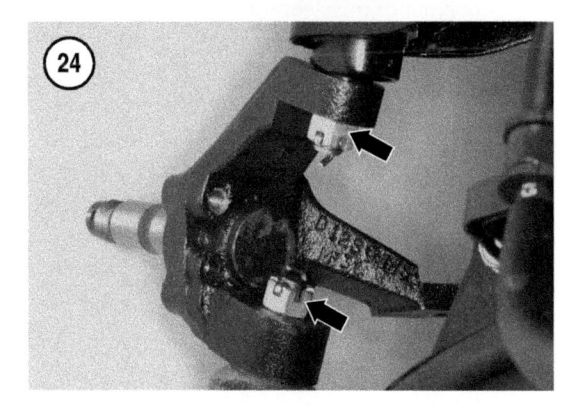

21 STEERING KNUCKLE AND CONTROL ARMS

1. Upper control arm
2. Cotter pin
3. Nut
4. Tie rod
5. Steering knuckle
6. Lower control arm

CAUTION
Do not suspend the brake caliper with the brake hose. The strain could damage the hose.

4. Remove the brake caliper bolts (**Figure 23**) and remove the brake caliper from the steering knuckle. Use a bunjee cord or wire to suspend the brake caliper from the frame. Do not twist the brake hose.
5. Disconnect the tie rod from the steering knuckle (**Figure 16**) as described in this chapter.
6. Remove the cotter pins and loosen the nuts (**Figure 24**) from the upper and lower control arm ball joints. Do not remove the nuts at this time.

CAUTION
Do not strike the ball joint or its stud when removing it. The ball joint becomes damaged.

7. Use the ATV ball-joint separator (part No. 08-0120 [**Figure 25**]) to disconnect the upper and lower control arm ball joints from the steering knuckle. Perform the following:
   a. Turn each ball joint nut so it is flush with the end of the stud.

b. Thread the pressure screw into the tool body.
c. Mount the ball-joint separator between the ball joints and run the pressure screw up against the upper-arm nut as shown in **Figure 26**.
d. Hold the tool body and turn the pressure bolt until the upper arm ball joint breaks loose from the steering knuckle.
e. If the ball joint feels tight and does not want to break loose, stop at this point. Do not try to force it with the ball-joint separator. Instead, place a 2 × 4 against the control arm, and strike it with a mallet. The ball joint should pop out of the steering knuckle.
f. Invert the tool and repeat this process for the lower control arm.
g. Remove the tool from the steering knuckle.
8. Remove each nut from its ball joint stud.
9. Remove the upper-arm ball joint from the steering knuckle (**Figure 27**), and remove the steering knuckle from the lower arm ball joint.
10. Inspect the steering knuckle as described in this section.
11. Install the steering knuckle by reversing these removal steps. Note the following:
    a. Position the steering knuckle on the lower control arm ball joint (**Figure 27**), and then install the upper control arm ball joint into the knuckle.
    b. Install the control arm ball joint nuts. Tighten each nut to 29 N•m (21 ft.-lb.).
    c. Install *new* cotter pins and bend the ends over completely.
    d. Install the tie rod to the steering knuckle as described in this chapter.
    e. Tighten the 6-mm and 8-mm brake hose guide bolts to 12 N•m (106 in.-lb.) and 29 N•m (21 ft.-lb.), respectively.
    f. Tighten the brake caliper bolts to 30 N•m (22 ft.-lb.).
    g. Check front brake operation before riding the vehicle.

Inspection

1. Clean the steering knuckle in solvent, and dry it with compressed air.
2. Inspect the steering knuckle (**Figure 28**) for bending, thread damage, cracks or other damage.
3. Inspect the spindle bearing surfaces for wear or damage. A hard spill or collision may cause the

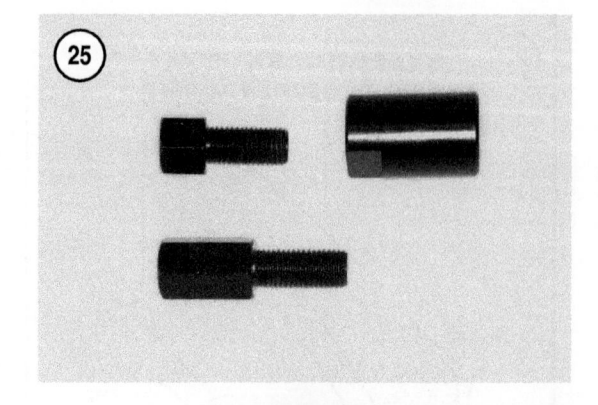

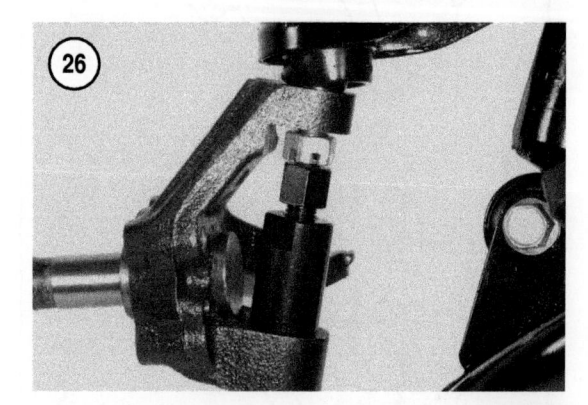

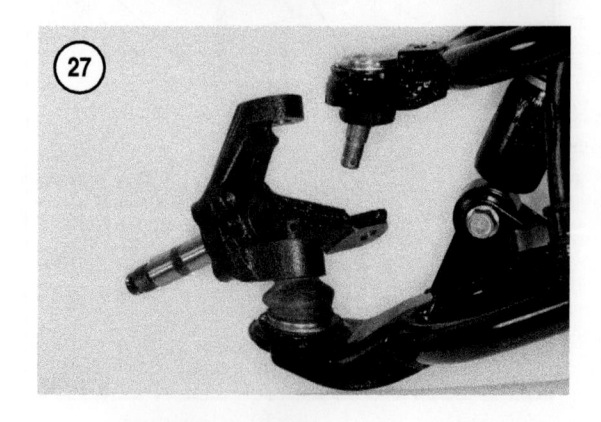

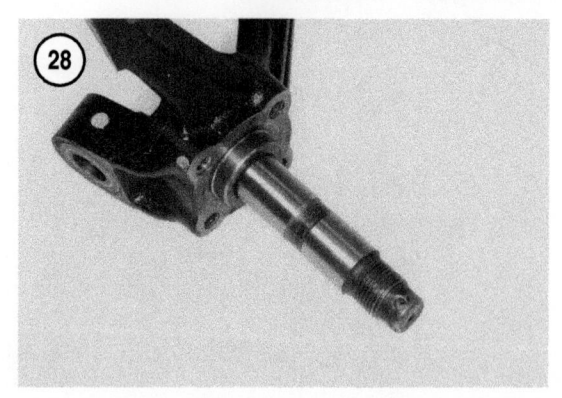

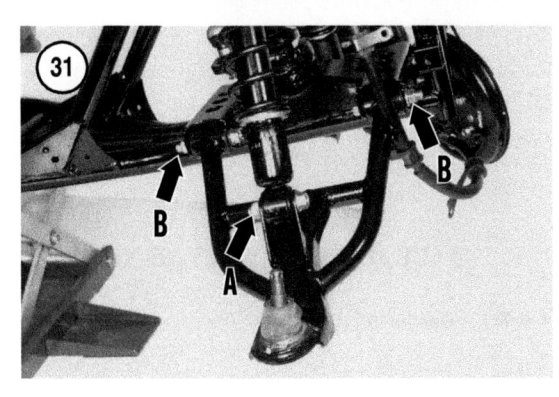

FRONT SUSPENSION AND STEERING

NOTE
When replacing the control arms separately, the tie rod does not have to be disconnected from the steering knuckle.

1. Remove the steering knuckle as described in this chapter.

WARNING
The control arm pivots and the shock mounts use self-locking nuts. Discard these nuts when they are removed. New self-locking nuts must be used during assembly.

2. Remove the upper control arm by performing the following:
   a. Remove the 6-mm brake hose guide mounting bolt (**Figure 29**) and separate the brake hose guide from the upper control arm.
   b. Remove and discard the control arm pivot nut (**Figure 30**) from each upper control arm pivot bolt.
   c. Remove the pivots bolts and lower the upper control arm from the frame.
3. Remove the lower control arm by performing the following:
   a. Remove and discard the shock absorber lower mounting nut (A, **Figure 31**).
   b. Remove the shock absorber lower pivot bolt and lower the control arm from the shock absorber.
   c. Remove and discard the lower control arm pivot nut (B, **Figure 31**) from each pivot bolt.
   d. Remove the pivots bolts and lower the control arm from the frame.
4. Inspect the upper and lower control arms as described in this section.

spindle to bend or fracture. If the spindle is damaged in any way, replace the steering knuckle.
4. Check the cotter-pin hole at the end of the spindle. Make sure there are no fractures or cracks leading out toward the end of the steering knuckle. If any are present, replace the steering knuckle.

CONTROL ARMS

Removal

Refer to **Figure 21**.

Installation

1. Lubricate the control arm pivot bolts with grease before installation.

NOTE
Install new upper and lower control arm pivot nuts, and finger-tighten these nuts during installation. The nuts are tightened to their specification after the front wheels are installed and the vehicle rests on the ground.

2. Set the lower control arm mounts into place in the frame brackets, and secure the arm in place with the pivot bolts and *new* nuts (B, **Figure 31**). Finger-tighten the nuts at this time.

3. Install the shock absorber lower mounting bolt and a *new* nut (A, **Figure 31**). Tighten the shock absorber lower mounting nut to 54 N•m (40 ft.-lb.).

4. Set the upper control arm mounts into place in the frame brackets, and secure the arm in place with the pivot bolts and *new* nuts (**Figure 30**). Finger-tighten the nuts at this time.

5. Secure the brake hose guide to the upper arm with the 6 mm bolt (**Figure 29**). Tighten the brake hose guide bolt to 12 N•m (106 in.-lb.).

6. Install the steering knuckle as described in this chapter.

7. Install the front wheels as described in this chapter.

8. Lower the vehicle so all four wheels sit on the ground.

9. Tighten the control arm pivot nuts to 30 N•m (22 ft.-lb.).

Cleaning and Inspection

CAUTION
*When cleaning a control arm, do not wash the ball joint (A, **Figure 32**) in solvent. This could contaminate the grease or damage the ball joint cover.*

1. Clean and dry the control arms.

2. Check each control arm for bending, cracks or other damage. Replace the control arm if necessary.

3. Inspect the ball joint and rubber boot (A, **Figure 32**) in each control arm. Pivot the ball joint by hand. It should move freely. The ball joint is permanently packed with grease. If the rubber boot is damaged, dirt and moisture can enter the ball joint and damage it. If the ball joint or boot is damaged, replace the ball joint as described in this chapter.

4. Check the cotter pin hole (B, **Figure 32**) in the ball joint stud. Make sure there are no fractures or cracks leading out toward the end of the ball joint. If any are present, replace the ball joint.

5. Inspect the threads in the ball joint stud. Dress the threads with a metric die or replace the ball joint as necessary.

6. Inspect the pivot bolts. Replace them if excessively worn or damaged.

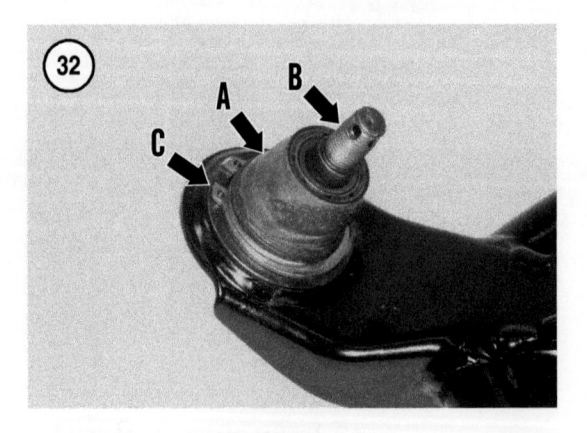

7. Inspect the pivot bushings (**Figure 33**) for excessive wear, separation or other damage. If damaged, replace the control arm. The bushings cannot be replaced separately.

BALL JOINT REPLACEMENT

Upper Control Arm

To replace the upper-arm ball joint, a ball joint remover/installer (Honda part No. 07JMF-HC50110), attachment, 28 × 30 mm (part No. 07946-1870100), attachment, 35 mm (part No. 07746-0030400) and a driver handle (part No. 07749-0010000) are needed.

1. Remove the snap ring (**Figure 34**) from the upper control arm ball joint.

2. Position the upper control arm and the ball joint remover/installer in a press. The side of the tool with the A mark must face the upper arm.

3. Install the 28 × 30 mm attachment and the driver.

4. Slowly lower the press arm (**Figure 35**), and press the ball joint from the upper control arm.

FRONT SUSPENSION AND STEERING

pletely visible so it can accept the snap ring. If necessary, press the ball joint further in.

11. Install the snap ring (**Figure 34**) so the flat side of the snap ring faces up away from the control arm. The snap ring must be completely seated in the groove.

Lower Control Arm

For ball joint removal, a ball joint remover/installer (Honda part No. 07JAF- SH20200), driver, 22-mm I.D. (part No. 07746-0020100), driver 40 mm I.D. (part No. 07746-0030100), attachment 35 mm (part No. 07746-0030400) and driver (part No. 07746- 0030100 or 07945-3710101) are needed.

1. Remove the snap ring (C, **Figure 32**) from the lower control arm.
2. Cut the ball joint rubber boot and remove the boot.
3. Position the lower control arm and the ball joint remover/installer in a press. The side of the tool with the A mark must face the lower control arm.
4. Install the 22-mm driver.
5. Slowly lower the press arm, and press the ball joint from the lower control arm.
6. Remove the tools and control arm from the press.
7. Clean the ball joint receptacle in the lower control arm with solvent. Dry it thoroughly.
8. Correctly position a new ball joint into the lower control arm.
9. Position the lower control arm and the driver into the press.
10. Install the 35-mm attachment and the 40-mm driver.

CAUTION
*If strong resistance is noticed when lowering the press arm, **stop immediately**. There is probably an alignment problem with either the ball joint or the tool. Realign the ball joint and tool and try again. The ball joint should press into place with a minimum amount of resistance.*

11. Slowly lower the press arm and press the ball joint straight into the lower control arm until the joint bottoms. The snap ring groove must be completely visible so it can accept the snap ring. If necessary, press the ball joint further in.

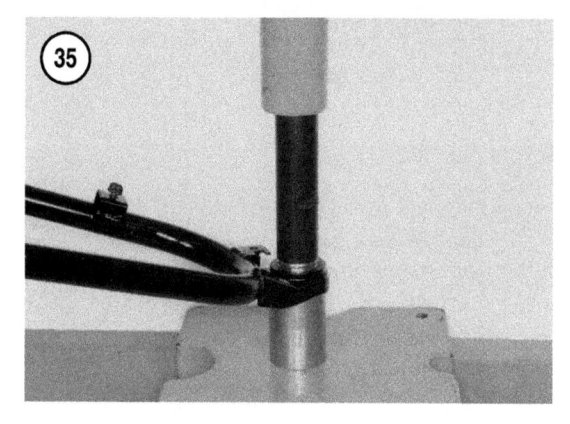

5. Remove the tools and control arm from the press.
6. Clean the ball joint receptacle in the upper control arm with solvent. Dry it thoroughly.
7. Correctly position a new ball joint into the upper control arm.
8. Position the upper control arm and the 35-mm attachment in the press.
9. Install the ball joint remover/installer in a press. The side of the tool with the A mark must face the upper control arm.

CAUTION
*If strong resistance is noticed when lowering the press arm, **stop immediately**. There is probably an alignment problem with either the ball joint or the tool. Realign the ball joint and tool and try again. The ball joint should press into place with a minimum amount of resistance.*

10. Slowly lower the press arm and press the ball joint straight into the upper control arm until the joint bottoms. The snap ring groove must be com-

CHAPTER ELEVEN

12. Install the snap ring (C, **Figure 32**) so the flat side of the snap ring faces away from the control arm. The snap ring must be completely seated in the groove.

SHOCK ABSORBERS

Removal/Installation

1. Support the vehicle with the front wheels off the ground.
2. Remove the shock nut (A, **Figure 31**) from the upper and lower shock absorber mounting bolt. Discard the self-locking nuts.
3. Remove the mounting bolts and shock absorber.
4. Inspect the shock absorber as described in this section.
5. Install the shock absorber by reversing the preceding removal steps while noting the following:

NOTE
The upper (10 × 55 mm) and lower (10 × 45 mm) shock mounting bolts are not interchangeable. Do not confuse them during assembly.

  a. Install the mounting bolt onto the front side of each mount.
  b. Install *new* self-locking nuts.
  c. Tighten the upper and lower shock absorber nuts to 30 N•m (22 ft.-lb.) and 54 N•m (40 ft.-lb.), respectively.

Inspection

NOTE
Replacement parts for the shock absorbers are not available. If any part is damaged or worn, replace the shock absorber.

1. Clean and dry the shock absorber.
2. Check the damper unit (**Figure 36**) for leaks or other damage.
3. Inspect the upper and lower rubber bushings for deterioration, excessive wear or other damage.
4. Inspect the shock spring for cracks or other signs of damage.

Table 1 FRONT SUSPENSION AND STEERING SPECIFICATIONS

Front suspension	
Type	Double wishbone
Wheel travel	150 mm (5.91 in.)
Caster	9.0°
Camber	-0.1°
Trail	40 mm (1 5/8 in.)
Toe-in	2-3 mm (3/32-1/8 in.)
Tie-rod length	325.7-327.7 mm (12.46-13.26 in.)

FRONT SUSPENSION AND STEERING

Table 2 FRONT SUSPENSION AND STEERING TORQUE SPECIFICATIONS

Item	N•m	in.-lb.	ft.-lb.
Brake caliper mounting bolts	30	–	22
Brake-hose-guide mounting bolts			
6 mm	12	106	–
8 mm	29	–	21
Control arm ball joint nut	29	–	21
Control arm pivot nuts	30		22
Handlebar lower holder nuts	39	–	29
Master cylinder clamp bolts	12	106	–
Shock absorber upper mounting nuts	30	–	22
Shock absorber lower mounting nuts	54	–	40
Steering shaft holder bolts	32	–	24
Steering shaft nut	108	–	80
Throttle housing cover screws	4	35	–
Tie-rod nuts	54	–	40
Tie-rod lock nut	54	–	40

CHAPTER TWELVE

REAR AXLE, SUSPENSION AND FINAL DRIVE

This chapter contains repair and replacement procedures for the rear axle, suspension and final drive unit. During inspection, compare measurements to the specifications in **Table 1**. Replace any part that is damaged or out of specification. During assembly, tighten fasteners as specified in **Table 2**. **Table 1** and **Table 2** are at the end of this chapter.

SHOCK ABSORBER

Removal/Installation

1. Raise the vehicle until the rear wheels just clear the ground. Use jack stands to securely support the vehicle.
2. Remove and discard the nut (**Figure 1**) from the upper mounting bolt.
3. Remove the upper shock mounting bolt. If necessary, raise or lower the vehicle to minimize the weight on the upper shock bolt.
4. Remove the shock absorber lower mounting bolt (**Figure 2**) and shock absorber.
5. Inspect the shock absorber as described in this section.
6. Install the shock absorber by reversing these removal steps. Note the following:

> *WARNING*
> *Self-locking nuts must be replaced when they are removed. The self-locking portion of the nut is weakened once the nut is removed and no longer properly locks onto the mating threads.*

   a. Install a *new* self-locking nut on the upper mounting bolt.
   b. Tighten the upper mounting nut and lower mounting bolt to 44 N•m (32 ft.-lb.) and 54 N•m (40 ft.-lb.), respectively.

Inspection

The shock absorber is spring-controlled and hydraulically damped. It cannot be serviced. If any part is damaged, replace the shock absorber.
1. Clean and dry the shock absorber.
2. Check the damper unit (**Figure 3**) for leaks or other damage.
3. Inspect the upper and lower shock bushings for deterioration, excessive wear or other damage.

REAR AXLE, SUSPENSION AND FINAL DRIVE

2. Remove the rear brake panel and brake drum as described in Chapter Thirteen.
3. Pull the axle from the right side. If necessary, tap the left end of the axle with a plastic mallet (**Figure 5**).
4. Inspect the rear axle as described in this section.

Installation

1. Apply molybdenum disulfide grease to the axle splines.
2. Align the splines on the rear axle with those in the final drive housing, and install the rear axle from the right side. If necessary, tap the right side of the axle with a plastic mallet until the axle bottoms in the final drive.
3. Install the brake drum and brake panel (Chapter Thirteen).
4. Install the rear hubs and wheels (Chapter Ten).

Inspection

1. Clean and dry the rear axle.
2. Inspect the axle splines (**Figure 6**) for twisting or other damage. Replace the axle if damage is noted.
3. Remove and replace the axle O-ring (**Figure 7**).
4. Check the axle cotter pin holes. Replace the axle if either hole is cracked, enlarged or damaged.
5. Place the rear axle on a set of V-blocks and measure runout with a dial indicator (**Figure 8**). Replace the rear axle if the runout exceeds the service limit in **Table 1**.

FINAL DRIVE

Removal

1. Remove the rear axle as described in this chapter.
2. Remove the right skid plate bolt (**Figure 9**).
3. Remove the front skid plate bolt (A, **Figure 10**) and the bolt (B), and then lower the skid plate from the final drive.
4. Drain the final drive oil as described in Chapter Three.
5. Support the final drive with a jack or wooden blocks.
6. Disconnect the breather hose (A, **Figure 11**) from on the left side of the final drive.

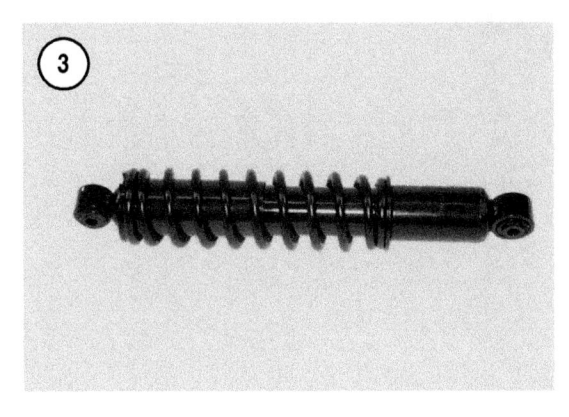

4. Inspect the shock spring for cracks or other signs of damage.

REAR AXLE

Removal

Refer to **Figure 4**.

1. Remove both rear wheels and hubs as described in Chapter Ten.

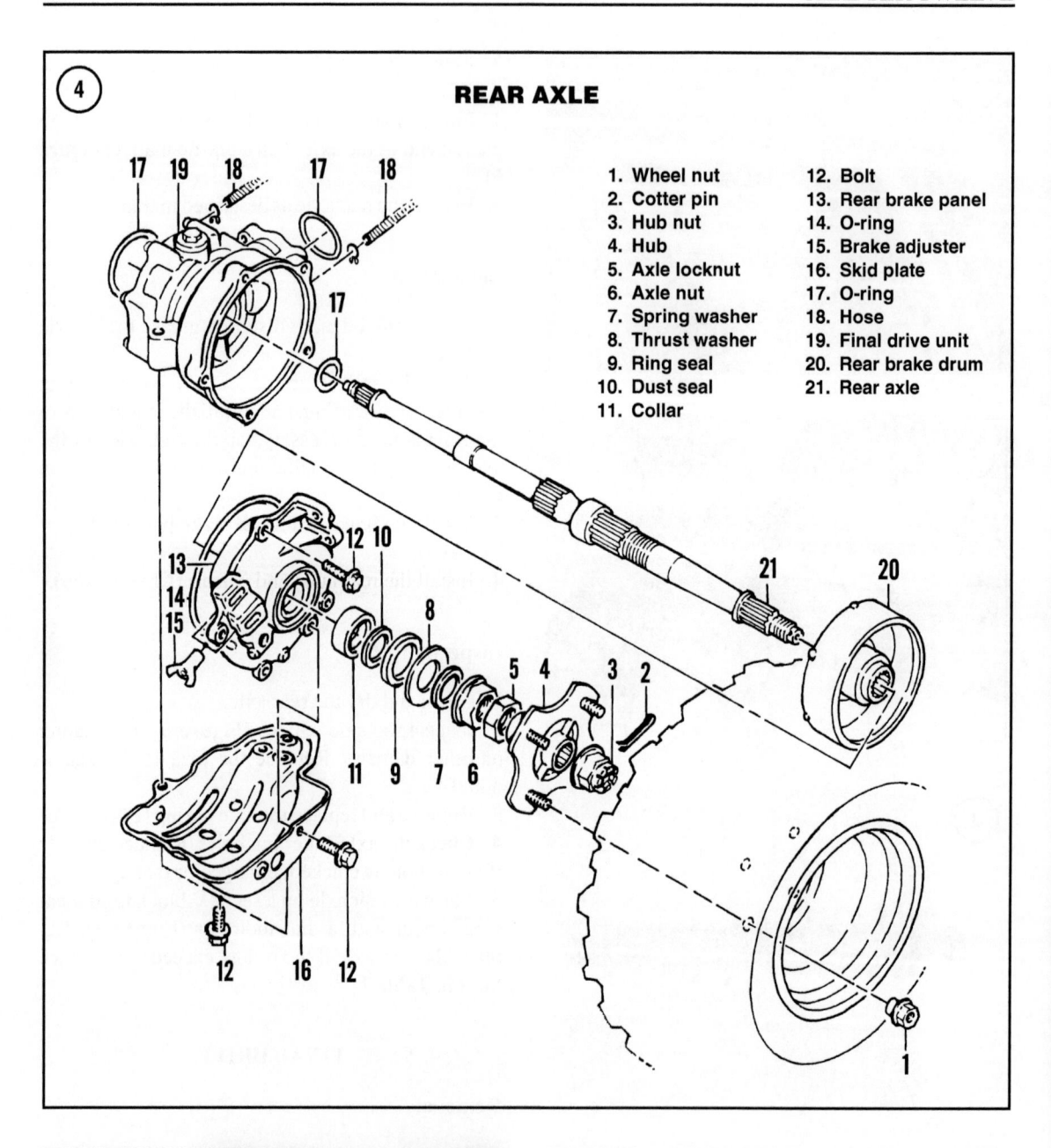

250

CHAPTER TWELVE

REAR AXLE

1. Wheel nut
2. Cotter pin
3. Hub nut
4. Hub
5. Axle locknut
6. Axle nut
7. Spring washer
8. Thrust washer
9. Ring seal
10. Dust seal
11. Collar
12. Bolt
13. Rear brake panel
14. O-ring
15. Brake adjuster
16. Skid plate
17. O-ring
18. Hose
19. Final drive unit
20. Rear brake drum
21. Rear axle

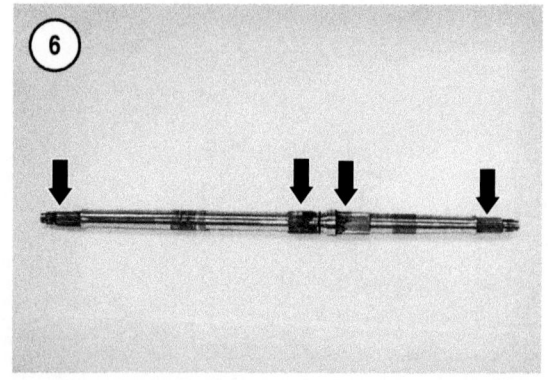

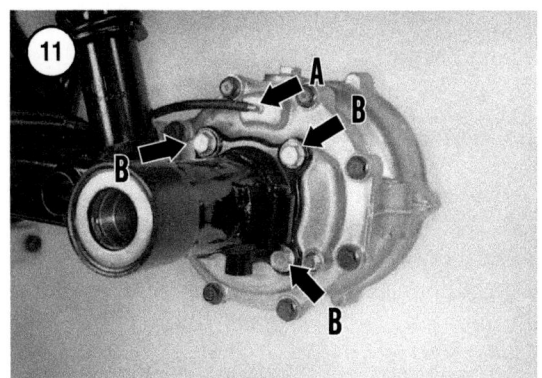

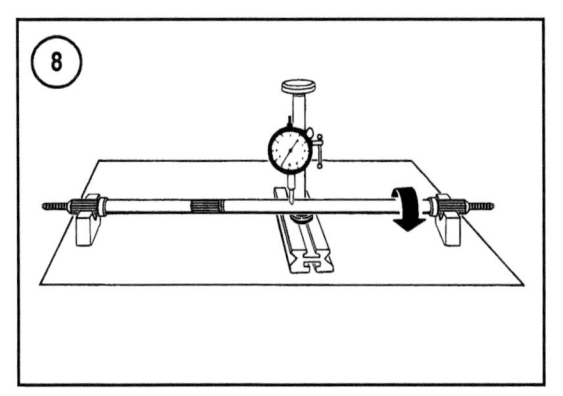

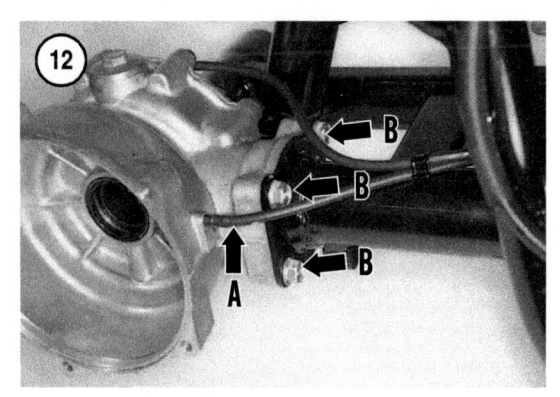

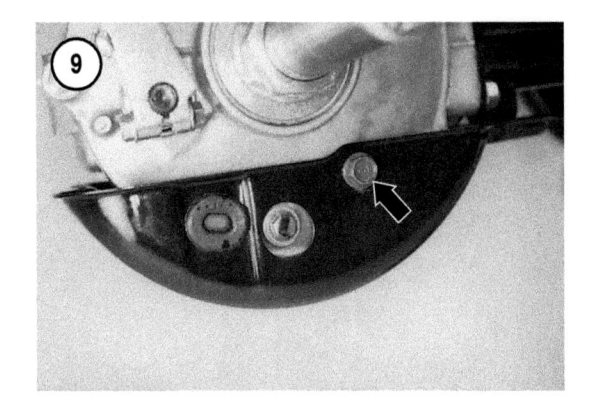

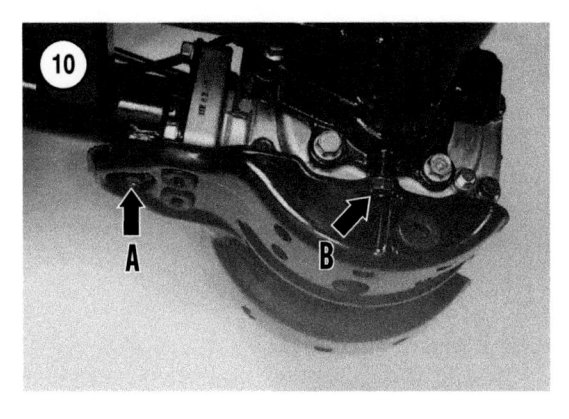

REAR AXLE, SUSPENSION AND FINAL DRIVE

7. Remove the four final drive mounting bolts (B, **Figure 11**) from the left side.

8. Disconnect the breather hose (A, **Figure 12**) from the right side of the final drive.

9. Remove the four final drive mounting bolts (B, **Figure 12**) from the front of the unit, and remove the final drive. Watch for the spring in the end of the drive shaft (**Figure 13**).

10. Remove and discard the two O-rings (A, **Figure 14**) from the final drive.

11. Inspect the final drive as described in this section.

Installation

1. Lubricate two new O-rings with lithium grease. Install each O-ring (A, **Figure 14**) into its groove in the final drive.
2. Lubricate the drive shaft spring with molybdenum disulfide grease and insert it into the end of the drive shaft (**Figure 13**).
3. Apply molybdenum disulfide grease to the splines of the pinion.
4. Set a wooden block onto the jack pad and place the final drive on the block.
5. Raise the jack and align the pinion with the splines on the drive shaft (**Figure 15**).
6. Install the final drive onto the swing arm so the pinion gear splines properly engages the drive shaft.
7. Install and finger-tighten the four mounting bolts (B, **Figure 12**) on the front of the final drive.
8. Reconnect the breather tube (A, **Figure 12**) to the fitting on the right side of the final drive.
9. Reconnect the breather tube (A, **Figure 11**) onto the left side of the final drive.
10. Install the four mounting bolts (B, **Figure 11**) on the left side of the final drive. Tighten the left bolts to 54 N•m (40 ft.-lb.).
11. Tighten the front mounting bolts (B, **Figure 12**) to 54 N•m (40 ft.-lb.).
12. Install the skid plate. Tighten the skid plate bolts to 32 N•m (24 ft.-lb.).
13. Install the rear axle as described in this chapter.
14. Refill the final drive with the recommended type and quantity of oil as described in Chapter Three.

Inspection

1. Check the final drive unit for oil leaks, cracks or other damage.
2. Inspect the exposed splines for excessive wear or damage.
3. Inspect the threaded holes for damage. Repair minor thread damage with a metric tap.
4. Inspect the O-rings (A, **Figure 14**) and oil seals (B) for wear, hardness and deterioration.
5. Turn the pinion gear (**Figure 16**) by hand. It should turn smoothly. If there is roughness or noise, refer to *Overhaul* in this section.

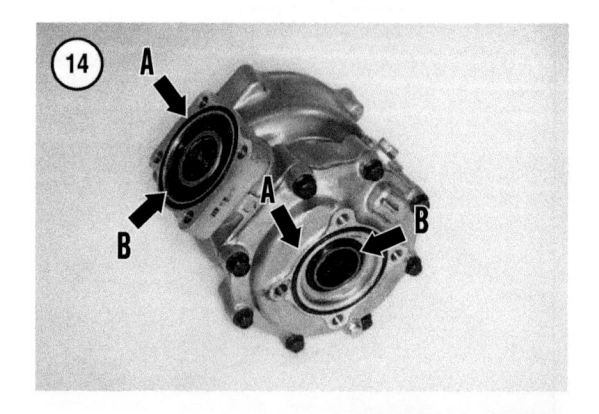

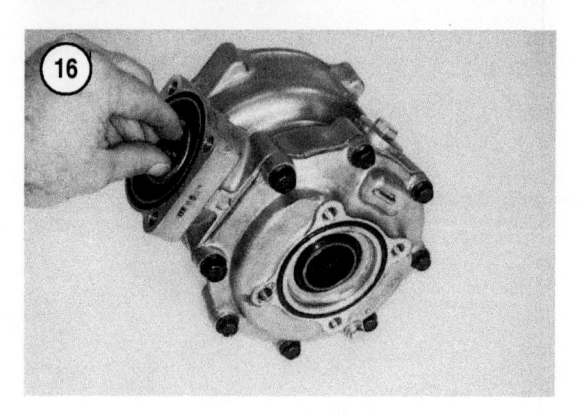

Overhaul

Tools

The following Honda special tools are recommended when servicing the final drive:
1. Pinion puller base (part No. 07HMC-MM80011A).
2. Puller shaft (part No. 07931-ME4010B).
3. Adapter (part No. 07YMF-HN4010A).
4. Special nut (part No. 07931-HB3020A).
5. Locknut wrench (part No. 07916-MB00002).

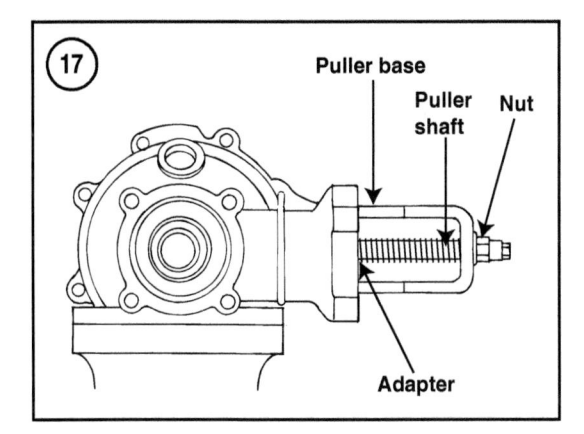

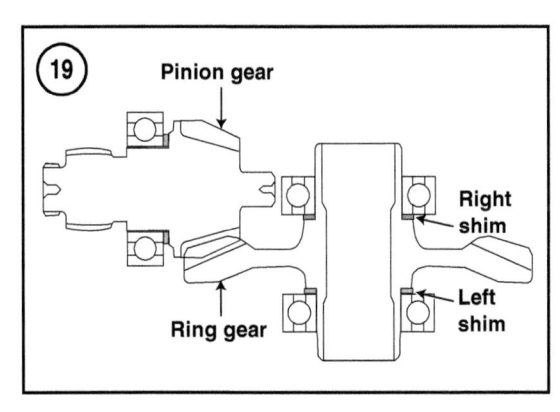

REAR AXLE, SUSPENSION AND FINAL DRIVE

Figure 17 (Puller base, Puller shaft, Nut, Adapter)

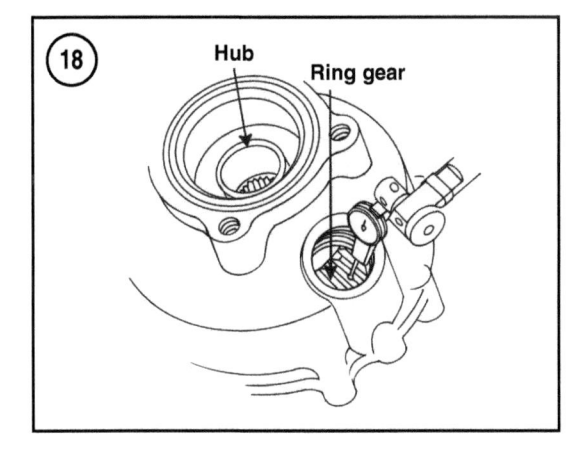

Figure 18 (Hub, Ring gear)

Figure 19 (Pinion gear, Right shim, Left shim, Ring gear)

6. Pinion bearing ring compressor tool (part No. 07YME-HN4010A).

Backlash measurement/adjustment

Perform gear backlash measurement before disassembly to determine if there is gear wear. Measuring gear backlash is also necessary after overhaul. If the backlash measurement is not within specification, the internal shim thicknesses needs to be adjusted.

1. Install the pinion puller base, puller shaft, adapter and special nut, as shown in **Figure 17**, so the pinion end play is removed and the pinion cannot rotate.
2. Place the final drive in a soft-jawed vice.
3. Remove the oil fill cap.
4. Insert a tool into the center splines of the ring gear hub so the ring gear can be rotated.
5. Position a dial indicator so the tip rests against a gear tooth (**Figure 18**).
6. To determine the gear backlash, gently rotate the ring gear while reading the dial indicator. Refer to **Table 1** for the specified backlash.
7. Remove the dial indicator, rotate the ring gear and take two additional backlash readings 120° from the original measuring point. If the difference between any two readings exceeds 0.2 mm (0.008 in.), note the following:
   a. The gear assembly is not square in the case, which may be due to the incorrect seating of a bearing.
   b. The housing may be deformed.
8. To correct the gear backlash, refer to **Figure 19** and note the following:

NOTE
When adjusting shim thickness, adjust the sides equally. For example, if the right shim is increased 0.10 mm (0.004 in.), decrease the left shim 0.10 mm (0.004 in.). Changing a shim thickness by 0.12 mm (0.005 in.) changes backlash 0.06 mm (0.002 in.).

   a. If gear backlash is less than the desired specification, reduce the thickness of the left shim and increase the thickness of the right shim.
   b. If gear backlash is greater than the desired specification, reduce the thickness of the right shim and increase the thickness of the left shim.

Disassembly

If the pinion gear, ring gear, gearcase, case cover, side bearings or pinion shaft bearing are replaced, perform the backlash and gear mesh pattern measurements before disassembly. If the oil seals or case cover seal need to be replaced, it is not necessary if the unit is otherwise operating correctly.

CHAPTER TWELVE

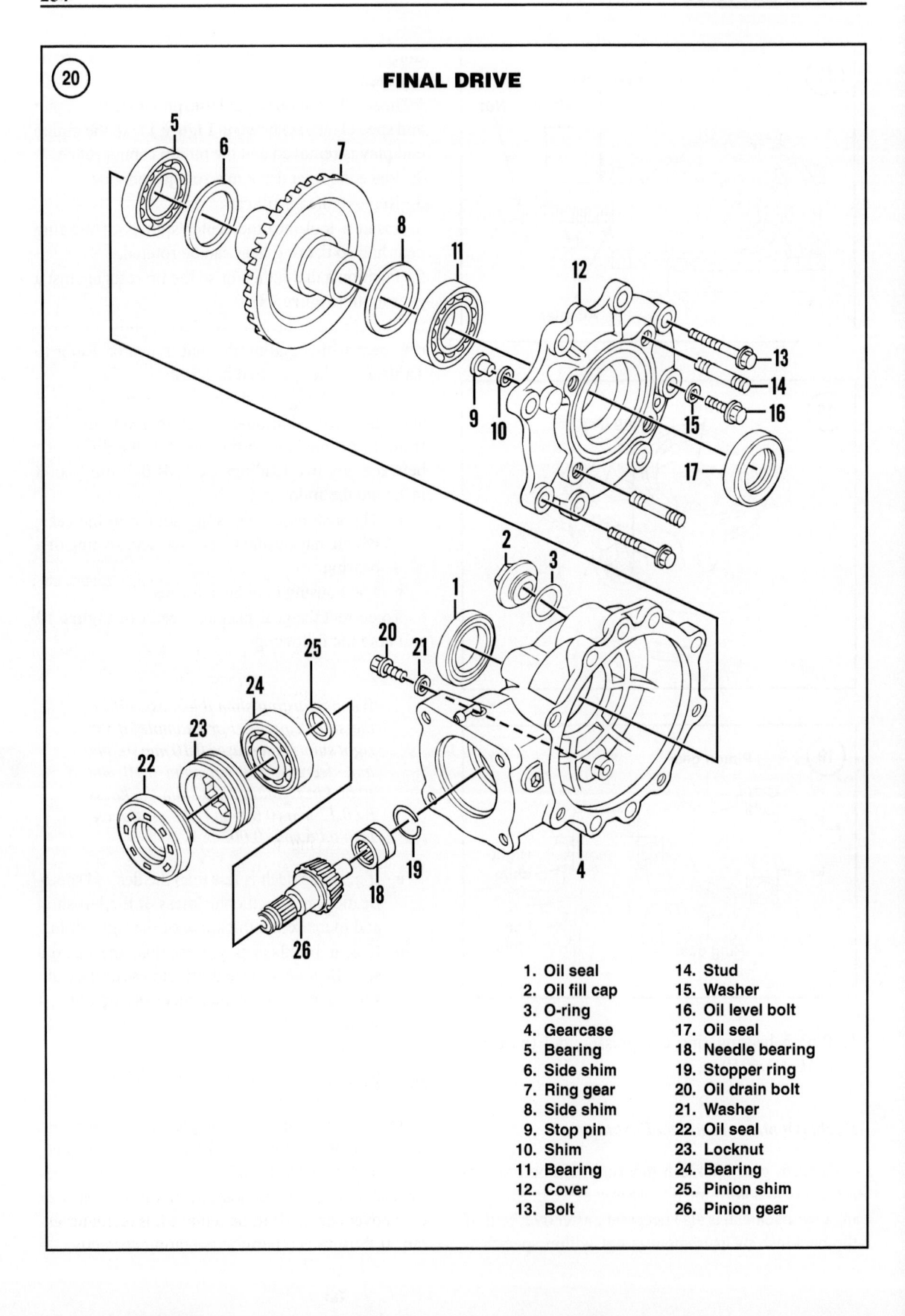

FINAL DRIVE

20

1. Oil seal
2. Oil fill cap
3. O-ring
4. Gearcase
5. Bearing
6. Side shim
7. Ring gear
8. Side shim
9. Stop pin
10. Shim
11. Bearing
12. Cover
13. Bolt
14. Stud
15. Washer
16. Oil level bolt
17. Oil seal
18. Needle bearing
19. Stopper ring
20. Oil drain bolt
21. Washer
22. Oil seal
23. Locknut
24. Bearing
25. Pinion shim
26. Pinion gear

REAR AXLE, SUSPENSION AND FINAL DRIVE

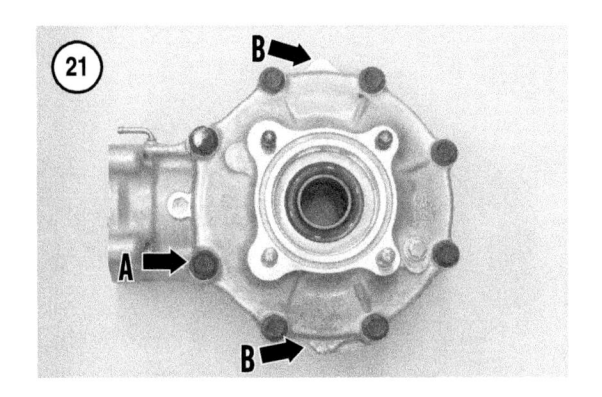

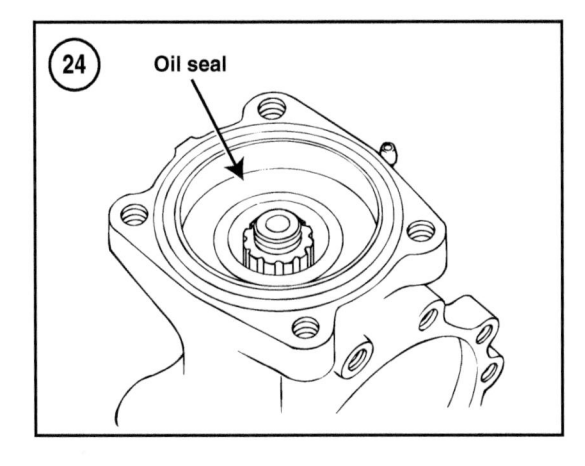

The final drive unit (**Figure 20**) requires a number of special tools for disassembly, inspection and reassembly. The price of these tools could be more than the cost of most repairs performed at a dealership. Read the procedure and determine the cost before undertaking the repair.

1. Remove the cover retaining bolts in a crossing pattern (A, **Figure 21**).
2. Insert a prying tool in the gaps between the gearcase and cover (B, **Figure 21**) and pry the cover off the gearcase.
3. Note the left-side shim on the ring gear (A, **Figure 22**). Remove the shim, label it and set it aside.
4. Remove the ring gear (B, **Figure 22**).
5. Note the right-side shim on the ring gear (**Figure 23**). Remove the shim, label it and set it aside.
6. Using a suitable seal puller, remove the oil seal (**Figure 24**).
7. Rotate the pinion shaft and check for noisy or rough pinion bearings.

NOTE
Cover the internal parts when unstaking the locknut in Step 8 to prevent the entry of metal debris.

8. Using a grinder or metal removal tool, remove the staked portion of the locknut (A, **Figure 25**).
9. Using the locknut wrench remove the locknut (B, **Figure 25**).
10. Assemble the tools as shown in **Figure 26**, and remove the pinion and bearing assembly.

Inspection

1. Clean and inspect all components for excessive wear and damage. Carefully remove gasket material from the mating surfaces on the gearcase and cover.

2. Remove the oil seals in the gearcase and cover using a suitable seal removal tool. Install a new oil seal so the closed side is out (**Figure 27**).

3. Turn the bearings (A, **Figure 28**) in the final drive and cover by hand. The bearings should turn freely and without any sign of roughness, catching or excessive noise. Replace the damaged bearings as described in Chapter One. The bearing must bottom in the final drive or cover bore.

4. Inspect the ring gear and hub (**Figure 29**). Inspect the gear teeth, splines and seal running surfaces on the hub. Replace them if they are excessively worn or damaged.

5. Inspect the pinion needle bearing (A, **Figure 30**). If it is damaged, replace the bearing using the following procedure:
   a. Rotate the pinion needle bearing until the end of the wire stopper ring is visible through the access hole. Use a punch to bend the ring upward by striking it near the end. Grip the end of the wire stopper retainer ring using needlenose pliers and pull it out through the access hole (B, **Figure 30**).

   CAUTION
   Do not use a flame to heat the gearcase; it can warp the final drive.

   b. Heat the gearcase in an oven to 80° C (176° F) and extract the bearing.
   c. Install a new wire ring into the groove on the outside of the new bearing.
   d. Install the bearing and ring into the ring compressor tool.
   e. Place the compressor tool with the bearing into the freezer for at least 30 minutes.
   f. Heat the gearcase in an oven to 80° C (176° F).
   g. Position the compressor in the gearcase and drive the bearing in the final drive. Only one blow should be required. Multiple blows may dislodge the wire ring, which requires the installation of a new ring and bearing. Make sure the wire ring is properly positioned as viewed in the access hole (B, **Figure 30**).

6. Inspect the pinion gear and bearing. If the bearing must be replaced, replace it as follows:
   a. Using a press or a puller, remove the bearing form the pinion shaft.
   b. If only the bearing is being replaced, use the original shim on the pinion shaft. If the gearcase cover or gearcase, ring and pinion gears or the side bearings are being replaced, install a 2.0 mm (0.79 in.) thick shim as a starting point for the gear position adjustments.
   c. Press or drive the new bearing onto the pinion shaft so the marked side of the bearing is toward the threaded end of the shaft.

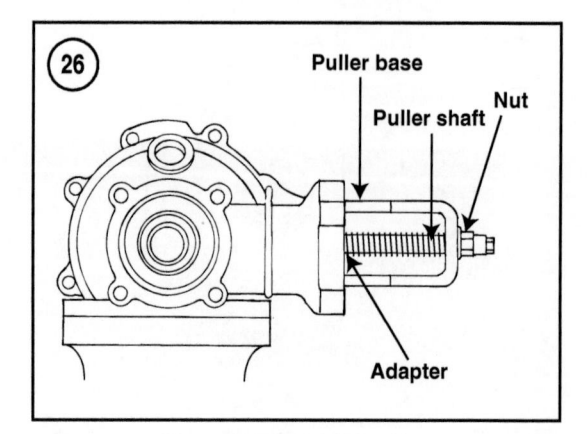

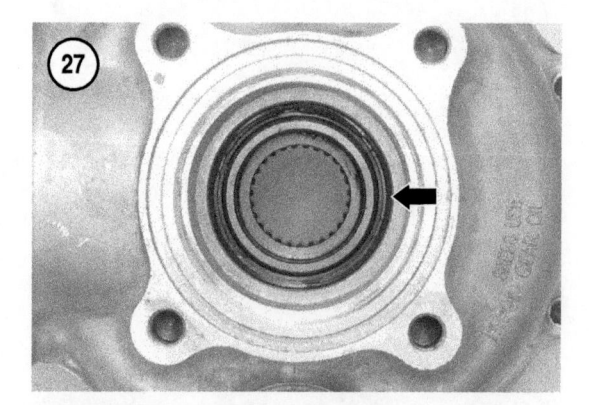

7. Check the ring gear side clearance using the following procedure:

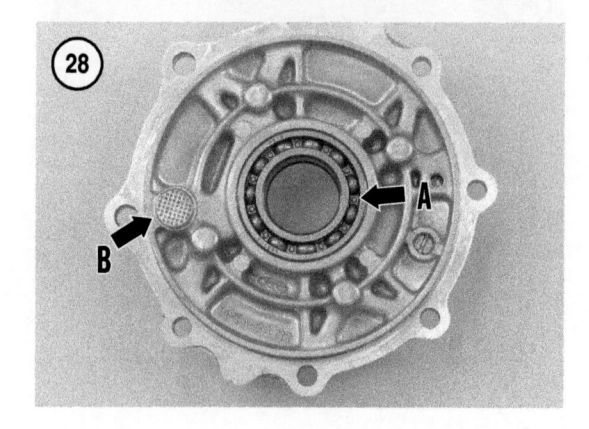

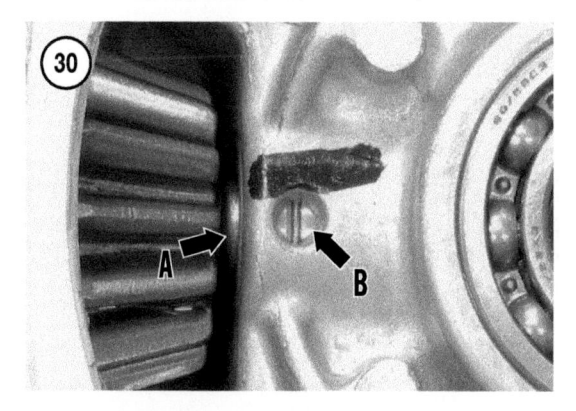

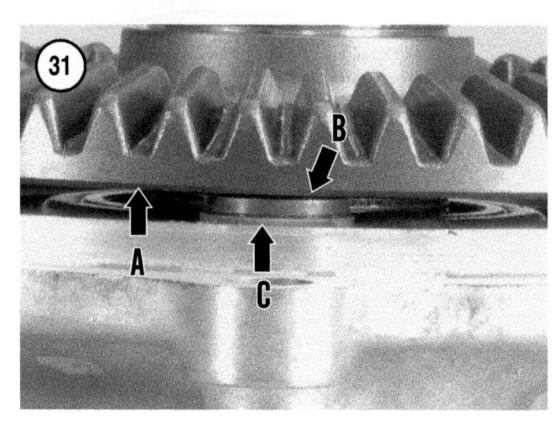

REAR AXLE, SUSPENSION AND FINAL DRIVE

d. Install or remove shims as necessary to obtain the desired clearance.
e. Drive the stop pin into the cover and recheck the clearance.

Assembly

Refer to **Figure 20**.

> *NOTE*
> *Lubricate all moving parts with SAE 80 hypoid gear oil.*

1. Install the pinion gear and bearing into the gearcase.

> *NOTE*
> *The torque wrench attachment point on the Honda tool specified in Step 2 increases wrench leverage. The actual torque is 98 N•m (72 ft.-lb.). Refer to **Torque Adapter** in Chapter One.*

2. Install the locknut (B, **Figure 25**). Using the locknut wrench, tighten the locknut to 89 N•m (66 ft.-lb.) as indicated on the torque wrench.

> *NOTE*
> *Do not stake the locknut when performing the gear mesh pattern check in Step 3. The pinion gear may still need to be reshimmed.*

3. If the pinion, ring gear, bearings, housing or cover have been replaced, check the gear mesh pattern using the following procedure:
   a. Apply a Prussian Blue or other gear marking compound to the ring gear teeth.
   b. Install the side shims (6 and 8, **Figure 20**) onto the ring gear, and then install the ring gear into the final drive.
   c. Install the cover on the gearcase.

> *NOTE*
> *While tightening the cover bolts in substep d, rotate the pinion shaft.*

   d. Install the cover bolts. Install the two 10-mm bolts in the locations shown in **Figure 32**. Tighten the bolts evenly in a crossing pattern in several steps until the cover is seated. Tighten the 8-mm bolts to 25 N•m (18 ft.-lb.). Tighten the 10-mm bolts to 49 N•m (36 ft.-lb.).
   e. Remove the oil fill cap.

a. Install the ring gear and side shim into the cover.
b. Using a feeler gauge, measure the clearance between the ring gear (A, **Figure 31**) and the stop pin (B). Refer to **Table 1** for the recommended clearance. The shim (C, **Figure 31**) under the stop pin is used to adjust the clearance.
c. To adjust the clearance, heat the cover in an oven to 80° C (176° F). Remove the stop pin (B, **Figure 28**).

f. Rotate the pinon shaft several rotations so a pattern is evident on the ring gear teeth. View the ring gear teeth through the oil fill hole (**Figure 33**).
g. Refer to the typical gear patterns in **Figure 34**. If the pinion is low, install a thinner pinion shim (25, **Figure 20**). If the pinion is high, install a thicker shim. The pinion and bearing must be removed to replace the shim. Changing the shim thickness 0.12 mm (0.005 in.) moves the contact pattern approximately 0.5-1.0 mm (0.02-0.04 in.).
h. Reinstall the pinion gear and bearing, if they were removed, as described in Step 10 and Step 11.
i. After obtaining a satisfactory gear contact pattern, check the gear backlash.
j. Remove the cover and continue with the final assembly procedure.

4. Stake the pinion locknut (A, **Figure 25**) into the notch in the final drive housing.
5. Install the oil seal (**Figure 24**) so it is bottomed. Lubricate the oil seal lips with grease.
6. Install the side shims (6 and 8, **Figure 20**) onto the ring gear.
7. Install the ring gear into the housing.
8. Apply a liquid sealant, such as Yamabond No. 4, to the mating surface of the cover and then install the cover.

NOTE
While tightening the cover bolts in Step 9, rotate the pinion shaft.

9. Install the cover bolts. Install the two 10-mm bolts in the locations shown in **Figure 32**. Tighten the bolts evenly in a crossing pattern in several steps until the cover is seated. Tighten the 8-mm bolts to

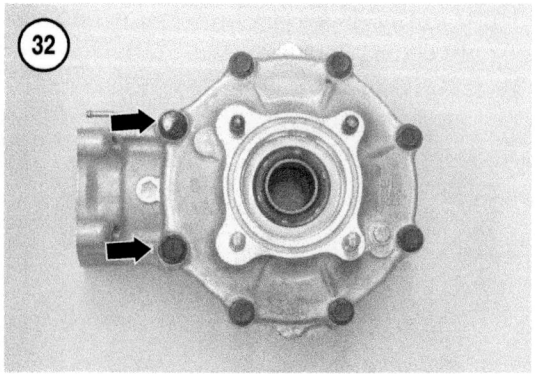

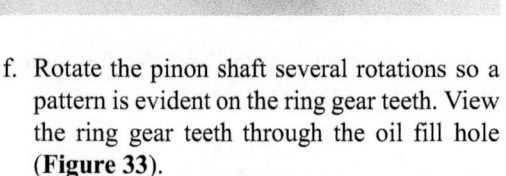

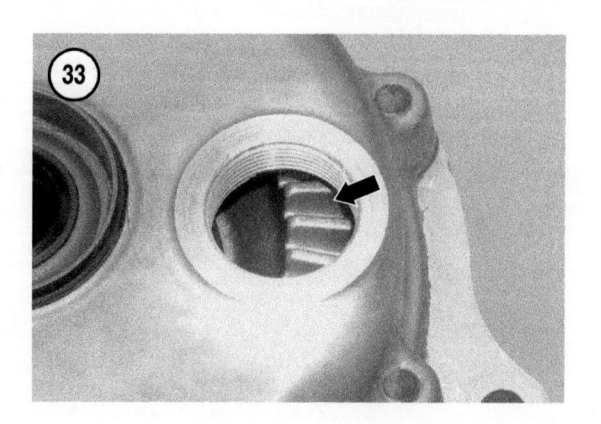

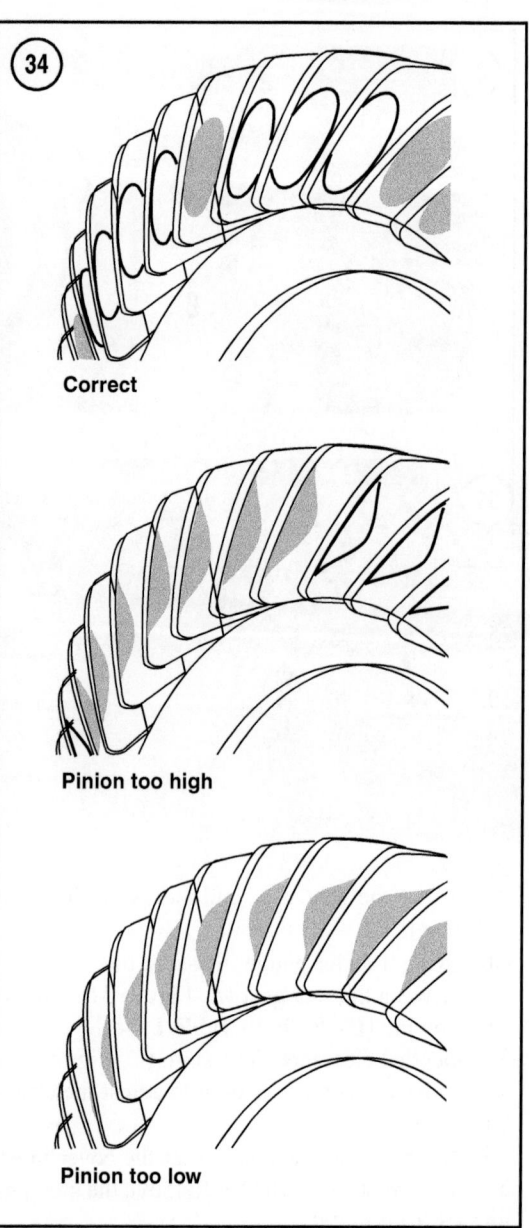

REAR AXLE, SUSPENSION AND FINAL DRIVE

SWING ARM

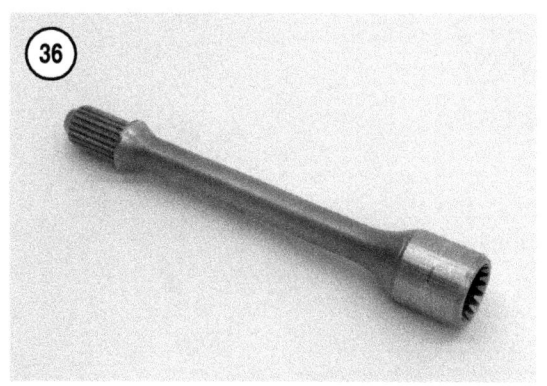

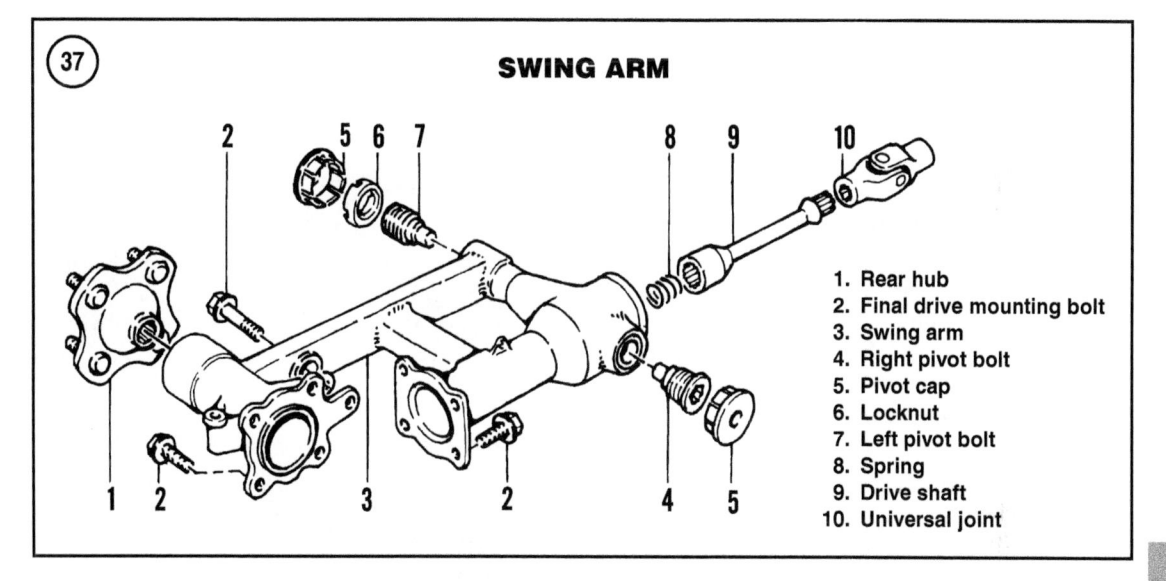

Figure 37

1. Rear hub
2. Final drive mounting bolt
3. Swing arm
4. Right pivot bolt
5. Pivot cap
6. Locknut
7. Left pivot bolt
8. Spring
9. Drive shaft
10. Universal joint

25 N•m (18 ft.-lb.). Tighten the 10-mm bolts to 49 N•m (36 ft.-lb.).

10. Make sure the gears rotate freely without binding.

DRIVESHAFT

Removal/Inspection/Installation

1. Remove the final drive unit as described in this chapter.
2. Remove the spring in the end of the driveshaft (A, **Figure 35**).
3. Remove the driveshaft (B, **Figure 35**).
4. Inspect the splines and seal contact surface on the driveshaft (**Figure 36**). Replace the driveshaft if it is excessively worn or damaged.
5. Before installation, apply molybdenum disulfide grease to the splines of the driveshaft.

6. Insert the driveshaft into the splines of the universal joint. Make sure the driveshaft is fully seated in the universal joint.
7. Install the spring into the end of the driveshaft (A, **Figure 35**).
8. Install the final drive unit as described in this chapter.

SWING ARM

Bearings are pressed into both sides of the swing arm, and seals are installed on the outside of each bearing to keep dirt and moisture out of the bearings.

Refer to **Figure 37**.

Tools

The Honda swing arm locknut wrench (part No. 07908-4690003 [A, **Figure 38**]) and a 17-mm Allen socket (B) are required to remove and install the swing arm.

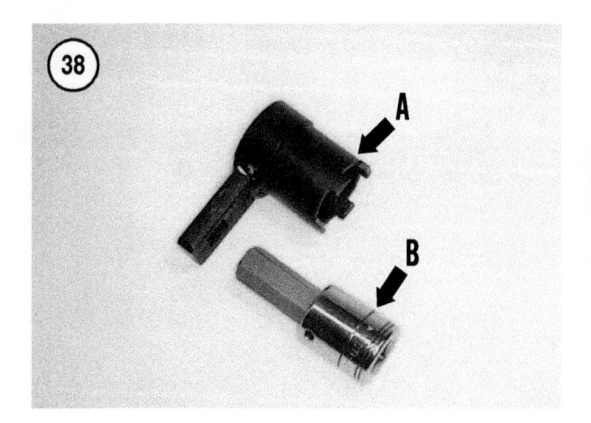

Swing Arm Removal

1. Remove the rear mud guards as described in Chapter Fourteen.
2. Remove the rear axle and final drive unit as described in this chapter.
3. Use a jack or wooden blocks to support the frame directly below the swing arm pivots.
4. Loosen the clamp (**Figure 39**) on the swing arm boot.
5. Release the breather hoses from the clamp (A, **Figure 40**) on the swing arm.
6. Remove the lower shock absorber mounting bolt (B, **Figure 40**).
7. Remove the pivot cap and right pivot bolt (**Figure 41**).
8. Remove the pivot cap and use the swing arm locknut wrench to remove the locknut from the left pivot bolt (**Figure 42**).
9. Remove the left pivot bolt (**Figure 43**) and pull the swing arm from the frame.
10. Remove the drive shaft (A, **Figure 44**) and universal joint (B) if they did not come off with the swing arm.
11. If necessary, loosen the remaining clamp and remove the boot (A, **Figure 45**) from the countershaft protector.

Swing Arm Installation

1. If removed, install the boot onto the countershaft protector. Position the boot so the tab marked HM8 faces up (A, **Figure 45**).

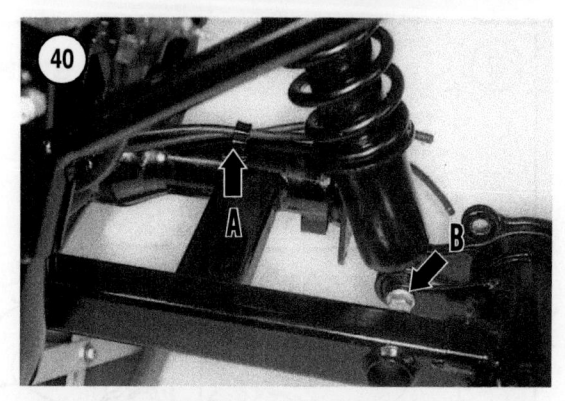

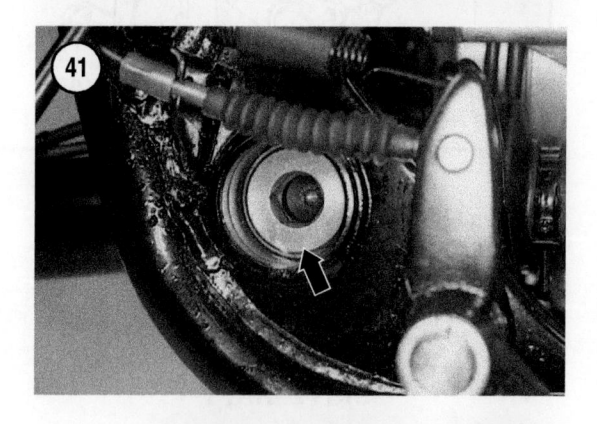

REAR AXLE, SUSPENSION AND FINAL DRIVE

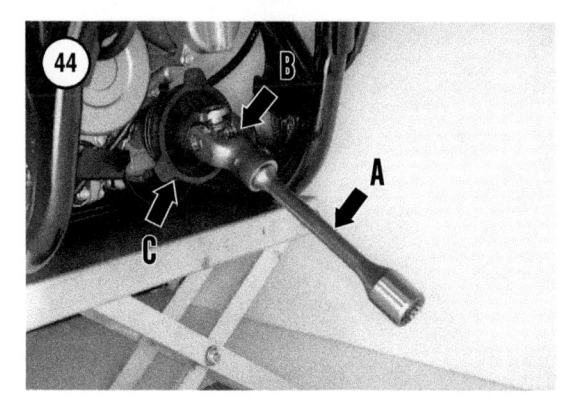

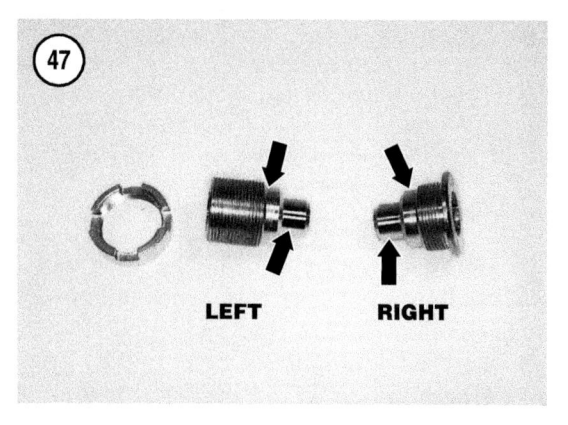

2. Lubricate the splines of the universal joint and drive shaft with molybdenum disulfide grease.
3. Install the universal joint (B, **Figure 44**) and drive shaft (A) onto the countershaft. Make sure the spring is installed in the end of the drive shaft.
4. Pack the grease retainer (A, **Figure 46**) and bearing (B) in each end of the swing arm bore with grease.
5. Slide the swing arm over the drive shaft and position the swing arm in the frame.
6. Raise the rear of the swing arm and secure the lower shock mount to the swing arm. Install the lower shock mounting bolt (B, **Figure 40**). Finger-tighten the bolt.

CAUTION
Do not apply grease to the pivot bolt threads. This causes the bolts to overtighten.

7. Apply grease to the shaft and shoulder on the end of each pivot bolt. Refer to **Figure 47**. Do not apply grease to the bolt threads.
8. Install and finger-tighten the right pivot bolt (**Figure 41**).
9. Install the left pivot bolt, and loosely install the locknut onto the left pivot bolt. Refer to **Figure 48**.
10. Tighten the right pivot bolt to 113 N•m (83 ft.-lb.), and then tighten the left pivot bolt to 4 N•m (35 in.-lb.).
11. Move the swing arm up and down through several strokes.
12. Retighten the left pivot bolt to 4 N•m (35 in.-lb.).

NOTE
Because the swing arm locknut wrench changes the effective length of

*the torque wrench, an adjusted torque setting must be used to compensate for the change in lever length. Refer to **Torque Adapters** in Chapter One to determine the adjusted torque setting needed to tighten the bolt to specification.*

13. Hold the left pivot bolt with the Allen socket and use the swing arm locknut wrench (**Figure 49**) to tighten the locknut to 113 N•m (83 ft.-lb.).
14. Install the swing arm pivot caps.
15. Tighten the lower shock mounting bolt to 54 N•m (40 ft.-lb.).
16. Secure the breather hoses in the clamp (A, **Figure 40**) on the swing arm.
17. Fit the boot over the swing arm and tighten the boot clamp (**Figure 39**).
18. Install the final drive unit and the axle as described in this chapter.
19. Install the rear mud guards (Chapter Fourteen).

Swing Arm Inspection

1. If still installed, remove the universal joint and drive shaft from the swing arm.
2. Clean and dry the swing arm and its components.
3. Inspect the welded sections on the swing arm for cracks or other damage.
4. Remove the dust seals (C, **Figure 46**) with a seal removal tool.
5. Inspect each pivot bearing by performing the following:
    a. Inspect the bearing for excessive wear, pitting or other visual damage.
    b. Make sure the bearing fits tightly in the swing arm bore.
    c. Check the movement of the inner race (B, **Figure 46**). It should turn smoothly.
    d. If necessary, replace the bearings as described in this section.
6. Check that each grease retainer (A, **Figure 46**) fits tightly in its swing arm bore.
7. Inspect the pivot bolts (**Figure 47**) for excessive wear, thread damage or corrosion. Make sure the machined end on each pivot bolt is smooth. Replace if necessary.
8. Check the threaded holes (B, **Figure 45**) in the frame for corrosion or damage.
9. Replace the boot (A, **Figure 45**) if it is damaged.

REAR AXLE, SUSPENSION AND FINAL DRIVE

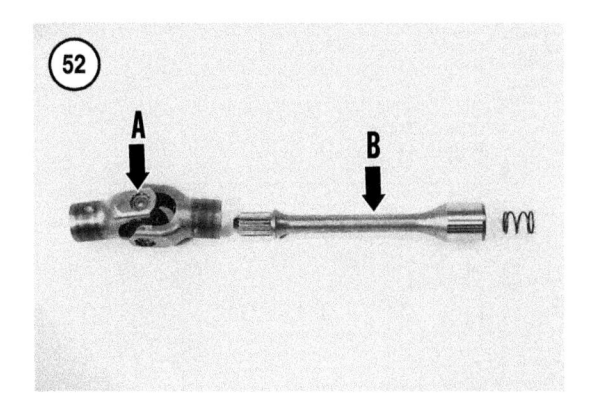

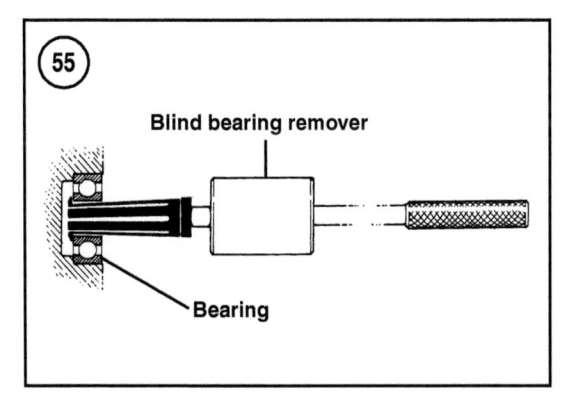

10. Inspect the axle bearing oil seal (**Figure 50**) for damage or signs of leaks.
11. Turn the axle bearing inner race. It should turn smoothly. Replace the axle bearing as necessary.
12. Make sure the axle bearing race fits tightly in the housing bore. Replace the bearing if necessary.

Drive Shaft and Universal Joint Inspection

1. If still installed, remove the spring (**Figure 51**) from the end of the drive shaft. Inspect the spring for cracks or other signs of fatigue.
2. Check that the universal joint (A, **Figure 52**) pivots smoothly with no binding or roughness.
3. Inspect the splines in both ends of universal joint. If these splines are damaged, inspect the splines in the drive shaft and transmission countershaft for damage.
4. Check the drive shaft (B, **Figure 52**) for bending, spline damage or other damage.

Pivot Bearing Replacement

Replace the left and right side bearings as a set.
1. Support the swing arm in a vise with soft jaws.
2. Pry out the dust seals with a seal remover (**Figure 53**).
3. Remove each bearing (A, **Figure 54**) with a blind bearing remover (**Figure 55**).
4. Check the grease retainer (B, **Figure 54**) for looseness or damage. If necessary, replace the retainer by performing the following:
   a. Drill a suitable size hole through one of the grease retainers.
   b. Insert a drift through this hole and drive out the opposite grease plate.
   c. Insert a drift through the open side of the swing arm pivot, and drive out the remaining grease retainer.
   d. Drive a new grease retainer into each side of the swing arm.
5. Lubricate the new bearings with grease.
6. Drive a new bearing (**Figure 56**) into each side of the swing arm. Use the appropriate size bearing driver or socket so pressure is applied only on the outer bearing race. Install both bearings with the manufacturer's marks facing out.
7. Apply grease to the lips of new dust seals, and install them into the swing arm with the closed sides facing out (C, **Figure 46**).

Axle Bearing Replacement

1. Pry the oil seal (**Figure 50**) from the bearing housing with a seal remover.
2. Remove the snap ring from the bearing housing.
3. Drive the bearing out of the left side of the bearing housing.
4. Pack the open side of the bearing with molybdenum disulfide grease.
5. Install the bearing with the appropriate size bearing driver or socket. Drive the axle bearing into the housing until the bearing is set to the depth specified in **Table 1**. Make sure the sealed side of the bearing faces in. Refer to **Figure 56**.
6. Install the snap ring so it is completely seated in the groove in the bearing housing.
7. Apply grease to a new oil seal, and drive the seal into place with the appropriate size driver or socket.

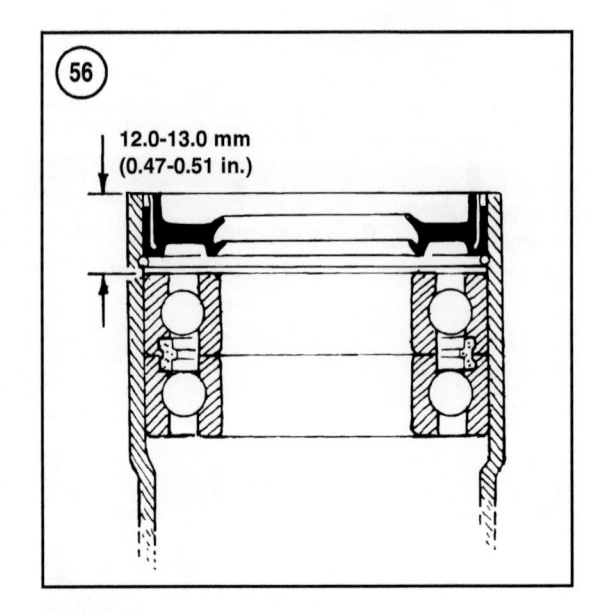

Table 1 REAR SUSPENSION AND FINAL DRIVE SPECIFICATIONS

Rear suspension	Swing arm
Wheel travel	125 mm (4.9 in.)
Rear damper	Double tube
Rear axle runout service limit	3.0 mm (0.12 in.)
Final drive gear backlash	
New	0.05-0.25 mm (0.002-0.010 in.)
Service limit	0.40 mm (0.016 in.)
Axle bearing depth	12.0-13.0 mm (0.47-0.51 in.)

Table 2 REAR SUSPENSION AND FINAL DRIVE TORQUE SPECIFICATIONS

Item	N•m	in.-lb.	ft.-lb.
Final drive cover bolts			
8 mm	25	–	18
10 mm	49	–	36
Final drive mounting bolts	54	–	40
Final drive oil drain bolt	12	106	–
Final drive oil cap	12	106	–
Final drive oil check bolt	12	106	–
Pinion gear locknut*	98	–	72
Shock absorber lower mounting bolt	54	–	40
Shock absorber upper mounting nut	44	–	32
Skid plate bolts	32	–	24
Swing arm left pivot bolt	4	35	–
Swing arm left pivot locknut	113	–	83
Swing arm right pivot bolt	113	–	83

*See text.

CHAPTER THIRTEEN

BRAKES

This chapter provides service procedures for the front and rear brake systems, including the brake pads, master cylinder, calipers, discs and brake pedal. Refer to Chapter Three for brake fluid level inspection, brake pad inspection and adjustment of the brake lever and pedal. The front brakes are actuated by the hand lever on the right side of the handlebar. The rear brake is actuated by the brake pedal and left brake lever. The left brake lever is also equipped with a lock that allows it to be used as a parking brake.

When inspecting the brake system, compare any measurements to the brake specification in **Table 1**. Replace any component that is damaged or out of specification. During assembly, tighten fasteners to specifications in **Table 2**. **Table 1** and **Table 2** are at the end of this chapter.

BRAKE SERVICE

The front brakes are hydraulically actuated. When pressure is applied to the brake lever, the brake fluid in the lines is compressed and pushes the brake pads against the brake disc. When pressure is relieved, the pads slightly retract from the disc, allowing the wheel to spin freely. As the pads wear, the piston in the caliper extends, automatically keeping the pads adjusted close to the disc.

Observe the following when maintaining or working on a hydraulic brake system:

1. Keep brake fluid off painted surfaces, plastic and decals. The fluid damages these surfaces. If fluid does contact these surfaces, flush the surface thoroughly with clean water.

2. Keep the fluid reservoirs closed, except when changing the fluid.

3. Replace brake fluid often. The fluid absorbs moisture form the air and causes internal corrosion of the brake system. Fresh fluid is clear- to slightly-yellow. If the fluid is obviously colored, it is contaminated.

4. Do not reuse brake fluid, and do not use leftover fluid that has been stored in an open container for any length of time.

5. When rebuilding brake system components, lubricate new parts with fresh fluid before assembly. Do not use petroleum-based solvents. These can cause rubber components to swell and damage them.

6. Bleed the brake system when a banjo bolt or other connector in the brake line has been loosened.

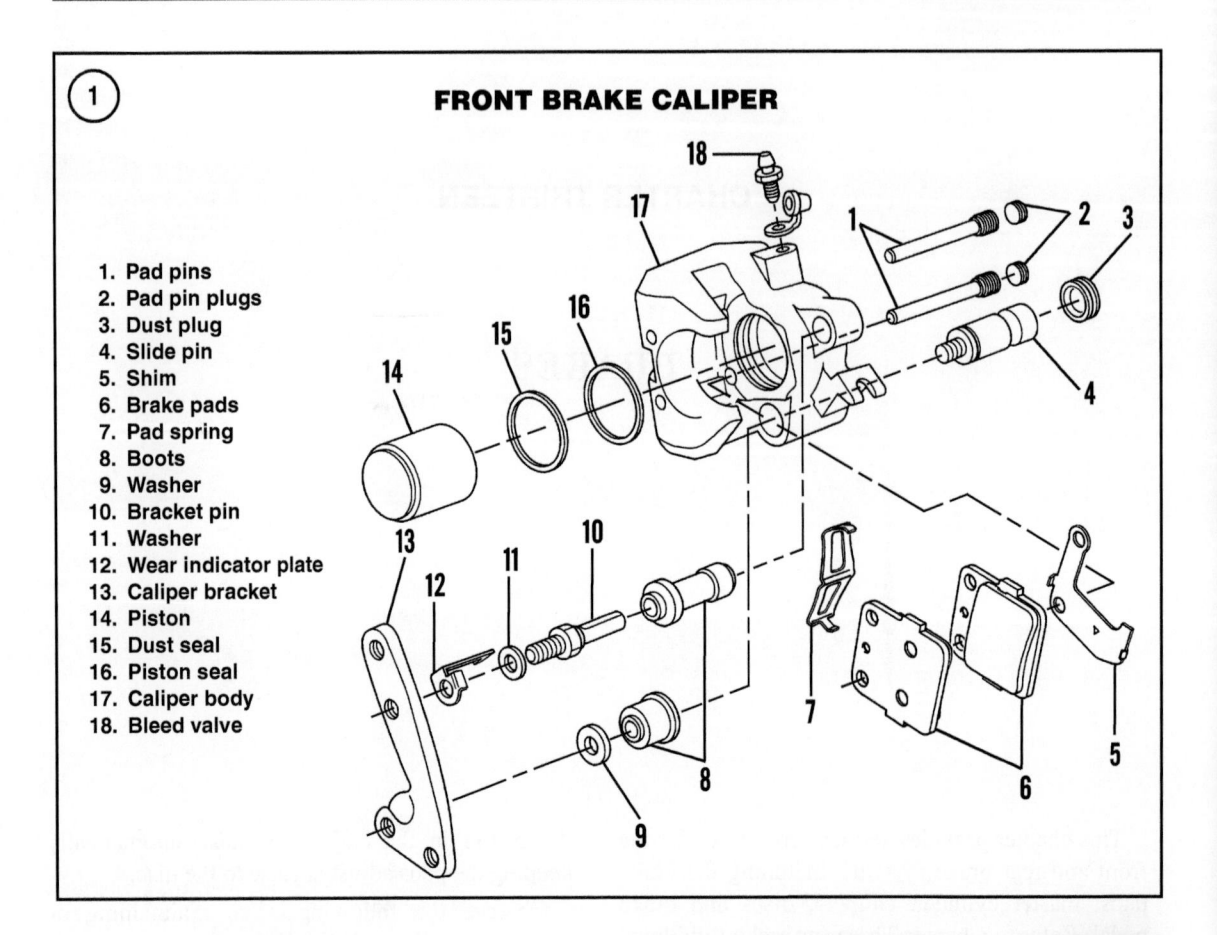

CHAPTER THIRTEEN

FRONT BRAKE CALIPER

1. Pad pins
2. Pad pin plugs
3. Dust plug
4. Slide pin
5. Shim
6. Brake pads
7. Pad spring
8. Boots
9. Washer
10. Bracket pin
11. Washer
12. Wear indicator plate
13. Caliper bracket
14. Piston
15. Dust seal
16. Piston seal
17. Caliper body
18. Bleed valve

FRONT BRAKE PADS

Brake pad life depends on riding conditions and the material used to manufacture the brake pads. Replace the pads when they are worn or have been contaminated with oil or other chemicals. Refer to Chapter Three for brake pad inspection. Always replace pads as a set.

Replacement

It is not necessary to drain the brake fluid from the brake lines when replacing the pads.

Refer to **Figure 1**.

1. Remove the front wheel as described in Chapter Ten.
2. Remove the pad pin plugs (A, **Figure 2**).
3. Loosen the pad pins (**Figure 3**), but do not remove them.
4. Remove the brake hose from the clamp (**Figure 4**) at the upper control arm.
5. Remove the caliper mounting bolts (B, **Figure 2**). 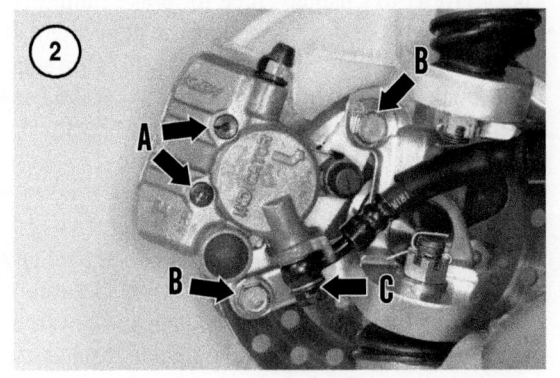
6. Inspect the fluid level in the front brake master cylinder. If overfilled, remove some of the fluid.

CAUTION
The prying action in the following step forces fluid back up the line and into the reservoir. While performing the next step, check the reservoir as the brake piston is pushed back into the caliper. The piston must be pushed back to make room for the new pads.

BRAKES

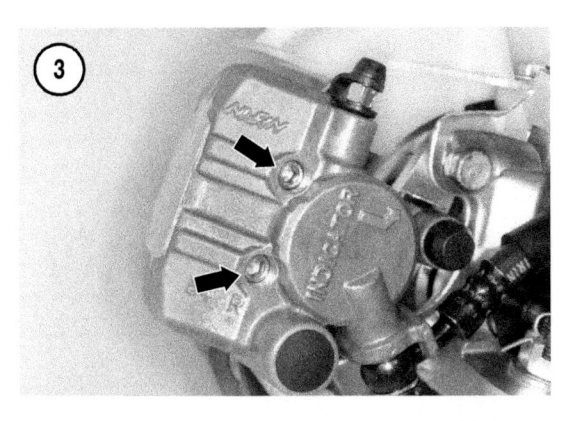

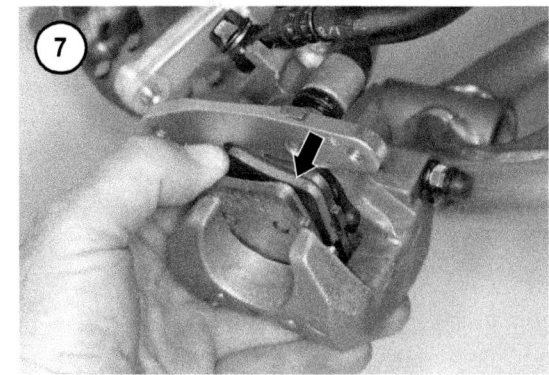

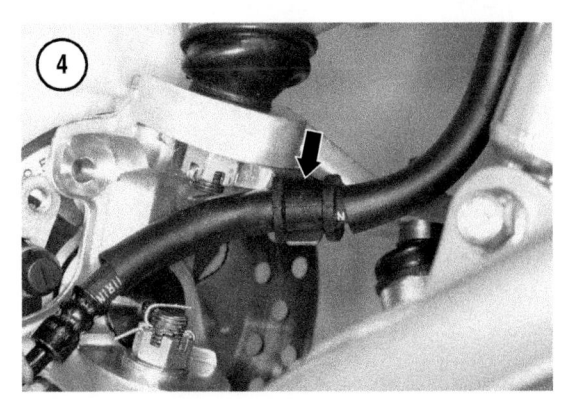

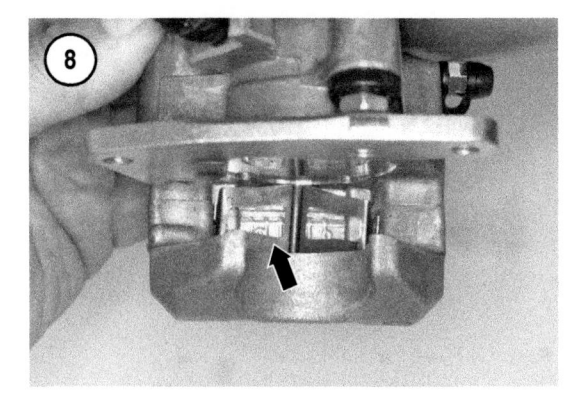

7. Place a large screwdriver between the old pads and push the brake piston into the caliper (**Figure 5**).

8. Press the brake pads against the pad spring and remove the pad pins (**Figure 6**).

9. Remove the loose brake pads (**Figure 7**).

CAUTION
Do not operate the brake lever with the pads removed. Without the pads in place, the piston can come out of the caliper housing.

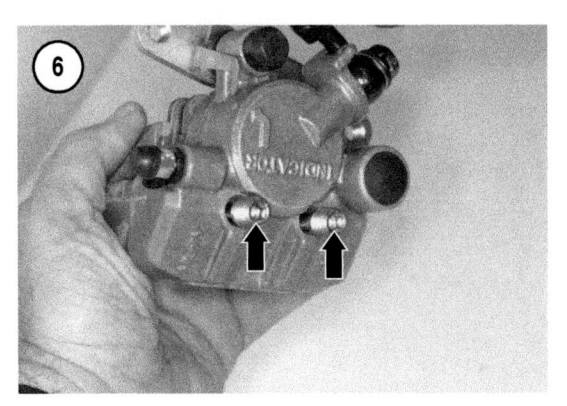

10. Make sure the pad spring is properly positioned in the caliper (**Figure 8**). If the spring is broken, rusted or missing, replace it.

11. Clean the interior of the caliper and inspect for leaks or damage.

12. Inspect the pad pins for wear and corrosion. Replace the pins if necessary.

13. Install the new pads into the caliper. The pad with the shim must be installed against the caliper piston (**Figure 9**).

14. Press the pads against the pad spring to align the pad pin holes.

15. Install the pad pins. Do not tighten the pad pins at this time.
16. Install the caliper over the brake disc and align the caliper mounting bolt holes (**Figure 10**).
17. Install *new* mounting bolts and tighten them to 30 N•m (22 ft.-lb.).
18. Install the brake hose (**Figure 4**) into the clamp on the upper arm ball joint.
19. Tighten the pad pins to 18 N•m (13 ft.-lb.).
20. Install and tighten the pad pin plugs to 3 N•m (27 in.-lb.).
21. Operate the brake lever several times to seat the pads.
22. Check the brake fluid reservoir and replenish or lower if necessary.
23. With the front wheel raised, make sure the wheel spins freely and the brake operates properly.
24. Install the front wheel as described in Chapter Ten.

FRONT BRAKE CALIPER

Removal and Installation

Refer to **Figure 1**.

1. Remove the front wheel as described in Chapter Ten.
2. Drain the brake fluid from the brake line as follows:
    a. Remove the rubber cap from the bleed valve (**Figure 11**).
    b. Attach a length of tubing to the valve so the brake fluid can be drained into a container (**Figure 12**).
    c. Loosen the bleed valve and drain the brake fluid. Squeeze the brake lever to aid the flow of fluid.
    d. Close the bleed valve and disconnect the drain tube.
3. Remove the banjo bolt and seal washers from the brake hose (C, **Figure 2**). Have a shop cloth and container nearby to catch the brake fluid that drips from the hose.

CAUTION
Wrap the hose end to prevent brake fluid from damaging other surfaces. Wipe up fluid spills and wash your hands to make sure brake fluid does not get on painted or plastic surfaces.

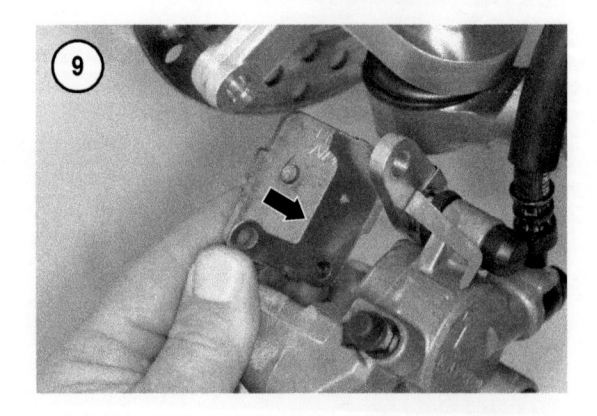

BRAKES

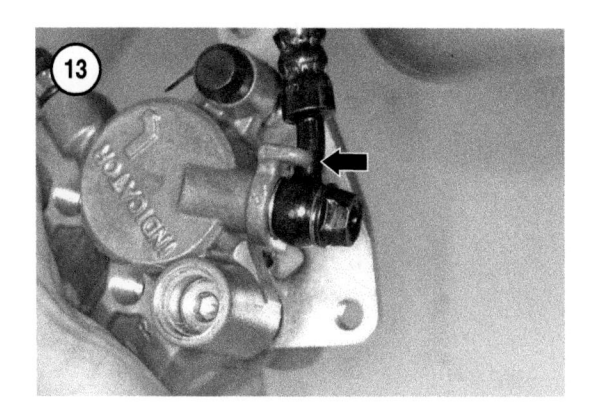

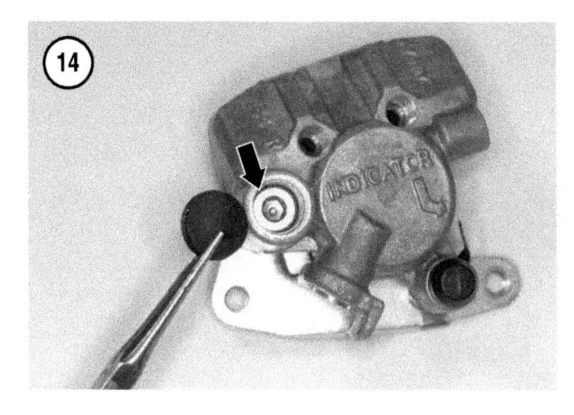

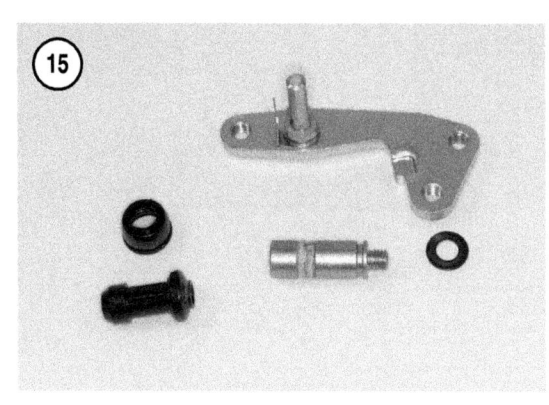

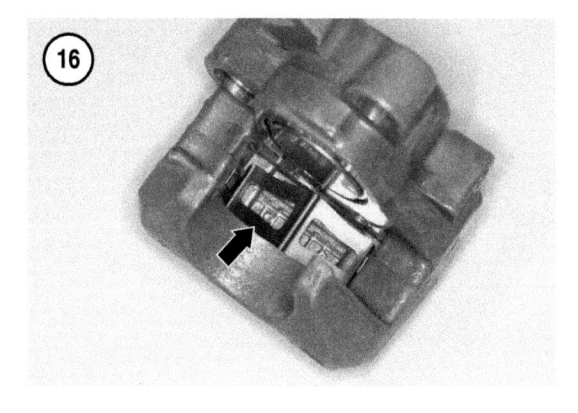

Dispose of fluid in an environmentally safe manner.

4. Remove the caliper mounting bolts (B, **Figure 2**) and then remove the caliper.
5. Repair the caliper as described in this section.
6. Reverse this procedure to install the caliper. Observe the following:
    a. Position the brake hose fitting so it lays flat and is seated in the groove at the back of the caliper (**Figure 13**).
    b. Install the *new* seal washers on the banjo bolt.
    c. Install new caliper mounting bolts.
    d. Tighten the caliper mounting bolts to 30 N•m (22 ft.-lb.).
    e. Tighten the brake hose banjo bolt to 34 N•m (25 ft.-lb.).
    f. Fill the brake fluid reservoir and bleed the brakes as described in Chapter Three.

Repair

Refer to **Figure 1**.

1. Remove the caliper as described in this section.
2. Remove the brake pads and pad pins as described in *Front Brake Pads/Replacement* in this chapter.
3. Remove the dust plug and slide pin (**Figure 14**), then remove the caliper bracket, washer, slide pin and boots (**Figure 15**).
4. Remove the pad spring (**Figure 16**).

WARNING
In the following step, an air nozzle is held tightly in the brake hose fitting and the air pressure pushes the piston out. Do not pry the piston out of the caliper. Read the following procedure entirely before beginning removal. Wear eye protection when using compressed air to remove the piston. Keep fingers away from the piston.

5. Remove the piston from the caliper as follows:
    a. Place the caliper on a padded work surface.
    b. Close the bleeder valve on the caliper so air cannot escape.
    c. Place a folded shop cloth in the caliper. The pad cushions the piston when it comes out of the caliper.
    d. Lay the caliper so the pistons will discharge downward.

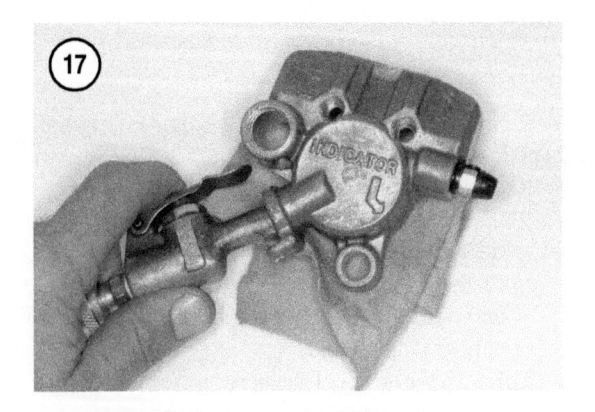

e. Insert an air nozzle into the brake hose fitting (**Figure 17**). If the nozzle does not have a rubber tip, wrap the nozzle tightly with tape to seal it and prevent thread damage.
f. Place a shop cloth over the entire caliper to catch any discharge from the caliper.
g. Apply pressure and listen for the piston to pop from the caliper (**Figure 18**).

6. Remove the bleeder valve and piston seals (**Figure 19**). When removing the seals, avoid contacting the piston bore with tools or other objects that could scratch the surface.

7. Inspect the caliper assembly as follows. Replace worn, corroded or deteriorated parts.
   a. Clean all parts to be reused with fresh brake fluid or isopropyl (rubbing) alcohol. Use a wood or plastic-tipped tool to clean the seal grooves.
   b. Inspect the cylinder bore for wear, scratches, pitting and corrosion.
   c. Measure the inside diameter of the piston bore (**Figure 20**). Refer to **Table 1**.
   d. Measure the outside diameter of the piston (**Figure 21**). Refer to **Table 1**.
   e. Inspect the caliper bracket, washer, slide pin and boots (**Figure 15**).
   f. Inspect the brake pads, pad pins and pad spring (**Figure 22**).
   g. Inspect the bleeder and cap. Check the threads and seat on the bleeder (**Figure 23**) for corrosion and damage.

NOTE
Use new DOT 4 brake fluid to lubricate the piston and seals in the following assembly steps.

8. Install the new seals and piston as follows:

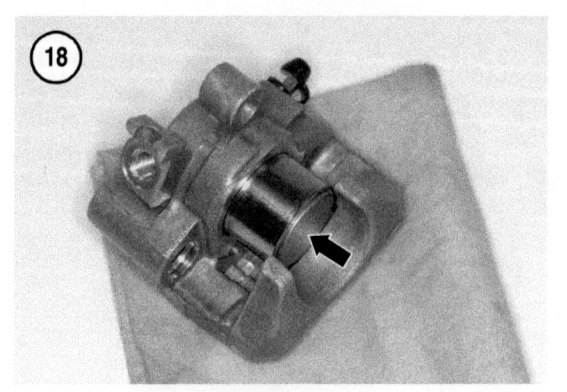

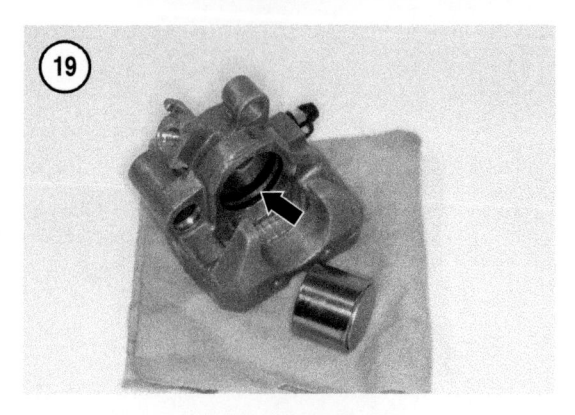

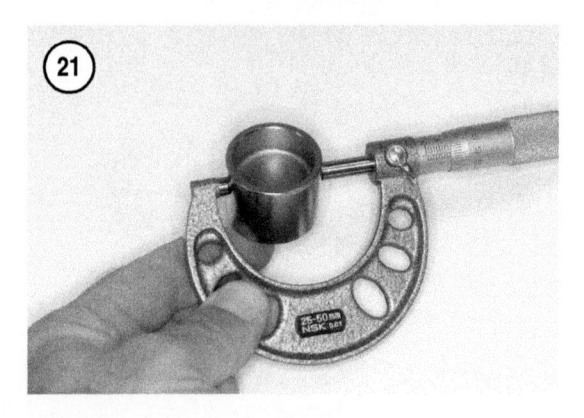

BRAKES

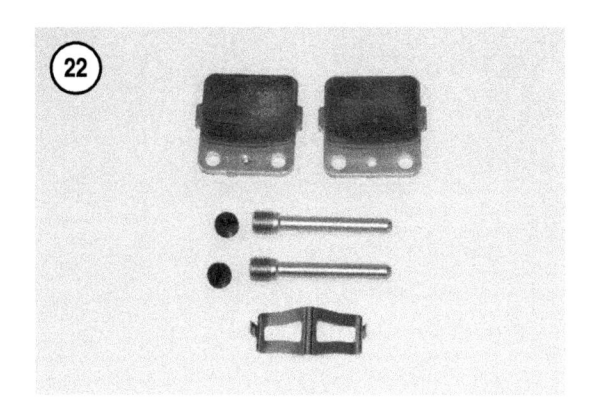

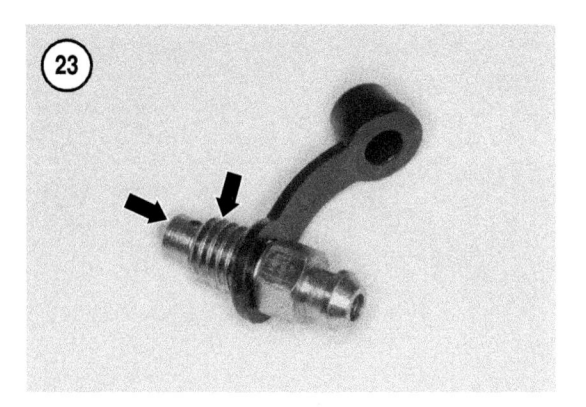

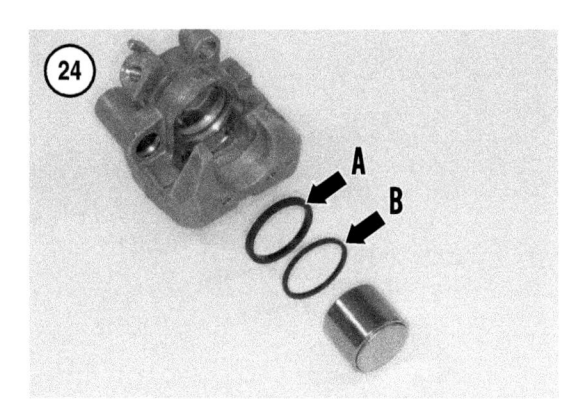

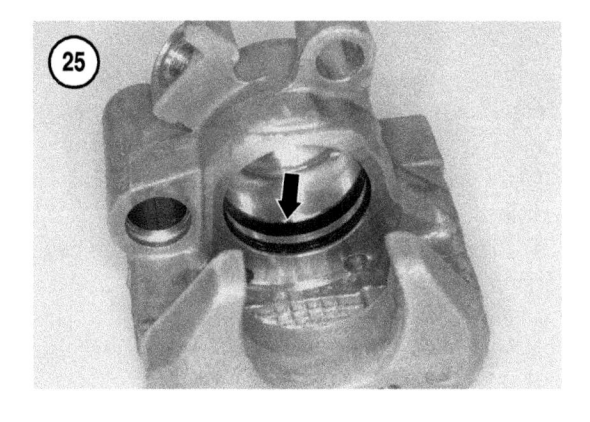

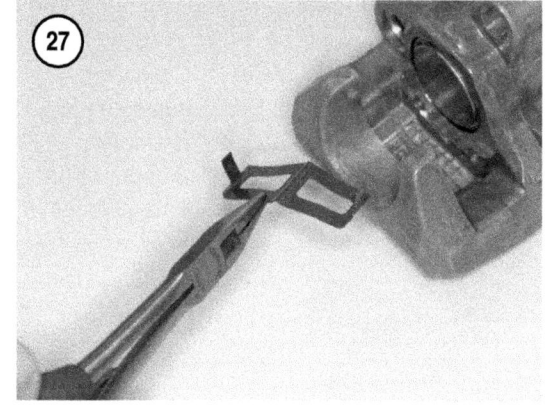

271

a. Soak the seals in brake fluid for 5 minutes.

b. Coat the caliper bore and piston with brake fluid.

c. Seat the piston seal (A, **Figure 24**), then the dust seal (B) into the caliper grooves. The piston seal goes in the back groove (**Figure 25**).

d. Install the piston with the flat end facing out (**Figure 26**). The piston does not go straight into the bore. Twist the piston past the seals, and then press the piston to the bottom of the bore.

9. Seat the pad spring into the mounting bracket (**Figure 27**). The tabs at the ends of the spring must face up.

10. Insert the boots into the caliper (**Figure 28**). Lightly lubricate the exterior of the boots with silicone brake grease to aid in installation. After the boots are installed, pack the interior of the bracket pin boot with silicone brake grease.

11. Pack silicone brake grease into the slide pin groove (**Figure 29**), and then install the pin. Make

sure the ribs on the slide pin boot are seated in the caliper and slide pin.

12. Place the washer over the end of the slide pin (**Figure 30**).

NOTE
The washer is a spring washer and should not be completely flat. Replace the washer if it is flat.

13. If necessary, assemble the caliper bracket (**Figure 31**), and then mount the bracket onto the caliper.
14. Screw the slide pin into the caliper bracket and tighten the pin (**Figure 32**) to 22 N•m (17 ft.-lb.).
15. Install the dust plug over the slide pin.
16. Install the bleeder valve.
17. Install the brake pads, pad pins and plugs as described in *Front Brake Pads* in this chapter.
18. Install the caliper as described in this section.
19. Fill the brake fluid reservoir and bleed the brakes as described in Chapter Three.

FRONT MASTER CYLINDER

Removal/Installation

Refer to **Figure 33**.
1. Park the vehicle on level ground and set the parking brake.
2. Remove the handlebar cover as described in Chapter Fourteen.

CAUTION
Brake fluid damages the finish on painted, plated or plastic surfaces. If brake fluid should spill on any surface, wash the area immediately with soapy water and rinse completely.

3. Drain the brake fluid as described in this chapter.
4. Cover the area under the master cylinder to prevent brake fluid from damaging any component that it might contact.
5. Remove the banjo bolt (**Figure 34**) and disconnect the brake hose from the master cylinder. Watch for the two sealing washers on either side of the brake hose fitting. Place the loose end of the brake hose into a reclosable bag so brake fluid does not drip onto frame components. Tie the brake hose to the handlebar.

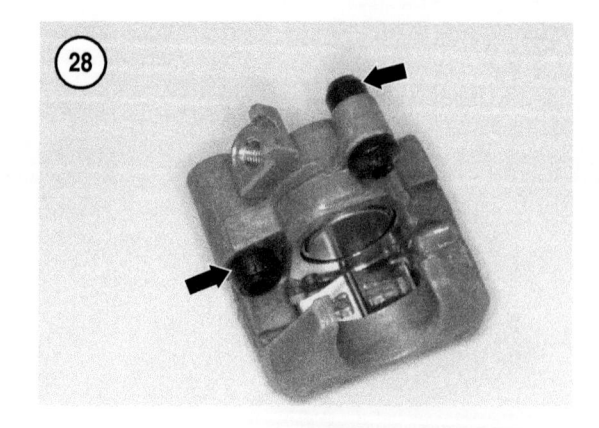

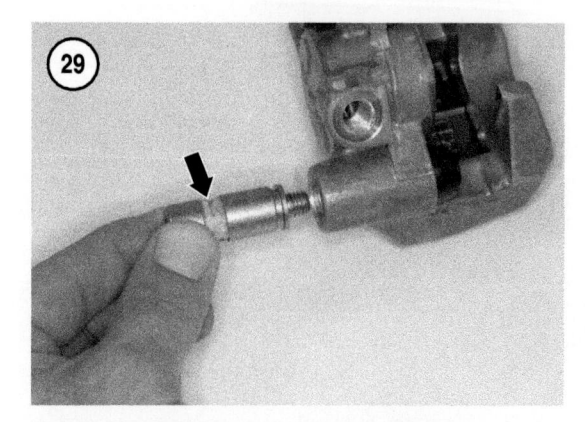

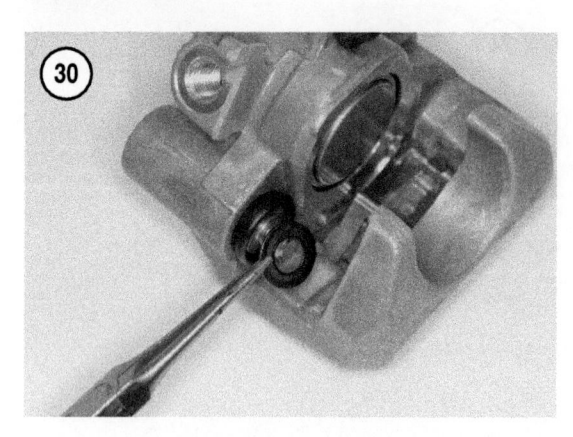

6. Unscrew the master cylinder clamp bolts (A, **Figure 35**). Remove the clamp and the master cylinder from the handlebar.
7. If necessary, service the master cylinder as described in this section.
8. Clean the handlebar, master cylinder and clamp mating surfaces.
9. Fit the master cylinder and its clamp into place on the handlebar. Position the clamp so its UP mark (B, **Figure 35**) faces up.

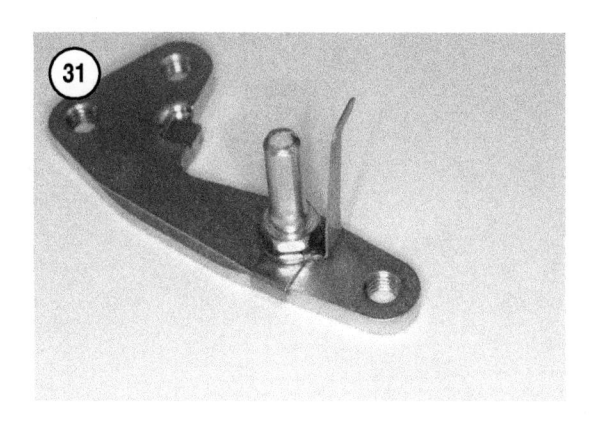

BRAKES

FRONT MASTER CYLINDER

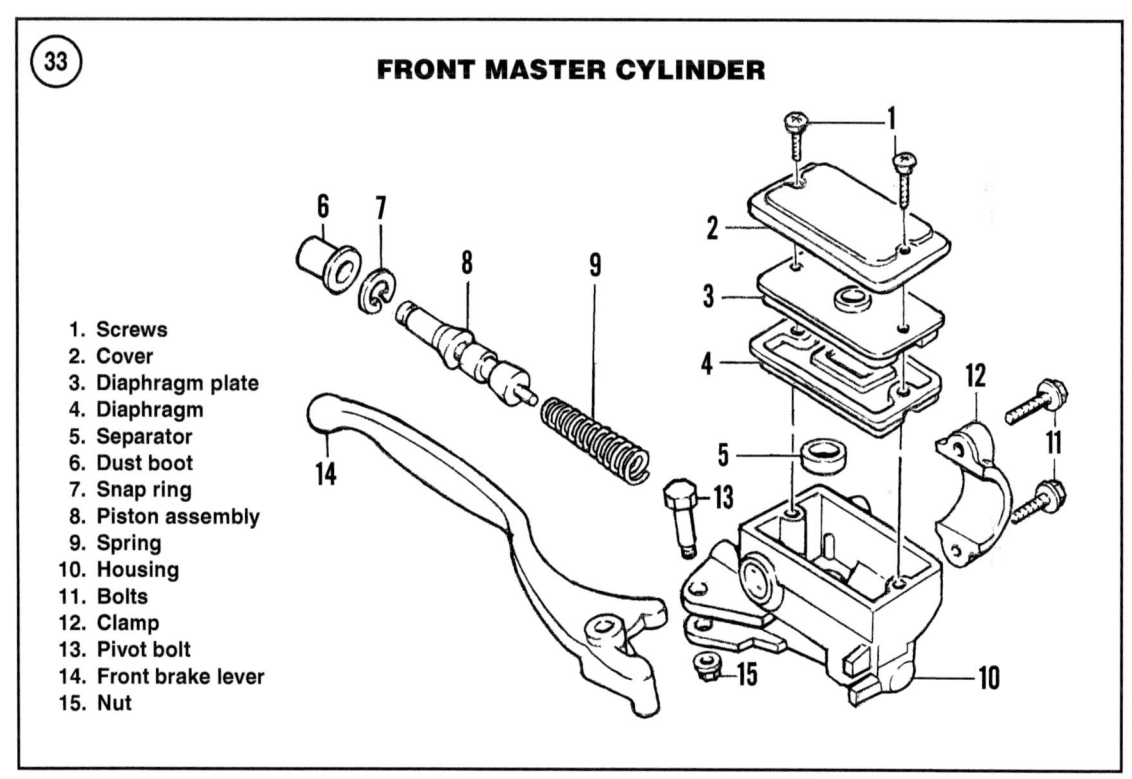

1. Screws
2. Cover
3. Diaphragm plate
4. Diaphragm
5. Separator
6. Dust boot
7. Snap ring
8. Piston assembly
9. Spring
10. Housing
11. Bolts
12. Clamp
13. Pivot bolt
14. Front brake lever
15. Nut

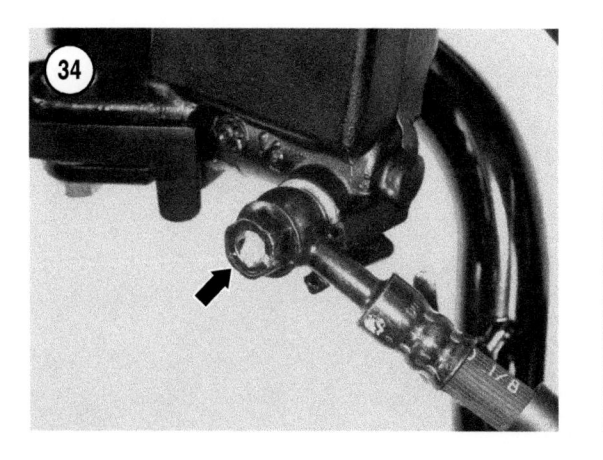

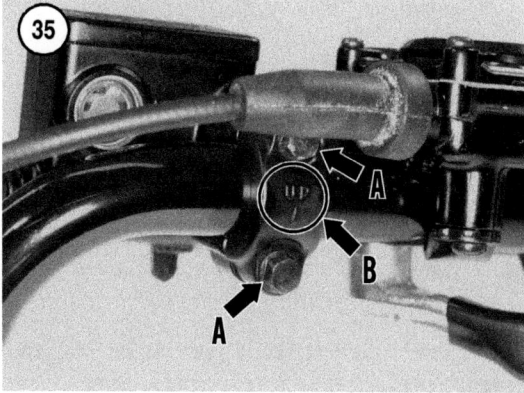

10. Align the edge of the master cylinder housing with the punch mark (**Figure 36**) on the handlebar.
11. Install the master cylinder clamp bolts. Tighten the bolts to 12 N•m (106 in.-lb.). Tighten the upper bolt first and then the lower bolt.
12. Connect the brake hose to the master cylinder with the banjo bolt and two new washers. Install a washer on each side of the hose fitting. Tighten the banjo bolt (**Figure 34**) to 34 N•m (25 ft.-lb.).
13. Refill the master cylinder reservoir with DOT 3 or DOT 4 brake fluid until the fluid level rises to the upper limit line (**Figure 37**).
14. Bleed the brakes as described in this chapter.

WARNING
Do not ride the vehicle until the front brakes are working properly. Make sure the brake lever travel is not excessive and the lever does not feel spongy. Either condition indicates the bleeding operation must be repeated.

15. Install the handlebar cover (Chapter Fourteen).

Disassembly

Refer to **Figure 33**.
1. Remove the master cylinder as described in this section.
2. Remove the nut, pivot bolt and front brake lever.
3. Remove the screws, top cover, diaphragm plate, diaphragm and float.
4. Pour out any brake fluid, and discard it properly.
5. Remove the dust boot (**Figure 38**) from the end of the piston and piston bore.

NOTE
If brake fluid leaks from the piston bore, the piston cups are worn or damaged. Replace the piston assembly.

NOTE
*To hold the master cylinder when removing and installing the snap ring, thread a bolt with a nut into the master cylinder. Tighten the nut against the master cylinder to lock the bolt in place, and then clamp the bolt and nut in a vise as shown in **Figure 39**.*

6. Compress the piston and remove the snap ring (**Figure 40**) from the master cylinder bore.

BRAKES

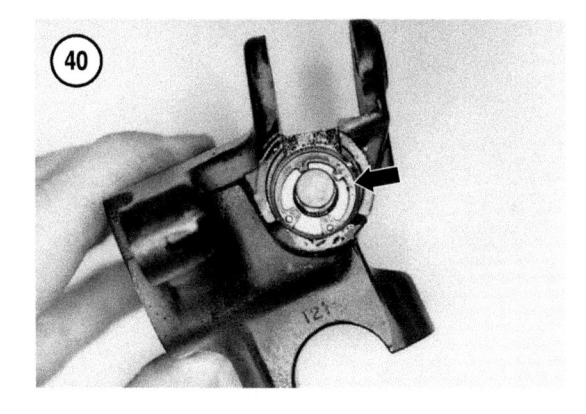

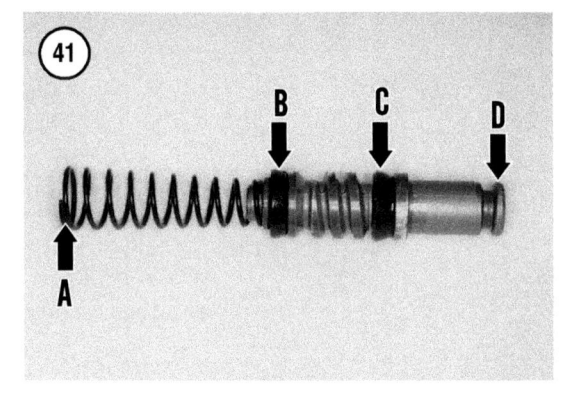

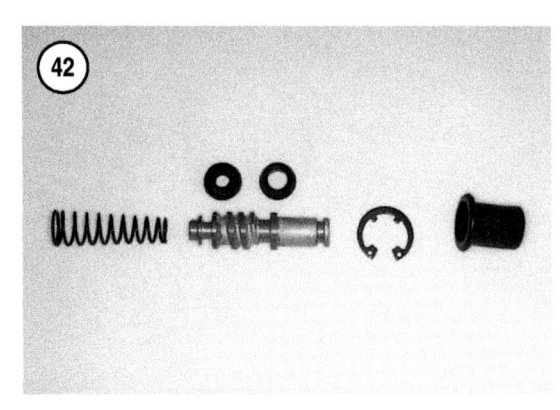

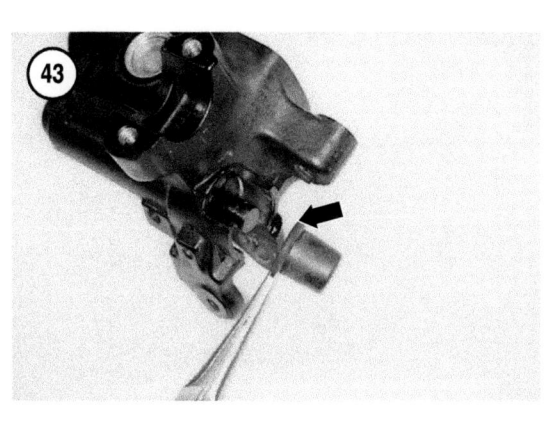

7. Remove the piston and spring assembly (**Figure 41**).

8. Inspect the master cylinder as described in this section.

Assembly

1. Use new DOT 4 brake fluid when brake fluid is called for in the following steps. Do not use DOT 5 (silicone based) brake fluid.

2A. When installing a new piston assembly (**Figure 42**), perform the following:
   a. Soak the new primary and secondary cups in new brake fluid for at least 15 minutes to make it pliable.
   b. Lubricate the new piston with brake fluid.
   c. Install the primary cup over the piston and seat it in the groove as shown in B, **Figure 41**.
   d. Install the new secondary cup and seat it in its groove in its piston. Refer to C, **Figure 41**.

2B. If reusing the original piston assembly, lubricate it with brake fluid.

CAUTION
When installing the piston assembly into the master cylinder bore, do not allow the cups to turn inside out. This damages them and allows brake fluid to leak out of the bore.

3. Assemble the spring/piston assembly as shown in **Figure 41**.

4. Install the spring/piston assembly into the master cylinder bore. Check that the cups did not turn inside out or fold over themselves.

5. Push the piston into the bore. Hold it in place, and then install the snap ring (**Figure 40**). Install the snap ring with its flat edge facing out (away from the piston). Check that the snap ring is fully seated in the bore groove. Push and release the piston a few times. It should move smoothly and return under spring pressure.

6. Slide the dust boot—shoulder side first—over the piston. Seat the small boot lip into the groove in the end of the piston (**Figure 43**). Make sure it is correctly seated in the cylinder bore (**Figure 38**).

7. Install the brake lever by performing the following:
   a. Install the brake lever and its pivot bolt. Tighten the pivot bolt to 6 N•m (53 in.-lb.).

Operate the brake lever, making sure it moves smoothly.

b. Install the brake lever pivot locknut. Hold the pivot bolt and tighten the locknut to 6 N•m (53 in.-lb.). Operate the brake lever again. It should move smoothly with no roughness or binding.

8. Temporarily install the master cylinder cover assembly.

9. Install the master cylinder as described in this section.

Inspection

When inspecting master cylinder components, compare any measurements to the specification in **Table 1**. Replace parts that are out of specification or damaged.

1. Clean the diaphragm, reservoir housing (inside) and the piston assembly with new brake fluid. Place the parts on a clean lint-free cloth.

NOTE
Do not remove the primary or secondary cup from the piston during inspection. If either is damaged, replace the entire piston assembly. Leave the cups in place for reference when installing the new cups onto the new piston.

2. Inspect the piston assembly for:
   a. Broken, distorted or collapsed piston return spring (A, **Figure 41**).
   b. Worn, cracked, damaged or swollen primary (B, **Figure 41**) and secondary cups (C).
   c. A scratched, scored or damaged piston (D, **Figure 41**).
   d. If any of these parts are worn or damaged, replace the piston assembly. Individual parts are not available separately from Honda.

3. Inspect the snap ring for corrosion, rust, weakness or other damage. Replace the snap ring if necessary.

4. Inspect the boot. Replace it if damaged.

5. Measure the piston outside diameter (**Figure 44**).

6. Inspect the cylinder bore (**Figure 45**) for scratches, pitting, excessive wear, corrosion or other damage. Do not hone the bore to remove nicks, scratches or other damage.

7. Measure the cylinder bore diameter (**Figure 46**).

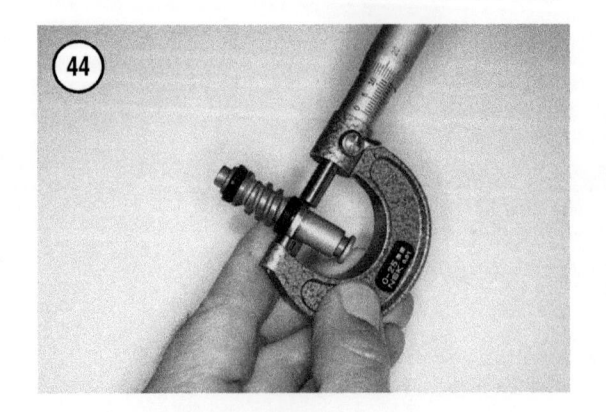

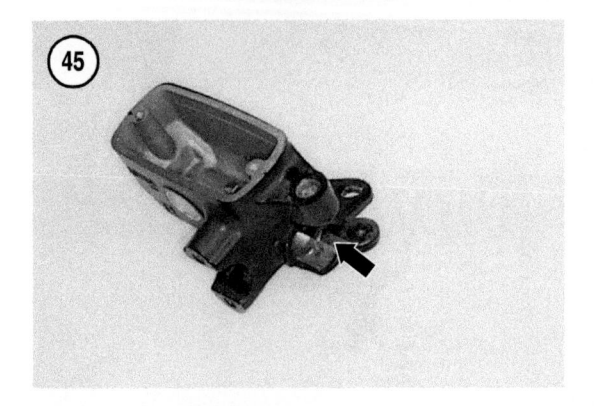

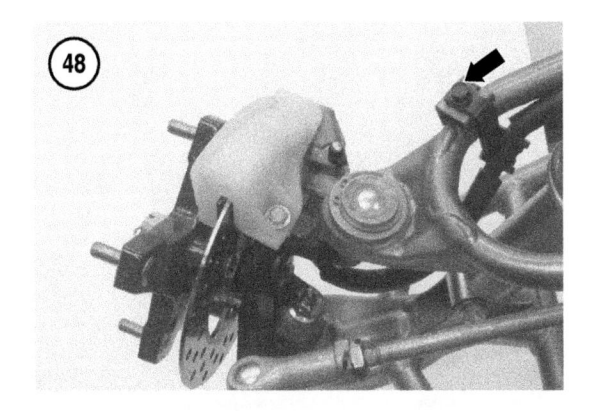

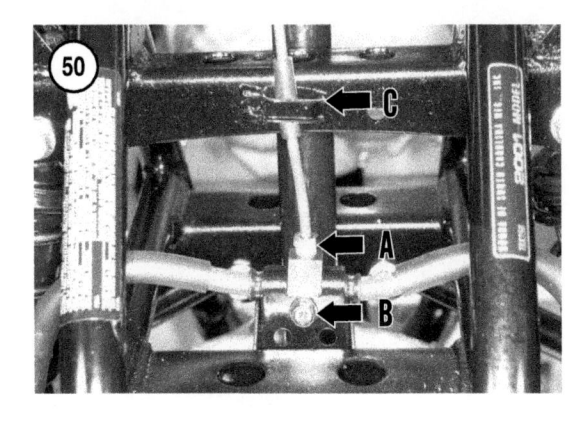

BRAKES

rect size metric tap or replace the master cylinder assembly.

12. Check the hand lever pivot holes and the mounting lugs on the master cylinder body for elongation or cracks. If damaged, replace the master cylinder assembly.

13. Inspect the hand lever and pivot bolt. Replace it if damaged.

BRAKE HOSE REPLACEMENT

NOTE
The following describes the procedure for replacing the caliper hoses, brake pipe and the master cylinder hose. If the entire brake line does not need replacing, perform just the appropriate part of this procedure.

1. Drain the brake fluid from the front brake system as described in this chapter.
2. Remove the handlebar and front cover as described in Chapter Fourteen.

CAUTION
Because some residual brake fluid remains in the lines, be careful when disconnecting and removing the brake hoses.

3. Remove the banjo bolts from one caliper (**Figure 47**). Watch for the sealing washers on either side of the brake hose fitting.
4. Insert the brake hose end into a reclosable plastic bag so brake fluid does not drip onto the suspension components.
5. Remove the brake hose clamp bolts (**Figure 48** and **Figure 49**), and disconnect each clamp from the hose.
6. Repeat Steps 2-5 for the brake hose on the other wheel.
7. Loosen the lower brake pipe nut (A, **Figure 50**) at the brake hose union.
8. Remove the union mounting bolt. Separate the union from the brake pipe, and insert the brake pipe end into a reclosable plastic bag.
9. Remove the brake hose/union assembly from the frame.
10. Loosen the upper brake pipe nut (A, **Figure 51**).
11. Release the master cylinder brake hose from the clamp (B, **Figure 51**) and insert the hose end into a reclosable plastic bag.

CAUTION
A plugged relief port causes the brake pads to drag on the disc.

8. Check for plugged supply and relief ports in the master cylinder. Clean the ports with compressed air.
9. Check the entire master cylinder body for wear or damage.
10. Check the cover and diaphragm assembly for damage.
11. Inspect the bolt threads in the brake fluid port in master cylinder. Repair minor damage with the cor-

12. Release the brake pipe from the lower clamp (C, **Figure 50**), and remove the brake pipe.
13. Remove the banjo bolt (**Figure 34**) and disconnect the brake hose from the master cylinder. Watch for the sealing washers on either side of the brake hose fitting.
14. Release the brake hose from the clamp (**Figure 52**), and remove the master cylinder hose.

WARNING
Do not ride the vehicle until the brakes are operating properly.

15. Installation is the reverse of removal. Note the following:
   a. Use new sealing washers on either side of the hose fitting when installing each banjo bolt.
   b. Apply oil to the threads and flanges surfaces of the brake pipe mounting hardware.
   c. Secure the hose/pipe with the clamps noted during removal.
   d. Tighten the banjo bolts, brake hose clamp bolts and brake pipe to the specifications in **Table 2**.

BRAKE FLUID DRAINING

An empty bottle, a length of clear hose (**Figure 53**) that fits tightly onto the wheel cylinder bleed valve and a wrench to open and close the bleed valve are needed for this procedure. A vacuum pump (**Figure 54**) can also be used to drain the brake system.

1. Turn the handlebar so the front master cylinder is level with the ground.
2. Remove the reservoir cover and diaphragm assembly (**Figure 55**).
3. Connect a hose to one of the wheel cylinder bleed valves (A, **Figure 56**). Insert the other end of the hose into a clean bottle.
4. Loosen the bleed valve and pump the brake lever to drain part of the brake system.
5. Close the bleed valve when fluid stops flowing through the valve.
6. Repeat Steps 3-5 for the other side. Because air has entered the brake lines, not all of the brake fluid drains out.

CAUTION
Because some residual brake fluid remains in the lines, be careful when disconnecting and removing the brake hoses during service.

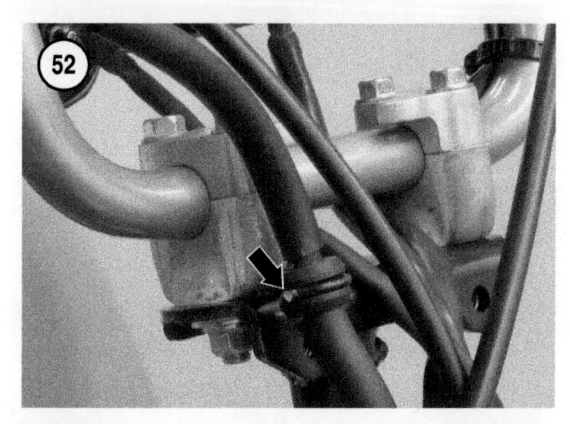

7. Reinstall the diaphragm assembly and reservoir cover.
8. Perform the required service to the front brake system as described in this chapter.
9. After servicing the brake system, bleed the front brakes as described in this chapter.

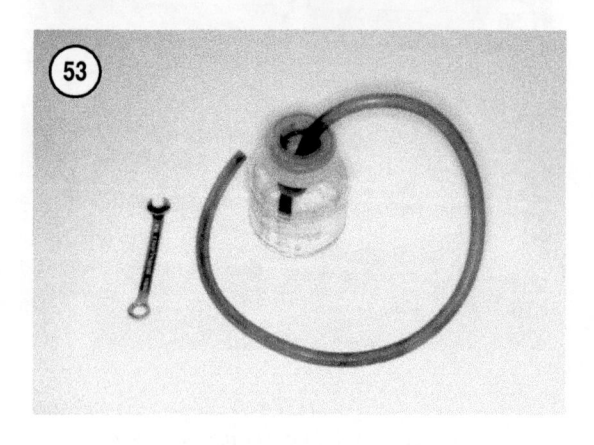

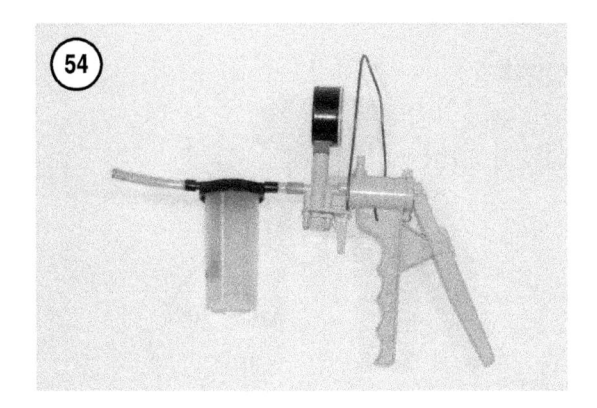

BRAKES

2A. If using a vacuum pump, assemble the pump by following the manufacturer's instructions. Connect the vacuum pump hose to the wheel cylinder bleed valve.

2B. If a vacuum pump is not being used, perform the following:

    a. Connect a piece of clear tubing onto the bleed valve (A, **Figure 56**).

    b. Insert the other end of the tube into a container partially filled with new brake fluid (B, **Figure 56**). Tie the tube in place so it cannot slip out of the container.

3. Clean all debris from the master cylinder cover.

4. Turn the front wheels so the master cylinder is level with the ground.

CAUTION
Brake fluid damages the finish on plastic, painted or plated surface. Wash any spilled fluid from these surfaces immediately. Clean the area with soapy water and rinse completely.

5. Cover the area under the master cylinder with plastic to protect the parts in the event of brake fluid spills.

6. Remove the cover screws (**Figure 55**) and master cylinder cover and diaphragm assembly.

WARNING
Use DOT 4 brake fluid from a sealed container. Do not mix different brands of fluid. Do not use silicone-based DOT 5 brake fluid because it can damage the brake components, leading to brake system failure.

7. Add DOT 4 brake fluid to the reservoir until the fluid level reaches the upper limit line.

NOTE
When bleeding the front brake, frequently check the fluid level in the master cylinder. If the reservoir runs dry, air enters the system. If this occurs, the entire procedure must be repeated.

8A. When using a vacuum pump, perform the following:

    a. Operate the vacuum pump several times to create a vacuum in the attached hose.

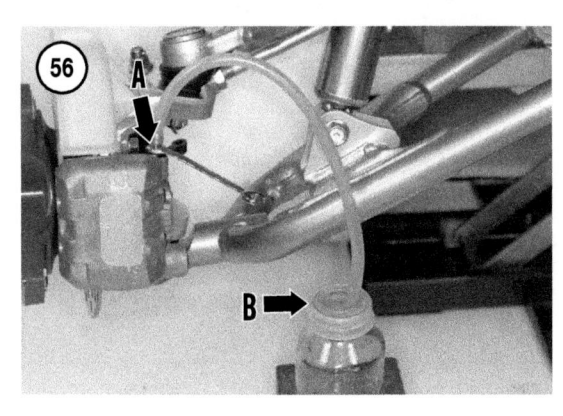

BRAKE BLEEDING

Bleed the front brakes when they feel spongy, after a brake hose has been removed, when replacing parts in the system or when replacing the brake fluid.

This section describes two methods for bleeding the brake system. The first requires a vacuum pump (**Figure 54**) and the second requires a container and a piece of clear tubing (**Figure 53**).

1. Remove the dust cap from the bleed valve on a wheel cylinder.

REAR BRAKE

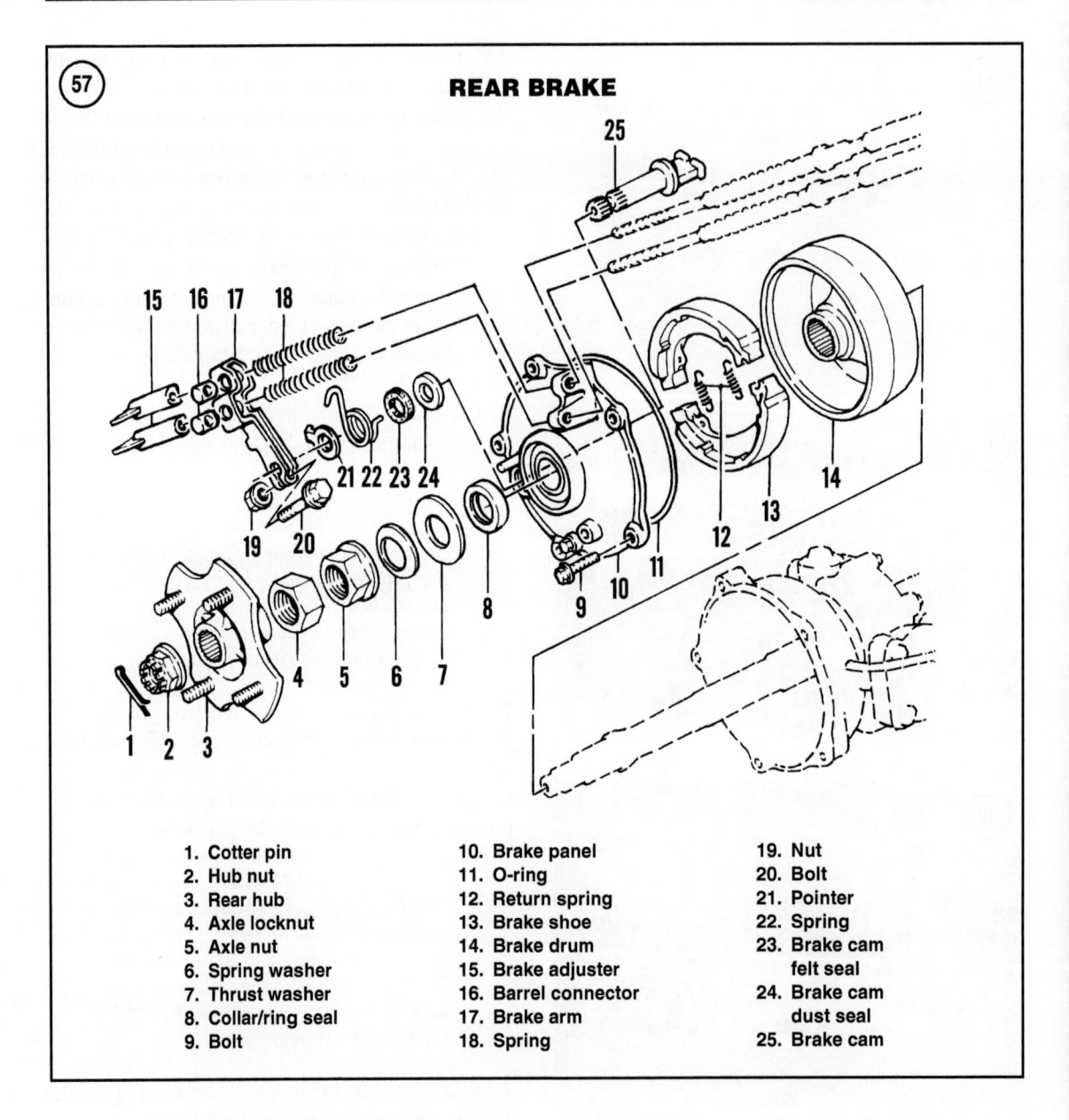

1. Cotter pin
2. Hub nut
3. Rear hub
4. Axle locknut
5. Axle nut
6. Spring washer
7. Thrust washer
8. Collar/ring seal
9. Bolt
10. Brake panel
11. O-ring
12. Return spring
13. Brake shoe
14. Brake drum
15. Brake adjuster
16. Barrel connector
17. Brake arm
18. Spring
19. Nut
20. Bolt
21. Pointer
22. Spring
23. Brake cam felt seal
24. Brake cam dust seal
25. Brake cam

b. Open the bleed valve 1/4 turn to allow extraction of air and fluid through the line. When the flow of air and fluid starts to slow down, close the bleed valve.

c. Operate the brake lever several times and release it.

d. Check the fluid level in the master cylinder. Refill the reservoir as necessary.

e. Repeat substeps a-d until no air bubbles emerge from the bleed valve and until a solid feel is noted when the brake lever is operated.

f. Repeat for the opposite brake line.

8B. If a vacuum pump is not being used, perform the following:

a. Operate the brake lever several times until resistance is felt, and then hold it in its applied position. If the system was opened or drained completely, there is no initial resistance at the brake lever.

b. Open the bleed valve 1/4 turn and allow the lever to travel to its limit. Close the bleed valve and release the brake lever.

c. Check the fluid level in the master cylinder. Refill the reservoir as necessary.

BRAKES

10. Tighten the bleed valve to 6 N•m (53 in.-lb.). Snap the dust cap onto the bleed valve.
11. If necessary, add fluid to the upper level line in the reservoir. It should be to the upper level line inside the master cylinder reservoir.
12. Install the diaphragm and cover. Tighten the screws securely.
13. Recheck the feel of the brake lever. It should be firm and offer the same resistance each time it is operated. If the lever feels spongy, check all the hoses for leaks, and bleed the system again.

REAR BRAKE DRUM

Brake Drum Removal

WARNING
When working on the brake system, never blow off brake dust with compressed air. ***Do not inhale*** *any airborne brake dust. It may contain asbestos, which can cause lung injury and cancer. As an added precaution, wear an OSHA approved face mask and thoroughly wash your hands and forearms with warm water and soap after completing any brake work.*

Two 41-mm wrenches are needed to remove the axle nuts.
Refer to **Figure 57**.
1. Park the ATV on level ground and set the parking brake.
2. Remove the right rear wheel and hub as described in Chapter Ten.
3. Remove the right skid plate bolt (**Figure 58**).
4. Remove the front skid plate bolt (A, **Figure 59**) and left bolt (B) and lower the skid plate from the final drive unit.
5. Note the differences between the axle nut and axle locknut. They must be reinstalled in the same relative positions. The axle locknut (A, **Figure 60**) has two internal shoulders. The side with the deeper shoulder faces toward the axle nut. The axle nut (B, **Figure 60**) has an external shoulder that faces toward the spring washer.
6. Use the 41-mm wrenches to remove the axle locknut (A, **Figure 60**) and then the axle nut (B).
7. Remove the spring washer (A, **Figure 61**) and thrust washer (B).

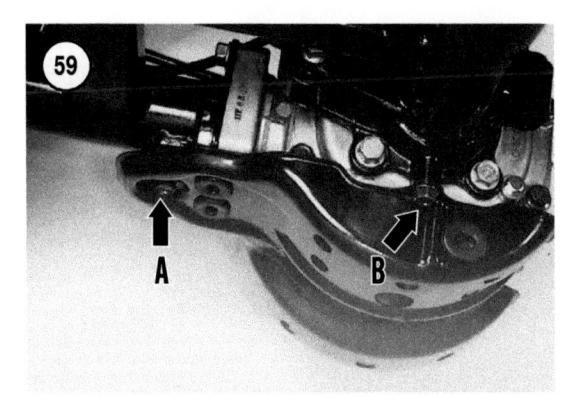

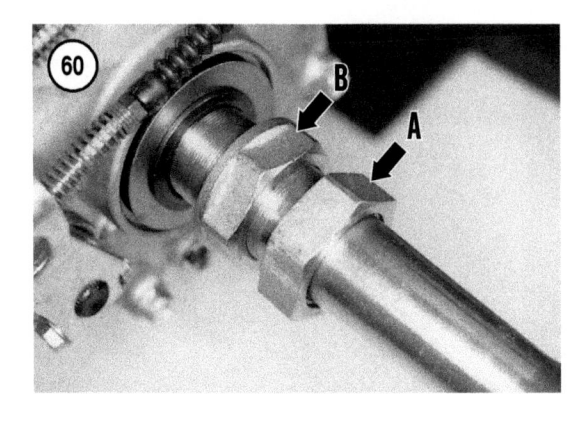

d. Repeat substeps a-c until no air bubbles emerge from the bleed valve and until solid feel is felt when the brake lever is operated.
e. Repeat for the opposite brake line.

NOTE
If you are flushing the system, continue Step 8 until the fluid expelled from the system is clean.

9. Remove the vacuum pump or the container and hose from the bleed valve.

8. Disconnect the rear brake lever/parking brake cable (upper cable) from the brake arm by performing the following:
    a. Unscrew the adjuster (A, **Figure 62**) from the end of the parking brake cable.
    b. Remove the barrel connector (B, **Figure 62**) and spring (C) from the cable.
    c. Remove the cable from the boss (D, **Figure 62**) on the brake panel.
9. Disconnect the rear brake pedal cable (lower cable) from the brake arm by repeating the procedures in Step 8.
10. Remove the five brake panel bolts (**Figure 63**).
11. Carefully pry the brake panel at the two pry points (**Figure 64**). If necessary, use a slide hammer to separate the brake panel from the final drive unit (**Figure 65**).
12. Remove the collar/ring seal (**Figure 66**) assembly from the brake panel oil seal, and then remove the brake panel. Discard the brake panel O-ring. A new one must be installed during assembly.
13. Slide the brake drum (**Figure 67**) from the final drive unit, and remove it from the axle.
14. Inspect the brake drum as described in this section.
15. Disassemble and inspect the brake panel as described in this section.

Brake Drum Installation

1. Clean all grease and threadlocking compound from the threads on the axle.
2. Align the inner splines of the brake drum (A, **Figure 68**) with those of the axle, and slide the drum (**Figure 67**) along the axle until it bottoms in the final drive gearcase.
3. Lubricate a new O-ring with multipurpose lithium grease and install the O-ring (**Figure 69**) onto the brake panel.
4. Slide the brake panel over the axle and seat it against the final drive unit.
5. Install and finger-tighten the five brake panel bolts (**Figure 63**). Using a crisscross pattern, evenly tighten the bolts in two or three stages.
6. Install the collar/ring seal (**Figure 66**) and seat it in the brake panel dust seal. Make sure the ring seal side faces away from the brake panel.
7. Connect the rear brake lever/parking brake cable (upper cable) to the brake arm by performing the following:

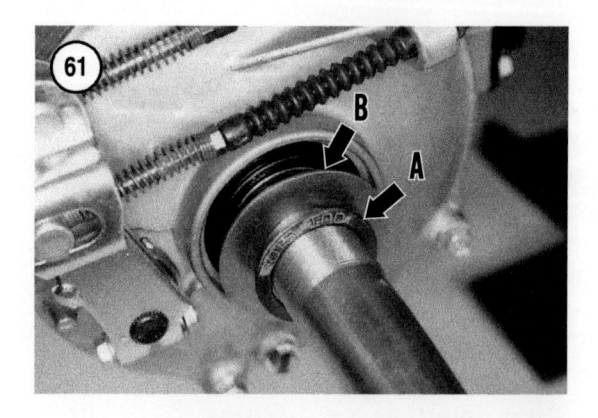

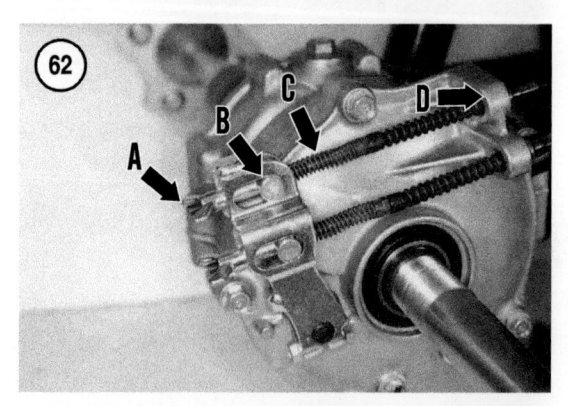

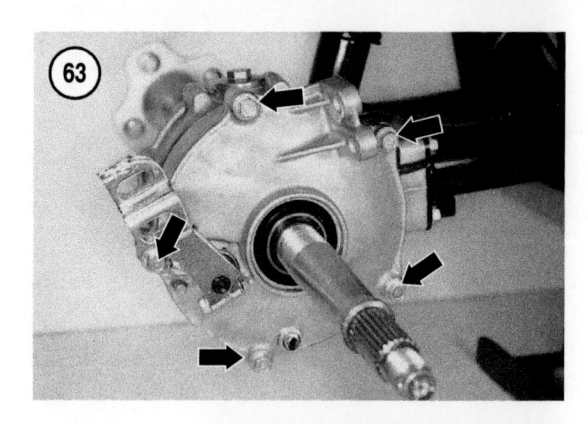

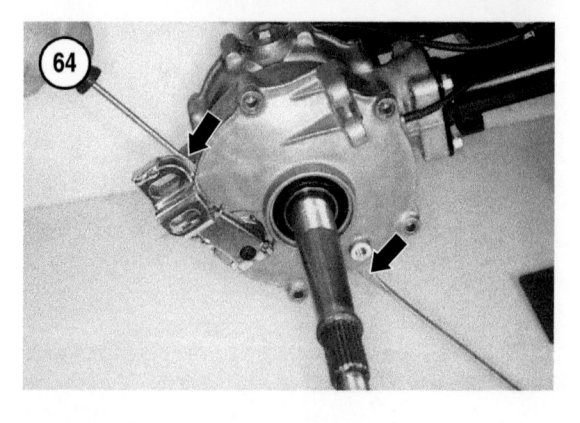

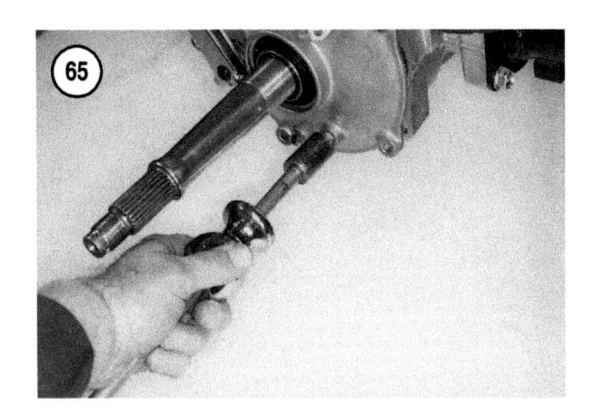

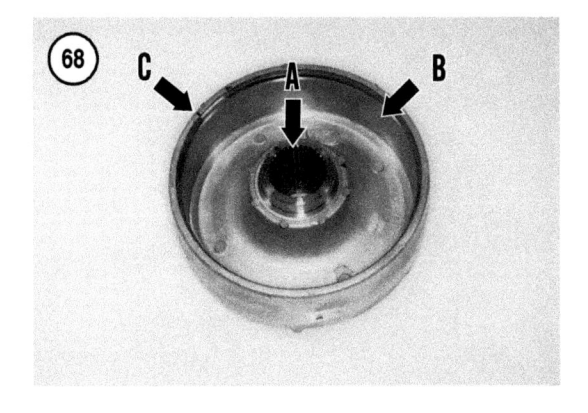

BRAKES

a. Route the cable through the boss (D, **Figure 62**) on the brake panel.
b. Fit the barrel connector (B, **Figure 62**) into place in the brake arm.
c. Slide the spring (C, **Figure 62**) over the cable end and feed the cable through the hole in the barrel connector.
d. Thread the adjuster (A, **Figure 62**) onto the cable end.

8. Connect the rear brake pedal cable (lower cable) to the brake arm by performing the procedures in Step 7.

9. Install the thrust washer (B, **Figure 61**) and spring washer (A). Make sure the side marked OUT faces away from the thrust washer.

NOTE
*Because the axle nut wrenches change the effective lever length of the torque wrench, use an adjusted torque setting to compensate for the change in lever length. Refer to **Torque Adapters** in Chapter One.*

10. Install the axle nut (B, **Figure 60**). The side with the external shoulder must face toward the spring washer. Tighten the axle nut to 39 N•m (29 ft.-lb.).

11. Apply ThreeBond 1303, or its equivalent, to the locknut threads and install the axle locknut (A, **Figure 60**). The side with the deeper shoulder must face toward the axle nut. While holding the axle nut, tighten the axle locknut to 127 N•m (94 ft.-lb.).

12. Install the skid plate. Tighten the skid plate bolts (A and B, **Figure 59** and **Figure 58**) to 32 N•m (24 ft.-lb.).

13. Install the right hub and wheel as described in Chapter Ten.

14. Adjust the rear brake as described in Chapter Three.

Brake Drum Inspection

When inspecting the brake drum, compare measurements to the specifications in **Table 1**. Replace the brake drum if any measurement is out of specification or if the drum is worn or damaged.

1. Inspect the rear brake panel as described in this section.

CAUTION
Do not clean the brake drum with any type of solvent that may leave an oil residue.

2. Check the brake drum surface (B, **Figure 68**) for oil or grease. Clean the surface with a rag soaked in brake parts cleaner. Check the brake shoe linings for contamination.
3. Check the drum contact surface (B, **Figure 68**) for scoring or other damage.
4. Inspect the brake drum for cracks or damage.
5. Inspect the drum splines (A, **Figure 68**) for twisting or damage.
6. Inspect the damper ring (C, **Figure 68**) for signs of wear or damage.
7. Measure the brake drum inside diameter (**Figure 70**).

Brake Panel Disassembly

NOTE
Checking the rear brake lining is addressed in Chapter Three. However, always measure the brake linings and check for uneven wear when the rear brake panel is removed.

1. Measure the brake lining thickness (**Figure 71**) at several places with a vernier caliper. Replace both shoes if uneven wear is noted.
2. If the brake shoes are reused, mark them left and right so each shoe can be reinstalled in its original location.
3. Carefully lift the outside of both shoes in a V-formation (**Figure 72**), and remove the brake shoes and springs as an assembly (**Figure 73**).
4. Remove both brake springs (A, **Figure 73**) and separate the brake shoes.

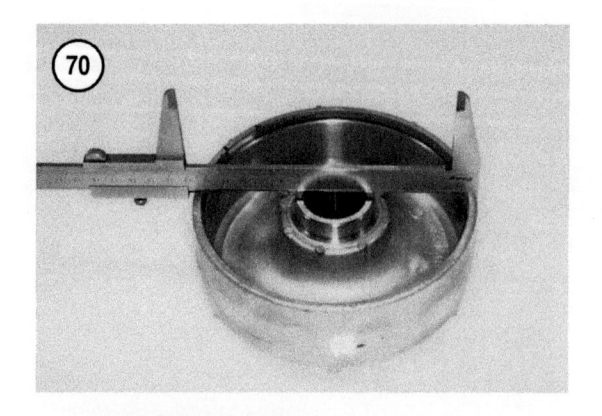

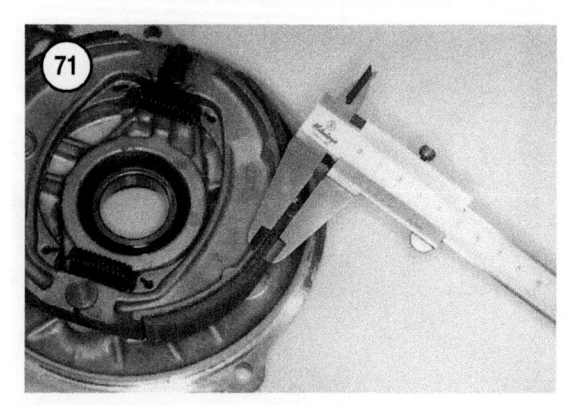

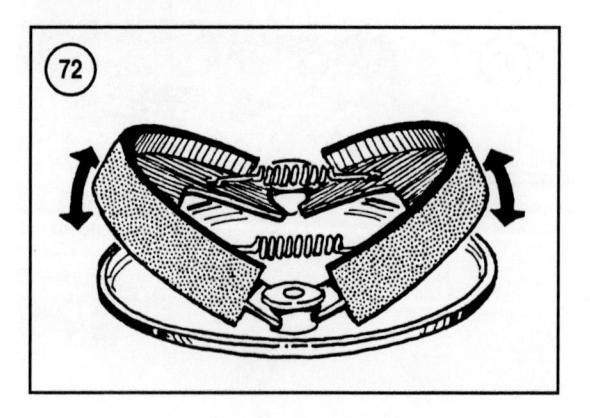

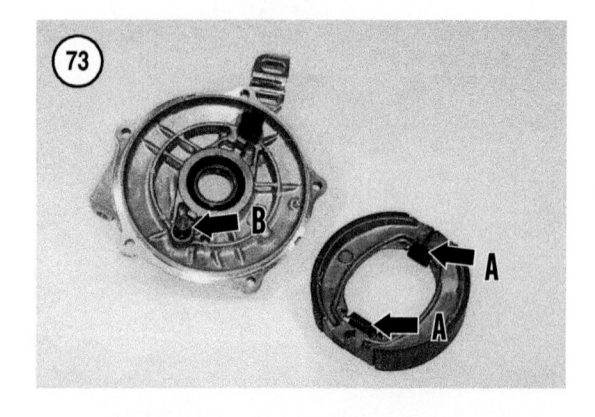

BRAKES

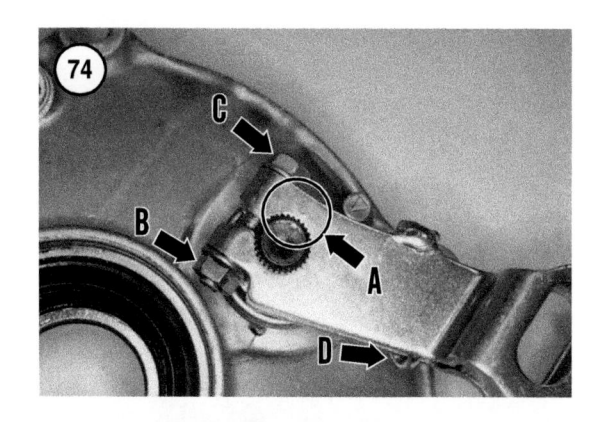

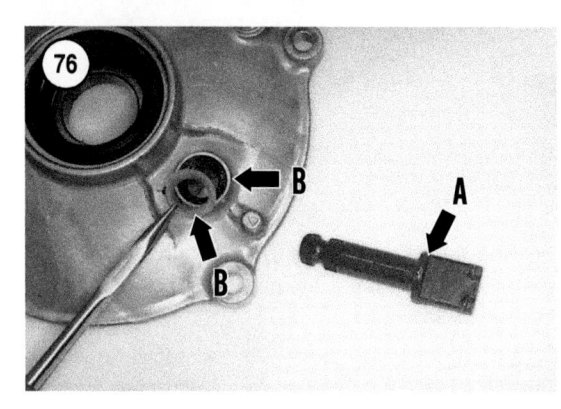

5. Note the indexing mark (A, **Figure 74**) on the brake cam and brake arm. These marks should align. If necessary, make punch marks on each part so they can be reinstalled with the same relative positions.

6. Remove the brake arm nut (B, **Figure 74**) and bolt (C), and lift the brake arm from the brake cam.

7. Lift the pointer (A, **Figure 75**) and the spring (B) off the brake cam.

8. Remove the brake cam (A, **Figure 76**) from the brake panel.

9. Remove the felt seal (B, **Figure 76**) from the brake cam dust seal.

10. Inspect the brake panel as described in this section.

Brake Panel Assembly

1. Apply a multipurpose lithium grease to the dust seals (A and B, **Figure 77**).

2. Apply oil to the felt seal, and set the seal (B, **Figure 76**) in place on the brake cam dust seal.

3. Apply a light coat of high-temperature brake grease onto the brake cam (A, **Figure 76**) and install the cam into the brake panel. Wipe any excess grease from the brake panel.

4. Install the brake cam spring (B, **Figure 75**). Make sure the tang on the spring sits in the hole (C, **Figure 77**) in the brake panel.

5. Install the pointer onto the brake cam. The tab on the pointer must engage the slot in the brake cam as shown in C, **Figure 75**.

6. Fit the brake arm onto the brake cam so the index marks are opposite one another as shown in A, **Figure 74**. Make sure the spring tang (D, **Figure 74**) engages the brake arm.

7. Install the brake arm clamp bolt (C, **Figure 74**) and clamp nut (B). Tighten the nut to 12 N•m (106 in.-lb.).

8. Apply a light coat of high-temperature brake grease to the anchor pin (B, **Figure 73**). Keep grease off any part of the brake panel that might come in contact with the brake linings.

9. Place the brake shoes opposite one another on the bench. If reusing the original brake shoes, position them so they are reinstalled in their original locations.

10. Attach the springs (A, **Figure 73**) to the brake shoes.

11. Hold the brake shoe/spring assembly in a V-formation with the shoes engaging the brake cam and anchor pin. Snap the shoes into place in the brake panel. Check that the ends of both springs are securely hooked onto the brake shoes. Refer to **Figure 69**.

Brake Panel Inspection

Replace any part that is worn or damaged.
1. Remove old grease from the brake cam (A, **Figure 76**), anchor pin (B, **Figure 73**) and brake panel.
2. Inspect the brake panel dust seal (A, **Figure 77**) and brake cam dust seal (B) for excessive wear or damage. Replace either dust seal if it is starting to harden or deteriorate. Refer to *Brake Panel Bearing Replacement* in this section.
3. Turn the inner race of the brake panel bearing (D, **Figure 77**) by hand. The race must turn smoothly. Also check that the outer race fits tightly into the brake panel. If necessary, replace the bearing as described in this section.
4. Inspect the O-ring (**Figure 69**) for excessive wear or damage.
5. Check the brake panel for cracks or other damage.
6. Inspect the splines on the brake cam and brake arm.
7. Check the brake cam spring (B, **Figure 75**) for cracks or signs of fatigue.

Brake Panel Bearing Replacement

1. Remove the brake shoes as described in *Brake Panel Disassembly* in this section.
2. Pry the dust seal (A, **Figure 77**) from the brake panel with the seal remover or other appropriate tool. Place a rag beneath the tool so the brake panel is not scratched.

NOTE
If only replacing the dust seal, go to Step 8.

3. Remove the snap ring from the bearing bore.
4. Use a suitable side bearing driver or socket, and drive the bearing from the bearing bore (**Figure 78**).
5. Inspect the mounting bore for cracks, galling or other damage. Clean the mounting bore thoroughly.

6. Inspect the snap ring groove for cracks or other damage.
7. Use a suitable size driver or socket and drive the bearing into the bore (**Figure 79**) until the bearing bottoms. The snap ring groove must be visible above the bearing.
8. Install the snap ring into the mounting bore groove. Make sure the snap ring completely seats in the groove.
9. Install the new dust seal (A, **Figure 77**) as follows:
   a. Pack the new dust seal lip with a multipurpose lithium grease.
   b. Align the dust seal with the mounting bore so the side with the manufacturing marks faces out.
   c. Use the appropriate size driver or socket to tap the dust seal into place until the upper surface of the seal aligns with the edge of the brake panel.

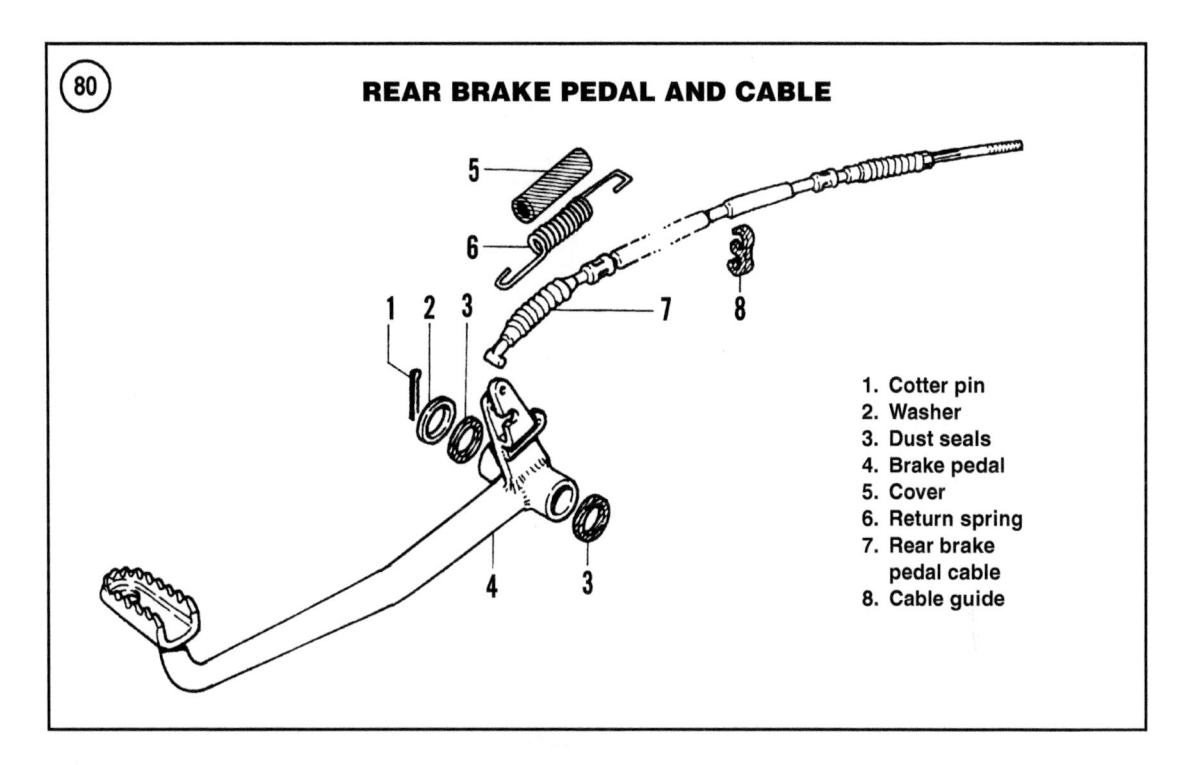

BRAKES

Figure 80 — REAR BRAKE PEDAL AND CABLE

1. Cotter pin
2. Washer
3. Dust seals
4. Brake pedal
5. Cover
6. Return spring
7. Rear brake pedal cable
8. Cable guide

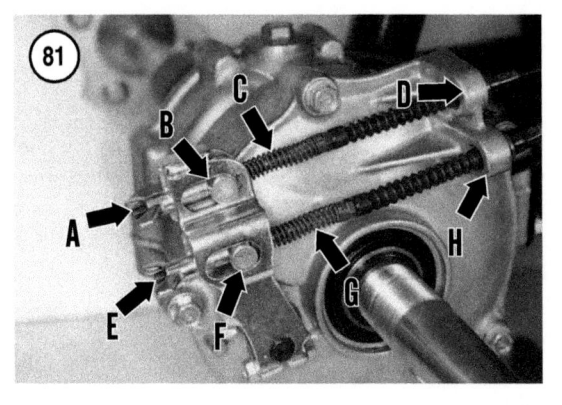

REAR BRAKE PEDAL AND CABLE

Removal/Installation

Refer to **Figure 80**.

1. Loosen and remove the rear brake pedal cable adjusting nut (E, **Figure 81**), barrel connector (F) and spring from the brake arm (G).
2. Disconnect the brake cable from the boss (H, **Figure 81**) on the brake panel.
3. Disconnect the brake return spring (A, **Figure 82**) from the brake pedal assembly.
4. Remove the cotter pin, washer (B, **Figure 82**) and brake pedal assembly from the frame pivot shaft.
5. Disconnect the brake cable (C, **Figure 82**) from the brake pedal.
6. When replacing the rear brake pedal cable, perform the following:
   a. Remove the rear brake cable from the frame, noting any cable guides or brackets that secure the cable in place.
   b. Lubricate the new brake cable as described in Chapter Three.
   c. Route the new rear brake pedal cable along the frame and through any cable guides or brackets.
7. Remove all old grease from the brake pedal pivot shaft.
8. Check the brake pedal dust seals. Replace them if excessively worn or damaged.
9. Pack the lips of the brake pedal dust seal with grease.
10. Apply lithium grease to the frame pivot shaft, brake pedal pivot bore and the brake cable end (brake pedal side).
11. Reconnect the brake cable to the brake pedal, and then install the brake pedal (C, **Figure 82**) onto its pivot shaft.
12. Install the washer (B, **Figure 82**), and secure the pedal to the shaft with a new cotter pin. Bend the cotter pin ends over to lock it in place. Operate the

brake pedal by hand, making sure it moves smoothly.

13. Reconnect the brake return spring (A, **Figure 82**) to the brake pedal.

14. Reconnect the rear brake pedal to the brake panel. Install the spring, collar and adjusting nut (E, **Figure 81**).

15. Adjust the rear brake as described in Chapter Three.

REAR BRAKE LEVER/ PARKING BRAKE CABLE

Removal/Installation

The handlebar mounted rear brake lever operates the rear brake and is also equipped with a lock that allows it to be used as a parking brake.

1. Remove the handlebar cover and front fender as described in Chapter Fourteen.

2. Loosen and remove the rear brake pedal cable adjusting nut (A, **Figure 81**), barrel connector (B) and spring from the brake arm (C).

3. Disconnect the brake cable from the boss (D, **Figure 81**) on the brake panel.

4. Roll the brake lever boot (A, **Figure 83**) off the lever housing.

5. Disconnect the brake cable (B, **Figure 83**) from the brake lever.

6. Tie a long piece of heavy string to one end of the brake cable. As the brake cable is removed, the string follows the cable's original path so the new cable can be installed correctly.

7. Remove any clamps or cable guides securing the brake cable to the frame.

8. Pull the brake cable from the frame making sure the string follows the cable's original path.

9. Lubricate the new brake cable as described in Chapter Three.

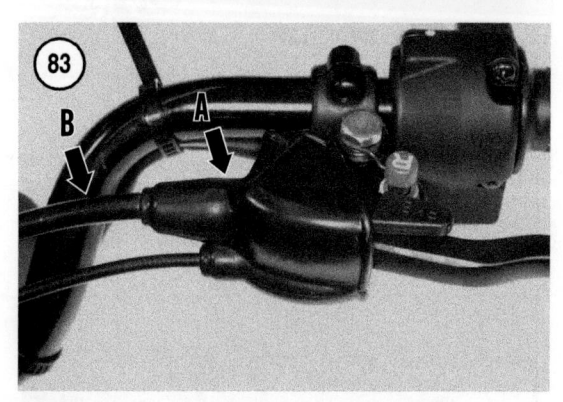

10. Cut the string and tie it to the end of the new brake cable. Pull the string through the frame and route the new brake cable along the path of the original cable.

11. Reconnect the brake cable (B, **Figure 83**) to the brake lever.

12. Secure the brake cable with clamps or cable guides.

13. Reconnect the rear brake lever/parking brake cable to the brake panel. Install the spring, collar and adjusting nut (A, **Figure 81**).

14. Adjust the rear brake as described in Chapter Three.

BRAKES

Table 1 BRAKE SYSTEM SPECIFICATIONS

Item	New mm (in.)	Service limit mm (in.)
Front brakes		
Caliper cylinder inner diameter	33.96-34.01 (1.337-1.339)	34.02 (1.34)
Caliper piston outside diameter	33.895-33.928 (1.334-1.335)	33.87 (1.333)
Disc thickness	2.8-3.2 (0.11-0.13)	2.5 (0.10)
Disc runout		0.30 (0.012)
Rear brake		
Drum inside diameter	140.0 (5.51)	141.0 (5.55)
Lining thickness	4.5 (0.18)	To the indicator
Master cylinder inside diameter	12.700-12.743 (0.5000-0.5017)	12.755 (0.5022)
Master piston outside diameter	12.657-12.684 (0.4983-0.4994)	12.645 (0.4978)

Table 2 BRAKE SYSTEM TORQUE SPECIFICATIONS

Item	N•m	in.-lb.	ft.-lb.
Brake hose banjo bolt	34	–	25
Brake hose clamp bolts			
6 mm	12	106	–
8 mm	29	–	22
Brake lever pivot bolt	6	53	–
Brake lever pivot locknut	6	53	–
Brake pipe	17	–	12
Front brakes			
Caliper bleed valve	6	53	–
Caliper bracket pins	18	–	13
Caliper mounting bolts	30	–	22
Caliper pad pins	18	–	13
Caliper slide pins	22	–	17
Caliper pad pin plugs	3	27	–
Front brake disc bolts	42	–	31
Front wheel hub nut	69	–	51
Master cylinder clamp bolts	12	106	–
Master cylinder reservoir cap screw	2	18	–
Rear brake			
Rear axle nut	39	–	29
Rear axle locknut*	127	–	94
Rear brake arm clamp bolt/nut	12	106	–
Rear brake panel drain bolt	12	106	–
Rear wheel hub nut	148	–	108
Skid plate bolts	32	–	24

*Apply threadlocking compound.

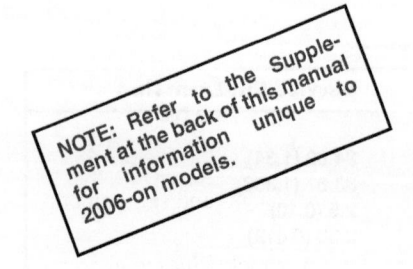

NOTE: Refer to the Supplement at the back of this manual for information unique to 2006-on models.

CHAPTER FOURTEEN

BODY

This chapter contains removal and installation procedures for the seat, side covers, upper fuel tank cover, front and rear fender and handlebar cover. During removal, reinstall mounting hardware to ensure the fasteners are reinstalled in their original locations.

RETAINING CLIPS

The TRX250EX uses plastic retaining clips to secure many body components to the frame or other body panels. Refer to **Figure 1** for clip removal and installation procedures. The clips are easily damaged, which can make removal and reinstallation difficult. Replace damaged clips as necessary.

RETAINING TABS

Some panels are equipped with directional tabs (**Figure 2**). The tab fits into a slot in the adjoining panel. Make sure to move the panel properly to disengage or engage the tab in the slot.

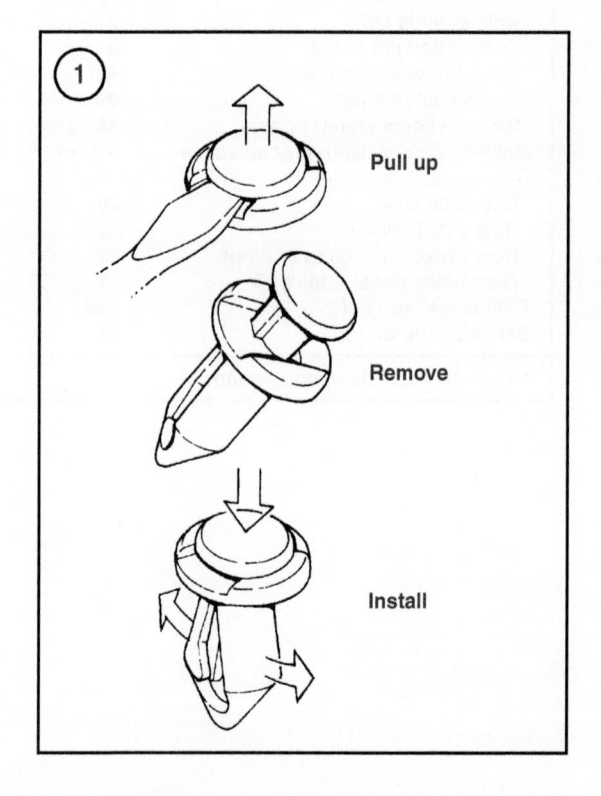

BODY

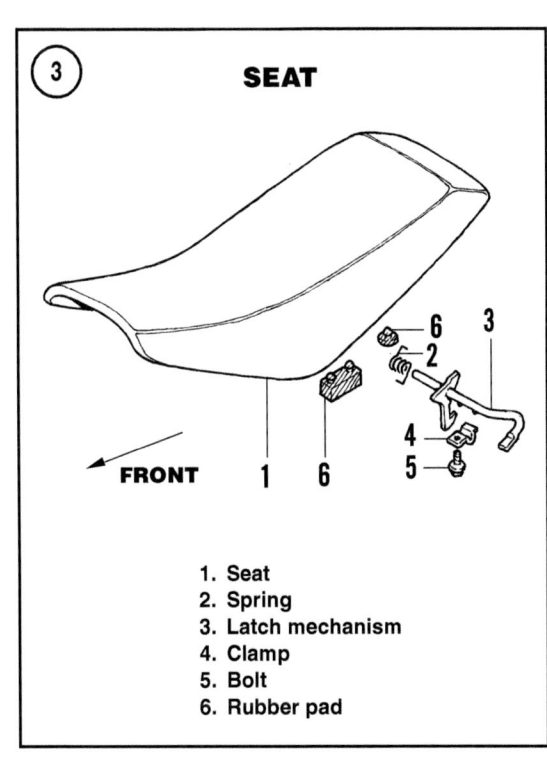

SEAT

Removal/Installation

Refer to **Figure 3**.
1. Park the ATV on level ground and set the parking brake.
2. Pull up on the seat lever lock (**Figure 4**) to release the seat lock.
3. Lift the rear of the seat to disengage it from the mounts. Then slide the assembly back to disengage the seat at the front. Lift away from the vehicle.
4. Inspect the underside of the bodywork for damage and hardware tightness. Check the seat prongs and latch area.
5. To install the seat, align the prongs and slot at the front of the seat with the front mount.
6. Press down firmly on the rear of the seat to lock it into place.
7. Lift at the rear of the seat to make sure it is locked in place.

WARNING
Do not ride the vehicle unless the seat is locked in place.

SIDE COVERS

Removal/Installation

Refer to **Figure 5**.
1. Park the ATV on level ground and set the parking brake.
2. Remove the seat as described in this chapter.
3. Remove the retaining clips securing the side covers. Do not miss the clip between the rear fender and the frame at the top of the mud guards (**Figure 6**).
4. Disengage the tab on the side cover from the front fender by lifting the lower part of the cover up and pulling the side cover away from the front fender.
5. Installation is the reverse of removal.

FUEL TANK COVER

Removal/Installation

Refer to **Figure 5**.
1. Park the ATV on level ground and set the parking brake.

---

③ SEAT

FRONT

1. Seat
2. Spring
3. Latch mechanism
4. Clamp
5. Bolt
6. Rubber pad

FRONT FENDER, SIDE COVERS AND FUEL TANK COVER

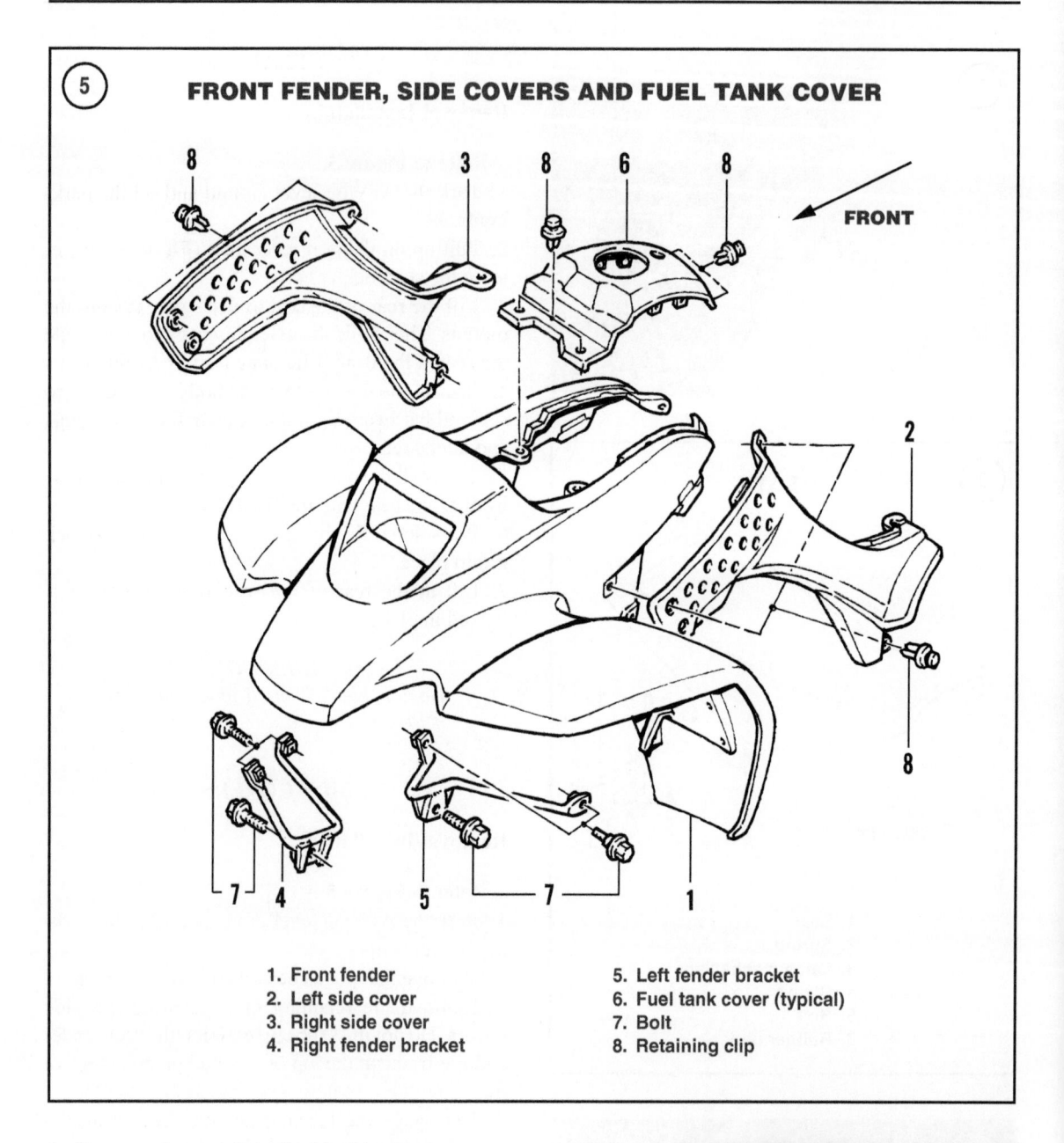

1. Front fender
2. Left side cover
3. Right side cover
4. Right fender bracket
5. Left fender bracket
6. Fuel tank cover (typical)
7. Bolt
8. Retaining clip

2. Remove the seat described in this chapter.

3. Remove the fuel tank cap (A, **Figure 7**) and breather tube (B).

4. Remove the retaining clips (**Figure 8**) securing the fuel tank cover.

5. Slide the cover rearward and release the tabs from the mounting slots in the front fender. Lift the tank cover from the fuel tank.

6. Reinstall the fuel tank cap and tighten it securely.

7. Installation is the reverse of removal.

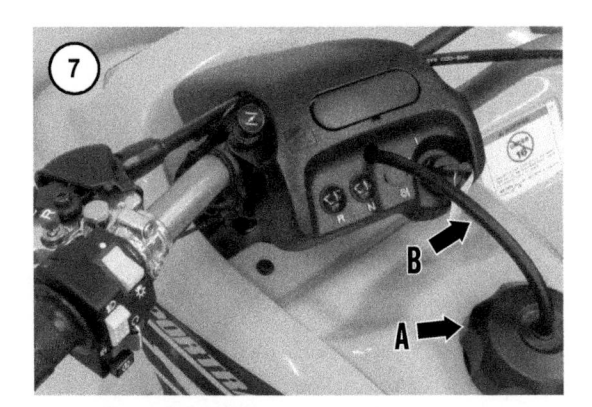

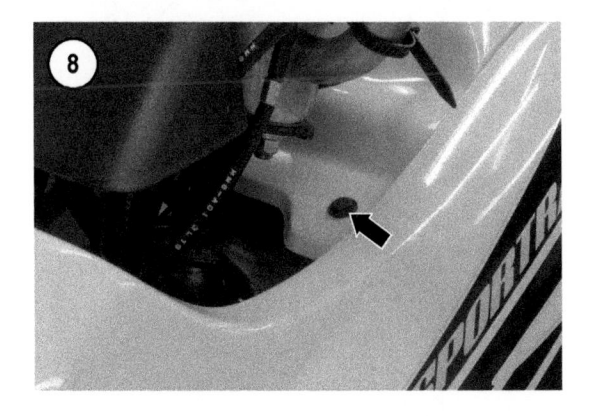

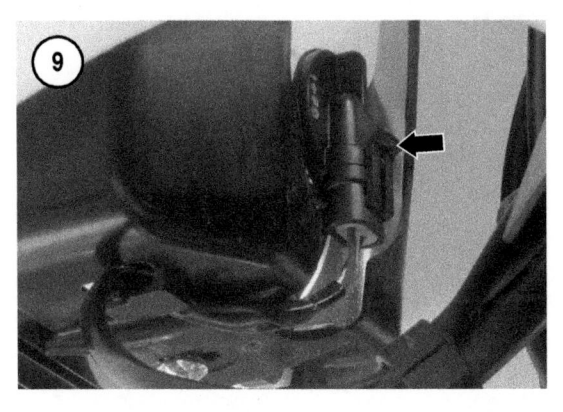

BODY

FRONT FENDER

Removal/Installation

Refer to **Figure 5**.
1. Park the ATV on level ground and set the parking brake.
2. Remove the fuel tank cover and side covers as described in this chapter.
3. Disconnect the headlight from the wiring harness (**Figure 9**).
4. Remove the two retaining clips holding the fender to the frame.
5. Remove the two retaining clips holding the fender to the fuel tank.
6. Remove the four bolts securing the fender braces in the front wheel wells (**Figure 10**).

FRONT AND REAR GUARDS

Removal/Installation

Refer to **Figure 11**.
1. Park the ATV on level ground and set the parking brake.
2. Remove the bolts securing the front and rear guards to the frame.
3. Installation is the reverse of removal.

REAR FENDER

Removal/Installation

Refer to **Figure 12**.
1. Park the ATV on level ground and set the parking brake.
2. Remove the seat as described in this chapter.
3. Remove the left and right side covers as described in this chapter.
4. Remove the battery as described in Chapter Three.
5. Remove the tool case (A, **Figure 13**).
6. Disconnect the battery lead and the starter cable lead connected to the starter relay as described in Chapter Nine.
7. Disconnect the taillight connector (**Figure 14**).
8. Remove the upper fender mounting bolts (B, **Figure 13**).
9. Remove the lower fender mounting bolts (A, **Figure 15**).

CHAPTER FOURTEEN

(11) FRONT AND REAR GUARDS

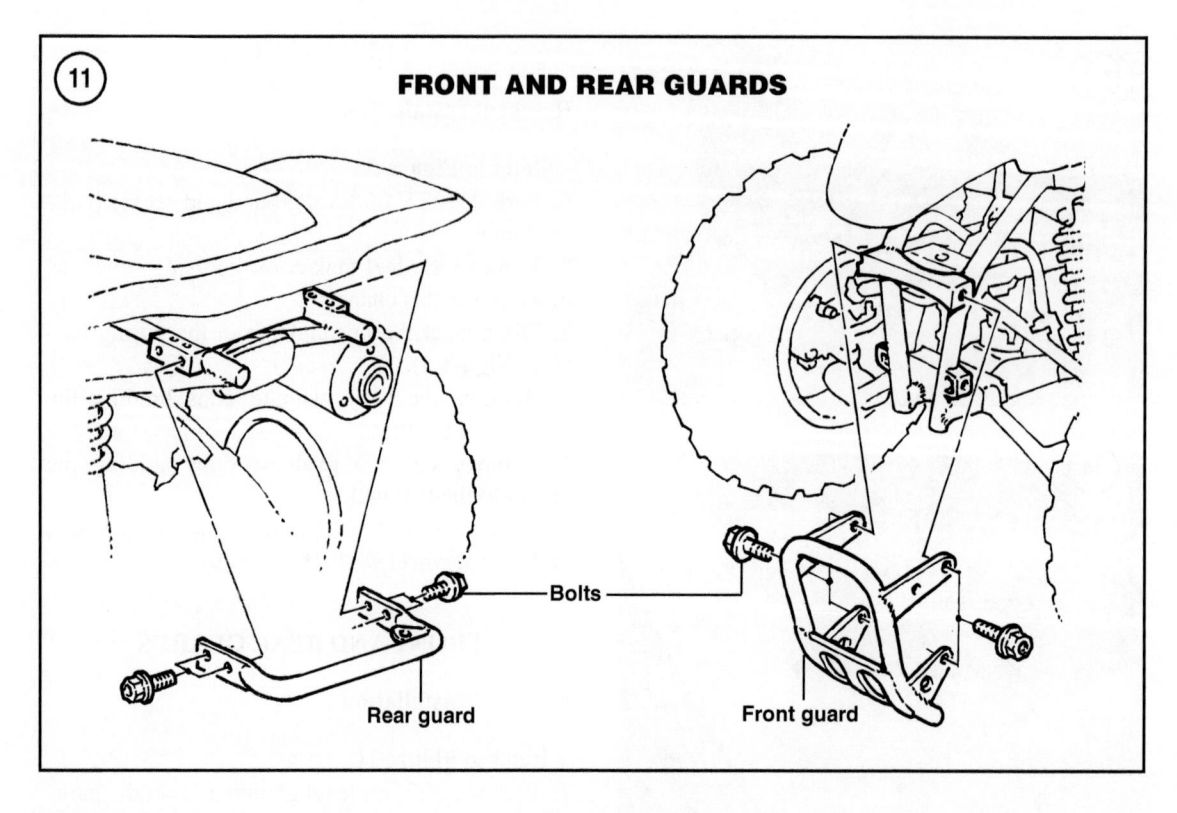

Bolts — Rear guard — Front guard

(12) REAR FENDER

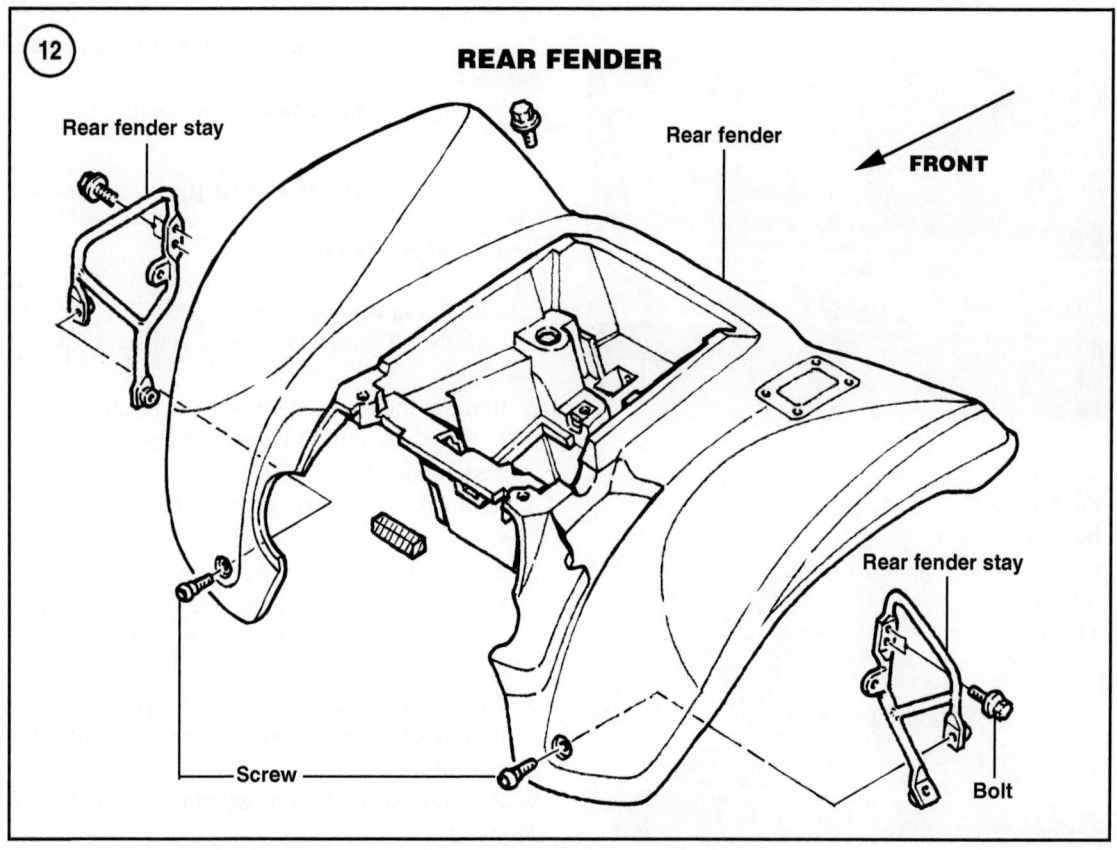

Rear fender stay — Rear fender — FRONT

Screw — Rear fender stay — Bolt

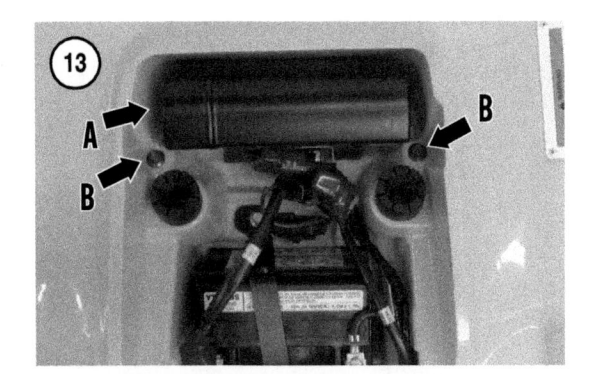

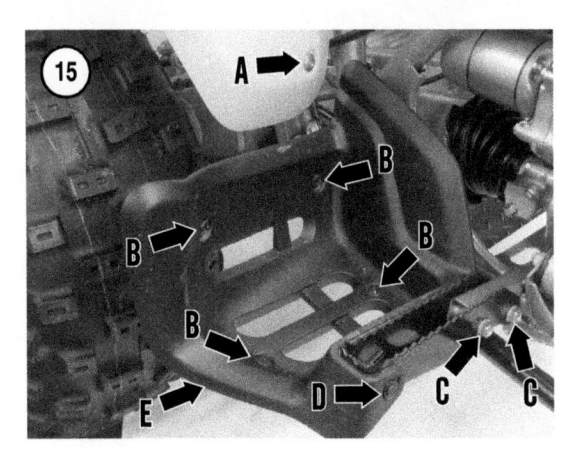

BODY

MUD GUARDS

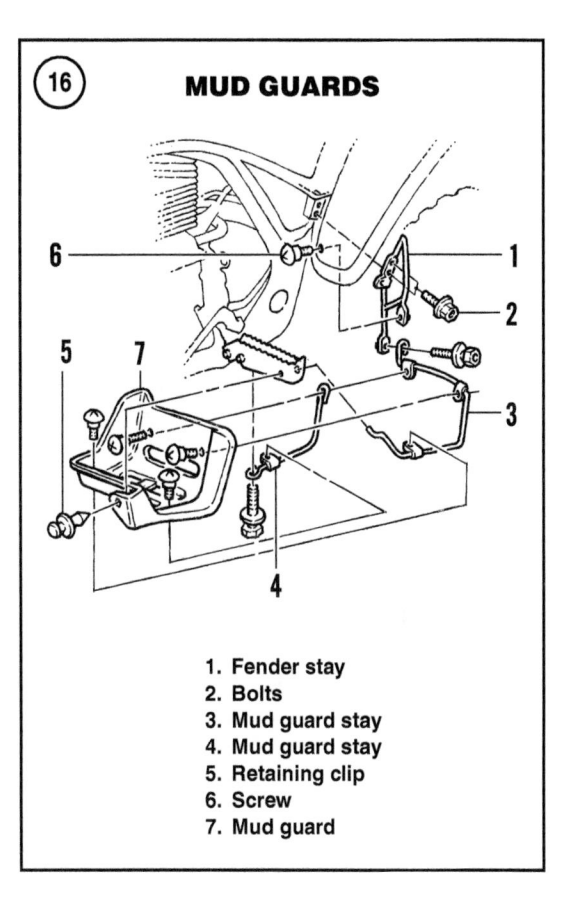

1. Fender stay
2. Bolts
3. Mud guard stay
4. Mud guard stay
5. Retaining clip
6. Screw
7. Mud guard

1. Park the ATV on level ground and set the parking brake.

2. Remove the screws (A, **Figure 15**) and retaining clip (D) securing the mud guards (E) to the mud guard stays.

3. Remove the bolts securing the mudguard stay to the frame (**Figure 17**).

4. Remove the bolt securing the mudguard stay to the footpeg (**Figure 18**).

5. Remove the two bolts securing the foot pegs to the frame (C, **Figure 15**).

6. Installation is the reverse of removal.

10. Lift the rear fender assembly up. Hold the wiring harness together while feeding it through the hole in the rear fender. Once the wiring clears the rear fender, lift the fender up and away from the frame.

11. Installation is the reverse of removal.

FOOTPEGS AND MUD GUARDS

Removal/Installation

Refer to **Figure 16**.

HANDLEBAR COVER

Removal/Installation

1. Park the ATV on level ground and set the parking brake.

2. Remove the fuel tank vent tube (B, **Figure 7**) from the handlebar cover.

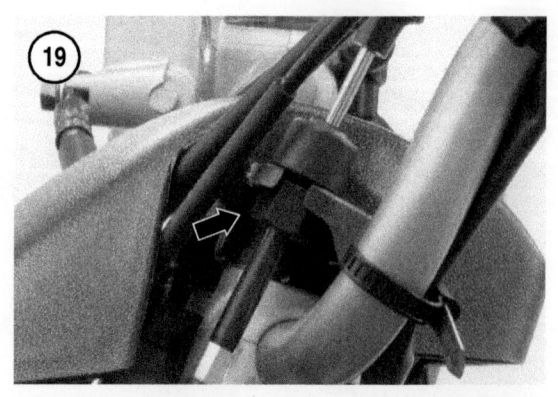

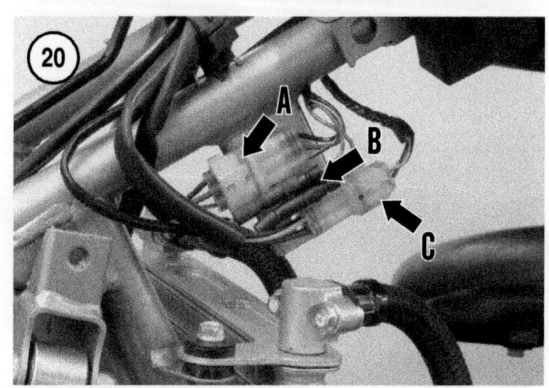

3. Loosen the choke knob locknut (**Figure 19**) and slide the choke knob from its mount on the handlebar cover.

4. Follow the ignition switch harness and disconnect the ignition switch 3-pin connector (A, **Figure 20**) and its bullet connectors (B) from the main harness.

5. Disconnect the indicator lamps from the wiring harness (C, **Figure 20**).

6. Pry the cap (**Figure 21**) from the handlebar cover.

7. Remove the handlebar cover mounting screws (**Figure 22**).

8. Check that all wires are disconnected from the main harness and released from the wire clamps securing them to the frame.

9. Release both ends of the handlebar cover from the handlebar, and then remove the handlebar cover assembly.

10. Installation is the reverse of removal. After assembly, check that the ignition switch and indicator lights work properly.

SUPPLEMENT

2006-2012 MODEL SERVICE INFORMATION

This Supplement contains all procedures and specifications unique to the 2006-2012 models. If a specific procedure is not included, refer to the procedure in the appropriate chapter in the main body of this manual

This Supplement is divided into sections that correspond to the chapters in the main body of the manual.

Tables 1-7 are at the end of the appropriate sections.

CHAPTER ONE

GENERAL INFORMATION

Refer to **Table 1** for specifications unique to later models.

Table 1 VEHICLE DIMENSIONS

Dry weight	
2006 and 2007 models	172 kg (379 lb.)
2008-on models	171 kg (377 lb.)
Ground clearance	
2008-on models	146 mm (5.7 in.)
Overall height	
2006 and 2007 models	1076 mm (42.4 in.)
2008-on models	1082 mm (42.6 in.)
Overall length	
2006-on models	1739 mm (68.5 in.)
Seat height	
2006-on models	797 mm (31.4 in.)

CHAPTER THREE

LUBRICATION, MAINTENANCE AND TUNE-UP

Refer to **Table 2** and **Table 3** for specifications.

BRAKE LIGHT SWITCH ADJUSTMENT

The front brake switch is not adjustable. If the taillight does not come on when the front brake is applied, replace the switch. The rear brake switch is attached to the rear brake pedal and is adjustable. To adjust the switch, hold the switch body and turn the adjusting nut (**Figure 1**) in the appropriate direction. The brake light should turn on just before the rear brake begins to engage.

CLUTCH LEVER ADJUSTMENT

The clutch cable must be properly adjusted in order to fully disengage/engage the change clutch when shifting.

1. Check the clutch lever for proper free play as follows:
    a. Measure the amount of free play at the end of the clutch lever (**Figure 2**). Refer to **Table 3** for the correct measurement.
    b. If free play is incorrect, adjust the cable as described in this section.
2. Pull the rubber boot away from the lever and adjuster.
3. Loosen the locknut (A, **Figure 3**) and turn the cable adjuster (B) to increase/decrease play in the cable and lever. Note the following:
    a. If correct play can be achieved with the adjuster, and the adjuster is close to the middle of its range of travel, tighten the locknut securely. Reposition the rubber boot and adjustment is complete.
    b. If correct play cannot be achieved with the adjuster, or if the adjuster is fully screwed in

2006-2012 MODEL SERVICE INFORMATION

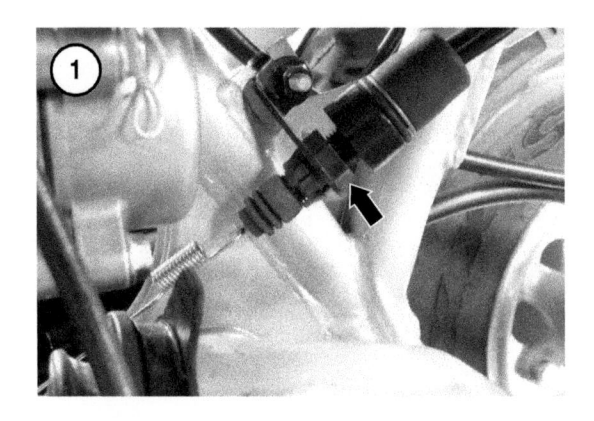

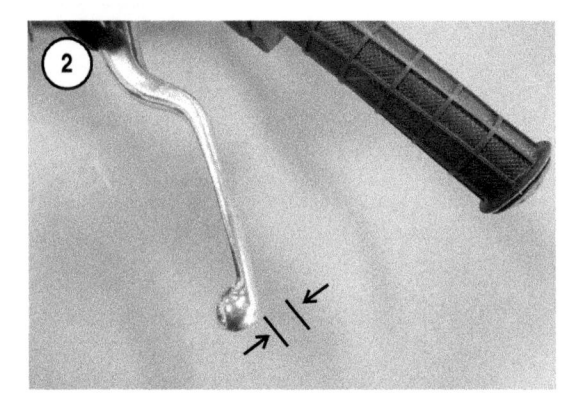

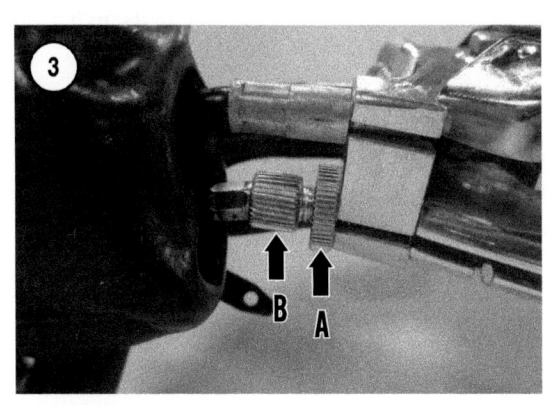

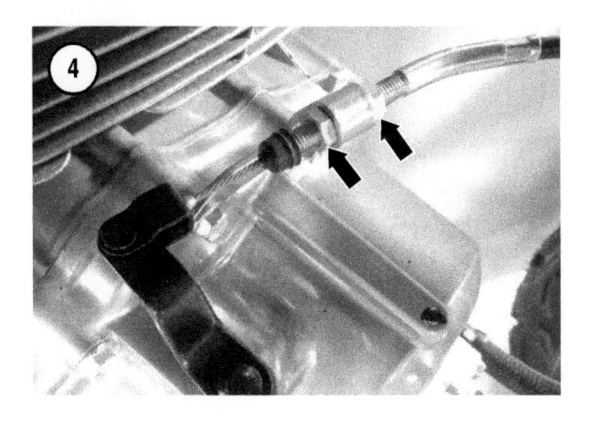

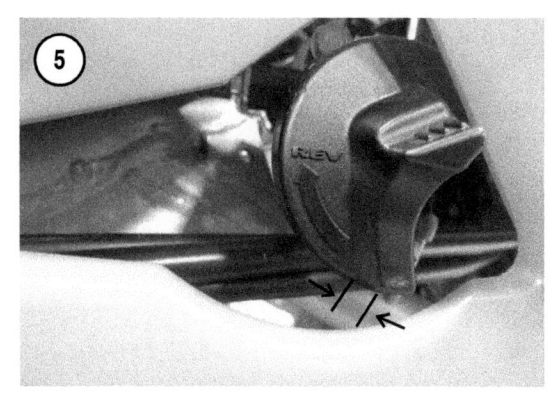

or out, screw the adjuster completely in. Then turn the adjuster out one full turn and make the adjustment at the engine.

4. At the engine, adjust the cable as follows:
   a. Loosen the locknuts (**Figure 4**) and adjust the cable housing so free play is correct at the lever.
   b. Tighten the locknuts securely.
   c. If necessary, make fine adjustments at the lever.
   d. Reposition the boot over the lever adjuster.

5. At engine startup, check that the clutch properly engages and disengages. If poor clutch operation continues, disassemble the change clutch and inspect for wear and damage.

REVERSE SELECTOR CABLE ADJUSTMENT

2006 and 2007 Models

The reverse selector cable must be properly adjusted to keep the transmission locked out of reverse without the use of the reverse selector lever.

1. Check the reverse selector lever for proper free play as follows:
   a. Measure the amount of free play at the reverse selector lever (**Figure 5**). Refer to **Table 3** for the correct measurement.
   b. If free play is incorrect, adjust the cable as described in this section.

2. At the engine, pull the rubber boot away from the adjusters (**Figure 6**).

3. Loosen the locknut and turn the cable adjuster to increase/decrease play in the cable and lever. Note the following:

a. If correct play can be achieved with the adjuster, tighten the locknut securely. Reposition the rubber boot and adjustment is complete.
b. If correct play cannot be achieved with the adjuster, or if the adjuster is fully screwed in or out, the cable is damaged or fatigued. Replace the cable.

4. In a safe location, start the engine and check the following:
   a. Without using the reverse selector lever, try to shift the transmission into reverse gear. The transmission should be locked out of reverse gear.
   b. Turn the reverse selector lever and shift the transmission into reverse gear. The transmission should be engaged with reverse gear.
   c. Disengage reverse gear without using the selector lever. The transmission should be locked out of reverse gear.
   d. If any of these safety checks fail, recheck adjustment. Also inspect the cable for pinching, fatigue or damage.

2008-on Models

NOTE
The cable is not adjustable and must be replaced if it doesn't properly operate the reverse selector lever.

The reverse selector cable must be in good condition to keep the transmission locked out of reverse without the use of the reverse selector lever. Check the condition of the cable as follows:

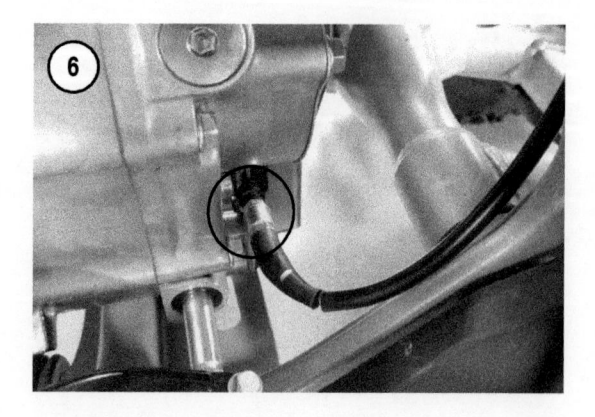

1. In a safe location, start the engine and check the following:

   a. Without using the reverse selector lever, shift the transmission into reverse gear. The transmission should be locked out of reverse gear.

   b. Turn the reverse selector lever and shift the transmission into reverse gear. The transmission should be engaged with reverse gear.

   c. Disengage reverse gear without using the selector lever. The transmission should be locked out of reverse gear.

2. If any of these safety checks fail, inspect the cable for pinching, fatigue or damage. Replace the cable if it fails to operate properly, or if damage is evident.

Table 2 RECOMMENDED LUBRICANTS AND FLUIDS

Fuel	
Octane	Regular unleaded
Tank capacity w/reserve	
2008-on models	9.5 L (2.5 gal.)
Tank reserve capacity	
2008-on models	2.6 L (0.69 gal.)
Engine oil	
Grade	
2006-on models	API SG or higher, or JASO MA
Viscosity	
2006-on models	10W-30

Table 3 MAINTENANCE AND TUNE-UP SPECIFICATIONS

Clutch lever free play	10-20 mm (3/8-3/4 in.)
Idle speed	1300-1500 rpm
Ignition timing	14° BTDC at 1300-1500 rpm
Reverse selector free play	
2006 and 2007 models	14-22 mm (1/2-7/8 in.)
2008-on models	Refer to text

CHAPTER FIVE

ENGINE LOWER END

GEARSHIFT LINKAGE

2006-on models no longer use gear shift pedal linkage to disengage the change clutch. The change clutch is disengaged by the clutch lever at the handlebar. The lever uses a cable, lifter arm and lifter to actuate the clutch. Therefore, this eliminates the linkage clutch lever and sub-gearshift spindle arm. All parts from the master arm inward are the same.

CHAPTER SIX

CLUTCH AND PRIMARY DRIVE

Refer to **Table 4** for specifications.

CLUTCH RELEASE MECHANISM

Refer to **Figure 7**.

2006-on models use a cable-actuated lifter arm and lifter to disengage the change clutch. The cable is attached to the left lever at the handlebar and all gear changing is done by hand. Honda calls this the SportClutch system. The benefit of this system allows for quick starts at high engine rpm without the possibility of stalling the engine. It also gives new riders experience in using a clutch lever if they intend to progress to larger machines that use a single manual clutch.

The SportClutch also eliminates the change clutch adjuster on the front of the clutch cover. All clutch adjustment is done at the handlebar lever.

CLUTCH COVER

Removal/Installation

Removal and installation of the clutch cover is essentially the same as described in Chapter Six, except for the differences noted in this section.

1. Disconnect the clutch cable as follows:
   a. At the handlebar, loosen the locknut (A, **Figure 3**) and turn the adjuster (B) in to create maximum slack in the cable.

CLUTCH RELEASE MECHANISM

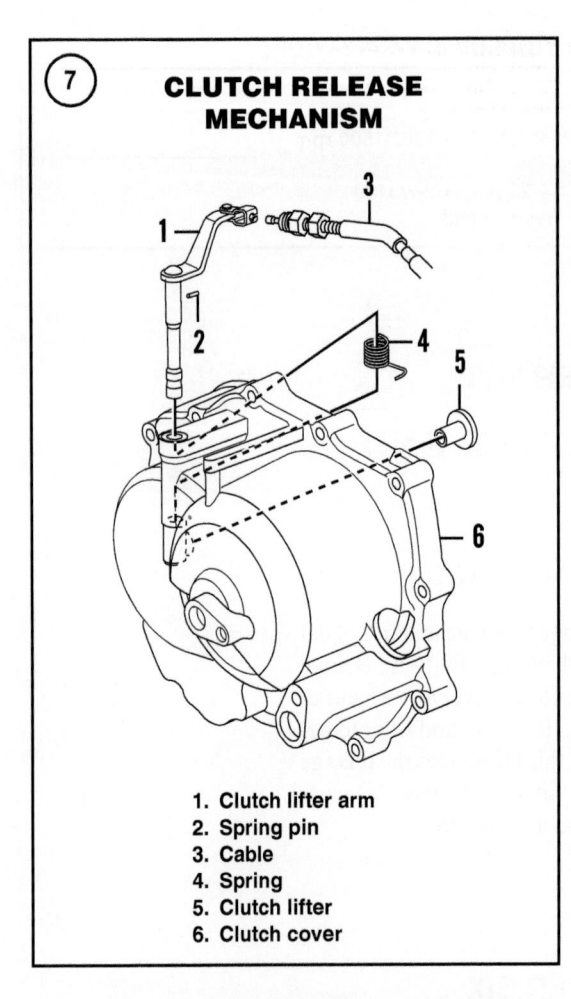

Figure 7

1. Clutch lifter arm
2. Spring pin
3. Cable
4. Spring
5. Clutch lifter
6. Clutch cover

b. At the clutch cover, remove the locknut nearest the cable boot (**Figure 4**) and remove the cable from the clutch lifter arm. Prevent turning the remaining locknut on the cable, as its location will aid in accurately installing the cable near its original position during assembly.

2. Account for the clutch lifter when the clutch cover is removed.

3. When installing the clutch cover, turn the clutch lifter arm so the cutout in the spindle is aligned with the hole in the cover. Insert the clutch lifter, engaging it with the lifter arm spindle. Release the lifter arm so it seats with the lifter.

4. After the cover is installed, install and adjust the clutch cable as described in this Supplement.

CLUTCH LIFTER ARM

Removal/Inspection/Installation

Refer to **Figure 7**.

Use the following procedure to remove the clutch lifter arm from the clutch cover.

1. Place the clutch cover face up on the workbench.
2. Turn the clutch lifter arm and remove the clutch lifter from the cover.
3. Carefully unhook the spring to prevent damage to it.
4. Use a small driver and tap the spring pin into the lifter arm spindle. The pin must be flush so the spindle can pass through the bearing and seal.
5. Inspect the parts as follows:
   a. Inspect the lifter arm, lifter and spring for excessive wear or damage. The spring must be in good condition to fully return the lifter arm to the engaged clutch position.
   b. Clean, lubricate and inspect the bearings and seal. Check for roughness, wear and corrosion. If the bearings must be replaced, refer to Chapter One. If a new seal is required, install seal so it is 0.5-1.0 mm below the top edge of the case.
6. Install the parts as follows:
   a. Lubricate the bearings and seal with engine oil.
   b. Place the spring in the cover so the spring pin hook is facing up.
   c. Carefully insert the lifter arm spindle through the cover and through the spring. Do not attempt to hook the spring at this time.
   d. Identify the side of the pin hole in the spindle that is chamfered. From this side, drive the spring pin out until it protrudes 3 mm.
   e. Slide the spring up the spindle and hook the ends of the spring to the pin and to the cover seat.
   f. Turn the clutch lifter arm so the cutout in the spindle is aligned with the hole in the cover. Insert the clutch lifter, engaging it with the lifter arm spindle. Operate the lifter arm and assure that the spring is under tension when the lifter is raised. Release the lifter arm and check that it returns to the engaged position.

Table 4 CLUTCH SPECIFICATIONS

Item	Standard mm (in.)	Service limit mm (in.)
Change clutch spring free length	38.9 (1.53)	36.0 (1.42)

CHAPTER EIGHT
FUEL, AIR AND EXHAUST SYSTEMS

Table 5 CARBURETOR SPECIFICATIONS

Identification number	PDC1G
Slow jet	#42 × #42
Pilot screw	
Initial setting	1 1/2 turns out
Final setting	5/8 turns out

CHAPTER NINE
ELECTRICAL SYSTEM

Table 6 ELECTRICAL SYSTEM SPECIFICATIONS

Ignition timing	14° BTDC at 1300-1500 rpm

Table 7 BULB SPECIFICATIONS

Item	Specification
Brake light/taillight	LED
Headlight	12 volt-39/39 watts × 2
Neutral indicator	12 volt-3.0 watts
Reverse indicator	12 volt-3.4 watts

CHAPTER FOURTEEN

BODY

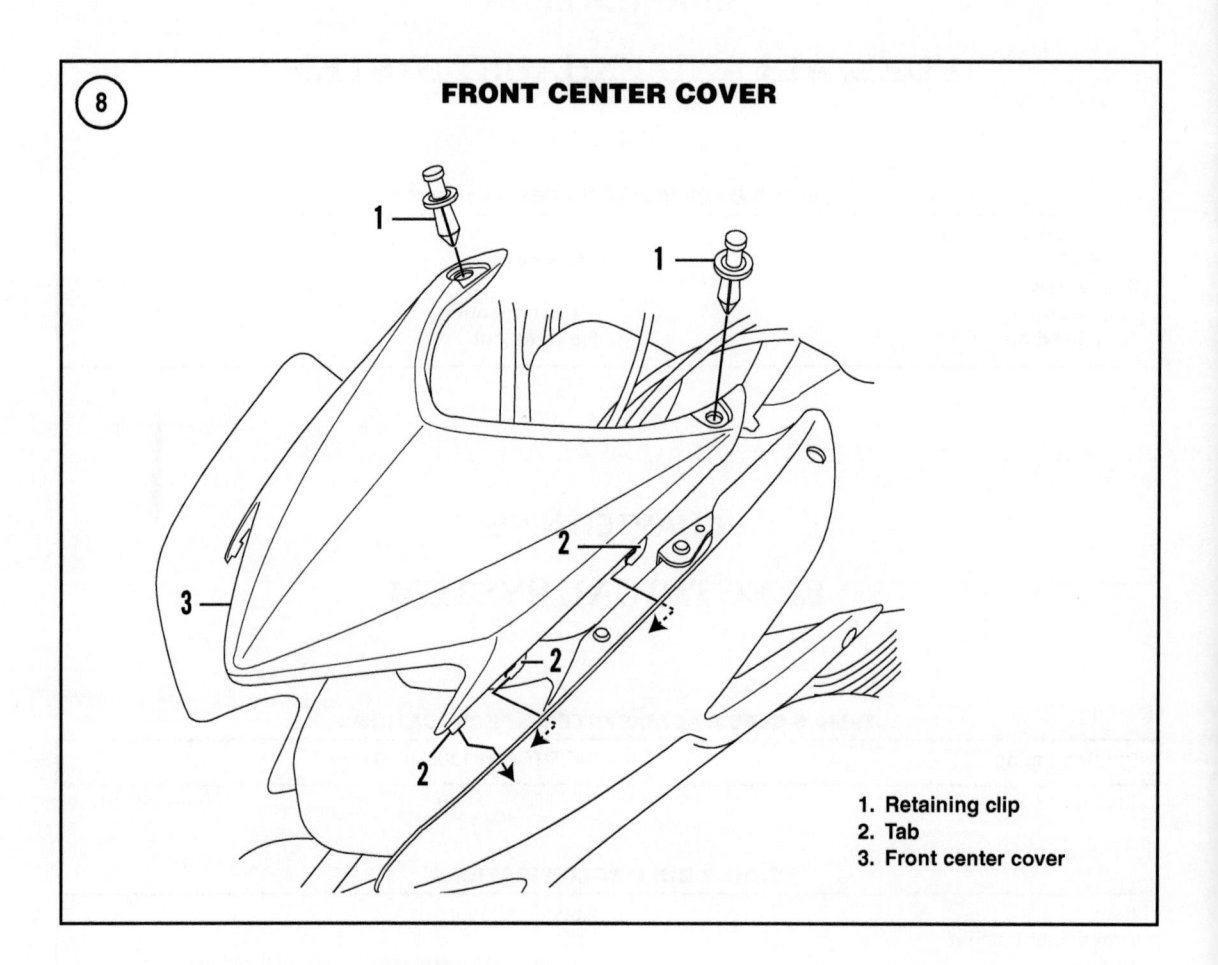

FRONT CENTER COVER

⑧

1. Retaining clip
2. Tab
3. Front center cover

FRONT CENTER COVER

Removal/Installation

Refer to **Figure 8**.

1. Remove the two retaining clips.

2. Pull the front center cover to the rear and release the tabs from the front fender.

3. Reverse the removal procedure to install the front center cover.

FRONT FENDER

Removal/Installation

Refer to **Figure 9**.
1. Remove the front center cover as described in this Supplement.
2. Remove the two retaining clips.
3. Remove the four bolts.
4. Release the fender from the mounting boss.
5. Reverse the removal procedure to install the front fender. Tighten the four bolts securely.

FRONT FENDER

⑨

1. Retaining clip
2. Bolt
3. Mounting boss
4. Front fender

FUEL TANK COVER

Removal/Installation

Refer to **Figure 10**.

1. Remove the seat as described in Chapter Fourteen.

2. Remove the front center cover as described in this Supplement.

3. Remove the four retaining clips.

4. Remove the four bolts.

5. Remove the fuel cap.

6. Release the tabs at each side of the cover and remove it from the machine.

7. Install the fuel cap.

8. Reverse the removal procedure to install the fuel tank cover. Tighten all of the bolts securely.

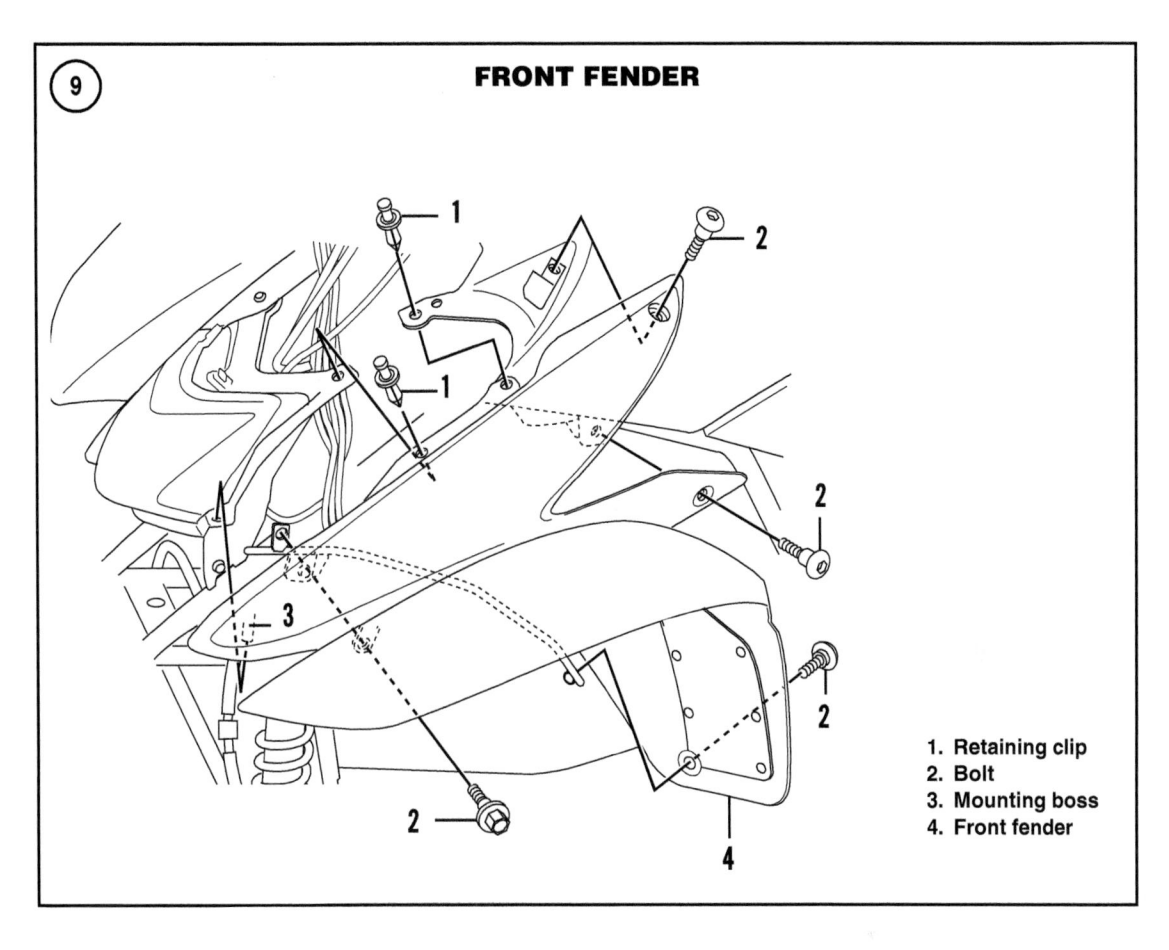

REAR FENDER

Removal/Installation

Refer to **Figure 11**.

1. Remove the fuel tank cover as described in this Supplement.
2. Disconnect the negative battery cable.
3. Disconnect the starter cable from the starter relay switch.
4. Disconnect the main fuse from the starter relay switch.
5. Disconnect the starter relay wire connectors and remove any clamps securing them to the fender.
6. Remove the eight bolts securing the fender.
7. Remove the rear fender from the machine.
8. Reverse the removal procedure to install the rear fender. Note the following:
    a. Tighten all of the bolts securely.
    b. Make sure all connectors are securely fastened.
    c. Install any clamps securing the starter relay wire connectors to rear fender.

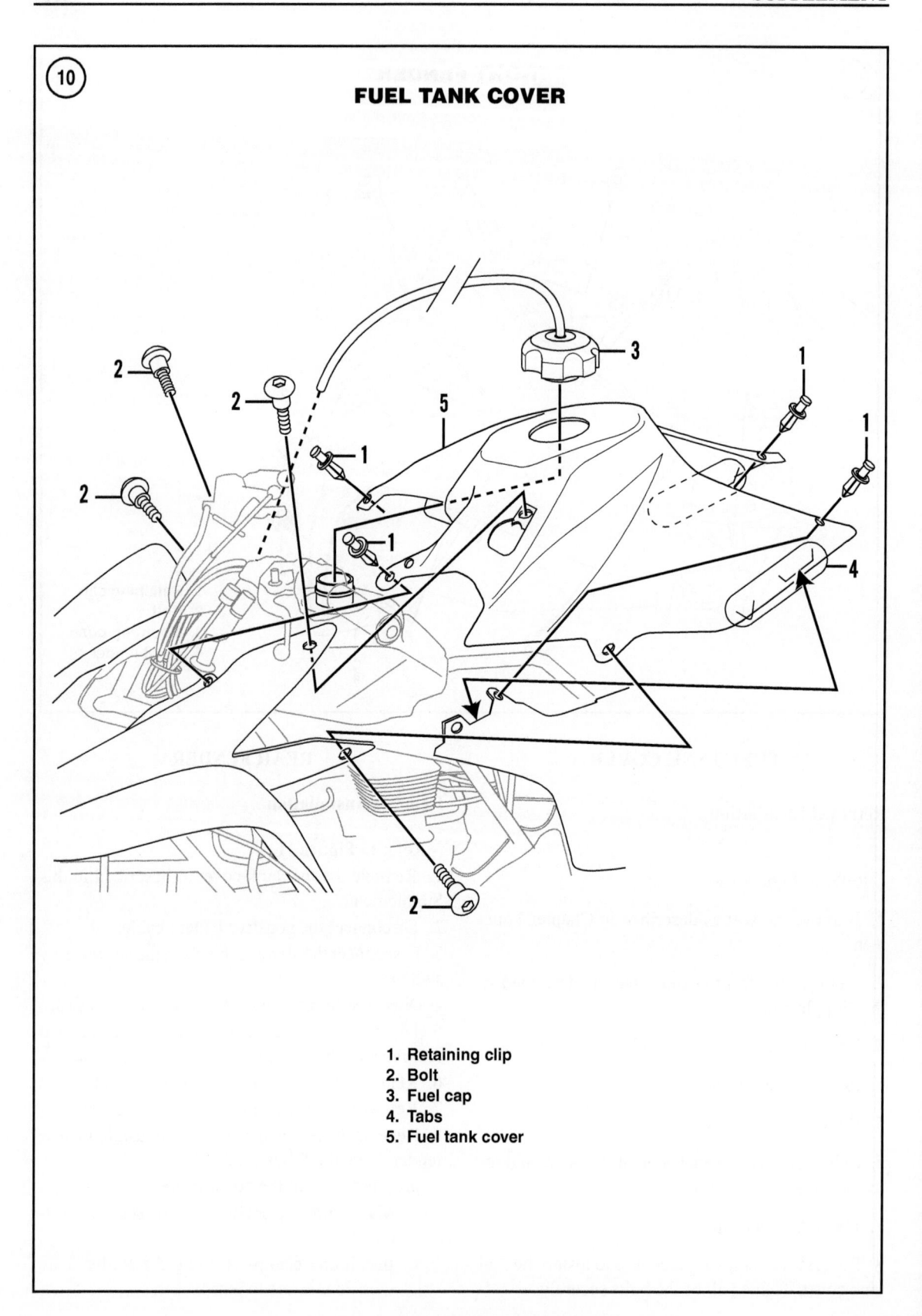

FUEL TANK COVER

1. Retaining clip
2. Bolt
3. Fuel cap
4. Tabs
5. Fuel tank cover

2006-2012 MODEL SERVICE INFORMATION

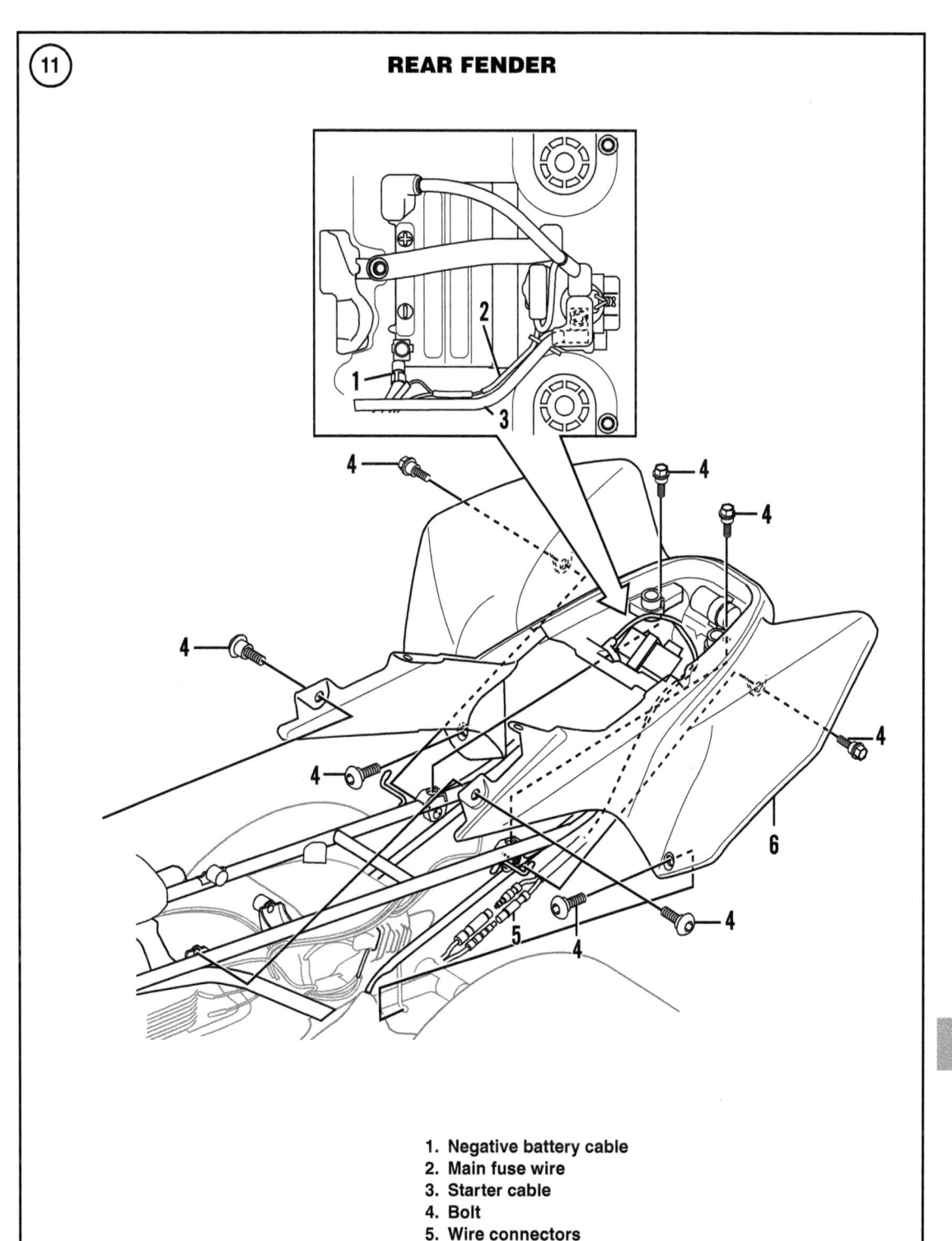

REAR FENDER

1. Negative battery cable
2. Main fuse wire
3. Starter cable
4. Bolt
5. Wire connectors
6. Rear fender

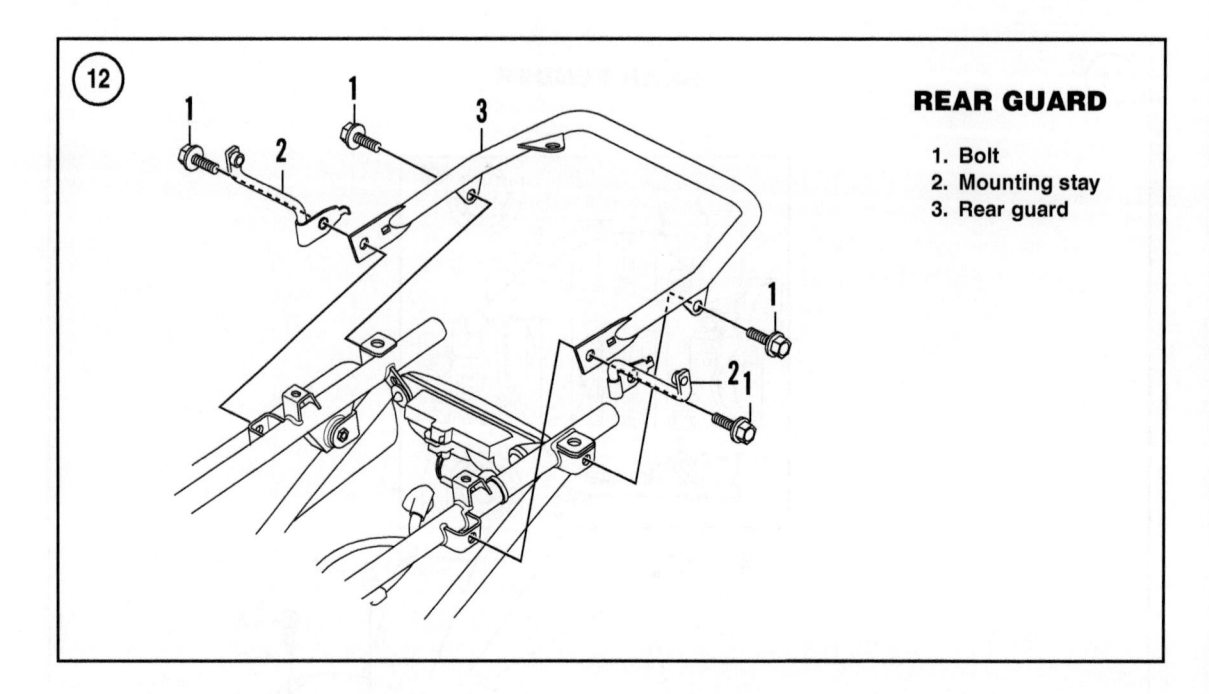

REAR GUARD

1. Bolt
2. Mounting stay
3. Rear guard

REAR GUARD

Removal/Installation

Refer to **Figure 12**.
1. Remove the rear fender as described in this Supplement.
2. Remove the four bolts and two mounting stays securing the rear guard.
3. Remove the rear guard from the machine.
4. Reverse the removal procedure to install the rear guard. Tighten all of the bolts securely.

HANDLEBAR COVER

Removal/Installation

Refer to **Figure 13**.
1. Remove the front center cover as described in this Supplement.
2. Disconnect the wire connectors leading to the ignition switch.
3. Release the wires from the clamps.
4. Remove the fuel cap vent hose from the bracket.
5. Remove the screw and washer securing the cover to the bracket.
6. Remove the handlebar cover from the handlebar.
7. Reverse the removal procedure to install the handlebar cover. Note the following:
   a. Tighten all fasteners securely.
   b. Make sure all connectors are securely fastened and the wires are secured in place by their clamps.

MUD GUARDS AND FOOTPEGS

Removal/Installation

1. Remove each mud guard **(Figure 14)** as follows:
   a. Remove the retaining clip.
   b. Remove the four screws from the mud guard.
   c. Remove the mud guard from the mounting stays.
   d. Reverse the removal procedure to install the mud guard. Tighten the four screws securely.
2. Remove each set of mud guard mounting stays **(Figure 15)** as follows:
   a. Remove the two bolts securing the stays to the machine.
   b. Remove the stays from the machine.
   c. Reverse the removal procedure to install the mud guard stays. Tighten the two bolts securely.
3. Remove each footpeg as follows:
   a. Remove the mud guards and mounting stays.
   b. Remove the two mounting bolts and nuts securing the footpeg to the machine.
   c. Reverse the removal procedure to install the footpeg. Tighte the mounting bolts and nuts securely.

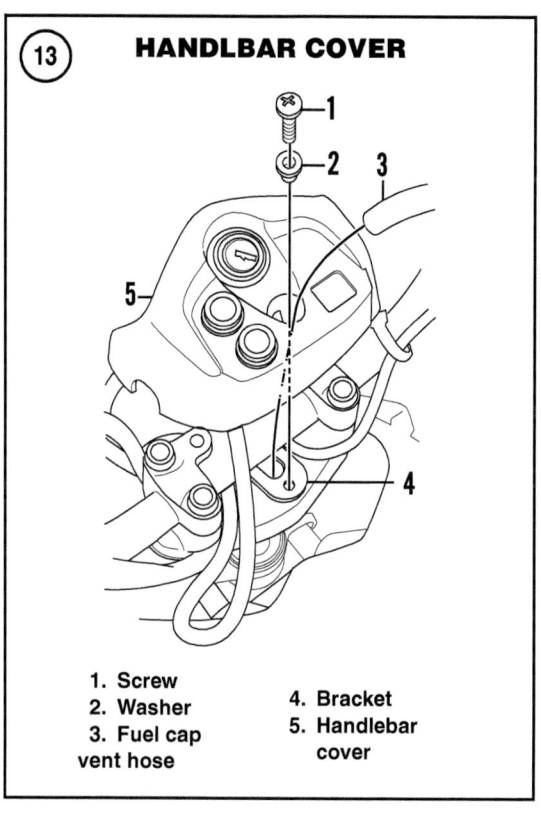

2006-2012 MODEL SERVICE INFORMATION

13. HANDLBAR COVER

1. Screw
2. Washer
3. Fuel cap vent hose
4. Bracket
5. Handlebar cover

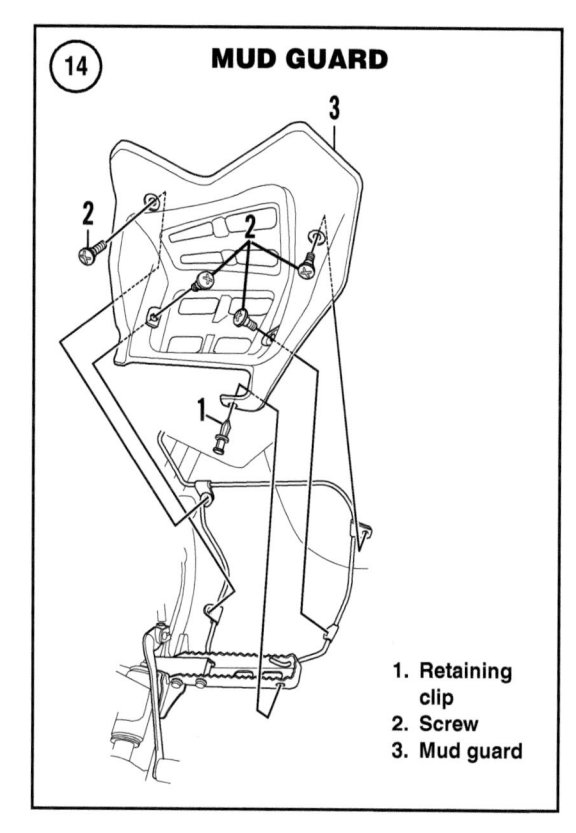

14. MUD GUARD

1. Retaining clip
2. Screw
3. Mud guard

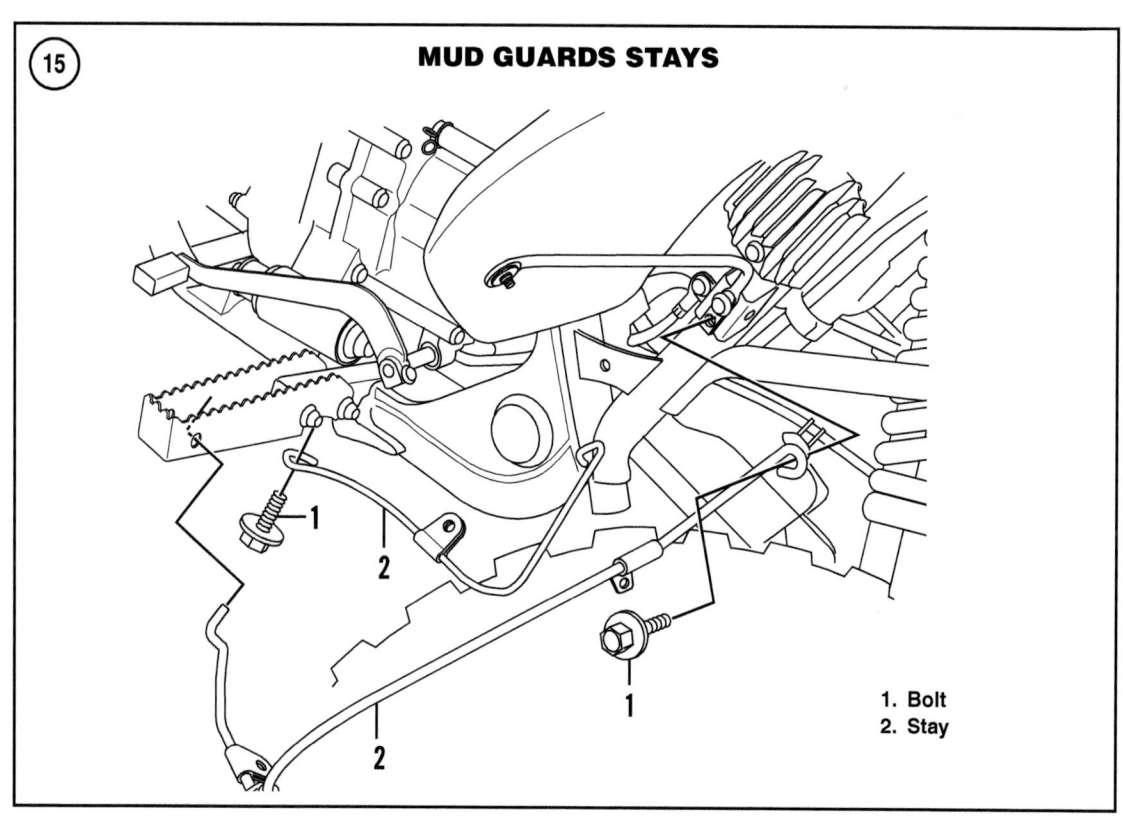

15. MUD GUARDS STAYS

1. Bolt
2. Stay

INDEX

A

Abbreviations, technical 29
Adjustment, clutch 70-71
Air and fuel system 64-67
Air box 198-199
Alternator 205-206
   cover 121-125
Axle, rear 249
   and final drive 249-259
   suspension and final drive 248

B

Ball joint replacement 244-246
Battery 57-60
   maintenance 57-60
   negative terminal 203
   voltage readings 84
      maintenance 84
Body 290
   cover
      front center 304
      handlebar 295-296,308
      side 291
      fuel tank 291-292
   fender
      front 293, 304
      rear 293-295, 305
   guards
      front and rear 293, 308

   mud, and footpegs 295, 308
   retaining
      clips 290
      tabs 290-291
   seat 291
Brake 54-55, 265
   bleeding 279-281
   cable
      and pedal, rear 287-288
      lever/parking, rear 288
   caliper, front 268-272
   drum, rear 281-286
   fluid draining 278
   hose replacement 277-278
   light switch adjustment 298
   master cylinder, front 272-277
   pads, front 266-268
   service 265
   system 68-70
      specifications 289
      torque 289
Break-in, engine 149
Bulb, and fuse specifications 222

C

Caliper, front brake 268-272
Camshaft 109-113
Carburetor 183-190
   adjustment 190-192

INDEX

fuel system 183-190
  specifications 201
Centrifugal clutch and primary drive gear . . 155-161
Change clutch. 161-167
Charging system 46, 203-205
Choke cable replacement 195-196
Clutch. 52
  adjustment 70-71
    lever 298-299
    maintenance and tune-up 70-71
  and primary drive gear 151
    centrifugal 155-161
    change 161-167
    cover 151-153, 301-302
    lifter arm 302
    release mechanism 151-153, 301
    specifications 167
    torque 168
Compression test, engine 77-78
Control arms 243-244
Conversion formulas 28-29
Cooler, oil 120-121
Countershaft, specifications 182
Crankcase and crankshaft 136-149
Cylinder 101-103
head
    and pushrods 89-91
    cover 85-88
    rocker arms 88-90
  front master 272-277
  leakdown test 51-52

D

Diode 215-216
Drill and tap size, metric 30
Driveshaft 259
Drum, rear brake 281-286

E

Electrical system 202
  alternator 205-206
  battery negative terminal 203
  charging system 203-205
  component replacement 202
  connectors 202-203
  diode 215-216
  fundamentals 20
  fuse 221
  ignition system 206-209
  lighting system 216-217

  specifications 222
    torque 222
  starter 209-214
    relay 214-215
  switches 217-221
  testing 39-43
  wiring diagrams 303-307
Engine 50-51
  break-in 149
  compression test 77-78
    maintenance and tune-up 77-78
  lower end 116
    alternator cover 121-125
    crankcase and crankshaft 136-149
    flywheel and starter gears 125-128
    gearshift linkage 128-133, 301
    oil
      cooler 120-121
      pump 133-136
    starter gears and flywheel 125-128
    specifications 149
    torque 149-150
  oil and filter 60-62
  noises 51
  operating requirements 33
  overheating 50
  removal/installation 116-120
  starting 33-35
    will not start 35-38
  top end 85
    camshaft 109-113
    cylinder head 101-103
      cover 85-86
      rocker arms and pushrods 86-91
    piston rings 103-109
    specifications
      general 114
      torque 115
    valve components 91-101
Exhaust system 199-201

F

Fasteners 4-6
  inspection, maintenance and tune-up . . . 75-76
Fender
  front 304, 293
  rear 293-295, 305
Filter and engine oil 60-62
Final drive 53, 249-259
  oil and lubrication 62-63

INDEX

Final drive (continued)
  specifications 264
    torque. 264
Fluid draining 278
Flywheel and starter gears 125-128
Footpegs and mud guards 295
Formulas, conversion 28-29
Fractional, metric and inch equivalents 30
Frame noise 54
Fuel system 50, 64-67
  air and exhaust 183
    torque specifications 201
  air box. 198-199
  carburetor 183-190
    adjustment. 190-192
    specifications. 201
  cable replacement
    choke 195-196
    throttle. 194-195
    tank 196-197
    throttle housing 192-194
    valve 197
Fuel
  tank 196-197
    cover 291-292, 305
    valve 197
Fuse 221
  specifications 222

G

Gears, starter and flywheel 125-128
Gearshift linkage 128-133, 301
General
  engine specifications. 114
  lubrication. 64
Guards
  front and rear 293, 308
  mud and footpegs 295

H

Handlebar. 234-236
  cover 295-296, 308
Handling 54
High speed, performance 39
Hose replacement. 277-278
Hub
  front. 224-228
  rear. 229

I

Idle gear assembly
  reverse 176
    specifications. 182
Idle speed
  adjustment. 81
    maintenance and tune-up 81
  poor performance 38-39
Ignition system 46-48, 206-209
Ignition timing inspection. 81
  maintenance and tune-up 81
Inch, metric and fractional equivalents 30
Internal shift mechanism 179-180

L

Leakdown, cylinder test 51-52
Lighting system 48-50, 216-217
Lubrication
  general. 64
  maintenance and tune-up 56
    specifications. 83-84
  oil
    engine and filter 60-62
    final drive 62-63
  recommended lubricants and fluids 83
  schedule 57

M

Mainshaft specifications. 181
Maintenance and tune up
  battery 57-60
    voltage readings 84
  brake light switch adjustment 298
  cables 71-73
  clutch adjustment 70-71
  clutch lever adjustment 298-299
  engine compression test 77-78
  idle speed adjustment 81
  ignition timing inspection 81
  pre-ride check list 56
  reverse selector cable adjustment 299-300
  schedule 57, 82
  spark
    arrestor service. 73
    plug 78-81
  specifications
    tire 83
    torque 84
  suspension 73-75

INDEX

system
    air and fuel 64-67
    brake 68-70
    tires and wheels 57
    valve clearance. 76-77
Master cylinder, front 272-277
Medium speed performance. 39
Metric
    inch and fractional equivalents 30
    tap and drill size 30
Mud guards and footpegs 295, 308

O

Oil
    cooler 120-121
    engine and filter 60-62
    final drive 62-63
    pump 133-136
Operating requirements, engine. 33
Overhaul, transmission 169-176
Overheating, engine. 50

P

Pads, front brake 266-268
Pedal, rear brake 287-288
Performance speed
    high 39
    medium 39
    poor idle 38-39
Piston, rings. 103-109
Poor speed performance
    idle 38-39
    medium and high 39
Pre-ride check list 56
    maintenance 56
Primary drive gear and clutch
    centrifugal. 155-161
    specifications 167
    torque. 168
Pump, oil 133-136
Pushrods, rocker arms, and cylinder head . . 86-91

R

Recommended lubricants and fluids 83
Retaining
    clips 290
    tabs 290-291
Reverse

idle gear
    assembly 176
    specifications. 182
    selector cable replacement . . 180-181, 299-300
Rings, piston 103-109
Rocker arms 88-89

S

Seat 291
Shaft, steering. 236-239
Shift fork specifications 182
Shock absorbers. 246, 248-24
Shop supplies 6-8
Side covers 291
Spark
    arrestor service 73
    maintenance and tune-up 73
    plug 78-81
Specifications
    battery voltage readings 84
    brake system 289
        torque. 289
    bulb 303
        and fuse 222
    carburetor 201, 303
        fuel system 201
    clutch 167, 303
        and primary drive gear 167
        torque. 168
    conversion formulas 28-29
    countershaft 182
    electrical system 222, 303
        bulb. 303
        and fuse 222
        torque. 222
    engine
        general 114
        lower end 149
            torque 149-150
        top end 114-115
            torque 115
    final drive and rear suspension 264
    fuel and exhaust system
        torque. 201
    general torque 31
    mainshaft. 181
    maintenance and tune up 83-84, 301
        schedule 82
        torque 84

15

Specifications (continued)
  metric
    inch and fractional equivalents. 30
    tap and drill size 30
    recommended lubricants and fluids . . . 83, 300
  reverse idle gear 182
  shift fork 182
  suspension
    front and steering 246
      torque 247
    rear and final drive 264
      torque 264
  technical abbreviations 29
  tire. 83
    and wheel 233
    maintenance and tune-up 83
  torque
    brake system 289
    clutch and primary drive gear. 168
    electrical system 222
    engine
      lower end 149-150
      top end 115
    exhaust system 201
    final drive 264
    fuel system 201
    general 31
    maintenance and tune-up 84
    suspension
      front, and steering 247
      rear 264
    transmission 182
    tune-up. 84
    wheel and hub 233
  transmission 181
    torque. 182
  vehicle
    dimensions 28, 298
    identification number (VIN). 3, 27
    weight 28
  wheel and hub
    torque. 233
Starter 209-214
  gears and flywheel 125-128
  relay 214-215
Starting
  engine 33-35
  system 43-46
Steering
  handlebar 234-236
  knuckle 240-243
  shaft 236-239
  specifications 246
    torque. 247
  tie rods 239-240
Storage 26-27
Suspension 73-75
  ball joint replacement 244-246
  control arms 243-244
  handlebar 234-236
  maintenance and tune-up 73-75
  specifications
    front 247
    rear 264
    torque 247, 264
  shock absorber 246, 248-249
  steering 234
    knuckle 240-243
    shaft 236-239
  swing arm 259-264
  tie rods 239-240
Swing arm 259-264
Switches 217-221

T

Tank, fuel 196-197
  cover 291-292
Tap and drill size, metric 30
Technical abbreviations 29
Terminal, negative battery 203
Testing, electrical 39-43
Throttle
  cable replacement 194-195
  housing 192-194
Tie rods 239-240
Tires 229-232
  and wheels 57, 229-232
    maintenance 57
  specifications 83
    maintenance and tune-up 83, 233
Tools 8-14
  precision measuring 14-20
Torque specifications
  brake system 289
  clutch and primary drive gear 168
  electrical system 222
  engine
    lower end 149-150
    top end 115
  exhaust system 201

INDEX

final drive	264
fuel system	201
general	31
maintenance and tune-up	84
suspension	
front, and steering	247
rear	264
transmission	182
wheel and hub	233
Transmission	52-53
and internal shift mechanism	169, 179-180
inspection	176-179
overhaul	169-176
reverse idle gear assembly	176
reverse selector cable replacement	180-181
inspection	176-179
overhaul	169-176
specifications	181-182
countershaft	181
mainshaft	181
reverse idle gear	182
shift fork	182
torque	182
Troubleshooting	
brakes	54-55
charging system	46
clutch	52
cylinder leakdown test	51-52
electrical testing	39-43
engine	50-51
noises	51
operating requirements	33
overheating	50
starting	33-35
will not start	35-38
final drive	53
frame noise	54
fuel system	50
handling	54
ignition system	46-48
lighting system	48-50
operating requirements, engine	33
performance speed	
high	39
medium	39
poor idle	38-39
starting	
engine	33-35
system	43-46
testing, electrical	39-43
transmission	52-53
water damage	32-33
Tune-up and maintenance	
cables	71-73
clutch adjustment	70-71
engine compression test	77-78
idle speed adjustment	81
ignition timing inspection	81
schedule	82
spark	
arrestor service	73
plug	78-81
specifications	83-84
torque	84
suspension	73-75
system	
air and fuel	64-67
brake	68-70
tire specifications	83
valve clearance	76-77

V

Valve	
clearance	76-77
maintenance and tune-up	76-77
components	91-101
fuel	197
Vehicle	
dimensions	28
identification number (VIN)	3, 27
weight	28
Voltage, battery readings and maintenance	84

W

Water damage	32-33
Wheels and tires	57
front	223-224
hub	223
maintenance	57
rear	228-229
specifications	233
torque	233
Wiring diagrams	316-323

2001-2005 TRX250EX SPORTRAX (USA)

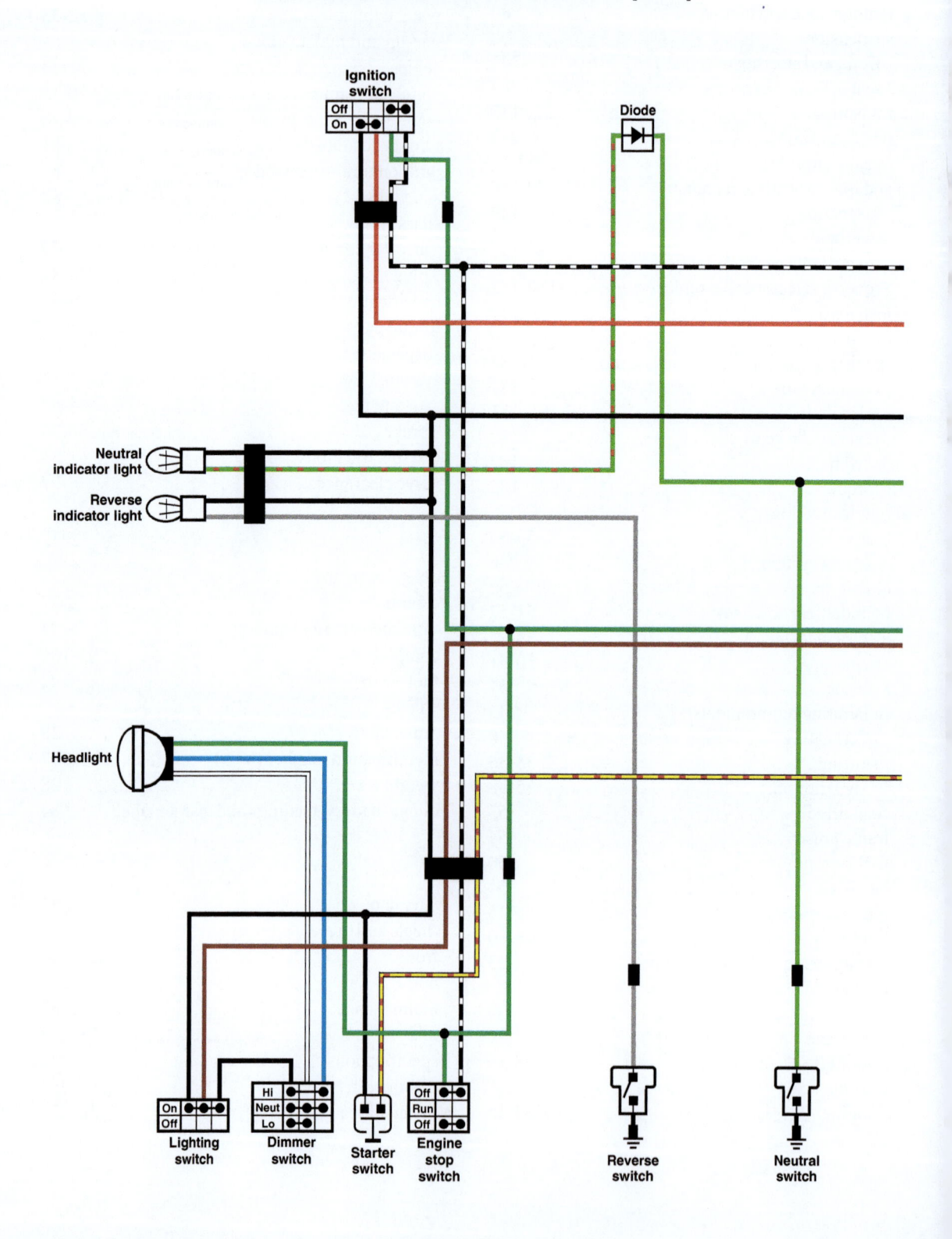

WIRING DIAGRAMS

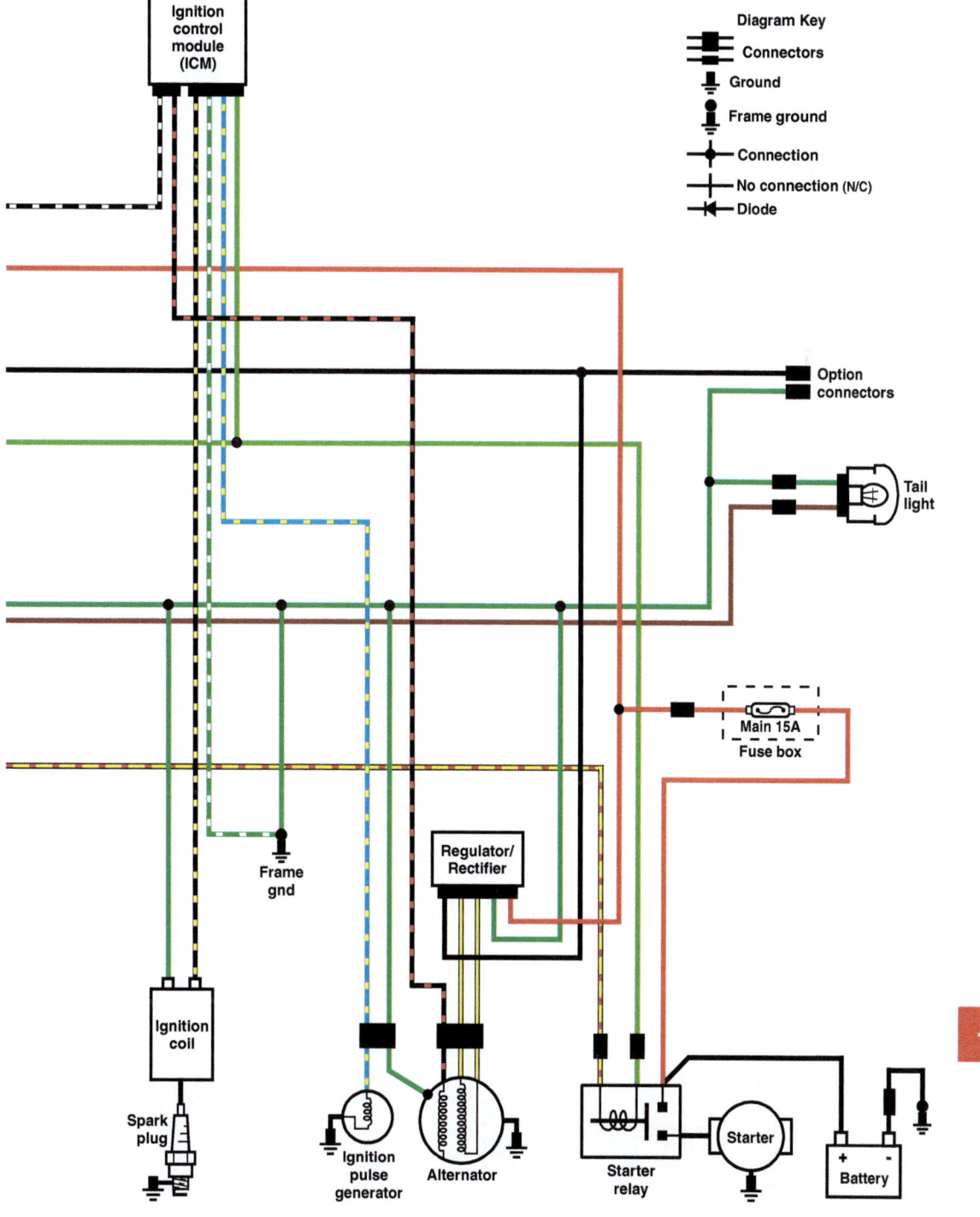

317

Diagram Key
- Connectors
- Ground
- Frame ground
- Connection
- No connection (N/C)
- Diode

Ignition control module (ICM)

Option connectors

Tail light

Main 15A Fuse box

Regulator/ Rectifier

Frame gnd

Ignition coil

Spark plug

Ignition pulse generator

Alternator

Starter relay

Starter

Battery

17

2001-2005 TRX250EX SPORTRAX (CANADA)

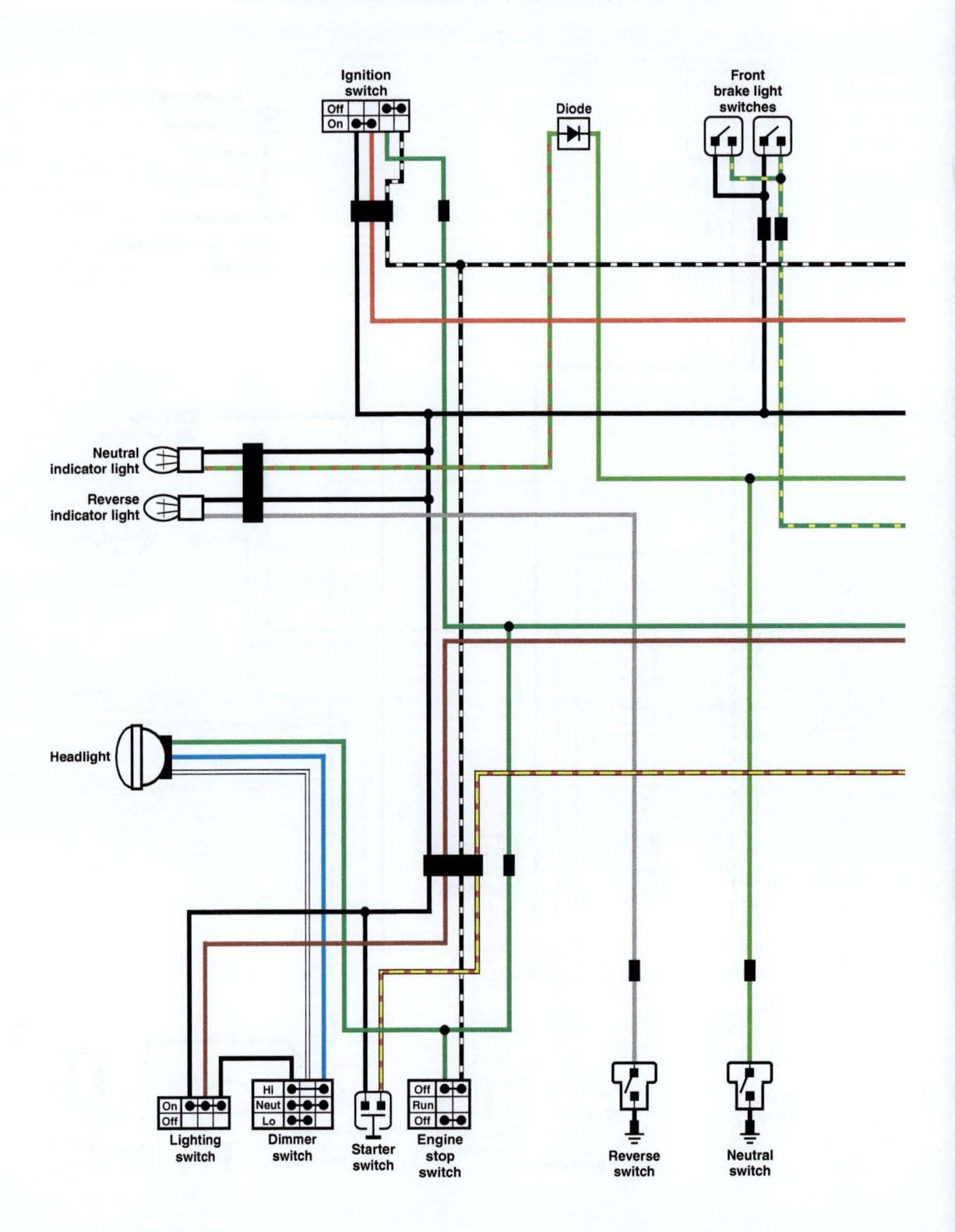

WIRING DIAGRAMS

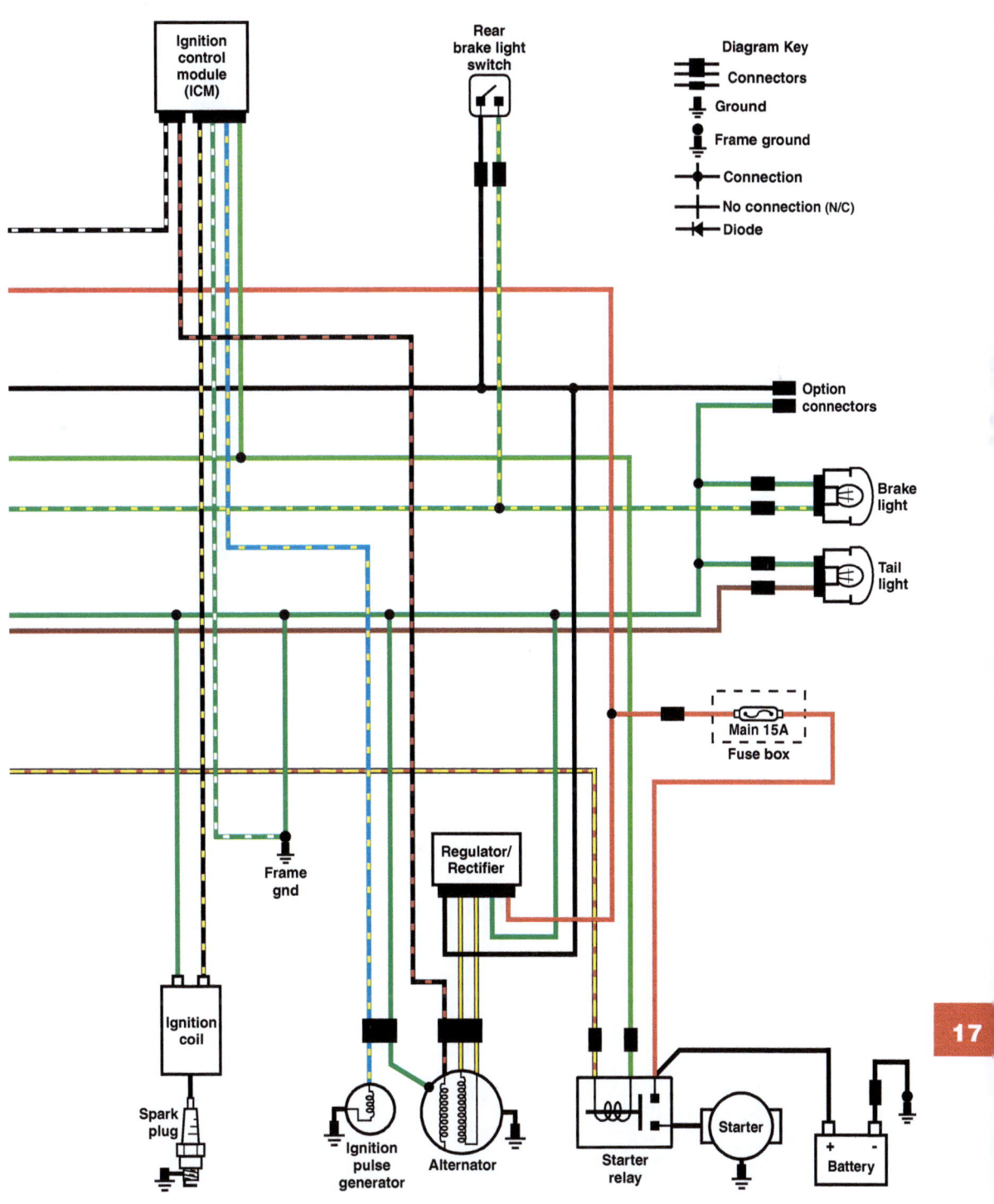

2006-2007 TRX250EX SPORTRAX

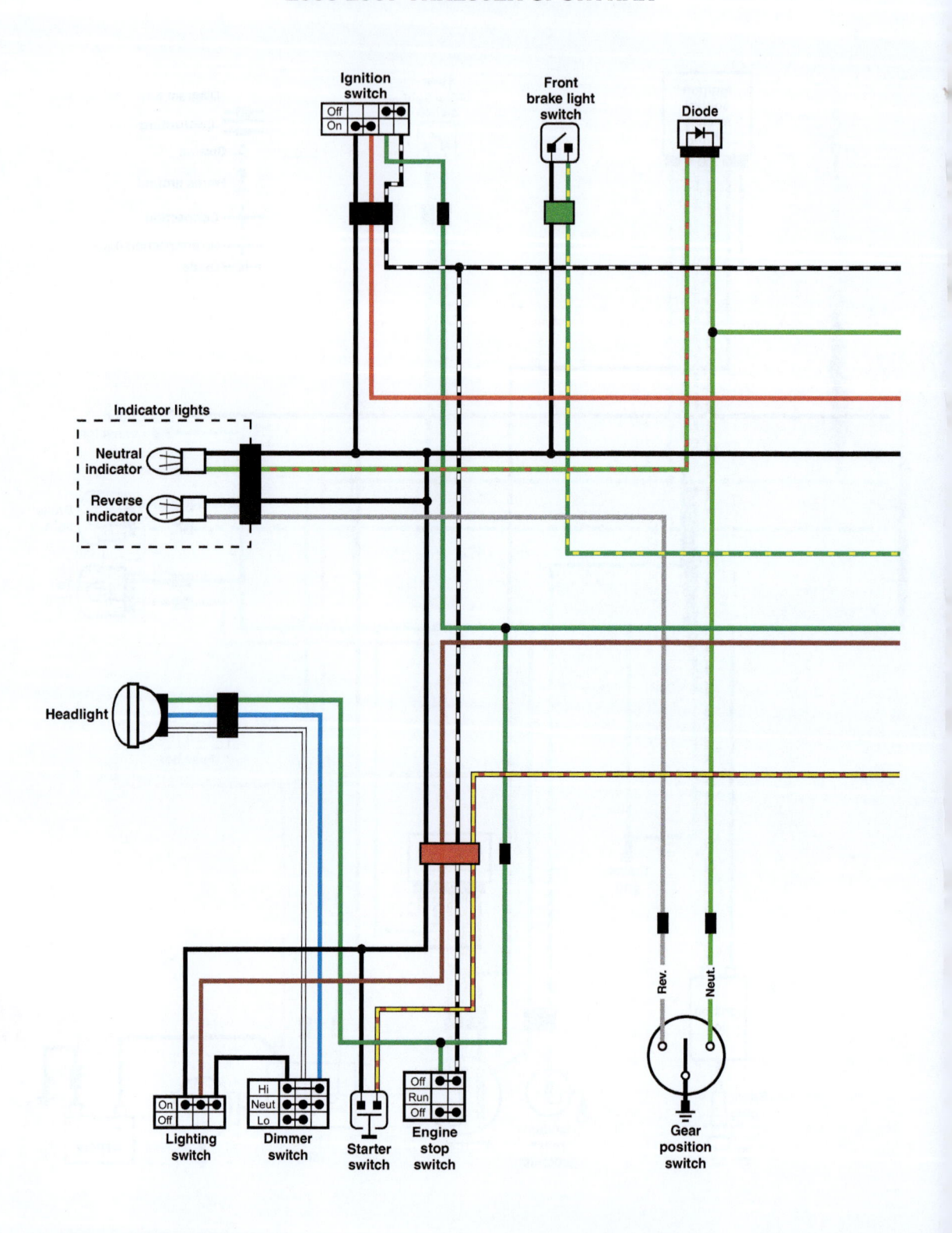

WIRING DIAGRAMS

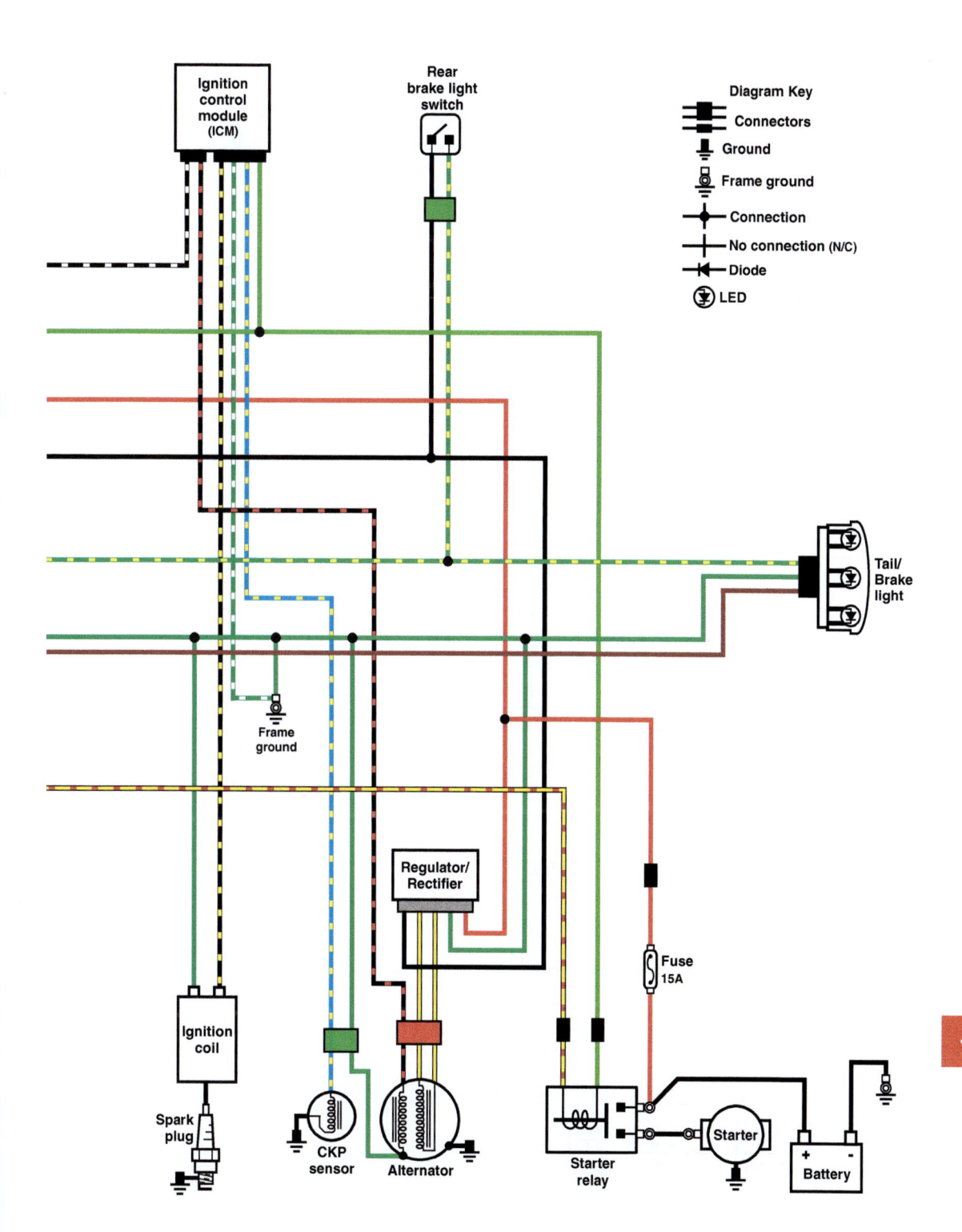

Diagram Key
- Connectors
- Ground
- Frame ground
- Connection
- No connection (N/C)
- Diode
- LED

WIRING DIAGRAMS

2008-ON TRX250EX SPORTRAX AND TRX250X

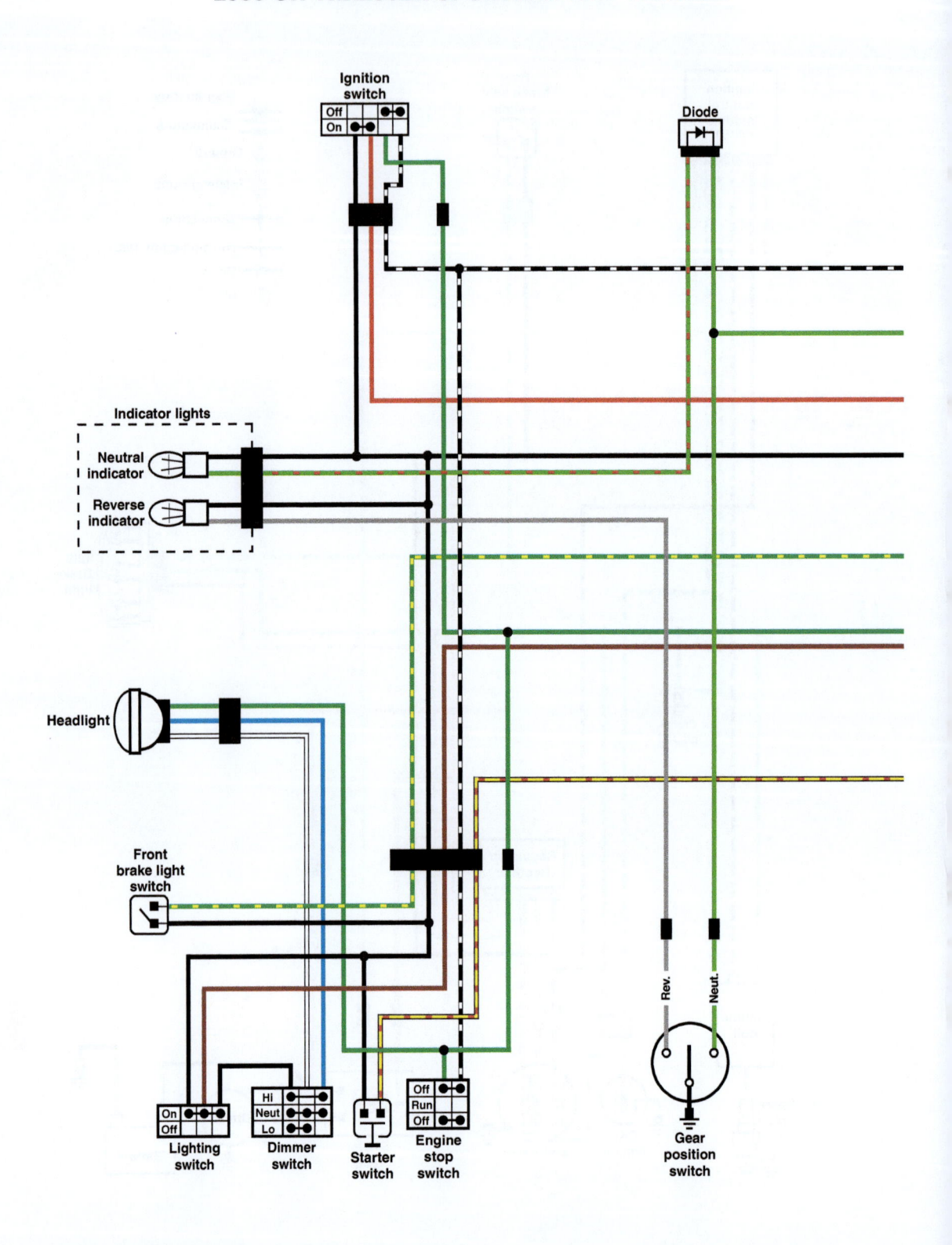

WIRING DIAGRAMS

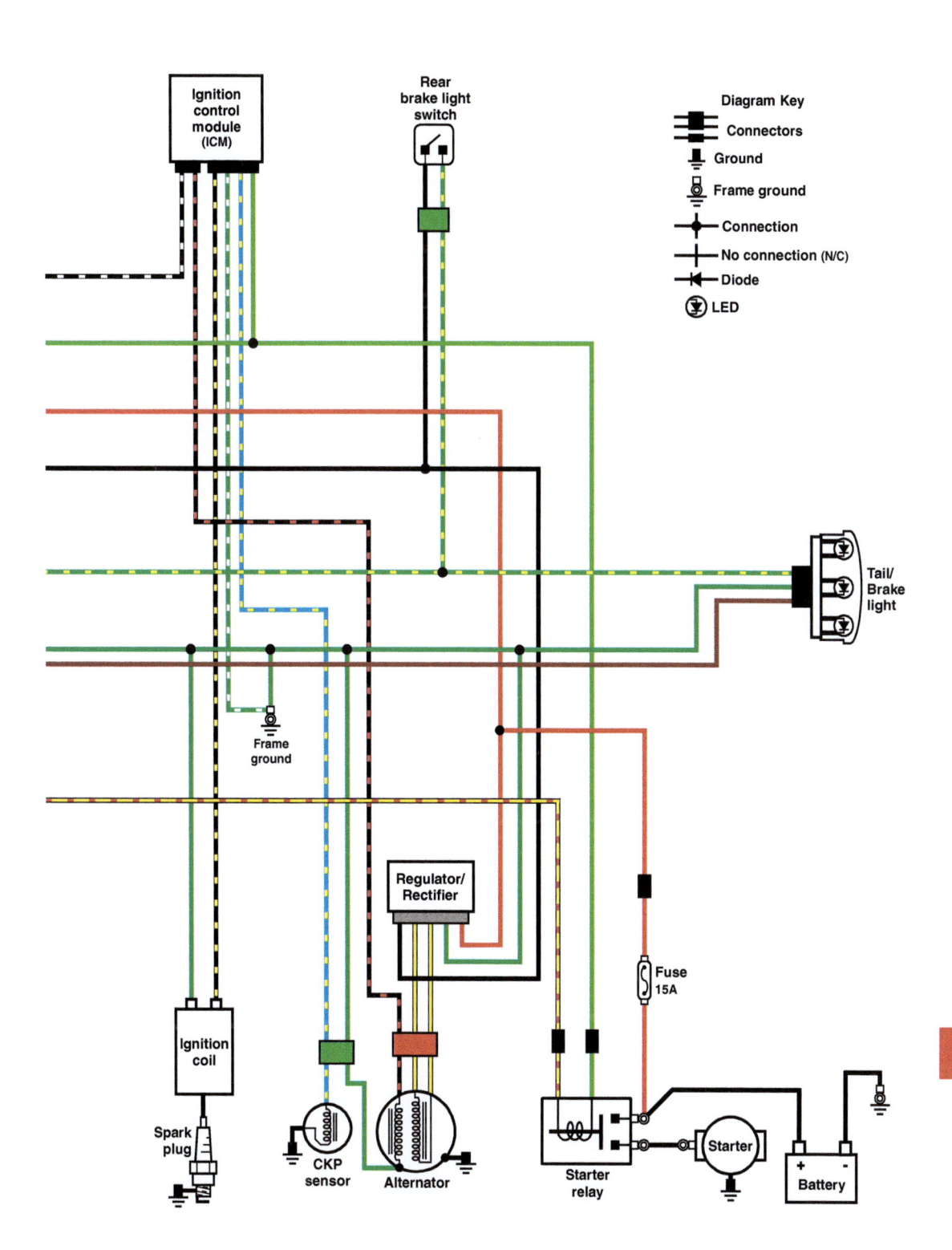

323

17

NOTES

NOTES

MAINTENANCE LOG

Date	Miles	Type of Service